RELIGION IN THE SOVIET UNION

RELIGION IN THE SOVIET UNION

BY

WALTER KOLARZ

ST MARTIN'S PRESS
1961

MACMILLAN AND COMPANY LIMITED
London Bombay Calcutta Madras Melbourne

THE MACMILLAN COMPANY OF CANADA LIMITED
Toronto

ST MARTIN'S PRESS INC
New York

PRINTED IN GREAT BRITAIN

PREFACE

THIS book does not deal with theology. It is an attempt to provide a fuller understanding of Russian reality by drawing attention to what might be called 'the other Russia', the Russia of the believers. I did not begin writing this book with any preconceived ideas about the strength of religion in the Soviet Union. In examining the available material and weighing up the evidence I have reached conclusions which have come as a surprise to me.

The book is not written for religious-minded people only, but for everybody anxious to come nearer to the truth about Russia and Soviet Communism. I believe it is an essential part of this truth that religious believers form the new oppressed class of the communist régime.

In a certain sense the writing of this book was a religious experience. At an early stage I found that the book could only be written if I approached every religious group of the Soviet Union with sympathy and charity. I must leave it to the reader to judge whether and how far I have succeeded in this endeavour, but I trust he will not mistake a criticism of political attitudes, especially towards Communism and nationalism, as an attack on the spiritual essence of a given faith.

People belonging to the most different religious persuasions have proved most helpful and have made a decisive contribution to the progress of the work. Several times I gave up this self-imposed assignment in despair. I thought I should never be able to conclude it for lack of time and, even more often, for lack of material. Whenever this happened I received a helpful letter or a pile of material from a Mennonite or a Catholic or a Seventh Day Adventist providing a sufficient incentive to continue the task, which became more and more an exercise in practical ecumenism. It was no longer necessary to rely on my own enthusiasm, but I found encouragement in the blessings and good wishes which I received from the most unexpected quarters. At the same time I contracted an obligation towards those who have lent me their assistance and I only hope that I have honestly discharged it.

The number of pages allocated to the various religious groups in the Soviet Union is no criterion of either their numerical importance or their spiritual significance for the peoples of Russia and I do beg the reader not to judge the book only on this 'arithmetical' basis. My main concern was to throw light on the less familiar aspects of the religious

v

situation in the Soviet Union, and those religious groups about which there is little up-to-date literature in the West had, therefore, a primary claim on my attention. In such instances it was the chief duty of the author to give information. With regard to those Churches about which there already exists a fair amount of literature in the West, interpretation rather than information seemed to be required.

In writing this book I have drawn wherever possible on Soviet sources, both religious and anti-religious, but it seemed to me that there was a good case for using material which the various religious groups of the Western world have issued about their co-religionists in Russia. As a rule, this literature is hardly read outside the religious circle which produces it. In a few cases the sources could not be quoted for fear of betraying the confidence of those who have spoken to the author confidentially. The author has also refrained from disclosing certain printed Soviet sources which are not officially available for export.

To a certain extent the book, although entirely self-contained, is a continuation of the author's previous works on the ethnic problems of the Soviet Union. He has, therefore, abstained from including in the present book certain facts about the pagan religions of Siberia which have already been covered, albeit inadequately, in *The Peoples of the Soviet Far East* (London, George Philip and Son, 1954).

As so many people have helped me in one way or another in writing this book it is difficult to draw up a complete list of acknowledgements and yet gratitude demands that an attempt, at least, should be made in this direction. The first to be thanked is my wife, Shura Kolarz. Were it not for her self-effacing attitude this book would not have been written. Special thanks are also due to my mother, J. M. Kolarz, and Miss Greta Hanel who at various times looked after my 'home front' whilst the book was being written. Books in large numbers, including a complete set of the *Large Soviet Encyclopaedia* were generously provided by my dear friends D. S. and L. V. Lipovsky, who left us so soon; and my father, A. Kolarz, helped me with the tedious task of keeping in order extensive files of Russian press-cuttings.

Miss Joan Ford gave me her most patient assistance with the manuscript and so did Miss Elisabeth Hunkin, who also put at my disposal a complete file of the *Journal of the Moscow Patriarchate*. For information on different aspects of the religious situation in the Soviet Union I am indebted to H. E. Cardinal Agaganian, Bishop Sipovich (Byelorussian Catholic), Fritz Penner (Mennonite), Mr Torma, the Estonian minister in London, Pastor Roemmich (German Lutheran from Russia), Pastor

Birks (Latvian Lutheran), Father Mutulis (Latvian Catholic), Archimandrite Shevich (Russian Orthodox), Father Abrikosov (Russian Catholic), Dr W. O. Lewis, the Baptist leader, who lent me a complete set of the Soviet Baptist journal and many others. To Emil Marmorstein I owe advice about the problems of Judaism in the Soviet Union. I have gained greater clarity about various aspects of the Russian religious situation in talks with the late Professor Hans Koch, Bishop Boleslav Sloskans and Dr Kurt Hutten. I am grateful to Miss Anna Holdcroft, Miss Mavis King and Mr John Lawrence for supplying me with various items of Soviet religious and anti-religious literature not available in Western Europe. Substantial help has also been given by the Council on Inter-Church Relations of the Church of England, the Institute for the Study of the USSR in Munich as well as by various libraries such as the London Library, the Westdeutsche Bibliothek in Marburg (Dr Witte) and the University Library in Bâle, where special thanks are due to Professor Fritz Lieb's unique collection.

As I have contracted a debt of gratitude towards persons so I have also to several countries where I have come into contact with the various religions whose fate in the Soviet Union is described in this book — to Tunisia, where I first became acquainted with Islam, to Hawaii, which brought me in touch with Buddhism, to the American West coast where I was able to study some of the sects described in the chapter 'American Seeds — Russian Harvest', to Yugoslavia where I had contact with Orthodox Christianity, to Spain where I got a vivid picture of the meaning of religious persecution and to the country where I was born — the Austro-Hungarian Empire — with whose destinies Catholicism, Lutheranism and Judaism were linked in varying degrees.

My gratitude also goes out to the Fellowship of St Alban and St Sergius and St Basil's House, when under the joint secretaryship of Helle Georgiadis and Joan Ford, and to *The Eastern Churches Quarterly* study group when under the guidance of the late Dom Bede Winslow. They provided much of the ecumenical atmosphere as well as that inspiration and encouragement which was essential for the progress of the work.

In paying all these tributes I do not wish to associate anybody mentioned with the views expressed in the book. The interpretations, views and mistakes are the author's sole responsibility.

London, Christmas 1960   WALTER KOLARZ

LIST OF MAPS

CONTENTS

VIII   WESTERN PROTESTANTISM I (LUTHERANS, CALVINISTS,
           MENNONITES)   245

           I. LUTHERANS   248
          II. CALVINISTS   270
         III. THE 'FOURTH PARTY OF THE REFORMATION'   274

  IX   WESTERN PROTESTANTISM II (EVANGELICAL CHRISTIANS
           AND BAPTISTS)   283

   X   AMERICAN SEEDS — RUSSIAN HARVEST   322

           I. SEVENTH DAY ADVENTISTS   322
          II. THE PENTECOSTAL MOVEMENT   330
         III. JEHOVAH'S WITNESSES   338
          IV. CHRISTIAN SCIENTISTS   345

  XI   GENUINE RUSSIAN SECTS: 346

           I. MOLOKANS   349
          II. DUKHOBORS   353
         III. THE SECT OF THE CASTRATED   356
          IV. THE FYODORIST CRUSADERS   358
           V. THOSE GLORIFYING THE HOLY NAME (IMYASLAVTSY)   362
          VI. IOANNITES   363
         VII. INNOCENTISTS   365
        VIII. OTHER 'RED DRAGON' SECTS   368

 XII   THE SECULARISATION OF SOVIET JEWRY   372

XIII   ISLAM   400

XIV   BUDDHISM   448

 XV   SCATTERED GROUPS   470

           I. BAHA'IISM AND COMMUNISM   470
          II. KARAITES   473
         III. YEZIDIS   476
          IV. ZOROASTRIANS   477
           V. THE SYRO-CHALDAEAN CHURCH   478

XVI   THE FUTURE OF RELIGION IN THE SOVIET UNION   480

          APPENDIX: THE PEOPLES OF THE SOVIET UNION AND THEIR
              RELIGIOUS BELIEFS   490

          INDEX   499

ILLUSTRATIONS

Acknowledgements for illustrations are due to *The Eastern Churches Quarterly*, *The Baptist Times*, *The Jewish Chronicle*, the Hon. Henrietta Bower, Mr Charles Thomas and Dr Charles Bawden, who owns the copyright of the photos taken by him in the Mongolian Peoples' Republic.

I

The Survival of Religion
in the Soviet Union

'Woe unto them that call evil good, and good evil; that put darkness for light, and light for darkness; that put bitter for sweet, and sweet for bitter!'

ISAIAH, 5.20.

Throughout the history of the Soviet Union religion has remained the most visible ideological alternative to Communism. It has remained the only opponent of Communism able to preserve at least some of its institutional forms. The recognition of this fact does not depend on one's own convictions. It imposes itself on the minds of both believers and unbelievers who want to arrive at a proper assessment of Russian reality. Any appraisal of the state of Russia is incomplete unless it takes the survival of religion into account.

The extent of the survival of religion in Russia cannot be expressed in terms of figures although some of the smaller Christian denominations of the Soviet Union publish detailed statistics about their membership. Survival of religion is not a question of formal church membership and not a question of religious rites publicly performed. Religion survives in the hearts of men who believe in God, it survives in prayers said and in pious thoughts. One would have to look into the depth of every human soul in Russia if one wanted to investigate how much religious thinking still exists after so many years of communist rule. Even if such an investigation were possible one would not obtain a clear statistical picture of the numbers of believers and unbelievers in the Soviet Union. There are many stages between a devout or even fanatical faith, on the one hand, and uncompromising atheism on the other. Such intermediate stages between total belief and total unbelief exist in every society and in Russia as everywhere else there are the masses of the indifferent who are lost or nearly lost to religion, though militant atheism has not won them. This group includes a large mass of Soviet citizens who practise religion neither publicly nor privately but who are nevertheless reluctant to describe themselves as 'unbelievers'.

1

(Religious believers, if this term is taken in the more precise term of church members, are only a minority of the population of the USSR) even if they still aggregate many million people. However, from this (one must not conclude that the majority of the inhabitants of the USSR have consciously embraced the atheist doctrine.(The advance of atheism in Russia is not exclusively a product of communist education, propaganda and terror. To a great extent it is part of the secularisation of life which has affected most parts of Europe as a result of the industrial revolution. The decline of religious belief in the USSR must be seen in connection with the general de-Christianisation of the European cities and especially of their proletarian inhabitants.)Moscow, St. Petersburg (Leningrad) and Yekaterinburg (Sverdlovsk) might include to-day only a minority of people practising their religion even if Russia were not ruled by communists but by a coalition government of constitutional democrats and social democrats. Such a government would have carried out the same industrialisation measures as the Soviets, in a more liberal and more humanitarian way, it is true, but it would have uprooted vast masses of people and so changed their traditional way of life and beliefs. One only has to look at the big cities in the non-communist countries to find an indirect confirmation of this hypothesis. In Paris or Marseilles only one out of seven attends church service on Sunday, and in certain French coal-mining centres it may be only one in twenty or even one in forty.[1]

A good deal has been written in many countries to explain why people have stopped being religious and why Christian Churches have failed in their apostolate. Many of these explanations are applicable, *mutatis mutandis*, to Russian conditions although they must be supplemented by the one factor which does not exist in a free society and which dominates the Soviet scene, namely the active persecution of religion by the communist régime.(However, for the purpose of our analysis it seems more important to ask how and why religion could survive under an oppressive atheist régime. This question is not only of interest to people outside the Soviet Union but the Soviet communists themselves have considered it of tremendous practical importance. They have spent much time and energy to find an answer or rather a whole series of answers supplementing each other.)

Leaving out of account reasons of a supernatural kind which make for the survival of religion in Russia, and limiting ourselves to a purely terrestrial horizon, (we can trace the communist failure to wipe out

[1] Adrien Dansette, *Destin du Catholicism Francais 1926–1956*, Paris 1957, p. 46.

religious beliefs to two main factors. These are the relative ineffectiveness of anti-religious propaganda and the communist inability to create a new civilisation and morality sufficiently solid and successful to put an end to the religious era in the history of mankind.)

I. THE FAILURE OF THE ATHEIST MOVEMENT

The ineffectiveness of atheist propaganda is the ineffectiveness of the atheist movement which conducted it. There have been two kinds of atheist movement in the Soviet Union. In a certain wider sense, the Communist Party and its subsidiary organisations such as the Young Communist League are part and parcel of the atheist movement, even if atheist propaganda is not their chief aim but only a side-line of their activity. In addition, however, an atheist movement has existed in Russia in a more narrow direct sense in the form of a special atheist organisation, which, during the pre-war period, was known successively as 'Society of the Friends of the Newspaper *Bezbozhnik*', the 'League of the Godless' and after 1929 as 'League of the Militant Godless'. In the post-war period certain functions of this League were taken over by the 'Society for the Dissemination of Scientific and Political Knowledge'.

1. *The Communist Party and the Young Communist League*

To define the atheist movement as the sum total of régime organisations is not fully satisfactory. The atheistic character of even the Communist Party is not a matter which can be affirmed without any reservations. Certainly, (on the ideological plane Communism and religion are at opposite poles. The leaders of the Communist Party are atheists. But when we look at the rank and file then we get a slightly different picture.) People have rarely joined the Russian Communist Party because of its anti-religious bias. They joined for a variety of reasons, some highly idealistic, and some of a purely opportunistic nature. (Quite a number of Russians became Party members without even accepting the atheistic ideology of Communism.) At first the Party turned a blind eye to such persons. In the years prior to the October Revolution, Lenin had no hesitation in admitting into the Party industrial workers who were religious believers. In 1909 Lenin wrote, 'We must not only admit into the Social-Democratic Party all those workers who still retain faith in God, we must redouble our efforts to recruit them. We are absolutely opposed to the slightest affront to these workers' religious convictions. We recruit them in order to educate them and not in order to carry on an active struggle against religion.'[1] On the same occasion Lenin said that even a priest could become a party member 'if he conscientiously performs party work and does not oppose the party programme'. Lenin fully endorsed Marx's dictum about religion being 'an opium for the people' but in practice he pleaded for an elastic and opportunistic attitude toward religious believers. For him the conquest of power and not dissemination of atheist views was the primary objective.

As a result of this opportunistic approach there were a number of devout Christians among the working-class rank and file of the Old Bolsheviks. Yaroslavsky, the Chairman of the League of the Militant Godless, once told the story of an old party member who even after the Revolution wrote on the top of a party questionnaire 'In the Name of the Father and of the Son and of the Holy Ghost, Amen'.[2] That this was hardly an isolated case may be gathered from the fact that as late as 1921 the Central Committee of the Party issued instructions to the effect that in exceptional cases tolerance may be shown towards believing party members provided they had worked in favour of the Revolution and defended it in time of danger.[3] This toleration clause was, of course, not applicable to new recruits to the Party although among them were again people who failed to accept the atheist doctrine.

Even at the time of the first Five Year Plan the problem of party members who were conciliatory towards religion was not yet solved. This was proved by the instructions which the sixteenth Party Conference issued in April 1929 for the perusal of purge commissions. The commissions were advised to expel all members from the urban party branches who had not finally broken with religious customs. In the countryside the purge was aimed at party members who had still kept friendly relations with local priests.[4] In deference to these instructions thousands of party members were expelled all over the Soviet Union, especially in rural areas, throughout the second half of 1929 and the first half of 1930. One single territorial party organisation, that of the Middle Volga region, expelled as many as 453 members for their conciliatory attitude towards religion.[5]

[1] *Proletarii*, 26 (13) May 1909 no. 45, V.I. Lenin, *Religion*, Little Lenin Library, vol. 7, London 1940, p. 22.
[2] Yaroslavsky, *Protiv Religii i Tserkvi* ('Against Religion and Church'), *Moscow 1932–35*, vol. iii, p. 201.
[3] Yaroslavsky, op. cit., vol. ii, pp. 35–6.
[4] *Kommunisticheskaya Partiya Sovetskogo Soyuza v Resolyutsiakh i Resheniyakh Sezdov, Konferentsii i Plenumov Tseka* (The Communist Party of the Soviet Union in Resolutions and Decisions of the Congresses, Conferences and Plenums of the Central Committee), vol. ii, pp. 488–9.
[5] *Bezbozhnik* August 20, 1930, no. 46.

Also during the subsequent purge, that of 1933, it was once again revealed how difficult it was for individual party members and even whole groups of communists to make a clear break with religious beliefs. As an extreme example of religious survivals within the Party during this period, one might mention the conditions which the Central Purge Commission discovered in Moldavia. There, certain Communist Party members were not only practising Christians but even took part in the collection of funds for the repair of churches. They sang religious hymns even when going to the meetings of the very Purge Commission which was to victimise them for their ideological backwardness.[1]

In examining the attitude of the individual Communist Party members towards religion one must not forget that the Party consisted in the early years of Soviet rule of a fairly small number of people who lived inside a predominantly Christian country. It stands to reason, therefore, that they could not ignore its rules and customs altogether. For instance, some Communist Party members had their children christened, others went on celebrating religious holidays and insisted on having the traditional Russian Orthodox Easter food — these used to be nicknamed 'Easter Cake Communists' ('*Kulichnye Partiitsy*'). Others again continued to have ikons in their homes to placate older members of the family.[2] These traditions seem rather innocent and yet a Party with a revolutionary and totalitarian philosophy could not tolerate such a pandering to 'the old way of life' but had to fight it with every means. The party authorities had to be constantly on the look-out for people paying lip-service to the official atheist doctrine whilst violating at the same time the atheist code of behaviour. This was bound to create an atmosphere of suspicion and distrust in the communist ranks.

Even in the period after World War II, the Soviet press continued to report about the presence of crypto-Christians within both the Communist Party and the Young Communist League. It usually spoke about such cases in terms of moral indignation about the alleged duplicity of the individuals concerned. In 1954, for instance, it was disclosed that an outstanding Leningrad physiologist working in the Academy of Medical Sciences was a secret believer despite being for twelve years a Communist Party member. His religious affiliation was discovered only by chance when he was asked to deliver a lecture about the incompatibility between science and religion.[3] Even party officials give a 'bad example'

[1] *Bezbozhnik*, October 10, 1934.

[2] A. A. Kostitsyn, *Rabselkorovskaya armiya na anti-religioznom fronte*, (The army of Workers' and Peasants' Correspondents on the anti-religious front), Moscow 1930, p. 18.

[3] *Literaturnaya Gazeta*, October 14, 1954.

to the rank and file members by observing religious rites and having their children christened and it is not always possible to keep this grave offence against party discipline secret. The problem of religious infiltration into the Communist Party and the Young Communist League exists not only in the crude form of a Christian joining the only legal political or youth organisation as a kind of camouflage but also in a more subtle form. The subconscious mind of the Soviet communist is still coloured by religious influences. His notions on morality are still drawn from the Christian, Jewish or Moslem heritage.

2. *The League of Militant Godless*

The failure of the Communist Party in the fight against religious leanings among its own members was a sufficient reason for the existence of an organisation specialised in attacks on Church and religion and in disseminating atheist ideas. The organisation was probably the most colourful one ever emerging at the periphery of the Soviet Communist Party — the League of Militant Godless (LMG).[1] To what extent was the League an atheistic organisation? This seems to be an absurd and superfluous question to ask, and yet it is not quite out of place. The atheism of the League was not something absolute. It was an atheism mitigated by opportunism. The leaders of the League always stressed that atheist propaganda must be related to the interests of the class struggle and the general political and economic programme of the Communist Party. The materialism of the League became, therefore, often a petty, economic materialism devoid of any larger ideological concept and vision. For instance, the League motivated its campaign for the removal of church bells by its desire to provide more precious ferrous metals for Soviet heavy industry, and it conducted the agitation against Christmas trees in the alleged interest of forest protection. As the atheism of the League was no aim in itself, a situation could easily arise in which the whole atheist organisation had to be sacrificed to a tactical manœuvre of the Soviet Government, and this is what finally happened.

[1] The League of Militant Godless attracted considerable interest in the West and a good deal has been published on its history, activities and objectives. The best documented of the earlier accounts is Adolf Ziegler's *Die russische Gottlosenbewegung*, München 1932. A good description of anti-religious propaganda in the first Five Year Plan period is given by Edmund A. Walsh, *The Last Stand*, Boston 1931. N. S. Timasheff's, *Religion in Soviet Russia 1917–1942*, London 1943, is a concise and well-written account of the godless movement from its beginnings to its eclipse at the beginning of the war. Valuable documentary evidence about the movement is further included in the series of pamphlets 'Life in Russia', no. 6. *Training for the Godless Ministry*, 1934, and no. 10, *Russia's Religious Future*, 1935, copyright by Paul B. Anderson.

But what about the membership of the League? Could their atheism be taken more seriously than that of the rank and file of the Party? It would seem logical that all members of a League of Godless should be genuine atheists, and yet the leaders of the League themselves were never really sure about this point. They were always haunted by the fear that some persons might join their organisation for ulterior motives, to prove their loyalty towards the régime, or even to undermine the League from within. Yaroslavsky asserted once that not only individual members of the organisation but even entire branches might have connections with religious groups.[1] There were in all likelihood members in the League who fundamentally sympathised with its aims but who time and again may have been tortured by doubts as to whether they were doing the right thing in giving support to a society for the promotion of Godlessness. In the early years of the League a discussion took place within its fold which clearly showed that the members suspected each other of harbouring religious feelings in secret. The question at issue was whether members of the League should enter church buildings to check on the number of believers and to assess the strength of religious feeling in a given locality. It was finally decided that no league member should go to church without consulting his local branch organisation beforehand — otherwise the impression might be created that he wanted to pray himself.[2]

When the League of Godless was first launched it was far from being popular with the bulk of party members. Many a Russian communist was reluctant to boast about his atheism in public and considered the League of Godless as an eccentric sect of the Party. The foundation congress of the League which was held on Easter Day, 1925, attracted hardly any attention. The principal Soviet newspapers devoted no comments to it, nor did they report its speeches and discussions. The Party and the Government did not wish to be associated officially with the new organisation. The leaders of the League, the members of its first Executive Committee, were people without any close contact with the important social forces of the country — the working class and the peasantry. They were mostly radical communist intellectuals who had a vested interest in the promotion of atheism, such as F. M. Putintsev the editor of the *Bezbozhnik*, Madame Kostelovskaya the editor of the journal *The Godless at the Bench* (*Bezbozhnik u Stanka*), Aleksandr Lukachevsky the head of the anti-religious sector of the Communist Academy, and a certain Mikhail Gorev, an orthodox priest who apostatised and became the theological expert of the organisation.

[1] Yaroslavsky, op. cit., vol. iv, p. 78.   [2] Yaroslavsky, op. cit., vol. iii, p. 230.

There were also a few politically more important figures on the Executive Committee, including the old Bolsheviks Skvortsov-Stepanov (1870–1928), the editor of *Izvestiya*, Peter Krasikov (1870–1939) who occupied high posts in the People's Commissariat for Justice as well as in the Supreme Court and above all, Yemelyan Yaroslavsky (1878–1943), the Chairman of the League. He was highly appreciated as a journalist and pamphleteer and served on the editorial board of both *Pravda*, the Party's central organ, and *Bolshevik* its principal theoretical mouthpiece. At one time he was Chairman of the *Society of Old Bolsheviks* and 'Elder' of the *Society of former Political Prisoners and Exiles*. His most important post was that of a secretary of the Central Control Commission of the Party, the body in charge of party purges. Although godlessness was never more than a sideline of his many-sided activities, it was mostly because of his influence that the League of Godless acquired recognition in party circles and that it succeeded in becoming a mass organisation, at least for a short period.

But this took years of very tough up-hill struggle. The whole idea of a League of Godless did not fit into the Soviet atmosphere of the middle twenties, when the Soviet Government was still out to appease the peasants by concessions and hesitated to show any open hostility towards their religious feelings. In certain districts the party authorities did not even allow the opening of branches of the League. In others, they prevented the distribution of its pamphlets among the rural population. Also, the Political Administration of the Red Army was at first unenthusiastic about the League, and confiscated some of its posters, fearing that their crudeness might incite religious fanaticism.

The turning point in the official attitude towards the League came in 1928–9, with the beginning of long-term economic planning and compulsory collectivisation of Soviet agriculture. The new course in the economic sphere was accompanied by a greater radicalism and by measures against religion in the first place. The de-Christianisation of rural Russia was to run parallel with its collectivisation and the League of Godless had, of course, an important part to play in this process. The tasks facing the League in this new situation were outlined at its second congress in June 1929. In the communist daily press the Congress received more publicity than its predecessor although it was somewhat overshadowed by the twelfth congress of the German Communist Party which took place at the same time. The Congress held its meetings in the Bolshoi Theatre which is reserved for important functions only; it was addressed by such distinguished figures as Bukharin, then still a member of the Politbureau, Lunacharsky, the

People's Commisar for Education and various prominent writers including Maxim Gorky.(About 2,000 people were present: it was the greatest and most representative Soviet gathering devoted to the cause of atheism ever held and was never to be repeated, for the League never held another congress.)

The leaders of the organisation could have been quite satisfied with the success achieved and yet one wonders whether they actually were. Inside the Bolshoi Theatre there were the delegates of Soviet Russia's atheist minority but outside in the country there still lived a religious-minded people. And not only outside — in some inexplicable way a spokesman of this other Russia had penetrated into the congress hall and had sent to the Praesidium a little piece of paper with a laconic message which said: 'Woe to him who goes against his Creator'. The message was read out to the delegates, who greeted it according to *Pravda*'s report 'with bursts of indignant laughter'.[1] Nevertheless, the religious message to the Godless Congress may have provoked not only laughter but also some serious thoughts. Perhaps the one religious voice of dissent in the hall had after all a greater weight than the atheist chorus of the other 1999? But if the delegates harboured such awkward feelings of embarrassment, they quickly dismissed them again. They did not deviate from the road on which they had embarked and even decided that the League's name should henceforward be enriched by the adjective 'militant'. This militancy required a mass recruitment of members which started soon after the second Godless Congress, along with a considerable increase of the League's bureaucratic apparatus.

(Like the Central Committee of the Communist Party, the Central Council of the 'League of Militant Godless' had its departments which were subdivided into sections.\ In 1930, there were as many as seven departments of which the most important one was that in charge of mass agitation. It had as many as twelve sections, the sphere of competence of which shows the all-embracing character of the atheist propaganda work conducted by the League. There was one section for mass campaigns which must have included the anti-Easter and anti-Christmas campaigns. Other sections dealt with atheist lectures, the press, radio, libraries, exhibitions and artistic forms of atheist propaganda (belles-lettres, theatre, cinema and music). A special section took care of schoolboys, another one of women and a third of Red Army soldiers. Section number 12 specialised in the creation of a new way of life. The Nationalities Department of the Central Council of the League consisted of three sections catering respectively for Western and

[1] *Pravda*, June 11, 1929.

Eastern nationalities and those of the Volga-Urals region and the Far North.[1] However, this organisational structure was changed several times, particularly with the purpose of connecting the work of the League more closely with the economic policy pursued by the Communist Party. Thus in 1934 new departments were created for 'work in villages' and 'work on railway transport'.[2]

(It seems that the League had to prove to the Party continuously its practical usefulness. It wanted to show that it was not just a society engaged in an ideological struggle but that it was able to make a direct contribution to the success of the plan.) Its main slogan became therefore 'the fight for godlessness is a fight for socialism'. Under the League's patronage, so-called 'Godless Collective Farms' were formed which were to excel by their economic efficiency whilst exercising at the same time ideological leadership over the countryside. It does not seem that there were at any time more than three hundred of such Godless Collective Farms, all over the Soviet Union. In collective farms where there were still believers and which could therefore not be given the title 'godless' the members of the League were expected to form special 'Godless Brigades' or sow 'Godless Acres' (hectares) in excess of the plan. In the towns the League established 'Model Godless Kitchen Gardens' and organised 'Godless Shock Brigades', of which as many as 3,200 seem to have existed at the time when they were in fashion.[3]

None of these special *ad hoc* institutions, in which the economic and ideological aspirations of the régime became inseparably intertwined, was of long duration. We mention them only as oddities of the communist fight against religion and not because they left a lasting mark on the history of the Soviet State. Nevertheless they were a characteristic feature of the early thirties when the ranks of the League of Militant Godless had increased to over five millions.

(This was the time when certain Russian communists thought that the LMG could become a kind of counter-church. Instead of theological training there was to be extensive anti-religious training. In 1933, in a period when the real Churches were not allowed to have a single seminary, the LMG had six anti-religious higher educational institutions, twenty-six Workers' Anti-Religious Universities, one Anti-Religious University for Red Army soldiers and one Anti-Religious Correspondence Institute with six departments.) In addition, there were various anti-religious working groups and seminars on a lower level.

---

[1] *Bezbozhnik*, July 15, 1930.   [2] *Antireligioznik*, 1934, no. 2, p. 48.
[3] *Antireligioznik*, Jan.–Febr. 1933, no. 1, p. 48.

What the parishes are for the Church the cells were to be for the LMG, only the cells were to outnumber the parishes at the ratio of sixty to one or so. The Five Year Plan of anti-religious propaganda which was adopted in 1932 and was to run until 1937 provided for the organisation of 400,000 cells in towns alone; not less than one cell was to be founded in each factory, government office and school. In addition, 600,000 cells were to be founded in the countryside, one cell in every inhabited locality, collective farm and machine tractor station. One need not say more about the fantastic anti-religious Five Year Plan, the most insane plan ever produced by a communist brain. It provided for the formation of one million atheist cells or one cell for every 160 or 170 Soviet citizens. Only people totally ignorant of the frame of mind of the Russian people could have fixed such a target figure. In actual fact, it does not seem that the fulfilment of the plan was ever seriously attempted. Far from gaining any ground the League lost a great deal of what it held in the first year of the plan.

It would appear from official statistical evidence that the League of Militant Godless declined from the 5,700,000 members which it had in the peak year of 1932, to about two million members in 1937. These membership statistics may however not convey a correct impression of the League's decline, since the 1932 figure may have been artifically inflated and included quite a number of merely nominal members whilst the 1937 figure may have been nearer to truth. In 1931 and again in 1938, the League supplied a geographical analysis of its membership which clearly revealed its weakness. In 1931 at least half the League's membership was in Moscow, Leningrad and in the heavily industrialised Ukraine.[1] Some of the provincial organisations produced only very round and approximate figures of their membership and they failed to give any data about the number of cells. In the remoter parts of the Soviet Union the League did not exist even nominally. As time went on, quite a number of regional organisations either closed down altogether or were virtually extinct. Fifteen regional organisations failed to send any returns when the League counted its members in 1938.

The League of Militant Godless was not only inefficient from a purely organisational point of view, it was also unable to cope with the task which it had set itself — the fight against religion. This does not mean that the League had no external successes. Many thousands of places of worship of every creed were closed on its initiative and instigation. The country was flooded with anti-religious pamphlets and posters

[1] *Antireligioznik*, 1931, no. 8, p. 101.

printed under the League's auspices. The League had also done its best to intimidate believers and to render the observance of religious holidays as difficult as possible.

(However, the aggressive propaganda and activities of the League did not wipe out religion. This was shown by the Soviet census of 1937. One of the purposes of the census was to demonstrate the triumph of atheism in Soviet Russia after almost two decades of communist rule. To prove this point every Soviet citizen filling in the census questionnaire had to state whether he was a believer or a non-believer.)No such question was asked in the first Soviet census of 1926 and Yaroslavsky himself stated at the time that the question was unconstitutional and at variance with the principle of freedom of conscience.[1] Nevertheless, this 'unconstitutional question' was included in the form used for the census of January 1937. It was obviously thought that as a result of both atheist propaganda and active terror only a small number of people would dare to proclaim their religious belief openly. This assumption proved mistaken. The census became an opportunity for believers, of all religious creeds, to demonstrate their attachment to their faith. It was also a great challenge to those who had wavered and even to those who had nearly abandoned religion altogether. These could not bring themselves to carry out the last step of apostasy and to write the ugly word 'non-believer' on the census form. So they entered 'believer' instead. No wonder that the census failed to sound the death-bell of religion and became its great triumph. According to reliable evidence about fifty million Soviet citizens proclaimed themselves as 'believers'. This caused such embarrassment to the authorities that they scrapped the census returns and arrested the census officials. In the subsequent Soviet censuses of 1939 and 1959 all reference to religion was omitted.

(The stubborn survival of religion in the Soviet Union suggested to the Kremlin and particularly to its police organs two parallel and seemingly contradictory courses of action: on the one hand, mass arrests and deportations of both ecclesiastical dignitaries and religious 'activists', and on the other, a purge of the League of Militant Godless. This dual persecution was not as illogical as it may seem at first glance.) The religious groups fell victims of increased police terror because the propaganda offensive against them had failed and the leaders of the godless organisation were arrested for having been so unsuccessful in their anti-religious campaign. Yaroslavsky personally was spared but his deputy Aleksandr Timofeevich Lukachevsky, the Vice-President of

[1] Yaroslavsky, op. cit., vol. iv, p. 320.

the League, was arrested and in all probability executed. The same fate was meted out to some of the most important provincial chiefs of the League, including Matorin, who was in charge of the Leningrad organisation, and Ignatyuk, the leader of the Ukrainian *bezbozhniki* Both had to pay the penalty for the particularly heavy membership losses of their organisations. The Leningrad branch, for instance, lost within less than six years eighty per cent of its supporters and the Ukrainian League had suffered even more drastic setbacks.

The charges against the hapless godless leaders were never made before a court of law, but they were neatly listed by Fyodor Oleshchuk the acting secretary of the League, in an article published in its journal *Antireligioznik*. This article is a real statement of bankruptcy of the League, although it must be taken for granted that it contains quite a number of exaggerations calculated to justify the purge. Oleshchuk said in substance that the League was very largely in the hands of 'enemies of the people', Bukharinists and Trotskyites who sabotaged its work in a dual way. They either deliberately put an end to anti-religious propaganda work or on the contrary, tried to discredit this propaganda by their extremism. This they allegedly did by staging various provocations such as the organised burning of ikons with the purpose of stirring up religious fanaticism and so creating among the people hostility towards the Soviet régime. Finally, the disgraced leaders were charged with having produced inflated statistics as to the number of so-called 'godless' factories, shock brigades and collective farms, a charge which throws grave doubt on the general accuracy of the statistics of the League.[1]

The purge of the League was not tied up exclusively with the problem of religion and the fight against it. It must also be considered within the context of wider political issues. From the point of view of the Soviet police it was not safe to have too many organisations in Soviet Russia. Even if communist in spirit, they were sources of potential danger. An inner-party opposition could easily use them as a tool for its ambitions. Such an organisation was the LMG. However unattractive its objectives to a believer, there was something to be said in its favour. In a way it was an alien element within the Soviet totalitarian state. It stimulated discussions and disagreements on certain philosophic and political subjects. Ideological conflicts which could not be argued out within the Party itself were debated inside the League. An extremist minority consisting mainly of functionaries of the Young Communist League

[1] F. Oleshchuk, '*Vrazheskaya agentura na antireligioznom fronte*' (The enemy agency on the anti-religious front), *Antireligioznik*, November 1937, no. 11.

went out to transform the godless organisation into the radical vanguard of Soviet Communism.

The eagle eyes of the NKVD saw in the League not only germs of a rival political party but also the potential bearer of a rival ideology. Right from its beginnings as a distinct organisation the League presented itself to the public as a vanguard of proletarian internationalism. The internationalism of the League appeared to be as spontaneous and sincere as the internationalism of Communist Party leaders was calculated and opportunistic. The League never dreamt of boosting Russian cultural and national interests under the cover of internationalism and in fact was the main prompter of Esperanto in the USSR. It organised a 'Central Bureau of Godless Esperantists' (*Bezbozhniki Esperantisty*) which translated the more important documents published by the Soviet godless movement and sent them to as many as twenty-nine countries. Esperanto also played a very important part in the correspondence between Soviet and foreign atheists. The keenness of the Russian 'Godless' on maintaining contact with people in foreign countries not only made them suspect in the eyes of the NKVD but also the medium used for the correspondence, the Esperanto language was frowned upon. In 1937, the Central Bureau of Godless Esperantists was closed down, together with all other Esperanto organisations in the Soviet Union.

After the purge of 1937 the League was given another chance and in a way it had its revenge. The NKVD proved no more successful in the fight against religion than the godless movement had been. To judge by external signs, the Churches had been virtually destroyed, it is true, but still atheism was not victorious. The communists had mistaken religion for the ikons, the church bells, the priests and the bishops. Now on the morrow of the purge it appeared that religion could exist quite independent of these externals and so there was once again a need for resuming anti-religious propaganda with those conventional weapons which the League of Militant Godless provided — atheist lectures, articles and pamphlets as well as membership recruitment campaigns. After the beginning of the war, during the short period when the atheist Soviet Union linked its fortunes with the anti-Christian and anti-Jewish Third Reich, the League even experienced a certain recovery. In 1940 the League's secretary claimed once again a membership of three million, a fifty per cent increase over 1937.[1] The increased activity of the League was favoured by the régime which was confronted with the necessity of pumping atheist propaganda into the newly annexed territories, Eastern

---

[1] *Sotsialistichekoe Zemledelie*, May 18, 1940.

Poland, the Baltic States and Bessarabia, where religion was a major factor in the life of the local nationalities. Also in the 'old' territories of the Soviet Union anti-religious propagandists had much to do, for, as the chairman of the Moscow godless organisation said in 1940, believers could be found among people of every walk of life, even among the intelligentsia of the Soviet capital.[1] What holds good of Moscow was, of course, even more true of smaller towns and of the Russian countryside.

Without the outbreak of the German-Soviet War the League of Militant Godless might have carried on for an indeterminate period but the invasion of Russia created a new state of affairs, and called for a thorough reappraisal of the communist anti-religious policy. On June 17, 1941, when the nazi troops were already poised for attack, Moscow Radio still broadcast an anti-religious lecture, but on June 22, when these troops crossed the Soviet frontier, the atheist Government was in dire need of the support of believers. This and no other reason prompted the disbandment of the League of Militant Godless and the suppression of its journals, the *Bezbozhnik* in particular. It has always been awkward for the Soviet communists to admit the real reason for these measures. They have therefore asserted that a special League of Godless had become unnecessary since the large majority of the population had joined the godless camp.[2] This however was only a self-deceiving afterthought.

3. *The All-Union Society for the Dissemination of Scientific and Political Knowledge*

When the war was over, the Soviet Government could easily have revived the League but it refrained from doing so. This omission was in a way an implicit judgment on the League's inefficiency, of which it had given ample proof in the sixteen years of its existence. The powerful resurgence of religious feelings during the war had shown the régime, and Stalin in particular, how little use there was in having a special militant atheist organisation in the Soviet Union. A new, more subtle approach to the problems of atheist propaganda seemed necessary. The open and brutal frontal attack against the Church was to be replaced by a skilfully camouflaged guerilla struggle. But it was difficult to decide by what organisational medium to wage it. During the first two post-war years nothing happened. Anti-religious propaganda was conducted so discreetly and on such a reduced scale that it was hardly noticeable to the outside observer.

[1] *Pravda*, July 9, 1940.   [2] *Nauka i Zhizn*, 1957, no. 11, p. 42.

The turning point came in June 1947 with the foundation of the 'All-Union Society for the Dissemination of Scientific and Political Knowledge'. Unlike the Godless League the Society is no mass organisation, it consists of the communist *élite* — professors, teachers, doctors, agronomists and other members of the intelligentsia. Nobody can become a member of the Society unless he is able to contribute directly to its objective, namely the spreading of scientific and political knowledge. The number of its members grew from year to year. By 1950 there were 130,000 of them, and in 1959 this number had increased to 850,000. The knowledge which the Society disseminates is most comprehensive; it includes biology, agriculture, astronomy, physics, literature, history and there is a particularly strong bias in favour of technical subjects. At the same time however, the Society serves, as its name indicates, political propaganda purposes. One of its foremost tasks is to acquaint the people with the long-term programme of the Communist Party and its ideology and it is in this context that the Society conducts its atheist propaganda.

The Society has a special 'scientific atheist section'. This term 'section' is very misleading. It conceals the existence of an entire organisation which has its branches all over the Soviet Union, in every republic and every province. The 'section' carries on in a new form the tradition of the League of the Militant Godless. It is significant that the first head of the section was the League's former secretary Fyodor Oleshchuk, whilst some of its principal collaborators are other former associates and pupils of Yemelyan Yaroslavsky who died in 1943. So in the fifties Soviet atheist propaganda was still very largely conducted by those very same people who had excelled in this activity already in the twenties: Sheinman, the expert in the fight against the Catholic Church, Klimovich, a veteran in the campaign against Islam, Shakhnovich whose speciality was orthodox Judaism and Uzkov who wrote about the 'sects'.

The scientific-atheist propaganda section tries to promote its objectives by organising atheist lectures and publishing atheist pamphlets. In 1954, for instance, as many as 120,679 lectures were read on antireligious subjects[1] and 100,000 atheist lectures seemed to be a fair annual average during the first post-Stalin years, but in 1958 their number was increased to 300,000. The lecturers are trained in special courses held in all parts of the Soviet Union and attempts have also been made here and there to set up permanent atheist evening classes.

As to the anti-religious pamphlets of the Society, they deal with such

[1] *Nauka i Religiya* (Science and Religion), Moscow 1957, p. 10.

subjects as *Contradiction between Science and Religion, Russian Revolutionary Democrats versus Religion, Religion in the Period of Imperialism, Origins of Religion and Belief in God, Darwinism and Religion, Christianity, its Origin and Essence, Atheist Education of Children in School and Family*, etc. The pamphlets produced by the Society's headquarters in Moscow are printed in editions ranging from 80,000 to 200,000 copies, whilst those printed locally are published in much smaller numbers (e.g. 30,000 in the Ukraine). The pamphlets at first appeared with uniform covers but as time went on their presentation became more imaginative to attract greater attention.

Almost since its inception the Society has encountered a good deal of criticism for its atheist propaganda work. It has been reproached with either not doing enough work on the 'anti-religious front' or performing this work badly and superficially. Even where quantity was sufficient, quality was challenged. Although Khrushchev himself, in a decree of November 10, 1954, on the mistakes in atheist propaganda, instructed the Society to keep its lectures on a high ideological level, this proved impossible in practice. In the light of Soviet self-criticism it would appear that many anti-religious lectures contain factual mistakes which the believers can easily discover, or else they defeat their purpose by their offensive and aggressive attitude. The main argument which the communists themselves put forward against their own lecture propaganda is that it does not reach believers to any major extent. Even the President of the Society, Academician Mitin, admitted that the very titles of lectures such as '*Religion, the enemy of the toilers*' or '*The reactionary essence of Christianity*' were bound to deter believers from attending them.[1] The same seems to apply to atheist pamphlets. The author of a pamphlet directed against the Christian sects, of which the Society issued 114,000 copies, admitted at the end of his work that people might consider his effort futile, for the believer would not read his pamphlet and to the unbeliever it was unnecessary. Nevertheless, the author hoped that the unbeliever would pass on its content to the believing sectarian.[2]

In the long run, the purely academic fight against religion as conducted by the Society proved as disappointing from the communist point of view as the robuster methods which characterised the activities of the League of Militant Godless before World War II. Doubts emerged in communist circles whether the Society should be allowed

[1] *Nauka i Religiya*, Moscow 1957, p. 15.
[2] I. N. Uzkov, *Chto takoe religioznoe sektantsvo?* (What is religious sectarianism?) Moscow 1956, p. 30.

to exercise a monopoly in anti-religious propaganda or whether one should not entrust it to other bodies and institutions and thus make for greater variety and vigour in the atheist campaign. Thus in a number of towns where the 'religious enemy' seemed particularly dangerous there were established in the late fifties special 'Houses of the Atheist' whilst an atheist youth organisation was founded in Moscow which was both to study religious survivals and to fight them, among the intellectual and working youth of the Soviet capital. A further symptom of the growing anti-religious offensive was the publication, after an interruption of 18 years, of periodicals specialising in atheist propaganda. In 1959 the Society published in Moscow the monthly *'Nauka i Religiya'* (Science and Religion) and in the following year it brought out another monthly in Kiev called *'Voiovnichii Ateist'* (The Militant Atheist).

II. INDIRECT ANTI-RELIGIOUS PROPAGANDA

Only a very small part of the communist fight against religion is carried out with the help of special atheist organisations and by direct anti-religious propaganda. In overcoming 'religious survivals' the Soviet communists count much more on what may be described as indirect propaganda. This includes the growth of a new society in which religion has no part, technological achievements which as the communists believe dwarf all Biblical miracles as well as the development of a new superior communist morality. Theoretically speaking, the indirect anti-religious propaganda which primarily consists in the creation of certain sociological and technological facts calculated to outflank religion, could be victorious even if the direct propaganda conducted through pamphlets, lectures and noisy atheist campaigns proved a failure.

However, neither the new social order created by the communists nor the most fantastic technical developments have been sufficient in themselves to oust religious thinking from the minds of the Soviet citizens and to make them conscious followers of the materialist philosophy. Of course, in Russia as everywhere else, there are many people who are greedy for material comfort and whose God is the motor car or the television set, or would be if these amenities were more widespread in the Soviet Union. Such people are of as little use to the Communist Party as they are to religion. As a well-known Russian proverb says they are neither a candle to God nor a pitchfork to the devil. The Soviet régime would wish to put in the place of religion philosophical materialism and the allegiance to the collective but this is an ambitious aim. In Russia as in the capitalist world many people cast off religion not because they embrace a non-religious philosophical concept but out of petty personal egotism. This Soviet egotism differs from capitalist egotism only in that its material objectives are less spectacular.

The Promethean Illusion

The idea of playing off the material against the spiritual is no communist invention; it has accompanied mankind throughout its history and it is the idea of the golden calf and the idea of Prometheus. The Soviet communists have consciously built on the Promethean tradition. A Soviet state publishing house issued Aeschylus' *Prometheus in Chains* in a mass edition of 150,000 copies, not because of its literary value but because it was considered useful from an anti-religious propaganda point of view. The preface drew attention to the attraction which Prometheus, 'the noble fighter against the gods,' exercised on Karl Marx and other 'progressive thinkers'.[1] Nevertheless, even Prometheus is of use to the Soviet atheist cause only if one suppresses the essential fact that the authentic Prometheus, unlike his communist successor, was not a rebel against the divine in the general sense. According to the ancient myth he revolted against a tyrannical and evil Zeus — not against the God of love and righteousness of the Bible or against 'Allah, the Merciful, the Compassionate'.

In anticipating that the Promethean concept would work atheist miracles, the Soviet communists greatly misjudged the human frame of mind and especially the mentality of the peoples with whom they had to deal directly, the Russians in the first place. They had expected that the poor Russian muzhik could easily be impressed by new machines and technical devices and fall for a primitive confidence trick. Modern technology, which in other countries had become a matter of daily routine, was to be exploited in the Soviet Union as evidence of the superiority of the Soviet system over any other social order and as an illustration of the power of Soviet man and so as an anti-religious argument. For instance, anti-religious propagandists thought that the appearance of tractors would have a magic effect in the Russian countryside. An anti-religious pamphlet printed in the first Five Year Plan period was entitled *Prayers or Tractor*[2] and a widespread poster crudely elaborated on the alleged contradiction between 'cross and tractor'.[3]

[1] Aeschylus, *Prometei Prikovannii* (Prometheus in Chains), Moscow, 1956, pp. 10-12.
[2] Quoted in *Antireligioznik*, 1933, no. 1, p. 4.
[3] The poster is reproduced in *The Last Stand* by Edmund A. Walsh ,Boston 1931, p. 190.

The alternative, 'religion or tractor' with which the communists operated, never existed in the minds of the people for whom this propaganda was intended. The illusions about the 'atheist tractor' were therefore soon shattered, especially when the peasants affixed crosses to them and when priests celebrated thanksgiving services at their arrival in the villages.

Another Promethean illusion, but one which the communists will hardly ever recognise as one, can be epitomised with the slogan 'assault on heaven'. This expression hails from Karl Marx who used it with regard to the Paris Communards of 1871 who with the help of balloons outwitted the besiegers. This Marx quotation was dragged out by the Soviet communists when Russia's aeronautical developments started to make headway. In the Russian language, as in many others, there is only one expression for both 'heaven' and 'sky' and 'assault on heaven' therefore meant both the technical conquest of the air and the conquest of space where God was supposed to live according to primitive ideas, which the communists themselves shared, albeit in a negative sense. By proving that there is no God in heaven, the communists thought an important battle in the campaign against religion would be won.

The aircraft therefore appeared to the Soviet communists a much greater asset in the promotion of atheism than the tractor. Peasants in the backwoods of Siberia were taken on a plane ride to show them that there were no angels and no God in heaven. The Soviet writer Victor Fink described such a plane trip in his book *Jews in the Taiga*, first published in 1929.[1] More important than such attempts at individual conversions was the general ideological use made of the more spectacular Soviet air records. Great hopes were pinned, for instance, on Soviet stratosphere flights of which the first took place in October 1933 and which it was hoped, would become a daily occurrence.[2] However, before atheist propaganda was able to exploit the 'conquest of the stratosphere' it suffered a tremendous setback when the stratosphere plane 'SSSR' crashed after having reached the height of twenty-two kilometers.[3] As the communists considered these flights as a challenge to religion it is not to be wondered at that the more simple-minded believers considered the accident and the death of all three pilots as an act of divine punishment. So from the standpoint of anti-religious propaganda there was at first more lost than gained by the stratosphere flights. A few years later, this propaganda obtained another chance when Valery Chkalov made his famous flight across the Pole in 1937. The event was immediately

[1] Victor Fink, *Yevrei v Taige* (Jews in the Taiga), Moscow 1932, pp. 190–4.
[2] *Pravda*, October 2, 1933.   [3] *Pravda*, February 1, 1934.

1. A cartoon in the Soviet humorous journal *Krokodil* (February 29, 1960)
The caption reads 'Oh Lord, send at least one anti-religious lecturer into our district.'

2. Stalin—the new Star of Bethlehem.
The front page of the Soviet illustrated journal *Ogonyok* on the occasion of
Stalin's 70th birthday and on the eve of the Orthodox Christmas of 1949.

endowed with an anti-religious meaning, as can be seen from certain passages of Lebedev-Kumach's well-known poem '*The Ordinary Soviet Man*':

> 'About the Pole he proudly paces,
> The flow of rivers shifts to plan;
> Towering mountains he displaces —
> The ordinary Soviet man. . . .
> Rejecting miracle and fable,
> Driving the gods from out the sky,
> These ordinary Soviet people
> Work wonders every time they try.'[1]

However, the impact of Chkalov's flight on the believers was once again nil. Almost two decades elapsed before the old claim about the Soviet man 'driving the gods from out the sky' was revived. This happened in connection with the launching of the artificial earth satellites, the 'sputniks'. 'Now that the first two sputniks have appeared in the cosmos,' said the director of the Moscow planetarium, 'it is possible to say that we have visited heaven.' 'We have been where the eyes of the believer are directed with religious awe.' He added that the border between the 'heavenly' and the 'terrestrial' was now being obliterated.[2] In other words, after the launching of the sputniks, the believers had no alternative but to admit their error and to renounce their faith. The real reaction of the believers to the sputniks was quite different. For them the sputniks were no argument against the existence of God. They probably expressed thoughts similar to those which a Moscow workman had when leaving the Planetarium. He said, 'Well, well, who would have believed how wisely God has organised the world!' Madame Krupskaya, Lenin's widow, once quoted this statement to show how easily anti-religious propaganda could misfire.[3] Moreover, some of the believers are so suspicious of any official Soviet claim, that they refused to take the existence of even the 'sputniks' for granted and whilst such sceptics were but a small minority, it is characteristic that they should have existed at all.[4] October 4, 1957, the day of the appearance of the first sputnik, may have been a turning-point for many things in the world, but certainly not in the fight between Soviet Communism and religion.

[1] Quoted by E. Ya. Fortunatova, *Kniga dlya chtenya*, a textbook for primary schools, 1938, p. 190. Translated by Dr. W. A. Morison.

[2] V. Bazykin, 'The artificial earth satellites and the religious legends about heaven', *Kommunist Tadzhikistana*, April 6, 1958.

[3] *Izvestiya*, April 27, 1937.   [4] *Literaturnaya Gazeta*, October 30, 1958.

B

If even the 'sputniks' cannot turn believers away from religion, one can well imagine how little influence some other achievements must have exercised, such as the so-called *Great Construction Works of Communism*, the building of hydro-electric power stations, dams and canals. In the early fifties it was thought in all seriousness that they would have 'great importance in propagating the scientific world outlook and be an inexhaustibly rich source for printed and oral scientific-atheistic propaganda'.[1] However, the 'inexhaustible' source dried up very quickly. After Stalin's death the ambitious term 'Great Construction Works of Communism' was abandoned and at least one of the schemes — perhaps the most sensational one — namely the irrigation of the Kara Kum desert, was temporarily suspended.

The point is, of course, not whether the Soviet régime succeeds or fails in carrying out its plans to the full and according to schedule. The point is that the fulfilment of even the most exciting construction project and economic plan is no argument against religion and not understood as such by even the most simple-minded religious believer. On the contrary, most of the Soviet projects may, from the point of view of the believers, be desirable in themselves. Reasonable objections can refer only to the use which is made of them and to the sacrifices exacted for their implementation. Moreover, the believers of the Soviet Union are by no means idle onlookers at the creation of material values. The latter are the result of the joint efforts of both unbelievers and believers and for this reason alone, they are ill-suited for anti-religious propaganda purposes.

Religion and Soviet Society

It is difficult for the communists to accept that technology has not vanquished theology, but it is even more arduous for them to cope with the fact that religion has survived all communist social engineering. This has involved anti-religious propaganda in very considerable difficulties and contradictions and compelled the revision of one of its main tenets, namely the thesis about the class character of religion. In the early years of the Soviet régime there was from the Marxist point of view perhaps some justification in stating that religion served the 'class enemy'. In the light of the Marxist analysis the situation became different from the very moment when the Soviet leaders claimed to have built up a socialist society without class differences. Had the Churches disappeared from this society, then the communist view of

[1] P. Pavelkin, *Religioznye sueveriya i ikh vred*, (Religious superstitions and the harm they do), Moscow 1951, p. 162.

the class character of religion would have found striking confirmation. In reality, they showed no signs of disappearing and, if they lost some members they recruited new ones, including persons born under the new régime. The religious groups of the Soviet Union must now be recognised for what they are, that is organisations representing no longer any 'alien' classes nor even their remnants, but the three groups of which Soviet society consists. These are according to the official terminology — workers, collective farmers and the 'toiling intelligentsia'.

Of these three groups, the collective farmers include the largest number of religious believers, whilst religious survivals may be weakest among the 'toiling intelligentsia' especially in its highest income group. The industrial proletariat takes an intermediate position between the two other groups. The persistence of religious beliefs among the collective farmers is at complete variance with the original interpretation which the communists gave to the collectivisation process. They did not consider it as something belonging to the economic-social sphere alone, but attributed to it a major ideological significance. The collective farms were regarded as bulwarks of atheism in the countryside. The individual peasant was a religious being, so the communists thought, but the collective farmer will be an atheist. However, they soon recognised their mistake. The drought of 1934 led to a powerful manifestation of religious feelings among the collective farm members, who bombarded the local Soviet authorities with requests to authorise processions for rainfall and better harvest.[1] Frequently such processions were headed by the chairmen of the collective farms themselves, but this happened not only in the thirties, when the collective farm system was still in its infancy but also much later, after the Second World War.

Not only has collectivisation not eliminated religion among the rural population, but the economic shortcomings developing in collectivised agriculture became, even according to the communist view, an important cause for the 'perseverance of religious prejudices' in the Communist State. A speaker addressing the large all-Union anti-religious seminar held in Moscow in 1957 admitted that religion survived because there were backward collective and state farms as well as entire rural districts with low agricultural yields. The speaker thought that this interdependence between religious survival and agricultural crisis in the Soviet Union came to an end with the year 1953 when Khrushchev began to take things in hand.[2] One cannot agree with this qualification since the most important of the new measures in agricultural policy, the development of the virgin soil areas, with their uprooted, disgruntled

---

[1] Yaroslavsky, op. cit., vol. i, p. 386.   [2] *Nauka i Religiya*, Moscow 1957, p. 59.

and homesick inhabitants, became once again fertile ground for the spread of religious beliefs.

However, the greatest anomaly and at the same time the greatest practical and ideological defeat of Communism in the struggle against religion is its survival among the younger generation, among the people who have grown up under the Soviet régime and who are products of communist education in the schools and in the Young Communist League. Even if only two or three per cent of the young Soviet citizens were religious, and the proportion is likely to be greater, this would have to be considered a very serious setback for the whole Soviet educational system, which has such immense facilities for the conduct of anti-religious propaganda at its disposal. Religion among the young has two roots, of which the Communists themselves would admit only one, namely the influence which the older members of the family, either the mother or more often the grandmother, exercise on the boys and girls in their charge. The other reason why young people in Soviet Russia either persist in those religious beliefs which they have held since early childhood or turn towards religion at a later stage must be traced to the frustrations created by the new Soviet society and its dominant ideology. In other words the unfulfilled hunger of the human soul awakes religious feelings in the young. We shall mention only one single aspect of this spiritual starvation, the one which is tied up with de-Stalinisation.

For many years Stalin was held up as the great educator of Soviet youth, the man who had an unrivalled knowledge of its needs and aspirations, giving it the intellectual equipment for the building of the new society. 'Be like Stalin' was the Alpha and Omega of communist education. The Komsomol, it is true, bore the official name of 'Leninist Young Communist League' but in its day to day work Stalin assumed an ever-increasing prominence. Posters and newspapers spoke of the Leninist-Stalinist Komsomol. In Chelyabinsk, the local newspaper called itself *The Stalin Generation*, in Minsk *Stalin's Youth* and in Saratov *The Young Stalinist*.[1] The Stalin cult injected a strong irrational element into an otherwise sober and matter-of-fact doctrine, and for many it made the doctrine more attractive and more understandable.

And then came March 6, 1953. Stalin died. There was a very short moment when it seemed that the dead Stalin could become a more powerful weapon in the hands of the communist régime than the living Stalin had ever been. Immediately after his death several enthusiasts suggested that Stalin should be made an 'eternal member' of this or

---

[1] *Large Soviet Encyclopædia*, second edition, Moscow 1951, vol. ix, pp. 342–6.

that Soviet body. But Stalin's successors refused to make the jump into the metaphysical. They stopped the more spectacular expressions of the Stalin cult and this created a vacuum in the minds of the younger generation reared in the spirit of adoration for the man who had moulded the destinies of Russia for a quarter of a century.

The situation became much worse with the express devaluation of Stalin after the twentieth Communist Party Congress in February 1956. Uneasiness and doubts grew into demoralisation. It produced what the communist youth leaders themselves described as 'nihilism'. This term as the communists understand it covers any form and any expression of an anti-régime frame of mind from the lowest — hooliganism and drunkenness — to the highest, return to permanent and in particular to religious values. Even in the extent to which the 'nihilism' of youth finds non-religious expressions it is of a certain relevance to our subject. It deprives Communism of its argument that Communism and youth are identical notions and that Communism is therefore the to-day and to-morrow of mankind, whilst religion is the yesterday.

There is yet another category of human beings in Soviet Russia which, like youth, cuts across all social groups, the women. Their life has been thoroughly affected by the economic and social upheavals which the Soviet régime has carried out. Many millions of women were drawn into the great Soviet industrialisation process which, as a by-product at least, was meant to bring about a basic change in the Russian women's ideological outlook, including their attitude towards religion. At the same time the women were the target of a great deal of direct anti-religious propaganda. There have been few anti-religious pamphlets and few anti-religious lectures which did not make the point that religion enslaved woman and approved her exploitation by man.

The two-pronged offensive of social transformation and anti-religious propaganda has left a large proportion of Russia's women unaffected as far as their attitude towards religion is concerned. According to the estimates of anti-religious propagandists the women provide at least seventy per cent of all believers in the USSR[1] and in some religious sects the women constitute eighty to ninety per cent of the membership.[2] It would again be wrong to consider the women's loyalty to religious beliefs only as a hangover of the past which has diminishing importance with every passing year. As in the case of the young people, the conditions inherent in Soviet reality continuously weaken and even nullify both the anti-religious arguments which the régime puts forward and the positive aspects of the communist women's emancipation. The

[1] *Nauka i Religiya*, p. 61.   [2] *Nauka i Religiya*, p. 411.

heavy work women have to perform in Soviet industry and transport and the lack of security which has resulted from the frequent changes of communist family legislation have made it difficult to believe that Communism is women's greatest friend and religion their worst enemy.

A New Morality?

Millions of women, but also millions of men, in the Soviet Union seek refuge and safety in the religious morality which the communist morality has been unable to replace. Herein lies another failure of the great communist outflanking attempt which aimed at making religion in the Soviet Union a superfluous and dispensable thing. Communism does not know any morality *per se* but only a morality related to the needs of a political system and a political party. Communist morality is, therefore, liable to be changed with the shifts in the political and sociological situation. In the Communist State the nature of morality was determined at first by the necessities of the struggle for the destruction of the old social order and later by the needs dictating the building of a new society and the consolidation of the political power of the proletariat and its driving force, the Communist Party. The continuous recasting of communist morality can best be studied by the development of the Soviet family legislation to which we have referred already.

Every consecutive change of this legislation corresponded from the orthodox communist point of view to a new phase in the social, economic and political development. Therefore every new family law, however different from its predecessor, was always hailed by official propaganda as a progress and a just and correct solution. The first Soviet family and marriage decrees, signed in December 1917 by Lenin himself, authorised one-sided divorce but they did not yet recognise unregistered marriages. At the time the régime was out to fight the Church marriage which therefore had to be opposed by a new orderly system of official marriage registration.[1] As the influence of the Church diminished the marriage problem could be considered from a different angle. This is why the Marriage Code of 1926 attributed legal validity both to the registered marriage and to the factual marriage. The unregistered marriage was presumably considered as a step towards fully-fledged Communism for, according to a view widespread in the twenties, not only the State but also the family were to wither away in a communist society.[2] The content of socialist morality has varied not only in time but also in space. In the

[1] G. M. Sverdlov, *Sovetskoe Semeinoe Pravo* (Soviet Family Law), Moscow 1958, p. 71.

[2] Jessica Smith, *Women in Soviet Russia*, New York 1928, pp. 91–2.

Ukraine, for instance, not only could one marriage partner get a divorce without the presence of the other, as in the Russian Federation, but one partner could even register a marriage in the absence of the other. The latter, it is true, had the right to contract out of such a unilaterally registered marriage within one month.[1]

In 1936 the construction of Socialism was concluded and a new era begun. Licentiousness was now out of place and the consolidation of the socialist family became necessary from the régime's point of view. From now on both parties to a divorce were summoned to the Registry Office and the more often a person divorced, the higher became the fee he had to pay. Eight years later family legislation was revised once again. The colossal losses the Soviet Union had suffered during the war and the interests of postwar reconstruction demanded a stable family life. An Ukaz which the Praesidium of the Supreme Soviet issued on July 8, 1944, therefore set itself the task of making the dissolution of a marriage as difficult as possible. This Ukaz permitted divorce only if there were serious grounds for it and made it a very costly and complicated matter. In addition, it withdrew recognition from *de facto* marriages. It even discriminated against illegitimate children, who from now on received incomplete birth certificates, where the name of the father was lacking, for it was no longer permitted to establish the paternity of such children.[2]

The revolutionary change of Soviet family legislation as expressed in the Ukaz of July 8, 1944, was greeted like its predecessors, as an act of supreme wisdom and a new triumph of socialist morality. After ten or twelve years it was once again outdated. The Soviet State was then in the period of transition to Communism, the post-war reconstruction was long completed and there was no longer any need for such a rigorous morality and such strict family legislation as that decreed under Stalin in a quite different situation. In discussing these matters, it is only too easy to adopt a pharisaic attitude. Family legislation even in non-communist states is the object of frequent experiments and it would be quite wrong to gloss over this fact, but the legislators in democratic countries do not regard themselves as the creators of a new morality. Whatever their legislation may stipulate, the representatives of religious morality are free to defend their point of view. In Soviet Russia, on the other hand, any open polemics with official morality are impossible.

The problem of morality cannot be confined to the sphere of family and sex. If we view it in the wider context of the simple and challenging

---

[1] Jessica Smith, op. cit., p. 113.
[2] A full English text of the Ukaz was published in *Soviet War News*, July 12, 1944.

question, 'What is a good man?' then we shall find even more how inadequate communist morality is. The question has been asked count-less times in the Soviet Union but the questioner has never received a straight and satisfactory answer. The question how to be a good man is usually transformed into the quite different question of how to be a good man devoted to the homeland and to the Party. The non-political good man cannot and must not exist in the Communist State.

Only a few particularly far-sighted communists have ever understood that the time-serving communist morality places Communism in a weak position *vis-à-vis* the Churches. One of these exceptions was Nadezhda Krupskaya. In 1937, the twentieth year of Soviet power, she gave a warning to her party comrades which may thus be summarised: Don't underrate religion as a source of morality. For centuries religion has taught people what is good and what is bad and you cannot eradicate it unless you do as the Church does. But we have not yet been able to supersede the Church satisfactorily and many parents are still impressed by the argument that children receiving religious education behave better than those without it.[1] This statement applies not only to the year in which it was made but in all probability to a later period as well, for the precepts of communist morality, always synchronised with the latest shifts of the party line, are still bound to produce the same feeling of frustration as they did on the eve of World War II.

The Communist Cultural Revolution

As Communism set out to produce a new morality it also claimed to carry out a cultural revolution and to create a new way of life. Both were expected to strike at the root of religious beliefs. There is no doubt that the Soviet cultural revolution has been in many ways successful if we look at it in the same way as the Soviet industrial revolution and judge it by the number of cultural and educational establishments which have been created since the communist régime took power. The success of the cultural revolution is also undeniable if the spread of literacy is to be considered the chief criterion. However, the communists them-selves would not be satisfied with such a superficial definition, which views the cultural revolution only in terms of statistics relating to schools, libraries and books. The cultural revolution as they originally understood it was to bring about very sweeping qualitative changes, and it is in this respect that it has failed. The content of the new communist culture was redefined in the same way as communist morality.

At first, the communist efforts were focused on building up a new

[1] Izvestiya, April 27, 1937.

proletarian class culture, growing as it were on a virgin soil. In the early thirties, proletarian culture was abandoned in favour of a 'socialist culture' claiming lineage with the great cultural achievements of the past. Despite the change of label, the value of Soviet cultural and artistic creation remained disappointing from the point of view of the communists themselves. The rhetorical question 'where are our Shchedrins and Gogols?', 'where are our own great writers?' became almost a cry of despair.

The less attractive the present, the more fascinating grew the past — the literary and artistic works of the pre-communist period. The Soviet communists claimed to be the custodians of these works irrespective of the religious elements woven into many of them. Certainly, they did try to distort them and they also tried to separate art from the spiritual roots of its inspiration. Nevertheless, the fact that the Russian communists had to operate with a religiously influenced national culture is one of the basic difficulties of Soviet atheism.

The communist anti-religious propagandists have always been painfully aware of the fact that the love of God has inspired many works of Russian literature and art, whilst the hatred and rejection of God has not left any mark on either of them. Anti-religious Soviet poetry is usually so dated and of such scanty literary merit that it is normally omitted from the collected works of the poet who produced it. The atheist bias in Soviet belles-lettres is usually implicit rather than explicit, and they are, therefore, of little use from a militant anti-religious point of view. Its outstanding representative during the period between the two wars, therefore, threw out a most eloquent challenge to the Soviet Writers when addressing their first congress in 1934. 'The revolution, he said, has overthrown the gods, the devils and the saints, but where is this doom of the gods described? Where can we find a description of the disintegration of this terrible power, a description of the fall and the dying of religion — this grandiose social phenomenon of the epoch of the proletarian revolution?'[1] The Soviet writers have never properly responded to Yaroslavsky's admonition, and the imaginary subject of the death of religion in Russia has never captivated their imagination.

Far from fighting religion, some writers have borrowed the titles of their books from the Bible so as to stimulate interest in them. Nicholas Virta's play *Our Daily Bread* and Vladimir Dudintsev's novel *Not by Bread Alone* may be cited here as cases in point. These writers may not have been aware what disservice they did to the atheist cause, but Soviet pedagogists are conscious of the fact that the Russian language

[1] Yaroslavsky, op. cit., vol. iv, p. 395.

with its Biblical, religious and ecclesiastical expressions continues to be an ally of religion in the fight against atheism. They believe that the danger of religious contamination of the young is always present as long as certain terms are not ousted from the Russian vocabulary. Indeed, a pamphlet which the Soviet mass education society published in 1955 warned parents not to use inadvertently words like 'God', 'angel' and 'devil' or expressions like 'God preserve', lest religious ideas should take root in the minds of the children.[1] Strangely enough some communist leaders have been the main offenders against this injunction of the anti-religious propagandists. Both Stalin and Krushchev have been fond of talking of 'God', the 'devil' and 'angels' not in a religious sense, of course, but in their desire to speak in a popular way even at the price of perpetuating 'religious prejudices'. A number of consistent atheists among Russia's linguistic scholars pleaded for the exclusion of the word 'God' from the dictionary, realising that the survival of religious terms might breed religious thinking. This idea was not adopted, for the strange reason that the word 'God' was needed for anti-religious propaganda.

There are some other ikonoclastic ideas of the communist cultural revolution which never got beyond the planning stage: for instance, the reform of the calendar. Many communists and especially the members of the League of Militant Godless, thought it intolerable that the Soviet régime should continue to count the years from the Birth of Christ. In 1929, several alternative proposals were submitted to the public as to how the Christian Era might be replaced. For instance, the introduction of a Proletarian Era was suggested to begin with the year 1890, the first in which the European working class celebrated May Day. The proletarian year was to begin, of course, on May 1 itself and not on January 1. Others recommended a Soviet Era to begin on November 7, 1917. A third suggestion was to bring the calendar year in line with the Soviet economic year, which began on October 1.[2] Also the days of the week were to change their names. One reformer wanted to call them 'Trade Union Day', 'Culture Day', 'Party Day', 'Soviet Day', etc. Another demanded the introduction of a special weekly 'Day of Godlessness', a third more prosaically suggested 'First Working Day', 'Second Working Day', etc. until the weekly 'Day of Rest' was reached. The more 'moderate' communists, including Oleshchuk, wanted to retain the old names of the days of the week except the two which in the

---

[1] E. I. Perovsky, *Ateisticheskoe vospitanie detei v shkole i seme* (Atheist education in school and family), Moscow 1955, p. 34.

[2] *Bezbozhnik*, March 10, 1929.

Russian language have a clear religious meaning, namely Saturday — in Russian *subbota* which is derived from the biblical sabbath — and Sunday — in Russian *voskresenie* or resurrection.[1]

Nothing came of these radical reforms. Having the rather short-lived experiment of the French Revolutionary Calendar before their eyes, the authorities shrank from throwing the Christian Calendar overboard. They also feared that the introduction of a new calendar might further complicate relations with the outside world and were probably also convinced that the masses of the people would not support such a daring venture which the members of the godless organisation propagated. Only in one point did the latter score a short-lived success. In 1929 the so-called uninterrupted working week was introduced and Sunday was abolished as the universal day of rest. On every day of the week five-sixths of the workers were working and one sixth resting. In the towns this made the religious observance of Sunday virtually impossible, but the Russian village was little affected by the 'uninterrupted week'. In 1940, Russia reverted to the seven-day week and Sunday came into its own again. The Russian communists could have avoided this loss of face, had they drawn a further lesson from the failures of the French Revolution, which tried to replace Sunday by the 'decadi'. When this reform was discussed in the revolutionary parliament the famous Abbé Grégoire told the deputy Romme, the inventor of the new calendar, 'Le dimanche existait avant toi, il te survivra.'[2] These prophetic words could have been addressed with equal validity to the Soviet Government.

The ousting of religious holidays also played an important part in the communist cultural revolution. They were to be replaced by new communist holidays 'in honour of the victory over the class enemy and in commemoration of the great class struggles of the past'.[3] In practice, there could be no question of any real replacement. All the authorities have achieved is a coexistence between religious and secular holidays. The celebration of Christmas and Easter, it is true, is no longer and can no longer be held as before but these feasts have remained for millions of people in Russia the most sacred days of the year.

As to the holidays introduced by the communists, they have undergone considerable changes even in the, comparatively and historically speaking, short period of Soviet rule. The Lenin Commemoration Day, January 22, ceased to be a public holiday in 1952. The Day of the

---

[1] *Bezbozhnik*, November 24, 1929.
[2] M. Grégoire, *Histoire des sectes religieuses*, Paris 1828, p. 122.
[3] *Bezbozhnik*, January 7, 1923.

Stalin Constitution, December 5, became the Day of the Soviet Constitution, thus losing one of its main original purposes, the glorification
of the leader. December 21, Stalin's birthday (in the last years of
Stalin rule a holiday *de facto* though not *de jure*) was ignored almost as
soon as he had closed his eyes for ever. On the other hand, the October
Revolution Anniversary and May 1 have genuinely become part of the
new secular communist civilisation. They tend to assume the character
of popular feasts like July 14 in France and so lose much of their
original ideological importance and sharpness. Even Church dignitaries
would refer to November 7 as an 'all-national holiday'.[1] May 1 too has
lost in the Soviet Union its previous traditional meaning. It has become
a travesty of what it originally was and what the initiators of the feast,
the leaders of the West European labour movement, originally foresaw.
In Russia, May 1 has long ceased to be the feast of liberated labour
and international brotherhood. Rather has it become a manifestation
for plan fulfilment, labour discipline, communist militarism and split-
ting the working class of the world. Soviet May Day propaganda was
frequently characterised by violent attacks against those sections of the
working class which refused to recognise Moscow's leadership.[2] The
ideological content of both the Soviet May Day and the October
Revolution Anniversary changes with every move of Soviet home and
foreign policy. These perpetual shifts of emphasis are faithfully reflected
in the slogans which the Central Committee of the Communist Party
issues on the eve of the two feasts. If one studies and compares these
slogans throughout the years one cannot help realising the opportunistic
tactical character and the inner poverty of the two principal Soviet
holidays. One can also understand better the attraction which religious
holidays continue to exercise.

Not only has the nation as a whole its great festive days, but also the
individual — the day of wedding, for instance, and, in a Christian
country, the day of baptism. These days too were to be brought within
the scope of the communist cultural revolution, but with even smaller
success than in the case of the public holidays. November 7 and May 1
are now being celebrated more ostentatiously than Christmas and
Easter, but the régime has found no substitute for Christian wedding
and even less for Christian baptism, despite many attempts and experiments in this respect.

[1] See Patriarch Alexis's telegram to Khrushchev, *Zhurnal Moskovskoi Patriarkhii*,
no. 11, 1958, p. 3.
[2] E.g. in 1932. May Day slogan no. 9 ran as follows 'Social-fascists-inciters of a
new imperialistic war of intervention against the Soviet Union and China! Down with
the Second International and its "left" agency!' *Pravda*, April 27, 1932.

In the early years of the Soviet régime so-called 'Red Weddings' were celebrated and some factories seemed to have worked out a regular ritual, with the head of the then existing factory committee acting as 'master of ceremonies'.[1] In place of the baptism the so-called 'Oktyabrina' was introduced at which the child was dedicated to the new era which started in October (in Russian Oktyabr) 1917. Instead of being christened, the child was to be 'octobered' and, if possible to receive a new revolutionary first name instead of the old-fashioned Christian name. A few revolutionary enthusiasts really called their children Oktyabrina, May, Svoboda (freedom), Komintern, Revolyutsiya (Revolution), Lenin, Ninel (meaning Lenin in reverse), Lentrozina (contracted from Lenin, Trotsky and Zinovev), Rem (the first letters of *R*evolution, *E*lectrification and *M*oscow) and Kim (the Russian abbreviation of Communist Youth International). Some of these names were out of date even before their recipients had grown up and the unfortunate 'Lentrozina' which glorified the 'enemies of the people' Trotsky and Zinovev, was quickly transformed from an expression of revolutionary enthusiasm into a manifestation of treason and counter-revolution.

These eccentricities of name-giving were soon abandoned and also the 'Red Weddings' and the 'Oktyabriny' fell into oblivion. After World War II the experiment with secular rites was resumed in new form. The 'Red Weddings', in particular were revived as 'Komsomol Weddings' and borrowed certain external features, especially the white bridal garments, from the religious marriage customs. Despite such efforts it is not very likely that the Party will ever score a complete victory in the 'battle of the wedding'. Even a registration office with flowers, cosy armchairs, good carpets and smartly dressed officials cannot exercise the same emotional attraction as a church service. Naturally, in the Soviet Union, as elsewhere, there are many people who cling to a religious wedding not for religious reasons but out of love for tradition and pomp. A church wedding in the Communist State is therefore not in every single instance a victory of religion over Communism, but it is in every single case a defeat for the materialistic philosophy.

III. FORMS OF RELIGIOUS SURVIVAL

Religion has survived in Soviet Russia in countless forms and also in many formless ways. As far as the religious bodies properly speaking are concerned, one might divide them into three groups, a division

[1] Jessica Smith, op. cit., p. 93.

which coincides with the one to which the Soviet authorities themselves have adhered ever since 1943–4 when they redefined their policy towards religion. The first group comprises one Church only, the Russian Orthodox Church which, as we shall see in the next chapter, occupies a unique and exceptional place.

The second group of religious bodies and Churches are those which fall into the competence of a Soviet State authority called the Council for the Affairs of Religious Cults. Official Soviet sources have never published a complete list of the denominations which the latter recognises and we know the scope of its activities only very approximately. The first official announcement referring to the Council said it would look after 'the following religious associations: the Armenian-Gregorian, Old Believers, Catholic, Greek-Catholic and Lutheran Churches; the Moslem, Judaic and Buddhist religions and sectarian organisations'.[1] It can be seen from this announcement that at the time of the formation of the 'Council' the authorities themselves had not yet made a proper up-to-date inventory of the religious forces of the Soviet Union. Some bodies were referred to as 'associations', others more vaguely as 'religions' and others were simply summed up as 'sectarian organisations'. The Greek-Catholics were soon officially 'unchurched' and deleted from the groups for which the Council for the Affairs of Religious Cults was responsible.

A somewhat fuller picture of institutionalised religious life in the Soviet Union after World War II could be obtained from the list of the participants in the so-called 'Conference in Defence of Peace of all Churches and Religious Organisations in the USSR' which was held in the *Troitse-Sergieva Lavra* (Monastery) of Zagorsk in May 1952. Although the official title of the conference expressly claimed that *all* Churches and Religious Associations were represented it must be clear that this claim was exaggerated, for it referred only to such bodies as were recognised at the time by the Soviet authorities. In addition to the Orthodox Churches of Russia and Georgia, these bodies were the following:

(1) Armenian Church
(2) Evangelical Lutheran Church (only the Churches of Latvia and Estonia were represented)
(3) Catholic Church (only its Latvian and Lithuanian dioceses were represented)
(4) All-Union Council of Evangelical Christians/Baptists

---

[1] *Soviet War News*, July 4, 1944.

(5) Old Believers (five groups were represented, namely two national bodies and three local groups from Moscow, Latvia and Lithuania)

(6) The All-Union Council of Seventh Day Adventists

(7) The Reformed (Calvinist) Church of the Transcarpathian Province

(8) The Methodist Church of Estonia

(9) The Community of Spiritual Christians (Molokans) of Baku and Tiflis

(10) Moslems (four different regional Moslem Councils were represented)

(11) Central Buddhist Council

(12) Jewish Communities of Moscow and Kiev.[1]

The list of the delegates to the Zagorsk religious peace conference greatly enhanced our knowledge of the officially recognised religious bodies in the USSR but at the same time it showed the limits of Soviet religious tolerance. Some religious organisations, for instance, Lutherans Catholics and Jews enjoy recognition locally but have no central organisation covering the whole country.

The third group of religious bodies in the Soviet Union comprises those which are either ignored by the authorities or persecuted as illegal organisations. We shall see later that this 'religion of the Catacombs' in the Soviet Union has many shapes and forms ranging from the Greek Catholic Church to the small conspiratoral circles of Jehovah's Witnesses. Finally, there is the wide range of personal religious beliefs, that personal living and walking with God, which is quite unconnected with any institutionalised church organisation, whether legal or illegal. This most intimate side of the religious life of Russia defies any factual description, but it must be present in our mind, otherwise our ideas about the survival of religion in Russia will be one-sided and incomplete.

---

[1] *Conference in Defence of Peace of all Churches and Religious Associations in the USSR, Documents and Materials*, published by the Moscow Patriarchate, Moscow 1952, pp. 12–19.

II

The Russian Orthodox Church

I. CHURCH-STATE RELATIONS

The Strength of the Church

The Russian Orthodox Church is the most important single spiritual entity in Russia.[1] Czarist statistics put the Orthodox proportion of the population as high as 69·9 per cent out of a total of 163 million inhabitants.[2] The percentage of the real Orthodox Church membership was smaller, since the Czarist régime considered as Orthodox everyone who belonged to the State Church as it were theoretically and historically. This included not only the Old Believers, whose ancestors had broken away from the official Church in the second half of the seventeenth century, but also the members of the sects who held theological ideas devoid of any connection with Orthodoxy. Nevertheless, despite all defections, the Russian Orthodox Church was Russia's Church *par excellence* and this she remained when Russia became the Soviet Union.

There are no statistics available as to the Church's numerical strength after World War II, only a wide range of conflicting and vague estimates.

[1] The Russian Orthodox Church is the one Church of the Soviet Union about which there is no lack of literature. The fullest account is the work of John Shelton Curtiss, *The Russian Church and the Soviet State 1917–1950*, Boston 1953. Other works on the subject written by Western and Russian emigré authors and likely to prove particularly helpful to the student include Efraim Briem, *Kommunismus und Religion in der Sowjetunion*, Basel, no date. Julius F. Hecker, *Religion and Communism, State of Religion and Atheism in Soviet Russia*, London 1933. Matthew Spinka, *The Church in Soviet Russia*, New York 1956. Paul Anderson, *People, Church and State in Modern Russia*, London 1944. *Il Christianesimo nell' Unione Sovietica*, Roma 1948 (edited by W. de Vries, SJ.) Gleb Rar, *Plenennaya Tserkov* (Captive Church), Frankfurt 1954, Wilhelm de Vries, *Kirche und Staat in der Sowjetunion*, München, 1959.

First-hand information about the state of the Russian Orthodox Church and her official attitude towards both the Soviet régime and world affairs must be primarily obtained from the 'Journal of the Moscow Patriarchate' — *Zhurnal Moskovskoi Patriarkhii* (*Zh.M.P.*), and from other publications of the Patriarchal Church, such as 'One Church' (*Yedinaya Tserkov*), the organ of the Moscow Patriarch's Exarch for North America.

[2] *Ezhegodnik Rossii za 1914*, St. Petersburg 1915, p. 99.

The Orthodox Church has not committed herself officially on this matter. She has only stated through her authoritative spokesmen that the number of her churches was about 20,000.[1] According to another statement, also from an authoritative source, the number of her parishes was 22,000. From this it has been concluded that the number of believers must be in the neighbourhood of 45,000,000 assuming that there are on the average 2,000 faithful per church.[2] A more realistic estimate puts the number of practising Orthodox Christians as somewhere between twenty and thirty million.[3] But even if the lowest estimate were accepted there is little doubt that the supporters of the Russian Orthodox Church are, after four decades of communist rule, much stronger than the members of the Soviet Communist Party and also more numerous than the adherents of all other religious communities put together. At the same time it is only fair to point out that the Orthodox Church is likely to include a much larger proportion of collective, sociological or traditional Christians and a much smaller number of personal Christians than some of the smaller Christian denominations of the Soviet Union.

From the very first day of its existence the Soviet régime considered the Russian Orthodox Church exceptionally important. It was the Church which the Communist Party found at its seats of power in Petrograd and Moscow. The Church which the communists were confronted with was, however, not quite the same as that which had served the last Romanov Czars. Two days before the Bolshevik *coup d'état* a Russian Church Council (*sobor*) elected a Patriarch, the first since 1721, when Peter the Great abolished the patriarchal dignity. It was under the leadership of this new Patriarch Tikhon that the Church fought and anathemised the communist Government, thus providing a kind of spiritual backbone to the counter-revolution. This interference of the Church in politics was only one aspect of Russian Orthodoxy, but it was the aspect to which the régime paid exclusive attention. The communists, unlike the believers, are unable to discriminate between the human and divine elements of the Church. They therefore failed to realise at first that the Orthodox Church could not be judged exclusively by the doings of political priests who supported extreme right-wing organisations and that the Church was something more than an instrument of the opponents of Communism. Only when the reminiscences of the Czarist régime and the Civil War receded into the

---

[1] Metropolitan Nikolay, *The Status of Religion in the USSR, One Church*, vol. ix 1955, no. 11–12, p. 244.

[2] *Vestnik Russkogo Studencheskogo Christianskogo Dvizheniya*, vol. iv, 1957, no. 47 p. 24.

[3] *International Review of Missions*, October 1958, pp. 442–3.

background did the communists arrive at a different assessment of the Church. They finally succeeded in regarding it as an expression of the cultural and political continuity of the Russian people.

From a purely legal point of view the Russian Orthodox Church lost its character of an established Church only by the decree about the separation of Church and State of January 19, 1918. The decree proclaimed the absolute equality of all religious communities in Russia and expressly abolished all the legal distinctions which had previously existed, with regard to the non-established religious groups. Nevertheless the Russian Orthodox Church never enjoyed a position of strict equality in the Communist State. Its outstanding importance on the 'religious front' always secured it a special status. At first it was singled out for special martyrdom and later benefited from special tolerance. The period of tolerance can only be seen in the right perspective if it is borne in mind that a period of violent persecution preceded it.

Seen in retrospect it almost seems a miracle that the Russian Orthodox Church did not disintegrate and that after a time of bitter trial it was able to reassemble the scattered sheep and rebuild the framework of its organisation. All prerequisites for its annihilation seemed in being. The assets which the Soviet régime held when fighting the Church were not only superior material power but also superior tactical skill, in which many ecclesiastical leaders were lacking. The Soviet régime succeeded in falsifying the issues at stake and manœuvred the Church into a position where it did not appear to be fighting for the defence of the faith against unbelief but for the retention of church property with the help of which the Government wanted to feed the starving people. The government decree which put the Church into this most awkward position was issued on February 23, 1922. It stipulated that churches must surrender all objects of value for the purposes of famine relief. The decree brought Orthodox religious resistance into the open. Bishops, priests and believers, following the injunctions of Patriarch Tikhon, the head of the Church, resisted the confiscation of church treasures. This resistance led to incidents and riots in various parts of the country and these again resulted in arrests and trials.

The Schism of the 'Renovators'

However, the question of the church treasures also divided the Church itself. A number of ecclesiastical dignitaries refused to accept the lead of the Patriarch and agreed that sacred vessels should be used to overcome a grave national emergency. This enabled the régime to play off one section of the clergy against the other. Bishops, priests and professors of canon law could be brought before the courts as witnesses for the prosecution, testifying against such bishops and priests as had taken a recalcitrant attitude towards the question of the church treasures. Whether the confiscation of the sacred vessels was a major help in fighting the famine is most debatable, but it is beyond dispute that the question had an enormous impact on further developments within the Orthodox Church. The division which it created undermined church discipline, prompted Patriarch Tikhon in May 1922 to surrender his functions to another Orthodox dignitary, Metropolitan Agathangel of Yaroslavl and finally led to a church schism.

From July 1922 a number of schismatic Orthodox bodies entered the Russian religious scene and were an important force in Russia's ecclesiastical life in the twenties. They melted away during the thirties and entirely disappeared at the beginning of the forties. The first schismatic group to make its appearance was the 'Living Church' which at first was only the name of a definite ecclesiastical group but later it became a popular collective term for the entire church 'reform' movement. In addition to the 'Living Church' proper a 'Union of Church Regeneration' was founded as well as a 'Union of Parishes of the Ancient Apostolic Church'. There were also some smaller, purely local, groups including one describing itself as 'Russian People's Church'. These groups were not new Churches but church parties. Between them they formed a kind of coalition, the main organ of which became the so-called 'Supreme Church Administration'. They all differed from the Patriarchal Church by their servile pro-Soviet attitude and a demonstratively-proclaimed sympathy for Communism. Their common political views were enshrined in an 'Address to the Government', which they adopted in 1923 at an 'All-Russian Church Council' (sobor) which was summoned by the 'Supreme Church Administration'. The address said that Soviet power was fighting for the ideals of God's kingdom and that every member of the Church should not only be loyal to the authorities but actually help them in the struggle against the evil in the world.[1]

People joined the reform movement — its supporters were later referred to as 'Obnovlentsy' or 'Renovators' — for a variety of reasons. Some welcomed it because they wanted a progressive Church dissociating itself from the Czarist past. Others approved of the liturgical reforms which it introduced. For instance, renovator-priests conducted services in Russian instead of the traditional Church Slavonic and celebrated the eucharistic ceremony openly before the congregation and

[1] W. C. Emhardt, *Religion in Soviet Russia*, Milwaukee–London 1929, p. 96.

not behind the altar-screen.[1] Many parish priests or members of the 'white clergy' as they were called in Russia, thought it advantageous to join a movement which clearly championed their interests against the 'black clergy', namely the monks, from whom the Old Church recruited its bishops. The movement demanded that married priests should be able to be made bishops, and the new schismatic Church had indeed a large number of married bishops, consecrated in a completely uncanonical way. Moreover, some of the parish priests who had in the past been extreme monarchists and anti-Semites sought safety by adopting a left-wing point of view which they demonstrated by their adherence to the new Church.

To the Soviet authorities, schism within the Russian Orthodox Church was highly welcome. The Agitation and Propaganda Department of the Communist Party stated frankly that the disintegration of the hostile camp must be used to bring about its full and final collapse. There was plenty of sarcastic communist comment about the Renovators and cartoons of its leaders, especially of Metropolitan Vvedensky, one of its most vocal personalities. In the view of the Party the Living Church remained an enemy even if it could be exploited for a time. Once this period was over it was expected to become a cover for counter-revolutionary anti-Soviet forces despite its frantic attempts to come to terms with the régime. As the communists saw it, the Old Church represented the counter-revolutionary upper class and the New Church the petty bourgeoisie, which was likewise bound to come into conflict with Soviet power.[2]

Nevertheless the Living or Renovated Church enjoyed, within limits, a privileged position. It was allowed to have a periodical, it was able to train priests both in Moscow and Leningrad, and the reformist 'Supreme Church Administration' was until 1927 the only officially recognised Orthodox Church body. What was even more important, the authorities strengthened the position of the 'Renovators' indirectly by arresting and deporting their rivals, the bishops who had remained loyal to Patriarch Tikhon. For a very short time it seemed as if the reform movement was about to win in the conflict within the Church. In Moscow, for instance, all the Orthodox churches except four or five were temporarily under its control.[3] In the whole of Russia the schismatic Church boasted at one moment 12,593 parishes, 16,540 members of the clergy and 108 dioceses. But although inaugurated with such aplomb, its appearance

---

[1] G. P. Fedotoff, *The Russian Church since the Revolution*, London 1928, p. 62.
[2] I. Stepanov, *O Zhivoi Tserkvi* (About the Living Church), Moscow 1922, p. 4.
[3] Emhardt, op. cit., p. 318.

on the Russian religious horizon was only an episode. The majority of Orthodox laymen viewed the 'Renovators' with suspicion and hostility, and it was their negative attitude which doomed the whole experiment to failure. At the same time, the Living Church lost its original usefulness to the régime because the Old Church adopted, gradually but surely, an attitude of loyalty towards Soviet rule.

Patriarch Tikhon and his Succession

The first move made by the Old Church in this new direction was the amazing *volte-face* of Patriarch Tikhon. The Patriarch, or Citizen Belavin as the Soviet press described him, was a prisoner of the GPU from August 5, 1922, and his trial was thoroughly prepared. The charges to be made against him were to include 'counter-revolutionary activities', connections with white emigrés, especially the emigré Russian Orthodox Church which had its centre in Karlovac (Yugoslavia) and his personal responsibility for the widespread resistance to the confiscation of church treasures. The Tikhon trial never took place. Instead, the press published a statement by the Patriarch in which he promised that he would no longer be an enemy to Soviet power.[1] He also disowned the monarchists, both in Russia and abroad, with whom he had 'completely and resolutely' broken off all relations. The statement secured the Patriarch's release from prison. This gesture by the Government in turn gave rise to a second statement in which Tikhon expressed in greater detail regret at his various anti-Soviet actions.[2]

Tikhon's recantation was the prelude to that new relationship between the official 'Old' Orthodox Church and the Soviet State which ultimately culminated in the *modus vivendi* of 1943. Even after Tikhon's statements the Orthodox Church had to endure much suffering and persecution, but they were nevertheless a turning-point. In the two years which the Patriarch had still to live he never went back on his profession of loyalty, but re-emphasised and extended it several times, the last time in a most explicit document which he signed on the day he died, April 7, 1925.

In return for Tikhon's statements of loyalty the Soviet Government formally renounced all judicial proceedings against him and allowed him to play an active part again in church affairs. Although Tikhon was not able to carry out the task he had set himself, namely to heal the church schism, at the end of his life he again acquired considerable prestige and his funeral was an impressive religious manifestation attended by five Metropolitans, sixty-three bishops, a large number of priests and vast crowds of people.

[1] *Izvestiya*, June 27, 1923.   [2] *Izvestiya*, July 4, 1923.

The death of Tikhon greatly increased the chaos within the Russian Orthodox Church. Not only did the fight between 'Renovators' and the Patriarchal Church continue, but even within the latter there were various groups fighting with one another for influence and leadership. The Soviet authorities did everything to increase this confusion, for instance by arresting in December 1925 Metropolitan Peter Polyansky, who had taken over the provisional direction of the Church and by suddenly releasing from exile in May 1926 the Metropolitan Agathangel, probably in the hope of creating a new pretender for the post of the Patriarchal locum tenens. From the unedifying struggle of Metropolitans and Archbishops fighting each other and intriguing against one another, Metropolitan Sergius Starogorodsky (1867–1944) of Nizhnii Novgorod finally emerged as victor and as the widely recognised acting or deputy locum tenens of the Patriarchal see. Metropolitan Peter Polyansky remained nominal locum tenens but he never exercised any effective jurisdiction again. Canonically however, he was the head of the Russian Orthodox Church until his death in 1936, and prayers were said for him during the Liturgy in all Patriarchal churches.

Metropolitan Sergius

When Metropolitan Sergius took over the government of the Church in December 1925, his position was precarious, not only inside the Church but even more so *vis-à-vis* the régime. He had no official recognition and was put in prison twice, once at the beginning of 1926 and again in December of the same year. It was during his second term of imprisonment, which lasted nearly four months, that a new and doubtful armistice was worked out between the régime and the prisoner. Indeed, the beginning of Sergius's effective jurisdiction must be dated not from December 1925 but from his second release from prison at the end of March 1927. It was only then that he was able to set up a proper ecclesiastical administration. But what really safeguarded the position of Sergius was his statement of July 29, 1927, which amounted to a total identification of himself with the Soviet Union. It was signed not only by Sergius but by all the members of the newly-formed Holy Synod. One of the signatories was Alexis Shimansky who later became Patriarch of Moscow and all Russia. The statement of Metropolitan Sergius and of his Holy Synod pledged not only loyalty to the Soviet State, as Tikhon had done before, but it was an unreserved profession of Soviet patriotism. The joys and successes of the Soviet State, so its most crucial sentence said, were the Church's joys and successes, the setbacks which the State suffered were the Church's own setbacks. Any blow directed against the

Soviet Union, the statement added, whether war, boycott or even treacherous murder, was a blow against the Church.[1]

The reference to treacherous murder in the statement was not a vague and general one. It alluded to the murder of Voikov, the Soviet ambassador to Warsaw, an event which occurred only about six weeks before Sergius's pronouncement and which may, at least to some extent, have determined its tenor. In a certain sense the Church was involved, albeit innocently, in the assassination. Voikov's murderer, a nineteen-year-old Russian emigré, was a devoted, though misguided, member of the Church. He had witnessed the Revolution as a little boy and he could never forget that the communists had converted into a dancing hall the church of Samara, where he was a server.[2] His soul was filled with such bitterness that he stooped to murder. His deed was bound to discredit the Church in Russia, and may have made it necessary for Sergius to issue a more outspoken pro-régime statement than he originally intended.

In return for his statement Sergius obtained from the régime the recognition of the central organisation of the Orthodox Church which he headed himself. He also obtained permission to move from Nizhnii Novgorod to Moscow and to publish the *Journal of the Moscow Patriarchate*. The armistice which Sergius concluded with the State was far from meeting with general approval within the Patriarchal Church. Whilst Sergius and those around him chose the road of collaboration and subservience to the State, there were others who preferred the road of martyrdom and who rejected his statement of July 29, 1927, and the frame of mind which it expressed. This opposition was weak in terms of power but it had great moral weight. It included most of the ecclesiastical leaders whom the communists had put into prison or exiled, especially a large group of church dignitaries interned in the ill-famed island camp of Solovki in the White Sea. Also Metropolitan Peter, the lawful locum tenens of the Church, disowned Sergius which has been interpreted as depriving the statement of the latter of its canonical validity.[3] Of more immediate concern to Sergius was the resistance which his policy and jurisdiction encountered among the Russian Church leaders who for the time being had still escaped arrest. The centres of active resistance against the Sergius administration were Leningrad, where Metropolitan Joseph led the opposition, Yaroslavl,

[1] *Patriarkh Sergii i ego dukhovnoe nasledstvo* (Patriarch Sergius and his spiritual heritage), Moscow 1947, p. 61.
[2] *The Times*, June 17, 1927.
[3] Matthew Spinka, *The Church in Soviet Russia*, New York Oxford University Press, 1956 p. 71.

the see of Metropolitan Agathangel, and various episcopal sees in the Urals and Siberia.[1] At first it seemed that the fight against this opposition would be arduous and protracted, especially in Leningrad where the 'Josephites', the supporters of Metropolitan Joseph, had the solid support of the 'reactionary groups of the clergy and the believers'.[2] Sergius entrusted a gifted young bishop, Nikolay Yarushevich, with fighting the Josephite schism. Although Nikolay was a great orator, his powers of persuasion might not have been sufficient to convince the dissenters had not the GPU silenced the anti-Sergius groups who refused to pray in their churches for the Soviet Government.

Although the Sergius Church appeared to the authorities a lesser evil than the right-wing opposition which challenged Sergius's leadership, it was not immune against persecution. Sergius obtained legal recognition which the anti-régime groups lacked, but this entitled neither his clergy nor the believers following his lead to special protection. Anti-religious agitators were little interested in questions of ecclesiastical jurisdiction when, in the years 1929–32, they engineered the closing of churches and the confiscation of church bells on a vast scale. On the contrary, Sergius's adoption of a pro-Soviet point of view, far from leading to a weakening of the atheist campaign, caused it to be intensified. The Soviet communists feared that people could easily misinterpret the fact that Sergius put religion into a pro-Soviet attire. They might have harboured the illusion that this made religion 'less harmful'. Such an erroneous view had to be fought by increased anti-religious propaganda, which was conducted as much by deeds as by words.[3]

The Plight of the Priests

Officially the League of Militant Godless always condemned the so-called 'anti-priest deviation' ('*anti-popovskii uklon*') in atheist propaganda but in practice it has always seemed to the Soviet communists a much more profitable line to launch personal attacks on priests than to conduct lengthy arguments against religious beliefs. The ordinary Orthodox parish priest felt very keenly the fallacy of Sergius's statement that the joys and failures of the State were also the joys and failures of the Church. Soon after these much quoted words were put on paper there began one of the most distressing periods in the history of the Russian Orthodox Church, for the authorities were determined to carry out its extermination in the Russian countryside, parallel with the collectivisation of agriculture which began in 1929. In many

---

[1] *Patriarkh Sergii i ego dukhovnoe nasledstvo*, Moscow 1947, p. 40.
[2] *Zh.M.P.*, 1945, no. 4, p. 53.   [3] Yaroslavsky, op. cit., vol. i, p. 155.

cases parish priests obstructed the sequestration of their churches and therefore came into bitter conflict with the authorities. However, even if they themselves exercised restraint, they were still held responsible for the resistance of their parishioners. They were dealt with as hostages, arrested and even shot. Such things happened over and over again especially in 1929 and 1930.

The priests of the Orthodox Church were persistently treated as the pariahs of Soviet society. This status, it is true, they shared with the servants of all other religious cults, but because the Orthodox clergy were more numerous than any others, they provided the largest number of second-class citizens. Up to the introduction of the 'Stalin Constitution' of 1936, priests were disfranchised. They belonged to the category of the so-called 'lishentsy' which included, among others, former factory owners, traders and other 'exploiting elements'. Not only were they disfranchised, but they were also excluded from membership of trade unions and co-operatives, were unable to obtain ration cards, and were barred from employment in most People's Commissariats. They could not become teachers and in Byelorussia they could not even become peasants. Their children were not admitted to higher educational establishments. Even if a priest tried to earn his living by manual labour whilst exercising his priestly functions in his spare time only, this made no difference to his status. Since 1926 at least, priests remained disfranchised irrespective of whether they received remuneration or not. The régime did not even trust priests who had broken with religion in a public and spectacular manner, and these cases were not infrequent in view of official terror and pressure. Their readmission to full citizenship was a protracted and complicated affair. Their voting rights were restored only after they had performed 'productive and socially useful work' for at least five years and proved their loyalty to the Soviet State.

Even the constitution of 1936, which abolished the category of 'lishentsy' did not alter the real status of priests. They were given voting rights but continued to be regarded as second-class citizens. They remained in communist eyes members of a profession 'exploiting the backwardness and ignorance of the toilers'.[1] The importance of this characterisation was not merely theoretical. It was of practical relevance whenever a priest tried to invoke in his favour the principle of equality which the Constitution promised to all citizens. For instance, priests who had all the necessary qualifications for teaching in schools were told very emphatically that servants of the cult could not be employed as

[1] *Komsomolskaya Pravda*, August 10, 1937.

educators. The pledge of article 118 of the Constitution that every citizen had a right to work did not apply to them.[1]

The Purge of 1937

It must be stated in fairness that the head of the Church, Metropolitan Sergius, was only the first among the pariahs. He did not undergo martyrdom in prisons and camps as many other Orthodox hierarchs did. His martyrdom was of a subtler kind. He had to cover up the plight of his Church by restating in even more outspoken terms his original statement of allegiance to the régime. This he did in particular in an interview he granted in 1930 condemning the protests which both the Pope and the Archbishop of Canterbury had issued against religious persecution in the Soviet Union. In 1934, it is true, the metropolitans, archbishops and bishops under his jurisdiction decided to bestow on him the title 'Most Blessed Metropolitan of Moscow and Kolomna' for until then he was still Metropolitan of Nizhnii Novgorod (Gorky) only. This promotion was of course only a gesture of courtesy on the part of his fellow-bishops, and brought him no increase in actual power, nor did it usher in a period of greater stability for the Church. On the contrary, a year after his elevation in rank, Metropolitan Sergius saw himself compelled to disband the Church's central government, the Holy Synod, and to allow the individual bishops much greater latitude in their dioceses.

This destroyed the administrative cohesion of the Church but nevertheless turned out to be a wise precautionary measure. As Metropolitan Sergius exercised very little effective jurisdiction over the other members of the Orthodox hierarchy he could not be held responsible for the various plots against the State of which the NKVD accused them. In 1937, such plots were discovered almost all over the Soviet Union. In Orel, Bishop Innokentii Nikiforov was accused of leading a clerico-fascist organisation in which sixteen of his priests and deacons were said to be implicated. In Smolensk, Archbishop Serafim Ostroumov was said to direct a 'counter-revolutionary band'. In Gorky, Metropolitan Feofan Tulyakov was unmasked as the leader of an 'organisation of terrorists and spies' in which two other bishops and many priests were said to have taken part. The NKVD asserted that they had apprehended other clerico-fascist plotters in Omsk and Vladivostok as well as in the Provinces of Leningrad, Yaroslavl, Kuibyshev and Kirov. In the coal mines of the Kuzbas the watchful eyes of Yezhov's police spotted Orthodox Church agents working on behalf of the Japanese intelligence service and organising accidents. In the Urals the police

---

[1] *Za kommunisticheskoe prosveshchenie*, no. 56, 1937.

arrested a bishop who had founded a group of spies and saboteurs and instigated explosions in Soviet ammunition dumps. During this great purge the NKVD showed itself most impartial with regard to the various ecclesiastical factions within Russian Orthodoxy and among those arrested on the most fantastic spy charges there were ar least two Metropolitans of the Living Church.[1]

In the years 1937 and 1938 Metropolitan Sergius must have lived in constant fear that to him would be meted out the same fate which had befallen others — arrest, deportation and perhaps even execution. No doubt the authorities must have seriously considered whether to arrest Sergius, and it seems that the case against him was already carefully prepared. The NKVD was very near to discovering a Moscow clerico-fascist centre headed by Sergius himself and a 'confession' by an orthodox priest called Krylov was lined up for this purpose. Another piece of 'evidence' kept in readiness against Sergius was a harmless exchange of telegrams between him and another Metropolitan Sergius (Tikhomirov) who was the head of the Orthodox Church of Japan. Sergius Tikhomirov (1871–1945) was a great Russian patriot who never severed relations with the Moscow Patriarchate and so occupied an almost unique position among the Russian churchmen outside the Soviet Union. For this reason he incurred a good deal of hostility on the part of the more extreme elements of the Russian emigration.[2] Nevertheless, Metropolitan Sergius Tikhomirov was denounced in Soviet Russia as 'one of the principal intermediaries between Japanese militarism and the White Guardist scum'. Consequently, the innocuous message of greetings of the Moscow Metropolitan Sergius to his namesake in Japan was really a 'message to the Japanese intelligence service'.[3] As such accusations were already being openly published in Soviet anti-religious pamphlets, the head of the Russian Orthodox Church seems to have had a very narrow escape. After all, other people were arrested and executed on even flimsier 'evidence' than that available against the Metropolitan of Moscow and Kolomna.

The Police could have arrested Sergius only with Stalin's express approval and Stalin had obviously decided that no harm should be done to him. Unwittingly perhaps the Soviet dictator showed a good deal of foresight, for soon he was to need the Metropolitan's help. One might say that this was no new role for Sergius and that he had been collaborating with the Soviet State at least since 1927 and in a certain sense this is so.

---

[1] Boris Kandidov, *Tserkov i shpionazh* (Church and Espionage), Moscow 1938, pp. 55–6.
[2] *Zh.M.P.*, no. 7, 1951, p. 52.   [3] Kandidov, op. cit., pp. 54–5.

But until 1939 this collaboration between the Metropolitan and the Soviet régime was completely one-sided. In all dealings with the Soviet Government the Metropolitan spoke from a position of weakness and the Government from a position of strength. It was only after 1939 that the Church was able to strike a bargain with the State and mutual relations therefore started to take a different shape. The Russian Orthodox Church gradually strengthened her hand, thanks to the annexation by the Soviet Union of new territories with an Orthodox population or at least with well-organised Orthodox minorities. In these territories the State required the Church's assistance to smooth the process of their absorption by the Soviet régime. A much more drastic change in Church-State relations came later in 1941 when the nazi army invaded Russia. Not till then was the Russian Church able to rid itself of the humiliating part of a despised servant and to become a co-belligerent if not an ally.

The Church as 'Co-Belligerent'

The régime took note of the steadfastness and loyalty which millions of Russian men and women continued to show to the Orthodox faith and became prepared to conclude, first an armistice with the Orthodox Church and later a kind of concordat. The authorities could not easily admit that religion had survived in Russia to the extent it did. To save their face they asserted that the war had given moribund religion a new chance. The war, so the Soviet anti-religious experts argued, 'broke weak-minded and ideologically unstable people.' As a result of tremendous tribulation, destruction and suffering, they began to seek consolation in Church and religion. A section of believers who on the eve of the war were already on the road to atheism went back into the bosom of the Church.[1] If this communist explanation is true, and it may certainly be true in parts, the communist case becomes not stronger but weaker. It implies that people accepted Communism as a fair-weather ideology and reverted to religion in time of emergency. Even the Communist Party itself could not afford a militant anti-religious attitude when this emergency came. In the dark days of the war it had every interest not to antagonise the masses of believers of the Soviet Union, but to enlist their co-operation in defending the country and ultimately in achieving victory over the invaders. It would have been nothing short of suicidal for the régime to conduct propaganda against the Orthodox Church at a time when the life and death of the communist régime, the Russian State and the Russian nation were at stake. Communist régime and

[1] S. N. Khudyakov, *Vsegda-li budet suchchestvovat religiya?* (Will religion always exist?), Moscow 1958, p. 17.

Russian nation were of course not *a priori* identical but they were made identical by the policy of Adolf Hitler, who did not fight against Communism alone, but tried to impose the rule of the Herrenvolk upon what he considered to be the inferior races of the East. Hitler's policy gave full justification to the Soviet slogan about the 'Great Patriotic War' which the Soviet régime claimed to wage, and it left the Russian Orthodox Church no choice but to observe a staunch patriotic attitude despite all the persecutions she had endured in the past.

Whilst Hitler's attitude alone went very far towards creating a truce between the Orthodox Church and the atheist State, there was also a more fundamental *rapprochement* between the two. The ideological content of Soviet Communism in 1941 or 1943 was infinitely more patriotic than it was in the twenties and early thirties. All sorts of nationalist contraband had infiltrated into the official communist ideology — pride in the Russian past, Slav brotherhood, and the worship of historical heroes, including saints of the Orthodox Church when they happened to be statesmen and military commanders, as for instance Dimitry Donskoy and Alexander Nevsky. The Church found Stalin's revised Communism attractive to its traditional way of thinking, and the régime, converted to patriotic ideas, was now able to appreciate the patriotic record of the Orthodox Church. Even if the Church had had no other merits in communist eyes her patriotism now stood above any suspicion and the Soviet communists continued to acknowledge her as a patriotic force long after the war emergency was over. The Soviet professor Rozental defined the new revised Soviet communist attitude towards Orthodoxy as follows: 'Only in one respect did the Orthodox Church definitely deserve to be preferred to the Catholic Church. Both in Russia and other countries the Orthodox Church was subordinate to the State. As a result, she linked by necessity her interests with the interests of the latter. Therefore the Orthodox clergy not infrequently lent its assistance to the secular power in the fight for political advancement and national independence.' Professor Rozental illustrated his point by mentioning a number of dignitaries of the Russian Orthodox Church who at various times proved their patriotism, and so played a positive role from the point of view of the Soviet concept of history. These included Sergius of Radonezh (1315–92) who had advised and inspired Dimitry Donskoy in his fight against the Tartars and Patriarch Hermogen (1530–1612) who led the national resistance against the Polish invasion at the beginning of the seventeenth century.[1] There is

---

[1] N. N. Rozental, *Iz istorii pravoslaviya, katolitsizma i protestantsva* (From the history of Orthodoxy, Catholicism and Protestantism), Moscow 1957, pp. 23–4.

no doubt that the examples of these great Russian churchmen of the past guided the patriotic Orthodox Church leaders of the Soviet Union during the Second World War. The most prominent of the latter were Metropolitan Alexis Shimansky who stayed in Leningrad throughout the siege of the city, Metropolitan Nikolay who spent the worst years of the war in Moscow and of course Metropolitan Sergius, the head of the Church.

Co-operation between Church and State was expressed from the very first day of the nazi aggression by the church administration issuing statements in favour of the Soviet war effort, which the official propaganda services publicised widely both in Russia and abroad. They were sent out by radio, printed in Soviet newspapers, distributed by Soviet embassies in the Western and neutral capitals and dropped as leaflets by Red Army planes over temporarily occupied territories. Metropolitan Sergius alone signed as many as twenty-three messages and proclamations which called upon the faithful to fight the invaders and expressed firm confidence in a Russian victory. Sergius and the other Orthodox Church leaders impressed upon the Christians that they must fight not only in defence of Russia but also in defence of Christianity which Hitler 'with his pagan theories and his cult of the pagan god Wotan was threatening'.[1]

The church leaders assisted the war effort not only in words but also in deeds. Shepherds and flock made tremendous material sacrifices and provided the means for a fighter squadron christened 'Alexander Nevsky' and a tank column called 'Dimitry Donskoy'. The latter was handed over to the Army at a solemn presentation ceremony during which Metropolitan Nikolay spoke of *sacred hatred against the fascist robbers* and referred to Stalin as *our common Father* (capital in the original) *Iosif Vissarionovich*.[2] Some people gave up their last savings in response to church appeals to contribute to the defence of the homeland. Patriotism was a strong motive in all this but there was also another, namely the hope of buying toleration and religious freedom for the future.

Although most of the patriotic initiatives of the Russian Orthodox Church were officially attributed to Metropolitan Sergius, his leadership was more nominal than real. He was ailing, and was evacuated to Ulyanovsk on the Volga, where the Moscow Patriarchate had its temporary seat from October 1941 to the autumn of 1943. The much younger Metropolitan Nikolay was more and more superseding him, if

---

[1] Sermon of Metropolitan Nikolay of August 8, 1941. Metropolit Nikolay, *Slova, Rechi, Poslaniya* (Words, Speeches, Pastoral Letters), Moscow 1947, p. 178.

[2] *Zh.M.P.*, no. 4, 1944, pp. 13-14.

not as church leader, at least as the principal ecclesiastical collaborator of the Soviet State. Nikolay became the first Orthodox dignitary whom the Soviet Government entrusted with an official position, at least since the famine of 1921–2 when certain 'liberal' churchmen were invited to sit on the Famine Relief Committee. On November 2, 1942, Nikolay was made a member of the Extraordinary State Commission of Enquiry into the crimes committed in Soviet territory by the 'German-fascist invaders and their collaborators'. This was, from every point of view, an important appointment. It showed first of all that the régime had to include a distinguished church representative in the commission in order to endow it with greater prestige in the eyes of the world, which had grown somewhat weary of Soviet propaganda statements.

Nikolay's inclusion in the Commission and the composition of the Commission in general had a still wider significance. It was the first formal attempt to create a Popular Front organ in the Soviet Union. In Soviet conditions a Popular or United Front could not be based on a coalition of parties as in other countries. It was simply an alliance of the Communist Party with the patriotic Church and with various prominent non-party figures. Thus the Commission included, besides the Metropolitan, such 'non-party patriots' as Academician Tarlé and the poet Aleksei Tolstoy (previously Count Tolstoy), in addition to such Communist Party chiefs as Zhdanov and Shvernik. Another expression of the United Front *à la soviétique* was the participation of Orthodox Church representatives in the All-Slav Committee and in All-Slav Conferences, where Metropolitan Nikolay was once again a prominent figure.

The 'Concordat'

Early in September 1943 came the reward for the patriotic conduct of the Russian Orthodox Church and its full identification with Soviet power. On September 4 Stalin received the three Metropolitans, Sergius, Alexis and Nikolay in the Kremlin. All the subsequent history of the Russian Orthodox Church must be traced back to this memorable meeting, in which the foundations of a concordat were laid. Stalin no doubt outlined at this meeting the extent and the limits of the concessions the Church could expect. These concessions meant a most remarkable step forward even if they did not add up to religious freedom in the Western sense. The Church was at last allowed to elect its Patriarch in the person of Metropolitan Sergius and to re-establish a proper ecclesiastical government — the Holy Synod. All this took place four days after the three Metropolitans had paid their visit to Stalin.

The Church Council (*sobor*) which put the canonical seal on the concessions granted by Stalin was surprisingly small. In addition to the 'Big Three' of the Russian hierarchy it was attended by only eleven archbishops and five bishops — nineteen people all told. A much larger number of Orthodox hierarchs could probably have been found at that time in Soviet prisons and concentration camps.

The other concessions which the Russian Orthodox Church was granted, either by the original concordat or as the result of its later application were: permission to recommence publication of the *Journal of the Moscow Patriarchate* which had been interrupted in 1936; the opening of theological seminaries, academies and courses in a rigorously restricted number of localities, and recognition of the Church as a 'juridical person' entitled to own property. The latter recognition, which acquired legal force in 1945 and was extended to all legal religious groups in the country, necessitated a tacit and no doubt desirable abrogation of Lenin's Decree about the Separation of the Church from the State and the School from the Church.[1]

As a result of the concordat the Russian Orthodox Church was also recognised as the principal religious body of the Soviet Union. The State even accepted the view of the Patriarchal Church that she alone is entitled to speak on behalf of the Orthodox Christians of the USSR. In other words, one cannot be Orthodox in the Soviet Union in any valid and effective way except by belonging spiritually to the Russian Orthodox Church. To this rule only one exception was made: in favour of the autocephalous Orthodox Church of Georgia. This attitude really put an end to the principle of equality of all religious creeds and bodies which the Soviet Union originally proclaimed.

The Living or Renovated Church, erstwhile favourite of the Soviet régime, was also sacrificed to the concordat with Sergius. Once he was elected Patriarch, the priests, bishops and metropolitans of the schismatic body made their submission to him in quick succession, whereupon each of them had to resume the ecclesiastical rank he held before joining the schism.[2] These submissions had the practical advantage for the Patriarchal Church that it gained control of a considerable number of important church buildings which until then were in the hands of 'renovated' priests. In Moscow and its suburbs alone, some of the finest churches returned to the Patriarch, including the Church of the Resurrection which now contains one of the most famous miraculous

[1] M. M. Persits, *Otdelenie Tserkvi ot Gosudarstva i Shkoly ot Tserkvi v SSSR* (The Separation of the Church from the State and the School from the Church in the USSR), Moscow 1958, p. 120.
[2] *Zh.M.P.*, 1944, no. 1, pp. 7–8; 1944, no. 4, p. 9.

3. Alexis, Patriarch of Moscow and All Russia.

4. Young Russian couples in Moscow taking their infants
to church for christening (1954).

5. A group of Russian Orthodox bishops attending the election of
Patriarch Alexis (February 1945).

6. Mr. Georgii Karpov, from 1943 to 1960 'Soviet government supervisor of the Russian Orthodox Church', addressing a session of the Russian Orthodox Church Council.

7. A delegation of the Orthodox Patriarchate of Antioch setting out to the
Lenin and Stalin Mausoleum. Left, Alexander III, Patriarch of Antioch and
all the East. The picture was produced by the official Soviet photo agency.

Russian ikons, Our Lady of Iberia. By the liquidation of the schism of the 'Renovators', churches were also regained in Leningrad, Tula, Tashkent, Sverdlovsk and other cities. One wonders whether these reconversions of the renovator-priests were altogether voluntary or whether official persuasion did not help to accelerate them. The régime had no interest in keeping the 'Living Church' in being once it had been realised that it represented only a minute proportion of the Orthodox believers. Whilst the 'Old Church' collected many millions for the defence of the country — 200 million roubles up to the beginning of 1945 — the contributions of the Living Church seemed insignificant by comparison.

'The People's Commissar for Opium'

The official recognition of the Patriarchal Church as the most important ecclesiastical body of the country and as the sole legal representative of the Orthodox Christians became fully operative in October 1943 when the Soviet Government created a special 'Council for the Affairs of the Russian Orthodox Church'. There could be no doubt that the Russian Orthodox Church, as the régime understood it, meant the Church of the Patriarch alone and not a sum total of groups claiming to hold the Orthodox faith. The Council and in particular its Chairman have played a very important part in Soviet religious policy. The latter has been nicknamed 'Narkombog' ('God's own Peoples Commissar') or 'Narkomopium' ('Peoples Commissar for Opium').[1] His position has also been compared half in joke, half in earnest with that of the Over-Procurator of the Holy Synod who acted as the eyes and the ears of the Czar in the supreme administration of the Orthodox Church. This comparison is in many ways incorrect. Whatever criticism one could make of the Over-Procurator and his tyrannical powers he was at least expected to be a Christian believer, whilst the Chairman of the Council for the Affairs of the Russian Orthodox Church must be a convinced atheist. Nor is the position of the latter as exalted as was that of the Over-Procurator, who held ministerial rank and was one of the most important men in the Emperor's entourage. The exact place which his approximate Soviet equivalent holds in the communist hierarchy is difficult to determine with any precision but he is certainly not in the top class of Soviet officialdom.

Nevertheless, the very establishment of a separate Council for the Affairs of the Russian Orthodox Church marked a return to a pre-revolutionary order and the abandonment of that hostile aloofness

[1] Alexander Werth, *The Year of Stalingrad*, London 1946, p. 248.

C

towards religious matters which the Soviet régime originally observed. Ever since 1918 there had existed special state organs to supervise and to fight the Churches, such as the Fifth and later the Ninth Department of the Peoples' Commissariat for Justice. Later, 'Commissions for the Affairs of Religious Cults' were established in the various Soviet republics and provinces, but until 1943 no state authority was in existence to deal with the Orthodox Church alone. The break in the continuity of official religious policy is perhaps more formal than factual. The various Soviet state bodies dealing at various times with church affairs were but a façade for the Cheka-GPU-NKVD-MVD and its ecclesiastical section. As early as the twenties the head of this section could be referred to with some justification as the 'underground Over-Procurator' of the Russian Church.[1] The Council for the Affairs of the Orthodox Church has likewise its close contacts with the police apparatus. Its first Chairman, G. G. Karpov, tried hard to keep his past record secret, but it has always been common knowledge in Moscow that before his new appointment he was a police official in charge of ecclesiastical matters.[2] Hence the considerable familiarity with theological and liturgical matters which he displayed both in public addresses and in conversations with visitors. This connection between the police and the new 'Council' does not invalidate the fact that the year 1943 marks a change in the régime's attitude towards the Church, but this change was as much one of police methods as of state policy.

The terms of reference of the 'Council' have never been published, except in a very vague and general manner. It is in charge of liaison between the Patriarchate and the state authorities. The Patriarch cannot directly approach any ministry or any other official body. The 'Council' acts as the indispensable go-between. To carry out its task also on the lower levels the Council has its plenipotentiaries in all republics and provinces. There is at least one 'plenipotentiary' for every diocesan bishop of the Orthodox Church. Up to a point the activity of the 'Council' is to the benefit of the Church. The Council has provided many licences for the opening and restoration of churches and has attended in many ways to the Church's material needs. It is also an important part of the 'Council's' duties to look after the personal interests and even the personal comfort of the hierarchs, especially the Patriarch and his closest collaborators who as the result of the concordat have moved up into the privileged classes of Soviet society. The prestige of the atheist State seems to require that 'its' Patriarch should not be

---

[1] G. P. Fedotov, *The Russian Church since the Revolution*, London 1928, p. 53.
[2] R. Magidoff, *The Kremlin and the People*, New York 1953, p. 74.

in a worse position than the church leaders of the non-communist countries. The Chairman of the 'Council' and the officials under his command also show a respectful attitude towards the Patriarch and the members of the hierarchy, at least in the presence of foreigners. On special occasions the Council even arranges receptions in honour of the Patriarch, usually attended only by minor Soviet officials and representatives of semi-official organisations with which the Church co-operates.

It is a natural task of the 'Council' to see how the Church can best be made to serve the Soviet State and its policy. By its day-to-day dealings with the Orthodox hierarchy the personnel of the 'Council' has acquired a unique knowledge of the various church personalities and their reliability from the régime's point of view. It is, therefore, in an excellent position to advise the Government which ecclesiastical figures should be allowed to travel abroad, who should be recommended and who vetoed for promotion. Herein lies a certain similarity between the Over-Procurator of the pre-revolutionary Holy Synod and his Soviet counterpart.

Patriarch Alexis

Metropolitan Sergius Starogorodsky was Patriarch for eight months only. He died on May 15, 1944. Following Sergius's death, the direction of the Church was taken over by the Metropolitan of Leningrad and Novgorod. He was the obvious choice for this task because for many years he had been closely associated with the late Patriarch's policy of loyalty towards the secular power. His very first statement as locum tenens showed once again the extent to which the Church had become a State Church. He assured Stalin of his 'profound affection and gratitude' and promised that he would 'safeguard the Church against mistakes and false steps'.[1]

During the period between Alexis assuming the temporary function of locum tenens and his election as Patriarch of Moscow and all Russia, the war situation had undergone a drastic change. Soviet troops were fighting on German soil and victory seemed within reach. Instead of struggling for its own survival the Soviet State was now imposing its will on other nations and occupying other peoples' territories. The war for the defence of the fatherland was turned into a war of conquest. As the Orthodox Church had linked her destinies with those of the State her status and her tasks had to be adapted to the new situation. In the days of victory it was no longer necessary for the Church to keep alive

[1] *Izvestiya*, May 21, 1944.

the flame of patriotism among the Russian people, as it was at the time of defeat and retreat, but this does not mean that the Church had exhausted its usefulness for the régime even inside the USSR. Church support was still needed to enhance the respectability of the Soviet Government in the eyes of Soviet citizens and it was particularly essential in the fight against centrifugal forces in the borderlands from the Baltic states to Bessarabia. Outside the new Soviet borders there was even more for the Church to do as an ally of the Soviet State. The Red Army was now operating in countries with an Orthodox population — Rumania, Bulgaria and Serbia — and the Russian Orthodox Church could therefore be of considerable assistance in promoting friendship and loyalty towards the Soviet Union among the Orthodox peoples of the Balkans. The Russian Orthodox Church was also able to perform for the State other tasks lying further ahead. Her authority could be displayed in order to reconcile with the Soviet régime the masses of the 'white' emigrés living in the West or, if not, at least to carry confusion into their ranks and to split them. Finally, the historical ties between the Russian Orthodox Church and the Orthodox Patriarchates of the Orient were an inestimable asset to Moscow in case Soviet diplomacy decided to conduct a more active policy in the Middle East.

Seen against this background it is obvious why the Soviet régime was determined to maintain its friendly attitude towards the Church, although military victory was won. The régime even had to enhance the prestige of the Russian Orthodox Church at home to enable her to play the part of a great ecclesiastical world power — to the ultimate benefit of the Soviet Government. This goes perhaps far to explain why the election of Patriarch Alexis in February 1945 and also the celebration of the five-hundredth anniversary of the foundation of an autocephalous Russian Orthodox Church, in July 1948, could be held with such splendour in the capital of atheist Communism.

The contrast between the election of Sergius and that of Alexis was most characteristic of the outward improvement in the situation of the Russian Church. The election of Sergius was carried out modestly and hastily by a handful of Russian bishops. The Church Council which elected Alexis was carefully prepared and attended by as many as 204 ecclesiastical dignitaries and laymen. Several distinguished guests came from abroad, including the Patriarchs of Antioch and Alexandria and the representatives of the Patriarchs of Serbia, Rumania, Jerusalem, as well as of the Oecumenical Patriarch of Constantinople. The representative of the Soviet State, G. G. Karpov, greeting the assembly, paid tribute to the patriotic role of the Russian Orthodox Church throughout history and especially to her most ardent participation in the defence of the fatherland during World War II. Karpov also indicated in an unmistakable way that the Soviet Government would wholeheartedly approve if the 'esteemed churchman and fervent patriot Alexis' were elected Patriarch.[1]

Moscow — 'The Third Rome'

The Russian Orthodox Church Council of 1945 made a deep impression on its Russian and foreign members. It seemed almost incredible that such a magnificent ecclesiastical manifestation could be held in a suburb of communist Moscow. It filled the Russian Orthodox leaders with great pride and hope for a happy future of their Church, and revived centuries-old Russian messianic ideas. Metropolitan Benjamin, who was then Exarch of the Moscow Patriarchate for North America, gave expression to these messianic expectations, current among his fellow-bishops, when he said that Moscow may yet become the 'Third Rome' and that in future Moscow would be the obvious meeting place for the entire Church. Perhaps, so the Metropolitan added, Moscow would even become the seat of an advisory central organ linking all Orthodox Churches the world over.[2] Such ideas met with a sympathetic echo in official Soviet circles, who were quite in favour of a Russian Orthodox Church imperialism and of Moscow becoming the world's most important ecclesiastical centre. Patriarch Alexis was given every support and encouragement to extend his foreign contacts and to claim for himself and his Church a leading position in the religious world.

Stalin himself assured Patriarch Alexis and Metropolitan Nikolay of this support at a meeting which took place on April 10, 1945. This was a continuation of the conference which the three Metropolitans, Sergius, Alexis and Nikolay had had with the Generalissimo in September 1943, and it was intended to define in a more precise manner the already existing *modus vivendi*, particularly with regard to the training of priests and the publishing activities of the Church. According to a short account of the meeting given by Metropolitan Nikolay, Stalin and the Patriarch also discussed the journey which the latter was to undertake in May and June 1955 to the countries of the Middle East.[3] Molotov, who at that time was First Deputy Premier and Foreign Minister, was present at the meeting. It fell to him and his subordinates to make the Middle East tour of the Patriarch as smooth and successful

---

[1] *Izvestiya*, February 6, 1945.   [2] *Zh.M.P.*, 1945, no. 3, p. 21.
[3] *Zh.M.P.*, 1945, no. 5, p. 26.

as possible. No leading churchman of a non-communist country was likely to receive more official assistance on his travels abroad than Alexis obtained from the Soviet Government, which put at his disposal a special aircraft piloted by a 'Hero of the Soviet Union'. The same solicitude was shown to the Patriarch and his suite by the communist diplomats in Teheran, Damascus and Cairo.

The Patriarch's visit to the Middle East, which lasted four weeks, had both religious and political importance. First of all, the head of the Russian Orthodox Church established closer relations with the Orthodox Patriarchs of the Orient. He also prepared the ground for the restitution to the Russian Church of the property in Palestine which had belonged to it before the October Revolution. This restitution materialised fully three years later, when Patriarch Alexis sent a permanent ecclesiastical mission to the Holy Land to take over various Russian church buildings which until then had been administered by Russian emigré clergy.[1] Last, but not least, the appearance of Patriarch Alexis in the Levantine countries made a tremendous impression on the local Arab Christians, and produced a spate of publicity favourable to the Soviet Union and still bearing dividends several years later.

The Middle-East journey of Patriarch Alexis was but one of many moves which the Russian Orthodox Church undertook to extend its influence under the protective wings of the Soviet State. The Moscow Patriarch and his Holy Synod were able to use to their advantage the fact that Soviet forces were in occupation of large parts of Central and South-Eastern Europe as well as of Manchuria. Within this vast new Soviet sphere the Patriarchal Church enjoyed a privileged position. Her envoys were received with honour wherever they went and were able to bring a considerable number of scattered Orthodox groups under Moscow jurisdiction. Many Russian emigrés were only too anxious to seize the opportunity of declaring their allegiance to the Moscow Church, for this submission could secure for them and their families forgiveness for collaboration with Nazis and Japanese, and so freedom from arrest and deportation. This accounted, for instance, for the speed and enthusiasm with which the Russian Orthodox hierarchy of Kharbin, that well-known centre of the Russian 'White Guards', proclaimed their attachment to the Patriarch once the Soviet Army had occupied the city. As a result of the *volte-face* of the Russian Orthodox Church in Manchuria, the ranks of the Muscovite episcopate were increased by one metropolitan, one archbishop and two bishops.[2] The Russian Orthodox communities in China proper, in Shanghai, Peking, Canton

[1] *Zh.M.P.*, 1950, no. 10, p. 32.   [2] *Zh.M.P.*, 1945, no. 11, pp. 14–17.

and other cities had still a few more years of respite. They accepted the jurisdiction of the Moscow Patriarch only after the communists established their rule over the whole of China.[1] At the other end of the new Soviet Empire, in the Russian zones of Germany and Austria, the emigrés showed the same eagerness to come to terms with the Patriarch-ate and the Orthodox parishes of Berlin, Potsdam, Dresden and Leipzig and also that of Vienna quickly accepted its authority.

Even in countries where the Soviet Union was not directly in control, indirect Soviet pressure worked in favour of the Moscow Patriarchal Church. Thus the atmosphere existing in France towards the end of the war and in the immediate post-war period was most favourable to both the Soviet Union and the Moscow Patriarchate. The communists were in the Government; the Soviet State, France's war-time ally, was at the height of its prestige; and a mighty wave of Soviet patriotism swept an important section of Russian refugees, many of whom applied for Soviet passports, hoping to return to their homeland. Under these circumstances there was a strong desire among them to leave the ecclesiastical orbit of the Oecumenical Patriarch of Constantinople, to which most Russian Orthodox emigré parishes belonged, and the Paris Metropolitan Eulogius recognised the Moscow Patriarch in August 1945, without severing his ties with Constantinople. Soon, however, affection for Russia subsided in France, the communists left the Government, the pro-Soviet Russian emigré organisations were closed down and their newspapers suppressed. This immediately decreased the chances of the Moscow Patriarchate in France and the vast majority of the Russian Orthodox parishes turned their back on Moscow once again.

The Moscow Patriarch was unsuccessful almost everywhere where his connection with the political Moscow were, in the eyes of the local power, a liability to him. The failure of the special emissary whom he sent to the United States in 1947 shows this in a particularly convincing way. This emissary, who was the Metropolitan of Leningrad, Grigorii, one of the most distinguished figures of the Russian Orthodox hierarchy at the time, was expected to bring back into Moscow's fold the large body of the Russian Orthodox of North America. After three and a half months, Grigorii returned empty-handed. The Russian Orthodox Church of America was ready to acknowledge the Moscow Patriarch as spiritual head, but without accepting his jurisdiction. Only a small group of American Russian parishes, representing about ten per cent of the total, remained under the Patriarch's Exarch for North America.[2]

[1] *Zh.M.P.*, 1950, no. 10, p. 29.   [2] *Zh.M.P.*, 1948, no. 1, pp. 16–17.

In the Soviet satellite countries of Europe, on the other hand, the Russian Orthodox Church scored a number of easy victories. The small Czechoslovak Orthodox Church with its Czech, Slovak, Russian and Ukrainian membership came under the wing of Moscow in 1946 and was supplied with a Russian Exarch. In 1951, the Czechoslovak Church received autocephalous status but Russian influence continued to be strong. After prolonged negotiations the Moscow Patriarchate recognised in the same year the autocephaly of the Orthodox Church of Poland, but as a birth gift appointed a Soviet metropolitan, Makarii Oleksiyuk.[1] He was nicknamed the 'Ecclesiastical Rokossovsky' since his appointment had some similarity with that of the Soviet Marshal Rokossovsky to the post of Polish Minister of Defence and Commander in Chief. In Hungary, where the Orthodox Church has a few parishes only, it was put under Moscow jurisdiction in 1949 at a time when the political Sovietisation of the country was virtually completed. A bishop from the Soviet Ukraine was allowed to enter Hungary and to carry out this ecclesiastical annexation, not without encountering the protests of the Serbian Orthodox Church, to which the parishes in question originally belonged.

With the Orthodox Churches of Bulgaria and Rumania the Moscow Patriarchate established most intimate contact. Patriarch Alexis visited Bulgaria in 1946 and Rumania in 1947. With Rumania, relations became closer than with Bulgaria, although the contrary should be expected in view of the cultural affinities and the historical ties linking Russians and Bulgars. In the first five post-war years, the Orthodox Patriarchs of Rumania — until 1948 Patriarch Nicodemus and since then Patriarch Justinian — undertook as many as five journeys to Moscow. Patriarch Justinian was a particularly fervent supporter of the communist régime in Rumania and of Soviet-Rumanian friendship, which may have been a primary motive for his endeavour to keep in close touch with the Russian Holy Synod.

The many moves which the Russian Orthodox Church made with the aim of strengthening its position throughout the world were overshadowed by one daring initiative which the Moscow Patriarch launched in the spring of 1947. With the obvious backing of the Soviet authorities he issued invitations for a Conference of the Heads of all Orthodox Churches to be held in Moscow in November 1947. To show the truly ecumenical character of the gathering, the Patriarch proposed that Russian, French, English and Greek should be the official conference languages. Among the topics of discussion the Patriarch suggested

---

[1] *Zh.M.P.*, 1951, no. 7, p. 4.

relations between the Orthodox Churches on the one hand and the Vatican and the ecumenical movement on the other.[1]

This Russian-sponsored pan-Orthodox Conference did not material-ise. The Oecumenical Patriarch of Constantinople declined the invitation and even urged Moscow to abandon the idea of summoning a conference altogether. The Patriarch of Alexandria joined Constantinople in reject-ing Moscow's initiative and so did the Churches of Greece and Cyprus. Under these circumstances the pan-Orthodox Conference could not take place, but the Patriarch of Moscow and all Russia did not give up easily. As he could no longer expect the Orthodox leaders of the world to come to an ecumenical conference he requested them to attend at least the celebrations which were to mark the five-hundredth anniversary of the canonical independence of the Russian Orthodox Church. The idea of the Conference was not given up altogether; it was still to be held in connection with the anniversary festivities.

Even this new modified invitation to Moscow met with only scant success. None of the heads of the autocephalous Orthodox Churches of the non-communist world came to Moscow although some sent representatives for the celebrations of the Russian Church autocephaly. However, with one exception they did not attend the ensuing Confer-ence. It was confined to the church representatives of the communist countries from Czechoslovakia to Georgia and from Poland to Albania. The only outsiders were the emissaries of the pro-Soviet Patriarch of Antioch. Thus it would not be unjust to describe the Conference as an ecclesiastical Cominform. The Conference adopted various statements, for instance, one attacking the Vatican and another somewhat less hostile about the ecumenical movement as well as an appeal to the Christians of the world which was critical of both Catholicism and Protestantism. These documents which bore the hallmark of communist Cold War propaganda, were unrepresentative of the entire Orthodox Church since they were signed by the Patriarchs and church leaders of the Soviet bloc supported only by the delegation from Antioch.

Strong anti-Vatican bias was the most distinct feature of the Con-ference and this was certainly most welcome to the Soviet Government. Nevertheless, the Government realised as much as the Moscow Patriarch that the Conference had fallen short of original expectations, and when Mr. Karpov addressed it he did not conceal his disappointment. He accused 'the heads of some ancient Greek Churches' of having boycotted the Moscow festivities for reasons of a non-ecclesiastical character.[2] The

---

[1] *Orthodoxia*, Constantinople 1947, no. 5/6 pp. 161–15.
[2] *Zh.M.P.*, Special number, 1948, p. 11.

failure of the 1948 Conference showed that Moscow's bid for leadership of the Orthodox world had suffered a severe setback. Having scored a number of initial successes, the ecclesiastical imperialism of the Moscow Patriarchate was unable to make any further advance. It was not different with the cruder imperialism of communist Moscow which by 1948 likewise found itself in an impasse.

The Church and the Peace Campaign

To overcome the deadlock in its struggle for domination of the world, the Kremlin embarked on a new venture on a vast scale. It was to be of all-embracing character. The Russian Orthodox Church and, to a lesser extent perhaps, all other Churches had to play a part in it. This new venture was the peace campaign. Ever since 1949 this campaign has absorbed a great deal of the public activity of the Orthodox hierarchy. If one examines the *Journal of the Moscow Patriarchate* of the period, one cannot help being impressed by the amount of space which it devoted to the 'defence of peace'; not only to the Church's own participation in it, but to the 'peace movement' as a whole, its meetings, congresses and statements. Some issues of the journal devoted one-third and some even up to half of their contents to the peace problem. This may serve as an indication that its strong involvement in the peace campaign was to a considerable degree forced upon the Church. Its leaders cannot have been enthusiastic about the waste of the valuable space of their only journal in the Russian language on the reproduction of messages and statements which everybody could have read much earlier in the secular press. The active contribution of the Church to the peace propaganda, which in practice turned out to be propaganda against the West, became a new way in which it could prove its usefulness to the State and buy tolerance from the communist Government. Church support lent to the peace campaign a respectability which it would not otherwise have possessed, and it misled many simple-minded people. But, on the other hand, the State had once again recognised the Church in the Soviet Union as an important social factor, which could not be overlooked if the movement of peace partisans was to have a genuine all-national character. By founding the movement of the peace partisans the Soviet communists resurrected the unofficial Russian Popular Front of the wartime period. Only this time it attained a more formal and organised character than the alliance between believers and unbelievers during the 'Great Patriotic War'.

The bodies where communists, church representatives and non-party people were brought together to demonstrate for common political objectives, were the 'Soviet Peace Defence Committee' and the 'All-Union Conferences for the Defence of Peace'. The Russian Orthodox Church sent very representative delegations to these conferences. The third conference of the Soviet peace partisans in November 1951, for instance, was attended by the Patriarch himself, two metropolitans, one archbishop, one bishop and one priest.[1] At the fourth Soviet peace conference this Russian Orthodox delegation had increased to eight men, again headed by the Patriarch.[2] The spokesman of the Church at these conferences was usually Metropolitan Nikolay who also represented his Church on the Soviet Peace Committee, a body comprising 110 Soviet personalities from all walks of life. In this capacity Metropolitan Nikolay frequently attended peace meetings and peace conferences abroad.

Metropolitan Nikolay's activities in the peace movement brought him considerable publicity not only in the foreign but also in the Soviet press and this created no small confusion in the minds of ordinary Soviet citizens. Even schoolchildren were puzzled by the Metropolitan's assiduous participation in peace congresses. They could not square this fact with what they were told about the harmfulness of religious beliefs.[3] So in a sense the participation of ecclesiastical dignitaries in the peace campaign set up the Church as an ardent champion of peace on earth. This was not an ideal way to publicise the Church but it was the only way open in the conditions prevailing in the communist totalitarian state.

Metropolitan Nikolay's speeches, and the peace statements of the Russian Orthodox Church, did not show it in the best possible light. They were oversaturated with human elements, they contained violent attacks on the Western world and reflected political passion. Strangely enough it was not the passion of the convinced fellow-traveller and enthusiast of the Soviet régime which permeated Metropolitan Nikolay's speeches in particular, it was the passion of the Russian nationalist for whom the Soviet State was nothing but a new expression of eternal Russia. In some of his speeches, Metropolitan Nikolay seemed deliberately to avoid mentioning the word 'Soviet Union', and instead spoke of 'my homeland' or 'our great fatherland'. His nationalistic mentality brought him close to that of the 'Union of the Russian People', the right-wing extreme nationalist party which before World War II enjoyed the support of a large section of the Orthodox clergy.

[1] *Zh.M.P.*, 1951, no. 12, p. 17.   [2] *Zh.M.P.*, 1952, no. 12, p. 21.
[3] *Organizatsiya i vospitanie uchenicheskogo kollektiva* (Organisation and education of the pupils' collective), Moscow 1954, p. 322.

It is not that the Church has not tried to give to the struggle for peace a specific Christian meaning. Indeed, the attempt to endow it with a non-political religious content was an essential feature of the Church's participation in the campaign. When Patriarch Alexis gave his blessing for the signing of the 'Stockholm Appeal' of the World Peace Council by Orthodox clergy and believers, he said that in so doing they would observe Christ's commandment of love.[1] Also in Metropolitan Nikolay's peace speeches there was not only nationalistic passion but much Christian fervour; for instance, when he said: 'As Christians believing in God the Creator, in God the source of peace, fight for peace with all the strength of your reason, heart and will-power — in the name of Christ.'[2]

There is still something else which must be considered when passing judgment on the peace appeals or any other statements on world affairs which are issued on behalf of the Russian Orthodox Church. Her leaders have suffered, like all other Soviet citizens, from the communist news blockade and from a total ignorance of the other side's point of view. They are familiar only with the Soviet version of international events, and this fact was at the root of many of their biased and one-sided utterances — for instance, when they charged America with conducting germ warfare against the Korean people.

The Death of Stalin

The death of Stalin did not at first make much difference to the mobilisation of the Church for the purposes of the peace campaign, but the tactical shifts in Soviet foreign policy which it gradually brought about changed the tone of the peace propaganda. It made it more subtle, more courteous and more acceptable from the Christian point of view. In the Stalin era peace propaganda had often had the character of a sledge-hammer; in the post-Stalin period it became a siren song.

Generally speaking, the death of Stalin was as important a landmark in the life of the Russian Orthodox Church as it was for any other aspect of Soviet reality. At first, the Church shared with the rest of the country the feeling of utter confusion which the sudden disappearance of the Soviet dictator provoked. Like everybody else in Russia, the Church had supported the Stalin cult most zealously. The Church bestowed on Stalin all the praise which it was customary to give to him in the last years of his life; only, when delivered in cathedrals and churches by the Patriarch and his bishops, this praise sounded more out of place than when expressed during the sessions of the Supreme Soviet or in meetings

[1] *Zh.M.P.*, 1950, no. 7, p. 7.   [2] *Zh.M.P.*, 1950, no. 7, p. 7.

of the Communist Party. Moreover, the Church added one more flattery to those which the communist press habitually showered on Stalin, namely that of a 'faithful defender of the Church'.

Seen from the point of view of Russian Orthodoxy, it was not entirely out of place to award Stalin this high-sounding title. Stalin could have crushed the Church or he could have denied it even that precarious existence which it enjoyed in the last ten or twelve years of his rule. For reasons of state he did not do either and for this the leaders of the Church must have felt a genuine gratitude. They expressed this in particular on Stalin's seventieth birthday when the whole episcopate signed a collective letter to him. Within the limits of the Soviet situation this letter was not undignified even if it addressed the dictator ritually as 'leader, teacher and friend of the toilers'.[1] Much more effusive was the Patriarch's statement, which he sent to the Soviet Council of Ministers on the occasion of Stalin's death. It said: 'His death is a heavy grief for our Fatherland and for all the people who inhabit it. The whole Russian Orthodox Church, which will never forget his benevolent attitude to church needs, feels great sorrow at his death. The bright memory of him will live ineradicably in our hearts. Our Church proclaims eternal memory to him with a special feeling of abiding love.'[2]

At the death of Stalin, the Church clearly acted like a state institution. Four of her representatives, including Metropolitan Nikolay and two archbishops, were among those who provided the guard of honour when the deceased leader was lying in state. It also seemed quite natural that church leaders from all over the world sent messages of condolences to the Moscow Patriarch.[3] The members of the Russian Orthodox hierarchy were in all probability sincere in their mourning, but they must also have harboured an anxious thought. They must have wondered to what extent the concordat with the Church and the policy of religious tolerance was Stalin's own personal policy and whether some of the concessions made in the war and post-war period might not be withdrawn by the new collective leaders.

The Church under the 'Collective Leadership'

The latter were so overwhelmed with problems of all kinds that they had no time to pay any attention to the Church. Things were allowed to drift and this meant in practice a somewhat greater latitude for all sides — the Church; its competitors, the sects; and its opponents, the anti-religious propagandists, who in the last years of the Stalin era had

[1] *Zh.M.P.*, 1949, no. 12, p. 7.   [2] *Izvestiya*, March 10, 1953.
[3] *Zh.M.P.*, 1953, no. 4, pp. 5–13.

been rather reticent since they never knew how far they were allowed to go in attacking religion. The comparative 'liberalism' of the post-Stalin period, with its greater freedom for anti-religious propaganda was from the Church's point of view by no means an undivided blessing, but the advantages of the new situation certainly outweighed the disadvantages. The diminished power of the secret police brought relief on every level of church life. It removed or at least reduced the feeling of fear among believers and clergy. It made contacts with foreign Christians more frequent and less inhibited.

On the other hand, the more relaxed atmosphere in the Soviet Union after Stalin's death also allowed attacks on the Orthodox Church, believers and clergy to become more vicious. Moreover, the return to Lenin and Leninism which the post-Stalin régime propagated also meant a return to the atheist militancy of the Lenin period. For the first time since the end of the religious persecution in the late thirties a crisis in Church-State relations occurred. This happened in the summer of 1954. For quite inexplicable reasons the entire Soviet press suddenly assumed a violent tone against the Church. This must have had the approval of high places since it was *Pravda*, the central organ of the Communist Party itself, which gave the starting signal to a campaign which lasted over a hundred days.[1]

During this short period the press not only produced its customary vague general attacks on religion, but it took up a number of specific individual cases of 'religious obscurantism' usually involving Orthodox believers, and thus created an atmosphere of hostility against the Church. Later it was officially admitted that in a number of instances local party organisations and party members tolerated 'administrative interference in the activities of religious organisations and groups' and also 'an ill-mannered attitude to the clergy'.[2] Mr. Georgii Karpov, speaking to a delegation of English churchmen, in June 1955, admitted that priests and citizens in various parts of the country had sent complaints to his office about such cases of interference and roughness.[3] Another church delegation visiting Moscow at the end of 1954 was told by a communist source that similar complaints were addressed to the Patriarch Alexis who under these circumstances might have lodged a protest with the Government.[4]

All this made it necessary for the Government to reaffirm the validity of the concordat. The leaders of the Kremlin, bitterly divided among

---

[1] *Pravda*, July 24, 1954.   [2] *Pravda*, November 10, 1954.
[3] Stanley G. Evans, *The Russian Church To-day*, London 1955, p. 8.
[4] Alex Horsley, *Russian Journey 1954*, Hull 1955, p. 15.

themselves, needed popular support, including that of the believers. They even seemed to have vied with one another in patching up the new conflict with the Church. Khruschchev, on behalf of the Central Committee of the Communist Party issued the decree entitled 'About mistakes in conducting scientific-atheistic propaganda among the population'.[1] It was not intended to put a stop to anti-religious propaganda but it certainly aimed at shielding from attack the Orthodox Church and especially the clergy, to whose loyalty to the régime tribute was paid. Although the decree did not actually discriminate between various religious groups subsequent developments showed that party officials epitomised its meaning as 'hands off the Orthodox Church'. They did not think that it also implied a go-slow policy towards other religious groups such as 'sects' or the Catholic Church. Khrushchev's main opponent, Georgii Malenkov, then still Chairman of the Council of Ministers, did not want to lag behind his rival in the struggle for power. On December 11, 1954, Malenkov received Patriarch Alexis. It was the first meeting between Premier and Patriarch since 1945. Its purpose was to reassure the Church and to re-emphasise the promise of a qualified religious tolerance which was implicit in Khrushchev's decree. When Malenkov received the Patriarch his days as Premier were already numbered. His successor Bulganin continued the policy of limited concessions to the Church, coupled with political exploitation.

This political exploitation of the Church and its identification with the régime was carried much further under Stalin's diadochs than under Stalin himself. Stalin's negative and aggressive foreign policy limited the role of the Church in foreign policy to the publication of statements supporting the Kremlin and to the appearance of spokesmen at peace conferences. The new more flexible policy of peaceful coexistence combined with the communist tactics of the 'united front' in the capitalist world gave the Church a tremendous chance to expand her activities. Instead of campaigning against the 'warmongers' and violently denouncing them, the Church was encouraged to make friends with everyone in the wide Christian world.

In response to this new Soviet attitude the *Journal of the Moscow Patriarchate* was either allowed or forced to suspend its attacks on the Vatican, which were a frequent feature in Stalin's time. Also the sceptical Russian Orthodox attitude towards the ecumenical movement was dropped and there was suddenly a keen interest on the part of the Holy Synod in collaborating with it as closely as possible. Previously it was sufficient from the régime's point of view, if the Orthodox Church

[1] *Pravda*, November 11, 1954.

maintained contact with various 'Red Deans' and 'Red Abbés', namely
with left-wing clerics devoid of prestige and influence in their respective
Churches. This was no longer adequate in the new post-Stalin situation.
Moscow was no longer content with a few Christian fellow-travellers to
whom peace prizes could be awarded, but it wanted the large representative bodies of Western Christendom and their legitimate leaders to
adopt a neutralist attitude. A maximum of contact between the Russian
Orthodox Church and foreign ecclesiastical circles was therefore
encouraged and Russian Church delegations no longer had any difficulty
in travelling to the countries of the free world. They went to Britain,
the United States and Western Germany on official visits and there
was an almost uninterrupted flow of Western ecclesiastical visitors to
the Soviet Union. Up to a point these contacts benefited the Soviet
cause, they tied the hands of the Western Churches in their criticism
of Soviet conditions, often resulted in ill-informed rosy descriptions of
Soviet reality and generally produced an attitude of gullibility among
Western Christians towards the problem of Communism. On the other
hand, it is equally certain that this extension of foreign contacts improved
the Church's bargaining position vis-à-vis the Kremlin.

In the new period of 'peaceful coexistence', it became particularly
clear that the foreign relations of the Russian Orthodox Church are
almost inseparably intertwined with the moves of Soviet diplomacy.
This is not a criticism of the Church but a statement of fact. In a state
which can be closed at any moment to any outgoing traveller and every
incoming visitor the Church has a priori no freedom to determine the
nature and extent of her foreign relations. This makes it inconceivable
for the Russian Church to maintain friendly or even normal relations
with the Church of a country with which the Soviet State finds itself
at loggerheads at a given moment.

Relations between the Russian and Serbian Orthodox Churches may
serve here as a particular case in point. No Russian churchman could
go to Yugoslavia and no Yugoslav bishop to the Soviet Union as long
as the Tito-Cominform conflict lasted. At the height of this conflict, in
1950, the Patriarch issued a statement denouncing Yugoslavia as having
joined the 'camp of the warmongers' and returned to Yugoslavia the
Order of National Liberation which he had received when Soviet
Russia and Yugoslavia were still close allies.[1] But once Khrushchev
made peace with the Yugoslavs the position changed. In October 1956
the Serbian Patriarch visited the Soviet Union and in October 1957
Patriarch Alexis paid him a return visit. The parallel between official

[1] *Izvestiya*, March 15, 1950.

policy and the attitude of the Patriarchal Church went even further. Both the Soviet Government and the Moscow Patriarch were anxious to reassure the Bulgars that the *rapprochement* with Belgrade was not to be carried out at their expense. Khrushchev stopped in Sofia after his reconciliation visit to Tito in May–June 1955 and the Patriarch went to the Bulgarian capital in September 1957, one month before his Yugoslavian tour.

Another similar example is provided by the relations between the Moscow Patriarch and the Orthodox Church of Finland. They too were an almost exact replica of the political relations between the Soviet Union and Finland. Finnish Orthodoxy stubbornly defended its independence of Moscow and finally compelled the Russian Orthodox Church to recognise both its autonomous status and its canonical links with the Oecumenical Patriarch in Constantinople. Even the two Orthodox parishes in Finland and the famous Valamo Monastery which in 1945 were put under Russian patriarchal jurisdiction, were handed back to the Finns in 1957. The Russian Orthodox Church here obviously emulated the example of the Soviet secular power, which two years before had given up the Finnish naval base of Porkkala.

The Church was intended to serve the State in its diplomatic offensive not only by entering into multiple ecumenical relations but also by helping to create among foreign statesmen an attitude of confidence in the Soviet régime. As from June 1955, the Soviet Government invited representatives of the Russian Orthodox Church to diplomatic receptions. This was an important new move, for which Belgrade had provided the inspiration. During their state visit to Yugoslavia, Bulganin and Khrushchev had noticed with some surprise that the Serbian Orthodox Patriarch Vikentije and some other ecclesiastical personages had graced the party which Marshal Tito had offered to his Soviet guests. Bulganin had a short friendly conversation with the Patriarch. After his return to Moscow he decided that in future the Russian Patriarch should not be treated worse than the Serbian. He imitated Tito's gesture and invited Alexis to a Kremlin reception in honour of Pandit Nehru. Since then the Patriarch's representatives have been frequent guests at receptions given in Moscow for foreign statesmen or government delegations.

As time went on the Soviet State found more and more uses for the Orthodox Church within the framework of its diplomatic manœuvres and political warfare. The Church was expected to express publicly its agreement with the Soviet stand on any major international issue, especially when countries with an Orthodox population were involved.

The Russian Orthodox Church, which was unable to utter a word of criticism of Soviet policy, was persistently encouraged to criticise non-communist régimes for their alleged lack of humanitarian principles and their imperialistic character. Thus the Patriarch, who had to remain silent about the persecution of the ethnic groups of the Soviet Union, called upon the British Government to respect in Cyprus the principle of self-determination for small nations.[1] The Patriarch also strongly condemned the British and French invasion of Egypt but at the same time defended Soviet intervention in Hungary. He attributed the Hungarian Revolution to 'forces hostile to the people' and considered it right that 'our Government' should help the Hungarian nation in its struggle against those fomenting revolt.[2] The Church was also used for Soviet Russia's attempts to draw the uncommitted Afro-Asian countries closer to the communist camp. Metropolitan Nikolay issued a statement for Soviet-Ceylonese friendship,[3] a Russian church delegation was sent to Ethiopia and a representative of the Church participated in the foundation of the Soviet Society for Friendship with the Peoples of Africa. The more the Church did in supporting the régime, the more the latter seemed to demand from her.

The Church under Khrushchev

It was under the premiership of Nikolay Bulganin that the Orthodox Church enjoyed the maximum degree of freedom. Both he and Marshal Zhukov, who from 1953 to 1957 played an ever-increasing role in Soviet politics, seemed opposed to any too violent anti-religious agitation, let alone anti-religious action, at least as far as the Orthodox Church was concerned. With the increase of Khrushchev's power things became different. The Party decree which Khrushchev himself signed in 1954, urging all communists to conduct anti-religious propaganda in a tactful and 'scientific' manner, became a dead letter once Khrushchev became the principal master of Russia's destinies. Towards the end of the fifties the Press seemed to drop every restraint in attacking the Orthodox Church. It became much more aggressive than during the 'one hundred days' of atheist excesses which had provoked the Khrushchev decree of 1954. Not only priests, but even bishops, came in for bitter and sarcastic attacks. Their private lives were closely scrutinised and their wartime record was investigated. All over the country, Soviet newspapers went out of their way to print as unsavoury disclosures as possible about bishops and priests allegedly indulging in

[1] *Zh.M.P.*, 1957, no. 3, p. 3.   [2] *Zh.M.P.*, 1957, no. 1, p. 37.
[3] *Zh.M.P.*, 1957, no. 10, p. 23.

immoral living, embezzlements and drunkenness.[1] Nothing like that had appeared in the communist press since the 'thirties. In addition to merely verbal attacks there was anti-religious action also. Several hundred Orthodox churches and a few monasteries were closed down under various pretexts in different parts of the country.

The deterioration of Church-State relations in the Khrushchev era found expression in several other significant events. There were important personnel changes on both sides. Early in 1960 Georgii Karpov, who seemed to have grown lenient during his long tenure of office as chief Soviet supervisor of the Orthodox Church, was replaced by a younger and presumably tougher man, Vladimir Kuroyedov. Until this appointment, he was known chiefly as an expert on Marxist-Leninist ideology and problems of Party agitation and propaganda. Along with Karpov, some of his closest collaborators in the Council for the Affairs of the Orthodox Church were dismissed and replaced by new people. A few months after Kuroyedov had taken over, Metropolitan Nikolay ceased to be the Church's spokesman on foreign affairs[2] and the deputy of the Patriarch. This was the end of an epoch, as for seventeen years Church-State co-operation, both in its negative and positive aspects, had at the highest level been conducted primarily by two persons: Georgii Karpov for the Communists and Metropolitan Nikolay for the Orthodox.

However, for once the Church was not a passive spectator of the new campaign conducted against it. It took at least one important dignified step of self-defence. On December 30, 1959, the Holy Synod issued a courageous decree which amounted to a wholesale excommunication of all apostates who had supplied anti-religious and anti-clerical material to the communists and who thus had committed 'public acts of blasphemy'.[3]

Khrushchev himself had given the signal for the harsher treatment meted out to the Church under his premiership, for in his speeches he attached a much greater importance to religious problems than any of his predecessors. Part of the explanation of this fact was certainly that Khrushchev had learned from his extensive travels to many parts of Russia a good deal about the vitality of religion. This may have made him less optimistic than his predecessors about the speedy disappearance of religious belief and shown him the need for more extensive action against the Orthodox Church. Khrushchev's constant preoccupation

---

[1] E.g. *Kazakhstanskaya Pravda* of February 20th 1959, attacked the Archbishop of Alma Ata; *Sovetskaya Rossiya* of July 11th, 1959, attacked the bishops of Astrakhan and Stalingrad and Smolensk and Dorogobuzh; *Sovetskaya Rossiya* of June 24th, 1960, reported about a trial of the Archbishop of Kazan.
[2] *Zh.M.P.*, 1960, no. 7, p. 6.　　[3] *Zh.M.P.*, 1960, no. 2, p. 27.

with the problems of Church and religion may call for psychological analysis in addition to purely political comment. A psychologist might ask whether the man Khrushchev, who like most Russians of his generation was baptised in infancy by an Orthodox priest, and who, as he said, was nurtured on the Scriptures in a parish school,[1] had really fully solved the problem of religion for himself. At any rate both Khrushchev and the writers and agitators at his service felt the constant need to strengthen their atheist convictions by drawing attention to all instances in which Christians fail to live up to Christian principles.

II. THE GEOGRAPHICAL AND ETHNOGRAPHIC PATTERN

When the *modus vivendi* was reached between the Orthodox Church and the Soviet State, this meant theoretically the re-establishment of a minimum of religious and church life throughout the country. In practice, however, conditions vary a great deal in the various republics and provinces of the Soviet Union but, on the whole, it would be true to say that the influence of the Church and its power as an institution diminishes from West to East. This statement needs a good deal of qualification. Nevertheless it can serve as an approximate guide for a Russian religious geography, even if there are Western territories from which the Church is being kept out and localities in the Eastern portion of the Soviet Union where she is influential.

The Church is strongest in those areas which at first were not covered by the concordat but only gradually fell within its scope, namely those Western and Southern territories of the Soviet Union which during the war were under German and Rumanian occupation. In some of them, such as the Baltic states, Eastern Poland, Bessarabia and the Northern Bukovina, Soviet rule was established only in 1939 or 1940 and for this reason alone Soviet anti-religious policy has made little impact there. But, in addition, Germans and Rumanians occupied large parts of the pre-1939 Soviet Union where by the outbreak of war religious life was almost entirely destroyed. There the population took advantage of the Soviet retreat and spontaneously re-opened the secularised churches. This happened in the German-occupied areas with the connivance of the local military authorities. The people turned towards the Church not only for religious reasons but also in the search for a political third solution, neither Soviet nor German.[2] In the Rumanian-occupied areas

---

[1] *Tass*, April 4th, 1960.
[2] Alexander Dallin, *German rule in Russia 1941–1945*, London 1957, p. 493.

the Orthodox Church enjoyed the official support of the Rumanian State, although the Church which they encouraged was not the Russian but the Rumanian. The Rumanian Orthodox Church established as many as three bishoprics in the South-Western Ukraine, the so-called Transdnistria territory which she considered as her mission field.[1]

When the Soviets re-established their rule over the formerly occupied territories, they could not possibly show themselves less generous than their enemies, they could not revert to the *status quo ante* and close the churches which the Germans and their allies had allowed to open. This is why the Western parts of the Soviet Union remained in the post-war period the strongholds of the Russian Orthodox Church and of religion in general. Not only have the Western territories a very developed parish and diocesan organisation, but they are virtually the only parts of the Soviet Union where monasteries and convents continue to exist. There are sixty-nine monastic institutions in the Soviet Union, with about 5,000 monks and nuns.[2] These monasteries are almost entirely concentrated in the belt of border republics stretching from Estonia down to the Ukraine and Moldavia. These same territories contain at least one half of all churches and parishes of the Soviet Union.

The Ukraine

Russian Orthodox Church life is particularly intense in the Ukraine, a fact which is the more remarkable as that country also boasts the largest number of sectarian organisations. The Orthodox Church of the Ukraine forms a special Exarchate under the Moscow Patriarchal see, the only one existing within the Soviet Union. It consists of nineteen dioceses, each of which contains a larger number of parishes than the average diocese of Russia proper. In the Ukrainian dioceses there are 8,500 churches served by 6,800 priests.[3] This means that the Ukraine contains at least two-fifths of all the Orthodox churches open for religious worship in the Soviet Union though she has less than one-fifth of the country's total population.

Kiev, the Ukrainian capital, the city where the Christianisation of the Russian-Ukrainian lands began, has re-emerged as an important ecclesiastical centre of the Orthodox Church, and certainly as its most important monastic centre. Before the German invasion, church life in Kiev was virtually non-existent. Practically all the churches were closed

---

[1] *Internationale Kirchliche Zeitschrift*, 1944, p. 66.
[2] *The Russian Orthodox Church, Organisation, Situation, Activity*, published by the Moscow Patriarchate 1959, p. 78. The number of monks and nuns was given in the *Church Times*, July 18, 1958.
[3] *One Church*, vol. xi, 1957, no. 11–12, p. 387.

and a number of church buildings outstanding for their historical importance and architectural value were destroyed in 1934–36 in connection with the transfer of the Ukrainian capital from Kharkov to Kiev.[1] In the post-war period as many as twenty-eight churches in Kiev were again open,[2] a number which corresponds exactly to the number of churches existing under the German occupation.[3] The most famous of the churches functioning in Kiev is the Cathedral of St. Vladimir, built in 1862 to commemorate the thousandth anniversary of the foundation of the Russian State. The Cathedral, which was closed in the thirties, was taken over during the war by the 'Autonomous Church', one of the ecclesiastical parties emerging under the German occupation, and has remained open ever since then. The Orthodox Church could, however, not restore her rights over the much more venerable Cathedral of St. Sophia, the most important monument of medieval Christian Kiev, officially known as the 'Sophia-Museum' ever since it was closed for services in 1934.

On the other hand, the State was not able to keep the Church out of another 'museum' erected in Kiev on sacred ground, namely from the famous Monastery or Laura[4] of the Caves ('*Kievo-Pecherskaya Lavra*)', the cradle of Russian monasticism. After the October Revolution the Laura with its churches, chapels and cells was gradually secularised and transformed into the 'Ukrainian Museum City' (*Horodok*). The last monks left the monastery in 1929 and from then until September 1941, when the Red Army evacuated Kiev, there was no monastery any more but only 'a remarkable scientific and anti-religious centre', whose officials were busy debunking the religious devotions which the Laura had encouraged, especially the veneration of relics. When the museum workers returned after the recapture of the city by the Soviets, they found that monks were once again installed in the Laura. In the words of a Soviet newspaper it became once again a 'centre of religious propaganda.'[5] In reality, the Laura is a striking symbol of the uneasy co-existence between religion and atheism which characterises Church-State relations in the country as a whole. In parts it is a state museum

[1] B. Mikorskii, *Razrushenie kulturno-istoricheskikh pamyatnikov v Kieve v 1934–1936 godakh* (Destruction of the cultural and historical monuments in Kiev during the years 1934–36), Munich 1951.

[2] *One Church*, vol. xi, 1957, no. 11, pp. 9–10.

[3] *Internationale Kirchliche Zeitschrift*, 1943, p. 31.

[4] Laura, in Russian Lavra, is the name used for the four large Russian monasteries, namely those of Kiev, St. Petersburg, Sergievo (Zagorsk) and Pochaev. Also the monasteries of Mount Athos and Mount Sinai are in the Lavra class. The term is derived from the Greek word 'lavros' meaning street or passageway and also a whole row of monastic cells.

[5] *Literaturnaya Gazeta*, September 2, 1954.

where 'religious obscurantism' is denounced and where a 'natural explanation' is given why the mummified bodies of Russian saints and churchmen of which the Laura boasts are so well preserved.[1] At the same time the caves of the Laura attract masses of pilgrims from many parts of Russia who pay their respects to the founders of the monastery and to other great representatives of the Russian Christian past who found their last resting place there. According to a delegation of the Russian Orthodox Church of the United States, there were about 100 monks in the Laura in 1955, whilst the three Kiev convents — the Presentation Convent, the Florovskii and Petrovskii Convents, had 735 nuns and novices between them.[2]

There is yet another little triumph which not only Orthodoxy but Christianity in general has scored in Kiev. The main thoroughfare of the city, through which, according to tradition, St. Vladimir led the people to the Dnieper to be baptised, has resumed its traditional name 'Kreshchatik' meaning 'Street of Baptism'. The communists at first found this ancient name intolerable, especially since the street carrying it housed many important party and government buildings. So they changed 'Kreshchatik' into 'Vorovsky Street' to honour the communist revolutionary and Soviet diplomat Vatslav Vorovsky (1871–1923), who was of Polish descent. Only after the old Kreshchatik was completely destroyed during the war, was it allowed to resume its former name.

By contrast to Kiev, Kharkov (930,000 inhabitants), the former capital of the Soviet Ukraine, was not able to build up an Orthodox church life which could even remotely be compared with that of Kiev. The city has but one large cathedral and two churches. Odessa, on the other hand, is even better provided with churches than the capital. There are twenty churches in Odessa, the same number as under the Rumanian occupation, or one church per 33,000 inhabitants. In Kiev the ratio is roughly one church per 40,000 inhabitants. In the neighbourhood of Odessa there are also two Orthodox monasteries; one is St. Michael's Convent with 137 nuns,[3] and the other the Monastery of the Holy Assumption. This seems a particularly privileged institution. Its monks are not just grudgingly allowed to occupy part of a state museum as they are in the Kiev Laura but are the rightful occupants of the place even from the official point of view. The reason why the monastery has enjoyed the particular benevolence of the authorities is not difficult to decipher. The Monastery is the summer residence of the Patriarch, where he often receives distinguished foreign churchmen.

---

[1] *Le Figaro*, May 29, 1959. [2] *One Church*, vol. xi, 1957, no. 7–8, p. 234.
[3] Stanley G. Evans, op. cit., p. 8.

A case apart is the Orthodox Church of the Western Ukraine, about which more will have to be said in Chapter VII which deals with the Eastern Catholics, including those of the Western Ukraine, which have been absorbed by the Orthodox Church. Of all the larger Ukrainian and Russian cities Lvov, the former centre of Eastern (Uniate) Catholicism, has now the largest number of churches per head of population. There are twenty-two of them, or one for less than 20,000 inhabitants.[1] The centre of West Ukrainian Orthodoxy is not so much Lvov as Pochaev, situated twelve miles south-west of the town of Kremenets, within easy distance of the border which until 1917 separated the Austro-Hungarian Empire from that of the Czars. Pochaev is the see of the famous Laura of the Assumption, the architecture of which seems a compromise between West and East. But instead of serving as a symbol of the synthesis between Eastern and Western Christianity, Pochaev has been an apple of discord between the two and helped to fan their mutual antagonism. Since 1945, Pochaev's primary importance is that of a most popular place of pilgrimage attracting vast numbers of people not only from the Ukraine proper but also from the central provinces of Russia. The number of pilgrims increases from winter to summer, reaching its climax on Ascension Day, the Feast of the Assumption and the feast day commemorating St. Job of Pochaev (1551–1651) the Orthodox saint who was abbot of the monastery for twenty years.[2]

The Soviet authorities originally welcomed the fact that the monks of Pochaev conducted anti-Vatican propaganda in Galicia and preached sermons against 'the errors of Catholicism' in former Uniate churches.[3] However, as time went on the Soviet authorities discovered that Pochaev as a place of pilgrimage and religious mysticism did more harm to the communist cause than all advantages ensuing from the anti-Catholic missionary activities of its monks.[4] The Soviet police always regarded the Laura of Pochaev with suspicion and considered it a centre of Ukrainian nationalist machinations. At least two former abbots of Pochaev were arrested and charged with having co-operated with the violently anti-Soviet 'Ukrainian Insurgent Army' and similar organisations.[5] The same diffidence has been observed in official communist circles towards the four Orthodox monastic institutions of the Transcarpathian Ukraine (which belonged to Czechoslovakia until 1939) of which the convent of Mukachevo is the most important.

---

[1] *Tygodnik Polski-Dziennik Polski*, London, April 4, 1959.
[2] *One Church*, vol. xiii, 1958, no. 5–6, p. 185.
[3] *Zh.M.P.*, 1953, no. 10, pp. 31–2.   [4] *Nauka i Zhizn*, 1959, no. 4, p. 50.
[5] V. P. Andrievskii, *Pro Pochaivsku Lavru* (About the Pochaev Laura), Kiev 1960, pp. 35–6.

They were accused in the communist press of engaging in lucrative business transactions and appeals were made to monks and nuns to return to secular life.[1]

Other Western Borderlands

In addition to the Ukraine, there are three other Western borderlands of the Soviet Union inhabited by people with a predominantly Orthodox background. These are the Kaliningrad Province of the Russian Federation (RSFSR) and the Byelorussian and Moldavian Soviet Republics. The situation in these territories varies greatly from one to another. In the Province of Kaliningrad, with its 600,000 Russian and Byelorussian inhabitants, no organised Orthodox religious life was allowed to come into being. The protestant churches of the former German Koenigsberg were either destroyed or used for secular purposes.[2]

In Byelorussia, the Orthodox Church was not able to recover to the same extent as it was in the Ukraine. This may have been due to the fact that no big ecclesiastical centres such as Kiev or Pochaev existed in Byelorussia and also to the fact that an important section of the Byelorussian population is Catholic. There are seven hundred Orthodox parishes in the Byelorussian republic, not a great number considering that its total population is 8,000,000.[3] Many churches in the Eastern Byelorussian countryside which were still functioning at the time of the collectivisation are closed. The parishes have become much bigger than they used to be and the faithful often have very long distances to cover to reach the nearest church. Minsk cathedral and the churches in other towns and district centres are still overcrowded on holy days but the number of Orthodox believers in the country as a whole has dwindled.[4] Also the monastic life of Byelorussia cannot be compared with that of the Ukraine. There is only one convent, near Grodno, and only one monastery, in the town of Zhirovitsy, where the Byelorussian theological seminary has its premises.

Moldavia, on the other hand, offers a very different picture and the situation of the Church there seems to be similar to, if not better than, that in the Western and Central Ukraine. The Bishop of Kishinev and Moldavia has more monastic institutions under his jurisdiction than any other bishop of the Soviet Union; a heritage, of course, of pre-war days, when most of the Moldavian Republic, which is roughly identical with

---

[1] *Partiinaya Zhizn*, 1959, no. 2, p. 70.
[2] *Ostkircheninformationsdienst*, 1958, no. 9.
[3] Information supplied by Metropolitan Pitirim to the author.
[4] *Sovetskaya Etnografiya*, 1957, no. 2, p. 55.

Northern and Central Bessarabia, belonged to the Rumanian State. In the Kishinev diocese there are seven monasteries and eight convents and the bishop even holds special conferences of abbots and mothers superior, a unique feature in the Soviet Union.[1]

European Russia Proper

The 'second zone' of Russian Orthodox Church activities comprises those parts of European Russia where Soviet rule was not interrupted during the war. There too the Church was allowed to recover some of the ground which it had lost at the time of the persecution but by no means to the same extent as in the Western territories. The reopening of the closed or secularised churches, which was a *fait accompli* in the Western territories, became a more complicated matter in the Central, Eastern and Northern parts of European Russia. The wish of the local population or at least of a sizeable body of believers to have a church reopened was not sufficient for the authorities to accede to the request. Many churches were used as storehouses or for other purposes. In order to restore such a church to its original use the believers had to build, by their own means, alternative accommodation so that no material damage should ensue to the State from the desecularisation of a house of worship. In places where the churches had been closed without being put to another use, it was even more difficult to get them reopened, for there the believers were not able to offer the State a material bribe in return for the 'concession'.[2]

Although Orthodox parish life in Russia proper remained on a reduced scale, most of the dioceses which existed before the Revolution had been resurrected after the conclusion of the *modus vivendi* with Stalin. In Czarist times the dioceses used to coincide with the boundaries of the then existing administrative units, the guberniyas. To-day they coincide with the Soviet provinces and autonomous republics. Some of the new episcopal titles sound rather strange and unhistorical, especially those of the bishops whose cathedral towns have been renamed by the Soviet authorities and called after the leaders of the communist atheist régime such as Lenin, Kirov, Kalinin and Sverdlovsk, the communist official associated with the execution of the Russian imperial family. Such titles as 'Bishop of Astrakhan and Stalingrad' or 'Metropolitan of Leningrad and Novgorod' tend to underline the anomaly of Orthodox-communist co-existence. Other bishops have

---

[1] *Zh.M.P.*, 1956, no. 12, p. 6.
[2] V. Tendryakov, *Chudotvornaya* (The Miracle-working Ikon), Moscow 1959, p. 63.

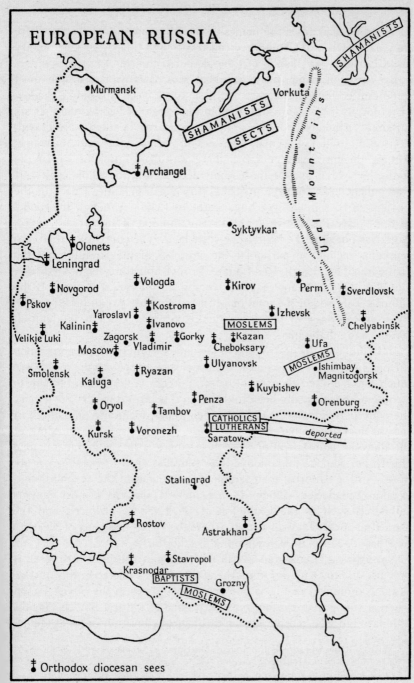

EUROPEAN RUSSIA

SHAMANISTS

•Murmansk

Vorkuta•

SHAMANISTS

SECTS

‡ Archangel

•Syktyvkar

‡Olonets

‡ Leningrad

‡ Novgorod

‡ Vologda

‡ Kirov

Perm•

‡ Sverdlovsk

‡Pskov

Yaroslavl ‡

‡ Kostroma

‡ Izhevsk

MOSLEMS

‡ Chelyabinsk

‡ Kalinin ‡

‡ Ivanovo

Velikie Luki

Zagorsk•

‡ Gorky

‡ Kazan

Moscow•

‡ Vladimir

Cheboksary

‡ Ufa

MOSLEMS

‡ Smolensk

‡ Ryazan

‡ Ulyanovsk

•Ishimbay

Magnitogorsk•

‡ Kaluga

‡ Kuybishev

‡ Oryol

‡ Penza

‡ Orenburg

‡ Tambov

CATHOLICS

‡ Kursk

‡ Voronezh

LUTHERANS

deported

Saratov•

Stalingrad•

‡ Rostov

‡ Astrakhan

‡ Krasnodar

‡ Stavropol

BAPTISTS

Grozny•

MOSLEMS

‡ Orthodox diocesan sees

Ural Mountains

79

included in their titles the names of the Autonomous Republics where they have their sees. Thus they call themselves 'Bishop of Cheboksary and Chuvashia' or 'Bishop of Izhevsk and Udmurtia'.

By virtue of being the Patriarchal see, Moscow is still the most important ecclesiastical centre of Russia but as such it is only a shadow of its former self. Before the Revolution, Moscow had as many as six hundred Orthodox churches. The vast majority of them were closed, destroyed, used for secular purposes or transformed into museums. Among the destroyed churches there was the Church of Christ the Redeemer which was the most richly decorated in the whole capital. It was pulled down in 1931 to make room for a gigantic 'Palace of the Soviets' to be topped by a huge statue of Lenin. Although the model of this Palace was shown at the Paris exhibition of 1937, construction work was not started even twenty years later. The churches turned into museums include in particular the churches of the Kremlin and the Cathedral of St. Basil in Red Square. In 1958 only thirty-eight Orthodox churches were open for religious worship in the Soviet capital.[1] If the suburbs were added the total of Moscow churches would be fifty-five.[2] Even on the basis of this larger figure, Moscow has but one church for 100,000 inhabitants.

In Leningrad, the destruction of Orthodox Church life has gone much further and its restoration after the conclusion of the *modus vivendi* was much more limited than in Moscow. Foreign ecclesiastical visitors to Leningrad have usually been told that in this second largest Soviet city there are between eleven and fifteen churches, including the church of the theological seminary and the house church inside the building of the diocesan administration.[3] At most, there is in Leningrad but one church per 200,000 inhabitants. The churches open to worshippers are mostly in the suburbs, for example the churches in the Smolensk and Serafim cemeteries.[4] They do not include the city's most famous cathedrals such as the Cathedral of St. Isaak of Dalmatia and the Cathedral of Our Lady of Kazan, where the Soviet Academy of Sciences now has its Museum of Religion and Atheism.

Nevertheless, Leningrad is still an important church centre, even if only because the 'city of Lenin, the cradle of the Proletarian Revolution' as the communists call it, is one of the two places in the Soviet Union where a young man can not only be trained as a priest in a theological seminary but also receive higher theological education in an academy.

[1] Moscow Radio transmission in Italian, December 11, 1958.
[2] *The Russian Orthodox Church*, etc., op. cit., p. 70.
[3] *One Church*, 1958, vol. xii, no. 9–10, p. 315.   [4] *Zh.M.P.*, 1958, no. 9, p. 18.

Leningrad's two theological training establishments are housed in the building which they occupied in Czarist times, namely the Laura of Alexander Nevsky, which also serves as a residence of the Metropolitan of Leningrad, but which is no longer used as a monastery.

The only other place to have both a theological seminary and an academy is Zagorsk, situated about fifty miles from Moscow. The place is named in honour of an Old Bolshevik, Vladimir Mikhailovich Zagorskii, but if one were to do justice to the spiritual importance of Zagorsk, one would have to revert to its old name, Sergievo. It is called after the great Russian Saint Sergius of Radonezh, who is buried there. He founded the Laura of the Holy Trinity, the *Troitse-Sergieva Lavra*. The monastery's long and glorious history was interrupted in 1921, when the Soviet authorities transformed part of it into a museum, another part into flats and the remainder into a teachers' institute. After the end of the war, the Laura was allowed to become a national shrine again. At Easter 1946 its bells, silent for many years, sounded anew. Monastic life was resumed in the Laura, albeit on a small scale. The theological teaching establishments, which were at first billeted in Moscow, took up their abode there and, above all, Zagorsk, or rather Sergievo, resumed its role as a place of pilgrimage to which many thousands of people flock each year from every part of the country. These pilgrimages reach their culminating point on great holy days particularly on St. Sergius Day and Trinity Sunday when the Patriarch himself celebrates the Liturgy in the presence of huge crowds. The many pilgrims who cannot find accommodation in the houses of Sergievo camp in the open air, often for three or four nights. On such occasions the crowds are so big and the queues so long that it is often difficult to get into the grounds of the monastery itself. The State has not entirely withdrawn from Zagorsk, for the Party maintains within the precincts of the monastery a so-called 'agitpunkt', a propaganda base; but this can hardly detract from the fact that Zagorsk is the most glorious expression of the other Russia, the Russia of the believers.

As far as the Russian provinces are concerned, the Church is comparatively strong in rural areas and those small and ancient towns which are only little touched by the social engineering of the Soviet era. On the other hand, the Church has lost ground in the industrial centres where the population became inflated during the Five Year Plan period. Even big industrial centres such as Sverdlovsk (777,000 inh.), Perm (628,000 inh.) or Kazan (643,000 inh.) have only two churches each. In the new 'socialist cities' built by the Soviet régime, no provision was made for the building of churches. The Government was firmly determined to keep Church and religion out of them. And yet the extremely materialistic atmosphere of these cities demanded a spiritual antidote. The pressure of the believers, all simple Russian workmen, for places of worship to be opened became so strong that official permission had to be given for the opening of Orthodox 'houses of prayer' in such places as Ishimbay, the new oil town of Bashkiria or Magnitogorsk, the seat of Russia's largest metallurgical plants.

News about religious life outside the places visited by foreign travellers is scant. The Church itself does not wish to boast about the fervour of believers in various parts of the country, for this might lead to an immediate increase of anti-religious propaganda in the areas concerned. Only very rarely and almost inadvertently does the *Journal of the Moscow Patriarchate* give some details about how the Orthodox faith is kept alive even in the more distant places of European Russia, or perhaps there even more than anywhere else. A glimpse of what the Orthodox religion still means in the vast territory of Northern Russia could be obtained from a description of an arduous journey which Bishop Theodosius of Archangel and Kholmogory made in 1955 to the remoter parishes of his diocese, which is the largest in the European part of the Soviet Union. Several localities to which he went had not seen an Orthodox bishop for over eighty years. No wonder his appearance caused tremendous excitement among the faithful. They welcomed him on their knees, with tears in their eyes. All churches where he celebrated the liturgy were overcrowded.[1] The zeal shown by the Bishop hardly pleased the authorities and the Holy Synod found itself compelled to recall him almost immediately after his memorable journey.

The Ugro-Finnish Peoples

The Bishop of Archangel and Kholmogory, when travelling across this vast diocese and in particular through the Komi Autonomous Republic, was the carrier of an important historical message which is still relevant in Russia to-day. He recalled the memory of the great Saint of the Russian North, St. Stephen of Perm, who was a most inspiring figure. In the fourteenth century, Stephen preached the Christian faith to the pagan people of the Zyryans, the Komi as they are now called, a nationality who together with the Mordvinians, Mari and Udmurts belong to the Finno-Ugrish group of peoples who live in considerable numbers throughout the Northern and Eastern parts of European Russia. The importance of St. Stephen's apostolate consisted in the fact that he did not come to the pagans in the wake of a military

[1] *Zh.M.P.*, 1955, no. 10, p. 12.

and political conquest, but was ahead of it. Those whom he converted became Christians before they became subjects of a Russian ruler. Stephen of Perm might be described as the first pioneer of a Russian Christian nationalities policy. He created a written language for the Zyryans into which he translated the Gospel and the liturgical books. In honouring Stephen of Perm the Russian Orthodox Church emphasises its claim that it is not a Church of the Russian people alone, but that it considers it its task to preach the Gospel, if not to all, at least to many of the peoples of the Russian Empire.

This part of the apostolate of the Russian Orthodox Church suffered tremendously under the Soviet régime. By weakening the Orthodox Church in the areas inhabited by peoples only recently or incompletely converted to Christianity the communist Government involuntarily brought about a certain pagan revival. As far as European Russia is concerned this revival occurred in particular among two Ugro-Finnish nationalities, the Mari (504,000) and the Udmurts (623,000). Among the Mari the pagan 'Kugu-Sorta' ('Big Candle') sect, which made its first appearance in the eighties of the nineteenth century, was particularly active. It was intensely nationalistic and opposed to technical progress and communist social reforms.[1] The rather elaborate Udmurt pagan religion which flourished particularly in the twenties and early thirties, caused the Soviet authorities even greater worries. This pagan religion of the Udmurts is a mixture of totemism, Christian influences and ancestor-worship, which provides the main ingredient. The Udmurt pagan cult is centred either around the 'kuala', the house-altar where people pray to their ancestors or the 'lud' which also played a part in the Mari pagan worship. It was to the 'lud', the sacred forest, that the Soviets took particular exception, because of the animal sacrifices offered and the mass character which the communal prayers in the forests took. In 1929, as many as 5,000 people attended an Udmurt pagan pilgrimage of this kind.[2] At least until 1931 there still existed pagan priests called 'bösyasi' in Udmurtia and quite a number of sacred forests were still 'in operation'.[3]

The extent to which the pagan worship in Udmurtia spread in the early years of collectivisation forced the anti-religious propagandists to soft-pedal the campaign against the Orthodox Church and to divert some of their energies to the fight against the 'old beliefs'.[4] Ultimately, the communists may have considered Christianity a lesser evil than

[1] A description of the Mari pagan revival under the Soviet régime is given in Walter Kolarz, *Russia and her Colonies*, London 1952, pp. 51-2.
[2] *Antireligioznik*, 1932, no. 17-18, p. 13.   [3] *Antireligioznik*, 1932, no. 4, p. 43.
[4] *Sovetskaya Etno rafiya*, 1932, no. 3-4, p. 213.

paganism particularly because of the latter's connection with nationalist trends. In the post-war period the Bishop of Izhevsk and Udmurtia was presumably able to recover the ground which the Church lost after the Revolution to the pagans.

Siberia

What happened in the land of the Mari and Udmurts gives us a foretaste of the kind of situation with which Russian Orthodoxy was faced in Soviet Asia. In this vast landmass the physiognomy of the Russian Orthodox Church has again its specific peculiarities. On the whole, Soviet Asia benefited less from the *modus vivendi* between Church and State than European Russia. In the whole territory between the Urals and the Pacific Ocean there is not a single Orthodox theological seminary — the nearest is in Saratov, nearly 150 miles inside European Russia. Whilst most dioceses of European Russia were resurrected, the Orthodox Church administration in Asia has been greatly cut down. The ten Siberian dioceses existing in the Czarist era — Omsk, Tobolsk, Tomsk, Yakutia, Yenisei, Transbaikalia, Irkutsk, Blagoveshchensk, Vladivostok and Petropavlovsk (Kamchatka) were reduced to five with their sees in Novosibirsk, Omsk, Krasnoyarsk, Irkutsk and Khabarovsk. Of these five dioceses only three were fully operative, as a rule, namely Novosibirsk, Omsk, and Irkutsk, whilst the other two were almost permanently vacant. The diocese of Khabarovsk and Vladivostok was usually administered by the Archbishop of Irkutsk and Chita, whose jurisdiction thus virtually extended over one-sixth of the entire territory of the USSR. He made periodic visits to the parishes in the far-flung territory along the Trans-Siberian Railwayline and even to places like Yakutsk and Olekminsk which are a considerable distance from any railway station.[1]

These deficiencies of church administration in Soviet Asia are not fortuitous. The régime seems to be out to make of 'socialist Siberia', the scene of so many new construction works and the country of the future *par excellence*, a land without Church and a land without God. In this the communist authorities have not entirely succeeded and from time to time they betray their disappointment about the vigour of Orthodox Church manifestations in an area from where the Church was supposed to disappear earlier than anywhere else in the Soviet Empire. They are dismayed to find that in these parts there are priests who do not behave as if they were representing a dying Church but are most active in defending their faith. A case in point was that of a humble village priest

[1] *Zh.M.P.*, 1952, no. 10, p. 48. *Zh.M.P.*, 1954, no. 3, pp. 8-9.

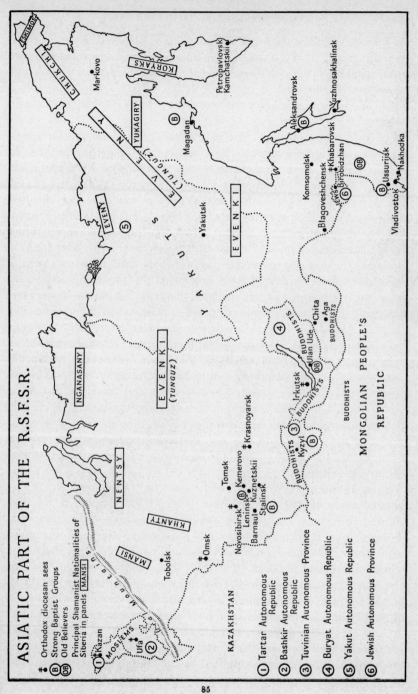

ASIATIC PART OF THE R.S.F.S.R.

⌗ Orthodox diocesan sees
● Strong Baptist Groups
Ⓑ
ⓄⒷ Old Believers

Principal Shamanist Nationalities of
Siberia in panels MANSI

⌗ Ⓑ ⓄⒷ

① Tartar Autonomous Republic
② Bashkir Autonomous Republic
③ Tuvinian Autonomous Province
④ Buryat Autonomous Republic
⑤ Yakut Autonomous Republic
⑥ Jewish Autonomous Province

ESKIMOS
CHUKCH
KORYAKS
YUKAGIRY
EVENY (TUNGUZ)
EVENY
EVENKI
NGANASANY
EVENKI (TUNGUZ)
NENTSY
KHANTY
MANSI
MOSLEMS

KAZAKHSTAN

MONGOLIAN PEOPLE'S REPUBLIC

BUDDHISTS

Markovo
Petropavlovsk Kamchatskii
Aleksandrovsk
Kuznosakhalinsk
Magadan
Komsomolsk
Khabarovsk
Birobidzhan
Ussurijsk
Nakhodka
Blagoveshchensk
Vladivostok
Yakutsk
Ulan Ude
Chita
Aga
Irkutsk
Kyzyl
Krasnoyarsk
Tomsk
Kemerovo
Novosibirsk
Leninsk
Kuznetskii
Barnaul
Stalinsk
Omsk
Tobolsk
Kazan
Ufa

85

in Buryat-Mongolia who was alleged to have delivered within a single year as many as 217 sermons containing religious instruction, apart from speaking dozens of times at weddings and funerals. He alone did more for religion than a hundred local communists and Komsomol members did against it, since their combined efforts resulted, in the same year, in only fifty lectures.[1]

There is, however, one part of Siberia from which the Orthodox Church has been successfully kept out by the Soviet authorities, its former mission areas in the Far North. At the time when the communists drove out the Orthodox Church from the tribal territories of the Arctic and Subarctic their evangelisation was still an unfinished business. Formally many of the tribes were Christian but in practice Christian baptism resulted in what is called in Russian 'dvoeverie' ('dual faith'), a co-existence of Christian and pagan beliefs. More frequently perhaps, the natives preserved pagan beliefs and added to them a number of the externals of the Christian faith. The things they took from the Orthodox Church included baptism, Christian names and especially ikons, which acquired in the nomadic tents the character of fetishes. Also some of the Christian saints were 'assimilated' to pagan beliefs, especially St. Nicholas whom the Tunguz (Evenki) regarded as a helpmate of the 'good spirit' of their own mythology whilst the Samoyeds (Nentsy) venerated him as the protector of the four-footed animals and therefore smeared reindeer fat and blood on his ikon. Given time, Christianity might have overcome the pagan beliefs but Soviet intervention put an abrupt end to this process of gradual transformation. By expelling the Christian missionary the régime strengthened in many places the authority of the Siberian witch-doctor, the Shaman.

Even in and after World War II, when the Orthodox Church was granted more elbow-room in other parts of the Empire, it was not allowed to resume work among the Siberian natives. The missionary dioceses, like Kamchatka, remained redundant despite all the good work they had once performed by building schools, hospitals and homes for nomad children.[2] On the other hand, it was not easy to eradicate Christian customs or even the wish among certain natives to be part of the Christian Church, a wish which was strong in areas where they had had close, permanent and prolonged contacts with the Russians. An anti-religious conference, which took place in 1938 in the Leningrad Institute of the Peoples of the North, supplied some interesting data in this respect. The reports submitted to the conference testified to the

[1] *Literaturnaya Gazeta*, Sept. 26 1956.   [2] *Zh.M.P.*, 1956, no. 11, pp. 13–14.

survival of Christian rituals among many nationalities of the Far North. The Evenki of the Markovo district of Chukotka in the north-eastern tip of Siberia went even so far as to demand the re-opening of an Orthodox church. This happened during the discussion about the new Soviet Constitution of 1936 which, amongst other things, held out the promise of freedom of religious worship.[1] Such demands were flatly refused, for the Soviet régime seemed to consider 'missionary' work among the small North Siberian nationalities to be its own exclusive prerogative.

These communist 'mission' activities often led only to the emergence of a new kind of syncretism in Northern Siberia, to the emergence of a 'triple faith' supplanting the dual faith of the Czarist period. Soviet customs and Soviet holidays were added to the pagan and Christian ones. Sergeev, a well-known Soviet expert on the Siberian peoples, tells how this 'triple faith' worked in practice in the case of an Ostyak (Khanty) family where a child was born. The child was first 'octobered', meaning that a kind of secular communist birth-celebration took place, then it was baptised by its grandmother, and finally some pagan amulets were attached to its cradle to preserve it against evil spirits.[2]

The Church in the Moslem Republics

In this regional survey about the situation of the Russian Orthodox Church, the eight Asian Soviet Republics have not yet been accounted for. Little can be said about Russian Orthodoxy in the three Transcaucasian Republics. In Armenia and Georgia the main religious forces are the two national Christian Churches — the Armenian Church and the Georgian Orthodox Church respectively, and in Moslem Azerbaidzhan Russian Orthodoxy represents a minority, not only among the religious-minded population as a whole, but probably also among the Christians of the country, except perhaps for the capital, Baku. No Russian Orthodox hierarch has his see in Transcaucasia, though one bishop of the North Caucasus region, that of Stavropol and Baku, betrays by his title that he claims jurisdiction over the Orthodox of the Azerbaidzhani republic.

In Central Asia, the situation differs greatly, not only from that of Transcaucasia, but also from the state of affairs in Siberia. In the Central Asian republics the Church may even have expanded in the post-revolutionary era as compared with the Czarist period. This is due to the large influx of Europeans, including many Orthodox Christians,

---

[1] *Antireligioznik*, 1938, no. 8–9, p. 38.
[2] M. A. Sergeev, *Nekapitalisticheskii put razvitiya malykh narodov Severa* (The non-capitalist way of development of the small nationalities of the North), Moscow–Leningrad 1955, p. 388.

especially into Kazakhstan. It would have been unwise from the point of view of the régime to deny them a certain minimum of religious freedom. Such a denial would have benefited only the various sects, which in this part of the Soviet Union are more active than anywhere else in the country, except for the Western border territories. During the period following World War II the number of Orthodox dioceses in Kazakhstan has increased from one to three. The local hierarchy now comprises the Archbishop of Alma Ata, the Bishop of Semipalatinsk and Pavlodar and the Bishop of Petropavlovsk and Kustanai. The foundation of the last-mentioned diocese took place at the beginning of 1957.[1] It was obviously connected with the arrival in the Provinces of Petropavlovsk and Kustanai of a large number of settlers participating in the opening up of the virgin soil belt of Northern Kazakhstan. The Orthodox Church now has its priests and houses of worship not only in all the towns of the Kazakh republic but also in a large number of the new workers' settlements.

Orthodox Church activities in the four other Central Asian republics are directed by the Bishop (since 1958 Archbishop) of Tashkent and Central Asia, whose diocese is probably more prosperous than many of the inner-Russian bishoprics. Priests under his jurisdiction serve in most Central Asian towns from Ashkhabad in Turkmenistan to Frunze in Kirghizia and Samarkand, the holy city of Islam, where there are three Orthodox churches. One of them, the church devoted to St. George, was built as late as 1946 by the voluntary labour of the local Orthodox believers. Building work went on for several months from the early morning until late at night.[2] The fervour and the spirit of sacrifice of the Christians of Samarkand and other Central Asian places may have made an impression on the local Moslems. There is, however, no direct evidence from Russian Central Asia that the Orthodox Church has been successfully proselytising among Moslems, although such evidence was forthcoming from the Chinese border province of Sinkiang (Eastern Turkestan) where there is a small number of Russian Orthodox Christians. There the Moslems of the Ili District, which is in close proximity to the Soviet border, were said to treat the Orthodox with particular respect. They visited the Orthodox Church and listened to the sermons of the Orthodox priest. There were even many instances of local inhabitants being baptised, along with their families. 'The light of Orthodoxy', said this report from Sinkiang, 'has not only been kindled, but continues to spread.'[3]

[1] Zh.M.P., 1957, no. 9, p. 7.   [2] Zh.M.P., 1947, no. 3, pp. 56–7.
[3] Zh.M.P., 1949, no. 3, p. 8.

This happened before the Chinese communists took over the Sinkiang Province, and what occurred there might not have been possible under Soviet conditions in Western Russian Turkestan. The Russian Church certainly has some experience in missionary activities in Moslem areas, and is still bound to give some thought to the matter, but cannot easily take any practical steps. The Missionary Council which the Holy Synod established in 1946 with a bishop as chairman, did not devote its visible efforts to Moslems and other non-Christians, but to Old Believers, sectarians and Catholics, and it also looked after certain missionary establishments abroad, especially the Palestine Mission. Little was heard of this Council, apart from the fact of its being established. In various official accounts listing the departments of the Russian Orthodox Church administration it has not been mentioned. From this one might conclude that either it has ceased to exist or that the Church is reluctant to advertise its activities.

III. THE PROBLEMS OF THE CHURCH

New Priests and New Bishops

We may agree with the French Cardinal Suhard that Constantine is a greater danger to the Church than Nero, and yet have to admit that the Russian Church has gained rather than lost from the *modus vivendi* with the Soviet State. Its survival as an institution has become more secure as the result of its reconciliation with the communist Government. This has guaranteed the exercise of religious worship, not only to the present generation but also to the next, by allowing the Church to resume the training of priests. This one concession of the State may prove to be more important than anything the Church conceded to Stalin and his successors. The concessions of the Church to the State affect only the present, whilst the opening of theological schools affects both the present and the future. Its effects can still make themselves felt in thirty or forty years' time or even longer. Even if one does not wish to look so far ahead, it is clear that the theological schools, as long as they exist, are an ideological challenge to the régime and its totalitarian aspirations. A young Russian upon reaching the age of eighteen, has, at least theoretically, the possibility of embracing an education and of leading a life which takes him far away from the Soviet pattern or, as a communist put it, which transplants him from the twentieth century, the century of Communism, to the Middle Ages.[1] Of course, the theological schools do have a certain contact with Soviet society. Their

[1] *Komsomolskaya Pravda*, March 24, 1957.

students celebrate the state holidays, and an official of the Council for the Affairs of the Russian Orthodox Church lectures them about the Constitution of the USSR, but otherwise they are 'alien bodies' from the communist point of view.

The theoretical possibility of entering a theological school is a practical possibility for at least several dozens of young Russians each year. This can be judged from such figures as are available, about the number of theological students. For instance, the Zagorsk seminary and academy, each running a four-year course, had in 1954–5 220 students altogether. The seminary alone had 140 students, so there could not be more than an average of 35 graduates per annum.[1] In the same year the Leningrad theological schools had 160 students not including those studying through correspondence courses. For this method of study only ordained priests and deacons are eligible.[2] The Odessa seminary had 150 students in 1956.[3] In the remaining five theological seminaries the number of students is comparatively small. Thus in 1955 there were 54 students in the Stavropol seminary and 74 in that of Kiev.[4] The total number of theological students throughout the Soviet Union was estimated in the same year as 1,500, but this may be on the optimistic side and include students of correspondence courses.[5] The number of theological graduates ordained each year is smaller than the demand for priests. In 1960 only 155 new graduates of the theological seminaries and academies became parish priests in the whole of Russia.[6] Nevertheless the new ordinations will render possible a certain continuity of orderly church life, particularly if the insufficient quantity is made up by the quality of the new clergy.

More important still is the question, what kind of bishops will take over from the old generation, the veterans of persecution who, sooner or later, will disappear from the scene. Under the rule of Patriarch Alexis the episcopate has been rejuvenated. It has been joined by people who have lived abroad for many years and who were either emigrés themselves or children of emigrés. Other bishops were promoted from the ranks of priests from the annexed Western territories who had received Orthodox theological training, for instance at the theological faculty of Warsaw University or at the Paris Theological Institute, at a time when no theological schools were open in the Soviet Union itself. Finally, more and more bishops are post-war graduates of the theological academies of Zagorsk and Leningrad. They are usually

---

[1] One Church, vol. x, 1956, no. 5–6, p. 150. [2] One Church, vol. xii, no. 9–10, p. 318.
[3] Moscow Radio, 'Return to the Homeland' transmission, May 21, 1957.
[4] Zh.M.P., 1955, no. 8, p. 18; One Church, vol. xi, 1957, no. 7–8, p. 233.
[5] Stanley G. Evans, op. cit., p. 11. [6] Zh.M.P., no. 1, 1961, p. 19.

people who have had a certain experience of practical Soviet life, acquired either in the army or in a secular profession. This knowledge of life may be a great asset to them both in their pastoral work and when facing the authorities.

Communist Infiltration into the Church

At this point it would be a grave mistake to overlook the human elements of the Church which are encouraged by the political environment, in other words by that infiltration of the régime into the ranks of the Orthodox Church which is the greatest problem it has to face. The Soviet authorities have a natural interest in knowing what is going on in the Church. They want to probe the loyalty of priests and believers. They want to push the religious groups in certain directions, partly to discredit them in the eyes of the believers, partly to enhance their usefulness to the régime. The Soviet police is an extremely versatile institution. It operates on the widest possible front and one must therefore accept *a priori* that the Churches, especially the largest of them — the Russian Orthodox Church, are an important field of its manifold activities. Of particular importance for the régime are the theological seminaries and academies. It must be most anxious to infiltrate its agents into them, for these are the institutions which will help the Church to perpetuate its influence. Every prospective student of a theological school, it is true, must present a letter of recommendation from his parish priest or his bishop, and in a democratic country this stipulation might keep out undesirable elements. In the Soviet Union, however, it is not beyond the power of the police to extort such recommendations when needed. So in addition to the *bona fide* students, the theological teaching establishments may be expected to include a certain number of people who look after the interests of the Party and the state security apparatus. This infiltration undermines the Church from within. It creates fear and deep distrust in the ranks of the clergy, who cannot know who is foe and who friend in their midst. Among believers it arouses fear and suspicion of certain priests and bishops. Some religious people even keep away from the Church for this reason or join one of the numerous sects.

Suspicions are strengthened by graduates and even lecturers of theological schools and academies suddenly abusing the Church and its institutions and proclaiming themselves champions of militant atheism. It is from the ranks of such renegades that the régime has recruited its most active anti-religious propagandists. They usually write the most sensational anti-religious newspaper articles and are the main attractions

of anti-religious meetings.[1] The question arises whether these people
have undergone a genuine 'conversion' to atheism or whether the Party
simply withdrew them from the Orthodox Church to make public use
of the knowledge they had acquired on religious and ecclesiastical
matters whilst being temporarily associated with the clerical profession.

Church Finances

Another source of danger for the Church is tied up with the fact that
it has become again a property-owning organisation. In addition to
the various forms of public and co-operative property in the Soviet
Union there exists, since the end of the World War II, church property
also. This is almost as great an anomaly as the existence of theological
schools in the Communist State. The church property does not amount
to much but it is nevertheless remarkable that it should be admitted at
all, especially since the Church is able to own even means of production,
albeit on a minute scale. The Convent of St. Michael in Odessa, for
instance, was allowed to acquire an electric corn-grinding mill, which
is proudly shown to foreign visitors. The Church is also an employer
of manpower and in December 1955 the Pochaev Laura alone had as
many as 106 hired hands on its payroll.[2]

The Church is entitled to organise the manufacture of church vessels,
vestments, altar bread and ikons, but of particular importance from the
point of view of church finances is the production of candles. The largest
church candle factories are those in the New Virgin Monastery in
Moscow and in the Laura of Pochaev, the former producing candles of
paraffin, the latter of bees-wax. Production of candles is inexpensive
but they are sold in the churches at a 'fabulous profit', as an American
Orthodox Church delegation put it.[3] The believers gladly pay the prices
charged, knowing that the candle offerings provide a large part of the
parochial income. Few believers, however poor, omit to buy one or
several candles at each service.

Generosity is in general a particular characteristic of the Russian
believer and it is one of the surest expressions of the loyalty of the
Orthodox Christians towards their Church. Nevertheless, this generosity
has the tremendous disadvantage of making the Church too wealthy and
rendering the calling of the Orthodox priest too remunerative. Thus
clerical salaries have become comparatively high, higher than the
earnings of skilled workers, teachers and the average civil servant. A

---

[1] A collection of their statements can be found in the symposium *Pochemu my
porvaly s religiei* (Why we broke with religion), Moscow 1958.
[2] *One Church*, vol. xii, 1958, no. 5–6, p. 184.
[3] *One Church*, vol. x, 1956, no. 10, p. 302.

senior priest in Moscow may earn 3,000 roubles per month and even a village priest may have a good income.[1] Only a comparatively small proportion of this is taken away by the State in the form of direct taxation — never more than fourteen per cent. An Anglican ecclesiastical dignitary visiting the Soviet Union in 1954 said that the Russian priests looked prosperous, their clothes were made of good material, their footwear was above average and a few had expensive cars.[2] If there is a similar belief in Russia that a clergyman can live a very decent if not comfortable life, then the seminaries may well attract not only devoted young men but also materialistically-minded persons. At the same time Soviet anti-religious propaganda is being enriched by an anti-clerical argument which always has greater popular appeal than statements about the incompatibility between science and religion. However, young materialists may be deterred from becoming priests by considering the comparatively high clerical salaries as 'danger money' which it would be unwise to accept.

Precarious Toleration

The gifts which the Church has offered to the Soviet Caesar have made no difference to his fundamental attitude towards it. In wartime he took the savings of the believers and used them for the national defence. In peacetime he was pleased to accept the statements of the clergy about 'progress' and 'peace in the whole world'. Nevertheless he has always felt that the Church has done more harm than good to the State, even at the time when it made the greatest moral and material sacrifices to the régime. From the long-term point of view, what the Church says and how it behaves towards the State is not decisive; what does matter is that the Church should continue to exercise an influence on the minds of the people. Nobody has formulated the essence of the true communist attitude towards the Church better than the young Soviet writer Vladimir Tendryakov in his anti-religious novelette *The Miracle-working Ikon*. In this work, which is remarkable for its frankness, a woman-teacher representing the communist side tells a priest 'Your very existence is enough for us'.[3] This indeed is the core of the problem. It is the very existence of the Church to which the régime objects and to which it can never be reconciled. The Orthodox Church has no right to exist in the Communist State. It is only tolerated, and the policy of toleration may be revoked at any moment if the party

---

[1] *One Church*, vol. xi, 1957, no. 3–4.
[2] Mervyn Stockwood, *I went to Moscow*, London 1955, p. 83.
[3] V. Tendryakov, *Chudotvornaya*, Moscow 1959, p. 65.

leadership so decides. This shows the precarious character of the material assets which the Church and her servants have again accumulated and the futility of both the positions of honour they have acquired in various régime organisations and the medals and orders which have been awarded to their leaders by the State.

The position of the Church also remains precarious because the State is clearly determined to starve it intellectually, to confine its influence to the field of worship and to prevent it from becoming a factor in the intellectual life of the country. The number of religious books which can be printed is insignificant, to say the least, and some of them are only partly religious and partly serve political propaganda, like the collections of sermons and statements by Metropolitan Nikolay, or the minutes of the ecclesiastical peace conference of Zagorsk. The complete edition of the Russian translation of the Bible issued by the Moscow Patriarchate in 1956 was printed in only 50,000 copies, or little more than two copies per parish. The only Russian periodical published by the Church, the *Journal of the Moscow Patriarchate*, appears in a monthly edition of 15,000 to 25,000 copies. The only other Church periodical, the *Pravoslavnii Visnik*, is published in the Ukrainian language in Lvov in an edition of 3,000 copies, and is obtainable in the Western Ukraine only.[1] As a rule scholarly works produced by the new generation of Russian theologians can be neither printed nor mimeographed; they can only be copied.

The result of all this is that the Church can do little to improve the intellectual level of its members in order to fight superstition and to counteract, by proper instruction, the growth of certain extremist sects which bring religion into disrepute. All this must be said as a warning against too optimistic an assessment of the present and future of the Russian Orthodox Church. And yet nothing can detract from the great religious mission the Church has discharged under the most difficult circumstances. Nor can any resurrection of terror ever nullify the spiritual power which the Church has radiated under Soviet rule and the consolation which her liturgy and her sacraments have given to millions of souls.

---

[1] *One Church*, vol. xii, 1958, no. 7–8, p. 262.

III

The Fight for National Orthodox Churches

'Not in the dogma, nor in the canon law, nor in the dominant historical practice of our Church is there any basis for tasks which are alien to her, namely, for encroachments on national freedom, language, culture, and the whole tenor of life of any nation. The history of the Eastern Church, it is true, has contradicted this norm—in the majority of cases because she found herself subject to the political power and in the second instance because she was sinfully attracted by national passions.'

Professor Kartashev, leading Russian theologian.[1]

The problem to be discussed in this chapter is somewhat different from those examined in the rest of the book. The church bodies whose history we are now to consider were forced to defend their existence not only against the Soviet State but also against the Russian Orthodox Church. The question of the national Orthodox Churches, or rather of aspirations towards national Churches, is therefore an extremely delicate one. It is easy to fall a victim to partisan passion on this issue and to pronounce firmly either for or against the Patriarchal Church of Moscow. It is not our task, however, to look for the guilty party. The crux of the matter is that Christian Churches, priests and laymen, have become deeply involved in a nationalist struggle and that the totalitarian atheist State in its communist and nazi incarnations has benefited greatly from their mutual lack of charity and understanding.

The strengthening of local nationalism which resulted from the collapse of the Czarist régime was bound to have repercussions inside the Russian Orthodox Church. The Church was unable to preserve her unity once Russia was dismembered. The Orthodox Churches of Georgia, Estonia, Poland and Latvia went their own way, and even among the non-Russian Slavs of the Soviet Union the desire for ecclesiastical independence grew. In a way this process of disintegration accorded with Orthodox tradition. The Orthodox world prides itself not on organisational unity but, on the contrary, on multiplicity. There is no limit to the number of autocephalous national Orthodox Churches that can come into being as a result of political and territorial changes.

[1] *Put*, September–October 1933, no. 40, p. 45.

With the development of national consciousness in Eastern and South-Eastern Europe and the establishment of new national states the number of autocephalous Churches has risen steadily. The nineteenth century saw the emergence of autocephalous Orthodox Churches in Serbia (1879), Rumania (1885) and Greece (1850); the twentieth century in Poland (1924), Albania (1938) and Bulgaria (1946). The foundation of such new Churches is not always to the liking of the older Orthodox Churches, which see their authority diminished. The Oecumenical Patriarch of Constantinople, for instance, long opposed the autocephaly of the Bulgarian Church and the Serbian Patriarch is unlikely ever to agree to the setting up of an autocephalous Church in Macedonia, a matter of bitter controversy in Yugoslavia. On the other hand, the nations belonging partly or entirely to the Orthodox faith have usually considered national independence incomplete without ecclesiastical independence. The demand for an autocephalous Church has therefore become an almost obligatory item of their political programme, a fact recognised by the Russian theologian, Professor Troitsky, when he said: 'For the people, belonging to another nationality than that of the Mother-Church is usually a motive for seeking ecclesiastical autonomy.'[1] It would be true to say that autocephaly has even become a nationalist obsession; to many people the autocephalous status of their Church became more important than the Church itself.

The Russian Orthodox Church has, wherever possible, answered the desire for autocephaly with a stern 'No'. This opposition need not necessarily be interpreted merely as an expression of a chauvinistic frame of mind. In the early years of the Soviet régime the Russian Orthodox Church had good reason to view the national Church experiments with suspicion, especially in the Ukraine. The Patriarchal Church there fought desperately to defend its organisational and doctrinal integrity against attempts at subversion. The political struggle against Soviet power demanded likewise a concentration of the Christian forces and not their atomisation, which the Autocephalists apparently brought about. On the other hand, the fact remains that the Russian Church's opposition to the idea of national Churches was guided as much by tradition as by calm reflection. The Russian Church's close ties with the centralist state of the Czars prevented it from having much understanding of the idea of national autonomy and independence of the non-Russian peoples. Historically it was too much identified with Muscovy to see the problems of Orthodoxy from the point of view of Kiev, Tiflis

---

[1] *Messager de l'Exarchat du Patriarchat Russe en Europe Occidentale*, Paris, July 1952, no. 11, p. 25.

or Tallin. As time went on, this opposition of the Russian Church to national ecclesiastical aspirations changed its character, becoming pro-Soviet, and the ecclesiastical Moscow of the Orthodox Patriarch lent a helping hand in the struggle which Soviet Moscow conducted against the federalist and separatist tendencies of the local nationalities.

I. THE GEORGIAN CHURCH

A Glorious and Tragic History

The Church of Georgia is both one of the oldest and one of the most unfortunate Churches existing in the Soviet Empire. According to legend, the beginnings of Christianity in Georgia go back to the Apostle Andrew, who preached in Western Georgia, chiefly in the region now known as Abkhazia. The actual conversion of Georgia, or Iberia to use the historical name, took place in about A.D. 330, over six and a half centuries before the Christianisation of Russia (988–89). The status of the Georgian Church, too, was for a long time superior to that of the Russian Church. The institution of the Georgian Catholicosate goes back to the fifth century. In the eighth century the Georgian Church acquired complete independence, apart from owing a purely theoretical allegiance to the Patriarch of Antioch: this came to an end in 1053, 536 years before the establishment of the Moscow Patriarchate.

But the ancient and exalted status of the Georgian Church failed to save it from Russian encroachments after Georgia's annexation by the Czar, in 1801. The independence of the Georgian Church was broughts to an end in 1811, when the last head of the Church, the Catholicos Anthony II, was exiled to Russia and the national Church of Georgia was transformed into a branch of Russian Orthodoxy. The independent Catholicos-Patriarch was replaced by an Exarch, a member of the Holy Synod of St. Petersburg. Only the first Exarch was a Georgian; his successors, sixteen altogether, were of Russian nationality. The Russian Exarchs not only brought a large number of Russian clergy into the country but they also substituted Church Slavonic for Georgian as the liturgical language. After the 1905 Revolution, demands for the re-establishment of the Georgian Church became more and more insistent. The Georgian nobility, in a moving letter to the Viceroy of the Caucasus, said that as a result of the suppression of the Georgian Church, faith had died and churches were empty even on holy days. The clergy lived in miserable poverty; the spirit that inspired their training was opposed to the aspirations of the people, with the result that the latter looked

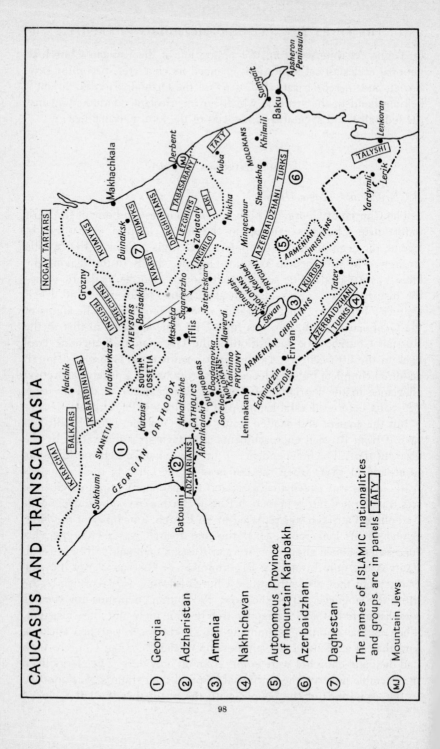

CAUCASUS AND TRANSCAUCASIA

① Georgia

② Adzharistan

③ Armenia

④ Nakhichevan

⑤ Autonomous Province
of mountain Karabakh

⑥ Azerbaidzhan

⑦ Daghestan

The names of ISLAMIC nationalities
and groups are in panels TATY

Ⓜ Mountain Jews

upon them merely as state functionaries. Only the re-establishment of an independent Church with an elected Catholicos at its head could deliver religion from its 'state of terrible agony'. A similar appeal was directed by Georgian priests to the Holy Synod. The petition was rejected and the leader of the movement for Georgian Church independence, Bishop Kirion, was forced to leave the country. He was confined in a Russian monastery.[1]

The state of religious life in Georgia and the plight of her Church, especially during the last years of Czarist rule, go far to explain the general situation in that country. The denationalised Church could be no friend of the Georgian national liberation movement. Her agony contributed to breed a generation of young people embracing anti-religious ideas. Among them was a student of the Tiflis Orthodox seminary, Soso Dzhugashvili, better known as Iosif Vissarionovich Stalin, the son of a simple pious Georgian peasant woman who wanted her boy to become a priest. It was in his Tiflis seminary that the tragedy of Stalin began. It was to become the tragedy of the peoples of Russia. The seminary which young Dzhugashvili entered in 1894 was part of that same Church which the letter of the Georgian nobility described in such alarming terms ten years later. It was a Church which had lost most of its soul. Transformed into a Russian institution, it was alienated from the Georgian people and could not even keep young Georgian seminarists under its spiritual spell. No wonder that the materialistic teachings of Marxism gained ground among the older pupils of the Tiflis seminary, including Dzhugashvili. Stalin's political development became to no small degree an indictment of the decay of the Georgian Church under Czarist Russian rule.

The Soviet Occupation

In the later course of events in Georgia Lenin's and Stalin's Bolshevik Party played at first a very minor role. The political driving force in the country were the Mensheviks, who founded the independent Georgian Republic which remained in being for over three years. This party, though not embracing the militant atheism of the Bolsheviks, had little use for the Church and failed to allocate her a significant role in the Menshevik state. The events of 1917 of course enabled the Georgian Church to shake off the yoke of the Russian Holy Synod: she became a Georgian national institution and was able to recover her autocephaly under a Catholicos. When in March 1921 armed Bolshevik aggression swept away the Georgian democratic republic and the Menshevik

[1] Michel Tamarati, *L'Eglise Géorgienne*, Rome 1910, pp. 393-6.

leaders fled the country, the Catholicos, Leonid Okroperidze, remained at his post. He had defended the rights of the Georgian Church under Czarist rule and no doubt he was determined to do the same during the Soviet occupation, but he died during a cholera epidemic in August 1921.

His successor, Catholicos Ambrosius Khelaya, occupied his high office for only a short time. He showed great courage and became the true spokesman of his people. In February 1922, he addressed a memorandum to the Conference of Genoa denouncing the communist oppression of the national and religious life of Georgia and demanding the setting up of an international commission to organise a plebiscite in the country. The communists could neither forgive nor forget this bold move of the Catholicos. In March 1924 he and eight other members of the Georgian clergy were put on trial. The trial took place in a theatre in Tiflis, to attract the maximum publicity. At its crucial stage a mass demonstration by four thousand workers was held in front of the theatre. The workers carried banners inscribed 'Down with the Catholicos', and demanding that the prisoners be condemned to death. The court proceedings were interrupted to hear the workers' delegates and to allow the presiding judge to address the manifestants, assuring them that exemplary punishment would be inflicted on the delinquents.[1] At the end of this ten-day travesty of justice, the Catholicos and his co-defendants were found guilty of treason and deserving of death. However, in view of the strengthening of the Soviet régime, said the verdict, it was possible to mete out milder punishment to the accused. The Catholicos was sentenced to eight years' imprisonment, four priests received prison terms of from two to five years, and the rest were acquitted.[2]

Deprived of its fearless leader, the Georgian Catholicosate could eke out in future only a shadow existence. The canonical independence of the Church of Georgia, so ardently desired by the clergy and the believers, became almost meaningless as a result of communist persecution. What was the use of autocephaly when Georgia's cathedrals, churches and monasteries were transformed into barns and communist clubs, or were pulled down altogether?

The Georgian Godless Movement

The anti-religious campaign was waged with greater intensity in Georgia than in many other parts of the Soviet Union. This was not so much because the Georgian communists were more militant atheists as because of the savage way in which political and ideological opposition

---

[1] *The Times*, March 13, 1924.   [2] *The Times*, March 22, 1924.

was crushed in a country that had become subject to Soviet rule only after a hard fight. It suffices to say that the man mainly responsible for the suppression of opposition in Georgia, including religious opposition, was L. P. Beriya, at first head of the Georgian GPU and from 1931 to 1938 supreme party chief of the Georgian Soviet Republic. In these positions Beriya did much for the anti-religious cause and greatly encouraged the building up of a strong atheist movement. Georgia's 'Militant Godless' organisation was one of the most efficient anywhere in the Soviet Union. In 1931 it reported 101,586 members, forming 1,478 cells. This statistical precision alone was significant, for most other regional branches of the League of Militant Godless produced only very round and vague membership figures.[1]

Not only was the League of Militant Godless in Georgia unaffected by the widespread decline that the League suffered in the thirties, but it succeeded in increasing its membership very considerably. In 1938 the Georgian League had 145,413 members, representing over four per cent of the total population of the Republic. This was an all-Union record. In the Ukraine, for instance, League membership had dropped by 1938 to one-sixth of the 1931 figure, and was much below one per cent of the total population. The Georgian Godless were also unrivalled in the number of atheist lecturers they were able to send regularly into the ideological battlefield, greater even than that at the disposal of the Province of Moscow.[2] It is not surprising therefore that the Georgian atheist organisation should have received particular praise at a conference in July 1938 on anti-religious work in the national republics, a conference otherwise devoted to the shortcomings and omissions of atheist propaganda. Yemelyan Yaroslavsky, the Chairman of the League of Militant Godless, delivering the main conference report, approvingly noted that Comrade Beriya gave his personal attention to the fight against religion.[3]

Pagan Revival in the Mountains

Although there are several religious minorities in Georgia (Armenian Christians, Moslems, Roman Catholics, Baptists and other 'sects'), atheist propaganda was concentrated first of all on Georgia's national Church. By their harsh treatment of the Orthodox Church the communist authorities even encouraged in some remote parts of the country the revival of ancient pagan beliefs which had never completely disappeared. There were three areas in particular where the pagan revival

---

[1] *Antireligioznik*, 1931, no. 7, p. 101.   [2] *Antireligioznik*, 1938, no. 12, p. 56.
[3] *Antireligioznik*, 1938, no. 7, p. 23.

assumed major proportions — in the South Ossetin Autonomous Province; in Khevsuria, less than ninety miles to the north of Tiflis, high up in the Caucasus; and in Svanetia in the mountainous part of Western Georgia.

In Southern Ossetia the Christian churches were closed after the Sovietisation of the territory, allegedly at the request of the local population itself. In 1932 there was not a single church left in the whole Autonomous Province. The place of the Christian Church had been taken by the cult of the old Ossetin gods, the Dzuary, to whom the people prayed and to whom they brought sacrifices. Some of these gods were not entirely pagan, being in the popular mind associated with certain Christian saints, chief among them the principal Ossetin god Uastrdzhi, the protector of cattle, who was identified with St. George. As the observance of this polytheistic Ossetin religion, and particularly of its numerous holy days, was very widespread, the communists began to take stern measures against it. Having eliminated Christianity in Southern Ossetia they considered the pagan beliefs the 'main danger' on the local religious front.[1]

In the almost inaccessible territory of Khevsuria the few existing churches were destroyed soon after the communist revolution, whilst the pagan religion survived at least until the middle of the thirties. The Khevsurs, a sub-group of the Georgian people, even practised two types of pagan cults presided over by two different types of priests, the 'black priests', who were magicians not unlike the Siberian Shamans, and the 'white priests', who administered the cult of the ancestors and were considered by the Soviet régime to be its main enemies.[2] As late as 1935 the Central Anti-Religious Museum in Moscow sent an expedition to Khevsuria to enquire into the social and property-owning position of the pagan priests and their assistants. This expedition predicted in its report that the Khevsurs, of whom there were but 3,600, would soon abandon their religion since the construction of a highway linking Barisakho, the centre of Khevsuria, with Georgia proper, would open the way to their re-education in a materialistic spirit.[3] Apparently the construction of the highway did not solve the Khevsur problem. Its solution was achieved only when the authorities resettled the Khevsurs from their mountain homes into the Georgian plain, a measure officially dictated by economic considerations, but no

[1] *Antireligioznik*, 1932, no. 10, pp. 39–40.
[2] Prof. V. A. Gorko-Kryazhina, *V Khevsurskikh Alpakh*, 'In the Khevsurian Alps', in A. Chzimbe, *Lyudi Ushchelii* (People of the Ravines), Moscow–Leningrad 1929, pp. 294–5.
[3] *Sovetskaya Etnografiya*, 1936, no. 1, p. 165.

doubt prompted by ideological reasons as well.[1] In Svanetia the main feature of the temporary pagan revival was the cult of the goddess of fecundity.

The Church under Catholicos Kallistrat

The primitive ancient paganism in the mountains was naturally only a very minor problem for the Georgian Church compared with the brand new communist paganism of the cities. The man who more than any other had to brave the permanent anti-religious offensive was the Metropolitan Tsintsadze. After the imprisonment of Catholicos Ambrosius he was at first locum tenens of the Patriarchal see and after the short reign of Catholicos Christofor II (1928–32) Tsintsadze himself was elected 'Catholicos and Patriarch of the whole of Georgia'. In this capacity he assumed the name of Kallistrat and the ancient title of 'Metropolitan of Mtskheta (Georgia's historical capital) and Tiflis'. Kallistrat's task as leader of a persecuted and vilified Church was difficult beyond description. Even in his own cathedral in Tiflis he and his Church were humiliated. As late as Easter 1939 whilst he was celebrating the solemn Easter liturgy a group of young communist hooligans staged a hostile manifestation against him.[2] Notwithstanding the plight of his Church and the strength of militant atheism in Georgia, Kallistrat believed in both a religious revival and a communist-Christian symbiosis based on the alleged identity of the communist and Christian world outlooks. Kallistrat even managed to get his views published in 'Bezbozhnik' to which he gave an interview.[3]

In a way, Kallistrat was right. The religious revival did come, though to a lesser degree in Georgia than in certain parts of European Russia. There also began an era of symbiosis, if not between Communism and Christianity, at least between the Soviet State and certain Churches. The re-shaping of relations between Church and State in the Soviet Union during World War II brought to the Church of Georgia not only greater toleration and security, expressed in such minor concessions as the publication of a Georgian Church calendar, but also a further normalisation of its canonical status.

Quite possibly the Kremlin suggested to the newly elected Patriarch of Moscow and all Russia that he should put his relations with the Georgian Church on a new footing. Relations between the Russian and the Georgian Churches had been unsatisfactory since the proclamation

[1] Academy of Sciences of the USSR, *Grunzinskaya SSR*, Moscow 1956, p. 54.
[2] *Bezbozhnik*, 1939, no. 21.
[3] N. S. Timasheff, *Religion in Soviet Russia 1917–1942*, London 1943, p. 112.

of Georgia's ecclesiastical independence in 1917. The Russian Orthodox Church did not accept the separation of the Georgian Church with a good grace, but refused to recognise the restoration of the *status quo* of 1811 for the purely formal reason that the Georgian Church had acted uncanonically in not asking for the blessing of the Russian Church when resuming its autocephalous status.

After the re-establishment by Stalin of the Moscow Patriarchate and the Holy Synod, the Russian Church changed her attitude towards the Georgians with surprising suddenness. On September 4, 1943, Stalin received the three Russian Orthodox Metropolitans in the Kremlin and on October 31 of the same year the Russian Orthodox Church solemnly recognised Georgian autocephaly. It is tempting to see a certain connection between these two events, the more so since Stalin had first-hand knowledge of the Georgian-Russian Church conflict from his seminary days. If he acted as a peacemaker between the two Ortho-dox Churches, he had certainly nothing to gain by advertising the fact, and all we know on the subject officially emanates from the Russian Patriarch Sergius, according to whom the initiative for the settlement of the conflict lay with the Georgian Patriarch. This he stated in a letter to the Oecumenical Patriarch and the three Orthodox Patriarchs of Antioch, Jerusalem and Alexandria. In that letter Sergius also stated with regret that the Russians had for too long assumed an attitude of resentment at the self-willed conduct of the Georgians.[1]

An indirect admission of government interference in the Russian-Georgian Church dispute can be seen in a statement which the Russian Holy Synod issued on November 14, 1943, on the problem of Georgian autocephaly. This document makes no mention of the special historical place that can be claimed by the Georgian Church, but recognises her autocephaly only in view of Georgia's constitutional position within the USSR. It refers to the radical change in Georgia's juridical status as compared with Czarist times, and so accepts with regard to Georgia the official Soviet thesis of the sovereignty of the Union republics. Georgia, says the Russian Holy Synod, had its own clearly defined state territory and state administration and the desire for Georgian autocephaly could therefore be fulfilled. This was in accordance with Orthodox canon law, which said that ecclesiastical boundaries should follow state boundaries.[2] On the same basis all other non-Russian Soviet Republics would be entitled to an autocephalous Orthodox Church of their own, if the Orthodox Christian people there so desire. Neither the Patriarchal Church nor the Soviet authorities wanted

---

[1] *Zh.M.P.*, 1944, no. 3, p. 11.   [2] *Zh.M.P.*, 1944, no. 3, p. 7.

anybody to draw this, in itself logical, conclusion. Georgia was to remain an exception, not a precedent.

The practical consequence of the reconciliation between the two Churches was that the Georgian Catholicos was able to exercise jurisdiction over the Russian parishes in Georgia whilst promising to respect their national peculiarities. He was also asked to do the same with regard to the Russian Orthodox congregations of Armenia, which until then, had been isolated and without any effective hierarchical supervision.

The Church under Kallistrats Successors

Despite canonical normalisation, the position of the Georgian Church remains most precarious. It has fewer churches and priests than an average diocese of the Russian Orthodox Church. Of the 2,455 Georgian churches of the pre-1917 period only about a hundred are still officially open, including eleven in Tiflis.[1] In 1960 the Georgian Church had eight bishops but only five of them were in charge of dioceses actually in existence. These were the bishops of Telavi (Eastern Georgia or Kakhetia), Kutaisi (Western Georgia or Mingrelia), Batumi (Adzharian Autonomous Soviet Republic), Sukhumi (Abkhazian Autonomous Soviet Republic) and Alaverdi (Northern Armenia where there is a strong Georgian minority). The Georgian bishops together with the clergy of the capital, as well as clerical and lay delegates from the provinces, form the 'All-Georgian Church Council'. One of its main functions is the election of the Catholicos-Patriarch, a duty which the Council discharged in April 1952 when, after the death of Kallistrat, Metropolitan Melchisedek (Pkhaladze) was made head of the Georgian Church. The Council met again in February 1960 after the death of Catholicos Melchisedek III to elect his successor Ephraim II (Sidamonidze) by secret ballot. He belongs to the family of the late Katholikos Leonid Okroperidze and is a man of considerable learning.

It appears that the Georgian nation has not fully reconciled itself to the shadow-existence to which its Church has been condemned. As the Church cannot fulfil the spiritual needs of the people, the Georgian rural population, in particular, has tried to replace institutionalised religion by new forms of spontaneous religious activity, for which they use the derelict and officially closed churches, especially during the great Christian holy days. As trained priests are lacking, the people are forced to resort on such occasions to the services of laymen whom the Soviet press has denounced as 'charlatans' and 'suspicious characters'.[2]

[1] *New York Times*, May 20, 1951.   [2] *Zarya Vostoka*, May 6, 1959.

Wherever religion is being driven out in one form in the Soviet Union, it is invariably returning in another, and usually in a form which the régime finds more difficult to combat. 'You may drive out Nature with a pitchfork, yet she will always hasten back,' said Horace.

II. THE UKRAINIAN AUTOCEPHALOUS ORTHODOX CHURCH

The Ukrainian Autocephalous Church was a child of the Russian Revolution, its foundation being perhaps the most serious attempt ever made to deny the Patriarchal Church of Moscow the right to speak on behalf of the non-Russian Christians of the Russian Empire and to limit its role to that of a purely Great Russian Church. Historically it could be argued that the separation of the Ukrainian Church from Moscow was only a return to a situation prevailing until 1686, for only in that year was the Metropolitan of Kiev put under Muscovite jurisdiction. In fact, that argument was used by the Ukrainian Autocephalists and it would have been valid had their Church really remained Orthodox in the traditional sense, but, as we shall see later, the establishment of a Ukrainian Autocephalous Church meant more than a mere regional secession from Moscow, for it became connected with doctrinal heresy. That heresy, it is true, was only an afterthought, and not an essential part of the Ukrainian autocephalist idea. Later events showed that a Ukrainian Autocephalous Orthodox Church could easily have existed within the traditional Orthodox theological framework.[1]

Foundation and Heyday

The Autocephalous Ukrainian Church came into being in the days of the Ukrainian National Republic under Simon Petlyura. Its birth-certificate was a decree which the Ukrainian nationalist directorate issued on January 1, 1919. In issuing it, the short-lived Ukrainian nationalist Government was guided by a consideration which in Eastern Europe has been shared by many founders of new national states, namely, that a State must be independent politically, economically *and* ecclesiastically. In short, a national State must have a national Church. That maxim has been defended not only by Christian politicians but also by those who attach little importance to religion, even by atheists. If there is to be a Church at all, so the latter seem to argue, let it at least be a national one. Had the Ukrainian nationalist régime remained in power, the new Church might have become a 'respectable'

---

[1] An indispensable guide to the history of the Autocephalous Church is Friedrich Heyer, *Die Orthodoxe Kirche in der Ukraine 1917 bis 1945*, Köln-Braunsfeld, 1953.

organisation recognised by the other Orthodox Churches, and in communion with them. But instead of a Ukrainian national régime interested in a Ukrainian national Church, the Ukraine acquired a Soviet régime aiming at the disintegration of the 'religious front'. In this new situation the Ukrainian Autocephalous Church changed its *raison d'être*. It became one of several factors allowing the Soviet authorities to split Orthodoxy and to weaken its influence. In this respect the Autocephalous Church was to play the same role as the Living Church, the Ancient Apostolic Church, and the other groups which had seceded from the official Patriarchal Orthodox Church in Russia proper.

The formal existence of the Ukrainian Autocephalous Church of the Soviet Ukraine dates from October 1921, when an All-Ukrainian Church Assembly (*sobor*) met in Kiev and remained in session throughout the second part of the month. It was attended by five hundred delegates from all parts of the Ukraine and gave the new Church its Constitution. There was no doubt that the members of the Sobor were honestly convinced that they were accomplishing a great act of national emancipation by freeing the Ukrainian national Church from Muscovite fetters. The statutes which they adopted showed, however, that their nationalist bias was stronger than their religious fervour. The Ukrainian national Church was to be founded at any price, even at the price of being uncanonically constituted. The statutes further made it clear that the Sobor acted very much under secular influence, by establishing not only a national Church but one with a modernist theology. Striking features of the statutes were the institution of a married episcopate, the introduction of lay-preachers, the transformation of all contemplative monastic communities into religious working collectives, and the decisive participation of laymen in the administration of the Church. The latter was assured by an entire network of diocesan, district and parish councils. The supreme organs of the Church were the All-Ukrainian Orthodox Church Council (Rada) which met twice a year, and the All-Ukrainian Orthodox Church Assembly, which met every five years. At all levels the lay element prevailed over the clergy. For instance, every diocesan council elected three people to the All-Ukrainian Church Council: of these, one belonged to the clergy, and two to the laity.[1]

Some of the most important and most controversial provisions of the statutes concerned the consecration of the bishops of the Autocephalous Church. These were dictated by reasons of emergency and not by

[1] The full text of the statutes of the Autocephalous Church is reprinted in *Orientalia Christiana*, Rome, June 1923, no. 3.

choice. The Ukrainian Autocephalists would have liked to preserve the apostolic succession and indeed tried hard to find a bishop who would consecrate any Ukrainian 'autocephalist' clergymen. However, such a bishop could not be found and so, as an emergency measure, the Autocephalists accepted the Protestant idea of the episcopate. The statutes stipulated that the All-Ukrainian Church Assembly was to act collectively as the consecrator of the first two bishops, after which consecration was to take place in accordance with the rites of the universal Orthodox Church. One of these first two bishops was the 'Archbishop and Metropolitan of Kiev and the whole Ukraine', Vasyl Konstantinovich Lypkivsky (1864–1938). Soon after his own consecration Lypkivsky consecrated no fewer than nineteen bishops.

Much of the activity of the new Church aimed at filling religious life with a nationalistic spirit. The anniversary of the death of Taras Shevchenko, the Ukrainian national poet, was included in the Church calendar, and the term 'Mother Ukraine' was widely used even liturgically. In every service prayers were said for 'Mother Ukraine, pious and divinely protected, her Government and the whole Ukrainian people'. Candidates for the priesthood were solemnly asked, 'Do you love Mother Ukraine, free and independent?' The Ukrainian language became a fetish of the new Church. Instead of being an accessory it was lifted to the level of an absolute value. It was given a status in theology. A special section in the statutes of the Church (VII 1–3) was headed 'The National Language of the Church', describing opposition to the Ukrainian language as an 'offence against the Holy Spirit' made punishable by expulsion.

In their relations with the Soviet authorities, the founding fathers of the Autocephalous Church seemed to have shared the illusions of many left-wing Ukrainian nationalists of the early twenties. They believed in the possibility of a reconciliation between Ukrainian nationalism and Communism and in the creation, by a merging of the two ideologies, of a kind of national communism under which Ukrainian national culture might flourish. Indeed, much of what happened in the first years of the Soviet régime, especially the determined Ukrainisation policy, seemed to lend body to this optimistic point of view. The Autocephalists also hoped that communist persecution would be directed only against the Patriarchal Orthodox Church as an instrument of autocracy and reaction, allowing the new Autocephalous Church to live in peace on account of its progressive character. It was in line with such considerations that the Constituent All-Ukrainian Church Assembly of October 1921 adopted the following resolution: 'The Assembly congratulates the Ukrainian Soviet Government on having promulgated the Law on the Separation of Church and State which guarantees freedom of belief in the Ukrainian Soviet Socialist Republic and gives the population the possibility of organising its ecclesiastical and religious life according to its wishes.'[1]

This loyalist and collaborationist attitude towards the Soviets continued during the next few years. In 1924 the All-Ukrainian Orthodox Church Council adopted a resolution clearly calculated to please the authorities. It said that the ruling circles of old Russia used the Church for oppressing the working class and non-Russian nationalities and it also protested against the persecution of the Orthodox Church of Poland and the oppression of the Ukrainians in that country. The resolution was handed to the Ukrainian Peoples' Commissar of the Interior (NKVD) by a delegation headed by Archbishop Lypkivsky himself.[2]

One particular aspect of autocephalist Church activities which pleased the Soviet authorities was Metropolitan Lypkivsky's attempt to propagate the autocephaly in America, and they gave a passport to the man he appointed bishop in the United States and Canada. The autocephalist propaganda destined for the Ukrainians of North America contained nothing that was directly pro-communist but it did create the impression that the Soviet Ukraine was the scene of a great national, and especially national-religious, rebirth in which Ukrainian brethren dispersed throughout the world were invited to take part. The autocephalist Metropolitan also addressed a special appeal to the Ukrainian Greek-Catholics of the United States, who were asked to break the chains that bound them to the Pope. 'Be as free as we are' — was the leitmotiv of Lypkivsky's message. 'Our Church is already completely free', it said, 'she administers all her ecclesiastical affairs in complete independence and makes her own decisions freely. Stop being Greeks and Catholics, become free children of the free national Church of the Ukraine. Break your chains, unite yourselves with us.'[3] Soon there was to be a terrible awakening for those who had believed in the illusion of the free national Ukrainian Church under Soviet rule.

Disintegration and Persecution

For a time the Ukrainian Autocephalous Church was a powerful body. In its heyday in the early twenties it had 26 bishops, 2,500 priests

---

[1] *Orientalia Christiano*, June 1923, no. 3, p. 47.   [2] *Pravda*, December 16, 1924.
[3] 'Dossier américain de l'Orthodoxie Pan-Ukrainienne', *Orientalia Christiana*, Rome, July–September 1923, no. 4, p. 178.

and deacons and 2,000 parishes.[1] However, it soon found itself under heavy attack from within and without. Having itself opened the doors to heterodoxy, the self-consecrated hierarchy of the new Church was soon faced with a new rebellious movement advocating a more radical departure from Orthodoxy, opposing fixed dogmas and rites and seeing the essence of Christian religion in action alone. The new movement described itself significantly as 'Diialnaia' or Active Church. We do not know how much support it enjoyed, but it may be indicative of its ephemeral importance that the Autocephalist Church Rada dealt on several occasions with the 'Diialnaia' heresy and on one occasion in July 1927 the Rada invited the secessionists to renounce their erroneous views and come back into the Church.[2]

The leaders of the Autocephalous Church made some opportunistic concessions at the expense of traditional Orthodox ideas, but there were limits beyond which they were not prepared to go. Metropolitan Lypkivsky may finally have recognised that the Autocephalous Church experiment and its defiance of tradition had brought grave danger to religion in the Ukraine. He may even have realised that the Church had been organised too hastily and that many members of the clergy were unworthy of their office. Former teachers, dismissed Czarist officials and frustrated intellectuals had entered the autocephalous priesthood, often with little preparation or qualification. Lypkivsky therefore began a dual reform of the Church by reducing the number of priests and by tightening up Church discipline and endowing the bishops with greater power. The All-Ukrainian Church Rada meeting of July 1927 adopted these emergency measures in the hope that they would lead to a consolidation of ecclesiastical life in the Ukraine and, indeed, for a moment it seemed as if the prestige of the autocephalous hierarchy was again on the increase. However, the Soviet régime had lost all interest in giving the Church a new lease of life. It had made up its mind that the Autocephalous Church, far from being 'progressive', was the counter-revolutionary organisation of the Ukrainian bourgeoisie. Official pressure was put on the local organisations of the Church for their representatives to insist on the removal of Metropolitan Lypkivsky. This took place at the Rada meeting of October 17, 1928, which deposed Lypkivsky by a large majority and elected a more pro-Soviet church head in the person of Mykola Boretsky, bishop of Yelizavetgrad (Kirovograd), or 'Zinovievsk', as the place was then called.

With or without Lypkivsky the Autocephalous Church had only a

---

[1] *Ukrainian Review*, Munich, 1956, no. 3, p. 20.
[2] *Questions Minoritaires*, Warsaw, March 1929, no. 1, pp. 36–7.

few months more to live, for it was too nationalistic to survive the purge of Ukrainian nationalists which started in 1929 and reached its peak in the trial of forty-five leading members of the *Spilka Vyzvoleniya Ukrainy* (SVU) (Union for the Liberation of the Ukraine) and the *Spilka Ukrainskoi Molodi* (Union of Ukrainian Youth). The very first official announcement of the new discovery of the SVU conspiracy incriminated the Ukrainian Autocephalous Church in the most categorical and unequivocal terms. It was asserted that the SVU had used the Church as its instrument and had appointed former officers of the Petlyura bands and Ukrainian insurgent organisations as bishops, priests and other ecclesiastical dignitaries.[1] Thus it was clear from the outset that the SVU trial would establish an intimate connection between the nationalist plot and the Autocephalous Church. The SVU was not a philosophically and politically homogeneous body, but in working out a Constitution for a free Ukraine its leaders agreed that the Autocephalous Ukrainian Church was to enjoy a privileged position, although other religions were to have freedom of worship. As far as the Ukrainian illegal nationalist youth movement was concerned, the communists looked upon it as a semi-religious organisation.

To forestall a persecution of church members an Extraordinary Church Assembly (*sobor*) met in January 1930 to sign the death-warrant of the Church. Its final statement was a self-accusation of its 'nationalist-counter-revolutionary and anti-Soviet activity', although an attempt was made to shift the responsibility on to Metropolitan Lypkivsky and five of his bishops, some of whom had shown themselves poor and incompetent churchmen.[2] The statement of the Extraordinary Assembly was not completely satisfactory from the point of view of the authorities, since it did not incriminate all the leading figures in the Church, but the public prosecutor found it nevertheless a useful document which he did not fail to exploit during the trial of the SVU, also called 'the trial of the forty-five', which started on March 9, 1930, and went on for nearly six weeks.

Only two of the defendants in the trial were directly connected with the Autocephalous Church, but these two sufficed to secure the Church a central place in the indictment and the proceedings. The two were the brothers Volodymyr and Mykola Chekhivsky; the latter was an ordinary autocephalist priest but the former was co-founder of the Church and its most distinguished lay-preacher. He was awarded the title All-Ukrainian Preacher and preached in St. Sophia's Church in Kiev. It was during Volodymyr Chekhivsky's long interrogation that the anti-

[1] *Pravda*, November 21, 1929.   [2] *Antireligioznik*, April 1930, no. 4, p. 18.

religious bias of the trial became evident. Chekhivsky was interrogated not by the Chief Public Prosecutor, Mikhailik, a communist of Jewish origin — this might have been bad propaganda in a country where anti-Semitism was rife — but by Panas Lubchenko, a communist with a Christian family background who was attached to the Prosecutor's office for the time of the trial. Lubchenko tried every means to trap Chekhivsky. Referring to the Christian maxim that one should love one's enemies, he asked Chekhivsky whether he prayed for Czar Nicholas II, who was after all an enemy of the Ukrainian people and its national aspirations. Chekhivsky answered in the affirmative. Then Lubchenko read extracts from the works of Marx and Engels to show that religion served the bourgeoisie and the capitalists. From this he concluded that the Autocephalous Ukrainian Orthodox Church too was an instrument of the bourgeoisie and wanted to re-establish capitalism in the Ukraine. Chekhivsky refuted this argument, pointing out that in the capitalist countries religion may well be used by the bourgeoisie but in the Ukraine the Autocephalous Church was the religious home of free men. Lubchenko answered that communist ideology did not recognise the term 'man', but divided mankind into proletarians and bourgeois. By speaking of a religion of free men Chekhivsky disregarded class differences. In the end Chekhivsky, together with thirteen other defendants, was sentenced to death but the sentences were commuted to life imprisonment. Several years after the trial Chekhivsky's accuser, Panas Lubchenko, became Prime Minister of the Ukraine; but his triumph was a short one, for at the height of the Ukrainian purge in the summer of 1937 he committed suicide in anticipation of his arrest.[1]

The 'trial of the forty-five' with all the incriminating material it produced against the Autocephalous Church and its alleged intention to prepare an armed rising against the Soviets in conjunction with the SVU, made impossible the revival of the Church in a new purified form. To safeguard themselves against its revival the Soviet authorities arrested all autocephalous bishops, even those against whom no political case could be construed. They were sent to various camps in Siberia, Central Asia and to the island of Solovki on the White Sea. The names of thirty-one deported autocephalist bishops are known, including of course the two successive heads of the Church, Lypkivsky and Boretsky. A similar fate befell many priests and lay-leaders.[2]

---

[1] *Questions Minoritaires*, August 1930, no. 1–2, p. 45.
[2] Dr. Lev Mydlowsky, *Bolshevist Persecution of Religion and Church in the Ukraine, 1917–1957*, London 1958, pp. 10–11.

The evidence suggests nevertheless that the Ukrainian Autocephalous Church was never completely vanquished, and that it continued to exist as a Church of the Catacombs in some rudimentary form until the beginning of World War II. Evidence of this survival of the Autocephalists was given at a meeting of the Central Council of the League of Militant Godless held in Moscow in April 1939. There the rapporteur on anti-religious work in the Ukraine, a man called Motusko, complained that the Autocephalous Church 'continued to the present day'. The Church, he added, did not exist as a mass organisation but there were nevertheless Ukrainian autocephalist priests. There were many churches where the liturgy was celebrated in the Ukrainian language. A number of autocephalist parishes using the Ukrainian language for their worship had joined the official Orthodox Church, but this, said Motusko, was only camouflage on the part of the Ukrainian nationalists.[1]

The autocephalist danger was almost an obsession with the Ukrainian communists. One wonders whether after the long years of terror the danger could be very acute in 1939. The great purge of 1937–8 must have inflicted a mortal blow on those former 'Autocephalists' who had tried to submerge themselves in the regular Orthodox Church of the Ukraine. The purge hit that Church with particular violence. The entire hierarchy, headed by the Exarch of the Ukraine, Konstantin Dyakov, was arrested and deported or executed. Practically all Orthodox churches except those in cemeteries were closed. The Soviet authorities did not then realise that they would soon need the Russian Orthodox Church to help them to keep in check Ukrainian separatism in the territories annexed from Poland in September 1939.

Ecclesiastical Separatism and Centralism in the Western Ukraine

For ethnographic and historical reasons there was considerable danger of an Orthodox ecclesiastical separatism in that part of Poland which later became the Western Ukraine. Before the inclusion of these areas into the Soviet Union, the Orthodox believers there came under the jurisdiction of the Autocephalous Orthodox Church of Poland. This was a strange body. It was a Polish Church in the sense that it was founded on the insistence of the Polish state authorities, who could not be reconciled to an Orthodox ecclesiastical organisation dependent on Moscow. It was a Russian Church in that its head, Metropolitan Dionys, and a large part of the hierarchy and priests were Russian. Finally, the Church was Ukrainian-Byelorussian because the bulk of its membership belonged to these two nationalities. The various parties involved

[1] *Antireligioznik*, no. 5, 1939.

produced contradictory statistical material about the ethnographic composition of the 3,787,000 members of the Polish Orthodox Church but all sources agree that Ukrainians and Byelorussians formed most of the flock. The Russians who played a leading part in the Church administration were a tiny minority and so were the Poles. In such a situation it was inevitable that the Polish Orthodox Church should become a battleground for rival passions. The struggle was particularly bitter between the Ukrainians and the Russians and at times it seemed as if the unity of the Polish Orthodox Church was no more than an administrative fiction. For instance, in June 1927 the Ukrainian section of the Church summoned to Lutsk an 'Orthodox Church Congress' which demanded the Ukrainisation of the ecclesiastical administration and of the liturgy as well as the appointment of Ukrainian bishops. This was an open rebellion against Metropolitan Dionys. Thereupon Dionys and his Russian supporters summoned a counter-congress to Pochaev which rejected the Ukrainian demands.[1]

There is no doubt that the Orthodox Ukrainians in Poland looked upon the Polish Autocephalous Church as a potential Ukrainian Autocephalous Church. The Soviet authorities, with the case of their own Autocephalists still fresh in their minds, were determined to nip in the bud all new autocephalist experiments when they occupied the Western Ukraine in 1939. They found an unexpected ally in the Russian Orthodox Church. That down-trodden, persecuted and martyred Church suddenly became useful to the Soviet communists. In the Western Ukraine they discovered for the first time that the Church had its uses not only in the issuing of isolated propaganda statements but also from the point of view of long-term political planning.

With the connivance of the authorities the Moscow Patriarchal Church almost immediately exploited the situation created by the temporary liquidation of the Polish State to restore its jurisdiction over the Western Ukraine and Western Byelorussia, which had been lost through the establishment of the Polish Autocephalous Church in 1924. In doing so the Moscow Patriarchal Church assisted the integration of the conquered territories into the Soviet Union and also prevented the emergence of any separatist church organisations, which might have caused considerable difficulties to the Soviet State. In 1940 the annexed Byelorussian and Ukranian territories were organised into a special Exarchate with headquarters in Lutsk; the Exarch was Metropolitan Nikolay Yarushevich.

The establishment of the Exarchate of the Western Ukraine and

[1] *Sprawy Narodowosciowe*, 1927, no. 4, pp. 399–400.

Western Byelorussia was one of the strangest episodes in Church-State relations in Soviet Russia. It meant that the Soviet Government gave permission for the setting up of a metropolitan see in the small town of Lutsk at a time when both the traditional see of the Exarch of the Ukraine in Kiev and the episcopal see in Minsk were vacant, their last occupants having been arrested by the authorities. The comparative tolerance which the Soviet authorities observed in the newly-annexed territories and the freedom of movement enjoyed by Metropolitan Nikolay during his travels to and from the new Exarchate made an interesting contrast to the persecution of the Church in Russia proper. Marxist dialecticians would have found no difficulty in explaining the discrepancy; in Russia the Patriarchal Church had until then played a 'reactionary' role and so deserved to be persecuted, but in the new territories the Church was a positive force as it was an ally in the fight against separatism. Consequently it was entitled to better treatment. The future showed how right that appraisal was from the Marxist and Soviet patriotic point of view.

The Return of the 'Autocephalists'

Under the German occupation the Ukrainian Autocephalous Church, defunct since 1930, saw a revival. This second Ukrainian autocephaly differed fundamentally from the first in being nationalistic only and not modernist. Unlike its predecessor, it did not come into being as a reform movement from below but had properly consecrated bishops, among them Bishop Polykarp Sikorsky who, with the title of 'Metropolitan', became the Administrator of the new Church. The new autocephalous ecclesiastical body held no monopoly in the German-occupied Ukraine. Side by side with the Autocephalous Church, there existed an Autonomous Church recognising the jurisdiction of the Moscow Patriarch, although this recognition remained in abeyance as long as he was under Communist control. The Autocephalous Church had fifteen bishops and the Autonomous Church sixteen, but these figures are no true guide to the relative strength of the two Orthodox groups. According to the most reliable accounts the majority of the Orthodox believers supported the Autonomists rather than the Auto-cephalists.[1] Nevertheless, a Ukrainian Autocephalous Church body, even if only the organisation of a militant minority, was likely to be a most dangerous centre of anti-Soviet nationalist tendencies. The supporters of the Autonomous Church were no ardent Soviet patriots but at least they were not all Ukrainian nationalists, for they included

[1] *Internationele Kirchliche Zeitschrift*, 1943, p. 31.

among their number the entire Russian ethnic group in the Ukraine, in so far as it consisted of religious believers. On the other hand, there could be no doubt that membership of the Ukrainian Autocephalous Church and adherence to a nationalistic programme went hand in hand. So the fight conducted during the war by the Moscow Patriarchal See against the Autocephalous Ukrainian Church met with the full approval of the Kremlin. The battle was conducted from a distance, mainly by pastoral letters to the Ukrainian Christians issued both by Metropolitan Sergius and by Metropolitan Nikolay in his new capacity of Metropolitan of Kiev and Exarch of the whole Ukraine. These pastoral letters, disseminated by the official Soviet propaganda services, threatened 'eternal damnation' to the ecclesiastical leaders of the Ukrainian Autocephalous Church.[1]

The Ukrainian Autocephalous Church disappeared together with the nazi occupation; but from this one need not conclude that it was no more than a tool of the invaders. As we have seen, its existence did correspond to the aspirations of such nationalistic groups as the Union for the Liberation of the Ukraine and, although many Autocephalists collaborated with the occupation authorities, there were others who were victims of nazi persecution. A number of them, including the leading autocephalist theologian Professor Ivan Vlasovsky, were arrested in the autumn of 1943 during the big nazi offensive against the Ukrainian national intelligentsia. The nazi authorities did not give any consistent support to the Autocephalists although the latter enjoyed the sympathies of the 'Ostministerium', which was almost completely powerless in the Ukraine. If there was a nazi ecclesiastical policy at all in the Ukraine it consisted in playing off the Autocephalists and the Autonomists against each other. At one time the nazi Reichskommissariat distinctly favoured the Autonomists, fearing that the nationalistic Ukrainian Church might become too powerful.[2] Any connection between the Nazis on the one hand and the Ukrainian Autocephalists on the other existed only a posteriori; it was a connection that confused the issue. A national Ukrainian Orthodox Church is unthinkable to-day in the Soviet Union not because it has been discredited by collaboration with the Nazis but primarily because it would be by its very nature a separatist body threatening the unity of the Soviet Russian State.

On the other hand, the Russian Orthodox Church remained, from the régime's point of view, the minor religious evil in the Ukraine even

[1] Metropolitan Nikolay, Slova, Rechi, Poslaniya (Words, Speeches, Pastoral Letters), Moscow 1947, p. 241.
[2] John A. Armstrong, Ukrainian Nationalism 1939–1947, New York, Columbia University Press 1955, p. 201.

after World War II. Its centralistic character and historical record seemed firm guarantees that it would continue the fight against Ukrainian local nationalism. The attitude of the Church towards the tercentenary celebration of the Russian-Ukrainian Union, the Union of Pereyaslav of 1654, which was celebrated throughout 1954, seemed to justify this expectation. On this occasion the *Journal of the Moscow Patriarchate* published three articles drawing attention to the ecclesiastical aspect of the Union, the contribution of the Church towards its success and the religious motives that prompted the Ukrainian hetman Bogdan Khmelnitsky to seek alliance with the Orthodox Czar against Catholic Poland.[1] The Exarch of the Ukraine and Metropolitan of Kiev Ioann issued a special pastoral letter describing the day of the Russian-Ukrainian Union — January 18 — as a great ecclesiastical holiday since it marked the end of the enslavement by the Vatican of the Orthodox Church of the Ukraine.[2] Believers were urged to commemorate the day of Union with special prayers and attendance at a solemn liturgy to be held in all Ukrainian churches.

Not all members of the Russian Orthodox Church in the Ukraine are likely to share its patriotic and anti-separatist sentiments. Ukrainian autocephalist trends may have survived in its midst and would no doubt come into the open again in a different political climate. The Russian Church has readmitted into its ranks a number of former autocephalist priests and there are even bishops with an autocephalist past. Despite having made a formal submission, certain ex-Autocephalists may not have renounced their former separatist views. Moreover, the Ukrainian Autocephalous Church continues to exist among the Ukrainians of the free world, especially in the USA, where it claims to have 85 parishes, 100 priests, and 50,000 faithful, and in Canada, where it numbers 120,000 faithful in 300 parishes.[3] If there were free contact between the Ukrainians in the world-wide diaspora and those of the motherland, the Autocephalists abroad would certainly try to 'reimport' their Church into the Ukraine. Ukrainian ecclesiastical independence from Moscow will remain an aspiration of Ukrainian nationalism, and as such it will always be a political rather than a religious demand. From a purely religious point of view, the question of autocephaly is a secondary consideration. The Ukraine's primary spiritual need is freedom of worship, not ecclesiastical autocephaly.

[1] *Rol Pravoslavnoi Tserkvi v Osvoboditelnoi Voine Ukrainskogo Naroda* (The Role of the Orthodox Church in the War of Liberation of the Ukrainian People), *Zh.M.P.*, 1953, no. 12, pp. 33–41.
[2] *Zh.M.P.*, 1954, no. 4, p. 12.
[3] Very Rev. Peter Bilow, *The Ukrainians and their Church*, Johnstown, Pa., 1953.

E

III. THE ESTONIAN APOSTOLIC ORTHODOX CHURCH

An Estonian Autocephalous Orthodox Church was in existence for nearly twenty-two years during the period between the two world wars and throughout most of World War II. It was the Church of nineteen per cent of Estonia's population. Like many Orthodox Churches it came into being for a political reason — the foundation of an Estonian national state. At the same time its existence corresponded to a real religious need of the Estonian people — provided of course that one accepts the Orthodox view that the division of Christendom into independent national Churches is necessary and desirable. At any rate the Autocephalous Estonian Church was a more solid and genuine institution than for example the present Autocephalous Orthodox Church of Czechoslovakia, which is an exotic plant grown in a Russian hot-house.

Before 1917 there was some ground for arguing that the Orthodox Church in Estonia was an artificial creation and that it owed its existence to a social protest movement rather than to a change in the spiritual outlook of the Estonian people. Indeed, when the mass conversions of Estonians to Orthodoxy began between 1842 and 1850, many regarded the acceptance of a new religious allegiance as a challenge to the German Lutheran landowners and the German pastors in their service. The Orthodox Church appeared to the destitute Estonian peasants to be a poor man's Church, as distinct from the Lutheran 'Herrenkirche', or landlord's Church. No doubt they also thought that conversion to the faith of the Czars would give them greater protection and would even put them in possession of land somewhere in orthodox Russia.

The bread and butter Orthodoxy of the Estonian peasants developed into genuine Orthodoxy. When Estonia became independent and when the Lutheran Church became a 'People's Church' (*Rahvakirik*) not only in name but in essence, the Estonian Orthodox ranks remained intact. The number of reconversions to Lutheranism was negligible, not least because the Orthodox Church in Estonia could claim to be predominantly Estonian in character. According to the official statistics, out of 212,000 Orthodox Church members in 1935, 125,000 were Estonians and 87,000 Russians. Perhaps the real strength of the Estonian membership was somewhat below these official figures but there was no doubt that the Russians were in the minority. Of the 156 Orthodox parishes in the country 119 were Estonian or mixed Estonian-Russian and the remaining 37 purely Russian. The main bulwarks of Orthodoxy in Estonia were the Baltic islands of Saaremaa and Muhu, where the Orthodox population was 39·7 per cent of the total, the Paernu district in South-West Estonia where it was 31·5 per cent, and the Valga district in Southern Estonia with 24·3 per cent Orthodox. A case apart was the Pechora (Petseri) district bordering on Russia. There the Orthodox formed 90 per cent of the whole population, but these were almost entirely Russians and Russianised Estonians.[1] During the period of Estonian independence this was the seat of a seminary, training priests for Estonia's Russian Orthodox churches, whilst Estonian priests were trained at the theological faculty of Tartu University.

The Autocephalous 'Estonian Apostolic Orthodox Church' (*Eesti-Apostlik Oigeusi Kirik*) was founded in 1923. The word 'Apostolic' was inserted in its title chiefly to make clear the distinction between it and the Orthodox Church of Russia. The new Autocephalous Church was recognised by the Oecumenical Patriarch, and it had a properly constituted government consisting of a synod of eleven members (four bishops and seven parish priests) and a church assembly which elected the Metropolitan. The existence of an Autocephalous Orthodox Church was in the national interest of the Estonian State, and also corresponded to the wish of the Estonian church members, but many Russian Orthodox people in Estonia accepted it only reluctantly. A split between the Estonian and the Russian element was only prevented by a virtual partition of the Church. The Metropolitan of Tallin looked after the Estonian parishes, while the Archbishop of Narva and Izhborsk was responsible for the Russian parishes. This settlement still left out of account the monastery of Pechora, whose abbot bore the title of bishop. The monastery became the scene of petty and undignified quarrels between Russians and Estonians. The dispute went on for three years and both the Oecumenical Patriarch and the Estonian Government were dragged into it. The latter appointed a special commissar for the monastery, a brother of the President of the Republic Päts, himself Orthodox.

Estonian and Russian Orthodox disagreed on more than questions involving national prestige. The Estonian Orthodox wanted to make use of the autocephalous status of their Church in order to westernise it; Western mentality was to be imposed under cover of an Eastern rite.[2] The Estonian Orthodox wanted fewer ikons in their churches, they tried to reduce ceremonies to a minimum, and attached greater

---

[1] J. Aunver, *Eesti Rahvakirku Ristitee*, Stockholm 1953, p. 71.
[2] Charles Bourgeois, sj., *A Priest in Russia and the Baltic*, Dublin–London 1953, p. 48.

importance to sermons than the Orthodox normally do. No wonder that Estonian and Russian Orthodox parishes differed more and more from one another. Estonian and Russian Orthodox also fought a hard ten-year battle over the question of the Calendar. The Synod of the Estonian Autocephalous Church tried to introduce the Gregorian Calendar as early as December 1923, but only in 1932 did the Russian parishes accept the abandonment of the 'old style', and even then there were still some recalcitrant elements left.

Another point of disagreement was the attitude of the two Orthodox national groups towards the Catholic Church. The Russian Orthodox of Estonia preserved the old hostility towards Catholicism inherited from the 'Czarist' Church; the Estonian Orthodox, on the other hand, were ecumenically minded. Their organ *Elutode* (September 1936) called for friendship with the Catholic Church and made the point that Orthodoxy and Catholicism formed a spiritual unity.[1] The Catholic Church itself regarded this situation with some hope and a small Catholic mission of the Eastern Rite tried to work for a *rapprochement*, but it would have taken many years of peaceful development to achieve any positive results.

From the point of view of universal Orthodoxy the establishment of an independent Orthodox Church in Estonia was an indisputable asset, for it removed from Estonian Orthodoxy the odium of being alien and 'imported'. For the Russian Orthodox Church, on the other hand, the 'Estonian schism' — as the foundation of the Autocephalous Estonian Church was described in circles close to the Moscow Patriarchate — meant a loss in power and prestige. Had it been official Soviet policy to give Estonia an independent Orthodox Church, the Moscow Patriarchal See would have accepted willy-nilly the Kremlin's point of view. But the Kremlin decided against independent Orthodox Churches in the Baltic countries, a decision which enabled the Moscow Metropolitan at the time of the first Soviet occupation of Estonia, to bring Estonian autocephaly to an end. The head of the Estonian Church, Metropolitan Alexander, acting under duress, made his submission to Moscow in March 1941, but when the Germans occupied Estonia a few months later the Church was immediately re-established by the same Metropolitan. The re-occupation of the country by the Red Army in 1944 sounded the death-knell of the Church as an independent body.

The *Journal of the Moscow Patriarchate* published a detailed account of the high-handed way in which the liquidation was carried out. In

[1] Helmut Risch, 'Die Estnische Apostolische-Rechtgläubige Kirche', *Kyrios*, vol. ii, zweites Heft, 1937, pp. 125–9.

February 1945 the Moscow Patriarchate entrusted the settlement of the 'Estonian question' to the Russian archbishop who was the nearest geographically, Grigorii of Pskov. Grigorii urged the Synod of the Estonian Church to send a letter of repentance to the Patriarchate with a request for re-admission into the Russian Mother-Church. On March 3, 1945, Archbishop Grigorii went to Tallin and two days later the schism was ended. The members of the Estonian Synod had to ask for pardon not only on their own behalf but also on behalf of all the clergy and faithful who belonged to the 'schismatic Church'. Archbishop Grigorii seemed to have some doubt about the motives of those repenting for he said he hoped that *this time* the action of repentance would be absolutely sincere.[1] The wishes of the faithful were not taken into account. Indeed, the *Journal of the Moscow Patriarchate* admitted that, to accelerate matters, the 'schism' was eliminated before the Orthodox parishes had had a chance to express an opinion on the matter.[2] No church assembly was summoned, not even a conference of priests. There was no need to consult the head of the Church, Metropolitan Alexander for he, together with one-third of all Estonian Orthodox priests, was in exile. The repentance and consent of five members of the Estonian Synod, three priests and two laymen, was all that was necessary to end Estonian autocephaly. Failing such a gesture of submission, the five might have been accused of collaboration with the Germans. Archbishop Grigorii dissolved the Estonian Synod and also ordered that all liturgical reforms introduced at the time of the Synod were to be discontinued. Archpriest Bogoyavlensky, a Russian who assisted Archbishop Grigorii in his mission, became Chairman of the Synod of the new Estonian diocese under the jurisdiction of the Moscow Patriarchal See, and in 1947 became its bishop.

It might be argued that the matter would not have been settled in such a precipitate manner had the Orthodox Patriarchate not acted under pressure from the Soviet secular authorities. The communist régime certainly had every interest in suppressing a Church which might easily have become an instrument of political separatism. It was much safer to have the Estonian Orthodox flock under Moscow's jurisdiction than under an independent Metropolitan of Estonian nationality. The Orthodox clergy and faithful of Estonia may have felt that their outward willingness to abandon their autocephalous Church would be considered a test of their loyalty towards the Soviet State. It was preferable from their point of view to accept Russian ecclesiastical overlordship and enjoy at least a restricted measure of freedom than to

[1] *Zh.M.P.*, 1945, no. 4, p. 3.   [2] *Zh.M.P.*, ibid.

remain independent and experience martyrdom — not for the faith but
for the sake of the form of the ecclesiastical organisation.

*   *   *   *

The Autocephalous Estonian Apostolic Orthodox Church continues
to exist among the Estonian emigrés in the United States and Canada,
and is particularly strong in Sweden. Its achievements during the
period of Estonian national independence have not been completely
lost. It would even seem that the Russian Orthodox Church owes a
debt of gratitude both to the Autocephalous Estonian Church and to
the independent Estonian state of the inter-war period. The Estonian
Church kept the Orthodox faith alive among both Russians and
Estonians, and the tolerant Estonian State protected its pastoral and
educational work. As a result, the Orthodox faith has been better
preserved in Estonia than in many other parts of the Soviet Empire.
Even in the exposed Baltic islands such as Saaremaa and Muhu quite
a number of parishes have survived all political upheavals.[1]

An important asset which the Russian Orthodox Church gained
through the absorption of the Estonian Orthodox Church is the
Convent of the Assumption in Pukhtitsa which, with 120 nuns and
novices, is one of the most famous in the Soviet Union. The convent
of Pukhtitsa — an Estonian word meaning 'holy place' — was only
founded in 1891 but it soon became one of the most important centres
of Estonian Orthodoxy.[2] The period of Estonian political and ecclesiastical independence can claim credit too for the preservation of the
famous Monastery of the Caves of Pskov ('Pskovo-Pecherskii Monastyr')
near Pechora. The monastery, founded in the fifteenth century, was
included in the Estonian Republic despite its Russian hinterland. Had
it belonged to the Soviet Union right from the beginning it might not
exist any more as a place of worship. Although the monastery grounds
and the town of Pechora were in 1940 incorporated into the Russian
Federation it continues to attract many Estonian pilgrims.[3]

IV. THE LATVIAN ORTHODOX CHURCH

In the independent Latvian Republic only 8·9 per cent of the total
population belonged to the Orthodox Church. Nearly two-thirds of all
Orthodox Church members were either Great Russian or Byelorussian.
Among the Latvian people the Orthodox formed a small minority of

[1] *Zh.M.P.*, 1956, no. 9, p. 13.   [2] *Zh.M.P.*, 1954, no. 11, pp. 11–12.
[3] *Zh.M.P.*, 1952, no. 10, pp. 28–9.

less than four per cent. There was obviously not, therefore, the same justification for an independent Orthodox Church in Latvia as there was in Estonia. In fact, formally and canonically the autocephaly of Latvian Orthodoxy existed for only four years, from 1936 when the Oecumenical Patriarch of Constantinople consecreatd the first Latvian autocephalous Metropolitan, Augustin Petersons, until 1940 when the same Petersons renounced the autocephaly after the Soviet occupation of Latvia.

Inside the Soviet State the Autocephalous Church of Latvia has been neither a political problem to the authorities nor a canonical problem to the Moscow Patriarchate. Nevertheless, the Orthodox Church of Latvia deserves a short epitaph for the honourable part it played in Russian as well as in Latvian ecclesiastical history. When it was still an autonomous body only, its head, Archbishop Ioann Pommer of Riga, spoke out in a situation in which the Russian Orthodox Church leadership in Moscow had been forced into taking sides with the oppressors of religion, against the entire Christian world. This was in February 1930, when Metropolitan Sergius of Moscow was compelled to issue a statement asserting that there was full freedom of worship in the USSR and rejecting the protests of the Pope and the Archbishop of Canterbury against Soviet religious persecution.[1]

In these circumstances Archbishop Ioann of Riga raised his voice on behalf of the silenced Church of Russia. He stated in an interview that the opinions attributed to Metropolitan Sergius could not be in form or in substance an expression of the real views of the spiritual leaders of the Orthodox Church in Russia. Indeed, said the Archbishop, who could believe a denial of church persecution after the Soviet authorities had closed hundreds of churches and monasteries, forbidden the ringing of bells to which generations of Russians had listened, publicly burned thousands of ikons, and defiled numerous sacred places.[2]

The Russian Orthodox Church is still reaping the fruits of Latvian Orthodox Church independence just as it still benefits from the defunct Estonian autocephaly. Latvia has still an orderly and well-organised Orthodox Church life. The majority of the Latvian parishes, 60 out of 78, have remained intact,[3] and the Convent of the Holy Trinity in Riga is the pride of the entire Orthodox Church.[4]

---

[1] *Izvestiya*, February 16, 1930.   [2] *The Times*, February 17, 1930.
[3] *Zh.M.P.*, 1957, no. 2, p. 11.
[4] *The Russian Orthodox Church, Organisation, Situation, Activity*, published by the Moscow Patriatchate 1959, p. 97.

V. THE BYELORUSSIAN AUTOCEPHALOUS ORTHODOX CHURCH

Tendencies towards an autocephalous Church in Byelorussia had not initially the same nationalist-chauvinistic flavour which marred their appearance in the Ukraine. Nor were they identified in any way with modernist and reformist currents. On the contrary, in the initial stage they were a conservative reaction against the Living Church movement Most documents referring to the setting up of the Byelorussian Auto-cephalous Orthodox Church have been destroyed in the years of church persecution and so its history cannot be traced with absolute certainty. In all likelihood, this history, or perhaps only prehistory, goes back to July 23, 1922, when the bishop of Minsk, Melchisedek (Payevsky), proclaimed the independence of the Byelorussian Church administration. Bishop Melchisedek himself assumed the title of Metropolitan of Byelorussia, with three bishops, those of Bobruisk, Mozyr and Slutsk, under his jurisdiction.

Nothing was further from Melchisedek's mind than the establishment of a Byelorussian national Church. He simply wanted to keep Byelorussia out of the church schism and to prevent the 'Living Church' from extending its influence to the Byelorussian dioceses. Indeed, Melchisedek's supporters consistently referred to themselves as 'Starotserkovniki' or 'People of the Old Church'. In the second half of 1925 Melchisedek went to Moscow and on the insistence of Metropolitan Sergius he renounced the title of 'Metropolitan of Byelorussia'.[1]

He died in 1931, apparently reconciled with the Patriarchal Church. After Melchisedek's departure from Byelorussia tendencies towards church independence took an even clearer shape. In August 1927 a conference of priests and laymen met in Minsk to reaffirm the autocephalous status of the Church of Byelorussia. A statement to this effect was signed by the bishop of Bobruisk, Filaret (Ramensky), the dean of the Minsk Cathedral, Ochanovsky, and a number of other priests. Unlike Melchisedek's initiative, this new move for a Byelorussian Church had a nationalist colouring. Whilst proclaiming its opposition to any doctrinal reform, the Minsk Conference of 1927 criticised the 'manifest hostility' of Moscow towards an independent Byelorussian Church. It underlined the 'right to national self-determination in the ecclesiastical sphere' and 'the right of every nation to free development as a living and active member of the universal body of Christ'.[2] In the same year, 1927, the

[1] Mgr. A. M., *Materiali da gistorii Pravoslavnae Belaruskae Tsarkvi* (Material for the history of the Byelorussian Orthodox Church), Germany 1948, p. 22.

[2] Kasyak *Z Iistorii, Pravoslavnai Tsarkvi Belaruskogo Narodu* (From the History of the Orthodox Church of the Byelorussian people), New York 1956, pp. 170-1.

Byelorussian Autocephalous Church published its statute under the title 'Statute of the Union of Orthodox Old Church Communities forming in their totality the Byelorussian Autocephalous Church'.

The Minsk Conference decided that an All-Byelorussian Church Council was to take place which was to give to the Autocephalous Church its final form. The Council was never summoned and there is little if any further evidence about the movement of the Byelorussian 'Autocephalists' between the end of the twenties and the beginning of World War II. Some of them were no doubt victimised by the Soviet authorities in the big offensive carried out in 1929 against the Byelorussian 'National-Democrats', for the demand for a national Church was automatically considered the hallmark of a counter-revolutionary frame of mind.[1]

The anti-nationalist campaign as well as the anti-religious campaign which the Soviet Government conducted in Byelorussia led between the late twenties and 1938 to the complete extermination of the Byelorussian Church. Its three bishops, Filaret of Bobruisk, Mikhail of Slutsk, and Ioann of Mozyr, died in prisons and concentration camps.[2] All the more prominent priests, including all the signatories of the Minsk statement setting up the Autocephalous Church, were also arrested. By July 1937 not a single priest continued to celebrate the liturgy in Byelorussia, and not a single church remained open.[3] In these difficult years, when the very survival of Christianity was at stake, the question of autocephaly was of only minor significance for both priests and believers.

In Western Byelorussia, which was Polish between the two world wars, the Orthodox Byelorussians looked upon the Autocephalous Orthodox Church of Poland in the same way as their Ukrainian brethren. They wanted to make it into a national Byelorussian body, at least in the dioceses of Vilna, Pinsk and Grodno, where the Orthodox believers belonged mainly to the Byelorussian ethnic group. With this aim in view two organisations were founded, the 'Byelorussian Democratic Orthodox Union' and the 'Byelorussian Orthodox Church Committee', both with headquarters in Vilna. After the Soviet occupation of Eastern Poland in 1939, the Byelorussians of that country were, with the connivance of the authorities, placed under the jurisdiction of two appointees of the Moscow Patriarchate, one of whom has already been mentioned. He was the new Metropolitan of Lutsk, Nikolay

---

[1] S. Krushibsky, 'Byelorussian Communism and Nationalism, Personal recollections', *Research Program of the USSR*, New York City 1953, p. 36.

[2] Mgr. A. M., op. cit., p. 23.   [3] Kasyak, op. cit., p. 42.

Yarushevich. It was an advantage for him, though hardly the reason for his appointment, that he himself was born in Russia's Western border areas of Byelorussian parents. Later he said of himself that he was a 'son of Byelorussia'.[1] A small number of Poland's Orthodox Byelorussians came under the Russian Archbishop of Vilna. In 1940, after Lithuania's annexation by the Soviet Union, he assumed the title of 'Exarch of the Baltic Countries' and one of his main tasks consisted in suppressing ecclesiastical separatism, whether Byelorussian, Latvian or Estonian.

The hopes of Byelorussian nationalists for an autocephalous Church of their own received a sudden though ephemeral revival in 1941 as a result of the nazi occupation of Byelorussia. It is remarkable that the nazi authorities, who never committed themselves in favour of an autocephalous Church in the Ukraine, should have shown an active interest in the establishment of an autocephalous Orthodox Church in Byelorussia. Of course, this was not to be the free autocephalous Church that certain Byelorussians wanted; it was to be but a willing tool of their policy. At the same time the Nazis executed one of the most ardent champions of the Byelorussification of the Church, Archpriest Koush, under the absurd pretext of his being a Soviet agent.[2] The Nazis granted permission for an All-Byelorussian Church Council to be held in August 1942, but they did not allow the head of the Church, Metropolitan Panteleimon (Rozhnovsky), to participate. So there was nobody to sign the letter to the Oecumenical Patriarch in Constantinople asking for acceptance of the new autocephalous status of Byelorussian Orthodoxy. Without such an acceptance the autocephaly was canonically null and void. The letter could not be dispatched until April 1943 after the release from internment of the Metropolitan.[3] But whether the German General Commissariat of Byelorussia actually forwarded the letter is not known. On the insistence of the Nazis the Church was forced to incorporate in its statutes a proviso at variance with fundamental Christian principles as it excluded Jews from baptism and church membership.

The sad chapter of the Byelorussian Autocephalous Orthodox Church by the grace of the Nazis ended with their retreat. As it had never achieved canonical status, its bishops had no wish to maintain the pretence of an autocephalous Church in emigration; least of all Panteleimon, the 'Archbishop of Minsk and Metropolitan of all Byelorussia', himself not a Byelorussian by nationality but half-Polish,

[1] *Zh.M.P.*, 1953, no. 8, p. 8.   [2] J. Kasyak, op. cit., p. 92.
[3] J. Kasyak, op. cit., p. 124.

half-Russian. He had lent himself with the utmost reluctance to the whole venture. Those Byelorussian Orthodox exiles who still insisted on autocephaly despite the attitude of the bishops, joined forces with the Ukrainian Autocephalists. In Byelorussia the tendencies towards ecclesiastical independence have not the dynamism that they have in the Ukraine, but they can nevertheless look back upon a certain tradition. Their future development will depend on the strength of Byelorussian nationalism.

Of all the autocephalous Churches which have existed at any time in the Western borderlands of the Soviet Union, a Byelorussian Church is the least likely to re-emerge in future. But the others, the Ukrainian, the Estonian and even the Latvian will, in all probability, re-enter the religious scene once full freedom of conscience is established in Soviet territory and the right to self-determination is granted to all peoples of the Soviet Empire.

IV

The Old Believers

The Old Believers or Old Ritualists occupy a unique position among the religious groups of Soviet Russia. They stand apart both from the official Orthodox Church and from that mass of heterogeneous groups which are usually termed 'sectarians'. In a way, the Old Believers are the most Russian of all religious bodies; they have no counterpart in any other country. They came into being in the second half of the seventeenth century as a national conservative Russian opposition to an Orthodox Church which was under Greek influence and had, according to a view, widespread at the time, distorted the ancient rites and liturgical books of Russian Christianity. The term 'Old Believers' does not stand for one single Church but is only the general name given to a large variety of religious groups and shades of religious belief tracing their origins back to the Great Russian Schism of 1666. Within the schismatic body of the Old Believers a further split soon arose on the question of whether the priesthood should be retained or not. Accordingly, two main groups of Old Believers emerged, the 'Priestists' (*popovtsy*) and the 'Priestless' (*bezpopovtsy*). Only the 'Priestists' retained a nationwide organisation. The priestless Old Believers disintegrated into a large number of isolated local communities, some of which are still in existence.

The question of the numerical strength of the Old Believers has always been a very puzzling one. The Czarist authorities in their endeavour to champion the cause of the official Church were never anxious to produce correct statistics showing the real weight of the Dissent. It is equally true however, that the authorities were not in a position to find out the exact number because many dissenters, especially the members of the more extreme priestless groups, were unwilling to disclose their true religious allegiance. The official number of Old Believers emerging from the 1897 census is 2,204,590 or 1·8 per cent of the total population of the Russian Empire. However, this figure has never been taken seriously by any student of the problem and has given rise to exaggerations in the opposite direction. Indeed, some have thought that the total number of 'dissenters' and 'sectarians' (the latter included Christian groups of a Protestant type unconnected with the Great Russian Schism) may have amounted at the beginning of the twentieth century to anything up to 25 million.

The Conflicting Views of Soviet Historians

The Soviet attitude towards the 'Old Believers' is somewhat complicated. The régime finds no difficulty in condemning them as it does all other religious groups, but it is not so easy to condemn their historical record. The question of whether the Old Believers are a progressive or a reactionary factor in Russian history has been answered differently during various periods of communist rule, and even by different historians and commentators of the same period. Two divergent views have been put forward. In the twenties and early thirties, the tone was set by Lenin's friend, the historian M. N. Pokrovsky. He paid to the original Old Believers the tribute that they were a 'People's Church' as compared to the official state-ridden Church. The 'People's Church', Pokrovsky added, had the respect and sympathy of the masses. It was wrong and a distortion of history to consider the original Dissent as a religion of the merchant class. Its founders were not merchants but came for the most part from the lower ranks of urban society, all kinds of artisans and the members of the lower clergy, the intellectuals of the period. There were also individual members of the upper classes in the movement, in the same way as, nearer to our own time, the offspring of aristocratic families joined the revolutionary movement. However, this could not affect the 'essentially democratic character' of the Old Believers' movement. Pokrovsky considered that the Old Believers became capitalists against their will. In the struggle against oppression by merchant capitalism, they themselves became accumulators of capital.[1] The progressive and democratic character of the Old Believers' movement is further borne out in his view by the participation of schismatics in the rebellions of Stenka Razin (1664) and Yemelian Pugachev (1773–4).

The social revolt which the original Dissent represented, at least in the Leninist view, is not the only link between Soviet Russia and the Old Believers. Another is the great personality of Protopriest Avvakum (1620–82), the greatest saint and martyr of the Old Believers. They still commemorate the day of his execution — April 14 — as a saint's day. Avvakum has a place in both the spiritual history of Russia and the

[1] N. N. Pokrovsky, *Brief History of Russia*, vol. i, Leningrad 1933, p. 95.

history of Russian literature. He is the author of the first Russian autobiography and played a pioneer role in the formation of the Russian literary style. Although Avvakum was not only a pious man but an outright religious fanatic, Soviet communist iconoclasm has never touched his work. In 1934, when no other religious literature could be published in the Soviet Union, the publishing house *Academia*, which served the Russian intellectual *élite*, brought out a most elegantly produced volume containing not only Avvakum's famous autobiography but also extracts from his comments on the Bible. The book, which also contained reproductions of seventeenth-century illustrations, was accessible to a small number of people; 7,300 copies were printed altogether. Avvakum's life-story was preceded by a long introduction not altogether unfavourable to the Old Believers' point of view.[1]

The reorientation of Soviet history writing under Stalin into a patriotic Russian genre did not affect the appraisal of Avvakum's literary genius but it led to a complete revision of Pokrovsky's views on the Dissent as a whole. Pokrovsky was accused of vulgarisation and falsification of the whole of Russian history. Therefore, his assessment of the Old Believers became suspect too. According to the Stalinist concept of history as it crystallised towards the end of the thirties, Pokrovsky had idealised the Dissent and supported the wrong side. Far from being democrats, so the Stalinist historians argued, the dissenters were reactionaries and unpatriotic. On the other hand, both Czar Aleksei Mikhailovich, the father of Peter the Great (in whose reign Avvakum was executed) and Patriarch Nikon were 'progressive', for, by introducing new liturgical books and new rites they endeavoured to consolidate the political and ecclesiastical centralisation of the State.[2] To strengthen his case against the dissenters a Stalinist historian would also identify them as an instrument of the exploiting classes, at first of the 'reactionary boyars and the heads of the streltsy' who opposed the reforms of Peter the Great, and later of the rich merchants.[3]

However, the problem of the historical past of the Old Believers was not of such importance to the régime as to make their condemnation an article of communist faith. Even during the period of the Stalinist patriotic distortion of Russian history, writings appeared which commented on the Dissent objectively and in a manner not unsympathetic to the Old Believers. For instance, the first volume of the standard work *History of Moscow* did not associate the Old Believers with the

---

[1] *Zhitie Protopopa Avvakuma im samim napisannoe i drugie ego sochineniya* (Autobiography and other works of Protopop Avvakum), Moscow 1934.
[2] *Large Soviet Encyclopædia*, first edition, Moscow 1948, vol. xlviii, p. 236.
[3] *Large Soviet Encyclopædia*, second edition, Moscow 1955, vol xxxvi, p. 35.

upper class and paid tribute to the stubbornness and fearlessness they showed in the defence of their faith.[1]

The fight against the personality cult which was launched by Stalin's successors was also carried into the historical field where it allowed for a qualified rehabilitation of Pokrovsky's concept. Historians were no longer obliged to pay exaggerated tribute to the role of the Czars and their merits in building a centralised state, and were urged to give more attention to the popular anti-government movements of past centuries. The emphasis was shifted from the 'leaders' to the 'masses'. This reorientation led to a reappraisal of the political and social role of the Old Believers. 'The fact that the Old Ritualists left the official Church', says one communist author, 'meant a hidden condemnation of the existing order of things and of the policy of the ruling class. The rank and file of the Old Believers, as distinct from the leaders of the Old Believer groups, adopted an irreconcilable attitude towards the official Church and governmental policy, thus reflecting the anti-feudal frame of mind of the bonded peasantry and the lower classes in the towns.'[2]

Old Believers and Atheist Propaganda

On the more practical level of atheist agitation the Old Believers have not attracted the same interest on the part of the communists. It is only too natural for the Old Believers to avoid the limelight. They show the reticence and discretion which characterise genuine martyrdom. They are not in the habit of engaging in the kind of propaganda which would make an impression on an unbelieving secular environment. They pray and worship God quietly and unobtrusively. They uphold a tradition and do not go out to make new converts. For this reason they have not caught the eye of the communist authorities to the same extent as the Evangelical and Baptist groups which have given the impression of much greater vitality. Nevertheless, a Soviet anti-religious propaganda pamphlet did say as late as 1955 that the Old Ritualists, although decreasing from year to year, were still the most numerous of all sects in the USSR and that they existed 'in many parts of the country' in the form of various groupings.[3]

To the Soviet mind, the phenomenon of the present day Old Believers is even less understandable than official Orthodoxy, Protestantism and Catholicism. Soviet writers on anti-religious topics hardly conceal their

[1] *Istoriya Moskvy* (History of Moscow), vol. i, p. 601, Moscow, 1952.
[2] A. M. Samsonov, *Antifeodalnye Narodyne Vosstaniya v Rossii i Tserkov* (Antifeudal popular risings in Russia and the Church), Moscow 1955, p. 111.
[3] E. A. Tuchkov, *Sektantsvo i ego ideologiya* (Sectarianism and its ideology), Moscow 1955, p. 21.

astonishment that anybody can keep as aloof from ordinary Soviet life as certain sections of the Old Believers have been able to do. Indeed, the Old Believers still live in a sort of internal exile, but they are not in opposition to the present Soviet régime as such. Theirs is a perpetual protest against a sinful environment which 300 years ago abandoned the true Orthodox faith and has fallen prey to the powers of evil. The 'behaviour pattern' of the Russian dissenters with which the communist régime is now faced, goes back 300 years. 'The Old Ritualists', says an atheist author from whom we have already quoted, 'even now stick fanatically to the old way of life and to outlived customs. Their leaders try to impress on their followers that going to the theatre, cinema or clubs, and consorting with people of another faith, is a great sin, and that one must live a separate and isolated life'. The author adds that the rank and file of the Old Believers and especially the youth 'by no means always' listened to the advice of their preachers.[1]

In addition to the total isolationism of the Old Believers, Soviet atheist literature also stresses the survival of their patriarchal family system. For instance, one writer makes the following assertions: 'In many Old Ritualist families there exists even now a patriarchal order based on the law of the fist and the despotic power of the head of the family. Religious beliefs in these families are maintained through compulsion, prohibition and fear. They are imposed by the fist and by threats.'[2]

To conduct atheist propaganda among the Old Believers is an almost hopeless task, for even Soviet sources would readily admit that Old Believers and other 'sectarians' do not usually attend lectures or read books on atheist themes.[3] To the extent to which there is anything written against the Old Believers in Russia, and such literature is rare, it aims at anti-religious propaganda in the broadest and most general sense and not at converting Old Believers to Communism.

After World War II the Russian public was given only one major opportunity to hear in greater detail about the Old Believers, and this was in 1955 and 1956, when a Soviet state publishing house republished the two novels *In the Forests* and *On the Mountainside* by Melnikov-Pechersky (1819–83). These two works of fiction, totalling 2,500 pages, are the longest ever devoted by a Russian writer to the problem of the dissenters. They depict with a wealth of folklore and historical detail the life of the Old Believers in the eastern part of European Russia,

---

[1] Tuchkov, op. cit., p. 21.

[2] I. N. Uzkov, *Chto takoe religioznoe sektantsvo?* (What is religious sectarianism?), Moscow 1956, p. 17.

[3] Uzkov, op. cit., p. 30.

their customs, holy days, and religious thought. To the author, the Old Believers symbolised the Russian spirit, and in writing his novel he wished to convince the Czarist Government that it was mistaken in assuming a hostile attitude towards the dissenters — an attitude which the writer himself had originally shared. The authorities, so Melnikov-Pechersky seems to have argued, could even have found an ally in the Old Believers in the struggle against revolutionary forces. Judged by Soviet standards this made Melnikov-Pechersky himself a 'reactionary'. Why then were his books reprinted in editions of 300,000 and 450,000 copies respectively, a considerable number even for Soviet conditions? In the first place, Melnikov-Pechersky's books are among the greatest works of Russian literature and as such could not be suppressed for ever. Moreover, the new Soviet editions of *In the Forests* and *On the Mountainside* were preceded by prefaces converting the author's praise of the Old Believers into documents of anti-religious propaganda. The preface to *In the Forests* asserted that Melnikov-Pechersky's great novel was *an indictment of religious fanaticism and hypocrisy*. The author, said the preface, tried to show that the Old Ritualist bourgeoisie was inseparably linked with the nation, but his attempt failed. In effect the reader could see what *shameless rapacious capitalists* emerged from the Old Ritualist environment.[1]

The 'Church of the Belo-Krinitsa Concord'

The largest of the Old Believer groups still existing in the Soviet Union is the Church of the Old Believers of the Belo-Krinitsa Concord. In Czarist times it was estimated that two-thirds of all Old Believers belonged to this Church. To-day it still appears to be larger than all other Old Believer organisations put together. Its membership is between 800,000 and 1,000,000, 50,000 of whom are in the city and province of Moscow.

The name of the Church, like all Old Believer terms, requires some explanation. Belaya Krinitsa, or, to give it its more romantic-sounding Rumanian name, Fantana Alba, is a village in the south-eastern part of the Bukovina, an Austrian province until 1918, and afterwards Rumanian territory. However, unlike other Bukovinian villages, Belaya Krinitsa was destined to play a tremendous part in Russian ecclesiastical history. Towards the end of the eighteenth century several hundred Old Believers had settled down in the Bukovina and made Belaya Krinitsa their centre. They were called 'Lippovans', a corrupted form of 'Philippians', after the Old Believer leader Filip Pustoswiat. The

[1] P. I. Melnikov, *V Lesakh* (In the Forests), Moscow 1955, pp. 8–9.

Austrian authorities treated them with kindness. Proscribed in their Russian homeland, they became an officially recognised community in the Hapsburg Empire. In 1844 they received permission from the Austrian Emperor to choose a bishop. This was an important concession not only for the small group of Old Believers in the Bukovina but also for the large masses of priestist Old Believers in Russia itself. For 180 years they had suffered greatly from the fact that there was no Old Believer bishop. This compelled them to recruit all their priests from among 'deserters' from the official Orthodox Church. But the permission of the Austrian Emperor opened new vistas. The next thing to be done was to find a candidate for the new office. This happened in 1846, when the Old Believers persuaded the deposed Orthodox Metropolitan of Bosnia, Ambrosius, to join their ranks. After an audience with the Austrian Emperor he took up residence in Belaya Krinitsa. Although he stayed there only two years, this short time was sufficient to bring the Belo-Krinitsa hierarchy of the Old Believers into being. Ambrosius consecrated two bishops, and ordained several priests.

The history of the Old Believer Church of the Belo-Krinitsa Concord under the Soviet régime is one of suffering and severe persecution. Several of its successive heads who had the title 'Archbishop of Moscow and all Russia' had serious difficulties with the communist authorities. They were denounced, either for counter-revolutionary activities or for common offences. In 1918, Archbishop Innokentii Usov fled to Rumania, one of the traditional sanctuaries of the Old Believers. There he lived very modestly in Kishinev as bishop of the local Old Believer community. The Old Believer Church in Rumania was in fact far too small to qualify for the legal status of an officially recognised religion and to receive subsidies from public funds. Nevertheless Soviet anti-religious propagandists charged Archbishop Innokentii with receiving assistance from the Rumanian intelligence service. 'The hangmen of the Rumanian people used Usov for the organisation of espionage in the USSR.'[1] Usov's successor Meletii died in 1934, otherwise he might have fallen victim to the Yezhov purge. He could only be charged posthumously with conducting a correspondence with General Denikin during the civil war and having 'close relations' with General Denikin's headquarters.[2] From the death of Archbishop Meletii until the German invasion of Russia the Old Believer Church had no Archbishop, only a locum tenens. One locum tenens, Gerontii Lakomkin, was arrested by

---

[1] Boris Kandidov, *Tserkov i Shpionazh* (Church and Espionage), Moscow 1938, p. 75.
[2] Kandidov, op. cit., p. 76.

the GPU under the pretext that he had embezzled ecclesiastical property. His successor, Vikentii Nikitin, who seems to have been in office from 1934 until the beginning of World War II, was charged in the Soviet press with immorality and drunkenness.[1] These charges were in all probability nothing but slander. The communist authorities were simply trying to render innocuous a church leader who exercised a considerable influence as a spiritual adviser and supreme arbiter of the Old Believer flock.

The Old Believer Church saw better days after Vikentii Nikitin's successor Irinarkh — whose secular name was Ivan Vasilevich Parfenov — took office in 1941. It fell to him to rebuild the Old Believers' Church after the years of persecution. During his term of office occurred the change in communist tactics towards institutionalised religion and even the Old Believers were allowed to benefit from it to a moderate extent. They were able to reopen and repair a number of churches, for instance those of Rostov-on-Don and Gorky, two important traditional Old Believer centres. Irinarkh appointed three new bishops and fifty new priests and deacons between 1942 and 1947. The new relationship between the State and the Old Believers was symbolised on the occasion of Irinarkh's sixty-fifth birthday on November 18, 1946, when Ivan Vasilevich Polyansky,[2] the head of the Council for the Affairs of Religious Cults, sent a telegram of greetings to the Archbishop. This was the first congratulatory message from a secular official ever received by an ecclesiastical dignitary of the Old Believers in the almost three hundred years which had elapsed since the Russian Church schism.[3] Irinarkh died in March 1952.[4] His successor was elected almost immediately by an Assembly of thirty-five Old Believer bishops and priests—Archbishop Flavian (Feofilakt Slesarev), since 1948 Bishop of Donets-Don and the Caucasus.

In the administration of the Church the Old Believer Archbishop is assisted by a Council, and under Irinarkh this was properly reconstituted. According to the latest known composition (1956) the Council consists of twelve members, the Archbishop himself, three bishops, the Dean of the Moscow Old Believers' Cathedral, six Old Believer priests from

---

[1] *Antireligioznik*, 1938, no. 12, p. 40.

[2] Ivan Vasilevich Polyansky (1898–1956) was Chairman of the Council for the Affairs of Religious Cults for as long as twelve years. It is not known what posts he occupied prior to this appointment. His official biography only says that he performed government work and carried out 'important state assignments' (*Pravda*, October 16, 1956). This reticence about Polyansky's past record may indicate that he was employed by the police like Mr. Karpov his opposite number in the Council for the Affairs of the Russian Orthodox Church.

[3] *Staroobryadcheskii Tserkovnii Kalendar na 1955 god*, Moscow, p. 45.

[4] *Izvestiya*, March 11, 1952.

various parts of the country, and the lay-secretary of the Moscow Archbishopric. One of the four Old Believer bishops acts as deputy to the Archbishop. This deputy was for a long time Bishop Gerontii who from 1942 until his death administered the diocese of Yaroslavl and Kostroma. Gerontii was one of the great Old Believer bishops of the first half of the twentieth century who in Czarist times, as Bishop of Petrograd and Tver, was responsible for the building of large numbers of churches and church schools. Between 1945 and 1949, as deputy to the Archbishop, he edited the Old Believer calendars, the only Old Believer publications which the Soviet Government allowed to be printed. Between 1951 and 1955, for unknown reasons, their publication was interrupted.[1] When Gerontii died in 1951 at the age of almost seventy-nine, the honour of deputising for the Archbishop passed to the Bishop of Donets-Don and the Caucasus and later to the Bishop of Kishinev, Odessa and Chernovtsy (Joseph Morzhanov).

Of all religious groups of the Soviet Union, the Church of the Belo-Krinitsa Concord is likely to be the most nationalistic. This nationalism is covered by the dust of centuries. It has little in common with the nationalism of the Orthodox Church which has persistently adapted itself to new political situations. The Old Believers still try to live mentally in ancient Holy Russia as it existed before the Great Schism, and to cultivate its memory. Of great importance to them is their Moscow headquarters, the Rogozhskoe cemetery. Much of the history of the Old Believers is enshrined in this cemetery where many priests, bishops and other distinguished figures of the Belo-Krinitsa Church are buried. In the midst of the cemetery is the Pokrovskii Cathedral ('Cathedral of the Protection of Our Lady') which can hold as many as 10,000 people. The significance of the Cathedral, however, lies not in its size but in the fact that it is a real museum of ancient Russian ikonography, containing as many as four hundred ikons of the pre-schism period presented to the Church by their owners, faithful Old Believer families.[2]

The Old Believer Church considers it one of its tasks to preserve the old religious art. It has been allowed to publish a book of reproductions of some of the ikons of the Pokrovskii Cathedral. Part of its income is spent on the restoration and purchase of ikons and also on the purchase of ancient religious books. The Church used to have within its fold many wealthy merchants and even to-day is not devoid of

[1] *Staroobryadcheskii Tserkovnii Kalendar na 1955 god*, Moscow, p. 47.
[2] *Drevnie ikony staroobradcheskogo kafedralnogo Pokrovskogo sobora pri Rogozhskom kladbishche v Moskve* (Ancient ikons of the Pokrovskii Cathedral at the Rogozhskoe cemetery in Moscow), Moscow 1956, p. 7.

means. Like the Orthodox Church it derives an income both from the offerings of the faithful and from the sale of candles. The administration of its temporal affairs is in the hands of a very experienced layman, Kirill Aleksandrovich Abrikosov, who, with a business background — the Abrikosovs were well-known sweet producers in Czarist Russia — is well versed in financial matters.

A Geography of Sufferings

The Belo-Krinitsa Church outside Moscow too, represents a phase of history which in some strange way has survived into our time. The very names of the bishoprics reflect both the history and the geography of the sufferings of the Old Believers. They show the direction in which the Old Believers fled from persecution by the Czarist authorities and the official Church. The Donets-Don-Caucasus diocese with its centre in Rostov-on-Don recalls the Old Believers' flight to the South, the country of the Don Cossacks.

The bishopric of Kishinev-Odessa-Chernovtsy indicates another region in which the Old Believers sought refuge — Moldavia and Bukovina. Most of Moldavia belonged to the Rumanian State during the period between the two wars. This enabled the Old Believers there to escape the persecution to which their brethren in Soviet Russia were exposed in the twenties and thirties. Soviet persecution caused particular havoc in the small area of Moldavia around Tiraspol which remained in Soviet hands, many of the Old Believers there being deported during the collectivisation period.[1] A second wave of persecution descended on the Tiraspol Old Believers in 1937, when fifty of them were arrested as 'counter-revolutionaries' for signing a petition for the re-opening of a church building. Alex Weissberg, the Austrian ex-communist and author of Conspiracy of Silence, met one of these Tiraspol Old Believers. He was eighty-eight years old, of handsome patriarch-like appearance, and in the absence of a priest he acted as head of the community. The NKVD tried to make him confess that the Old Believer Bishop of Kiev was a Rumanian spy and that he himself was to act as go-between with the Rumanian authorities.[2] The Old Believer community of Tiraspol survived all storms and its priest is even a member of the Archbishop's Council in Moscow.

Strangest of all must seem the existence of an Old Believer Bishop of Klintsy and Novozybkov. Klintsy and Novozybkov are two small

[1] W. E. D. Allen, The Ukraine, A History, Cambridge University Press 1950, p. 328.
[2] Alex Weissberg, Conspiracy of Silence, London, p. 454.

townships on the borders of Russia proper and Byelorussia. These two places are further reminders of the special Old Believers' geography of escape. Klintsy and Novozybkov were among seventeen places which the Old Believers founded in the forests of Starodub near the Polish frontier at the end of the seventeenth and beginning of the eighteenth century, when the intolerance of the authorities forced them out of Moscow and other places in Inner Russia. The special importance of Klintsy was that it was the site of the first printing works belonging to the Old Believers in Russia, which produced new copies of the ancient liturgical books used in Old Believer services.

In addition to the bishoprics mentioned, the Old Believers of the Belo-Krinitsa Concord have retained their other traditional centres, in the Urals and the Middle and Lower Volga Region. Often the Old Believer strongholds are hidden deep in the Russian countryside as they always were and we learn only by chance of their continuing existence. Easily the most picturesque and romantic of these hidden Old Believer bulwarks is no existing town or village but the legendary city *Grad Kitezh*. Legend has it that this city existed until about 1237 when the Mongol Khan Baty invaded and pillaged Russia. When Baty approached Kitezh, so the legend says, the Lord did not permit the city to be ransacked by the enemies of Christendom, so it disappeared and Baty's men looked for it in vain ten days and ten nights.[1] According to the legend the city still exists but it is invisible. It is concealed from the human eye by the waters of the little Lake Svetloyar near the village of Vladimirskoe, only 120 miles north-east from Gorky, the fifth largest city of the Soviet Union.

It is hardly surprising that Lake Svetloyar became a place of pilgrimage. People believed that with the Lord firmly in one's own heart one could hear the sound of the bells of Grad Kitezh. It was the Old Believers who above all cultivated the beautiful legend since it belonged to ancient Holy Russia. Even after many years of communist rule the legend did not die. On the contrary, Soviet sources throughout the fifties disclosed how widespread the belief in the holy city still was then. Every year, in July, Old Believers came to the lake and brought their ancient liturgical books with them. At improvised altars, they held religious services. People continued to expect from a pilgrimage to the lake fulfilment of their dearest wishes and even children reared in Soviet schools thought that a pilgrimage might help them to pass examinations. Healing qualities too have been attributed to the lake and this also has attracted pilgrims from near and far. Those who made the pilgrimage

---

[1] P. I. Melnikov, *V Lesakh*, Moscow 1955, p. 13.

often exposed themselves to great physical hardship, they walked around the lake on their knees, a practice viewed with great disfavour by the authorities.[1] At one time the latter considered whether they should not keep pilgrims away from the lake under the pretext that they interfered with fishing. Even a Moscow newspaper took up the case of Lake Svetloyar and urged that special lectures be delivered to destroy belief in *Grad Kitezh* and the lake.[2]

The hinterland of Lake Svetloyar is traditional Old Believer territory. Even long after World War II there were still villages in the Gorky Province where the social and religious activities of the Old Believers made an infinitely greater impact on the population than communist cultural work. In the provincial capital Gorky itself the parish priest of the Belo-Krinitsa Church dismayed the communists with his zeal in urging people to put crosses around their children's necks and teach them psalms and prayers.[3]

The Belo-Krinitsa Church has also had a certain following in Siberia where it had three bishoprics until the late twenties — those of Tomsk, Minusinsk and the Far East. At that time Soviet sources complained bitterly about the actively anti-communist attitude of the Belo-Krinitsa clergy. The clergy called for the boycott of elections; in 1926 they urged Old Believers not to let census officials into their homes and they tried to open illegal schools because they said Soviet schools produced communists and godless people.[4] It is probably this resistance which led to particularly ruthless suppression of the Siberian Belo-Krinitsa Church. The three bishoprics Tomsk, Minusinsk and the Far East seem to have disappeared.

The Church of the Fugitive Priests

The Church of the Belo-Krinitsa Concord has never been recognised by all priestist Old Believers. Even after the hierarchy of Belo-Krinitsa had come into being one Old Believer faction continued to use runaway priests of the official Church. It was, therefore, usually called the Church of the Fugitive Priests — the 'Beglopopovtsy'. One reason for the non-recognition of the Belo-Krinitsa bishops was their formal connection with a foreign country — Austria — a connection which the official Orthodox Church did not fail to exploit. The Belo-Krinitsa Old Believers were officially referred to as 'Austrians' or as the 'Church of

---

[1] Zvezda, 1958, no. 12, pp. 110-112.
[2] *Komsomolskaya Pravda*, December 18, 1953.
[3] *Komsomolskaya Pravda*, ibid.
[4] A. Dolotov, *Tserkov i Sektantsvo v Sibiri* (Church and Sectarianism in Siberia), Novosibirsk, 1930, pp. 56-73.

the Austrian Concord', certainly a considerable handicap for a religious group which laid great store by its national-Russian character.

The Beglopopovtsy too, survived the Revolution and it was only after the establishment of Soviet power that they were able to become a 'respectable' Church with a proper hierarchy. This was possible because two bishops had gone over to them, one being Bishop Nikolay Pozdnev of the 'Living Church', who joined them in 1923 and the other Bishop Stephen of the Orthodox Church proper who became an Old Believer in 1930. In 1935 the ex-Beglopopovtsy had five bishops altogether, and their hierarchical head assumed the title of 'Archbishop of Moscow and all Russia'. The old nickname 'Beglopopovtsy' had become an anachronism and the group called itself the 'Old Believer Church of Ancient Orthodox Christians'. The group produces no literature and it is difficult therefore to get a picture of its geographical distribution. However, the fact that it has its headquarters in Kuibyshev seems to indicate that its centre of gravity is still in the Middle and Lower Volga region. The Beglopopovsty also have their strongholds in Siberia, especially in the Buryat-Mongol Autonomous Republic where in the late twenties a Soviet source estimated their number at 40,000.[1]

'Priestless' Old Believers — the Recognised Groups

The priestless Old Believers were never inclined towards firm organisational ties, and Soviet religious persecution encouraged their natural tendency to split into ever smaller groups. As far as Soviet Russia within the pre-1939 frontiers is concerned, only the Moscow priestless Old Believers felt the need for a coherent organisation with official recognition. The group calls itself the 'Preobrazhenskoe Community of Old Believers of the Staropomorsk Concord'. This rather complicated title is derived on the one hand from the Cemetery of the Transfiguration of Our Lord (Preobrazhenskoe) in Moscow, an important centre of the priestless Old Believers since 1771, and on the other from 'Pomore', meaning the maritime region near Archangel, one of the remote areas where the Old Believers found refuge from persecution. The group, which is also known as 'Fedoseevtsy' after its founder Feodosii Vasilev claims a total membership of 90 to 120,000 in Greater Moscow and its surroundings. In the fifties the Moscow 'Fedoseevtsy' were one of the few religious organisations of the Soviet Union allowed to publish an annual calendar. It emerges from its content that the priestless Old Believers of the Soviet capital are in touch with other communities of the same faith in various parts of the country including

[1] Dolotov, op. cit., p. 58.

a group in Leningrad as well as those Old Believers who, towards the
end of the seventeenth century, settled along the shores of Lake Peipus
which forms the border between Russia and Estonia. The island of
Piirisaar which is situated in the Estonian part of the lake is almost
entirely inhabited by Old Believers.[1]

Through the annexation of the Baltic countries and Poland, two
more organised Old Believers' groups were added to the religious map
of the Soviet Union, one in Latvia, the other in the Vilnius region now
belonging to Soviet Lithuania. In pre-communist Latvia the Old
Believers were the fourth largest religious community after Lutherans,
Catholics, and Orthodox. They numbered over 107,000, forming more
than five per cent of Latvia's total population. Over 11,000 of them
lived in the capital, Riga, itself, but the majority — 78,000 — settled
in villages of the Latgale province close to the borders of Russia proper.
In independent Latvia the Old Believers lived a separate life. They
even had their own political party whose leader (Meletii Kalistratov)
was from 1922 to 1934 a member of the Saiema, the Latvian parliament.
He was one of the Latvian ex-MPs whom the Soviets deported in
1940–41. Nevertheless, the Old Believers of Latvia proved a comparatively pro-Soviet element. Under German occupation they gave
more support to the red guerillas than any other ethnic and religious
group. This may account for the benevolent treatment they enjoyed
after World War II. In 1952 they could still boast over a hundred
parishes.

The Old Believers' group which now lives in Lithuania looks back on
two hundred years of uninterrupted settlement in the Vilnius region —
longer than any other Russian inhabitants of pre-war Poland. In 1929,
the forty-nine Old Believer communities of Poland, with their 40,000
members, were organised into an 'Eastern Orthodox Church of the
Ancient Rite.' Of these all but 5,000 who continued to live in Poland
came under Soviet domination after World War II.

Being conservative and utterly devoid of any irredentist ambitions,
the Old Believers' attitude towards Poland was in striking contrast to
that of the unruly Ukrainians and Byelorussians. The Pilsudski and
post-Pilsudski régimes, which were not remarkable for their fairness
towards minorities, considered the Old Believer community a shining
example of loyalty. The most famous Old Believer in Poland was Boris
Pimenov who, until the outbreak of World War II, was a Russian
deputy of the Polish Sejm, and also a leading figure in the 'Union of
Russian Minority Organisations' (SRMO), of which he was for a time
chairman. The co-operation of the Old Believers of the Vilnius region

with the Polish 'bourgeois and landowners' state' must have discredited them in Soviet eyes. But to what extent they have suffered on this account is not known except that they have been forced to display public support for the régime on various occasions. Nevertheless, it seems that their community has remained more or less intact. A report about an Old Believers' peace meeting held in Lithuania said it was attended by thirty-eight spiritual leaders and community chairmen. This may indicate the number of parishes still in existence. Unlike the Latvian and Moscow Old Believer branches the Lithuanian is still referred to as a Church, the name it acquired under Polish rule.

Lost Tribes in Siberia and Central Asia

The three groups, of Moscow, Latvia, and Lithuania, participated in the 'Conference in Defence of Peace of all Churches and Religious Associations in the USSR' which was held in May 1952. Each group was represented by two delegates.[1] That no other priestless group was invited indicates that there were no other priestless organisations in the country to be exploited by the Soviet peace propaganda campaign, but it does not mean that no other priestless groups exist. 'Priestless Old Believers' and 'organisation' are to some extent contradictory notions and it is probably the absence of external organisation which has enabled the Old Believers to avoid the more drastic forms of anti-religious persecution and to survive. In their escape from the religious oppression of Czarist Russia the priestless Old Believers went to the most remote and inaccessible places. In the case of many, it was not only a flight from persecution. There was something more positive and spiritual about the great trek of the Old Believers. It was not simply a running away, it was also a seeking for a land of promise. They sought a legendary country where the Antichrist did not rule and where the true Orthodox Church remained in being. The Old Believers called that land *Belovode*, (literally 'land of the white water') and they sought it in the East. Some believed they had found it in the valleys of the Altai Mountains, with their majestic beauty. There two groups of Old Believers of the priestless faction have lived since the middle of the eighteenth century, one on the river Uba, the other on the river Bukhtarma, both tributaries of the Irtysh. Soviet political geography has divided the first group between Kazakhstan and the Altai Territory, whilst the whole of the second group, the Bukhtarma Old Believers, belongs to Kazakhstan.

[1] *Conference in Defence of Peace of all Churches and Religious Associations in the USSR*, Moscow 1952, p. 15.

The Altai Old Believers have presented an interesting problem to the ethnographers, for they are different from the usual type of Russian Siberian colonists. Their villages have broad clean streets, their houses are built with an artistic taste, embellished with carvings, coloured glass windows, and flowers in pots. The women are distinctive in their elaborate attire and their picturesque headgear. They are a poetic people with a rich store of songs, old Russian peasant songs brought from European Russia, which are sung at weddings.[1] The Bukhtarma Old Believers in particular have struck all travellers by the simplicity of their customs, their dignity, their courage and intelligence.[2]

What we know of the Old Believers' character generally, their steadfastness and their ability to brave the overwhelming power of the State, makes it unlikely that the communist hurricane could have swept the Altai Old Believers away. Had they been living in a more accessible part of the Russian Empire they might have been deported, but as it happened they already lived in a territory used for exile and deportation. In fact, the Uba Old Believers are themselves exiles. Early in the seventeenth century they lived in the town of Vetka on the Polish-Russian border. From this, their first place of refuge, they were deported to Siberia in 1764. The older settlers in Siberia called these newcomers 'Poles' despite their pure Russian origin, and this name stuck to them until the twentieth century. This great tradition of suffering makes them no easy victim, even of the most oppressive régimes. As everywhere in rural communities, the period of trial came probably only at the time of collectivisation, and about the Bukhtarma Old Believers we know definitely that their traditional way of life was still intact in 1927. In the summer of that year an expedition from the Soviet Academy of Sciences visited the villages of the Bukhtarma valley and discovered them, almost as one discovers a new tribe in the wilds of tropical Africa or in the interior of New Guinea.

The expedition, which published a compendium of fascinating folklore material, gave a picture of a closed community which, as yet untouched by Soviet power, lived a life of its own. The authority of Bible-readers (*Nachotchiki*) was very great, and all secular education was held in contempt. Parents refused to send their children to state schools because these failed to provide what Old Believers considered essential parts of the curriculum — hymn-singing and Church Slavonic. They preferred to entrust their boys to a good Bible-reader, who taught them to read the books necessary for liturgical purposes. A gifted boy

[1] Rossiya, *Zapadnaya Sibir*, S.P.B. 1907, vol vi, pp. 506–7.
[2] Rossiya, op. cit., p. 513.

was then able to become a Bible-reader himself. The Bukhtarma Old
Believers avoided contact with persons of other faiths as much as possible, referring to them as *Mirskie*, people of the world.[1]

Even the collectivisation which in other parts of the Soviet Union led
to a disruption of the traditional way of life may not have had the same
destructive results in the seven Bukhtarma Old Believer villages.[2] Up-
to-date Soviet maps of the Altai and North-East Kazakhstan show that
the Old Believer villages lying almost in a row, about 120 kilometres in
length, are still the only inhabited points in what seems otherwise an
unpopulated area. Situated at altitudes ranging from 1,850 to 3,600 feet
these villages are so remote from the lines of communication that the
great upheavals in Russian agriculture may have made little difference
to them.

Another Old Believer group which had to be re-discovered by a
scientific expedition are the so-called Uraltsy, who now live in Western
Kazakhstan and the Karakalpak Republic. A team of three people
was sent out in the autumn of 1945 to investigate their customs and
way of life. The expedition had to admit that this forgotten branch of
the Russian people still adhered to the 'Old Faith' which has its origins
in the great Russian schism.

The Uraltsy are the descendants of the Ural Cossacks who were
removed from the Ural Cossack force for insubordination in 1875–7,
expelled from their native villages and exiled to the newly conquered
territories of Central Asia. All were Old Believers and their faith was
the primary cause which brought them into conflict with the state
authorities. To-day there are several thousand Uraltsy families. They
live at Turtkul and Nukus — the former and present capital respectively of the Karakalpak Republic — in the whole of the delta of the
Amu Darya river, in the town of Kazalinsk near the mouth of the Syr
Darya river, and on the islands of Lake Aral. This geographical
distribution indicates the nature of their work. They are fishermen and
as such have been able to withstand the impact of the communist régime
to an even greater extent than the farming Old Believers. The expedition
sent by the Soviet Academy came to the conclusion that time had stood
still for the Uraltsy. They preserved the old style both in their way of
life and in their outlook. Funeral ceremonies were still performed
'according to a centuries-old canon' and until the beginning of World
War II weddings were celebrated according to an 'ancient complicated

---

[1] *Bukhtarminskie Staroobryadtsy* (The Old Ritualists of Bukhtarma), Leningrad
1930, pp. 33–4.

[2] Korobikha, Pechi, Belaya, Fikalka, Berel, Archaty, Yazovaya.

ritual', meaning the ancient ritual of the Old Believers. 'Godly verses' were still current among the Uraltsy, a kind of spiritual poetry once widespread among the Russian people, but which has now completely disappeared from most parts of the Soviet Union. The expedition collected twenty spiritual poems of the Uraltsy Old Believers bearing such characteristic titles as 'Noah's Ark' or 'How the Soul took leave of the Body'.

Although obviously unable to stamp out the 'Old Faith' among the Uraltsy, the Soviet régime has made some impact on them, particularly on the education of the younger generation. This used to be in the hands of pious women or Bible-readers, but 'after the Revolution' — we are not told how long after the Revolution — their work came to an end.[1] The findings of the expedition to the Uraltsy were published only in very short extracts. The promised longer monograph on 'The Uraltsy of Central Asia' never appeared, nor will it appear in view of the death of the main participant in the expedition, Madame Blomkvist.

Evidence of a different kind is available about a further Old Believers' 'tribe' living in the Far East near the Chinese border, in the midst of a jungle infested by tigers. In 1931 when these Old Believers were 'found' they were 400 kilometres away from the nearest railway station and 100 kilometres from the nearest telephone. The source revealing the existence of these Old Believers was not a scholarly publication but a play, *The Bikin river falls into the Ussuri*. The action of this play takes place in the spring of 1932. There can be no doubt that it describes real events, for the playwright has given most precise geographical data. The theme of the play is the difficulties which the Soviet authorities encountered on the Soviet-Chinese frontier which became the Soviet-Japanese frontier on the transformation of Manchuria into the Japanese puppet state of Manchukuo.

The plot can be roughly summarised thus: the Japanese are determined to have another Manchukuo in the Soviet Far East. Amongst other things they recruit Old Believers as spies and agents, and with their help they try to dislodge Soviet power from a strategically vital frontier zone. It is therefore not surprising that the local representative of the Soviet régime, symbolically called *Robinzon* — the civilised man among savages — speaks bitterly of the Old Believers. 'How many years have they plundered us, have they sneered at us. They do not want and they cannot live an honest life. They gave help to the Kolchak people, the

---

[1] Ye. E. Blomkvist, *Etnograficheskaya Rabota sredi 'Uraltsev'* (Ethnographic work among the 'Uraltsy'), Akademiya Nauk SSSR, Institut Etnografii, *Kratkie Soobshcheniya*, no. iii, 1947, pp. 49–54.

interventionists and all the other scum of imperialism.'[1] Whilst Comrade *Robinzon* appears to speak very knowingly about the past of the local Old Believers, the commander of the Red Army unit stationed in the area admits in all humility that until 1931 nobody even suspected the existence of these 'idiotic' Old Believer villages, there was no Soviet power there. They were discovered only when a technical reconnaissance party carried out some preparatory work for the fixing of telegraph communications. Only then was Soviet power established in their villages.[2] This belated but no doubt forceful introduction of the Soviet administration and collectivisation must have given rise to considerable tension between the Old Believers and the authorities. The play does not tell us how this tension is solved, it only records the failure of the Japanese intrigues and the arrest of the principal Old Believer spy. It would be in line with usual Soviet practice if they had been deported from the frontier area as a risk to security.

These Old Believers in the Ussuri forest, with whom the play deals, are only a small fraction of the Old Believers of the Far East. In 1926 they still numbered 18,500. As the Soviet Far East lived in permanent expectation of a Japanese attack, it was natural that these Far Eastern Old Believers, together with all other religious-minded people in the region, should constantly be suspected of working for the Japanese intelligence service.

Many years later, long after World War II and even after the death of Stalin, evidence reached the outside world that there were still some priestless Old Believers deep in the Far Eastern taiga. They were discovered by a Polish 'régime Catholic' Dominik Horodynski whom the Soviet authorities had allowed not only to visit Soviet Asia but even to go on a Far Eastern hunting expedition. It was on this occasion that he met priestless Old Believers who after four decades of communist rule retained not only their faith but also the code of behaviour which this faith imposes. They neither drank spirits nor smoked. Those who were not members of their sect were still not allowed to touch their cups and plates. Although living in the midst of a forest rich in game they did not engage in hunting but modestly earned their livelihood by collecting nuts and keeping bees — a favourite occupation also of the Altai Old Believers. The Polish visitor greatly praised the high moral principles of the Old Believers of the Far Eastern forest, their kindness and their generous hospitality.[3]

---

[1] M. Chumandrin, *Bikin vpadaet v Ussuri* (The Bikin falls into the Ussuri), *Novy Mir*, no. 6, p. 146.

[2] *Novy Mir*, 1939, no. 6, p. 165.   [3] *Swiat*, November 30 1958, no. 48, p. 19.

Old Believers and the 'Official' Church

From time to time, the Council for the Affairs of Religious Cults enlists the support of the Old Believer hierarchy and even that of the leaders of the priestless Old Believer groups to serve the aims of Soviet foreign policy. On such occasions the heads of the Old Believers are required to sign statements in support of Soviet government policy.[1] It is probably desirable from the point of view of the régime that the dissenters should not compromise themselves less than the 'official' Orthodox Church. If the Old Believers were allowed to desist from identifying themselves with the atheist state, they might easily gain in popularity and attract the most intransigent elements of the Patriarchal Church. Such a development would not be in the interests of the régime. The communists seem to favour a clarification on the 'religious front' by the absorption of smaller groups and sects by larger bodies, for the larger can be more easily supervised. For this reason, the authorities may be expected to view favourably the attempts of the Patriarchal Church to proselytise among the Old Believers. Such attempts were undertaken actively after the war. They took the form of direct appeals to the 'Old Ritualist brethren' to realise that no dogmatic differences separated them from the Orthodox Church, and efforts were made to revive the so-called 'Yedinoverie' movement.

This 'Yedinoverie' movement, the literal translation of which would be movement for a 'single faith', was inaugurated by the Orthodox hierarchy itself as a means of bringing the dissenters back to official Orthodoxy. The 'Yedinoverie' started in 1800 when permission was granted to former dissenters to use the old ritual in the liturgy, while being subject to the authority of the Orthodox Church. It was never a Church in its own right, but remained a missionary department of the Orthodox Church. Although there were yedinoverie parishes, church buildings and even monasteries, the hierarchy of the Yedinovertsy was the official Orthodox hierarchy. The Yedinoverie remained a despised branch of the Church, and several bishops considered it rather contemptuously as 'semi-dissent'. Such successes as the Yedinoverie movement had were mostly due to official backing. Its members were most

---

[1] One such statement was signed for instance by the Belo-Krinitsa hierarchy in 1950 in support of the so-called 'Stockholm Appeal' of the World Peace Council, and another in 1955 in favour of the Council's campaign against atomic and hydrogen weapons. The statement of 1955 was particularly violent. It denounced the 'imperialists' who 'yearn for the death of many people and, not fearing our Lord, threaten mankind with atomic weapons' (Tass message in English, March 26, 1955). A similar statement was signed by the 'Presidium of the Supreme Old Believers' Council' in Lithuania (*Soviet News*, March 23, 1955).

numerous in the reign of Nicholas I, under whom new discriminatory measures were proclaimed against dissenters, especially against those belonging to the merchant class.

Little is known about the development of the Yedinoverie in the Soviet period. The first edition of the *Soviet Encyclopaedia* said in 1932 that it had almost disappeared and that its members had either gone back to the Dissent or joined the Orthodox Church.[1] In the post-war period the Orthodox Church tried to use its enhanced prestige in order to revive the Yedinoverie. A long article devoted to its 150th anniversary by the *Journal of the Moscow Patriarchate* gave readers to understand that the Holy Synod still considered it a means of doing away with the Dissent. The author of the article mentioned two yedinoverie churches, one in the city of Moscow and the other in the Moscow Province. He added that he did not have at his disposal any 'precise statistical data about the present state of yedinoverie parishes' in other parts of the country. He only assumed that there were both yedinoverie and mixed parishes, namely parishes where the liturgy is celebrated both according to the old and the 'new' rites.[2] The yedinoverie movement has had one notable success in the post-war period; in 1949 three Old Believer priests joined the Orthodox Church. It was stated that this was achieved by the efforts and care of the Metropolitan Nikolay of Krutitsy and Kolomna, an indication of the importance which the Orthodox Church attached to the event.[3] However, the three priests belonged to the less well-organised 'Beglopopovtsy' group.

* * * *

What the future of the Old Believers will be is difficult to say: we know too little of their present. Few foreign visitors to Russia have seen anything of the Old Believers except for their Church at the Rogozhskoe Cemetery in Moscow, and their impressions are rather contradictory. A French diplomat described both priests and congregation as 'old with an air of decay' adding, 'here all was tatters, ruins and decrepitude.'[4] But such appearances may well be deceptive. The Old Believers have seemed old-fashioned and decaying to several consecutive generations, and still they have survived. Besides, other visitors have received a different impression of Rogozhskoe. They have found greater devotion and piety there than even in Orthodox churches. They have seen not

---

[1] *Large Soviet Encyclopædia*, first edition, vol. 24, 1932, p. 452.
[2] *Zh.M.P.*, 1950, no. 6, p. 41.   [3] *Zh.M.P.*, 1950, no. 6, p. 40.
[4] Rear Admiral Peltier, *Soviet Encounter*, London 1955, p. 123.

8. Flavian, the Old Believer Archbishop of Moscow and All Russia (1879–1960) addressing the ecclesiastical peace conference in Zagorsk in 1952. Behind him from left to right, the Lutheran Archbishop of Latvia, Turs, the Soviet writer Tikhonov, Melchisedek III, the Catholicos-Patriarch of All Georgia, and Kevork VI, the Armenian Catholicos.

9. Two communist 'Anti-Bibles', Yaroslavsky's *Bible for Believers and Unbelievers* and Kryvelev's *Book about the Bible*. Whilst the real Bible can be printed in the USSR in very small quantities only, the 'Anti-Bibles' appear in mass editions.

10. Khoren I, Catholicos of Echmiadzin and Patriarch of All Armenians, who died mysteriously in 1938.

11. Vazgen I, Catholicos of Echmiadzin and Patriarch of All Armenians, after his election in November 1955.

only the past but the future — the christening of little children according to the ancient Old Believer rites. The Old Believer children will, of course, grow up in Soviet schools, and communist indoctrination may prove successful in many cases, but the moral values which surround them closely in the religious life of the family will induce others to preserve their loyalty to the ancestral faith. And even the humblest member of the Old Believer communities feels that there is behind him a great historical tradition. He is part of a society which has survived despite all pressure exercised by a hostile world. To contract out of such a society, to which one belongs by right of birth, is neither easy nor dignified. It may bring material advantages, but no gain in a deeper sense.

V

The Armenian Church[1]

Two events have determined the fate of the Armenian Church since the beginning of the century, the Armenian massacres in Turkey during the First World War and the coming to power of an atheist régime in Russia. The Armenian massacres were a classic case of genocide. A whole nation ceased to exist, all its members being either killed or forced into exile. The end of the Armenian nation in Turkey was the end of the Armenian Church in that country, a Church which before 1914 had fourteen archbishops, twenty-seven bishops, six abbots and as many as 1,700 parishes and 1,600 churches. Only the Armenian Patriarch of Constantinople, who has not more than forty-two parishes and thirty-eight churches under his jurisdiction, has survived the extermination of the Armenian Church and nation in Turkey.[2]

In Soviet Russia no such catastrophe befell the Armenians. Soviet policy towards them might best be characterised by saying that the communist régime has tried to preserve the body of the Armenian nation whilst destroying its soul. One might even go further and say that the communist Government has endeavoured to make the body of the Armenian nation fit and healthy. But the Armenians are to become what Soviet jargon calls a 'socialist nation', a nation which has thrown off all survivals of the past, including religion.

The Communist Attitude to Echmiadzin

Soviet policy aims at wiping out the so-called religious prejudices of the Armenians of Russia and undermining their most venerated national institution — their Church, the 'Holy Apostolic Church of Armenia'. This is the strategic objective which the communist rulers pursue in

---

[1] Substantial parts of this chapter were first published in the *Eastern Churches Quarterly* under the heading 'The Armenian Church under Soviet Rule' (vol. ix, Summer 1956, no. 6).
[2] Malachia Ormanian, *The Armenian Church*, second revised English edition London 1955, p. 205.

relation to the Armenians, especially those living in the small territory in Transcaucasia known as the 'Armenian Soviet Socialist Republic'. Everything else, including the apparent official tolerance shown to the Armenian Church at certain times, belongs to the realm of tactical manœuvres.

There are very good reasons why the Soviet régime should show particular tolerance towards the Armenian Church. The Armenian Church is not so much a Church of the Soviet Union as a Church of the diaspora which has its supreme hierarchical head, the Catholicos of Echmiadzin, in Soviet territory. The bulk of Armenian Church members live scattered all over the globe, from France to Indonesia, from California to Persia. Nearly three-quarters of all Armenian churches in the world are outside the USSR and of the twenty-seven bishops, archbishops and patriarchs which the Armenian Church had in 1954 only five had their permanent residence in Soviet territory.[1] In this, the Armenian Church is very different from the Russian Orthodox Church whose members outside the USSR only amount to a very small proportion of the total membership. But the difference between the two Churches goes further than that. The Echmiadzin Catholicos or 'Supreme Patriarch of All Armenians', as he is officially called, is not only the spiritual head of a Church, but he is also a national symbol respected by Armenians throughout the world. The secular political power controlling Echmiadzin holds a key position which, if skilfully exploited, can enable it at least to some extent to dominate Armenian national life and Armenian communities all over the globe. That power must always take into account, however, that Echmiadzin is not an Armenian equivalent of Rome.

Echmiadzin, although referred to by pious Armenians as 'Holy Echmiadzin' has never played the unique part in the destinies of the Armenian Church which the Vatican has played in the history of Catholicism. Rome has an unbroken record as an ecclesiastical centre — except for the short spell in which the Popes resided at Avignon. Historians speak of the 'Babylonian captivity' of the Popes to denote that their absence from Rome was an exceptional state of affairs. There is no such compelling historical reason for the Armenian Church to be centred in Echmiadzin. Until the fifteenth century the location of the Armenian Patriarchal see was always changing along with the residence of Armenian kings and princes and in accordance with the ups and downs of Armenian history. There are at least seven places besides Echmiadzin from which the 'Patriarch of All Armenians' has exercised his jurisdiction at one time or another. So, in our time

[1] Ormanian, op. cit., pp. 205-12.

too, the Patriarchal see could be moved away from Echmiadzin if this were required by special and extraordinary circumstances. Moreover, the Catholicos of Echmiadzin has a traditional rival in the Catholicos of Cilicia, or Catholicos of Sis, who resides in the Lebanese village of Antilias and exercises jurisdiction over the Armenians of Syria, the Lebanon and Cyprus. The Catholikoi of Echmiadzin and Cilicia are co-equal, the Catholicos of Echmiadzin having a primacy of honour only. The Catholicos of Cilicia is entitled to bless the Holy Chrism and to consecrate bishops. In view of all these circumstances the leaders of the Soviet State had to reckon with the possibility of the centre of gravity of the Armenian Church being shifted beyond Soviet control if the Catholicos of Echmiadzin were cut off from the Armenian congregations in other countries. It was not in the Soviet interest to let this happen and so the Soviet authorities kept in being as much of the Armenian ecclesiastical structure as the Church required for the fulfilment of its world-wide tasks.

As long as the Catholicos is able to operate from Soviet territory, there is always a chance of influencing, with the help of the Church, Armenian public opinion in the Balkans, Western Europe, the Middle East and the Americas. At the same time the Soviet leaders were determined to see to it that the exploitation of the Armenian Church abroad should not lead to unnecessary concessions to Armenian Christians living in Russia. So it became Soviet policy to reduce to a minimum the influence of Echmiadzin inside the Soviet borders, whilst giving the Catholicos the maximum of support in his endeavours to maintain his influence over the Armenian diaspora. Within the borders of the Soviet Union the communists not only closed the majority of Armenian churches but also denied Echmiadzin a position of honour and dignity in present-day Armenia. In a book on Armenia which was awarded a Stalin Prize in 1951 and which was written by Marietta Shaginian,[1] a well-known Armenian-born Soviet writer, there is a passage about Echmiadzin which is characteristic of the official Soviet approach.[2] Madame Shaginian referred to the religious aspect of Echmiadzin as a matter belonging to history. 'In centuries gone by',

[1] Marietta Shaginian (born 1888) had religious sympathies in her youth, and her early poems published under the title 'Orientalia' are imbued with religious ideas. A collection of short stories Shaginian published in 1914 is still based on Christian premises and the hero of her first great novel *One's own Destiny* is a Christian for whom the dogma of the Christian Church is the highest law on earth. She abandoned her faith under the influence of the victory of communism and her first revolutionary novel, symbolically entitled *The Change* is openly anti-religious (A. Margarian, *Marietta Shaginian*, Erivan 1956, pp. 7–8, 12–13, 31).
[2] Marietta Shaginian, *Puteshestvie po Sovetskoi Armenii* (Travel through Soviet Armenia), Moscow 1951, p. 231.

she said, 'Echmiadzin used to be the centre of the national and religious unity of the Armenians and the highest person of the ecclesiastical hierarchy used to live there.' There was no suggestion in the book that Echmiadzin had continued to be an ecclesiastical centre and that it was still the residence of the Catholicos. The same attitude was taken by a textbook on Armenian geography published several years after the death of Stalin. It said that *before the revolution* Echmiadzin was known as the residence of the Catholicos of all Armenians.[1]

For the communists the ecclesiastical Echmiadzin belongs irrevocably to the past, and even if the monastery and the cathedral are occasionally the scene of impressive ceremonies, including the election of a new Catholicos, this has little importance from the communist point of view. It is only a kind of re-enactment of historical pageantry, most useful for enhancing Soviet prestige among the Armenians in the non-communist world. The new Echmiadzin, as the communist rulers of Armenia see it, is synonymous with atheism and economic efficiency. The district of Echmiadzin has become famous for its advanced agricultural methods. The inhabitants of the locality of Echmiadzin itself form a large and prosperous collective farm whose fields and farmhouses face the monastery. It is called *Anastvats*, in English, 'The Godless'.[2]

Though all Armenian communist leaders have been hostile to religion, being adherents of the doctrine of materialism, some at one time showed a certain respect for the Armenian Church as a national institution. Some may even have been inclined to shield it from the worst persecution. But after a while such moderate figures among the Armenian communists were usually swept away in one of the periodic purges. Charges of opportunism and collaboration with the class enemy were made against them. A case in point was the Armenian party secretary, Khandzhan, who was ousted from his post and committed suicide in 1936. He was alleged to have been in correspondence with an Armenian emigré politician of the Ramgavar Democratic Party, known for its clerical connections. It was significant that the Armenian Khandzhan was denounced by the Georgian Beriya, who was then the head of the Party and secret police for the whole of Transcaucasia. The fate of the Armenian Soviet Republic and its policy, including its policy in ecclesiastical matters, was usually determined by Georgian and Russian communists who had none of the traditional emotional attachment to the Armenian national Church such as Armenian communists were sometimes unable to throw off.

[1] *Armyanskaya SSR* (Armenian SSR), Moscow 1955, p. 155.
[2] Marietta Shaginian, ibid.

Khoren Muradbekian, or the Period of Active Persecution

Before the communists discovered the uses which could be made of Echmiadzin, they tried to disintegrate the Church by supporting an allegedly democratic reform movement within its ranks. A 'Reformed Church' was founded in Armenia in 1924–5 in obvious imitation of the 'Living Church' which split off from Russian Orthodoxy. It had the support of several bishops, and even published a magazine. The 'Armenian Reformed Church' experiment was of short duration. It enjoyed little support from Armenian Christians. The Soviet authorities themselves soon realised that it was more profitable from their point of view to penetrate the official, traditional Church rather than to build up a rival body which, being a Soviet instrument, was suspect from the outset. A former GPU agent, Gregorii Agabekov, a Transcaucasian by nationality who defected in 1930, has written a book *The Cheka at Work* which asserts that the Soviet secret police were highly successful in their attempts to infiltrate into the ranks of the Armenian hierarchy. The allegations of Agabekov refer, of course, to the twenties, but they are not without interest. In France, the GPU relied at that time on an Armenian archpriest whom it wanted to transfer to Persia and India where he could do more useful work. In Constantinople, the GPU was able to read the entire correspondence of the Armenian Patriarch of that city. In Greece, the Armenian bishop (then Garabed Mazloumian) was at the disposal of the GPU and carried out certain tasks on its orders.[1]

One may assume that such cases of Armenian priests and prelates acting as direct Soviet agents were the exception. The real service which the Armenian hierarchy rendered to the Soviet State did not take the form of participating in the cloak-and-dagger operations of the GPU but in its general pledge of loyalty towards the communist régime. This pledge was a *sine qua non* of the survival of the Church both in Russia and Armenia. In Russia, the main representative of the loyalty policy in the inter-war period was Metropolitan Sergius, the locum tenens of the Patriarchal see, and in Armenia it was Khoren Muradbekian. Until 1930, Muradbekian was the power behind the aging Catholicos Kevork V, who had been in office since 1912. From 1930 to 1932 Muradbekian was the locum tenens in Echmiadzin and at the end of 1932 he himself became Catholicos under the name of Khoren I. Muradbekian was a shrewd diplomat who was able to extract certain

[1] Gregorii A. Agabekov, *Die Tscheka an der Arbeit*, Stuttgart, Berlin, Leipzig 1932, pp. 154–60.

concessions from the communists, especially the re-opening of a number of churches which had been forcibly closed, and the return of some church property which guaranteed the maintenance of the monastery of Echmiadzin. The political loyalty which the régime received in return was not so much the loyalty of the Armenian clergy in Soviet Russia as the benevolent neutrality of many Armenian priests and bishops abroad. This meant in practical terms that the diaspora Church gave a lead in recognising the Armenian Soviet Republic as the State of the Armenian nation, in observing the foundation day of Soviet Armenia — November 29 — as an Armenian national holiday, and in respecting the red flag of Soviet Armenia as the Armenian national flag.

Every one of these symbolical recognitions was a most controversial issue for the hundreds of thousands of Armenians living abroad, and the fact that the Church came out in support of Soviet Armenia and its symbols was therefore a tremendous asset from the Soviet point of view. Many Armenians of the diaspora followed the example of the hierarchy and themselves assumed a positive attitude towards the Soviet régime in Armenia. But many others remained adamant in their opposition to Communism and went into schism rather than make the slightest compromise with the Soviet Government. In some countries the Armenian Church became a scene of rival political passions in which anti-communist nationalists and the supporters of a Soviet Armenia, who were not necessarily communists, fought each other with unbridled fanaticism. This struggle reached its tragic climax on Christmas Eve, 1933, when the Archbishop Levon Turian, denounced as pro-Soviet by his opponents, was murdered in Holy Cross Church in New York. The problem of the responsibility for this assassination has divided the Armenian community in the United States ever since.[1] But whoever was the immediate culprit there can be no doubt that a great deal of the moral guilt for the crime lies with the Soviet Government. For it was they who had forced the Armenian Church into a position where it had ceased to be the traditional guide of the nation and had become a fighting ground for political factions.

Throughout the whole inter-war period the Armenian Church had only one proud moment, the solemn election of the Catholicos in November 1932. The Soviet authorities hesitated a long time before allowing the election to take place, and two and a half years lapsed between the death of the old Catholicos Kevork V and the appointment

---

[1] Conflicting versions of the event are given in K. S. Papazian, *Patriotism Perverted*, Boston 1934, pp. 61–5 and Sarkis Atamian, *The Armenian Community*, New York 1955, pp. 367–73.

of his successor. Finally, it was decided that the election could not be further postponed if the communists wanted to maintain their control over Echmiadzin. The fact that the election could take place at all was in itself an unusual concession, considering that at that time the Orthodox Church had not been permitted to normalise its organisational life. There were three candidates for the Catholicosate of whom one was Mesrop, Archbishop of Persia and India, a most controversial figure whom the Persians had expelled as a Soviet agent.[1] The first ballot was inconclusive but in the second Khoren Muradbekian, the most distinguished Armenian Churchman of the period, was elected by sixty votes to nineteen. The election was the occasion of a great religious manifestation by the Armenian people. Thousands of Armenians flocked to Echmiadzin to witness the enthronement of the Catholicos and thus to demonstrate their attachment to their ancient national Church.

Khoren I exercised the office of Catholicos for just over five years under the most difficult circumstances. He died suddenly on April 6, 1938. The most charitable explanation is that he died because proper medical attention was denied to him but there is good ground to believe that he was in fact assassinated by the Transcaucasian NKVD of which Beriya was then in command. According to evidence reaching the Armenian Archbishop of Tabriz at the time, Khoren was strangled in his Palace by a group of five NKVD men because he refused to surrender church treasures. The burial of Khoren was carried out in great haste without any solemnities or even the usual church rites.[2] What is in doubt is not so much the manner in which Khoren lost his life but rather the motives which prompted the NKVD to carry out their crime. The Catholicos was too important a man to be assassinated over such a comparatively trifling matter as the question of the remnants of Armenian church property. His violent death — if it was violent — must be seen within the context of Soviet internal developments of the period of the so-called Yezhovshchina. In 1937–8, under Stalin's general instructions, under Yezhov's immediate command and with Beriya's most active assistance in Transcaucasia, the NKVD exterminated everybody, both in Moscow and in the republics, who could have provided an alternative government or who might have supported an invading foreign army. So the NKVD did away with ambitious generals, 'Old Bolsheviks' enjoying popular prestige, 'bourgeois nationalists', and also 'dangerous' ecclesiastical leaders. The Catholicos may well have

---

[1] *The Times*, October 13, 1930.
[2] *Armenian Review*, vol. x, December 1957, no. 4, p. 11.

been one of these. As a national and spiritual leader of the Armenian people he could too easily have played an important part in a time of political crisis.

In the atmosphere of terror which existed in the late thirties in the USSR, including Soviet Armenia, there could be no question of summoning a National Ecclesiastical Assembly to elect a new Catholicos. Soon the outbreak of the war supplied an excellent and respectable reason for the postponement of the election. The Soviet Government made ample use of this delay to transform the Armenian Church into a more reliable instrument of the régime than it had ever been before. It was to become more subservient to the communist rulers than the Russian Orthodox Church.

In this new period the destiny of the Armenian Church became closely connected with the name of Kevork Cheorekchian, who from 1938 was locum tenens of the Echmiadzin see. Cheorekchian was seventy years old when he became the acting head of the Church. He had had a good theological training, having studied divinity and philosophy at Leipzig University. In 1917, he became bishop, and from then on he occupied various high church offices, including that of Exarch of the Armenian Church in Georgia. Armenian nationalists abroad have judged Cheorekchian rather harshly; they have often described him as a puppet of the communist régime, but this seems to be an unfair over-simplification. Cheorekchian well knew what harm the communists had inflicted on the Armenian Church — the closing of churches, the arrests of priests — and also the truth about the death of Catholicos Khoren. Being rather old, and having gone through so many bitter experiences, he may have thought that only an attitude of total and unqualified subservience could preserve the Church from future persecution.

Communists and Armenian Church History

The reconciliation between Church and State in Armenia at which Cheroekchian aimed was assisted by various external circumstances. In the first place there was a certain reorientation of the Soviet communists towards Armenian history. The Armenians benefited from the reassessment of values which took place in Russia itself in the late thirties. We have already mentioned that various distinguished figures of Russian history, including certain Orthodox saints who were great patriots, were again recognised as important national figures worthy of the respect of the present generation. The Soviet Government could not refuse the Armenians what it had granted to the Russians.

F2

In Armenia, this rewriting of history had a more immediate impact on the religious question than in Russia, for the history of the Armenian nation is very largely the history of the Armenian Church. The rehabilitation of the Armenian past meant at the same time rehabilitation and recognition of the great historical role of the Armenian Church. The heroic resistance of the Armenian people against its pagan and Moslem enemies could not be recalled without tribute being paid both to the inspiration derived from the Christian faith and the leadership exercised by the Armenian Patriarchs.

By revising its concept of Armenian history, the régime unwittingly allowed religion to return through a back door at a time when it seemed to have reached the lowest level of its external influence. This return of religion in the guise of history might best be illustrated by the re-publication in Armenia of the works of Raffi (1835–88), the greatest Armenian novelist of the nineteenth century. Until 1940, Raffi's works were not reprinted in the Soviet Union and could not even be obtained in public libraries. Raffi was persistently denounced as a 'bourgeois nationalist'. The situation changed after the outbreak of the Second World War. The Soviet régime was interested in propagating a militant patriotic spirit in Armenia, especially by recalling the courage and steadfastness which Armenians had shown in the past in the struggle against foreign invaders. In this new atmosphere it was thought that the works of a patriotic writer such as Raffi might serve a useful purpose. They were reprinted by a Soviet state publishing house. The first new edition was sold out within a few hours.

Among Raffi's historical novels there is one which deserves our special attention — *Samuel*. It gives an insight into Armenia's historical development in the second half of the fourth century when certain Armenian aristocrats abandoned the Christian religion and embraced the Persian faith of Mazdeism. Raffi dwells at length on the fight waged by the Armenian people and the Armenian Church against this betrayal of Christianity. There are many passages in the novel which almost compel the contemporary reader to draw a parallel between the 'Godless heresy of Mazdeism' threatening to engulf Armenia in the fourth century and the 'Godless heresy of Communism' which at the present time is the official ideology of the country. If in reading Raffi's book one translates 'Persians' as 'communists' and if one replaces the names of the treacherous Armenian aristocrats by those of the communist leaders, the novel acquires a fascinating topicality. Such a sentence as 'They have destroyed the state, now they want to destroy religion and the people' is as true of Armenia to-day as it was 1,500 years ago.[1] Raffi's novel also contains in parenthesis a whole treatise about the Armenian Church in the early Middle Ages, especially about the cultural and social role of the monasteries. 'The monastery', Raffi says at one point, 'gave bread and fed the poor; it looked after orphans and widows and it educated the children of the nation.'[2] This positive appraisal is in striking contrast with what communist historians say about Christian monasteries.

These examples show that Raffi's works contained most dangerous religious contraband. No wonder there was much regret in leading Soviet circles at the rehabilitation of Raffi, and after the war attacks against Raffi, stressing his reactionary character, reappeared in the Soviet press.[3] However, the régime could not disregard Armenian national feeling to such an extent as to re-issue the original ban on Raffi's works. It rather tried to undermine the historical prestige of the Armenian Church by other means. For instance, Soviet authors commended the Paulician heresy[4] which in the ninth century acquired considerable importance in Armenia and which, if successful, might have destroyed the Christian Church in that country. They praised the heresy as a great social movement which aimed at social equality and opposed the exploitation of the people by ecclesiastical and feudal lords.[5] Also nineteenth century Echmiadzin was attacked by the protagonists of the Soviet régime especially in connection with the 150th anniversary of the birth of Khachatur Abovian (1805–48), an Armenian anti-clerical writer and educationalist. A pamphlet published by the Soviet Mass Education Society in 1955 described him as a 'merciless unmasker of Echmiadzin'.[6] Abovian came from a profoundly religious family and spent his whole life in a religious environment. The fact that he clashed with certain backward clergymen in no way implies that he was anti-Church.[7]

Kevork Cheorekchian, or the Period of Relative Tolerance

Whatever second thoughts the Soviet authorities may have had about their new view of Armenian history, there can be no doubt that at least

---

[1] Raffi, *Samuel*, Moscow 1946, p. 30. [2] Raffi, op. cit., p. 160.
[3] *Pravda*, October 5, 1951.
[4] The Paulicians considered St. Paul the only true apostle, rejected the Old Testament, claimed that the world was created by a spirit at enmity with the God of the New Testament and reproached the universal Church with worshipping the former. An Armenian Catholicos denounced the Paulician heresy as early as 553.
[5] Voprosy Istorii, no. 1, 1955, p. 161, quoting a book on the *Paulician Movement in Armenia* by Melik-Bakshian, published by Erivan University in 1953.
[6] Ruben Zaryan, *Khachatur Abovian*, Moscow 1955, p. 14.
[7] The Soviet Interpretation of Khachatur Abovian by V. Shahuni, *Caucasian Review*, no. 2, Munich 1956, p. 107.

externally and superficially it produced an ideological rapprochement between the Armenian Church and the Soviet State at the beginning of the Second World War. The outbreak of the war between Russia and Germany also resulted in a more practical co-operation between Echmiadzin and the Kremlin. Faced by a foreign invasion, the Soviet Government made an effort to enlist the material and moral assistance of the Churches for the defence of the motherland, and among others, it counted on the help of the Armenian Church. The head of the Armenian Church, Cheorekchian, supported the war effort as whole-heartedly as the Russian Orthodox bishops and called upon the Armenian people to sacrifice part of their savings to build a tank column called after the Armenian national hero, David of Sasoon. Although a number of Armenian priests in the Crimea and the North Caucasus region went over to the Germans, the loyalty of the Church as a whole was not in doubt, and the authorities had every confidence in the locum tenens.

At last the war came to an end and it was possible to normalise church administration by arranging for the election of a new Catholicos. It was a foregone conclusion that there was to be only one candidate — Kevork Cheorekchian. The last doubt about this was removed on April 19, 1945, when Stalin received the locum tenens in the Kremlin.[1] The reception took place at a crucial moment in the history of the war — on the very eve of the capture of Berlin. That the Soviet generalissimo should have found time to discuss ecclesiastical problems with a seventy-seven-year old Armenian archbishop is in itself remarkable. Throughout the period when he was supreme leader of the Soviet State, Stalin had had very few talks with church personalities — perhaps four or five altogether. The fact that he deigned to meet Cheorekchian had, therefore, its significance. No official record of the meeting is available but one may assume that Stalin outlined to the Catholicos-to-be what he expected him to do in his new office and what assistance he was to give to Soviet policy in the immediate post-war period. Stalin may also have used the opportunity to announce a number of concessions by which the position of the Armenian Church was to be consolidated.

Two months after his meeting with Stalin, Cheorekchian was duly and unanimously elected Catholicos with the name of Kevork VI. The election was carried out in accordance with Armenian canon law by the National Ecclesiastical Assembly, to which 111 delegates came from various parts of the Soviet Union and from all Armenian colonies abroad except South America. Countries represented at the Assembly included USA, Britain, France, Bulgaria, Greece, Rumania, Egypt,

[1] *Soviet War News*, April 23, 1945.

Persia, Iraq, Syria, Palestine, India and Turkey. From Turkey the Armenian Patriarch of Constantinople arrived in person. The Soviet authorities gave every facility to foreigners to reach the Assembly in time. Many of the foreign delegates, including those from the United States, had their long journeys paid for out of Soviet state funds, and in Armenia they were guests of the Armenian Soviet Government.[1]

However, the majority of the delegates were Soviet citizens from various walks of life — eighteen employees of various Soviet organisations, several collective farmers, six doctors, four engineers, four housewives and several scientists and artists.[2] Many of these delegates, no doubt, represented primarily or even exclusively the interests of the Soviet State and the Communist Party. But their presence at the Armenian Ecclesiastical Assembly did not mean that the election of the new Patriarch was invalid from a canonical point of view. In the Armenian Church, the laity has a decisive say in ecclesiastical affairs. From the very first Armenian Church Assembly in the year 365, power (*'potestas ecclesiastica'*) in the Armenian Church has belonged to the Armenian nation and not to the clergy.[3] This provision of Armenian canon law worked well enough throughout the many centuries when the Church and the nation formed a political, moral and spiritual entity in the midst of alien, hostile surroundings. As long as there was an independent Armenian state, the rulers of Armenia were in most cases inseparably linked with the faith of the Armenian Church. When Armenia lost her independence the Supreme Patriarch became the ruler of the nation. But to-day when the principal official spokesmen of the Armenian nation are the leaders of an atheist government the situation is obviously different. These leaders may perhaps have no real mandate to represent the nation but officially they are the nation and, therefore, the bearers of the *potestas ecclesiastica* — of course, only to the extent to which they care to exercise it. Moreover, Armenian canon law assumed its present shape at a time when every Armenian was a Christian believer. The Armenian nation was the sum total of the faithful. This is no longer true to-day. Officially, the Armenian nation has become a purely secular ethnographic notion. The so-called 'nation' which elects the Patriarch through delegates is, in part at least, an agnostic, if not atheist nation. The Catholicos thus elected is only to some extent the head of the Church. His true position is so paradoxical and contradictory that it defies description in any conventional or legal

---

[1] Vertanes, *Armenia reborn*, New York 1947, pp. 73–4.
[2] *Soviet News*, June 30, 1945.
[3] Dr. Abel Abrahamian, *The Church and Faith of Armenia*, London 1920, p. 32.

terms. In Soviet Russia he is occasionally referred to as the 'Catholicos of both Believers and Unbelievers', which probably comes nearest to the truth.

But let us revert again to the chronological sequence of events. We are still in 1945 when the Armenian Church Assembly elected Kevork VI Catholicos and Supreme Armenian Patriarch. The blessings and greetings of the Moscow Government were given to this Assembly by Polyansky, the head of the Council for the Affairs of Religious Cults. He paid the following tribute to the Armenian Church: 'From the very beginnings of the Armenian nation, this people which has seen so many failures, has suffered so much and has lost so much, the Armenian Church has always stood by the people, has helped to revive its national autonomy, has reared its children in national consciousness and has contributed to the nation's cultural advancement.' The Assembly itself responded to the 'kindness' of the Soviet Government by addressing a complimentary message to Stalin, who was credited with the 'liberation of the Armenian people' and the rebirth of the Armenian State.[1]

Subsequent events threw light on the terms of the bargain between Stalin and Kevork Cheorekchian. First of all the Armenian Church was allowed to replenish its hierarchy. The Patriarch's first action after his election and enthronement was to consecrate ten new bishops, including six for the diaspora. Then in September 1945 a theological seminary was opened in Echmiadzin. Finally, the Armenian Church was authorised to publish a religious journal under the title *Echmiadzin*. This took the place of the journal *Ararat* which had been suppressed before the war.

In return, the new Patriarch was to render two important services to the Soviet State; the first was to assist in the repatriation to Soviet Armenia of Armenians living abroad, and the second was to support the Soviet claim to the Turkish territory of Kars and Ardahan in North-Eastern Anatolia. Theoretically, neither of these services was a 'concession' on the part of the Armenian Church. On the contrary, one might argue that the return of the refugees to their Armenian homeland and the annexation of Kars and Ardahan, which historically speaking is part of 'Turkish Armenia', were both in the Armenian national interest and in the interest of the Armenian Church. This was indeed believed by many Armenian non-communists abroad. For a people living scattered in many parts of the world, a people decimated by the massacres which a former Turkish Government had inflicted on them, it was difficult to reject out of hand the dazzling promises of the Soviet

[1] *Soviet News*, June 26, 1945.

régime. Even the most anti-Soviet Armenian organisation, the Armenian Revolutionary Federation or Dashnaktsutyun, at first succumbed to the temptation, and for a while supported the repatriation campaign. The very words 'Return to the Homeland' and the claims to ancient Armenian lands stirred up such patriotic passion that the motives of the Soviet Government were entirely overlooked. Many Armenians did not realise that the launching of the repatriation action and the voicing of territorial demands against Turkey were not meant to promote the Armenian national cause and even less the cause of the Armenian Christian Church. They were intended to strengthen the might of the Soviet State and to enhance the striking power of the atheist-materialist doctrine.

It would have been utterly unfair to have expected the Armenian Catholicos to give a lead to the Armenian people by exposing the Soviet manœuvres. Living in Soviet territory and dependent on the good will of the Soviet authorities, he could not have refused to lend assistance to the Soviet Government on the two burning Armenian national questions. The communist leaders would have denounced him at once as a traitor to the Armenian nation and, worse than that, as a Turkish agent. So willy-nilly, he had to go the way of total collaboration. In his proclamations and pastoral letters to Armenians abroad he appealed to them to return to Soviet Armenia. In the articles published in *Echmiadzin* he and his collaborators called upon the 'patriotic Armenian clergy' to support pro-Soviet organisations and to fight 'all traitors' and 'enemies of Armenia and the Armenian Church'.[1] Those denounced as traitors and enemies were not the enemies of Christianity but the enemies of the Soviet régime, in the first place the nationalistic Dashnaktsutyun movement.

The most important single move of the Catholicos was a memorandum on the Armenian question which he addressed to the Big Three on November 27, 1945. In this document the Catholicos described himself as 'Patriarch of All Armenias' and not, as is usual, as 'Patriarch of All Armenians'. He claimed to speak as the traditional 'protector' of the Armenian people. He traced the main stages of the persecution of the Armenians by the Turks and stated emphatically that there was no difference between the old Turkey of the Sultans and the new Kemalist Turkey. The Armenian problem could only be solved by annexing Turkish Armenia to Soviet Armenia. The memorandum ended with the following stirring appeal to the Big Three: '... we ... implore that the Turkish Armenian provinces be united to Soviet Armenia, so that

[1] *Echmiadzin*, October-November-December, 1948.

the Armenian nation may be complete and, gathered in the national home in peace and security, continue their interrupted cultural and educational work. For the success of this just and lofty work we appeal and pray for the help of Almighty God. May the Most High bless you and guide your mind and will to the fulfilment of the good; and, meanwhile, move the conscience of the leaders of present-day Turkey into atoning for their and their predecessors' heavy crimes so as to efface that greatest injustice perpetrated in this most enlightened and civilised century upon this peace-loving, industrious and creative people.' If judged by its phraseology alone, the memorandum of the Catholicos seemed to be permeated with national and religious sentiments. Certainly, the words of the appeal were chosen by the Catholicos or one of his advisers. But the idea behind the appeal, namely, to supply ammunition in the Soviet war of nerves against Turkey, came from the Soviet Government. At any rate, the Catholicos, who is a private Soviet citizen, was bound to consult the Kremlin before embarking on a venture which, after all, affected Soviet foreign policy.

Echmiadzin's Relations with the Moscow Patriarchate

In his relations with other Christian Churches Kevork showed friendliness towards Russian Orthodoxy and hostility towards the Vatican. During his term of office relations between Echmiadzin and the Moscow Patriarchate became much closer. Although much of the co-operation took place under the auspices of the government-sponsored peace campaign it was not altogether devoid of an ecumenical meaning.

The Catholicos met the Patriarch of Moscow and all-Russia on at least three occasions. The first time was in Moscow in July 1948, when the Russian Church celebrated the fifth centenary of its autocephalous status; the second time was in August 1950, in Tiflis and Echmiadzin; and the third time in May 1952 on the occasion of the ecclesiastical peace conference which was held in the Holy Trinity Monastery in Zagorsk. The most important of these three meetings was the second: it has already entered Russian ecclesiastical history as 'The meeting of the three Patriarchs' for, apart from the Catholicos and the Russian Patriarch Alexis, it was attended by the Georgian Patriarch Kallistrat. Officially, the three Patriarchs met to sign a peace manifesto to the Christians of the world, but as they spent a whole week together it is likely that they dealt with other subjects as well and that the meeting served the cause of a genuine ecumenism. For instance, it seems that the Catholicos and the Russian Patriarch discussed the possibility of

Armenian priests undertaking post-graduate studies at the Zagorsk Theological Academy, and in fact a first batch of eight graduates of the Echmiadzin Academy went to Zagorsk in 1952 to study Orthodox theology.[1]

The Catholic Competitor

Unfortunately, Catholicos Kevork VI was not equally anxious to improve relations with the Roman Catholic Church. His first public statement after his election attacked the Vatican. Having referred to the contributions of the Armenian, Orthodox and Anglican Churches to the war effort, he added: 'It is particularly painful to think that there is a Christian Church which did not join our blessed cause. More — that Church supported the nazi enemies of the Lord.'[2] This attack on the Vatican was as much in line with Soviet wishes as the statements of the Catholicos about the repatriation campaign. But in all likelihood he spoke against the Catholic Church not in order to please the Soviet authorities but primarily because he regarded it as a competitor.

This competitor is not so much the universal Roman Catholic Church as the Armenian Catholic Church which is in communion with the Holy See in Rome. Although the number of its followers may be small it represents an important intellectual and moral force. Its very existence is a perpetual challenge to the Catholicos of Echmiadzin and a denial of his title of Patriarch of *All* Armenians. This challenge is underlined by the fact that the head of the Armenian Catholic Church, who is under the supreme authority of the Pope, carries the title of Patriarch and Catholicos.

The present Armenian Catholic Church goes back to the year 1740, but parts of the Armenian Church were in communion with Rome at the time of the Crusades. The Armenian Catholic Church has played a vital part in the development of Armenian national culture, in particular the Armenian Catholic Order of the Mekhitarists whose Monastery on the island of San Lazzaro, near Venice, has become the most important Armenian intellectual and educational centre in the Western world. The Armenian Catholic Church shared the grim fate of the Armenian people both in Turkey and in Russia. In Turkey her priests, nuns and laymen were massacred with the rest of the nation. In Russia under Soviet rule she was much worse treated than the Armenian Apostolic Church. Russia's Armenian Catholic groups were mostly situated in what is now the Georgian Soviet Republic. Their total number did not exceed 30,000 of whom 10,000 lived in the region of Akhaltsikhe and

[1] *Zh.M.P.*, 1954, no. 6, p. 69.   [2] *Soviet News*, June 30, 1945.

Akhalkelek.[1] It is in these areas that Catholic activities are recorded even in Soviet times, including the presence of a missionary from Rome as late as 1927.[2] The Armenian Catholic community of the Soviet Union was under an Apostolic administrator of Armenian nationality, who, like the rest of Russia's Catholic hierarchy, was arrested and deported.

Although liquidated in Turkey and the Soviet Union, the Armenian Catholic Church still remains a force in the world-wide Armenian diaspora, where it commands the support of tens of thousands of faithful. The small Armenian Catholic Church has produced one of the most remarkable figures of universal Catholicism in Lazarus Agaganian, who in 1937 became the 'Patriarch of the Catholic Armenians', under the title of Petros XV. Agaganian was born in Georgia and started his priestly career as curate of the Armenian Catholic Church in Tiflis. Although he has lived abroad for many years, mostly in Rome, he has never ceased to identify himself with the Armenian people. In 1946, his prestige was further enhanced by the fact that he was created a cardinal — the second Armenian to be thus honoured. When Kevork VI called upon the Armenians to 'return home' he found that only one prominent Armenian figure abroad stood in the way of the repatriation campaign — the Catholic Patriarch. With pastoral letters and encyclicals Agaganian warned the faithful against the pitfalls of the repatriation campaign and the unscrupulous propaganda by which the Soviet authorities tried to encourage it. In a pastoral letter of July 6, 1946, his warning was gentle and reticent; it became more forceful in another pastoral letter issued in 1947 on the Feast of the Immaculate Conception. There the Patriarch spoke of the 'bitter reality and material misery' in Soviet Armenia and denounced especially the negation of elementary human rights, such as freedom of conscience and freedom of speech.[3]

The Armenian Church at the Death of Kevork VI

Agaganian's general statement about the 'bitter reality' in Soviet Armenia was only too easy to substantiate. Despite the Kremlin's new religious policy the Armenian Church was unable to recover to any noteworthy extent the ground she had lost in the period between the wars. In this respect the Armenian Church was in a much worse position than the Russian Orthodox Church. The number of Orthodox parishes and churches dropped to between a quarter and a third of what it used to be in Czarist times. The decline of the Armenian

---

[1] Ormanian, op. cit., p. 208.   [2] *Bezbozhnik*, January 26, 1929.
[3] *Lettre Pastorale de Son Eminence le Cardinal Grégoire Pierre XV Agaganian*, Beyrouth 1947, p. 6.

Church was incomparably more tragic. Of a total of 1,446 Armenian churches existing in Russia in 1914 only 89 remained in 1954. In the Armenian Soviet Republic alone the number of parishes was reduced during the same period by 400 — from 459 to 59, and the number of Armenian churches from 491 to 38. In the two neighbouring republics — Georgia and Azerbaidzhan — Armenian church life declined even more drastically. Formerly there was an Armenian Archbishop in Tiflis and two bishops, one in Gori, Stalin's birthplace, and the other in Akhaltsikhe near the present Turkish border. Between them these three hierarchs cared for 235 parishes with 287 churches. In 1954 there was only one Archbishop in Georgia in charge of 20 parishes and 14 churches. In Tiflis, the Georgian capital, as many as 28 Armenian churches used to exist, but now only two survived.[1] In Azerbaidzhan before the Revolution there were two Armenian archbishops and three bishops. These five Azerbaidzhanian bishoprics comprised 430 parishes with 473 churches. Under the Soviet rule they were amalgamated into a single diocese with 32 parishes and 30 churches. However, this new diocese, which has its centre in Baku, includes not only the parishes of Azerbaidzhan but also the Armenian diaspora in the whole of Siberia and Central Asia. Before the First World War these scattered Armenian parishes had the Archbishop of Astrakhan as their ecclesiastical head. Astrakhan was then a very important Armenian centre; it had six Armenian churches, including a Cathedral, and there was also a seminary for Armenian priests. The Armenian Archdiocese of Astrakhan is not the only one north of the Caucasus range which has been abolished. The archdiocese of Bessarabia, which cared for the Armenian faithful in Western Russia — it had nineteen parishes with thirteen churches — was amalgamated with the bishopric of Novo-Nakhichevan or Nakhichevan on Don — the Armenian suburb of Rostov. In 1954 this diocese called the 'Diocese of Novo-Nakhichevan and the North Caucasus' comprised only eight parishes and seven churches though before 1917 there were four churches in the town of Novo-Nakhichevan alone.[2]

The Election of Vazgen Balgian

When Kevork VI died in May 1954 at the age of eighty-seven he left a Church which, despite years of collaboration with the régime, was still in a very sore state and yet there was some indication that the

---

[1] Archbishop Derenik Poledian, *Yerkir Haireni* (The Fatherland) quoted in *Armenian Review*, Winter 1956, vol. ix, p. 74.

[2] Unless otherwise stated the figures about the strength of the Armenian Church are taken from Malachia Ormanian, op. cit., pp. 205-12.

situation might soon improve. New men had taken over the leadership of the Armenian Communist Party who were more inclined to respect national Armenian traditions. It was reasonable to expect that the Armenian Church could benefit, within limits, from this new situation especially if it was prepared to render greater service to Soviet foreign policy than the old Catholicos could do. The new era, which was soon to be characterised by daring diplomatic initiatives, needed a young Armenian Patriarch who was able to make an impact on the Armenian communities especially in the Middle East which became to an ever-increasing extent, an objective of Soviet ambitions.

The Armenian Church Assembly electing this new Patriarch met in Echmiadzin in September 1955. The number of delegates to this new Assembly was larger than in 1945 — 137 Armenian laymen and clergy participated in the vote compared with 111 in the elections ten years before. Nevertheless, the Assembly was less representative than its predecessor. Those absent included the Armenian Patriarch of Constantinople, the locum tenens of the Catholicosate of Antilias and the locum tenens of the Armenian Patriarchate of Jerusalem. The absence of the latter was particularly significant, for originally there had been a widespread desire among Armenian church-people to elect him Catholicos, in accordance with what were believed to be the wishes of the late Kevork VI. But the locum tenens refused to be a candidate, for an Armenian ecclesiastical dignitary living outside the area under Soviet control is not likely to put himself at the mercy of the Soviet Government by assuming the thankless post of Catholicos. Moreover, the election of a prelate coming from outside the Iron Curtain would have been an affront to the Soviet régime and would have jeopardised the position of the Church in Soviet Armenia.

So the delegates assembled in Echmiadzin had their hands tied; they had to elect a man who enjoyed the confidence of the Soviet Government and who was known to that Government for his loyalty. One hundred and twenty-five out of the hundred and thirty-seven delegates voted for Vazgen Balgian, the head of the small Rumanian-Bulgarian diocese of the Armenian Church. The remainder of the votes were cast for the Armenian Patriarch of Constantinople and the Armenian Archbishop of North America.

The Ecclesiastical Assembly which elected Vazgen was packed with Soviet citizens to an even greater extent than the Assembly of 1945. Ninety-seven delegates represented the Armenians of the Soviet Union and only forty came from abroad. One may take it for granted that none of the ninety-seven delegates from the Soviet Union was a free agent —

but how many of them were true Christians is impossible to ascertain. Some no doubt attended the Assembly with the firm intention of supporting the Soviet communist cause — others were probably torn by a great internal conflict: they wanted to do their duty as Christians and at the same time they found it necessary to submit to the atheist Caesar. This was probably the case of the most distinguished Armenian layman participating in the Assembly — Avetik Isaakian (1875–1957) then the greatest living Armenian writer. The photographs taken during the festivities at Echmiadzin usually showed him sitting next to the Patriarch himself. Isaakian, who was Chairman of the Union of Soviet Writers of Armenia and a member of the Armenian Soviet Parliament, symbolised the dilemma facing the non-communist Armenian living under Soviet rule. On the one hand he was determined to adhere to the Christian tradition of his people, and, on the other, he was forced, or saw fit, to write poems in praise of the communist rulers to whom this tradition is anathema. Isaakian's tragedy did not end even with his death. Although he played such a great part in the affairs of the Armenian Church it was not associated with his funeral, which was purely secular.

Most of the details which the Soviet press published about the biography of the new Catholicos were as reassuring from the communist point of view as they were disquietening for the non-communist Armenian flock throughout the world. The Catholicos was only forty-seven years old at the time of his election and until then he had occupied a very junior position in the Armenian hierarchy. At first he had embarked on a secular career. Having graduated in 1936 from the Faculty of Philosophy and Literature of Bucharest University, he became a teacher at the Armenian school in the Rumanian capital. In 1943, he switched over to theology. After a year's study at the Theological Faculty he was ordained priest. In 1951 he was consecrated bishop and, in 1954, only a year before being elected Catholicos, he was made a member of the Supreme Spiritual Council of Echmiadzin, the central government of the Armenian Church.[1]

There were many Armenian archbishops and bishops who by their past services to the Church and their standard of theological learning would have deserved the honour of becoming Catholicos much more than Balgian. Why then was he chosen? The only conceivable answer was that his was a political rather than an ecclesiastical appointment. It was known to the electors that Balgian was *persona grata* with the Soviet régime and refusal to elect him would have meant to risk

[1] *Izvestiya*, October 4, 1954.

provoking a new conflict between Church and State in Soviet Armenia. It was understandable that few were prepared to shoulder such a responsibility. Vazgen Balgian earned Soviet and communist support in the first place because for years he had collaborated most wholeheartedly with the Rumanian communist Government. He was one of the active functionaries of the peace movement in Rumania, an activity for which he was awarded in 1954 the order of the 'Star of the Republic'.

At the time of his election to the Catholicosate Vazgen Balgian was known as the author of two books the contents of which stood in a certain contradiction to one another and threw light on the two sides of Balgian's personality — the Armenian patriot and the man serving the Soviet cause. The first book of Balgian was called *Father Khrimian as Pedagogue.*[1] It was not a bad omen that the new Catholicos should have chosen Father (in Armenian *Airik*) Khrimian as hero of his first book. Khrimian was one of Balgian's predecessors. He was Catholicos at the beginning of the century, an ardent churchman and an ardent Armenian nationalist. One of his principal claims to fame was his steadfast resistance to the Czarist Government in 1903 when it attempted to deprive the Armenian Church of its property and especially of its schools. Khrimian, sure of the support of the entire Armenian nation, refused to hand over the church property and in the end the Government had to give in and withdraw the confiscation order. Those who thought that Khrimian, the uncompromising defender of the Church against the secular power, might be Balgian's example must have been disappointed by his travel book *Beneath One's Native Sky* which contained the most enthusiastic tribute to the Soviet Union. For instance, it included the following appeal to Armenians living abroad: 'Armenians abroad should realise once and for all that it is Soviet rule and the Russian people alone that are the ultimate guarantors of our national life . . . and of the realisation of a golden future for the Armenian nation.'

After his election Vazgen I announced that he would become a Soviet citizen. The announcement was made in the following terms at the final meeting of the Armenian National Ecclesiastical Assembly of 1955: 'I am extremely pleased to announce that, following my election as Supreme Patriarch and Catholicos of All Armenians, I have submitted to the Government of the Soviet Union a request that they grant me Soviet citizenship, which has been my dream now for years. To-day the Armenian nation is stronger and more powerful than it has ever been in its age-long history. Shoulder to shoulder with

[1] *Zh.M.P.*, 1955, no. 12, p. 66.

the great Russian people and other Soviet peoples the Armenian people is creating its own happy and joyous life.'[1] The official report added that the last words of the Catholicos were greeted by 'loud cheers and applause'. One is tempted to ask who cheered and applauded a statement which so obviously served the propaganda purposes of the Soviet State.

Vazgen and the Middle East

When Vazgen became Catholicos he must have found a good many unsettled problems in the Armenian Church of the Soviet Union to which his predecessor had been unable to attend because of his advanced age. But, instead of tackling them, he went on a long trip abroad almost immediately. This journey of the Catholicos lasted nearly three months. Its general purpose was to increase the authority of Echmiadzin among the Armenians of the diaspora, first amongst those of the Middle East and secondly amongst those of Western Europe.

The Soviet authorities were vitally interested in the Middle-Eastern part of Vazgen's mission, for Russia's great diplomatic and political offensive in the Arab world had just begun. In planning and implementing this offensive the Kremlin was bound to devote particular attention to the 300,000 Armenians living in the Middle East. It was somewhat unlucky from Moscow's point of view that, out of this total, two-thirds were not under the jurisdiction of Echmiadzin but under that of the Catholicos of Cilicia. Under these circumstances it became a matter of no small interest to Moscow that the Catholicosate of Cilicia should be put into reliable hands. To achieve this was the main reason for which Vazgen undertook his Middle Eastern journey so soon after his election.

The Cilician Catholicosate had been vacant since 1952 because the Armenian community in the Levantine states, deeply divided into rival factions, could not agree about the person of the new Catholicos. The majority wanted a nationalist and anti-communist Catholicos and the minority, supporting a candidate acceptable to the Soviets, tried to delay the elections as long as possible. But at last the election date was fixed for February 14, 1956, and the bishop of Aleppo, Zareh Payaslian, who enjoyed the support of the nationalist Dashnak party, seemed to have the greatest hope of being elected. The threatened election of a 'Dashnak' as head of the 'Great House of Cilicia' precipitated Vazgen's trip to the Middle East. Vazgen arrived in Beirut two days before the election and contrived to delay it for a few days. Negotiations took place between Vazgen and the various groups inside the Catholicosate

[1] Erivan Radio, October 11, 1955.

during which the Echmiadzin Catholicos vetoed the election of Zareh Payaslian and Khoren Paroyan, the two Armenian churchmen who were generally known to be anti-communist. All Vazgen achieved was the boycott of the election by the pro-Soviet faction, but their members amounted to less than one-third of the laymen and clerics entitled to vote. The whole electoral college had fifty-one members. Of these, thirty-six turned up at the meeting and, all except four, gave their vote to Zareh.[1] Seen in political terms, the election was a victory for the West and a setback for the Kremlin. From a strictly ecclesiastical point of view the election and the quarrels which preceded and followed it were a blow to the unity of the Armenian Church.

Vazgen did not wait for the failure of his mission, but left Beirut for Cairo on the very day of the election. He did not recognise Zareh's accession to the Cilician Catholicosate, and during his stay in Egypt he convened an assembly of Armenian bishops and archbishops which declared the Patriarchal election in Beirut 'irregular and unacceptable'. However, those who came to this grave decision did not take it very seriously themselves, for they declared at the same time that they were prepared to accept the irregular election provided that the new Catholicos was willing to abandon the elevated status which Antilias had held for centuries and accept a subordinate position under Echmiadzin. Catholicos Zareh refused to accede to this demand. Relations between Echmiadzin and Antilias have remained critical ever since and 'Holy Echmiadzin' and the 'Great House of Cilicia' have continued to accuse one another of being subservient to political influences.

The remaining part of Vazgen's journey abroad was less sensational. It was presumably mainly concerned with obtaining financial support from wealthy Armenians in the free world. In London, Vazgen had the satisfaction of being received in Lambeth Palace as the guest of the Archbishop of Canterbury. The reports which had reached the Kremlin meanwhile about Vazgen's visits to Middle-Eastern and European capitals were bound to have been favourable. Although a very new Soviet citizen, he had already proved his loyalty to the communist régime and had well deserved Moscow's trust. In the Middle East, in particular, he had done good work from the Soviet point of view, if only by appearing as a living example of religious freedom in the USSR. The failure in Beirut could not be held against him. He could not have been expected to succeed within a few days where the prolonged efforts and intrigues of the Soviet diplomats on the spot had proved fruitless. As Vazgen had managed to obtain an audience with

[1] Arab News Agency, February 20, 1956.

President Nasser of Egypt, then the Arab statesman most courted by the Soviet Union, he was sure to be received on his return to Moscow by his own Prime Minister, then still Marshal Bulganin.

Soviet Concessions to Vazgen

The meeting took place on May 12, 1956, and it led to a more far-reaching *modus vivendi* between the Armenian Church and the Soviet State than that previously in force. Vazgen submitted to Bulganin a petition consisting of seven points. Its text was not published but, from Vazgen's own hints as well as from later developments, it is not difficult to gather what the document contained. Vazgen's points concerned, in the first place, the opening of more churches, the return of Armenian church property to its rightful owners, and the extension of the training of Armenian priests at the Echmiadzin seminary. No doubt he also sought permission to accept financial help from abroad. One further point of the petition dealt with suggestions about the development of Echmiadzin's contacts with foreign Armenians. These proposals met with enthusiastic response on the part of Bulganin who said, 'Very good! This is in full accord with the Soviet Government's present policy.'[1]

It was soon apparent that the Soviet Government had acceded to Vazgen's requests, for the situation of the Armenian Church clearly took a turn for the better. Money from the Armenian faithful abroad was allowed to pour into the Catholicos's treasury. It was used for the restoration of churches, the extension of the seminary and the establishment of a new printing press, for which the Armenian community in the United States provided the funds. The Echmiadzin seminary was able to increase its teaching staff and the number of students. Within two years the number of students went up from twenty to fifty and various remarks of the Catholicos indicated that the Government was prepared to admit a further increase in the seminary's intake provided the total number of students did not pass the hundred mark.[2] Under the previous Catholicos the seminary had suffered greatly from the shortage of teaching staff but Vazgen obtained permission to recruit teachers abroad without their having to change their citizenship. A curious feature of the new enlarged seminary was that two of its professors were at the same time lecturers at the State University of Erivan. The Echmiadzin seminary trains priests not only for the Armenian Church in the Soviet Union but also for the diaspora, and

[1] Erivan Radio, 'Armenian for abroad', May 21, 1956.
[2] Erivan Radio, 'Armenian for abroad', January 6, 1957.

the Soviet Government wished to put it into a position where it could successfully compete with Armenian seminaries in the free world.

It is clear that the Catholicos can be of use as a moral authority for the scattered Armenian people only as long as his Church enjoys a certain prosperity in Russia and as long as Echmiadzin, the great centre of attraction for foreign Armenian pilgrims, is surrounded with a certain splendour. This may explain why the communist régime has handed back to Vazgen some of the confiscated church land of Echmiadzin and several buildings previously belonging to the Catholicos. The greatest treasure of old Echmiadzin, the library with its priceless ancient Armenian manuscripts, confiscated in 1931, was not returned to the Church. On the other hand permission was granted to surround the new Armenian miniature Vatican with a wall 1,000 metres long and five metres high.[1] The importance of this symbolic gesture must not be under-rated. Holy Echmiadzin, however small, was once more a reality, although outside the walls protecting the residence of the Catholicos there was no peace between religion and State, not even in the district of Echmiadzin where anti-religious propaganda is conducted with particular intensity.[2]

And yet even outside Echmiadzin Armenian church life in the Soviet Union has experienced a certain recovery. Already in the first months of his Catholicosate Vazgen was able to announce that the Government had authorised the opening of ten to fifteen new churches and of four monasteries.[3] In 1959 he secured the return to the Church of several particularly ancient and venerated monasteries, especially the Tatev monastery whose history can be traced back to the ninth century, and the Haridj Monastery where the Armenian Catholicos used to spend his holidays.[4] These monasteries were of little use to the communist State, which for years had allowed them to decay. The Haridj Monastery was used as a store-house and Tatev Monastery was in a state of dilapidation, especially since the earthquake of 1931.[5] Both the State and the Church expected that the gifts of foreign Armenians would make possible the restoration of these and other ancient ecclesiastical monuments of Armenia. The revenues which the Catholicos receives from the five Soviet dioceses of the Church would be utterly insufficient for such vast expenditure. They cannot even cover the normal administrative expenses of Echmiadzin and the costs of maintaining the seminary.

---

[1] Erivan Radio, 'Armenian for abroad', January 6, 1958.
[2] Kommunist, Erivan, June 18, 1959.
[3] Erivan Radio, 'Armenian for abroad', July 22, 1956.
[4] Tass, June 12, 1959.
[5] *Armenian Review*, Winter 1956, vol. ix, no. 4, p. 75.

The normal annual income of Echmiadzin derived from internal resources is in the neighbourhood of two million roubles only.[1]

Although the situation of the Church under Vazgen has greatly improved in comparison with its situation under his predecessor, Echmiadzin's authority among the Armenians of the non-communist world suffered considerable setbacks during the first years in which he held his high office. The ancient Armenian communities of Persia put themselves under the jurisdiction of Vazgen's rival, Catholicos Zareh, of Antilias.[2] This was a grievous loss, for the three Persian dioceses of the Armenian Church — Tabriz, Teheran and Ispahan — have almost as many parishes as the five Armenian dioceses of the Soviet Union. The Armenian Christians in the United States split into an Antilias and an Echmiadzin faction and the small Armenian community in Greece accepted a new archpriest from Antilias although it belongs traditionally to the Echmiadzin jurisdiction. The stigma of being pro-Soviet evidently remained attached to Vazgen despite all the positive achievements he had to his credit. As to these achievements, they might have been on a much smaller scale but for the schism existing between Antilias and Echmiadzin. It was in the obvious interest of the Soviet régime to strengthen Echmiadzin's backbone in the struggle against the rival anti-communist Catholicos of Cilicia.

To strengthen Vazgen against his anti-Soviet opponents the authorities allowed him to undertake another long journey in 1960. He spent four months in the United States, Canada, Argentina, Uruguay, Portugal and France. The main purpose of this journey was to inspect the Armenian parishes and dioceses of the Western hemisphere and to make sure that they would not join those which had already withdrawn from his jurisdiction. The Catholicos also established contact with the pro-Soviet 'patriotic and cultural organisations' of the Armenian diaspora.[3]

---

[1] Erivan Radio, 'Armenian for abroad', January 6, 1958.
[2] Tass report, May 28, 1958.   [3] *Tass* report, October 10, 1960.

VI

Moscow and Rome

Most religious groups of the USSR have seen periods of tolerance alternating with periods of persecution, but this has not been so in the history of Catholicism in Russia. Catholicism shared the persecution of Orthodoxy in the early years of Soviet communist rule but unlike the Russian Orthodox Church it has not benefited since from a concordat. The reasons for this persistently hostile attitude of the Kremlin towards Rome are threefold. The first is the role which, in the communist view, has been played by the Roman Catholic factor in Soviet policy; the second is the impact of the Catholic Church on world politics and the third reason, of a more imponderable nature, lies in the influence of Russian national tradition on the Soviet mind.

The most immediate motive for the Soviet fight against the Catholic Church is bound up with the situation on the Soviet home front. Here anti-Catholicism is simply an integral part of Soviet nationalities policy. The Catholic Church in Russia has always been predominantly a Church of national groups with a Western orientation — Poles, Lithuanians, Latvians and Germans. Every aspect of the incorporation of these peoples into the Soviet Union, their political Sovietisation, their participation in the communist 'cultural revolution' and the collectivisation of their agriculture has seemed impeded by their loyalty to the principles of the Catholic Church. Moreover many Catholics of the Soviet Union have lived, and still live, in border areas which has made them a possible threat to security.

Although Soviet authorities have devoted their attention to the Catholic Church in Russia as a force which obstructs the internal consolidation of the communist régime, they have rated her even higher as an external danger. The Catholic Church and the Pope appear to the Soviet leaders primarily as tremendous obstacles both to the spread of world Communism and to the attainment of certain objectives of Russian diplomacy. In Rome, Moscow faces a truly universalist force and concept, a world-wide community bound together by one doctrine and allegiance to one supreme authority. Communism, it is true, has penetrated into many parts of the globe, but it still has not equalled the width and depth of the world-wide Catholic expansion. This Catholic and Christian universalism is disturbing the communists, particularly the more idealistic among them who consider internationalism an essential part of the communist message. They believe in the 'International' which, in the words of the famous song, unites the human race but their 'International', always limited to the proletarian section of human society, has proved a most fragile and time-serving institution. The existence of an institutional international communist brotherhood depended on a number of opportunistic considerations. The disbandment of the Communist International in 1943 and then again the liquidation of the Cominform in 1955 were expressions of this opportunism. Although the challenge of universalist Rome is perpetually present the Kremlin is bound to feel it more acutely at times when its own international communist apparatus is going through a crisis. This challenge would be a mighty one even if not a single Catholic were left in the territory of the Soviet Union.

But Soviet communist anti-Catholicism is also based on tradition. Anti-Catholicism in Russia has centuries-old roots. Fear and hatred inspired the attitude of the Russian Grand-Dukes and Czars of the pre-Petrine period towards the Catholics. The Catholic Church appeared to them as the powerful rival of their own Orthodox Church. Any healing of the church schism between Eastern and Western Christians was undesirable to the Russian rulers if it meant the establishment of papal jurisdiction over the priests and bishops of Russia. This would have led to a quite different relationship between Church and State from that obtaining in Muscovy. An Archbishop of Moscow holding the rank of Cardinal and defending supra-national church interests, if necessary against the Czar himself, would seriously have limited the powers of the Autocrat of All the Russias.

The fate of Orthodoxy in the Catholic Polish Commonwealth was also such as to encourage Russian anti-Catholicism. However, it would be a mistake to explain this attitude only in logical and rational terms. Every anti-emotion, be it anti-Semitism, anti-Catholicism or an anti-Negro attitude, always contains a strong irrational element. Olearius, a German who lived in Russia at the time of Czar Aleksei Mikhailovich, the father of Peter the Great, wrote that: 'The hatred of the Russians towards the Latin Church is primordial and somehow inborn; their ancestors took it over from the Greeks and passed it on as a heritage to their offspring.' The Jesuit Antonio Possevino, who visited Moscow in 1581 in the hope of furthering the cause of the Catholic Church in Russia, admitted frankly, 'The Muscovites dislike the Latins so much that if they wish evil to somebody they say, "May they make a Latin of you".'[1]

Soviet propaganda deliberately set out to revive and encourage these anti-Catholic prejudices of the past. It even tried to use them as a common ground on which the *rapprochement* between the Soviet State and the Russian Orthodox Church could be built. The old Orthodox fear of Catholic proselytism was brought into the service of an outwardly patriotic but ultimately anti-religious campaign. The following quotation from a Soviet book on the history of the Jesuits examplifies the communist use of traditional Latinophobia: 'For nearly 1,000 years there has never been any lack of words about the love of the Pope for the Russian people, but behind this have been hidden all sorts of intrigues, plans of military expeditions, dreams of conquest, robbery and extermination of the Russian people, and at times Russian blood has in fact been shed with arms blessed by the Vatican.'[2] In short, the communist slogan 'The Vatican — the chief stronghold of world reaction' has been supplemented by another patriotic slogan 'The Pope — the eternal enemy of the Russian people'.

It was important for the Soviets to play on the anti-Catholic trend of Russian history so that the pro-Catholic tendencies which had accompanied official anti-Catholicism like a shadow should not be able to gather strength. Rome did have some friends in Russia. There were not many of them but they were of such quality as to leave their mark on Russia's history. Under favourable circumstances the influence of a small pro-Catholic group might have grown. To prevent this the Soviets not only used administrative means of coercion but also renewed the old axiom that Catholicism and Russian nationality were irreconcilable.

II. THE CATHOLIC CHURCH IN PRE-REVOLUTIONARY RUSSIA

Russia's opposition to Rome is an attempt to escape the logic of geography and history. The Catholic Church may be alien to Russia in

---

[1] Prof. M. Krasnozhen, *Inovertsy na Rusi* (The Non-Orthodox in Russia), Dorpat 1900, p. 77.
[2] D. E. Mikhnevich, *Ocherki po istorii katolicheskoi reaktsii* (*Yezuity*) Essays on the History of Catholic Reaction (Jesuits), Moscow 1953, p. 196.

that it is a Church of non-Russian peoples, but it is only alien to Muscovy and not to all the territories which became part of Russia in the eighteenth and nineteenth centuries. However, the history of relations between Russia and the Catholic Church begins well before the later annexations of the Russian Empire. Whenever Russia established contacts with the West, she was bound to come in touch with Catholics. There were 'Latins' in Kiev as early as the twelfth century. When Czar Ivan III captured Novgorod in 1475 he already found a Catholic church there; it was closed down on his orders nineteen years later. In Moscow too there were Catholics in the embassies of Catholic countries quite apart from the Catholic foreigners who were being increasingly recruited into the service of the Russian State. For a long time the Czars hesitated to grant the Catholics the same rights as the Protestants. Only on December 12, 1705, did Peter the Great sign a charter authorising the Catholics to build churches in Russia although the first Catholic church of St. Peter and Paul had actually been erected in Moscow a few years prior to this formal permission.[1]

Whatever the hostility of the Czars towards the Catholics, they conceded them, nevertheless, a fair measure of tolerance from the days of Peter the Great onwards. This tolerance, it is true, was confined to the Latin Rite and to those nationalities of the Russian Empire which by tradition wholly or partly belonged to the sphere of Catholic influence. Within these limits the Catholic Church was even allowed to expand beyond the Catholic areas. She was not confined to the two Archbishoprics of Mohilev and Warsaw, which were incorporated into the Russian state as a result of the partitions of the Polish Commonwealth, but could extend her scope, for example by the foundation in 1848 of the huge diocese of Tiraspol reaching from the river Prut to beyond the Volga and including the whole Caucasus region. Tiraspol was a strange place to choose for the see of a Catholic bishop, for it did not even have a Catholic church. It was selected as a nominal episcopal see with the intention of giving no offence to the Orthodox Church which watched so jealously the growth of 'Latin influence'. The actual jurisdictional centre of Catholicism in the Russian South was never Tiraspol, but first Odessa and later Saratov where there was also a Catholic seminary. Three-quarters of the faithful of the Tiraspol diocese were Germans, mostly peasant colonists from the Black Sea and Volga region, but there was a sprinkling of other nationalities and given time and unrestricted religious freedom the diocese might have become more international still.

[1] Count Dmitry Tolstoy, *Romanism in Russia*, London 1874, pp. 140, 144.

On the eve of World War I the Catholic Church was present in many parts of the Russian Empire. In the capital, St. Petersburg, there were the Catholic Cathedral of the Assumption, the churches of St. Boniface and St. Catherine for the German-speaking Catholics, the Church of St. Stanislas for the Poles and Notre Dame de France for French-speaking foreigners. Here at least Catholicism was not more alien than Orthodoxy. The city contained Catholic worshippers right from the days of its foundation. The same may be said of Odessa, the big Russian city in the south founded in 1794. French Catholics played a considerable part in Odessa's early history; the Duc de Richelieu was its first mayor and the Jesuit Father Nicolle in 1816 founded a famous *lycée* later to be transformed into the University of New Russia (*Novorossiiskii Universitet*). In Moscow, the Church of St. Louis des Français was added at the end of the eighteenth century to the already existing church of St. Peter and Paul. Throughout European Russia from Polotsk, Vitebsk and Mohilev in the West to Orenburg and Ufa in the East, from Archangel in the North to Vladikavkaz in the South there was hardly a large town without its Catholic church or chapel. In Astrakhan, the gateway to Asia, was one of the oldest Catholic houses of worship, founded with the purpose of bringing the Armenians into the fold of the Church of Rome. In Russian Asia there were Catholic churches in such major urban centres as Tashkent, Tomsk, Tobolsk, Irkutsk and Vladivostok. These churches were erected for members of 'Catholic nations' such as Poles and Lithuanians but neither for Russians nor for the natives of Siberia. And yet in the reign of Alexander I the Jesuits very nearly obtained permission to evangelise there. The idea of a Jesuit Siberian mission was supported by Pestel, Russian Governor General of Siberia at the beginning of the nineteenth century, as well as by Kochubei, Minister of the Interior, but the opposition of other members of the government, notably Derzhavin, Minister of Justice, frustrated this plan.[1]

In the Ukraine there were facilities for Catholic worship even in smaller places. In the Crimea, the Catholic Church could boast both of many thousand members and of a colourful tradition going back many centuries. In fact, Catholicism in the Crimea had been established not only before Russian rule but even before the coming of the Tartar Khans. The churches which the latter destroyed or transformed into mosques, baths and private houses after the second half of the fifteenth century did not belong to Orthodox Christians but had been founded by Franciscans and Dominicans. In the nineteenth and the beginning

[1] Count Dmitry Tolstoy, op. cit., vol. ii, p. 176.

12. A service in the Moscow Roman Catholic church, St. Louis des Français.

Ежедневные молитвы.

1. Крестное знамя.

2. Во имя Отца и Сына и Духа Святаго. Аминь.

3. МОЛИТВА ГОСПОДНЯ.

Отче наш,иже еси на небесах,да святится имя Твое,да приидет царствие Твое,да будет воля Твоя,яко на небе -так и на земле; Хлеб наш насущный дай нам днесь и прости нам долги наши,как и мы прощаем должником нашим и не введи нас во искушение,но избави нас от лукавого. Аминь.

4. АНГЕЛЬСКОЕ ПРИВЕТСТВИЕ.

Радуйся,Мария,благодати полная,Господь с Тобою! Благословенна Ты между женами и благословен Плод чрева Твоего,Иисус! Святая Мария,Матерь Божия,моли о нас грешных,ныне и в час смерти нашей. Аминь.

5. АПОСТОЛЬСКИЙ СИМВОЛ ВЕРЫ.

Верую в Бога Отца,Всемогущего Творца неба и земли и в Иисуса Христа,Его Сына,Господа нашего,который был зачат от Духа Святого,родился от Девы Марии,страдал при Понтии Пилате,был распят,умер и погребен.Сошел в ад.В третий день воскрес из мертвых.Взошел на небеса,сидит одесную Отца Всемогущего,отгуда придет судить живых и мертвых.Верую в Духа Святого,Святую Католическую церковь,Святых общение,оставление грехов,воскресение плоти, жизнь вечную. Аминь.

6. Слава Пресвятой Троице,Слава Отцу и Сыну и Духу Святому, ныне и присно и во веки веков. Аминь.

7. АНГЕЛ ГОСПОДЕНЬ.

Ангел Господень благовестил Марии и Она зачала от Духа Святого. Радуйся,Мария!...Се раба Господня,да будет мне по слову Твоему!

14. First page of a hand-typed catechism used in the Moscow Roman Catholic church.

АКАДЕМИЯ НАУК СССР

НАУЧНО-ПОПУЛЯРНАЯ СЕРИЯ

М. М. ШЕЙНМАН

КРАТКИЕ ОЧЕРКИ ИСТОРИИ ПАПСТВА

ИЗДАТЕЛЬСТВО АКАДЕМИИ НАУК СССР

1952

13. One of many Soviet anti-Vatican pamphlets—'Short Essays about the History of Papacy' by M. M. Sheinman—published in 1952 by the Soviet Academy

of the twentieth century the revived Catholic Church of the Crimea
was as polyglot as befits the Crimean melting pot of races. The Crimean
Catholic parishes served Poles, Germans, Armenians and, to a lesser
extent Italians and Czechs.[1]

Another part of the Russian Empire with an old Catholic tradition is
Georgia. The Latin Catholic diocese of Tiflis was founded in 1328 by
a papal bull issued from Avignon. After that there were, albeit with
interruptions, close contacts between Rome and Georgia as evidenced
by the voluminous correspondence between the Popes on the one hand
and the heads of the Orthodox Church, the Catholikoi and the Georgian
Kings, on the other. Several Georgian Catholikoi (e.g. Nicholas VII
1742-4 and Anthony I 1744-88) were in sympathy with a union with
Rome, and the Catholic Church, working through Theatin and Capucin
missions, made numerous converts in Georgian high society, including
royal princes and members of the Orthodox hierarchy.[2] When in 1800
Georgia and the Georgian Church lost their independence to Russia
and the Russian Orthodox Church, limitations were put on Catholic
pastoral work among the Georgians, who were considered part
of the Orthodox sphere of influence. The Czarist Government was
particularly anxious to impede the work of the Roman Congregation de
Propaganda Fide; but it nevertheless authorised the building of some
beautiful new Catholic churches even if it later made sure that the
Georgian language would not be used in the services there. The Catholic
Church in Georgia was to be limited to Armenians, Poles and Germans.
The Czars did not wish to have any Georgian Catholic subjects. The
places of worship of Georgia's Catholics on the eve of the Russian
Revolution included the Church of the Holy Family in Gori, the
Church of St. Peter and Paul in Tiflis and the Churches of the Im-
maculate Conception in Batumi and Kutaisi.

III. MOSCOW AND THE UNIVERSAL CATHOLIC CHURCH

In defining its attitude towards the Roman Catholic Church of the
non-Soviet world Moscow has never paid the slightest attention to the
core of the problem, namely, the spiritual significance of the Church.
Moscow always looked at peripheral issues and factors such as the
clerical parties in the capitalist countries and the attitude of the Vatican

---

[1] *Ueberblick ueber die topographische und politische Geschichte und kurzer Abriss der
Kirchengeschichte Tauriens von Bishof Anton Zerr*, Saratov 1908.

[2] Michel Tamarati, *L'Eglise Georgienne des origines jusq' à nos jours*, Rome 1910.

G

towards world affairs. In the twenties and early thirties, until Hitler's rise to power in Germany, the picture which Moscow had of Roman Catholicism in Europe was more or less as follows. The Roman Catholic Church was a major obstacle to the spreading of the world revolution; it was the ally of capitalism, reaction and fascism; it was a driving force behind the war of intervention of the capitalist world aiming at over-throwing the young Soviet régime; and it never ceased to be a major element in the anti-Soviet front.

It was easier to put forward these general assertions than to substantiate them in detail and in some cases even anti-religious agitators had to admit the fallacy of their own generalisations. For instance, it proved impossible to establish a connection between the Catholic Church and the dictatorship of the twenties which seemed the most obnoxious from the Soviet point of view, that of Marshal Pilsudski in Poland. The Catholic episcopate appeared even to the biased Soviet observer as 'more than cool' towards the Marshal and his colonels. Indeed, it looked upon pro-Pilsudski priests as traitors.[1] Nor could the Catholic Church be made responsible for Italian fascism led by the atheist Benito Mussolini, nor for the Hungarian Horthy-régime whose most outstanding representative, Admiral Horthy himself, belonged to the Calvinist Church. On the other hand, Moscow could justifiably claim that Catholic parties and Catholic organisations of a number of countries such as Austria, Hungary, Germany, Czechoslovakia, Belgium and France regarded it as a major task to stop the advance of Communism and its atheist ideology.

Russian Bezbozhniki and German Freethinkers

The Catholic Church appeared such a redoubtable opponent that Moscow considered it desirable to have all over the 'capitalist world' fighting detachments specialised in the struggle against religion and, in the first place, against Catholicism. In other words, the Russian godless organisation was anxious to recruit allies abroad and in this quest for allies it came into contact with the movement of the Proletarian Freethinkers in Central Europe. To the uninitiated this may seem a natural alliance; in reality it was anything but natural. Russian Bezbozhniki and Central European Freethinkers vaguely agreed in their negative attitude towards religion and the Church, but differed greatly in outlook and motive. Underneath lay all the difference between Russian and German left-wing thinking, for the Proletarian Freethinkers

[1] *Antireligioznik*, December, 1931, no. 12, p. 104.

were mostly German-speaking — Germans, Austrians and Sudeten Germans. The Russian Bezbozhniki in their fight against religion were imbued with an almost religious fervour, whilst the German Freethinkers looked at the problem from a more rational angle. The origins of the two movements were different, for the Russian godless movement came into being as an auxiliary force of an atheist state in which Churches had ceased to wield any political power and were in fact oppressed. The Proletarian Freethinkers' movement, founded in countries where Churches were politically powerful, was a reaction against Central European clericalism. Instead of fighting God as the Bezbozhniki proclaimed by the very name they had chosen, the Freethinkers mainly fought the clergy and especially their involvement in the political scene. The beginnings of the Freethinkers' movement went back to the times of the Hapsburgs and Hohenzollerns. The 'North-Bohemian Union of Freethinkers' was founded in 1906 and the German Proletarian Freethinkers formed their first organisation in 1908. So they were much older than the Russian Bezbozhniki who set up their first organisation as late as 1922. Finally, the Russian Bezbozhniki were communists whilst the majority of the 'Proletarian Freethinkers' were Social-Democrats and it was this political difference above all which made the alliance between the two so unnatural and ultimately so futile.

Nevertheless, it was the most important attempt made by the Russian godless movement in the period between the wars to infiltrate into Roman Catholic countries and to determine there the nature and methods of the anti-religious struggle. With Soviet participation, an International of Proletarian Freethinkers came into being on June 1, 1925. Its first congress was held in Teplitz-Schoenau, a town in Northern Bohemia where the majority of the population belonged, nominally at least, to the Roman Catholic faith. Most organisations affiliated to the new International were in Catholic countries — Austria, Poland, France, Belgium and Czechoslovakia, which was represented by both a German and a Czech Freethinkers' body. The largest Freethinkers' organisation outside Russia was in Germany and the ex-Protestant members of it were probably more numerous than the ex-Catholics. In deference to the importance of the German Freethinkers' movement the second congress of the International took place in Protestant Leipzig (December 1928) and the third in Catholic Cologne (June 1929); the fourth was held, like the first, in Catholic Northern Bohemia, in Bodenbach (November 1930).

Although the communists exercised a considerable influence over the Freethinkers' International they were not able to transform it into a really effective weapon against religion and the Catholic Church. Direction of the International was largely in the hands of Social-Democrats who were committed to the support of coalition governments in which Catholic parties were represented. In these circumstances Social-Democrats could not adopt an intransigent anti-clerical attitude and even had to make concessions to the Church. In Prussia, in 1929, a government under social-democratic direction concluded a concordat with the Vatican, whilst the Czechoslovak social-democratic deputies voted budgetary allocations to all recognised religious bodies. The Russian godless movement and the communist minorities in the freethinker organisations denounced this as 'treason' and Soviet attacks on social-democratic Freethinkers therefore became increasingly violent.

As the anti-religious campaign in Russia became more savage Moscow felt a pressing need for a vigorous and militant anti-religious organisation on an international scale to fight the world-wide movement of Christian solidarity which the persecutions had provoked and in which the Pope had played a leading part.

The Climax of the Conflict

On February 8, 1930, Pope Pius XI addressed a letter to Cardinal Pompili protesting against the 'horrible and sacrilegious outrages' perpetrated in Russia and announcing his intention of celebrating a Mass of expiation in St. Peter's, Rome. It was to be on March 19, the Feast of St. Joseph, and was to be a Mass 'for the salvation of so many souls put to such dire trials and for the release of our dear Russian people and that these great tribulations may cease'. This announcement was made only after a period of prolonged hesitation and reflection when all hopes of an improvement in the religious situation in Russia had proved vain, and it is noteworthy that the Pope raised his voice not simply against the plight of Russia's Catholics but against the indignities to which Christianity in general, and particularly the Orthodox Church, was exposed under Soviet rule. In his letter the Pope mentioned some of the worst excesses of the atheist campaign — the closing of churches, the burning of ikons, the abolition of Sunday and the desecration of Christmas; and he expressed the hope that the whole Christian world, and not only the members of the Roman Catholic Church, would join his supplication in a world-wide Day of Prayer.

The Pope's letter provoked a response both in the Christian world and among the Soviet communists. The movement of protest was joined, as the Pope had hoped, by other Christian Churches, especially the Lutheran Church of Germany and the Church of England.[1] On February 12 the Convocations of Canterbury and York put on record their 'indignant protests' against the persecution of 'all who profess any form of religion in Russia'.[2] Both the Anglican Church and the Free Churches fixed the last Sunday in Lent, March 16 that year as a day of prayer for those suffering oppression in Russia as a result of their loyalty to their religious faith. This Christian protest against persecution took place on the level of prayer and spirituality, a level inaccessible to the materialistic mind. As Moscow could not understand the true essence of the protest, it did its best to denounce it as a purely political action. Many years afterwards the Soviet communists still spread the legend that 'at the beginning of 1930 . . . Pius XI proclaimed a crusade against the USSR'.[3] The word 'crusade' was not understood in a metaphorical but in its literal mediaeval sense.

When the great Mass of Expiation was celebrated in St. Peter's Basilica it was not an anti-Soviet manifestation, as it appeared to the communists. The Christian Mass can never have such a trivial secular and negative meaning. If it was a manifestation at all, it was only one on behalf of a Christian Russia. The Creed and certain other parts of the Mass were chanted in Church Slavonic by the alumni of the various Slav colleges in Rome. At the end they sang the Pope's invocation for Russia — 'Spasitel Mira, Spasi Rossiyu' — 'Saviour of the World, Save Russia'. The music for this was composed by a seminarist from Djakovo, once the see of Bishop Strossmeyer, a great pioneer in promoting union of the Churches and Slav brotherhood.

The Soviet régime met the Christian challenge not only with furious

---

[1] Soviet Communists have only shown a sporadic interest in the Anglican Church, but fundamentally they regard it with almost as much hostility as they regard the Vatican. This accounts for the fierce attacks on Anglicanism in Soviet works of reference as well as in Soviet political and anti-religious literature. The *Large Soviet Encyclopædia* may be mentioned as an example. It says that the Anglican Church 'is actively engaged in missionary work in the interest of the colonial robbery of the English bourgeoisie' and that its ecclesiastical apparatus 'supports all the most reactionary measures of British imperialism both in home and foreign policy' (*Large Soviet Encyclopædia*, second edition, volume ii, Moscow 1950, p. 364). The leading Soviet economist, Evgenii Varga, on the other hand, was of the opinion that the Anglican Church conducted a 'very subtle reactionary policy'. This subtlety consisted in talking of 'social justice' and establishing closest contact with the Labour Party (E. Varga, *Osnovnye Voprosy Ekonomiki i Politiki Imperializma* (Fundamental Questions of the Economics and Politics of Imperialism) Moscow 1953, p. 474). Soviet anti-religious experts consider that 'in the period of imperialism' differences between Anglicanism and Roman Catholicism are dwindling and state with regret that High Church dignitaries refer to the 'Catholic heritage' of the Anglican Church (M. M. Sheinman, *Religiya v Period Imperializma* (Religion in the Period of Imperialism), Moscow 1955, p. 13).

[1] *The Times*, February 13, 1930.

[3] M. A. Zaborov, *Krestovye Pokhody* (The Crusades), Moscow 1956, p. 276.

denials of any religious persecution in Russia, but also with meetings of protest in all major cities of the country held to denounce the 'slander' of the 'enemies of the Soviet Union headed by the Pope'. The peaceable and dignified action of the Supreme Pontiff was exploited for the strengthening of the Soviet military potential. A new campaign 'Our Reply to the Pope', much like the campaign of 1927 conducted under the slogan 'Our Reply to Chamberlain', was now launched. Its aim was the collection of money for Russia's air and chemical defence. The Deputy People's Commissar for Defence, Unshlikht, issued an appeal to the public to support the 'Our Reply to the Pope' fund. At the same time there was some grudging recognition in official circles of the power of the Catholic Church, even if that recognition was confined to the material-political world. This is how an editorial in *Izvestiya* commented on the Day of Prayer: 'The idiots and simpletons who underrate the political significance of the most reactionary force of present-day capitalist society have received an object lesson. . . . The Catholic Church is a powerful motor capable of inducing journalists to write, politicians to deliver speeches and organisers to go into action.'[1]

These words were perhaps more than an ill-humoured compliment to a powerful opponent. They were also indirectly an attempt to explain the retreat of the Soviet Government on the religious front after the Papal announcement. On March 15, the very eve of the Day of Prayer in England, and four days before the Mass of Expiation in Rome, the Soviet rulers published a decree which put a brake on the closing of churches and the de-Christianisation of the Soviet countryside. The Catholics were grateful for any relaxation of religious persecution, but have continued to consider Russia as an object of special anxiety having a primary claim on their prayers. On June 30, 1930, Pope Pius XI ruled that prayers after Low Mass should henceforth have as their main intention the deliverance of Russia from the evils afflicting her. Previously these prayers had been offered principally for the restoration of the civil independence of the Holy See and a satisfactory solution of the Roman question.

A Militant Anti-Catholic International

It is against this background that we must consider the Soviet communist attempts to establish a Militant Godless International with the Holy See in Rome as its main enemy. This was at last achieved in November 1930. The communist delegates walked out of the Free-thinkers' Congress of Bodenbach, which did not accept their extremist

[1] *Izvestiya*, March 27, 1930.

point of view, and held a rival congress in Tetschen, situated opposite
Bodenbach on the right bank of the river Elbe. Here an international
organisation was set up fully in line with the programme of the Russian
Bezbozhniki. It claimed to be the lawful successor to the socialist-
communist Freethinkers' International. This claim was hardly challenged. Very soon the remaining social-democratic Freethinkers joined
forces with 'bourgeois' freethinkers or gave up their international
affiliation altogether. The new communist Freethinkers' International
was made up of organisations from seven countries; four of them were
predominantly Catholic (Belgium, France, Poland and Czechoslovakia),
and in two countries (Germany and Switzerland) Catholics formed
substantial minorities.[1] Numerically, these various Western atheist
bodies did not add up to very much, they were dwarfed by the League
of Militant Godless which at the time of the Bodenbach and Tetschen
congresses had reached a membership of 3,500,000. Nevertheless, the
Soviet delegation allowed their foreign and especially their German
comrades to take the limelight. This Soviet delegation consisted of only
two men, the Vice-President of the League of Militant Godless,
Lukachevsky, and Sheinman who has remained for three decades the
chief expert of the Soviet Communist Party on the Roman Catholic
Church. The number of his anti-Vatican pamphlets, books and articles
is legion.

Not only the new International as a whole, but also each of its sections
engaged in violent attacks on religion and the Catholic Church. The
French Revolutionary Freethinkers' organisation, for instance, put
forward such demands as the rupture of diplomatic relations between
France and the Vatican, the dissolution of all religious orders and the
confiscation of their property, the prohibition of all religious teaching
in schools and the withdrawal of all subsidies to the Church in Alsace-
Lorraine.[2] The International could not be satisfied, however, with the
small number of organisations which belonged to it at the time of its
foundation. Serious attempts were made to branch out to other
countries. One of the first new recruits was the Liga Anticlerical
Revolucionaria in Mexico founded at Easter in 1931. For the first time
the communist Freethinkers had gained a foothold on the Latin

---

[1] The following organisations joined with the League of Militant Godless as
foundation members of the new International: Union of Proletarian Unbelievers of
Czechoslovakia, Union of Proletarian Freethinkers of Switzerland, Union of Freethinkers of Poland, Union of Materialists of Belgium and Union of Revolutionary
Freethinkers of France. In addition, there were seven regional German Freethinkers'
organisations, two of which — those of the Ruhr and Rhineland–Westphalia —
represented predominantly Catholic areas.

[2] *Antireligioznik*, 1933, no. 2, p. 44.

American continent and the accession of the Mexican League was therefore hailed as a prelude to the further growth of the anti-religious movement in the Americas.[1] In the following year the Freethinkers' International made a further important acquisition in another Catholic country when it secured the affiliation of the Spanish communist 'Liga Atea'. This body published a journal *Sin Dios* in conscious imitation of the Russian *Bezbozhnik*, and half of its first issue was devoted to atheism in the USSR.[2]

Hitler's Impact on Communist anti-Catholicism

Whilst the Soviet atheist leaders were dreaming of a world-wide atheist movement to counter Catholicism on every continent, an event took place almost at Russia's door which had a disturbing and, at the same time, sobering effect on the Soviet atheist mind. This was the victory of Nazism in Germany. It shook the confidence of the communists in their own evaluation of the Catholic Church and raised three important issues for the atheist movement:

(1) It showed that not Catholicism but Fascism was the main enemy of the 'revolutionary working class' and made the fight against the Roman Catholic Church somewhat pointless, at least for the time being;

(2) It confronted the Russian godless movement with the awkward task of explaining away the anti-Church campaign of the Nazis;

(3) It posed the problem of a united front between the communists and the Catholic victims and opponents of Nazism.

The Soviet communists became aware of these three issues only gradually and reluctantly. At first they were unwilling to accept the fact that there was a serious conflict between Christianity and the nazi totalitarian State. Commentators either minimised it or wrote about it in ironical and unsympathetic terms. Mikhail Koltsov, perhaps the most prominent Soviet journalist of the period, poured ridicule on the obscurantist religious opposition to Hitler when he wrote in *Pravda*: 'In solitary villages and in the skyscrapers of the towns people whisper mischievously and fearfully about the Antichrist, about the end of the world and the last judgment. But the Government firmly sticks to its guns.'[3] However, this same article credited the Catholic Church with having braved the nazi onslaught more successfully than the Lutherans. Koltsov attributed this to 'iron discipline, rigid centralisation, cunning

[1] *International Press Correspondence*, May 13, 1931, pp. 467–8.
[2] *Antireligioznik*, 1933, no. 3, p. 38.
[3] *Pravda*, January 1, 1934.

and the organising ability of the papal generals in cassocks'. As to the Soviet periodicals specialising in the fight against religion, they took the line that the Churches in Germany, especially the Catholic Church, were trying to inflate their conflict with Hitler, but that in reality both Fascism and the Church were serving the interests of capital.[1]

Such statements were no more than self-deceptive, if they were not a deliberate attempt to mask the fact that events in Germany had shattered the Soviet-sponsored international godless movement to its foundations. It was compelled to redefine its objectives and finally its leaders decided to disband the organisation altogether. In 1934, the executive committee of the 'Proletarian Freethinkers' International', strange as it may seem, really relinquished the intransigent fight against religion in favour of a united front which was to appeal to religious-minded members of the working class. The primary aim was no longer to transform Catholic workmen into atheists but to draw them into a joint struggle against economic exploitation and political oppression.[2] At the same time the sections of the Freethinkers' International, particularly those working in countries with a dictatorship (Italy, Germany and Austria), urged their followers to work 'to a greater extent than hitherto in the mass organisations of the Church and of Fascism'. This meant in particular that the communist freethinkers were to infiltrate the branches of 'Catholic Action' — for political purposes and not to propagate atheism. The Freethinkers' International even warned its supporters that it was an 'erroneous' and 'reformist' concept to concentrate one's militancy entirely on Church and religion.

From all this it was obvious that the Kremlin, which guided every step of the Freethinkers' International, had for the time being lost all interest in the anti-Church campaign, which could only irritate the mass of believers in Europe. It had even lost all interest in the existence of the International itself and looked for an early opportunity to dissolve it. The International had convened its fifth congress for the first half of 1935 and had announced that it would become 'a powerful manifestation of militant atheism'. Suddenly the communist policy-makers curbed the zeal of the Russian Bezbozhniki and their allies in other countries. The idea of the congress was dropped and instead the communist Freethinkers started negotiations for the formation of a Freethinkers' International to include Liberals and Social-Democrats whom they had previously vilified as 'opportunists', 'bourgeois' and 'social-fascists'. These negotiations led to a 'Unity Congress' held in

[1] *Antireligioznik*, 1934, no. 3, p. 35.
[2] *International Press Correspondence*, June 22, 1934, p. 947.

Prague at Easter 1936, at which it was decided to amalgamate the Proletarian Freethinkers' International, or rather its remnants, with the Brussels Freethinkers' International, which was pledged to a liberal anti-clericalism rooted in the French Revolution. The Soviet godless movement was represented at the congress by a delegation of three, again headed by Lukachevsky, who appeared in the minutes as 'Professor Lukachevsky'. In a long statement he said that thanks to the formation of the new International the 'liberated science of the USSR' would be able to give its 'valuable aid to the ideological struggle of the Freethinkers against Fascism and clericalism'.[1]

The position of the new International was most equivocal. On the one hand it was strongly anti-Catholic, most of its officials came from Catholic countries and one item on the agenda of its foundation congress was the 'International Policy of the Vatican'. On the other hand, the new body accepted the Soviet thesis that Fascism, not the Church, was the main enemy and that there should be a united front with religious workers against reactionary ecclesiastical leaders. The new International actually played a very minor part in communist ideological and political warfare. At its congress in London in the autumn of 1938 no Soviet delegation was present. The Soviet vice-president of the organisation, 'Professor' Lukachevsky, was meanwhile arrested and so could not attend.

From the middle of the thirties communist policy towards the Catholic Church was no longer determined to any noteworthy extent by the Russian Bezbozhniki and the Proletarian Freethinkers in the capitalist world. It was the communist leaders themselves who took the initiative. Very appropriately, their main spokesman was the communist leader, Maurice Thorez, secretary-general of the French Communist Party, then the strongest in Europe. His French party comrades have described Thorez as 'Stalin's best disciple in France' and one may assume that he has never taken an important policy step and never changed the tactics and ideology of his party without prior consultation with Moscow. This, no doubt, applies to his sensational statement of April 17, 1936, with its first offer to the Catholics of peaceful co-existence. This new French communist policy became known as the policy of the outstretched hand, 'la politique de la main tendue'. At first Thorez's readiness to give his hand to the Catholics could be dismissed as an election manœuvre, since it was made on the eve of the parliamentary elections which brought the Popular Front to power. However, after the elections he repeated his appeals. Thorez made every point which he thought might please the Catholics: he compared the builders of the

[1] *International Press Correspondence*, May 2, 1936, p. 582.

medieval cathedrals with the modern Stakhanovites, paid tribute to the progressive character of Christianity and to the 'Communism' of the religious orders, recalled the role of the French lower clergy in the French Revolution of 1789 and drew attention to the things which the 'Communist Manifesto' had in common with the Papal Encyclical 'Rerum Novarum'.[1]

These statements showed the extent to which the communists were prepared to compromise with their atheist principles and conclude an armistice and even an alliance with Catholics, provided this suited the ends of the world revolution or even only the interests of the first proletarian state, the Soviet Union. It emerged clearly that the United Front was to be extended not only to all Catholic workers but even to such members of the parish clergy as were ready to give the communists the benefit of the doubt. There was no indication whether the united front was to be extended to the Catholic hierarchy, but Thorez certainly left the door open even for this.

The 'policy of the outstretched hand' was not confined to France. Similar offers were extended to the Catholics by other communist parties, those of Germany and Belgium in particular. The Soviet anti-religious press not only approved these attempts to form a united front, it claimed that they had been highly successful. 'Millions of believing Catholics in Germany, Italy, Austria, France, Spain and all countries of the world' were said to have joined the 'communist struggle against Fascism and war, for bread, peace and freedom'.[2]

It would be wrong to see in all this only a tactical manœuvre and not also an admission that the original communist analysis of the relations between Catholicism and Fascism had been wrong. In the second half of the thirties the communists no longer seriously believed that the Catholic Church had sold itself to Mussolini by the Lateran Treaty of 1929 and to Hitler by the Concordat of 1933. They also realised at last that the persecution of the Catholic Church in Germany was as genuine as the persecution of the German Communist Party itself. The persecution of the German Catholics was denounced by Moscow as 'cruel' and 'shameful' and was said to have attracted the attention of the whole world.[3] It does not detract from the significance of such statements that they were made at a time when anti-religious persecution was rife in the Soviet Union itself. But this persecution of religion at home doomed to failure all overtures to the Catholic masses outside the Soviet Union,

---

[1] Oeuvres de Maurice Thorez, Paris 1954, vol. xiv, pp. 165–9.
[2] Antireligioznik, 1937, no. 7, p. 27.
[3] Antireligioznik, 1937, no. 8, p. 15.

despite all communist claims to success. Moreover, the difficulties which the Catholic Church underwent when Hitler and Mussolini were in power did not weaken its resistance to the communist form of totalitarianism and Pope Pius XI's Encyclical letter *'Divini Redemptoris'*, published on March 19, 1937, was an express condemnation not only of the theory of Communism but also of the Popular Front policy. The Encyclical therefore brought a very decisive setback to the 'policy of the outstretched hand'; it also caused particular embarrassment to communist propaganda in that it virtually coincided with what may be described as an anti-fascist statement from the same source, namely, the Papal Encyclical *'Mit brennender Sorge'* of March 14, 1937. The Soviet communists saw themselves compelled to give qualified approval to the Pope's denunciation of 'the idiotic racial theories of Fascism'.[1] On the other hand, the Encyclical *'Divini Redemptoris'* was bound to increase communist hostility to the Pope as a 'saboteur of the United Front'. He was accused of aiming at a peaceful solution of the conflict with Fascism, and the new charge was put forward that he had become an ally of Japanese imperialism.[2] A further absurd accusation was that the Catholic hierarchy, whilst rejecting the united front with the true communists, fought hand in hand with the Trotskyites.[3]

The political events in Europe which had preceded the outbreak of the war were not really helpful to Moscow's anti-Vatican propaganda, for in this period the Soviet communists considered it of primary importance to draw attention to Catholic resistance to Fascism. Communist denunciations of Catholic support for reaction were always matched by a stress on Catholic anti-Fascism. The pro-Hitler attitude of the Slovak priests was contrasted with the democratic outlook of the Czech Catholic party and of the Archbishop of Prague, Dr. Kašpar.[4] The ready acceptance of the Hitlerite Anchluss by Cardinal Innitzer of Vienna was emphasised and was a welcome gift to the Soviet godless movement, but the arrest of hundreds of Austrian Catholic priests by the Nazis was likewise registered as an important event.[5] Even Soviet reports about Spain, with their strong anti-Catholic bias, paid tribute to the anti-Fascism of the Basque priests and believers. In short, the Soviet communists, whilst not abandoning their fundamental hostility towards the Catholic Church, at that time realised that Catholicism was a complicated phenomenon and their approach to it in the past had been too superficial.

---

[1] *Antireligioznik*, 1937, no. 7, p. 24.   [2] *Antireligioznik*, 1938, no. 8–9, p. 66.
[3] *Antireligioznik*, 1937, no. 7, p. 24.   [4] *Antireligioznik*, 1938, no. 7, p. 25.
[5] *Antireligioznik*, 1938, no. 5, p. 38.

Stalin and the 'Pope's Divisions'

What the principal Soviet leader in this era thought of the Catholic Church was never made public. Stalin no doubt approved the attempts to extend the united front to the Catholics without perhaps attaching too much importance to them. As far as the Soviet Union was concerned he was not yet interested in coming to terms with the Vatican. Stalin worshipped naked power and bowed to a hostile power wherever necessary, as he did in the case of Hitler, but unlike some subtler thinkers in his own party such as Bukharin he underestimated moral and spiritual factors. When the French Premier of the time, Pierre Laval, during his visit to Moscow in 1935 tried to convince Stalin of the merits of a *modus vivendi* between the Vatican and the Kremlin, the Soviet leader countered the Frenchman's skilful diplomatic arguments with the ironic question: — Has the Pope a strong army?[1] Years later Stalin was said to have talked to President Roosevelt in a similar vein about Pius XII, asking how many divisions the Pope had.

And yet the day came when Stalin realised that the Pope did have 'divisions' after all and that a *modus vivendi* between the Kremlin and the Vatican might therefore be desirable. He realised this when Soviet Russia came into physical contact with Catholic countries and especially with Poland, the most staunchly Catholic of all the territories which the Red Army occupied in the pursuit of the retreating nazi forces. It must have occurred to Stalin that the passage of the Soviet troops through Poland could be smoother if a new relationship could be established between communists and Catholics. Perhaps he even anticipated that this might be of significance too for Russian policy in other Catholic countries which would sooner or later fall into Soviet hands. These considerations were the background to one of the strangest meetings Stalin ever had, namely, his conversations with Father Orlemansky, a well-meaning but naïve Roman Catholic priest of Polish extraction.[2] Orlemansky was an American citizen and paid a short visit to the USSR in 1944. Stalin met Orlemansky twice and it did not take him long to discover the American's political inexperience and to launch through him a *ballon d'essai*. Orlemansky gave the world the amazing message which the Kremlin wanted him to convey: that Stalin would in future prove very friendly towards the Roman Catholic Church.[3] This was the nearest approach to an offer of peace made to

[1] *Le Monde*, January 23, 1958.
[2] Robert Magidoff, *The Kremlin versus the People*, New York 1953, p. 81.
[3] *Soviet Monitor*, May 6, 1944, No. 4622.

the Vatican during Stalin's lifetime. Its purpose was no different from
that of the offers of peace the Kremlin has made from time to time to
secular powers, namely, to disarm an opponent and gain time for the
implementation of Soviet policy. Stalin, who had only just concluded
his agreement with the Russian Patriarch Sergius, probably considered
that the moment had come to repeat Thorez's coup of eight years
ago — only on a much larger scale. As Stalin's insincere peace feelers
met with no response, his own Government as well as those of the new
satellite states treated the Catholic Church as one of their most
dangerous opponents.

The Post-War Period

Soviet propaganda throughout the immediate post-war period
regarded the Catholic Church as the main enemy on the world-wide
religious front and the number of anti-religious books and pamphlets
directed against the Catholic community remained larger than that
devoted to any other religious group. The main argument of Soviet
anti-Catholic propaganda was that the Vatican was 'on the side of
international reaction headed by the United States' and was an active
supporter of American aggressive policy. All moves of the Vatican and
even changes in the internal organisation of the Roman Curia were
explained as serving but one purpose, namely, to please the ruling
circles of the USA.[1] Strangely enough, there were also some zealous
anti-religious propagandists who tried to prove the very opposite. A
book entitled *The Vatican in the Service of Reaction*, published in Minsk
by the Byelorussian Academy of Sciences, instead of showing the
dependence of the Vatican on American policy, asserted that it was the
Pope who tried to impose his will on the White House. This, it seemed,
was a grave mistake from the communist point of view, for it represented
the Vatican as an independent factor in international politics.[2]

In the years of the Cold War Soviet attacks on the Vatican, 'the
Catholic branch of the State Department' as Sheinman called it,
became increasingly crude. In the end the anti-religious propagandists
imputed to the Vatican motives which had no longer even the remotest
connection with actual facts. The Catholic Church was defined simply
as 'an organisation for spying and subversive activities'.[3] It was also
asserted that the Vatican 'was sympathetically inclined towards fascist

[1] M. S. Vozchikov, *Sovremennii Vatican, yego ideologiya i politika* (The Vatican at
the present time, its ideology and politics), in *Nauka i Religiya* (Science and Religion),
Moscow 1957, pp. 254–9.
[2] *Sovetskaya Belorussiya*, June 29, 1951.
[3] Moscow Radio, home service, April 4, 1951.

organisations everywhere, in France, Britain, Italy, the United States, and in the countries of South America'.[1] It was alleged too that with the help of the Jesuits, 'close co-operation' was established between the Vatican hierarchy and the 'Fascist-Tito clique'.[2]

The twentieth Congress of the Soviet Communist Party, which affected communist thinking on virtually every issue, also influenced Moscow's attitude towards the world-wide Catholic Church. From then on the Kremlin again attached major importance to a united front with the Catholics of the capitalist world, hoping for a split in the Catholic camp into a right wing which supported 'reactionary Vatican policy' and a left wing with which the communists could co-operate. Even before the twentieth Party Congress the Soviet press was eagerly on the look-out for a split within the Catholic camp and every Catholic priest or Catholic layman who expressed disagreement with what was thought to be the official Roman Catholic line on world affairs was certain to be given considerable publicity. Developments in connection with the worker priests in France and the tensions within the Christian Democratic Party in Italy were eagerly followed. In June 1955, for instance, *Pravda* published an interview with the Christian Democratic mayor of Florence, La Pira, who expressed a wish for better Soviet-Italian relations,[3] and there was satisfaction in Moscow when the interview provoked unfavourable comment in other Catholic quarters. These inter-Catholic controversies have always aroused exaggerated expectations in Soviet circles, where it was not realised that they dealt with peripheral and ephemeral matters, and even helped the Catholic Church to arrive at a more up-to-date appreciation of social, economic and political problems. The communists have never fully grasped that political disagreements between Catholics, though momentarily embarrassing to the hierarchy, matter little from a religious point of view as long as the Church's doctrinal unity remains firm.

The twentieth Communist Congress also ended the entirely negative attitude towards the Pope as the head of the Vatican State. The Kremlin became more anxious to acquaint the Vatican with the Soviet thesis on world affairs; it also began to display a certain respect for the Pope as a potential factor for peace. Pontifical statements condemning the armaments race from then on received at least a limited publicity in the Soviet press. The first contact between a Soviet diplomat and a Vatican dignitary was made in August 1956 when the Soviet chargé d'affaires

---

[1] M. M. Sheinman, *Vatikan vo Vtoroi Mirovoi Voine* (The Vatican in the Second World War), Moscow 1951, p. 346.
[2] Sheinman, ibid.   [3] *Pravda*, June 21, 1955.

in Rome, Pozhidaev, called on Mgr Giuseppe Fietta, the Apostolic Nuncio to the Italian Government. Pozhidaev presented two documents, a Supreme Soviet memorandum on disarmament and the Soviet Government's declaration on the Suez Canal dispute. Since then Moscow has despatched copies of diplomatic statements to the Vatican on various occasions, and in January 1958 the Soviet Foreign Minister Gromyko told a delegation of Italian peace partisans that his Government was anxious to have 'official contacts' with the Vatican on all problems concerning peace. He added that, in spite of ideological differences, an accord between the Vatican and the Soviet Union was possible, and the agreement could be not just temporary but a stable and enduring one.

These overtures did not mean the end of anti-Vatican propaganda at home. The Hungarian Revolution produced a new spate of anti-Catholic invective, and fresh evidence of 'close ties between Washington and the Vatican' was found when Cardinal Mindszenty obtained sanctuary at the American Legation in Budapest. Nevertheless these attacks did not alter the fact that for the post-Stalin régime in Russia the Vatican was not only a target for abuse but also a factor to be considered seriously if the world was to attach weight to the Kremlin's propaganda for peace and co-existence. Within limits the Pope was even recognised as the spiritual head of the Catholics of the Soviet Union. At the beginning of 1958 a group of seven Lithuanian Catholics received permission 'to visit the Vatican and other places which are sacred to Catholics'.[1] The pilgrims were received by the Pope in a public audience and in Venice they saw Cardinal Angelo Roncalli, who later became Pope John XXIII. Although this permission was primarily a propaganda gesture *pro foro externo* it was nevertheless the expression of a more imaginative Soviet policy quite unthinkable in Stalin's day.

The extension of Soviet ambitions to new areas is likely to influence the Kremlin's future policy towards the Vatican. As world Communism, under Soviet or Chinese auspices, attempts to penetrate deeper into the African and Latin American continents it is bound to come into greater conflict with the Church of Rome. The communists themselves seem to be aware of the fact that they must clash with the Catholic Church in Uganda, Kenya, the Congo, Ruanda Urundi, the Cameroons and other African territories.[2] The clear stand which the Catholic Church has taken against South African 'apartheid' is a disadvantage from the

---

[1] Tass in 'Russian for abroad', February 11, 1958.
[2] See I. V. Lavretsky, *Nekotorye Voprosy Politiky Vatikana v Afrike* (Some questions of Vatican policy in Africa), in *Voprosy Istorii Religii i Ateizma*, Moscow 1958, vol. vi, pp. 105–29.

communist point of view since it may make the struggle for Africa more difficult for the communists. This struggle will have its ups and downs and new united front manœuvres will no doubt be undertaken to draw the Catholics of the new states into the communist orbit.

IV. CATHOLICISM AS AN INTERNAL PROBLEM OF THE SOVIET UNION
1917–39

The Annihilation of the Hierarchy

The most remarkable feature of Soviet communist practice with regard to the Roman Catholic Church in the Soviet Union itself has been the struggle against the Catholic hierarchy. To the communists, the Catholic bishops in the USSR were primarily representatives of a supra-national power and this alone would have made them liable to persecution. Besides, their spiritual authority was such that they were a serious obstacle for the winning over of Catholic citizens to the point of view of the Communist Party.

Both these reasons prompted the Soviet régime in its three moves to exterminate the Catholic hierarchy. These three waves of persecution were not confined to isolated dramatic events but were each spread out over several years. The first series of blows was inflicted on those Catholic bishops who found themselves under Soviet rule as a result of the communist *coup d'état* of November 1917, the second struck the new Catholic hierarchy created in 1926 and the third was directed against the bishops of the territories annexed by Soviet Russia between 1939 and 1945. The three groups differed greatly in their racial composition. The first was almost entirely Polish, the second may be described as multi-national, and Lithuanians and Ukrainians predominated in the third.

Most of the Polish Catholic bishops in the Soviet Union were removed from their sees by arrest and subsequent expulsion. The first to suffer this fate was the Catholic primate Edward von Ropp, Archbishop of Mohilev who, after several months of imprisonment, was able to leave in exchange for a Polish communist in October 1919. More such exchanges of Catholic bishops and priests for Polish and Lithuanian communist functionaries were to take place later in the twenties and early thirties. Before 1925 the Soviet Government removed from their sees the bishop of Minsk, Mgr. Lozinski, the bishop of Zhitomir, Mgr. Dubowski and the bishop of Kamenets, Mgr. Makowski. Mgr. Sliwowski, of the small Valdivostok diocese established as late as 1923, fled to China.[1] In one case, however, that of the new Archbishop of Mohilev, John Cieplak, who took over Mgr. von Ropp's difficult office, the Soviets staged a trial. It was the climax in the first wave of persecution against the Roman Catholic Church.

The Cieplak trial, as it was usually called, took place from March 21 to March 26, 1923, nearly a year after Cieplak's arrest. Altogether there were sixteen defendants, fourteen priests and two devout Lithuanian peasants. The main allegation against them was that they had conspired to 'found a counter-revolutionary organisation having for its object a revolt against the laws and ordinances of the Soviet Government'. No such organisation in fact ever existed unless one were to identify the Catholic Church itself as the 'counter-revolutionary organisation'. As far as the 'laws and ordinances of the Government' were concerned, the Catholic priests did indeed oppose those of them which they thought incompatible with the laws of God, especially the decree of January 21, 1921, prohibiting religious instruction to all persons under eighteen years of age.

The defendants at the trial were not only priests but also human beings, and those of Polish nationality among them were bound to hope that Polish national interests would prevail over those of Russia. Nevertheless, the crucial and central issue was not such human problems as the defendants' relations with the Polish Government; it was a question quite beyond the competence of the Soviet court or any other court, namely, whether the laws of God should prevail over the laws of man. The issue was prejudged by the Public Prosecutor who during the trial made the statement which has become the Alpha and Omega of the whole Soviet approach towards religion, namely that the laws of God do not apply to the Soviet Union. This alone established the guilt of the defendants, who supported a 'foreign legislation' not recognised by the Soviet State in despite of the laws and decrees which (in the communist view) alone are valid. The trial ended with two death sentences, one on Archbishop Cieplak himself and the other on his vicar Constantin Budkiewicz; the other defendants were sentenced to terms of imprisonment ranging from six months to ten years. Budkiewicz was executed on Good Friday 1923 but Cieplak's sentence was commuted to ten years' imprisonment. A year later the Soviet Government dealt with him as it had done with his predecessor; it exchanged him for a Polish communist.

The Cieplak trial was a devastating blow to Catholicism in Soviet Russia, but once it was over there was hope that Soviet persecution

---

[1] Albert Galter, *The Red Book of the Persecuted Church*, Dublin 1957, p. 45.

would relax and that Catholic Church life would be able to continue in Russia. These hopes were the background to the mission to Moscow in 1926 of the French Jesuit Michel d'Herbigny, President of the Pontifical Commission for Russia. He arrived with far-reaching powers and proceeded to a sweeping reorganisation of the Catholic administration. In the place of the Mohilev Archbishopric and the Tiraspol Diocese he created nine ecclesiastical administrative districts:—Moscow, Mohilev-Minsk, Leningrad, Kharkov, Kazan-Samara-Simbirsk, Odessa, Saratov, the Caucasus region and Georgia. For each of these districts an apostolic administrator was appointed and four of them were consecrated bishop. The only survivor of the old administration was the diocese of Kamenets near the Polish border.

Among the new apostolic administrators were priests of Latvian, Lithuanian, German and Russian nationality. The administrator for Moscow, Bishop Neveu, was a Frenchman who had been doing pastoral work in Russia, especially among Don Cossacks, for three decades. Bishop Anthony Malecki of Leningrad was a Pole with a flawless command of the Russian language, a saintly and unworldly type of priest who, as a defendant in the Cieplak Trial, impressed even his communist accusers.[1] Bishop Boleslav Sloskans was Latvian, but as apostolic administrator in the Mohilev-Minsk ecclesiastical district he showed particular respect for the national aspirations of his Byelorussian parishioners whose language he spoke freely and used in his sermons. Bishop Alexander Frizon of Odessa, though of German extraction, was born in Russia and trained at the Saratov theological seminary. The number of nations represented in the new hierarchy was a fine illustration of the universalist character of the Catholic Church in Russia, but also made her a greater danger to the secular authority than a predominantly 'Polish' Church might have been.

The Soviet authorities were quick to perceive the challenge implied in d'Herbigny's mission and the appointments he had made. Every one of the new apostolic administrators was singled out for martyrdom as soon as he assumed office. They were arrested one by one and it was only a question of time before all had disappeared in Soviet prisons or had left the Soviet Union, usually under police escort. Of the four bishops, Malecki and Sloskans, after several years of imprisonment, were allowed to return to their countries of origin. Malecki, who was over seventy, survived his release from imprisonment only a few months. Bishop Frizon was several times arrested and finally executed at the

[1] Captain Francis McCullagh, *The Bolshevik Persecution of Christianity*, London 1924, p. 180

height of the purges in August 1937. Bishop Neveu lived in Russia until 1936 when illness compelled him to leave for France, temporarily as he thought, but he was refused a return visa. Mgr. Swiderski, apostolic administrator for the Kamenets diocese, was imprisoned in January 1930 and expelled in September 1932. The same tale of arrest and exile could be told of the other Catholic dignitaries of Russia, not only of the apostolic administrators, but also of the simple village priests about two hundred of whom were forcibly separated from their flock between 1929 and 1932. The consequences of the second annihilation of the Catholic hierarchy could never be repaired. Individual parishes could be restored, it is true, but no proper church organisation was allowed.

Soviet Régime and Catholic Minorities

Most of the bishops and ecclesiastical dignitaries whom we have listed here combined and symbolised in their person the particular strength of the Catholic Church, namely, her universalism and her nearness to the people. The fact that they gave allegiance to a supra-national ideal did not prevent these men from championing the national interests of the ethnic group into which they were born. Some of them, though not all, were therefore persecuted on two accounts, as pastors of their spiritual flock and as leaders of an ethnic minority.

In the first years of Soviet power this role of the Catholic Church as a protector of minorities was perhaps most obvious with regard to the Poles. It is significant that the resolution adopted by the twelfth Congress of the Russian Communist Party held at the end of April 1923, only a few days after the execution of Mgr. Budkiewicz, drew attention to 'the growth of nationalist-clerical influence among the Polish minority in the USSR' and denounced the Catholic clergy for gaining influence over schoolchildren.[1]

The Polish minority in the Soviet Union — comprising some 476,000 in the Ukraine and nearly 100,000 in Byelorussia — presented great difficulties to the Soviet authorities because being staunchly Catholic it could not be fully integrated, either ideologically or politically, into the Soviet State. Moreover, the failure of Soviet Russia to absorb her 'own' Poles was a continual setback to her prestige in Poland. How could the Polish nation be won over to Communism if even the small Polish minority in the Ukraine and Byelorussia remained obedient to its Catholic priests? Moreover the 'Soviet Poles', and thus the Catholics,

---

[1] *KPSS v Resolyutsiyakh i Resheniyakh Sezdov, Konferentsii i Plenumov Tseka* (The CPSU in the Resolutions and Decisions of Congresses, Conferences and Plenary Sessions of the Central Committee), Moscow 1953, vol. i, p. 742.

were concentrated in the strategically vital border areas. In the Soviet part of Volhynia the Poles formed 14·3 per cent of the total population, in the Proskurov district 10 per cent, in the Shepetovka district 9 per cent and in the Korosten district 8 per cent. These percentages give at the same time the approximate numerical strength of the Catholics in these areas for, if not all, at least the vast majority of Poles were Catholics. In 1926, among the half million Ukrainian Poles there were only 3,000 Communist Party members and 8,200 members of the Young Communist League.

Until that time the Polish Catholics of the Ukraine had a fearless champion in the person of Mgr. Theophil Skalski, dean of the St. Alexander Church in Kiev, and for a short while Apostolic Administrator of the Zhitomir Diocese. But he was arrested in June 1926 and tried eighteen months later by the Military Collegium of the Supreme Court of the USSR which moved to Kiev for this purpose. Presiding over the proceedings was the Supreme Court President Ulrich who later played a major part in the purge trials of 1936–8. Mgr. Skalski was charged with counter-revolutionary activities and espionage. The latter charge could not be substantiated, Mgr. Skalski was found guilty of 'counter-revolutionary activities' only, and the details about it in the indictment show how successful he must have been in his pastoral work among the Ukrainian Poles. In his sermons, so ran this indictment, he urged his listeners not to allow communist ideas to spread among the youth. Apart from sermons in church he had private talks with his parishioners, especially with those of the younger generation, whom he tried to sever from Soviet life. Owing to his skilful and energetic propaganda several young people agreed to leave the Soviet Ukraine for Poland to be trained there in theological seminaries, and he gave such persons letters testifying their political reliability. Another more general charge was that Skalski paralysed the official efforts to educate the Polish minority of the Ukraine in a communist spirit.[1]

Skalski was sentenced to ten years imprisonment. The trial and the sentence were greatly exploited in order to intimidate Catholics in the Ukraine. A number of priests were reported to have signed statements of loyalty addressed to the Ukrainian Soviet Government, even alleging that Polish priests had been guilty of spying and smuggling people across the frontier. However, the Soviet source which publicised these statements, extorted in all likelihood under duress, admitted that the persecution of Skalski was nevertheless a failure for the Government,

---

[1] M. Chudnovtsev, *Politecheskaya Rol Tserkovnikov i Sektantov v SSSR* (The political role of church-people and sectarians in the USSR), Moscow 1930, pp. 78–9.

for 'people surrounded him with the nimbus of a martyr of the Church and the Catholic religion'.[1] Early in 1930 a leading official of the League of Militant Godless of the Ukraine could still complain of the great influence Catholic priests continued to exercise on the masses.[2] Both in the Ukraine and Byelorussia the Catholic villages stubbornly defended their faith. As long as the villagers had the opportunity of regular worship they not only celebrated the Catholic holy days but also went on pilgrimages, held processions, especially on the feast of Corpus Christi, and observed May and Advent devotions.[3] Even when all this became impossible they assembled in cemeteries for prayer.[4] This does not apply only to Catholics of Polish nationality but also to Latvian and Byelorussian Catholics who were much more numerous in Byelorussia than the Poles. However, the Poles were certainly the authorities' greatest single 'Catholic problem'; that is proved by the quantity of anti-religious literature printed in the Polish language and the publication of a bi-monthly Polish communist journal entirely devoted to fighting the Catholic Church.

Next to the Poles, the Germans were the most important ethnic group of the pre-1939 Soviet Union to find in the Catholic Church a strong support for the preservation of their individuality and for their rejection of atheist Communism. The German case however was different from the Polish. Polish nationality and Catholicism were virtually identical in the USSR as they are in Poland itself, but the German colonists in the Ukraine, the Crimea and the Volga regions were divided in their religious allegiance as they are in Germany, the majority being Protestant and a substantial minority Catholic. Also, as in Germany, there were areas in Russia where the German Catholics were more numerous than the German Protestants, for instance the Kherson Province. The Soviets themselves considered the German Catholics a somewhat more dangerous force than the Lutherans because they were more conservative, and in the first years of communist rule the ranks of the Catholic priests were less depleted than those of the pastors, many of whom had departed for Germany. For instance, thirty out of the thirty-nine Catholic villages of the Volga German Autonomous Soviet Republic still had their priest in 1926, whilst only fourteen pastors remained in the 190 or more Lutheran villages where before the Revolution there had been forty.[5]

---

[1] Chudnovtsev, op. cit., p. 76.   [2] *Antireligioznik*, May 1930, no. 5, p. 123.
[3] *Bezbozhnik*, August 25, 1930, no. 47.
[4] *Sovetskaya Etnografiya*, 1932, no. 1, p. 106.
[5] E. Gross, *Avtonomnaya Sotsialisticheskaya Sovetskaya Respublika Nemtsev Povolzhe* (Autonomous Socialist Soviet Republic of the Volga Germans), Pokrovsk 1926, p. 98.

Communist sources themselves show that it was the humble parish priest who kept the faith alive among the Catholic German villagers and at the time of the collectivisation of agriculture his power was still unbroken. Indeed, it was in this collectivisation period that the Catholic priests seemed to the régime a particular danger, not because they opposed the setting up of the collective farms but rather because they tried to infuse a religious spirit into them. They opposed the class hatred fomented by the communists in the countryside, preached mercy to the class enemy, the 'kulak' whom the régime drove from his house and field, and urged that 'God and the Pope' should not be forgotten in the new 'kolkhozy'. In their sermons they underlined the unique role of the Church as a body uniting without difference rich and poor.

The régime tried to rely on a small number of 'activists' to fight the influence of the priests, but this was usually in vain. Only the priests' arrest and deportation could pave the way to the victory of Communism in the German Catholic village. The history of the large German village Rosental in the Crimea, which was the main theme of a Soviet anti-religious pamphlet in the German language, shows this very convincingly. In Rosental the authority of the priest was such that 'there could be no question of Soviet cultural work'. Whenever the 'activists', assisted by the local teacher, organised a cultural evening, it ended in a fiasco. The priest gave illegal religious instruction, spread religious knowledge through leaflets, spoke the decisive word in all matters of morality, induced the German farmers to boycott the Soviet schools, and did all this in such a clever 'Jesuitical' way that the authorities found it difficult to undertake anything against him. They got rid of him only by imputing to him the most unbelievable crimes and immorality.[1]

Both in the Ukrainian Soviet Republic and the Crimean Autonomous Republic, as it then was, the régime made every effort to extirpate both the Catholic and the Protestant religion among the German farmers by propaganda. The All-Ukrainian organisation of the League of Militant Godless published an entire 'Anti-religious Library for the German Village' made up of such pamphlets as *Does the Peasant need God's Help in Agriculture?*, *Socialist Construction and Religion*, *How does faith come about?* There were also atheist journals in the German language. For the benefit of the urban workers of German nationality there existed a periodical, *Der Gottlose an der Drehbank*, and there was yet another more general anti-religious journal, *Neuland*. The impact of this literature was insignificant. In six German National Districts in the Ukraine

---

[1] Neurer, *Der Klassenfeind in der Sutane*, Krimer Staatsverlag, Simferopol 1930.

with a total population of 140,000 the journal *Neuland* had 234 sub-
scribers and not all of them may have been atheists.[1]

Throughout the thirties the Soviet authorities systematically 'liberated' Soviet Poles and Soviet Germans from the influence of the
Catholic Church by forcibly reducing the number of priests working
for these two nationalities. The final and decisive blow came in 1937
when the NKVD 'uncovered and destroyed quite a number of spy
nests' directed, as they said, by 'holy' ksendzy, as the Catholic priests
are called in the Soviet Union. 'Under cover of the cross and the
cassock', it was asserted, many Catholic priests had turned out to be
'spies and intelligence agents of foreign countries', primarily of Poland
but also of Japan. The blowing up of factories, the destruction of
bridges and railwaylines, and the organisation of anti-Soviet bands,
were among the crimes imputed to Catholic priests and believers.[2] The
gravity of these charges indicates that the measures taken for the
suppression of the remnant of the Catholic clergy must have been
sweeping and thorough.

V. THE CATHOLIC CHURCH AFTER 1939

Soviet Russia's territorial annexations in 1939–40 completely changed
the position of the Catholic Church in the USSR. Until 1939 Catholicism
in the Soviet Union was the religion of small and scattered minorities
which, by the outbreak of the war, were themselves being gradually
annihilated. After 1939 there was an entirely new situation. By moving
its frontiers further to the west the Soviet régime extended its direct
rule over millions of Catholics. Catholicism in its Latin and Slavo-
Byzantine form became, after Orthodoxy and Islam, the third largest
religious group in the Soviet Union. The next chapter will deal specifically with the Slavo-Byzantine Catholic Christians; here we are
concerned only with Catholics of the Latin rite. The Lithuanians were
the largest single group. They were the first Catholic nation to be
brought in its entirety under Soviet dictatorship.

It is fair to point out that Lithuania is not a Catholic country in quite
the same sense as Italy, Spain or Portugal. It includes important
religious minorities, but Catholicism is the principal spiritual force of
the country and was professed by eighty per cent of its 2,900,000
inhabitants at the time of the first Soviet occupation in June 1940. To

---

[1] *Deutsche Zentralzeitung*, April 12, 1931.
[2] F. Oleshchuk, *Borba Tserkvi protiv Naroda* (The Fight of the Church against the
People), Moscow 1939, p. 55.

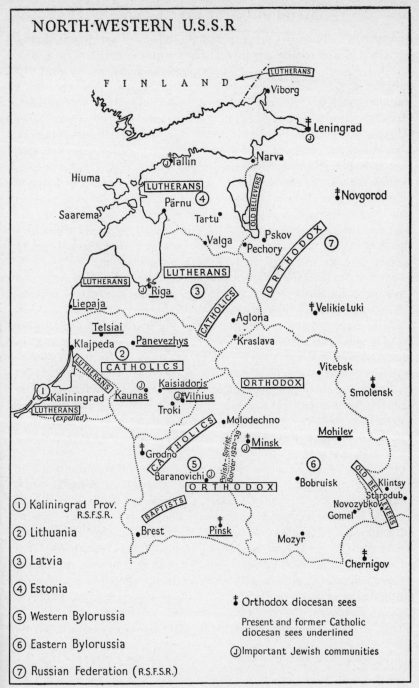

NORTH·WESTERN U.S.S.R

LUTHERANS

FINLAND

Viborg

‡Leningrad
Ⓙ

‡Tallin

Narva

Hiuma

LUTHERANS
Pärnu ④

Tartu

Saarema

Valga

OLD BELIEVERS

Pskov
Pechory

‡Novgorod

ORTHODOX ⑦

LUTHERANS
‡Riga ③
Ⓙ

Liepaja

CATHOLICS

Aglona

‡Velikie Luki

Telsiai

Panevezhys

Kraslava

Klajpeda ②

CATHOLICS

Vitebsk

LUTHERANS

Kaisiadoris

ORTHODOX

‡Smolensk

① Kaliningrad

Kaunas

Ⓙ

Ⓙ Vilnius

Troki

LUTHERANS
(expelled)

Molodechno

CATHOLICS

Polish–Soviet
Border 1920–'39

Mohilev

Ⓙ Minsk

⑥

‡Grodno

⑤

OLD BELIEVERS

Baranovichi Ⓙ

Bobruisk

Klintsy
Starodub

ORTHODOX

Novozybkov
Gomel

BAPTISTS

Mozyr

‡Chernigov

Brest

‡Pinsk

① Kaliningrad Prov.
R.S.F.S.R.

② Lithuania

③ Latvia

④ Estonia

⑤ Western Bylorussia

⑥ Eastern Bylorussia

⑦ Russian Federation (R.S.F.S.R.)

‡ Orthodox diocesan sees

Present and former Catholic
diocesan sees underlined

Ⓙ Important Jewish communities

205

this mass of Lithuanian Catholics must be added half a million Catholics who live in a compact territory in the south-eastern part of Latvia called Latgalia, possessing a folklore and language of its own. In addition to the Lithuanian-Latgalian Catholic bloc there is also a sizeable Latin Catholic population in Byelorussia. Most Byelorussian Catholics live in those Western border areas of the Byelorussian Republic which were Polish until 1939. The Orthodox Metropolitan of Minsk, Pitirim, in a personal conversation with the author in 1958, said that thirty per cent of the Byelorussian population (i.e. 2,500,000 people) were Catholics. His estimate far exceeded that given by Roman Catholic sources.[1] In two of the seven provinces of Byelorussia, those of Grodno and Molodechno, the number of Catholics was, according to the Metropolitan, higher than that of the Orthodox. Despite their numbers the Byelorussian Catholics are without bishops. The episcopal sees of Minsk, Mohilev and Pinsk remain vacant.

After the occupation of Lithuania and Latvia by the Red Army the situation of the Catholic Church almost at once became very precarious. The communists did their best to bring conditions in the newly annexed Catholic regions into line with the rest of the country. This meant that all religious instruction in school ceased, all Catholic organisations closed down, and no Catholic literature could be printed. Church property was confiscated, priests were turned out of their presbyteries and bishops had to relinquish their palaces. However, religious life in the restricted sense of religious worship continued. The homeless priests were billeted in the homes of the faithful or lived in sacristies and church towers, but they continued to say Mass and to administer the sacraments.

However great the losses which the Catholic Church suffered in Lithuania and Latvia during 1940–1, it was still in a much better position than the Orthodox Church or any other Church in Russia proper. In Lithuania parish priests were allowed to keep three hectares of land each. This was an unjust discrimination, for an ordinary peasant could own thirty hectares of land, but compared to the state of affairs in the 'old' Soviet Union, it was an unusual concession. Priests and bishops were closely supervised and suffered heavy taxation, intimidation and every form of chicanery that could be employed against them, but the régime did not feel sufficiently strong in the Baltic states to embark immediately upon open persecution of the

---

[1] According to L. Haroshka the number of Byelorussian Catholics in 1956 was about 800,000. (L. Haroshka, The Roman Catholic Church in the Belorussian SSR, Institute for the Study of the USSR, Religion in the USSR, Münich 1960, p. 100.)

clergy, which would antagonise the population. Such persecutions only started on any scale when the Soviet-Nazi war had broken out and the Soviet authorities were in a state of confusion. Then they no longer cared about popular reaction. In Lithuania alone fifteen priests were murdered by the retreating communists, ten were arrested and deported to the interior of the Soviet Union, and eighteen more were earmarked for the same fate but managed to escape from prison in the general chaos which ensued as the Nazis advanced.[1] In Latvia ten priests were either executed in the country itself or deported.[2] Those victimised in Lithuania and Latvia were humble parish priests; the hierarchy itself remained unscathed. Only the Apostolic Administrator of the small Catholic community in Estonia, Mgr. Profittlich, who was of German nationality, was arrested and disappeared without trace. The final tragedy of both the Catholic hierarchy and the Catholic Church in Lithuania and Latvia as a whole came after the end of World War II, after the Soviets had reoccupied the Baltic states.

The Hierarchy

This time the Lithuanian Catholic hierarchy suffered particularly severely. Four of the five bishops who had remained in the country were arrested, tried and deported. They were Bishop Borisevicius of Telshiai, his auxiliary Ramanauskas, Bishop Matulionis of Kaishiadorys, and Archbishop Rainys of Vilnius. The one bishop who was spared, Paltarokas of Panevezhys, owed his kinder fate to his advanced age alone. Particularly tragic was the case of Bishop Matulionis. He had as long an 'acquaintance' with the Soviet authorities as it is possible to have. He had been another of the defendants in the Cieplak trial, at which he had been sentenced to three years' imprisonment. After his release he was re-arrested, spent several years in Arctic labour camps, and in 1933 was at last allowed to go to Lithuania. He arrived there with a party of thirteen Roman Catholic priests who were exchanged for twenty-six communists.[3] He even survived a third period of Soviet imprisonment which lasted nine years, from 1946 to 1955. As a result of the amnesty he was sent back to his homeland at the age of eighty-two. His reappearance in Lithuania seemed almost a miracle, for it was generally believed that he was dead. He was not able to resume his episcopal jurisdiction but was allowed to celebrate Mass, a fact reported

[1] A. Trakiskis, *The situation of the Church and religious practices in occupied Lithuania*, New York 1944, pp. 34–6.
[2] Report on the Latvian Catholic Church by Rev. Richard Mutulis, Expulsus, Koenigstein, June–July 1957, no. 6–7.
[3] *The Times*, October 20, 1933.

by the Soviet propaganda services as an illustration of religious liberty in the USSR. In 1956 another deported bishop, Mgr. Ramanauskas (1873–1959) returned to Lithuania, but he too was unable to exercise his office in his former diocese.

In Latvia only the oldest member of the Catholic hierarchy, Archbishop Anthony Springovics (1875–1958) was left when in 1944–5 the Soviets again took control of the country. As the Nazis had forced three other Latvian bishops to leave, the Soviets were saved the trouble of themselves taking any measures against them. In June 1947 Springovics tried to replenish Latvia's Catholic hierarchy by consecrating two new bishops, Bishop Peter Strods and Bishop Kasimir Dulbinskis. Not long after his consecration Dulbinskis was arrested and sent to a labour camp in the Komi Republic. As a result of the post-Stalin amnesty he was allowed to return to Latvia.

Although the bishops released by the amnesty and allowed to return were still considered 'second-class citizens' and prevented from resuming their former positions, the situation of the hierarchy nevertheless took a turn for the better in the years following Stalin's death. In Lithuania, it became possible for three new bishops to be consecrated with the permission of the Holy See — two in 1955 and one in 1957. In Latvia Mgr. Peter Strods was able to take over the direction of the Catholic Church after the death of Archbishop Springovics in 1958. What the régime gave with one hand, however, it in part took away with the other. The members of the hierarchy were made the object of attacks in the Soviet press, which had previously completely ignored them. In Latvia the communist newspapers tried to undermine the great reputation of Springovics, even after his death, by denouncing him for an alleged predilection for the wealthy, for taking guidance from foreign broadcasts, and for encouraging anti-Soviet activities among the clergy. Even the nationalist argument that he preferred the Polish to the Latvian language was used.[1] His successor, Strods, who could not be accused of an anti-Soviet bias, was charged with being an ambitious careerist interested only in his own material prosperity.

Like all other church leaders, the Roman Catholic bishops and diocesan administrators of the Soviet Union are compelled from time to time to issue statements in favour of communist foreign policy. However, the two aged hierarchs were as a rule very reticent. Springovics' peace statements to the press were so 'short and obscure' that nobody could grasp their meaning.[2] Paltarokas' pronouncements were dignified

---

[1] *Cina*, June 17–18, 1959.   [2] *Cina*, June 18, 1959.

and his peace speeches propagated the Church's love of peace rather than the Soviet peace campaign. Some younger Catholic Church dignitaries, on the other hand, used all the clichés of the régime about the 'Anglo-American warmongers'.[1] This was not the full price which the Church had to pay, particularly at the time when it was suspected of being the ally of 'counter-revolutionary bourgeois nationalism'. The administrators of the Catholic Church were not only expected to sign personally statements in support of the régime but they had also to issue to parish priests texts of sermons 'exposing the Anglo-American imperialists and their henchmen' and 'praising the achievements of the democratic states, led by the Soviet Union'.[2] A particularly obnoxious statement by a leading Catholic Church dignitary was published soon after the Hungarian revolution. It condemned the Anglo-French Israeli aggression in Egypt whilst at the same time denouncing Western 'slander' about Hungary.[3]

The Priests

In the years of the Stalinist terror many Lithuanian and Latvian priests shared the fate of their bishops. Of 1,470 Catholic priests in Lithuania in 1945, only 741 were performing pastoral work in 1954. This means that in the space of ten years the Church lost almost half her priests, most of them probably through deportation.[4] Indeed, the Lithuanian Catholic priest was a familiar figure in many an Arctic and Siberian labour camp.[5] In Latvia the losses were not so great. Nevertheless of 187 priests as many as fifty appear to have fallen victim to communist terror, and others fled the country.[6] In 1959 the number of priests in Latvia had been reduced to 126. There were almost twice as many parishes.

To a certain extent the ranks of the Roman Catholic priests in Lithuania and Latvia can be replenished, thanks to the existence of the two Catholic seminaries in Kaunas and Riga, but the number of students is strictly limited. The Kaunas seminary is not allowed to exceed a total of seventy-five. It seems that the communist régime

[1] *Conference in Defence of Peace of all Churches and Religious Associations in the USSR*, Moscow 1952, p. 220.
[2] *Conference in Defence of Peace of all Churches and Religious Associations in the USSR*, Moscow 1952, ibid.
[3] *Izvestiya*, November 25, 1956.
[4] 'Die Römisch-Katholische Kirche in Sowjetlitauen', *Forschungsdienst Osteuropa*, Düsseldorf 1958, p. 4. Gelzinis estimates that 675 Catholic priests suffered martyrdom. Gelzinis, *Christenverfolgung in Litauen*, Koenigstein, no date, p. 50.
[5] Joseph Scholmer, *Vorkuta*, London 1954, p. 31.
[6] Albert Galter, op. cit., p. 62.

cannot close these two Catholic teaching establishments without making a mockery of the 'freedom of religious worship' guaranteed by the constitution. The Catholic seminaries are obviously exposed, like their Orthodox counterparts, to the danger of infiltration by government agents, and among several dozen students one or another can be found who will be willing to abandon the difficult life of a Catholic priest in the Soviet Union for material blandishments, or a good job, or the honour of becoming a local communist celebrity — as apostasising priests and seminarists invariably do. However, such renegades are few.

The Catholic priests in all three Catholic or part-Catholic Soviet Republics still enjoy considerable prestige, which the Soviet régime tries to reduce by every propaganda means at its disposal, from anti-religious pamphlets to belles-lettres. A novel *In the Shadow of the Altar* by Nikolaitis-Putinas 'laid bare the hypocrisy and egoism' of the priests as well as their 'indifferent and even hostile attitude to the people'.[1] The play *Western Frontier*, performed on the Lithuanian stage, purported to show that a Catholic priest might even commit vile murder.[2] Even the first full-length Lithuanian colour film, *Daybreak over the Nemunas*, showed 'a treacherous Catholic priest sowing discontent and doubt, spreading rumours and dissuading people from joining collective farms'.[3] In Byelorussian literature the anti-Catholic element also plays a significant part, which is the more surprising as the number of Catholic priests in Byelorussia is very small. Various Byelorussian communist writers such as Chernyshevich and Piestrok have depicted Catholic priests engaged in spying and sabotage.[4]

Notwithstanding the most violent anti-clerical propaganda the priest in the 'Soviet' Catholic village is 'powerful' as the communists themselves would admit.[5] He is powerful not only because his sermons influence the parishioners but also because he 'attracts young people to church' thanks to 'traditions hallowed by time, the solemnity of marriages, the stern magnificence of the Mass and the brilliance of (Catholic) festivals'.[6] Attempts have been made to replace these festivals by new Soviet feasts such as a 'Day of Harvest' and the 'Winter Feast'. Both were introduced in Lithuania. Naturally, the Catholic priest, especially in Lithuania and Latgalia, is not a religious figure only: he

---

[1] *Sovetskaya Litva*, December 11, 1958. This novel was first published in 1933, but only under the communist régime did it become a state sponsored best seller.
[2] *Sovetskoe Iskusstvo*, April 29, 1951.
[3] Moscow Radio, home service, September 20, 1953.
[4] *Byelorussian Review*, Munich 1956, no. 3, pp. 113–14.
[5] *Komsomolskaya Pravda*, July 8, 1956.   [6] *Komsomolsaya Pravda*, ibid.

represents the continuity of the nation, he is the link, the only link perhaps, with the nation's non-communist past. It is this dual religious and national significance which gives the clergy such great authority.

The Laity

The work of the priests is greatly facilitated by the faithfulness of the laity. It is they who provide the funds for the support of the priests and the repair of churches and who make it possible for Sunday and the Catholic holy days to be observed in the traditional religious way. In both Lithuania and Latvia there have frequently been powerful manifestations of religious vitality, especially since the death of Stalin. In the small Lithuanian town of Panevezhys a crowd of 15,000 attended the consecration of the two new Lithuanian bishops on September 11, 1955.[1] On July 1, 1957, an even greater crowd of 20,000 witnessed the solemn opening of a Catholic church in the port of Klajpeda (Memel).[2] The cost of building the church — over 3,500,000 roubles — was, of course, borne by the faithful themselves. However, even the Klajpeda gathering was dwarfed in January 1958 when many thousands of believers and over two hundred priests participated at the funeral of the eighty-three-year-old Bishop Kazimieras Paltarokas who, through-out his long life, had given to Lithuanian Catholics a great example of steadfastness and piety. His very last words on his death-bed were an appeal to his successors to show courage in the face of all adversity. Latvia witnessed a similar impressive religious gathering when vast masses of the people and a large number of priests joined the funeral procession of Archbishop Springovics on October 6, 1958.

Even more characteristic of the fervour of the Catholic faith in Latvia are the pilgrimages to the shrine of Our Lady in Aglona, undertaken regularly by vast crowds of believers especially during Whitsun and on the Feast of the Assumption. Even in the years of Stalinist persecution both Aglona and Kraslava, the other Latvian place of Catholic pilgrim-age, saw tens of thousands of faithful. To a Latvian communist the very word 'Aglona' is an irritant. In public, he would use the argument that the Aglona pilgrimages take place at the height of agricultural work, but his real objection is of a more fundamental nature. As long as Aglona enjoys popularity, communist ideology in Latgalia rests on shaky foundations. Certainly, the communists console themselves with the thought that not all the people thronging to Aglona go there to

---

[1] Tass in 'Russian for abroad', September 12, 1955.
[2] The figure is supplied by authoritative Catholic circles abroad. A Tass message simply speaks of 'thousands of believers'. Tass in 'Russian for abroad', July 1, 1959.

pray; some visit the place because it is a pleasant change from routine, and others make the pilgrimage because it is a deep-rooted tradition.[1] Nevertheless, the communists have no doubt that Aglona is primarily a symbol of the spiritual longings of the Latgalian people. What irks them particularly is the universal character of the Aglona pilgrimages, for the pilgrims include not only 'old folk and social misfits' but also 'cheerful boys and girls, healthy men and young children'.[2] The communists do all they can to reduce the spiritual significance of the pilgrimages. Until 1958 many priests were able to come to Aglona at Whitsun to hear confessions and to celebrate Mass. In 1959 only the parish priest of Aglona, the priest of a neighbouring parish and Bishop Strods were allowed to be there. So the pilgrims were not able to make their confessions individually, but the bishop with raised hands gave them a general absolution.[3]

Lithuania also has a great place of pilgrimage which has caused worries to the authorities. It is called Kalvariya and is situated near Lake Platyalyai in a remarkably picturesque landscape in North-Western Lithuania. Many thousands of believers flock to Kalvariya each year. In view of the popularity of the Kalvariya pilgrimages the Lithuanian Communist Party in 1959 started to organise secular 'counter-pilgrimages' during which traditional games and dances are performed.[4]

To see huge crowds of believers one does not need to attend an extraordinary event such as the funeral of a popular Church leader, the consecration of a new church or a pilgrimage. Ordinary Sunday or feast day services, whether in the Cathedral of St. James in Riga, the Church of St. Raphael or the Cathedral of St. Peter and St. Paul in Vilnius, or the Cathedral in Kaunas, are extremely well attended. Even the Tass agency admitted that a Christmas congregation in the latter comprised as many as 10,000 people.[5] Nor is the religious life of the Catholics in the Western borderlands of the Soviet Union confined to attendance at Mass on Sunday, for they observe all the typical Catholic religious practices dear to their brethren in other countries, the Sacred Heart devotions in June and the devotions to the Virgin Mary in May and October.[6]

The great handicap faced by the Communist Party in its struggle against Catholicism in Lithuania, Latgalia and Western Byelorussia is

[1] *Sovetskaya Molodezh*, September 6, 1957.
[2] *Sovetskaya Kultura*, September 5, 1959.
[3] Rev. R. Mutulis, 'Derzeitige religiöse Situation in Lettland', typescript, 1959.
[4] Sovetskaya Kultura, January 12, 1960.   [5] Tass for abroad, December 26, 1955.
[6] *Conference*, etc., op. cit., p. 174.

15. Exarch Leonid
Fedorov (1879–1935).

16. Metropolitan
Andrew Szeptycki
(1865–1944).

Odessa Province.

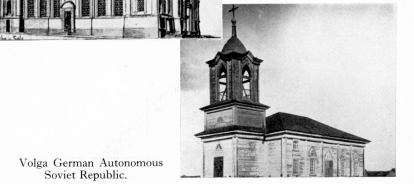

Volga German Autonomous
Soviet Republic.

Wooden Greek Catholic churches in the Carpathian Ukraine, 'Baroque' and
'Gothic' style.

17. Former Catholic churches in various parts of the Soviet Union.

the lack of really reliable anti-religious cadres. The usual policy of playing off the young against the old, the town against the country, the intellectuals against the uneducated, often proves unsuccessful in the Catholic areas. The communist newspaper published in the Lithuanian port of Klajpeda told the story of a chemistry teacher who was directed to give his fellow teachers a lecture on 'Atheist Education in Chemistry Lessons', but apparently did his best to undo the task entrusted to him. It was later discovered that he was himself a religious believer.[1] 'Religious infiltration' into communist organisations seems particularly common in the Catholic areas of the USSR. Thus in the Brest Province where the Catholic element has always been important, as many as 138 young people were expelled from the Young Communist League within a single year 'for carrying out religious rites'.[2]

The Catholic Diaspora

Only a handful are left of the many Catholic churches which existed in Czarist times throughout the Russian Empire, outside the areas with a compact Catholic population. The most important of them is the Church of St. Louis des Français in Moscow. It was founded in the reign of Catherine II and completed under Alexander I. It continued its existence unmolested throughout the years of Czarist rule, even at the time of the Napoleonic invasion. The little church in the very heart of the Soviet capital has had a tremendous significance for Catholicism in the Soviet Union. For a long time it was the only link between the oppressed Catholics of Russia and the universal Catholic Church. The Church of St. Louis of the French was able to play this part thanks to the Roosevelt-Litvinov agreement of 1933, as a result of which an American Assumptionist Father, Leopold Brown, went to Moscow and for twelve years ministered to the spiritual needs of both the Catholic members of the diplomatic corps and Soviet citizens of the Catholic faith. He was replaced in 1945 by another American, George Antonio Laberge, who spoke Russian and French fluently as well as English. As he was able to preach in Russian his services were always crowded.[3] The Soviet authorities did not like the idea of a foreigner preaching to Soviet citizens and were most anxious to sever all contacts between Russian and foreign Catholics. Their opportunity came when Father Laberge went home on leave in 1949. He was granted both an exit and a re-entry permit but, when he wanted to return to Russia, the latter

---

[1] *Sovetskaya Litva*, December 9, 1958.
[2] *Komsomolskaya Pravda*, March 13, 1975.
[3] Walter Bedell Smith, *Moscow Mission 1946–48*, London 1950, p. 270.

H

was cancelled. The parish then remained in the charge of a French Catholic priest, Jean Thomas, but not for long. The 'Council for the Affairs of Religious Cults' staged a little *coup* in the Moscow Catholic parish and one day a representative of the Council, accompanied by two women, called upon Father Thomas asking him to hand over the keys. To support the request the 'delegation' produced a petition signed by many members of the congregation demanding a Russian-speaking priest.[1] For a short time Father Thomas was able to officiate at one Mass a day but in 1950 he was expelled.

From that time on there was no more contact between Soviet and foreign Catholics in Moscow. The American Assumptionist Fathers Brassard (1950–3) and Bissonette (1953–5) never said Mass in the Church of St. Louis. They had a private chapel of their own exclusively attended by members of the diplomatic corps. But a devout congregation, up to a thousand people every Sunday, continues to flock to the Church of St. Louis, where they have a recognised priest under the jurisdiction of the Archbishop of Riga. During Archbishop Springovics' lifetime the parish used to be visited once a year by his auxiliary; in 1954 he confirmed almost four hundred persons.[2] A large section of the congregation is Polish, the epistle and gospel are read from the pulpit in both Polish and Russian, and the preaching is in Russian.[3]

The only Catholic church in Leningrad open to worshippers is, like that of Moscow, a French foundation — Notre Dame de France. A picture of Joan of Arc graces its main altar. As it is not so much before the eyes of foreign diplomats much less is known about the changing fortunes of the parish. Throughout the Leningrad blockade it was without a priest, but a small nucleus of faithful used to congregate on Saturday evenings and Sundays to pray together. In 1945 a Russian-speaking Jesuit, Father Bourgeois, went to Leningrad with the intention of taking charge of the parish but after ten days he was summoned by the police and had to leave the city within twenty-four hours.[4] Later the parish was again provided with a priest and ultimately with two priests. The Leningrad congregation seems to be larger than that of Moscow. It consists of Latvians, Lithuanians, Poles and Armenians, and as many as four Masses must be celebrated each Sunday to accommodate all the faithful.[5]

---

[1] Bedell Smith, op. cit., p. 271.
[2] Georges Bissonette, *Moscow was my parish*, New York–London–Toronto, 1956, p. 261.
[3] *Tygodnik Powszechny*, March 22, 1959.
[4] Charles Bourgeois, SJ, *A Priest in Russia and the Baltic*, Dublin–London 1953, p. 136.
[5] *Tygodnik Powszechny*, May 26, 1959.

The West Ukrainian city of Lvov has also now become part of the Catholic diaspora, although it was once a major Catholic centre where three Catholic Archbishops, a Greek Catholic, a Latin Catholic and an Armenian, held office. There are three Latin Catholic churches left in Lvov — a concession to the local Polish minority. An American visitor attending a service in one of these three churches expressed amazement at the large number of young members of the congregation.[1] In Tiflis there still exists the Catholic Church of St. Peter and St. Paul with a Georgian priest and an Armenian-Georgian congregation, and there are a few other cities where Catholic believers meet with official permission but without a priest to look after them. At the time of Father Bissonette's stay in Moscow these cities included Kishinev and Odessa.[2] In Odessa the Catholic Church was revived for a short time towards the end of World War II, thanks to the courage and devotion of the Italian Jesuit Pietro Leoni and the French Assumptionist Jean Nicholas. In September 1943 the two arrived as missionaries in Odessa, which was then still under German-Rumanian occupation. When the Soviets took the city in April 1944 the Catholic missionaries stayed and the military authorities allowed them to continue with their pastoral work among the local Catholics. They served a small church of the Slavo-Byzantine rite and a large one of the Latin rite. For a year they were able to celebrate Mass and to deliver sermons defending the existence of God, the Catholic Church, and the primacy of the Pope. The congregation included not only Catholics but also Orthodox. It was obvious that these activities could not go on for long, and at the end of April 1945, a few days before the end of the war, the two priests were arrested and charged with 'spying for a foreign power'. This was, at least for the time being, the end of the Catholic revival in Odessa. The eight thousand Catholics of the city were deprived of their pastors.[3]

In addition to the official Catholic diaspora in a few cities there existed in Stalin's time an unofficial or underground diaspora in the forced labour camps. In Siberia and the European Arctic, and especially in the Vorkuta area, captive priests improvised religious services, heard confessions and even baptised a number of people and received non-Catholic Christians into the Church of Rome. Mass was celebrated in the most impossible places, in mine-shafts, in a corner of a prison barracks, and even in offices staffed by prisoners. Those who could not attend the services themselves received the Host from their fellow-

[1] New York Times, September 20, 1957.   [2] Bissonette, op. cit., p. 165.
[3] Egon Sendler, sj, Zwölf Jahre Priester in der Sowjet-Union, Petrusblatt, July 23, 1955.

prisoners. Chalices and altar cloths were of the most primitive kind, eucharistic wine was made out of dried grapes, if it could not be smuggled into the camp, -and the Hosts were made out of wheat meal.[1]

The post-Stalin amnesties which brought freedom to most of the imprisoned Catholic priests terminated this heroic chapter in the Catholic Church's history. The Church of the catacombs came to an end, but a new unofficial Catholic diaspora assumed increasing importance. Throughout the vast expanses of the Soviet Union, in Siberia in particular, there were thousands of Catholics, in many cases ex-prisoners of Lithuanian, Polish and German nationality. They were now free workers, but free only in a purely physical sense; full freedom of religious worship was still denied them. As a rule they had no spiritual leader though it happened that priests appeared in their midst in areas far away from any railway line and from that civilisation to which they were used in better days.[2]

*   *   *   *

The Catholic Church in Russia has survived two great waves of terrible persecution, but its trials may not be over yet. As long as it fulfils its dual mandate as a branch of a universal Church and a champion of oppressed Catholic or part-Catholic ethnic groups the danger will remain, and any attempts to buy a safer existence would mean the abandonment of the Church's great mission. The relations between the Catholic Church and Soviet Communism remain full of difficulty, but the difficulty is not all on one side. The Soviet communists are not facing reality, nor are they truly sincere when they dismiss the Catholic Church as 'reactionary' and its teaching as 'unscientific'. In fact the communist anti-religious propagandists are really less disturbed by the Vatican's 'reactionary policy' and outlook than by the Vatican's interest in social problems as expressed in the social encyclicals 'Rerum Novarum' and 'Quadragesimo Anno', or in the institution of the new Feast of St. Joseph the Workman which coincides with International Labour Day on May 1. It seems that this new St. Joseph cult has quickly taken root in the Catholic areas of the Soviet Union.[3]

[1] Bissonette, op. cit., pp. 165–6: Scholmer, op. cit., pp. 129–31; Egon Sendler, SJ. ibid.
[2] Sovetskaya Rossiya, October 19, 1958.
[3] Nauka i Religiya, 1959, no. 2, p. 32.

As to communist denunciations of the Roman Catholic Church for its alleged 'unscientific' teaching, they must be contrasted with the secret awe the communists feel for Roman Catholic scholarship. An outspoken Hungarian communist, Professor Lukacs, dared to express this awe in public when he said in a lecture delivered on June 28, 1956, at the Budapest Communist Party School: 'If we put ourselves in a free debate against these Catholic theologians, where we have no organisational backing and where we cannot rely on anything except our knowledge and our arguments, we shall certainly be defeated.'[1] Lukacs' 'we' applied to communists in general, but one may apply it more particularly to the Soviet communists; they, longer than others, have been accustomed to talk to their religious opponents from a position of organisational strength masking ideological weakness.

[1] Tarsadalmi Szemle. no. 6–7 1956, pp. 68–87.

VII

Eastern Catholics

The importance of a religious group cannot be measured by the number of faithful who support it, but only by the greatness and significance of the idea which it represents. Catholics consider that a great idea is served by those small 'Uniate' Churches in Eastern Europe, the Middle East and India who have set themselves the task of bridging the ecclesiastical schism between West and East by being both 'Western' and 'Eastern' at the same time. They are 'Western' in that they pay allegiance to the Pope, head of a universal, but owing to the distribution of its members mainly Western, Church. They are 'Eastern' in respect of their rites and canon law. The Orthodox, on the other hand, see the Uniate Churches in a different light. They regard them as an impediment to Christian unity, and even such Orthodox as are inclined to be friendly towards the Catholic Church of the Latin Rite look upon the Uniates with hostility and suspicion. It may be argued that it is neither the Uniate Churches nor Orthodoxy as such which obstruct the cause of unity but the nationalist and political elements which have crept into the Churches. It is these which deprive Christianity in Eastern Europe of much of its freedom of action and make it difficult to approach the problem of Christian unity from a purely religious point of view. Be this as it may, our primary concern is not the Catholic-Orthodox antagonism but the fate of both Churches under the Soviet régime.

I. THE RUSSIAN CATHOLIC EXARCHATE

The Beginnings

Among the many Eastern Catholic Churches now in existence the one which the Soviets found in their territory on coming to power was probably the smallest. This was the Russian Catholic Church of the

Slavo-Byzantine Rite.[1] Under the Czarist régime this Church was an aspiration rather than a reality. This régime, the defender of the Orthodox faith, could not be expected to tolerate a group which could only grow at the expense of Orthodoxy. And yet the beginnings of such a Church may be traced back to the year 1905 when the October Manifesto of Czar Nicholas II granted a limited freedom of worship. This was the prelude to the opening of the first Catholic church of the Slavo-Byzantine Rite in the imperial capital of St. Petersburg, on the fourth floor of a private house in Polozov Street. The first to celebrate the liturgy there was Father Alexis Zerchaninov, an orthodox village priest of the Guberniya of Nizhnii Novgorod who had been converted to Catholicism.

It was the conversion to Catholicism of another simple Russian priest in 1909 which enabled the Russian Catholic Church to emerge from its semi-illegality. The name of the priest, who was to play such a significant part in the history of Russian Catholicism, was Father Susalev, and the place he hailed from was a town not far from Moscow with the beautiful name Bogorodsk — 'Birth of God'. The communists called it later after Nogin, a minor leader of the Revolution. Susalev did not belong to the official Russian Orthodox Church, he was a priest of the Old Believers of the Belo-Krinitsa Concord. His conversion to Catholicism created for Rome a problem which had never been posed before. Should his ordination as priest of the Old Believer Church be considered valid? Pope Pius X decided that it should. This made it clear that from Rome's point of view no greater gulf separates Catholics from Old Believers than from Orthodox. A Russian Catholic Church of the Slavo-Byzantine Rite could therefore become the bridge not only to one Church, as it had hitherto seemed, but to two, to both the Orthodox and the Old Believers.

However, apart from this wider perspective which Susalev's conversion opened, it brought one immediate advantage. It paved the way to the official recognition of Russian Catholicism under the strange name of 'Russian Old Believers in Communion with the Holy See'. The Czarist Government would never have granted recognition to a Russian Catholic Church, but it saw no harm in another Old Believer

---

[1] In writing a short account of the development of the Russian Catholic Church of the Slavo–Byzantine Rite, I was fortunate to be able to draw upon the first-hand knowledge of Father Vladimir Abrikosov who took an active part in the history of the Russian Catholic Exarchate. I have also used Prince P. Volkonsky's 'Aperçu sur l'origine del'Eglise Gréco-Russe' published in the periodical *L'Unité de l'Eglise*, 1930, no. 42; a monograph about Mother Catherine Abrikosov by de Regis published in Rome in the review *Unitas*, 1946, no. 3, as well as the unsigned article *Katolicheskaya Tserkov vostochnogo obryada v Rossii* (The Catholic Church of the Eastern Rite in Russia) published in the journal *Slaviya*, Moscow, July–October 1918, no. 6, p. 12.

group being added to the many existing ones. Having been received
into the Catholic Church, Father Susalev went to St Petersburg
where he celebrated the liturgy in Polozov Street, and as it was Easter,
this was an appropriate moment to send a telegram of greetings to the
Emperor. The Minister of the Court sent a telegram of thanks to the
'Old Believers in communion with the Holy See'. This became the
official birth-certificate of the new Church, and it was a most precious
document — a shield against all awkward police enquiries. In a sense
the little church in Polozov Street was indeed an Old Believer church,
some of its ikons came from an Old Believer shop and Father Susalev
officiated according to the Old Believer rites. It was nearly four years
before the Russian Eastern Catholic Church could move out of the
private apartment into a more appropriate special building. However, the
Eastern Catholic chapel which was opened in 1912 was in being only
four months, then it was closed down on the orders of the authorities.

Exarch Fedorov

This oddity of the Catholic Old Believer Church was the forerunner
of the Russian Catholic Exarchate which was set up in 1917 after the
downfall of Czarism. Its short history is inseparably linked with the
one and only incumbent of the office of Russian Exarch, Father Leonid
Fedorov (1879–1935). When a student at the St Petersburg Orthodox
Academy, he became favourably inclined towards Catholicism and
therefore left both the Academy and Russia. At first he went to Lvov
to Metropolitan Szeptycki, who received him into the Catholic Church
and became his spiritual father and director. Then he went to Rome
where he studied in the Collegium de Propaganda Fide, and finally to
Fribourg where he completed his theological training. In 1911, he
became a Catholic priest of the Eastern Rite but until the beginning of
the First World War he remained abroad, though paying short visits
to Russia each year. Having returned to his homeland at the outbreak
of hostilities he was arrested and exiled to Siberia. This was the first
of his many contacts with the Russian police authorities.

Time for action came for Leonid Fedorov only after the February
Revolution of 1917 when the Provisional Government established full
freedom of worship. In May 1917, the first Synod of Russian Catholics
took place under the chairmanship of Metropolitan Szeptycki. It was
held in a festive atmosphere in the presence of four Latin Catholic
bishops and several priests. A decree of the Metropolitan establishing
a Russian Exarchate was read out in the Russian and Latin languages,
whereupon the Metropolitan himself conferred the title of Exarch on

Father Fedorov. Szeptycki had full powers for the establishment of the Exarchate and the appointment of the Exarch; Pope Benedict XV officially confirmed his action four years later.

As Exarch Fedorov saw it, the main task of his group was not to proselytise individual members of the Orthodox Church but rather to propagate the idea of the Union of the Eastern and Western Churches. Its aim was to begin to remove the psychological and historical obstacles to this Union by patient explanation. The small Russian Catholic parishes of the Slavo-Byzantine Rite existing in Petrograd and Moscow served for Fedorov a dual purpose. They were a living proof that Russian nationality and allegiance to Rome did not exclude one another and were also convenient bases for work for the *rapprochement* between the Catholic and Orthodox Churches. In Petrograd, where the Exarch had his secretariat in the heart of the city, on the Nevsky Prospect, he celebrated the Liturgy himself every Sunday. It was regularly attended by 500 persons and on specially solemn occasions by as many as 2,000. The congregation always included Orthodox Christians, even priests.[1]

It was no intention of Exarch Fedorov to have the Petrograd and Moscow parishes inflated by mass conversions which might only create a further obstacle to reconciliation with the Orthodox. It was much more important to enter into a dialogue with the Orthodox and dispel the old misunderstandings about Catholicism. Exarch Fedorov was a man of great erudition and endowed with exceptional rhetorical powers. This together with his conciliatory nature, contributed greatly to the success of the Catholic-Orthodox meetings in which the representatives of the two Churches came together in the early years of the Soviet régime to discuss religious problems. The Orthodox priests participating in them did so with the approval of Patriarch Tikhon. These meetings resulted in friendly and cordial relations between the Orthodox ecclesiastics on the one hand and the Exarch and other Russian Catholics such as Father Abrikosov, the priest of the Moscow Catholic parish, on the other.[2] Prominent among high Orthodox churchmen who showed active interest in coming to terms with Rome was Bishop Ilarion Troitsky, a member of the Supreme Ecclesiastical Administration. He was arrested together with many other bishops and priests and implicated in the 'Trial of the fifty-four', all Orthodox

---

[1] Bishop Boleslav Sloskans, *Vospominaniya ob Exarkhe Fedorove* (Recollections about Exarch Fedorov), *Rossiya i Vselenskaya Tserkov*, 1958, no. 40, p. 4.

[2] The work of Father Vladimir Abrikosov came to an end when he was expelled from Russia in September 1922 together with a large number of other Moscow intellectuals.

churchmen, which took place in April–May 1922. As Soviet anti-religious legislation sharpened, Exarch Fedorov's meetings with the Orthodox assumed a more matter-of-fact character and explored the possibility of a joint protest against communist Church persecution.

The Exarch and Byelorussia

There was, however, one part of the Soviet Union where Exarch Fedorov had not simply a long-term, almost academic mission to perform, but where his task might have been of an urgent practical nature had the communist régime allowed him freedom to act. This was Byelorussia, a country with Catholic and Uniate traditions of longer standing. The official conversion of the Byelorussian Uniates to Orthodoxy had taken place only eighty years before the Russian Bolsheviks took power. It dated back to the Synod of Polotsk of February 12, 1839. This Synod consisted of three bishops and twenty-one priests, which, as A. M. Ammann, the Catholic historian of the Russian Church, put it laconically, is not much to represent two and a half million faithful.[1] About two-thirds of the Uniate secular clergy, but only one-quarter of the members of the monastic orders, subscribed to the 'Act of Union' drawn up by the Polotsk Synod.[2] Priests who persisted in remaining hostile to the liquidation of the Uniate Church were put into special monasteries under supervision— prison monasteries would be the right term.[3] Many of these imprisoned Uniate priests later made their submission to the Orthodox Church but some chose secular professions rather than become Orthodox priests. However, not all conversions were sincere and many of those who joined the Russian Orthodox Church outwardly, were actually 'papist agents within Orthodoxy'.[4] Various reports by the Over-Procurator of the Holy Synod, K. P. Pobedonostsev, bear witness to the survival of the Uniate outlook in Byelorussia right to the end of the nineteenth century. In his report to the Czar for 1884, Pobedonostsev denounced the drift towards the Catholic Church in the Russian West. Some of those attracted to Catholicism, he complained, belonged only formally to Orthodoxy and were waiting for the moment to leave its fold altogether. In the nineties of the nineteenth century the same Pobedonostsev spoke of a new *rapprochement* with Catholicism on the part of the descendants of former Uniates. According to him there were even priests belonging to an ex-Uniate milieu who were trying to reintroduce rites and methods

---

[1] A. M. Ammann, SJ, *Storia de la Chiesa Russa*, Torino 1958, p. 446.
[2] Prof. I. Shabatin, *Iz istorii vossoedineniya belorusskikh Uniatov* (From the history of the Byelorussian Uniates), *Zh.M.P.*, 1951, no. 11, pp. 53–5.
[3] Shabatin, op. cit., p. 58.   [4] Shabatin, op. cit., p. 59.

peculiar to Catholicism. After 1905 when there was a certain relaxation of Pobedonostsev's own rigid 'religious policy', attempts were made at an outright re-establishment of the Uniate Church. The Pyrrhic victory of Orthodoxy in Byelorussia had a direct bearing on the work of Exarch Fedorov. In fact, the shortly outlined historical background alone explains the extraordinary success of the Exarch in June 1922 when he paid a visit to the Byelorussian town of Mohilev, once one of the most important centres of the Uniate Church.

At first Fedorov's appearance in Mohilev caused amazement. Here was a priest who with his beard and Orthodox attire looked like a 'pop' and yet he gave his blessing to Latin Catholic priests who knelt down before him. But when the local people learned who this 'pop' was, amazement changed to joy and the rumour *'Uniya vernulas'*—'The Union has returned' went from mouth to mouth. The Exarch Fedorov celebrated the Liturgy according to the pure Slavo-Byzantine Rite in the presence of a vast number of people, mostly Orthodox. Even Orthodox priests came to hear the sermon and the singing was by the Orthodox Church choirs. A delegation of Byelorussian Orthodox intellectuals came to see the Exarch, asking him to visit Mohilev again and not to forget that there was a widespread desire 'for the speedy re-establishment of the Union'.

We have described things as they appeared to Exarch Fedorov himself and as he reported them immediately after his return to Petrograd on June 27, 1922, in a letter to Metropolitan Szeptycki. The welcome the Exarch received from the Byelorussian ex-Uniate Orthodox entitled him to believe that his Church could have a great future in Byelorussia. Support for the re-establishment of the Union may have been dictated not only by religious but also by national motives. The Byelorussian intellectuals must have thought that a resurrected Uniate Church would become a Byelorussian National Church in the same way as the Uniate Church was a Ukrainian National Church in Eastern Galicia. Exarch Fedorov was certainly sympathetic to the spiritual renaissance of the 'unhappy people', as he once called the Byelorussians, and he also felt that the Catholic Church, within the framework of its universal mission, should give encouragement to the Byelorussian national cause. In his correspondence with Metropolitan Szeptycki we find a strong insistence on the use of Byelorussian instead of Polish priests in Byelorussia.

The Trial of the Exarch and the End of the Exarchate

Fedorov's plans for following up and consolidating his first success in Byelorussia were foiled by the wave of persecution which broke on the Catholic Church in the summer of 1922 and which halted all his activities. This persecution culminated in the Cieplak-Budkiewicz Trial in which the Exarch himself was a prominent and, in the eyes of the communist Public Prosecutor Krylenko, even the most outstanding defendant. Indeed, it must be recognised that Krylenko showed great perspicacity in assessing properly the Exarch's potential significance despite the smallness of the ecclesiastical organisation at his command. He saw in him, and rightly so, the promoter of a Catholic-Orthodox religious united front which, as a communist, Krylenko was unable to interpret in anything but a political sense. This is why in the court room he made the strange but significant statement that Fedorov must be judged not only for what he had done but also for what he might still do.[1] For this Fedorov was sentenced to ten years' imprisonment.

Exarch Fedorov did not serve his full sentence but nevertheless in various forms his martyrdom continued until his death. When he was released from prison after three years under an amnesty, he could have led a quiet life in some provincial town, for his release was made conditional on his not going to Russia's six largest cities. However, this quiet life would have meant a betrayal of his mission. Although he could not go to the Exarchal see in Petrograd, which meanwhile had become Leningrad, he went to the place where he had seen his greatest triumph and where he was needed most — Mohilev. In fact as soon as the Mohilev Catholics knew about his release they invited him to their city, but shortly after his arrival there he was arrested and sent to the ill-famed Solovki island in the White Sea. There were a large number of other priests in Solovki and one of his fellow-prisoners tells how Fedorov took this opportunity to continue even as a prisoner the dialogue and the *rapprochement* with the Orthodox.[2] From Solovki he was sent to Kotlas in the Vyatka Province in the northern part of European Russia. Finally the GPU gave him permission to move to Vyatka itself, where he died in 1935. In the last weeks of his life he shared a room with a railwayman, his wife and his three children, and it was from this good-natured and semi-literate railwayman that the Red Cross, and ultimately the world at large, learned about the death of the Russian Catholic Exarch.

By ordinary human yardsticks this was a sad end, but it was not so from the Exarch's own point of view. It was his deep conviction that the Union of the Eastern and Western Churches to which his life was

[1] Captain Francis McCullagh, *The Bolshevik Persecution of Christianity*, London 1924, p. 231.
[2] Boleslav Sloskans, op. cit., p. 5.

devoted would not come in an easy way, but only as the result of great sacrifices and martyrdom. No doubt, he saw his lonely death in exile without receiving the Last Sacraments and without a friend about him, as a contribution to a great cause.

Leonid Fedorov was not the only martyr to die for the Union of the Churches in Russia, one of the great and seemingly hopeless causes for which men and women have lain down their lives on Russian soil, or to be more precise in Russian prisons, Russian labour camps and places of exile. Another person whose name will figure in the spiritual history of Russia and certainly in the history of the efforts to reconcile Russian Christians with the Church of Rome was Catherine Abrikosov, foundress of the first and only Eastern Catholic Russian order for women, a community of Dominican tertiaries. It came into being shortly before the October Revolution but the number of its members grew continuously during the first five years of Soviet power. Almost all of them were Russian by nationality and some were highly educated women. Mother Catherine herself came from a rich and well-known Russian family; in November 1923 she and all the sisters were arrested for belonging to an 'illegal organisation' and giving religious instruction to children. Finally, they were tried and sentenced to long terms of imprisonment, Mother Catherine herself to ten years. From then on they were scattered all over the prisons of Russia but wherever two found themselves together they tried to carry on a community life of prayer. As to Mother Catherine, she was released from prison one year before the expiration of her punishment but was re-arrested for conducting religious propaganda among communist girls. She died in July 1936 in the hospital of the Butyrka prison.

A further victim of the persecution of the Russian Catholic Church was Father Potapii Yemelyanov, parish priest in the Eastern Ukrainian village of Nizhnaya Bogdanovka in the Guberniya of Kharkov. His was an extraordinary case. By his own theological studies he had found the way to Catholicism. The large majority of his parishioners followed him and Nizhnaya Bogdanovka thus became a small Eastern Catholic island in Orthodox surroundings. It was the communists who released him in 1919 from the prison where he had been confined during the Civil War, since the 'white' administration considered him a deserter from Orthodoxy and a political criminal. It was the communist régime also which decided that the church of Nizhnaya Bogdanovka should be handed over to the Uniates since they were the largest local religious group. However, it did not take long before communist intolerance destroyed the small Ukrainian Uniate peasant community. In 1927 Yemelyanov was arrested and sent to Solovki and from there he never returned.[1]

So the Russian Catholic Church of the Slavo-Byzantine Rite was destroyed as an institution by the Soviets and those who might have perpetuated it as an ideal were physically exterminated. This could have been the end of Eastern Catholicism in the Soviet Union, but it was not. The territorial annexations carried out by the Soviets during World War II confronted them once again with an Eastern Catholic Church. The Soviet communists considered these new Eastern Catholic communities with even greater suspicion and hostility than the Church of Exarch Fedorov because they regarded them as an expression not only of religious but also of national opposition. The occupation of Eastern Poland, which became Western Byelorussia and Western Ukraine, brought Soviet power into contact with two Eastern Catholic communities of quite different numerical size and historical, religious and political significance — the small and scattered Byelorussian Eastern Catholic group and the large and compact Greek Catholic Church or Uniate Church of Eastern Galicia.

II. THE GREEK CATHOLIC CHURCH OF BYELORUSSIA

In Western Byelorussia the majority of the Byelorussians were Catholics of the Latin Rite. The problem of the Union was, therefore, not of the same importance as in Eastern Byelorussia with its orthodox population. When the Red Army marched into Western Byelorussia there was no real Church of the Slavo-Byzantine Rite there, but only two or three small monastic communities propagating this rite, and a few isolated Eastern Catholic parishes under the jurisdiction of Latin Catholic bishops, a fact which greatly impeded their development. The total number of Eastern Catholics did not exceed 30,000. It is a strange irony of fate that the foundation of an Eastern Catholic Byelorussian Church took place only under the Soviet régime, that most cruel oppressor of Eastern Catholicism.

It was once again Metropolitan Szeptycki who added a new chapter to the history of the Catholic Church in Eastern Europe by founding the Byelorussian Exarchate and appointing an Exarch in May 1940 in the person of Father Anton Nemantsevich (1893–1943). He was a well-educated priest who in the early twenties had shared the martyrdom of the Catholic Church in Russia — he had been a prison inmate in both Moscow and Petrograd — after which he was allowed to leave for Poland. After studies in Rome he became the leading champion of

[1] *Rossiya i Vselenskaya Tserkov*, 1957, no. 36, pp. 27–34.

Eastern Catholicism among the Byelorussians and even published a newspaper to propagate the idea of the Union. He was the obvious choice for the post of a Byelorussian Exarch. The appointment was kept secret and only under the German occupation of Byelorussia was Nemantsevich's position legalised. He was then able to issue pastoral letters to the Byelorussian people as well as various decrees: for instance, one on the use of the Byelorussian language in sermons. This nazi benevolence was of short duration; in the autumn of November 1942, the Gestapo arrested Nemantsevich. After that he was not heard of again. Either he was killed by the nazis or he died in prison.[1]

With the Exarch gone, the Byelorussian Greek Catholic Church ceased to exist in Eastern Europe. The Nazis saved the Soviets the trouble of liquidating it when they returned to Byelorussia in 1944. Such isolated Greek Catholic parishes as still survived were soon disbanded. Communist persecution of the Byelorussian Uniates had an epilogue, as it were, at the other end of the communist world—in Kharbin, in Manchuria. There was a small branch of the Marian Fathers, who before 1939 had upheld the cause of the Union in Poland's Byelorussian districts. Its members were arrested by the Chinese and extradited to the Soviets.

The next important event affecting Byelorussian Eastern Catholicism also happened outside the borders of Russia. This was the appointment by the Pope in 1960 of a Byelorussian Catholic bishop of the Eastern Rite—the first since 1838. He was entrusted with the task of looking after the spiritual welfare of the Byelorussian emigration in Western and Central Europe. The consecration of this bishop was a definite indication that Rome believed that the Byelorussian Catholics of the Eastern Rite still have a future.

III. THE GREEK CATHOLIC CHURCH OF THE UKRAINE

The ordeals which were to befall the Greek Catholic Church of the Western Ukraine were, of course, infinitely greater than the sufferings of the small Byelorussian Greek Catholic groups. Indeed there are few religious groups in the whole of the Soviet Union which have been so ruthlessly persecuted as the Ukrainian Greek Catholics or Uniates.

Metropolitan Andrew Szeptycki

The extension of Soviet rule to the Western Ukraine brought the Soviets in contact not only with the largest single body of Eastern

[1] A. Haroshka, *Aitsets Anton Nemantsevich, Bozhym Shlyakham*, no. 70–5, pp. 49–54.

Catholics existing anywhere in the world, but also with a great church-man, the like of whom could not exist in Russia proper — Metropolitan Szeptycki (1865–1944). We have already mentioned him several times in this chapter but we have not yet properly appraised this great personality and his spiritual and ecclesiastical significance. Without such an appraisal, his life and work and also his Church cannot be seen in proper perspective.[1]

The ideal which Szeptycki primarily served as Metropolitan of Lvov was the healing of the split between the Eastern and the Western Church. Szeptycki belonged to the West, but he understood and loved the East. He felt very strongly that the Christian East and the Christian West differed not in beliefs but only in their ways of applying their beliefs to their worship. He was deeply convinced that he himself had a great mission to perform in bringing the Churches closer to one another and many things happened in his lifetime to confirm him in this. Szeptycki acceded to the Metropolitan see of Lvov in 1901. A few years later, the Russian Revolution of 1905 brought a weakening of the Russian Caesaropapism which was such an obstacle to any new approach towards a *rapprochement* of the Churches. Later, in 1917, this Caesaro-papism was swept away entirely and the great opportunity seemed to have come to reconcile the Orthodox East and the Catholic West, with the help of Szeptycki's bridge-church which was both Catholic and Orthodox. But the emergence of a new Russian autocracy more tyrannical than that of the Czars made this impossible.

Metropolitan Andrew Szeptycki pursued no ambitions and aims of his own which were not the ambitions and aims of Rome. The Holy See had given him extraordinary and unprecedented powers of canonical jurisdiction over all Eastern Rite Catholics in the whole of widespread Russia. Pope Piux X granted Szeptycki the powers of a Patriarch for a sixth of the earth's surface. He could nominate and consecrate bishops without asking Rome's confirmation of his decisions.

Szeptycki's was not a national but a supra-national mission and the Metropolitan was indeed a cosmopolitan and not a nationalist. His aristocratic family background was at least as much Polish as Ukrainian and of his two brothers one became a Ukrainian like himself and the other a Pole. At the age of six Count Roman Szeptycki, as he was

[1] The fullest biography of Szeptycki is Dr. Gregor Prokoptchuk's, *Der Metropolit*, Muenchen 1955. I have had the opportunity of discussing the personality of the Metropolitan with a number of people of different faiths who had an insight into his mind, such as Professor Hans Koch, historian and protestant theologian, who met the Metropolitan in his capacity as German army officer during World War II, and Lev Gillet, who was Szeptycki's secretary in the twenties and later became an archimandrite of the Orthodox Church.

originally, already had a fluent command of French, a language he often used in later life. As a Galician he was also an Austrian, which brought him close to the German cultural sphere and further strengthened the cosmopolitan streak in him.

All this has to be pointed out because of the attempts to make of Szeptycki a local Eastern Galician figure and spokesman of Ukrainian nationalism. It should not be denied that Szeptycki was this too, but the Ukrainian national role he played was as it were a by-product of his greatness as an outstanding personality of the Church. The Metropolitan of Lvov was the natural leader of the people of Eastern Galicia, the poor Ukrainian peasant people who had such a hard struggle for national and cultural survival. It greatly added to the splendour of the Metropolitan that he belonged to a noble family for, as a rule, the Galician aristocrats were Poles and enemies of the Ukrainian people. Szeptycki was an exception; he could speak with Counts and Princes, with generals and ministers, on a basis of equality. And when in later years he talked to Polish officials, nazi gauleiters and Soviet commissars, it was the aristocrat who addressed upstarts and usurpers. It was not only the prestige of his high office but also his erudition, his diplomatic skill and his knowledge of the ways of the world, which made him tower above the local Ukrainian politicians of Eastern Galicia who looked to him for help and guidance. In these circumstances it was unavoidable but highly regrettable from the point of view of the Church, that Church and politics had become, in the Metropolitan's person, inextricably intertwined. He was confronted with the perpetual dilemma either of disappointing the masses of the Ukrainian people by avoiding those political responsibilities which, in the general belief, were part of the Metropolitan's office, or of discharging the secular duties he was expected to perform as President of the Ukrainian National Council in Lvov and so jeopardising the Church's future chances.

In this dilemma lies the tragedy of Metropolitan Szeptycki, which was also the tragedy of many priests of his Church throughout Eastern Galicia. In many villages and townships the priests were the leaders of the Ukrainian national movement without, of course, having the wide cosmopolitan background of the Metropolitan. As their horizon was limited, one wonders whether the Church's universality was not sacrificed in many cases to local national aspirations. In any case, the strength of the human, political element which was bound to permeate the Church of an oppressed and frustrated nation like the Western Ukrainians made it most vulnerable to the attacks of its enemies.

The First Soviet Occupation

During the first Soviet occupation of the Western Ukraine the communists were still so overawed by the prestige of Metropolitan Andrew that they did not dare to touch him. In a way, Szeptycki was protected by historical precedent. In September 1914 when the Czarist armies captured Lvov, then an Austrian city, Szeptycki was arrested and deported first to Nizhnii Novgorod, later to Kursk and finally to Suzdal. This deportation was intended to inflict a mortal blow on both Ukrainian nationalism and the Greek Catholic Church of Eastern Galicia. A quarter of a century had elapsed since this deportation of Szeptycki, but the people of Eastern Galicia had not yet forgotten it. Despite all its hostility to Szeptycki, the Soviet régime was not at liberty to carry out an action against him which in everybody's mind would have evoked memories of the Czarist anti-Ukrainian oppressive policies. In addition, any violent action against the Metropolitan would have stirred up active and passive opposition to the régime and rendered the Sovietisation of Eastern Galicia more difficult.

The losses which the Greek Catholic Church itself suffered during the first Soviet occupation, which lasted twenty-two months, were comparatively small. Of course, the Soviet authorities carried out most of the anti-religious measures implemented in the Soviet Union proper, especially the elimination of all religion from the schools, and the closing of all monasteries. But pastoral work was allowed to go on and the Metropolitan was able to preserve close contact with his priests and to issue to them a large number of instructions on how to fulfil their duties under the new difficult circumstances. For instance, he urged them to visit hospitals in civilian attire since priests were officially prohibited from entering them. He also empowered them to look after the spiritual welfare of Orthodox believers if they requested it. It must be realised that Eastern Galicia, despite Soviet occupation, was from a religious point of view infinitely better off than the Eastern Ukraine. Many East Ukrainians tried to take advantage of this, and had their children baptised, or themselves received Holy Communion, in Lvov, Stanislav, Drogobych or even in smaller West Ukrainian towns and villages. Often they had only the modest wish to get holy pictures ('paper ikons') or little crosses. For all this they frequently turned to Greek Catholic priests. So the first Soviet occupation was not merely a time of trial for the Greek Catholic Church of Eastern Galicia but also one of hopes of expanding her spiritual influence. Nevertheless, the Church had her losses; forty priests were arrested and deported and about a hundred left their parishes to escape Soviet persecution. Some of them emigrated with the help of the German resettlement commission which, by agreement with the Soviets, evacuated the entire German minority from Eastern Galicia.

The end of the first Soviet occupation came as a great relief to Szeptycki and his Church. However, the nazi occupation which followed brought neither national freedom for the Ukrainian people nor freedom for Greek Catholic missionary activities in the Central and Eastern Ukraine. Szeptycki as a prince of the Catholic Church was naturally an opponent of nazi neo-paganism and racialism and as a Ukrainian he was disappointed in Hitlerite Germany from the very first moment of occupation. He had given his support to Jaroslav Stetsko, the son of a Greek-Catholic priest who, between the Soviet evacuation and the German take-over, was Prime Minister of a short-lived Ukrainian Government.[1] Stetsko's removal from premiership and arrest by the Germans was at the same time an affront to the Metropolitan who had acted as Stetsko's chief sponsor. From then on relations between Szeptycki and the German overlords remained difficult. Still, it would be correct to say that the Germans were for him a lesser evil than the Soviets. He could find no common ground with nazi and Gestapo functionaries but it was different with army officers, especially those of Austrian origin, who showed understanding of Szeptycki's point of view and had a proper appreciation of both the importance of the Ukrainian factor and the significance of the Metropolitan of Lvov for the Ukrainian people.

The Official Liquidation of the Church

Szeptycki just lived to see the second Soviet occupation of the Western Ukraine, without himself experiencing its bitter fruits for his clergy and his Church. The soldiers of the First Ukrainian Front entered Lvov on July 27, 1944, but only on October 15 was Soviet control re-established in the whole of the Western Ukraine. Szeptycki died little more than two weeks later, on November 1, 1944. His funeral was celebrated with considerable pomp; it was attended by the Prime Minister of the Soviet Ukraine, Nikita Sergeevich Khrushchev himself. Even the enthronement of Szeptycki's successor, Metropolitan Joseph Slipy, could still be carried out with dignity.[2]

For a few months both the State and the Moscow Patriarchate seemed

[1] John A. Armstrong, *Ukrainian Nationalism 1939–1945*, Columbia University, New York, 1955, p. 36.
[2] *Die ersten Opfer des Kommunismus, Weissbuch über die religiösen Verfolgungen in der Ukraine*, Muenchen 1953, p. 36.

to accept the existence of the Greek Catholic Church. A delegation from the new Metropolitan was allowed to go to Moscow, where the locum tenens of the Patriarchal see received it kindly. More than that, Alexis sent both greetings and books to the Metropolitan of Lvov.[1] The delegation was also received by Soviet government officials. During this meeting it became clear that the Kremlin wanted the Uniate Church to make an active contribution in the fight against the nationalist guerillas then taking place in the Western Ukraine. This the Church could not and would not do, apart from insisting on the observance of the commandment 'Thou shall not kill'.[2] As the Church did not support the Government in this respect, a savage persecution started.

Faced by a recalcitrant and hostile Ukrainian population, the authorities believed that they must act quickly against every form of local resistance. They turned their primary attention to the Greek Catholic Church, historically the bulwark of Ukrainian nationhood in Eastern Galicia, which, in the absence of any legal Ukrainian nationalist organisations, was bound to assume particular importance. The new Greek Catholic Metropolitan might have become the real leader of the West Ukrainian people, as Szeptycki had been. Thus the Greek Catholic or Uniate problem with its strong historical roots created for the communist authorities an entirely new situation on the Soviet 'religious front', a situation not to be mastered with the conventional methods of atheist and anti-clerical action. Certainly, these methods too were used. On April 11, 1945, the NKVD arrested Metropolitan Slipy and four other Ukrainian bishops, and the most active members of the Greek Catholic parochial clergy suffered the same fate either immediately or soon afterwards. But at the same time it was felt that in addition to arrests, trials and deportations, something had to be done for which there was no precedent in Soviet practice and for which only Czarist Russian policy could be taken as a guide. Indeed, Stalin and Khrushchev, his viceroy in the Ukraine, followed the examples of Empress Catherine II and Emperor Nicholas I and exploited the human elements in the Russian Orthodox Church to eliminate another Church which was considered a source of disaffection and separatism in Russia's Western border regions.

This is the background to the emergence of a strange movement which between 1945 and 1950 was at work within the Greek Catholic Church and which, with visible official Soviet backing, advocated the Church's self-liquidation and its reunion with the Orthodox Church of the Moscow Patriarch. This movement, if so it may be called, was not

[1] *Zh.M.P.*, 1945, no. 2, p. 24.   [2] A. Galter, op. cit, p. 90.

confined to Eastern Galicia with its 3,500,000 Catholics of the Eastern
Rite, but also affected the Transcarpathian Ukraine which Czechoslovakia ceded to the Soviet Union in July 1945, and the Ukrainian-
speaking part of Slovakia which has tendentiously been described as
'Pryashovskaya Rus'. This might be translated as the 'Pryashov
Ukraine'.[1] In these two territories where there were 350,000 and
200,000 Greek Catholics respectively, the Greek Catholic Church
played the same part of a champion of Ukrainian national aspirations
as she did in Eastern Galicia. In the Transcarpathian Ukraine, in
particular, the Greek Catholic clergy exercised a decisive influence on
the Ukrainian national movement, and one of its members, Father
Augustin Voloshin, became Prime Minister of the autonomous Ukrainian
Government, which was set up soon after the Munich crisis of 1939 in
the township of Hust. In both these territories, with the exception of a
few Slovaks and Hungarians, the members of the Greek Catholic
Church were of Ukrainian nationality.

The three branches of the Greek Catholic Church of the Ukrainian
people were abolished and joined to the Orthodox Church by three
different methods. In Eastern Galicia the end of the Union with Rome
was decided in March 1946 by the self-appointed Synod of Lvov,
almost all 216 participants in which were Greek Catholic priests. They
represented less than ten per cent of the original number of Galicia's
Greek Catholic clergy. The Synod, which virtually coincided with the
trial of the Greek Catholic bishops arrested the year before, was a result
of official terrorism and blackmail. Attendance at the Synod was an
almost certain guarantee against further persecution by the authorities
and it is not to be wondered at that some of the Greek Catholic priests
were prepared to pay this price for their safety and that of their families.

Orthodox and Catholic sources differ greatly as to how popular the
decisions of the Lvov Synod were with the priests and believers of
Eastern Galicia. The Orthodox consider that the movement for union
with the Patriarchal Church was later joined by the vast majority of the
Uniate priests, but even they admit that 'a certain percentage of hard-
bitten Uniates' were left, chiefly Basilian monks, who having refused to
join the Orthodox Church, engaged in secular work.[2] The Catholics, on
the other hand, state that nearly 900 priests remained faithful to the
Church of Rome, whilst as many as 300 protested in a message to
Molotov against the so-called 'Committee of Initiative for the

[1] Pryashov, in Slovak Prešov, in Hungarian Eperies, is a small town of 20,000
inhabitants. It has a Ukrainian-speaking hinterland and is now the see of an Orthodox
bishop.
[2] *One Church*, vol. xii, 1958, no. 7–8, p. 261.

Transference of the Greek Catholic Church to Orthodoxy', the Committee instrumental in summoning the Synod.[1]

The nucleus of this Committee consisted of three priests, Dr. Kostelnyk, Melnyk and Pelvetsky, each representing one of the three East Galician dioceses — Lvov, Peremyshl and Stanislav. If personal ambitions guided the three chief promotors of the union with Orthodoxy, they were indeed amply fulfilled. Melnyk and Pelvetsky became bishops and Kostelnyk received the lesser, though infinitely rarer, title of 'Protopresbyter'. There was only one other 'Protopresbyter' in the whole Russian Orthodox Church, namely the priest in charge of the Patriarchal chancellery in Moscow. However, in the case of Gavriil Fyodorovich Kostelnyk (1886–1948) at least, personal gain may not have been the primary motive. The case was much more complicated. In the first place, Kostelnyk was exposed to particularly heavy pressure. Already during the first occupation of Galicia the Soviet authorities had arrested one of his sons to make the father more pliable.[2] Whilst this son was a Soviet prisoner his two other sons had served with the Ukrainian SS division and had fled to the West. This was, of course, no small liability for Kostelnyk once the Soviets returned to Lvov. On the other hand, he was genuinely a man of Eastern ecclesiastical orientation and he viewed with anxiety certain 'Latinising influences' in the Greek Catholic Church. It is further relevant that he was not born in Galicia but in a Ruthenian village of Southern Hungary, now part of Yugoslavia. Therefore he was not attached to the West Ukrainian soil to the same extent as other members of the local clergy and he may have found it easier to renounce the Greek Catholic Church in so far as it was Ukrainian.

In the Transcarpathian Ukraine the authorities dispensed with the comedy of a pseudo-synod. The end of the union was simply proclaimed at a church ceremony in Uzhgorod in August 1949. No pretence was made that a majority of the Carpatho-Ukrainian clergy had renounced the Union with Rome. In fact, the *Journal of the Moscow Patriarchate* admitted that, by 1948, only one Uniate priest had gone over to Orthodoxy and that the question of a reunion then appeared to some people 'almost hopeless'.[3] The quick change of heart within one year must be explained within the context of political developments.[4]

[1] Albert Galter, op. cit., pp. 95–9.
[2] *Die ersten Opfer des Kommunismus*, op. cit., p. 32.
[3] *Zh.M.P.*, 1949, no. 10, p. 5.
[4] In October 1948, the large Greek Catholic Church of Rumania with its one and a half million faithful was forcibly incorporated in the Rumanian Orthodox Church. Clearly, there was an over-all Soviet directive for the liquidation of a Church with close ties with Rome in all countries under communist control.

Soviet rule in the Transcarpathian Ukraine was very much tightened in 1948–9 especially in connection with the collectivisation of agriculture there and the sharpening of the Cold War. In this situation the position of the Greek Catholic Church became untenable not only because of its national-Ukrainian character but also because of its connections with the West — West meaning not only Rome but also the large Carpatho-Ukrainian emigration in the United States of which the vast majority belongs to the Greek Catholic Church. The authorities 'assisted' its liquidation not only by granting great latitude to the Orthodox in proselytising, but also by promising freedom to imprisoned Uniate priests on condition that they recognised the jurisdiction of the Moscow Patriarch.

As in Eastern Galicia, the unification of Greek Catholics and Orthodox in the Transcarpathian Ukraine could only be implemented after the removal of the legitimate church leader. The head of the Greek Catholic Church of the Transcarpathian Ukraine, Mgr. Romzha (1911–47) died on November 1, 1947, in mysterious circumstances, after a carefully engineered 'accident'.[1] The death of this young and popular bishop became the object of pious local legends which in themselves prove the survival of his Church in the hearts of the people. Later it became known that Mgr. Romzha, in premonition of his death, had appointed a successor, Mgr. Chira, whom he had secretly consecrated bishop. Chira was arrested in 1948 and spent ten years in a Siberian camp.

Lastly, the Greek Catholic Church of Eastern Slovakia was abolished in April 1950 by a Conference held in Pryashov at which priests formed only a small minority of the 820 'delegates'. How many of them were really church people and how many attended on the orders of the communist authorities it is impossible to say. This event took place outside the political frontiers of the Soviet Union but inside the jurisdictional boundaries of the Moscow Patriarchal Church, for only a year later did the Orthodox Church of Czechoslovakia acquire autocephalous status. It is significant that the Pryashov Synod met two years after the communists had established totalitarian rule over Slovakia and after the arrest of both the Greek Catholic bishop of Pryashov, Mgr. Hojdich and his vicar, bishop Hopko.

Voluntary or Forced Unification?

It was the communist atheist State rather than the Orthodox Church authorities which post-factum provided a religious motive for the Greek Catholics to join the Patriarchal Church, for it simply prevented the

[1] A. Galter, op. cit., pp. 107-8.

Uniates from continuing a legal existence even as a minority body. The decisions of the Synods of Lvov and Pryashov and the proclamation made at the Uzhgorod rally were in this way given the binding legal force of state laws. Any Greek Catholic desirous of attending the liturgy and receiving the sacraments had therefore to become Orthodox.

In view of all this it may be tempting to take an uncharitable attitude towards the Orthodox Church for lending such a willing hand in the destruction of another Christian body and co-operating to this effect with an atheist government. This reproach may indeed not unjustly be made to the Russian Orthodox hierarchy, and yet one can put forward some extenuating circumstances. In the first place, the Patriarchal Church may have been forced to assist the communist plot against the Greek Catholic Church in self-protection. Secondly, as Russian patriots the Orthodox Church leaders may have approved the dissolution of a Church which they, as much as the Soviet authorites, considered an expression of Ukrainian nationalism. Thirdly, the revocation of the Union of Brest of 1596 and the dissolution of the Greek Catholic Church have always been a cherished aim of the Russian Orthodox Church. Both remained desirable objectives even if a godless government helped to bring them about. Furthermore, the Orthodox hierarchy may have been honestly convinced that the reunion was at least to a certain extent voluntary and that many Greek Catholics recognised the Patriarchal jurisdiction of their own free will.

Indeed such a hypothesis is not unreasonable and should not be rejected *a priori*. The Greek Catholic Church of Eastern Galicia is a comparatively new Church. At the time of its dissolution it was exactly 350 years old and could hardly have the same power of resistance as other branches of the universal Catholic Church. Throughout the nineteenth century, and even at the beginning of the twentieth century, there have been a certain number of conversions from the Greek Catholic to the Russian Orthodox Church, conversions which could not be attributed simply to compulsory measures of the secular state.

When Eastern Galicia was still under Austrian rule Orthodox missionaries from Russia brought a number of people into the Orthodox fold; several Uniate priests even went over to Orthodoxy. In one case an entire Galician village situated not far from the town of Ternopol changed its faith.[1] Such conversions were not always prompted by religious considerations; they were often dictated by personal ambition

[1] Dr. Anton Korczok, *Die Griechisch-Katholische Kirche in Galizien*, Leipzig–Berlin 1921, pp. 138–40.

and more frequently even by political motives. Those who embraced Orthodoxy wished to manifest their allegiance to Russia, the great Slav State. Such 'Moscophiles' as they were called, were only a small minority in Eastern Galicia and for the Ukrainian nationalist majority the Russian Orthodox Church had little attraction.

In the Transcarpathian Ukraine Orthodoxy was likewise identified with a Great Russian orientation and something approaching a mass conversion to Orthodoxy took place in that territory in the early twenties when it was under Czechoslovak domination. The Orthodox Church then received 100,000 new supporters from Uniates claiming Russian nationality but all nationally-minded Ukrainians retained their membership of the Uniate Church. It is also true that many Ukrainian Greek Catholics who had emigrated to North America became Orthodox for quite different reasons, such as lack of Uniate priests, quarrels of Uniate priests with Latin Catholic bishops, the prolonged absence of a Uniate bishop or the financial difficulties of the Greek Catholic parishes, difficulties from which the Russian Orthodox parishes, heavily subsidised by the Czarist government, did not suffer.

In the light of such historical precedents, it cannot be said that voluntary conversions from Catholicism to Orthodoxy are beyond the realm of the possible. However, they were less likely to happen in the middle of the twentieth century than they were at an earlier period. If it could at one time have been argued that the Greek Catholic Church was the *parent pauvre* of the Latin Catholic Church, this could no longer be maintained after a number of Popes — Leo XIII, Pius X and Benedict XV had devoted their special attention to the Uniates. Moreover, the strengthening of Ukrainian nationalism throughout the first half of the twentieth century, a nationalism with a pronounced Western orientation, was a powerful safeguard against the Galician Ukrainians embracing a Church which in the nationalist Ukrainian view is identified with the Great Russian nation. An autocephalous Ukrainian Orthodox Church with headquarters in Kiev might have presented some attraction, but a Muscovite Church had no chance of winning the hearts of the Western Ukrainians. As the alternative in 1946 was not Lvov or Kiev but Lvov or Moscow, one could not expect a sizeable body of Galician and Transcarpathian Ukrainians to abandon voluntarily a Church in which they saw a champion of Ukrainian nationhood. But if any doubt is still left about the brutal, compulsory character of the Orthodox-Catholic ecclesiastical unification, it must subside in the light of the events which followed. They showed that the Synod of Lvov was not the end of the Greek Catholic Church.

Kostelnyk and Galan

The most striking though indirect evidence of the survival of the Greek Catholic Church throughout the late forties and early fifties was the campaign of anti-Vatican propaganda which began in Eastern Galicia in connection with the violent deaths of two prominent local East Galician figures who, for quite different reasons, must be included among the promoters of the Lvov Synod. We have already mentioned the first of the two, namely Dr. Gavriil Kostelnyk. He conducted the campaign against the Greek Catholic Church from the religious and ecclesiastical side. However, he had an unsolicited helper in the person of a communist pamphleteer, Jaroslav Galan, whose printed anti-Uniate diatribes were distributed at the same time as Kostelnyk's popular theological treatises. One of Galan's pamphlets, full of the most vicious attacks on the late Metropolitan Szeptycki, was published under the title *With the Cross or with the Knife?* a few days before the arrest of the Uniate bishops. Its appearance seemed deliberately timed as an ideological preparation for the impending blow against the Greek Catholic hierarchy.

Both Kostelnyk and Galan were assassinated in the city of Lvov. Kostelnyk was the first to die; he was killed by two revolver shots on September 20, 1948, on his way from the Church to his home. The authorities did not wait for the results of the investigation but proclaimed right away that the murder was instigated by the Vatican and carried out by one of its agents. Kostelnyk's funeral was used for a demonstration. The communist police for once did not object to a large street procession, which, externally at least, had a religious character; on the contrary, in view of its anti-Vatican bias, it was encouraged. As many as 50,000 people took part. Among the speakers at the cemetery were two convinced atheists, P. S. Khodzhenko, the plenipotentiary of the Council for the Affairs of the Orthodox Church for the Ukraine, and A. A. Vishnevsky, his Lvov representative. Nobody, they said in their funeral speeches, had known so well and unmasked with such power as Kostelnyk the lies of Papism. This was why the Vatican had sought ways and means to stop his activities. A 'despicable degenerate' had been found among the German-Ukrainian nationalists to carry out the Vatican assignment.[1]

The Orthodox Church leaders echoed these anti-Vatican charges. Macarius, the new Orthodox 'Archbishop of Lvov, Ternopol, Uzhgorod

---

[1] *Zh.M.P.*, 1948, no. 10, p. 22.

and Mukachevo'[1] signed an obituary in which he described Kostelnyk's death as the Vatican's revenge for the loss of the Greek Catholic Church of Eastern Galicia. The death of Kostelnyk was used to discourage and intimidate the die-hards among the Greek Catholic priests and believers who by September 1948 had still not joined the fold of Orthodoxy. Indeed, Archbishop Macarius expressed the hope that the 'martyr's blood' would wash away the blindness of those 'who still await salvation from the Vatican' and still look to the Pope with respect.[2]

No trial of Kostelnyk's murderers ever took place, or if it did take place, it was held in secret. The real background of Kostelnyk's assassination therefore remains mysterious. The question must be left open whether Kostelnyk was assassinated by the NKVD in an attempt to accelerate the destruction of the Greek Catholic Church or whether he was the victim of a genuine political murder. There is much to be said for either of these possibilities. The NKVD was then under the direction of Beriya, a man who certainly did not shrink from ordering a murder which was to be attributed to somebody else. On the other hand, Lvov has always been a city where political passions have run high and the extreme Ukrainian nationalists have always looked upon the killing of opponents as a legitimate continuation of the political fight. In 1907 in this same city of Lvov a Ukrainian student assassinated the Austrian Governor of Galicia, a Pole, Count Andrzej Potocki. In 1934 a Ukrainian nationalist murdered Pieracki, the Polish Minister of the Interior. Konovalets, the head of the Ukrainian national movement, was shot in Rotterdam in 1938 by a fellow-countryman. In March 1947 Ukrainian nationalists killed from an ambush the Polish communist Vice-Minister of War, General Swierczewski. Kostelnyk may have met his fate from a like hand, for Ukrainian nationalists may have considered him a Soviet collaborator and traitor to the Ukrainian cause. There could have been no genuine religious motives behind the murder. Even if the assassins were formally Catholics of the Eastern Rite this would have meant no more than the fact that the terrorists of the Irish Republican Army are usually Catholics of the Latin Rite. In either case the Christian faith is being abandoned for a nationalist heresy.

The death of Yaroslav Galan occurred more than a year after that of Kostelnyk, on October 24, 1949. He was not shot but murdered with

---

[1] Archbishop Macarius (Oksiyuk) had a chequered career. As a young man he was professor of theology in Kiev. Under the Soviet régime he at first taught languages and history in secondary schools, later he was employed in local government. Under the nazi occupation he worked in a library. He was ordained priest and consecrated bishop at the end of World War II.

[2] Zh.M.P., 1948, no. 10, p. 14.

an axe in his house, which makes it more likely than in Kostelnyk's case that he was the victim of a political vendetta. In addition to being a communist journalist, Galan was a city councillor of Lvov and a ferocious enemy of Ukrainian nationalism. He wrote a large number of anti-Vatican articles and pamphlets — the full bibliography of his anti-Vatican 'works' contains thirty-four items, though some of them were published only under pseudonyms and others only posthumously. The pamphlet which he produced as a kind of literary prelude to the persecution of the Greek Catholic Church was written under the pen-name 'Rosovich', and people in the Western Ukraine were ignorant of the real identity of the author.

The trial of Galan's murderers took place two years later in October 1951. It was conducted by the well-known Soviet Public Prosecutor, Roman Rudenko, who later became Chief Public Prosecutor of the USSR. Rudenko attributed the Galan murder to the OUN organisation ('Organisation of Ukrainian Nationalists') which seemed quite credible since OUN was known to engage in terrorist activities using methods identical to those employed by similar bodies in other countries, such as the Algerian FLN or the Cypriot EOKA. However, Rudenko was not satisfied with this explanation; at the same time he tried to implicate the Vatican. He stated that the assassins had spent the night after the murder in the home of a Uniate priest and that the sons of two priests had assisted in the preparations for the crime. To the uninitiated this was to suggest a connection between the Greek Catholic Church and the murder. In reality however, sons of priests were not *ipso facto* the Church's zealous supporters. On the contrary, they often embraced Orthodoxy or became atheists.[1] The murderer himself had no clerical connection, Rudenko simply described him as a 'kulak son who grew up under the influence of nationalistic and Uniate propaganda'.[2]

Rudenko's attacks on the Vatican and the Uniates in the Lvov court room, though proving nothing about Galan's murder, did show that the Greek Catholic Church was still a live issue in Eastern Galicia and that the campaign against it had still to be fed by atrocity stories and accusations of the wildest kind. The authorities may have suspected that the Church continued as an underground body under a provisional administrator and they may not have been far wrong. However, as long as the Stalinist terror lasted, no definite news about the Uniate Church could penetrate to the outside world.

---

[1] Korczok, op. cit., p. 148.
[2] Stalinskoe Znamya, October 18, 1951, quoted in *Voprosy Religii i Ateizma*, vol. ii, Moscow 1954, p. 273.

A Crypto-Catholic Church

However, in connection with the relaxations during the post-Stalin period, much more evidence about the continued vitality of the Uniate Church and the Uniate outlook has been forthcoming. In the first place, as the result of the post-Stalin amnesties, various Uniate priests returned from their places of banishment in Vorkuta, Karaganda and other distant areas. They were still popular with their former parishioners and the communist authorities regarded their presence in the Western Ukraine as no small danger. The Soviet Ukrainian press accused these priests not only of conducting oral propaganda among the population in favour of the Uniate Church, but also of 'fabricating' various miracles. Two priests, in particular, were charged with having organised the 'Miracle of Serednia', namely the appearance of Our Lady in the Galician village of Serednia in the Stanislav Province.[1] The Virgin Mary was said to have appeared to a peasant woman to whom she promised that the Greek Catholic Church would soon be re-established. Soviet sources indicate that Serednia has become a place of pilgrimage, a kind of Galician Lourdes or Fatima, but as the Catholic ecclesiastical authorities exercise no legal jurisdiction in Galicia, they have no possibility of investigating reports of the miracle, which seems to be widely believed. In general, the population of Eastern Galicia seeks comfort in the belief in miracles, some of which are attributed to the late Metropolitan Andrew Szeptycki, still a much beloved and even venerated figure in the country.[2] Even the Orthodox Archbishop of Lvov seems to have had some respect for the Szeptycki cult. In the former Uniate archiepiscopal palace Metropolitan Szeptycki's bedroom remained untouched and ten years after the Orthodox-Uniate 'reunion' his portrait was still hanging there.[3]

To stop the Uniate revival the régime re-deported some of the Uniate priests who had been released under the amnesty but, from the communist point of view, it was already too late.[4] The 'harm' was done. Somehow a Uniate movement had come into existence again. This is the more remarkable as it was a movement without proper leaders. For several of the Ukrainian Greek-Catholic bishops the amnesty came too late. They had perished in their places of banishment. Two, however, died in Galicia soon after their release and the funeral of at least one of them, Bishop Mykola Charnetsky (1884–1958), was attended by large crowds of faithful who were officially regarded as 'Orthodox' but had remained Greek Catholics at heart. The head of the Greek Catholic

[1] *Kommunist Ukraini*, July 1959, no. 7, p. 82.   [2] *Kommunist Ukraini*, ibid.
[3] *One Church*, vol. xii, 1958, no. 3–4, p. 107.   [4] Galter, op. cit., pp. 453–4.

Church in the Transcarpathian Ukraine, the 'secret' bishop, Mgr. Chira, was also allowed to return as a private citizen, but after a few months he was assassinated by 'persons unknown'; this was in 1958. Metropolitan Slipy was not allowed to return from exile even in a private capacity. He was kept in the Krasnoyarsk Province of Siberia carrying out the humble work of a caretaker in an Old People's Home.[1] A further indication of the survival of the Uniates came from Poland in connection with the internal upheavals taking place in that country in October 1956. These emboldened the association of the Ukrainian minority to take up the defence of Poland's Greek Catholic community and to demand that the Greek Catholic churches confiscated by the State should be restored to the believers.[2] It is very likely that the real frame of mind of the West Ukrainian Uniates in the Soviet Union is identical with that of the Ukrainian Uniates across the border, only with the difference that the latter are not free to make their true feelings heard. Nevertheless the existence of Greek Catholic Ukrainian parishes in various towns of Poland must be an encouragement to those in the Western Ukraine who have remained loyal to Rome.

The Orthodox Church in Eastern Galicia has remained very largely a crypto-Catholic Church. The Orthodox hierarchy is as much aware of this as the communist régime. From an ecclesiastical and theological point of view the Catholic-Orthodox unification was a purely mechanical one. It failed to transform the Greek Catholics into good Orthodox but only forced them to bow to another jurisdiction. The difference between the 'they' and the 'we' remained. The Lvov Archdiocese of the Russian Orthodox Church had to set about purging the religion of the Eastern Galicians of various Latin practices and beliefs, such as the Catholic doctrine of purgatory, the cult of the Uniate saint Josaphat, of whom there existed countless ikons throughout Galicia, and also the Sacred Heart devotions. Priests and 'diaki' (choir-directors) as well as the laity had to be 'freed' from the Latin-Uniate heritage. The priests found it hard to abandon the liturgical and ritual practices of the Greek Catholic Church and various conferences had to be held with the purpose of removing the Uniate survivals from the liturgy.[3]

Although Soviet secular power supported and encouraged the Orthodox Church in the fight against the Uniates, it had no desire to become involved in theological subtleties. Apart from permitting the West Ukrainian Orthodox Church to print a small journal and to

[1] *Osservatore Romano*, February 8, 1958.
[2] *Nashe Slowo*, Warsaw, March 10, 1957.
[3] *Zh.M.P.*, 1956, no. 11, pp. 10–11.

issue a church calendar, the Soviet State has not made easy the consolidation of its gains. For instance, the new Orthodox churches in
Galicia and the Transcarpathian Ukraine still have to use Uniate
liturgical books. Nor is there any kind of Orthodox devotional literature
available, and for this reason the faithful are still reading the Uniate
publications kept from pre-war days. The authorities also refused
permission to open an Orthodox theological seminary in Lvov although
they had more or less promised this on two occasions.[1] This was a poor
reward for the loyalty of the West Ukrainian Orthodox hierarchy and
must have entailed a considerable loss of prestige for them, considering that the Uniates had as many as three seminaries in Galicia before
the war. In general, the Orthodox Church in Galicia does not occupy
even to a remote degree the position which the Greek Catholic Church
previously held. For instance, the number of parish priests has dropped
to less than one-third of what it was in 1939.

All this seems to indicate that the Soviet authorities are full of
distrust towards the new Orthodox Archdiocese of Lvov-Ternopol
which was created with their connivance. They somehow feel that the
ex-Uniate priests are still Catholics and Uniates under their skin and
occasionally they still call them 'ksendzy', the name usually given to
Catholic priests. They see the survival of their Catholic outlook in their
militancy, which contrasts with the more pliable behaviour of the
Orthodox clergy in other parts of the Soviet Union. The Galician
Orthodox priests have been charged in particular with trying to keep
a grip on the younger generation and even with agitating against the
Komsomol, something an Orthodox priest in Russia proper might have
done only in the early years of the Soviet régime. One priest was said
to have gone so far as to call Komsomol membership cards a thing of
the devil.[2] In attacking the West Ukrainian ex-Catholic priests the
Soviet press has seen them as skilful opponents exploiting all inaccuracies
and mistakes made by anti-religious propagandists in their lectures. So
the régime has gained little by suppressing the Ukrainian Catholic
Church of the Slavo-Byzantine Rite, the more so since the communist
dictatorship could only exterminate it in the territory of the Soviet
Union itself and that of its more obedient satellites.

*   *   *   *

Throughout the world the Church continues to exist, in Western
Europe, Australia, in many Latin American States and especially on the

---

[1] *One Church*, vol. xii, 1958, no. 7-8, p. 361.
[2] *Molodoy Kommunist*, 1957, no. 9, p. 79.

North American Continent. The world-wide emigration of the Ukrainians was due to economic misery and political oppression, and the writer Ivan Franko was therefore right in saying that the Ukrainian misfortune spread 'all across the ocean'. Dozens of Ukrainian villages have sprung up in North America, and in Manitoba alone as many as sixty localities have Ukrainian names such as Ukraina, Halich (Galicia), Shevchenko or Khmelnitsky. It is in these Ukrainian settlements of the New World that a free Ukrainian nation and a free Church has found a refuge. There are no Ukrainian Greek Catholic bishops in the Ukraine itself but there are eight in the United States and Canada. There are no Greek Catholic churches in Lvov, the capital of the Western Ukraine, but there are nine such churches and a Greek Catholic cathedral in Winnipeg. The Greek Catholic orders, the Basilians and the Eastern Rite Redemptorists, have been banned from Galicia but they now exist in Alberta and Manitoba.[1] There are no Greek Ukrainian parishes in the Carpathian Ukraine, but the Carpathian Ukrainian immigrant parishes in the United States are strong and flourishing. They aggregate over 300,000 faithful, not so many fewer than the number of Greek Catholics in the old homeland. This survival of the Greek Catholic Church in free democratic countries is yet another promise that it will return one day to the Ukraine itself.

[1] Paul Yuzyk, *The Ukrainians in Manitoba*, Winnipeg 1953, p. 75.

VIII

Western Protestantism I

(Lutherans, Calvinists and Mennonites)

_____

And take they our life,
Goods, fame, child and wife
Let this all be gone,
They yet have nothing won,
The Kingdom ours remaineth.

MARTIN LUTHER

Western Protestantism owes its spread in Russia to a fundamental miscalculation on the part of the Czars. They were on their guard against the Catholics who, they feared, threatened 'Greco-Russian piety', to speak in the officialese of the sixteenth century. However, they saw no danger from the Protestant side. The heresies of Luther and Calvin were, so they thought, so far away from Orthodoxy that there could be no contamination. Whenever possible, and almost as a matter of policy, the Muscovite Government summoned Protestant foreigners to Russia in preference to Catholics. As a remarkable illustration of Russian tolerance towards Protestantism it may be mentioned that in 1575 Ivan the Terrible permitted the building of a Protestant church in Moscow, at a distance of only one mile from the Kremlin. This was three years after the horrors of the Massacre of St. Bartholomew in France. On the other hand, a petition for the building of a Catholic church in Moscow was rejected as late as 1695.[1] Contrary to the expectations of the Czars, Protestantism finally became a proselytising religion in Russia, even if it did not spread to the Orthodox in its original Lutheran and Calvinist forms. It was a naturalised and nationalised Protestantism, and although the Great-Russians remained comparatively immune to it, the same cannot be said of the Ukrainians and other nationalities whom the Holy Synod

[1] Prof. M. Krasnozhen, _Inovertsy na Rusi_ (The Non-Orthodox in Russia), vol. i, Dorpat 1900, pp. 86-7.

245

I

in Moscow regarded as coming under the spiritual sphere of influence of the Russian Orthodox Church.

Western Protestantism and Communist Ideology

The Soviet régime shared the view of its Czarist predecessors that Catholicism was more objectionable than Protestantism. This view was modified only after Hitler's seizure of power in Germany, when Catholic resistance to Nazism appeared to be on a larger scale than Protestant opposition. Towards the end of World War II the Soviets reverted to their original estimate of the Catholic Church, and it was grudgingly admitted that the Protestants were 'more progressive', although at the same time they were accused of drawing too close to the Catholics. The *rapprochement* between Protestantism and Catholicism is to the Communists something very real and dangerous.

In their view it is characteristic of the period of imperialism that the bourgeoisie, including its Protestant sector, should become increasingly reactionary and intolerant in the religious sphere. Therefore, Protestant Churches were taking from Catholicism what they had previously rejected as superstition and paganism because they believed that in doing so they would be better equipped to fight materialism and Communism.[1] In other words, the Soviet anti-religious propagandists are accusing the Protestants of betraying the Reformation for the sake of anti-Communism.

The communist attitude towards the religious side of the Reformation is negative. The communists sympathise only with certain of its political and social aspects, especially with the extremist movements which emerged under the general banner of the Reformation. The leaders of the Reformation are judged by the attitude they took towards their extremist contemporaries. It is obvious therefore that Luther receives very bad marks. He is accused of having invented a new kind of spiritual slavery. This assessment goes back to Karl Marx himself. 'Luther', said Marx, 'conquered slavery based on piety by replacing it with slavery based on conviction. He destroyed faith in authority by re-establishing the authority of faith. He transformed priests into laymen whilst at the same time transforming laymen into priests. He freed man from external religion but made religion the inner world of man. He emancipated the body from fetters but put the fetters on the human heart.'[2]

Soviet scholars have expressed themselves in a less sophisticated way

---

[1] M. M. Sheinman, *Religiya v Period Imperializma* (Religion in the Period of Imperialism), Moscow 1955, p. 14.

[2] *K. Marx i F. Engels o religii* (Karl Marx and F. Engels on Religion), Moscow 1955, p. 37.

than Marx. For them Luther's Reformation is simply an 'all-national movement for the liberation of Germany from the alien yoke' of papal Rome.[1] However, Martin Luther did not want the movement to go beyond a purely religious framework. He refused to make it the basis of social and political transformation. Ultimately Luther went over to the side of the princes and this was 'nothing else but a betrayal of the all-national cause by the conservative majority of the bourgeoisie'.[2] Thus Luther's life and work are divided into two periods, his earlier 'progressive' and his later 'reactionary' period. This distinction was particularly important for communist propagandists in Germany who were thereby enabled to make the 'early Luther' a champion of German unification.[3]

No such division exists in the life of Calvin. His teachings are simply dismissed as a 'religious justification of bourgeois accumulation of capital and bourgeois activity in general'.[4] At the other extreme in the communist appraisal are 'progressive' figures like Thomas Muenzer, of whom more will have to be said later, and the Czech reformer Jan Hus, praised as 'the great Czech patriot, 'fighter against Catholic obscurantism', and 'founder of a genuine national-popular heretical movement'.[5]

In Soviet Russia Communism has encountered Western Protestantism first and foremost in its Lutheran form. It has also had to deal with the difficult problem of a spiritually though not numerically important Anabaptist Mennonite group. The Calvinist Church in the Soviet Union, though small in numbers, has grown in importance since the war as a result of the annexation of territories with Calvinist religious minorities. Anglicanism enters the Soviet horizon only as an ideological opponent in the world-wide struggle between Communism and religion. In Russia itself Anglicanism has been the religion only of a small number of Englishmen temporarily or permanently living in the country. In Czarist times, there were Anglican churches in Moscow, St. Petersburg, Odessa and Archangel but these were closed after the Revolution, as was the Anglican church in Riga after Latvia's occupation by the Red Army. Methodism interests Soviet Communism mainly because of its role in the 'capitalist world', because it is an important religious force in the United States and in view of its extensive missionary

---

[1] *Voprosy Istorii*, 1954, no. 1, p. 76.
[2] *Voprosy Istorii*, 1954, no. 1, p. 77.
[3] *Neues Deutschland*, September 2, 1952.
[4] *L.S.E.*, vol. xix, 1953, p. 459.
[5] B. T. Rubtsov, *Gusitskie Voiny* (The Hussite Wars), Moscow 1955, pp. 3, 85.

activities in colonial territories.[1] The Methodist following in the Soviet Union has always been very small.[2]

The importance of Western Protestantism in the Soviet Union does not lie in the number of its followers — except in the Baltic republics where it is the leading religion. Its main significance lies in its contribution to the emergence of a native Ukrainian-Russian Evangelical movement. Lutheran churches and Mennonite houses of prayer may have disappeared from most parts of European Russia but the spirit which radiated from them has survived and continues to influence the religious situation in the Soviet State.

I. LUTHERANS

The Lutherans before the October Revolution

When considering the Lutheran Church in Russia we must distinguish between those areas where it has always been a diaspora Church and those where it has been the national Church of the bulk of the population. Before 1914 it could be found as a diaspora Church almost everywhere in the Russian Empire but was a national Church only in Estonia, in the greater part of Latvia and in the Grand-Duchy of Finland, only a small portion of which belongs to the Soviet Union to-day.

Under Soviet rule the Lutheran Church survives in an organised form only in Latvia and Estonia, and there are a few remnants in other parts of the country. However, in fairness it must be said that the plight of Lutheranism in Soviet Russia proper is due not only to religious persecution but also to the Soviet nationalities policy. The Lutheran Church in Russia is a Western Church, and its followers were originally Germans or belonged to other Western nationalities. The liquidation of the

---

[1] *Large Soviet Encyclopædia*, second edition, vol. xxvii, Moscow 1954, p. 315.

[2] There are known to have been Methodists at one time or another in Leningrad, the Soviet Far East and Western Byelorussia. The Soviet Far Eastern Methodists — about 1,500 Koreans — were transplanted in 1937 to Central Asia together with the entire Korean population of the Vladivostok region. Since then nothing has been heard of them. The Methodists of Western Byelorussia flourished during the period between the wars. They had a periodical in the Byelorussian language and a Byelorussian Methodist hymn-book was also printed (*Bozhym Shlyakham*, 1956, no. 70–5, p. 46). No further news of them has reached the outside world since the Soviet occupation. The only part of the USSR where Methodism is known to have survived is Estonia. In that country there is a small and faithful Methodist community headed by a superintendent. Two representatives of the Estonian Methodists were invited in 1952 to take part in the Peace Conference of the Churches in Zagorsk. Although it is so small, the Methodist community of Estonia has not been spared either from having to make the usual effusive statements of loyalty to the atheist régime or from vicious attacks in the press.

German minority as an organised community which the Soviet authorities carried out in 1941 would have meant the end of Lutheranism in many parts of Russia, even if it had not already suffered from the onslaught of communist atheism. The elimination of Lutheranism from the Karelian Isthmus and especially from Viborg, once the second largest Finnish town, was chiefly the result of migration to Finland of the entire Finnish and Lutheran population of the area. Also the liquidation of the once-flourishing Lutheran parishes in Moscow and St. Petersburg must be seen in connection with the disappearance of the Western minorities from the two cities.

To give an account of the fate of Western Lutheran Protestantism in Soviet Russia is to speak primarily of its losses. Before the October Revolution the Lutherans had eight consistorial districts. Two of them covered more of less the territory of the Soviet Union within the inter-war frontiers and the six others exercised jurisdiction over what to-day are the Baltic Soviet Republics, and over most of Byelorussia, where there were only a few Lutherans. In the Baltic consistorial districts the German Balts formed small but influential minorities and there were little Lutheran groups of Swedes, Lithuanians and Poles. All eight consistories formed the General Consistory with its seat in St. Petersburg.

Russia, less the north-western coastal and border areas, was divided between the consistorial districts of St. Petersburg and Moscow. St. Petersburg had the oversight of Western and Northern Russia, most of the Ukraine, Bessarabia and the Crimea. The consistorial district of Moscow had a smaller number of faithful but was much larger in size as it included the central and eastern parts of European Russia and the whole of Asiatic Russia. Between them the two districts were responsible for the spiritual welfare of 1,136,000 Lutherans, seventy per cent of whom, or 801,000, were Germans, according to the church statistics of 1904–5. The rest consisted of 136,000 Finns, 105,000 Estonians, 48,000 Latvians, 7,300 Swedes, 1,000 Armenians, and 1,400 'others'. The 'others' concealed a number of Russians who for one reason or another preferred to join the Western Protestant Church rather than one of the Evangelical sects which had a more marked Slav flavour.

The two consistorial districts comprised 184 parishes and 287 churches, 93 of them in towns and 194 in rural areas. The churches were almost evenly divided between the two districts, but those in the consistorial district of Moscow were usually smaller in size and more than half of them were wooden buildings. In the consistorial district of St. Petersburg, to which the more advanced provinces of Russia belonged, over three-quarters of all Lutheran church buildings we in stone.

The most important Protestant centre was the imperial capital, S Petersburg, itself. It had no fewer than sixteen Lutheran parishes, a the number of faithful exceeded 92,000. In fact, it would be true to s that St. Petersburg was Lutheran even before it became Orthodox. S Petersburg was founded in 1703 and no Orthodox Church life exist there before that date, although a Lutheran parish had existed in t territory which became St. Petersburg ever since 1632. The parishione were Swedes and Finns, inhabitants of the Swedish fortress of Nyenscha which then stood where St. Petersburg was later to be built. This pari was incorporated into the new Russian city, and Peter the Great hims endowed it with a new statute. In 1734 the two national groups separat and until the October Revolution there existed side by side the Swedi Lutheran parish of St. Catherine, with 5,500 parishioners, and t Finnish parish of St. Mary, with 16,500 parishioners, living either St. Petersburg itself or in the Finnish-speaking villages in the neighbou hood. The parish of St. John, which with 22,000 parishioners was t largest, consisted mostly of Estonian servants and workmen. Jes Church catered for a mixed Latvian-German congregation. T remaining parishes were German. The oldest of them, the parish St. Peter, was founded almost simultaneously with St. Petersburg itse and most of its first members were officials in the service of Czar Pete

In the first Russian capital, Moscow, Lutheranism is even older, b in that traditional Russian and Orthodox centre it found less favourab conditions for its growth and development than in the internation city on the Neva. Nevertheless there were three Lutheran parishes Moscow at the beginning of the twentieth century. The oldest, wit 4,500 parishioners, mostly German, used the church of St. Michae Then came the large German-Latvian-Estonian congregation of 17,00 with its church of St. Peter and St. Paul. Finally there was the sma parish of St. John, remarkable for the fact that the pastor preached onc a month in Russian.

Outside the cities of St. Petersburg and Moscow the main centres Lutheranism were in the German colonies in the Ukraine and th Crimea and on the Volga, as well as in the Finnish and Estonia countryside of the Guberniya of St. Petersburg. However, there wer Lutheran churches in practically every large town of European Russi including Tula, Kazan, Kursk, Nizhnii Novgorod, Voronezh, Rostov on-Don, Yekaterinburg, Kostroma, Archangel (1660), Yaroslav Vladimir, Rybinsk, Penza, Zlatoust, Sevastopol, Novorossiisk, Astrakha

(1702) and Vladikavkaz. The largest single urban parish outside the capitals was Saratov with 12,500 parishioners. A particularly interesting Lutheran parish existed on the Murman coast in the European Far North. It consisted of twenty-eight Finnish fishermen's settlements and had a Finnish pastor, but sermons were also preached in Norwegian.

Protestantism in its Lutheran form even crossed the Caucasus. The majority of the Transcaucasian Lutherans were Swabian peasant colonists, many of whose ancestors had come to Russia as followers of apocalyptic sects and had remained somewhat sectarian in outlook. They formed a special 'Transcaucasian Evangelical-Lutheran Synod' independent of St. Petersburg. Only under the Soviet régime did they join up with the rest of Lutheran Protestantism in Russia. However, there were other Lutheran groups in Transcaucasia less separatist-minded — for instance, Estonian Evangelical colonies in Kutaisi in Georgia, and in Kars which was Russian until 1920 and now belongs to Turkey. An international congregation of Germans, Swedes and Armenians, about 6,000 parishioners in all, existed in Baku. The ancient city of Shemakha, to-day in the Azerbaidzhani Soviet Republic, was the cradle of the small Armenian Evangelical movement and had an Armenian Lutheran church.

Lutheranism also penetrated to Siberia. The first Siberian Lutherans were Swedish prisoners of war who founded the parish of Tomsk. Other Siberian parishes owed their existence to Lutheran convicts and exiles, particularly to those of Finnish nationality. Some of the Siberian Lutheran congregations were among the most polyglot of the entire Lutheran Church of Russia. In the parishes of Tomsk and Vladivostok sermons were preached in four languages, and in the parish of Irkutsk even five — German, Estonian, Latvian, Finnish and Russian. Most of the eight Siberian parishes were very extensive and the work of a Lutheran pastor in those parts was exacting and strenuous. For instance, the pastor in Vladivostok spent three months there at the centre of his parish and nine months travelling to visit those of his 3,000 parishioners who were living in Sakhalin Island, Khabarovsk and even in Kharbin in Manchuria. The pastor of Irkutsk had to travel up to 6,500 miles a year, and the pastor of Tomsk-Barnaul had to cover nearly 8,000 miles and visit seventy-three widely scattered localities.

Hopes and Disillusion 1917–41

Under the Soviet régime Lutheranism at first enjoyed greater tolerance than the Orthodox Church. The communist authorities usually showed greater respect towards Protestant ministers than towards Orthodox priests. Rightly or wrongly the average communist looked upon the pastor as a well-educated man towards whom he felt animosity as an ideological opponent, whilst the Orthodox 'pop' was not only hated but also despised.

The Lutheran Church and its pastors had suffered losses in the Revolution and the Civil War, but when the time of trial was over, there was again some prospect of a normal ecclesiastical and religious life. The holding in Moscow of a Lutheran General Synod in June 1924 gave some grounds for optimism. It was prepared by various regional synods which elected delegates, twenty-seven pastors and twenty-nine laymen. The General Synod appointed for life two bishops, Arthur Malmgren for the Leningrad consistorial district, and Theophil Meyer for the Moscow district. A third bishop of Estonian nationality — at first Bishop Palsa, later Bishop Jürgensson — looked after the Estonian, Latvian and Finnish members of the Lutheran Church, which at this time was anxious to grant a kind of national-ecclesiastical autonomy to the non-Germans. Of the seventeen (later eighteen) synodal districts set up within the Moscow and Leningrad consistories, one served the Finns and Ingermanlanders with their 26 parishes, one the Latvians and one the Estonians.[1]

In addition to the three bishops the Lutheran Church had in 1924 thirteen provosts and sixty-six pastors. The total number of Lutheran ecclesiastics was thus less than half what it had been in 1917, but it could nevertheless serve as a basis for further development, particularly as a pastors' seminary was opened in Leningrad in September 1925.

At first the Bishops of Leningrad and Moscow had reasonably good facilities for keeping in touch with their parishioners. Bishop Meyer, for instance, undertook a lengthy journey through Siberia visiting the scattered evangelical groups there — an experience about which he even published a book in Germany.[2] Moreover, in 1927 the German Lutherans were given permission to publish a newspaper, *Unsere Kirche*. Early in 1928 the Lutherans held their second General Synod, which was to be the last one.

Although the situation of the Lutherans in the twenties seemed almost idyllic compared with the later period, they were already

---

[1] *Kirchenordnungen der Evangelisch-Lutherischen Kirche in Russland*, Eingeleitet und herausgegeben von Robert Stupperich, Ulm, 1959, p. 243. See also Hermann Maurer, *Die Evangelisch-Lutherische Kirche in der Sovetunion 1917–1937*, Kirche im Osten, Band II, Stuttgart 1959, pp. 74–5.

[2] Theophil Meyer, *Nach Sibirien im Dienste der Evangelisch-Lutherischen Kirche*, Leipzig 1927.

labouring under difficulties. The shortage of pastors made it impossible to provide appropriate spiritual care for the Lutheran population in many parts of Russia. This was particularly true of the Volga-German Republic where the number of pastors was reduced from forty in 1917 to fourteen in the middle of the twenties.

In the absence of pastors several Volga German congregations were taken over by schoolteachers with left-wing leanings, who organised them into a pro-régime ecclesiastical organisation describing itself as the 'German Living Church'. The idea of such a pro-Soviet Lutheranism and even the name of the organisation were borrowed from the 'Living Church' movement which split off from Russian Orthodoxy. In the Volga German Republic the 'German Living Church' had 4,000 members and controlled ecclesiastical life in six villages. It also became dominant in twelve German villages in the Ufa region and in thirty villages in Siberia.[1] Like most of such ecclesiastical reform movements launched under Soviet auspices, the 'German Living Church' was only a short-lived creation, but at one time it did make the existence of Lutheranism in Russia more precarious.

Even in the twenties the life of a Protestant pastor was a hard one. He was disfranchised, received no ration cards, and had to buy food on the black market. His pastoral activities were curtailed, he was not allowed to hold confirmation classes for children unless he was prepared to confine his teaching to groups of three people. Heavy, often ruinous taxation was imposed on him and he was under constant GPU supervision. All this was only a prelude to the much worse state of affairs after 1929, when the practice of religion in the Protestant villages was step by step eradicated. First came the arrests and deportations of the pastors. This by itself was not sufficient to destroy religious life altogether. Lay preachers, vergers, organists and chairmen of parish councils continued to conduct some sort of religious service, often consisting of Bible reading only. Children were still baptised and prayers were said at funerals. Soon these new 'religious agitators' were arrested too, but the members of Protestant congregations continued to come together for the singing of hymns. In the end the authorities made even this impossible by arresting the cantors. After this the churches and prayer-houses of the Lutherans remained deserted even on Sundays, and were closed down one by one. The family remained the last bulwark of religious life.[2] Prayers continued to be said and

---

[1] E. Gross, *Avtonomnaya S.S.R. Nemtsev Povolzha*, Pokrovsk 1926, p. 98.
[2] Pastor J. Föll, *Geschichte einer Kirche unter dem Kreuz, Heimatbuch der Deutschen aus Russland*, 1958, p. 116.

hymns were sung within the family circle. This too became dangerous, as schoolteachers enquired from the children the nature of the 'religious survivals' in their homes. Many parents who did not wish to expose their children to the grim dilemma of either lying or denouncing their families stopped teaching them religion or even praying with them.[1]

The campaign against the Protestants was closely linked with the collectivisation of the countryside. A large part of the Lutheran population lived in prosperous villages which could be collectivised only through the display of a great deal of pressure and terror, which in turn provoked popular resistance. Such was the case, for instance, in the Leningrad Province with its multi-national Lutheran population consisting of Finns, Estonians, Latvians, Germans and Ingermanlanders. To discredit the resistance movement official Soviet propaganda asserted that it was inspired by the 'rich peasants and Lutheran ecclesiastical circles (*tserkovniki*) of the white Baltic republics', meaning clearly the neighbouring republics of Finland, Estonia and Latvia. At the same time 'dozens of cases of provocation and savage murder, as well as arson of barns, hay-lofts and cattle-sheds' were attributed to rich peasants and Lutheran church people in the Leningrad Province itself.[2] The Lutheran Church in the Ukraine and in the Volga-German Republic was similarly charged with serving German imperialism and Fascism, more especially after Hitler had come to power in Germany.

By the summer of 1936 the number of pastors still in office was reduced to ten in the whole of the Soviet Union. Of these, five were Germans, four Finns and one Estonian. Forty-nine pastors lived in exile and twenty-six were 'prevented from holding office'.[3] For all practical purposes the two consistorial districts ceased to exist. The last Synod of the Moscow District was held in the autumn of 1933 when Bishop Meyer ordained seven graduates of the Leningrad seminary. That seminary was never officially closed; teaching simply became impossible in the atmosphere of terror created by the authorities. The two German Lutheran bishops were not themselves victims of the wave of persecution. Bishop Meyer died in April 1934, before it was properly under way, and Bishop Malmgren, gravely ill and unable to take any active part in church affairs, left Russia in 1936.

The fight against Lutheranism was conducted not only by such violent means as the arrest of pastors on trumped-up charges but also with the help of propaganda. The most important centre of anti-

---

[1] H. Römmich, *Die Evangelische Kirche Russlands, Ihr Leidensweg seit 1914 bis zur Gegenwart*, Stuttgart 1957, mimeographed, p. 5.
[2] *Kommunisticheskoe Prosveshchenie*, August 5, 1931, pp. 33-4.
[3] *Osteuropa*, vol. xii, October 1936, no. 1.

Lutheran propaganda was a party school in Leningrad, attended by German, Estonian and Finnish-speaking communists. The school course lasted three years, and in the last year as many as eighty hours were devoted to anti-religious indoctrination. The items in the curriculum included 'Origins of Christianity and of Christian cults', 'History of the Christian Church (with special reference to Lutheranism)', 'The political role of religion in contemporary capitalist states', and 'Forms and methods of anti-religious work'. There were also one-year courses for officials of collective farms and village soviets attended exclusively by people of nationalities whose leading religion was Lutheranism, namely Germans, Finns, Estonians and Latvians. In this shorter course forty hours were set aside for anti-religious work. The pupils of the Leningrad school, which seems to have had its heyday in the early thirties, not only attended lectures, but immediately imparted to others the anti-religious 'knowledge' which they had acquired. They formed anti-religious brigades which visited Finnish, Latvian and Estonian villages in the neighbourhood of Leningrad, especially at Christmas time, and also fought 'religious prejudices' among Latvians and Germans in the city of Leningrad itself.[1]

It might seem that by 1937 the Lutheran Church was so completely wiped out that no further measures were required for its suppression. Yet terror against the pastors flared up again, even against those who no longer engaged in any religious activity. Although the arrest of pastors seems to have been initiated by some central directive the charges made in each individual case showed considerable ingenuity on the part of the police, especially with regard to the last ten pastors, against whom accusations were hard to find. Pastor Suomalainen in the Kingisepp District of the Leningrad Province was charged with organising the blowing up of a railway line in the border area. Pastor Korbelainen, also a Finnish Lutheran working in a parish of the Leningrad area, was found guilty of having prayed in public for the health of a foreign spy, whilst his wife had praised the Trotskyite-Zinovievite bandits.[2] The alleged spy was another Finnish Lutheran pastor, Laurikkala of Gatchina. He at least could not be arrested — as a Finnish subject he had to be expelled. At the other end of the Soviet Union, in Tashkent, another pastor, Reichwald, also one of the last ten, was arrested for, amongst other things, having worked for the Czarist police before the October Revolution.[3] By the end of 1937 no Lutheran

---

[1] *Antireligioznik*, August 1931, no. 8, pp. 48–9.
[2] *Kandidov, Tserkov i Shpionazh* (Church and Espionage), Moscow 1938, p. 90.
[3] *Kandidov*, op. cit., p. 91.

pastor was in office and no Lutheran parish in existence anywhere in the Soviet Union.

Soviet Power and the Baltic Lutherans

Nevertheless, the history of Western Protestantism in the Soviet Union had not yet reached its end; far from it. In 1940 two million Lutherans became subject to Soviet rule through the annexation of Estonia and Latvia. In Estonia over three-quarters of the inhabitants delonged to the Lutheran Church. In Latvia those nominally of the Lutheran faith accounted for 56·6 per cent of the total population. In round figures there were 880,000 Lutherans in Estonia and 1,094,000 Lutherans in Latvia. These figures, like most religious statistics, denote a theoretical maximum and not the actual number of practising believers. Many who had virtually broken with religion were included among the Lutherans if their parents were church members. Such ex-Lutherans were particularly numerous in the Baltic cities, among the working class. In Latvia, for instance, there existed even at the time of the independent Latvian Republic an anti-religious organisation called 'The Free Word' ('Brivais Vards') which published the journal *The Freethinker (Brivdomatajs)*.[1] Nevertheless, the Lutheran Churches of Latvia and Estonia commanded mass support, not only at the time of their annexation by the Soviets, but also afterwards. Even in 1957, after years of communist persecution, the Estonian Lutheran Church could still claim a total of 350,000 active, not nominal, members[2] and the Latvian Lutheran Church 600,000 members. In addition to these two major Lutheran groups in Latvia and Estonia the Soviets brought under their rule several tens of thousands of Lutherans forming a minority Church in Lithuania as well as a small number of Ukrainian Lutherans in Eastern Galicia, which the USSR annexed as early as September 1939.[3]

1. *The First Occupation.* The history of the relations between Soviet Communism and Lutheranism in the Baltic countries started not in

---

[1] *Baltische Kirchengeschichte*, herausgegeben von Reinhard Wittram, Göttingen 1956, p. 279.
[2] Ecumenical Press Service, November 8, 1957.
[3] The Ukrainian Lutheran Church of Galicia, unlike Lutheranism in the three Baltic countries, is not a direct produce of the Reformation. It owes its existence to belated missionary efforts by Galicia's German Lutherans. The Lutheran Catechism was not printed in Ukrainian until 1929. The centre of the small Ukrainian Lutheran movement was Stanislav and its obvious recruiting grounds were certain disaffected elements of the Uniate Church. After the Soviet occupation Ukrainian Lutheranism completely disappeared, partly through communist persecution, partly because it lost its source of inspiration when the Galician Germans were evacuated from the country and their own Lutheran Church ceased to exist.

1940 but much earlier, for in 1918-19 the communists were for a short period in occupation in both Latvia and Estonia. This was a period of violent persecution, where many pastors were arrested, deported, or killed, and churches destroyed and desecrated. There exists a very interesting Soviet testimonial of communist 'ecclesiastical policy' in the short-lived Soviet Latvia of 1918-19. It is the work of the Latvian communist leader Stuchka and was printed in *Tserkov i Revolyutsiya* (*The Church and the Revolution*), an organ of the Soviet People's Commissariat for Justice. Stuchka refers to a significant number of pastors sentenced by communist revolutionary tribunals in Latvia and also mentions the execution of five pastors as hostages on May 22, 1918. He speaks approvingly of the executions as an 'act of popular wrath' which, he says, 'produced a favourable impression on the masses in Riga and Latvia'.

On the fate of the church buildings under the first Soviet occupation, Stuchka is not less outspoken. Churches were requisitioned for communist meetings. Even Latvia's first Congress of Soviets was held in a church in the town of Valmera. It is only fair to add, however, that the communists themselves felt a little uneasy when addressing meetings in churches. They sensed that they were out of place there. Stuchka himself said, 'Even I must confess that the first time it seemed strange to me when my listeners, ordinary parishioners, old men and women, received me with applause in a Lutheran church.' Another communist speaker who addressed a gathering in Riga Cathedral had this to say: 'It was not without embarrassment that I mounted the pulpit, which was surrounded by the wooden figures of the twelve apostles, and delivered a short address of greetings to the brotherly people of liberated Latvia. Both the Russian language and the revolutionary slogans sounded so strange within these ancient gloomy walls that had witnessed so many things in the past.[1]

2. *The Second Occupation.* Had Latvia and Estonia remained communist in the inter-war period the Lutheran Church, together with all the other Christian Churches and groups of the two Baltic countries, would have gone through a martyrdom of blood. But by the mercy of Providence this martydom came later and not in that violent form which it might have taken had the Soviets ruled over the Baltic states in the twenties. By 1940 the communists had become more civilised, and no longer boasted openly of the execution of pastors and the desecration of churches as they had done in the years of revolutionary

[1] P. Stuchka, *Tserkov i Shkola v Sovetskoi Latvii* (Church and School in Soviet Latvia), in *Tserkov i Revolyutsiya*, 1919, no. 2, pp. 2-5

exuberance. Still uncompromising enemies of all religion, they never-theless refrained on the whole from spectacular action, and their anti-religious measures were implemented coldly and legalistically. During the second Soviet occupation, which took place in June 1940, church life in the Baltic countries — and this applies to all Churches and not only to the Lutherans — was brought on to a level with conditions in Russia proper. This meant that article 124 of the Soviet constitution on 'freedom of religious worship and of anti-religious propaganda' was incorporated into the new Soviet Constitutions of Latvia and Estonia. Translated into practical terms this hypocritical article spelled the end of all religious instruction and confined the Churches exclusively to the sphere of worship. Religious teaching and morning prayers disappeared from the schools a few weeks after the establishment of the Soviet régime. Confirmation classes, Sunday schools and church choirs of children were stopped by law. The theological faculties of the universities of Riga and Tartu — the latter over three hundred years old — were closed. All religious youth organisations were suspended, and a ban was proclaimed on religious literature. On August 22, 1940, only two months after the annexation, the Soviet State security organs issued an order that religious literature of any kind was to be 'confiscated from all bookshops, publishers, and libraries'.[1] The same thing happened in Latvia.[2]

The new rulers in the Baltic states also attempted to reduce religious activities through economic pressure. Church buildings, vicarages, and all church property, were nationalised. This proved ruinous, particularly to clergymen and organists. As persons not engaged in work of social importance, to quote communist legal terminology, they had to pay rents which were six to eight times higher than those exacted from the ordinary citizen. The authorities hoped that parsons, faced with im-possible financial burdens, might give up their ecclesiastical profession, and in some cases they really forced them to look for jobs in factories or on farms. Public utility plants discriminated heavily against churches. Electric current for churches in Estonia cost fourteen times the usual tariff.[3]

In the short period between the annexation of the Baltic states by the Soviet Union and their occupation by the Nazis there was not much time for a great deal of anti-religious propaganda. Sections of the League

---

[1] Rahva Hääl, August 23, 1940, quoted by H. Perlitz, *The Fate of Religion and Church under Soviet Rule in Estonia, 1940–1941*, World Association of Estonians, New York 1944, p. 35.
[2] Dr. Alfred Bilmanis, *The Church in Latvia*, New York 1945, p. 23.
[3] H. Perlitz, op. cit., p. 41.

of Militant Godless (LMG) were, it is true, organised in Latvia and Estonia, but their membership must have been very small since it could only be recruited from among active supporters of the communist régime, of whom there were few. Anti-religious propagandists in the Baltic countries could not simply reproduce the arguments employed by the LMG in Russia proper; they had to take into account specific local conditions. For instance, the observation of Reformation Day (October 31) by Latvian and Estonian Lutherans faced them with a new problem. The Soviet *bezbozhniki* had conducted anti-Christmas, anti-Easter, anti-Passover and anti-Kurban Bayrami agitation but an anti-Reformation Day campaign was something new. The central organ of the Estonian Communist Party on October 31, 1940, published an attack on Martin Luther 'the zealous lackey of oppressors and exploiters' who had made of the new 'reformed' Church 'the same instrument of exploitation and oppression as all other Churches'. No official ban on the observation of Reformation Day was issued, but the Estonians were exhorted to commemorate not Martin Luther but 'the peasants who fell for the liberation of the oppressed rural people'.[1]

In the practical application of their religious policy the communist rulers of the Baltic states considered the Churches not only as ideological but also as political opponents. From the Soviet point of view both the Lutheran and the Catholic Churches were important political factors championing a Western orientation in countries which historically and culturally are in any case linked with the West. Soviet police organs devoted special attention to Lutheran pastors and to Catholic and Orthodox priests, less as church representatives than as leaders of the community with considerable knowledge of the mood of the population. A joint memorandum by a prominent Lutheran and an Orthodox church leader of Estonia gives a good picture of the cruel dilemma to which the Estonian clergy were exposed from the beginning of the Soviet occupation. The following is a quotation from it: 'A considerable number of the clergy soon fell victims to the NKVD. They were constantly summoned for questioning, mostly at night, and hard pressed by threats and violence to give information concerning the thoughts and beliefs of their flock; the Soviet Secret Police tried every means to force them to give evidence on the negative attitude of members of their congregations, as well as other citizens, towards the Soviet régime, and thus to make them join the ranks of the secret informers. These methods put the clergy under an almost unbearable strain and called forth sharp conflicts — as the possibility of their own annihilation and that of the

[1] Rahva Hääl, October 31, 1940, quoted by H. Perlitz, op. cit., p. 38.

members of their families in the event of refusal was kept always before their eyes by the Soviet authorities.'[1]

Although this is a description of conditions in Estonia only, there can be little doubt that the situation in Latvia was almost identical. It was the hope of the Soviet authorities to intimidate the servants of religious cults in the Baltic countries and if possible to use them in the interest of the Soviet State. Had the Soviet-German War not broken out in June 1941 the Soviet régime would have continued to fight the Churches of the Baltic countries by means of countless petty vexations rather than by any large-scale persecution. But the nazi invasion, the defeats of the Soviet armies in the first days of the war, and the confusion and panic in the Soviet rear made things different. At the end of June and the beginning of July 1941 mass arrests and deportations were carried out in Latvia and Estonia. Lutheran pastors were among the many distinguished citizens who were forcibly exiled to the East. Eight pastors from Latvia, including two professors of the Theological Faculty, were deported and seventeen prominent churchmen, including Professor Dr. Ramahägi, retired bishop of the Estonian Evangelical Lutheran Church from Estonia. In addition, seven Estonian pastors were drafted into the army as ordinary soldiers. Three Latvian and two Estonian pastors were killed at the time of the Soviet retreat.[2]

3. *The Third Occupation.* The end of the war found the Lutheran Churches of Estonia and Latvia in a most precarious situation. Many churches were destroyed and a large number of pastors had either fled the country or been forcibly removed to Germany by the nazi authorities. In Estonia only 77 out of the previous total of 250 clergymen stayed behind. Those who left the country in 1944, shortly before its re-occupation by the Soviets, did so for fear that they might have to share the fate of those pastors deported to the interior of the USSR three years before. Few of the more prominent churchmen stayed in the country. Bishop Köpp, Ramahägi's successor, sought safety in Sweden, some members of the Consistory went with him and most of the professors of the Lutheran Theological Faculty either went abroad or disappeared in Soviet camps.[3] From Latvia 134 pastors either fled to Germany or were deported by the Nazis, 14 left for Sweden, and

[1] Memorandum by the Dean of the Evangelical Lutheran Church of Estonia, Aleksandr Täheväli and the Dean of the Orthodox Church of Estonia, Juri Valbe, quoted by Aleksandr Kaelas, *Human Rights and Genocide in the Baltic States*, Stockholm, Estonian Information Centre 1950, p. 24.

[2] *The Lutheran Churches of the World, 1952*, published by the Lutheran World Federation, Geneva 1952, pp. 187, 196.

[3] Jaak Survel, *Estonia To-day*, London 1947 p. 46.

94 remained in Latvia. As in Estonia the majority of the more distinguished church dignitaries had left, including Archbishop Teodors Grinbergs, whom the Gestapo compelled to leave for Germany. The damage caused to church buildings by the war was also very considerable. In Estonia 10 churches were destroyed and 42 damaged during the military operations of 1941 and 20 more churches were destroyed in the operations of 1944. The total of damaged and destroyed churches may be very near the 100 mark.[1] In Latvia 42 churches were destroyed and about 80 heavily damaged.[2] It does not appear that the communists desecrated church buildings or used them for secular purposes once hostilities were ended. Only in the course of actual military operations did they use churches as ammunition dumps and for the storage of grain; afterwards they returned them to the congregations.[3]

After peace was restored the two Lutheran Churches tried to rebuild their administrative framework as well as they could with their reduced possibilities. In Estonia these attempts did not proceed smoothly. Pastor August Pähn, who was made bishop in 1945, had considerable difficulties with the Soviet authorities. He disappeared from his post, was accused of having collaborated with the Germans and was deported in 1951 to a forced labour camp in Vorkuta. Pastor Jaan Kiivit succeeded him, and later assumed the title of Archbishop. Under his leadership the Estonian Lutheran Church recuperated only very slightly from the losses which it suffered during the war. In 1956 the Church had again 170 church buildings[4] but there were only 122 pastors. The balance had to be made up by untrained or inadequately trained auxiliary pastors and lay-preachers. Urban parishes are large and often prosperous but in rural areas church attendance on Sundays is small, particularly in the winter. Many churches are unheatable and the distances to be covered by the parishioners are in many cases considerable.

In Latvia church life was normalised in March 1948, when the Evangelical Lutheran Church summoned its ninth General Synod. The Synod elected a new Archbishop, as well as a Supreme Church Council, and adopted new statutes for the Latvian Lutheran Church. The pastor elected Archbishop was Gustavs Turs, parish priest of Bauska, a small town near the Latvian-Lithuanian border. He had not completed his theological training, and was admitted to the clerical profession with the proviso that he could not aspire to offices above the level of parish priest. During the independent Latvian Republic he was suspended

[1] Jaak Survel, op. cit., p. 46.   [2] *Baznicas Kalendars*, Riga 1948, p. 33.
[3] Endel Kareda, *Estonia in the Soviet grip*, London 1949, p. 44.
[4] *One Church*, vol. x, 1956, no. 5–6, p. 167.

from office for a time.[1] Turs was elected Archbishop only because he was *persona grata* with the Soviet régime and because the latter had eliminated from the scene all rival candidates, being especially careful to remove those whom Archbishop Grinbergs had personally designated to succeed him. The first among these was Provost Irbe, who returned from Siberia to Latvia only after the post-Stalin amnesties. According to a trustworthy source the Soviet police early in 1948 arrested four pastors who opposed Turs's formal elevation to the dignity of Archbishop.

All this may not be very much to Turs's credit. Nevertheless, on those who have met him abroad he produced the not unfavourable impression of an unpretentious person conscious of his weakness, and a sincere churchman trying to cope as well as he can with great difficulties both inside the Church and in the field of Church-State relations. The extent of the purely internal difficulties of Latvian Lutheranism can be gathered from the report which he himself delivered at the ninth General Synod. The report noted the existence in Latvia of 322 Lutheran parishes but in many of them there could be no regular religious services because of the lack of pastors.[2] This precarious situation has not undergone a major change. In 1956 the number of Lutheran pastors in Latvia did not exceed 120. The Archbishop has carried out a few ordinations from time to time, just sufficient in number to fill the vacancies in those parishes where the incumbents have died.

The Lithuanian Lutherans

The problem of the Lithuanian Lutheran Church differs in several respects from that of the Estonian and Latvian Lutheran Churches. One might be inclined to dismiss Lithuanian Lutheranism as of very minor consequence, considering the enormous weight of the Catholic Church in Lithuania's national life. However, Protestantism played a notable part in the history of the Lithuanian national awakening which started among the Lithuanians of East Prussia, in particular the so-called Lithuania Minor, known as the Memelland or the territory of Klajpeda, in the period between the two wars.

On the eve of the Second World War there were two Lutheran Churches within Lithuania's present boundaries, one in the Memelland, the other in Lithuania proper. In the former, Lutheranism was the

---

[1] Harald Biezais, 'Das lettische Luthertum unter dem Kommunismus', *Der Remter* 1957, no. 5, p. 10.
[2] *Baznicas Kalendars*, Riga 1948, p. 33.

religion of the great majority. The 153,000 Lutherans of the area had 64 churches, in the care of 68 pastors. The Lutheran Churches of Lithuania, with 75,000 members, had 30 pastors. The head of the Memel Lutherans was a general superintendent, that of their brethren in Lithuania a bishop.

The Memelland Protestants were incorporated into German East Prussia in March 1939: thus when the Soviet authorities occupied Lithuania fifteen months later they found only one Lutheran Church there. Soon its ranks were to be greatly depleted. In February and March 1941 a transfer of population was carried out on the basis of a Nazi-Soviet agreement. Evacuated from Lithuania to Germany were nearly 52,000 people, the overwhelming majority of whom belonged to the Protestant faith. Officially the transfer was of ethnic Germans only, but quite a number of Lithuanian-born Protestants eager to escape Soviet rule managed to get themselves included in the lists of the re-settlers. In this way Lithuania lost the majority of its Lutheran believers and over two-thirds of its Lutheran pastors. Some had already been arrested and were released only when it was their turn to be removed to Germany.[1]

After a spell of nazi occupation Lithuania in 1945 came again under Soviet rule, which this time extended also to the Memelland. The majority of the Memellanders fled to Germany. Others perished, but a nucleus of 40,000 Lutherans stayed behind. These built up their Lutheran Church again in the face of great handicaps, for many church buildings had been destroyed, few pastors had remained on the spot, and there were no facilities for a proper training for the Protestant ministry. The newly organised congregations found a way out of these difficulties by ordaining capable and devout laymen from their midst. These new pastors came from all walks of life. Often they retained their secular jobs, which they performed during the week, confining their pastoral activities to Sundays. In one place the pastor would be a locksmith, in another the storekeeper of a state farm. Other recruits to the new Lutheran clergy in Lithuania were a postman, a former customs officer and a teacher.[2] Outside the Memelland the Lithuanian Lutheran Church is likewise recruiting lay preachers, as only eight pastors survived the war. The Evangelical Lutheran Church of Lithuania is directed by a consistory consisting of four pastors and three laymen. The chairman is a Kaunas lawyer who is said to have tolerable relations with the authorities.[3]

---

[1] M. Gelzinis, *Christenverfolgung in Litauen*, Koenigstein, no date, p. 68.
[2] M. Gelzinis, op. cit., pp. 70–72.   [3] *Der Remter*, 1959, no. 4, p. 241.

Baltic Lutheranism and Soviet Diplomacy

As everywhere in the Soviet Union, relations between Church and State were profoundly affected in the Baltic countries by the participation of the Churches in the peace campaign. The campaign made heavy demands on both Archbishop Turs in Latvia and Archbishop Kiivit in Estonia. Apart from taking part in peace conferences and signing peace manifestos themselves, they had to see to it that the pastors under their jurisdiction took their full share in propaganda work and that the peace theme figured prominently in all sermons. The theme could not be treated in an abstract sense, as a Christian might fittingly have treated it: the Government's chief concern was that the servants of the cult should denounce the so-called 'enemies of peace', the Western powers. The zeal which the Lutheran archbishops and pastors displayed in the peace movement became the touchstone of their loyalty towards the Soviet State. The Soviet authorities attached importance to the presence of the Protestant clergy in the peace movement, chiefly in the interests of Soviet and communist propaganda abroad. Archbishop Turs of Latvia became one of 110 members of the Soviet Committee for the Defence of Peace.

The more flexible diplomacy and in particular the new Soviet policy of increased contacts with the West which the Kremlin pursued after Stalin's death gave the Lutheran Churches a further opportunity to co-operate with the régime. The Soviet Government showed interest in obtaining the support of the German Evangelical Church for the idea of a neutralist, if not anti-Western Germany — support which would also strengthen Russian prestige in the Soviet-occupied zone (the so-called 'German Democratic Republic'). The first tentative contacts were made even in Stalin's lifetime, with Niemoeller's visit to Moscow in January 1952. The first official German Evangelical Church delegation, however, came to the Soviet Union only in June–July 1954. It was headed by Dr. Gustav Heinemann, Chairman of the German Evangelical Synod, and the majority of its members came from Eastern Germany.[1] The Orthodox Patriarch acted as formal host to the German delegation, but, of course, the visit would have been impossible without the active co-operation of the Soviet authorities. Indeed, the German pastors and professors of divinity were ushered round by the plenipotentiaries of the State Council for the Affairs of the Orthodox Church, and were received by Valerian Zorin, a deputy Foreign Minister who took a special interest in German affairs.[2] The German guests went to

---

[1] *Izvestiya*, June 18, 1954.   [2] *Zh.M.P.*, 1954, no. 8, 63–75.

Leningrad, Kiev and Odessa, but they had no opportunity of visiting their Lutheran brethren in Latvia and Estonia. In 1954 it still seemed preferable to the Soviet régime to send foreign Lutheran dignitaries to the flourishing centres of Orthodox Church life in Russia and the Ukraine rather than to the Baltic Republics, where the Lutheran Church leads a precarious existence. Nevertheless, the German Lutherans had to be given some opportunity of meeting the Lutheran Church leaders of Soviet Russia, and the two Baltic Lutheran arch-bishops were therefore asked to go to the Soviet capital.

From 1955 on, the Lutheran Churches of the Baltic countries and their hierarchy have made frequent appearances on the international scene. In June 1955 Archbishop Kiivit made his first trip abroad, to attend the Helsinki peace conference. In the following month both Lutheran Baltic bishops were allowed to leave the Soviet Union as members of an Orthodox-Lutheran-Baptist delegation visiting Scotland and England. The members of the delegation were able to establish extensive contact both with the Church of England and with Non-comformist bodies. They made numerous speeches and statements which conveyed, mostly by their omissions, a favourable picture of the situation of the Churches under Soviet rule. The presence of the two Lutheran bishops on the delegation enhanced its prestige and was one reason for its success — success, that is, from the point of view of the Soviet Government. In allowing an important delegation of ecclesiastical dignitaries to travel to Britain the Soviet Government hoped to deceive British public opinion and to lull its vigilance.

Soon after their return to the Soviet Union, in August and September 1955, a new German Evangelical delegation came to Russia under Dr. Heinrich Held, Chairman of the Evangelical Church of the Rhineland. This delegation was more representative than its predecessor. Most of its members were from Western Germany. This new delegation was authorised to visit Riga and to attend Lutheran services there. Now the ice was at last broken. In November 1955 another representative delegation visited Riga, this time from the Evangelical Lutheran Church of Denmark, more unequivocally Lutheran in its theology than the German Protestant delegation. It was headed by Fuglsang-Damgaard, Bishop of Copenhagen, and included the Bishop of Aarhus, Erik Jensen. The German Protestants had participated only in the singing of psalms when attending a Riga church service.[1] Bishop Fuglsang-Damgaard was given permission to preach in the packed Lutheran Cathedral.[2] To be addressed by such a foreign guest, not by

[1] *Zh.M.P.*, 1955, no. 10, p. 79.   [2] *Zh.M.P.*, 1956, no. 2, p. 31.

a fellow-traveller but by a Lutheran bishop of a democratic country, must have given tremendous satisfaction to the Latvian Lutheran Christians. The Iron Curtain was lifted for them, if only for a brief moment.

In the years which followed the Iron Curtain was lifted repeatedly. Numerous foreign ecclesiastical visitors were permitted to go to Riga and finally even to Tallin, for many years a city prohibited to foreigners. The two Baltic Lutheran archbishops were allowed to go abroad on several occasions, even to the United States. No doubt, the Soviet Government felt that these contacts between Soviet and foreign ecclesiastical dignitaries would be advantageous to the USSR, and so it proved. The foreign Protestants who toured the Soviet Union usually commented on the religious situation in that country in a way which was not unfavourable to the régime. Indeed, no other course was left to them if they did not wish to aggravate the situation of the various Russian church leaders who had acted as their hosts. There is a price for every concession which the Soviet State makes to a religious body and political neutrality is the price which the Kremlin is trying to exact from world Protestantism for being able to maintain relations with the Churches of the Soviet Union.

Lutheranism under the post-Stalin Régime

The post-Stalin régime has also granted the Lutherans a few concessions at home. A number of pastors have returned from Siberia. The training of pastors, assistant pastors and organists, which until 1955 was virtually impossible, can now again be undertaken. There are still no theological training colleges, but theological evening classes can be held. Church calendars are published in both Latvia and Estonia. These publications are not free from propaganda in support of the régime but they nevertheless contain much that is valuable for the believer. In 1954 permission was also granted for the printing of a Latvian Lutheran hymn book, the first to appear since the establishment of the Soviet régime, in the Baltic states. It is a well-produced book, with stiff covers and on good-quality paper. It comprises 417 pages and contains 475 hymns. Five thousand copies were printed.[1] One can well imagine with what enthusiasm the appearance of this book must have been greeted by the Latvian Lutherans. That the book could be published at all is certainly a sign of improved Church-State relations and it might even be considered as proof of greater communist tolerance

---

[1] *Dziesmu Gramata* (Hymnbook), Riga 1954, published by the Supreme Church Council of the Evangelical Lutheran Church

towards religious groups. However, this optimistic assessment is somewhat marred by the omissions which a more thorough scrutiny of the
hymnal reveal. These are significant omissions and show very clearly
how difficult and precarious church life has remained for the Lutherans
in the Soviet Union. For instance, from a well-known hymn which
starts with the words 'Praise the Almighty, my soul adore him' (in
German 'Lob den Herrn, o meine Seele . . .', in Latvian 'Slave to
Kungu ak Dvēs'le Mana') the following lines have been cut:

> 'Trust not in princes, they are but mortal
> Earth-born they are and soon decay,
> Naught are their counsels at life's last portal,
> When the dark grave doth claim its prey.
> Since, then, no man can help afford,
> Trust ye in Christ, our God and Lord.'[1]

The verse may have been omitted on the order of the Soviet censorship or by the frightened Lutheran Church Council itself. The reason
in either case can only be guessed. The hymnal was published very
soon after Stalin's death and although the verse about the mortal,
earth-born and soon-decaying princes is two hundred years old, some
people might have seen in it a topical allusion.

Even more significant was the censoring of Martin Luther's most
famous hymn, 'A mighty fortress is our God' (in German 'Ein' feste
Burg ist unser Gott', in the Latvian translation 'Dievs kungs ir mūsu
stipra pils'). Lutherans know this hymn by heart, and any omission
from the full text is sure to be noticed at once and to draw attention to
the deleted passages. These are the verses which were not included
in the hymn as published in the Latvian Lutheran hymn book:

> 'Tho' devils all the world should fill,
> All eager to devour us,
> We tremble not, we fear no ill,
> They shall not overpow'r us.
> The World's prince may still scowl fierce as he will,
> He can harm us none,
> He is judged; the deed is done;
> One little word can fell him.

[1] The other verses of the same hymn appear in *Dziesmu Gramata* on page 204. The
English version is taken from the *Lutheran Hymnal*, authorised by the Synods con-
stituting the Evangelical–Lutheran Synodical Conference of North America, Concordia
Publishing House, Missouri, 1941. (Hymn 26.)

The word they still shall let remain
Nor any thanks have for it;
He's by our side upon the plain
With his good gifts and spirit.
And take they our life,
Goods, fame, child and wife,
Let all this be gone,
They yet have nothing won,
The Kingdom ours remaineth.[1]

The authorities who censored Luther's famous hymn must have feared that those who sang it would make it a song of defiance against the Soviet régime, which has certainly taken the life, goods and fame of many a Latvian, and has also taken a good deal away from the Churches. Even the post-Stalin period cannot be described as a period of restoration, but has been in some respects one of deterioration in the situation of Baltic Lutheranism. In May 1959, the régime confiscated the historic cathedral of Riga, seven centuries old, although it had served as a useful show-place testifying to communist religious tolerance. There was no preliminary announcement. One day the people of Riga simply read in their newspapers that from now on there was only a 'cathedral-museum' which the Latvian Philharmonic Orchestra would use as a concert hall.[2]

More serious than the confiscation of Riga Cathedral are the attempts of the post-Stalin régime to drive a wedge between the Protestant Churches and the younger generation. The communists of Estonia and Latvia, like their East German comrades, have created a ceremony intended as a secular rival to the Protestant confirmation service. In Latvia and Estonia, this new communist ceremony has become known as 'Coming of Age Festival'. (*Prazdnik Sovershenoletiya*). It has a blatant anti-religious character and its celebration is usually timed in such a way as to coincide with the confirmation service in church. The Komsomol which organises the 'Coming of Age Festival' relies on the fact that participation in it is free whilst the pastors are forced to demand a modest sum from the parents of the confirmation candidates. The Komsomol even gives presents to those taking part in the Festival as well as special 'Coming-of-Age Certificates'. Every attempt is made to make the occasion no less solemn than the church ceremony. The girls are dressed in white and the boys in dark suits. There is usually a

[1] *Dziesmu Gramata*, p. 288; *The Lutheran Hymnal*, Hymn 262.
[2] *Sovetskaya Latviya*, May 13, 1959.

procession with banners and an orchestra and guards of honour formed by the communist pioneer organisation.[1] The 'communist confirmation' has met with scepticism and even opposition from the Lutheran villagers and the functionaries of the régime have to argue a great deal with them to try and prove that the 'Coming of Age Festival' is really something fine and useful.[2]

A positive development of the post-Stalin era as far as the Lutheran Church is concerned is its revival outside the Baltic republics. For instance, news reached the outside world that the Lutheran Estonians and Finns living in the Russian Federation south of Leningrad still continue some sort of Lutheran church life under the direction of three old pastors and some lay preachers. In one place confirmation of young people and baptism were carried out in the open in the absence of a building for worship.[3] More important is the religious revival among the one and a half million Germans of Siberia and Central Asia. The vast majority of them came to Soviet Asia as deportees during and after World War II. For years they enjoyed no community life whatever. They were unable to engage in any cultural and political activities and were reduced to the status of pariahs. It was one of their many disabilities that they were deprived of even that measure of precarious religious freedom which is granted to the other nationalities of the USSR. Only the amnesty of September 17, 1955 created a more normal situation for the German minority in Soviet Asia and led to a re-emergence of the Evangelical Lutheran Church. Groups of Lutheran Christians formed in various Siberian and Kazakh towns, such as Barnaul, Pavlodar, Slavgorod, Omsk and Karaganda. In one place, Akmolinsk, they were even allowed to attend services conducted by an ordained pastor, a graduate of the Leningrad theological seminary. Elsewhere their services are conducted by lay preachers. Freed from concern for their physical survival, the members of the German colony turned their attention to their spiritual recovery. They became aware of their deep need for the Bible and the sacraments, and desired to meet for prayer and worship.[4] It is difficult to imagine how charged with emotion must have been the atmosphere in these improvised Lutheran parishes, especially during the first services held in 1956 and 1957. One eye-witness report describes a service that took place in a barn, and lasted from nine o'clock in the morning to four in the afternoon. Such was the length of time needed to perform all the baptisms,

[1] *Molodoy Kommunist*, 1959, no. 2, p. 99.
[2] *Molodoy Kommunist*, 1959, no. 2, p. 98.
[3] Ecumenical Press Service, November 8, 1957.
[4] Ecumenical Press Service, September 6, 1957.

confirmations and marriage ceremonies. A gap of twenty to twenty-five years had to be made good in a single day. Some families had all their children baptised, and the older ones confirmed, whilst father and mother had their marriage bond solemnised by the Church all at the same time.[1]

II. CALVINISTS

As Protestantism is, for good or ill, abandoning what Protestants themselves call 'confessionalism', the divisions of the Protestant camp become less important. This is due not only to the growth of an ecumenical sense in Protestantism but also to an increase in religious indifference, for the theological differences between Lutherans and Calvinists are very real. Lutherans believe in the real presence of Christ in the eucharistic bread and wine, but the 'Lord's Supper' of the Calvinists is quite devoid of such significance. Inter-communion between Lutherans and Calvinists would therefore seem impossible. When these two main branches of Protestantism first penetrated into Russia the differences between them were much felt and even the authorities never confused the two groups. In the legislation of the Czars dealing with religious matters the two creeds always find separate mention.

The history of the Reformed Calvinist Church in Russia may be said to have started in 1629 when its first house of worship was opened in Moscow, fifty-three years after the first Lutheran church. The Lutherans at first regarded their reformed brethren with a certain envy as they enjoyed the support of powerful foreign sovereigns such as the King of Holland. By contrast the patrons of the Lutheran churches were the politically insignificant German Lutheran princes. Only the beginnings of the German peasant colonisation of the Volga region and the Russian South brought the Lutherans a clear advantage over the Calvinists. Very few of the many Protestant parishes which these colonists founded belonged to the Reformed Church — no more than four in the entire Black Sea region. Naturally, spiritual forces cannot be measured in numerical terms alone, and among the few Reformed parishes there was one that exercised tremendous influence on its Ukrainian surroundings. This was the parish of Rohrbach-Worms, not far from Odessa. Its pastor, Karl Bonekemper, was closely associated with the beginnings of Ukrainian 'Shtundism' which later developed into the Baptist movement.[2]

[1] Ostkircheninformationsdienst, March 27, 1958.
[2] *Bratskii Vestnik*, 1957, no. 3, pp. 10–11

The colonists adhering to the Reformed creed came originally from Alsace, the Palatinate, and Switzerland. Some of them preserved their independence right to the end, but this independence existed only on the parish level; there was no special central organisation of the Reformed Protestants in Russia. There existed only Reformed Departments within the Consistories of Russia's Evangelical Church. During the years of communist persecution of religion the division between Lutherans and Reformed Christians dwindled further in importance. By 1930 there was probably only one Reformed church left, that of Odessa, and this too was soon closed. In fact, Russia's Reformed Church might have died altogether had it not been strengthened during and after the Second World War by the incorporation into the Soviet Union of thousands of Calvinists.

1. The Calvinist Church of the Transcarpathian Ukraine

The most important single Reformed group to find itself within the Soviet Empire as a result of Soviet territorial annexations in Eastern Europe was the Calvinist Church of the Transcarpathian Ukraine. It grew up in Hungary, a country where the Calvinist-Lutheran division has deep roots and real significance. Lutheranism in Hungary has always been multi-national Hungarian-German-Slovak, whilst Calvinism has been almost purely Magyar. Transcarpathian Calvinism, like that of the Hungarian Mother-Church, is Hungarian in national character. In Soviet conditions it is the only organisation of the Hungarian minority in the Ukraine. It has about 95,000 members, divided among ninety parishes and served by sixty-seven ministers.[1] Its hierarchical head, at first called 'Dean', later assumed the title of Bishop.

It would appear that the Calvinists of the Transcarpathian Ukraine made no converts among the Ukrainians themselves. However, there was an organised group of Ukrainian Calvinists in existence on the other side of the Carpathians in Eastern Galicia, when the Soviet troops occupied that territory in September 1939.

2. The Ukrainian Evangelical Reformed Church

The history of Galicia's Ukrainian Calvinism began in 1925 when a conference in Stanislav decided to set up an Evangelical Ukrainian

---

[1] *Izvestiya*, November 25, 1950.

Church. The leading Ukrainians at the conference were Pastor Basil Kusiv and Pastor Paul Crath.[1] Kusiv (1887–1958) later became Superintendent of the Ukrainian Evangelical Reformed Church founded in 1935 in Kolomea.[2]

At one time it was uncertain whether Ukrainian Protestantism would become predominantly Lutheran or Calvinist, but the Calvinists had from the start a certain advance over the other party. The Reformed Heidelberg Catechism appeared in the Ukrainian language in 1927, two years before the Lutheran Augsburg Catechism. Moreover, Ukrainian Calvinism already existed among the Ukrainian emigrants in North America where a Ukrainian Evangelical Alliance was founded in 1922 and its representatives (Presbyterians) exercised no small influence on the strengthening of the Protestant movement in Galicia.

One may, of course, dismiss Ukrainian Calvinism as altogether artificial and alien to the Ukrainian people and their traditional form of religious life. Yet a case can be made for considering the Ukrainian Evangelical-Reformed Church as a Ukrainian national institution, despite its numerical insignificance. From a national Ukrainian standpoint, Orthodoxy may be broadly identified as the religion of the Great Russians and Latin Catholicism as that of the other 'hereditary enemy' of the Ukrainians — the Poles. The Ukrainians have tried hard to find a national Church of their own, and the nearer we come to the present day, the more intense has this search become. To many Ukrainians the alternative to Muscovite Orthodoxy and Polish Catholicism has been not a 'new religion' but a brand of Orthodoxy and Catholicism more congenial to the Ukrainian national character. Such Churches acceptable to Ukrainian nationalism were the Ukrainian Autocephalous Orthodox Church and the Catholic Church of the Slavo-Byzantine Rite in Galicia and the Transcarpathian Ukraine.

However, a small minority among the Ukrainians sought a more radical answer to the problem of the Ukrainian national Church, and one answer was the Ukrainian Evangelical Reformed Church. Its leaders do not think of it as a creation of the twentieth century. They claim lineal descent from some of the great Ukrainians of the past who, in so far as they were critics of the official Church, may be considered forerunners of the Protestant movement. These include the first Ukrainian secular philosopher Skovoroda (1722–94) and the two poets

---

[1] Hans Koch, 'Über Ukrainischen Protestantismus', *Die Evangelische Diaspora*, vol. xiii, 1931, p. 107.
[2] *Ekklesia*, Band 5, 'Die Europäischen Länder, Die Evangelischen Kirchen in Polen', Leipzig, 1938, p. 199.

Ivan Franko (1856–1916) and Taras Shevchenko (1814–61). Ukrainian Protestants would quote in particular Shevchenko's poem 'The Heretic' which is a tribute to Jan Hus, the Czech reformer. These three Ukrainian writers can of course be interpreted in various ways, and the Soviet régime also claims them as its intellectual ancestors and as champions of materialism and atheism.[1]

When the Soviets took over in Galicia, the Ukrainian Reformed, Church had thirty congregations and fifteen ordained priests. A number of new candidates for the Reformed ministry were being trained in various West European universities.[2] The Soviet authorities suppressed the Church, perhaps chiefly because of its staunch nationalist character. Its ministers and lay readers stood high on the list of suspected persons. A number of them were arrested and deported, others escaped to the West. Among those who escaped was the Superintendent Kusiv, who later became President of the Ukrainian Evangelical Alliance of North America. This organisation continues the tradition of the Ukrainian Reformed Church of Galicia, which, however, has not been entirely swept away by communist persecution. The post-Stalin amnesties resulted in the return to Galicia of a number of its members.

3. The Reformed Church of Lithuania

Ukrainian Calvinism, a creation of such recent date, forms a direct contrast with the third Reformed Church to fall under Soviet rule as a result of World War II, that of Lithuania. This Church looks back on four hundred years of history, and an impressive history it is. In the middle of the sixteenth century the whole of the Lithuanian nobility tended towards Calvinism and for a short period Lithuania had as many as two hundred Calvinist parishes. The success of the counter-Reformation brought this Calvinist advance almost to nothing, and only a small residue was left. In the independent Lithuanian Republic of the period between the World Wars the Reformed Church comprised only twelve parishes, seven pastors and two superintendents. The two superintendents and all but two pastors left with the German resettlers in 1941. These two remained in the country even when the Red Army occupied it for the second time.[3] Thanks to them the small Reformed Church of Lithuania has been able to weather all storms. It is now once more administered by a superintendent.

[1] I. F. Fessak, *Klassiki Ukrainskoi Literaturi pro Religiyu* (The Classics of Ukrainian literature about religion), Kiiv 1960, pp. 6, 8, 23.

[2] *News Bulletin* No. 1, The Ukrainian Evangelical Alliance of North America, 1957, p. 2.

[3] M. Gelzinis, op. cit., p. 72.

III. THE 'FOURTH PARTY OF THE REFORMATION'

Communists and Anabaptists

It is the generally accepted view that three religious parties existed in the Reformation period, Catholics, Lutherans and Calvinists. It may however be argued that there existed not three parties but four, the fourth being the Anabaptists with all their off-shoots. The spiritual descendants of the Anabaptists at least claim for their ancestors the honour of being the fourth great party of the Reformation. The communists readily endorse this view, for up to a point the 'fourth party' is their party, the only one they view with favour and sympathy and which they even regard as their forerunner. Luther was a traitor to the people and a servant of the princes, Calvin was the ideologist and theologian of merchant capitalism, but Thomas Muenzer (1490–1525), the outstanding figure of the Anabaptist movement, is in communist eyes a 'great revolutionary'. The communists find Muenzer an attractive figure not only because he led the plebeian camp in the Reformation, not only because he had a 'dim presentiment of Communism', but also because he was the nearest approach to a rationalist and agnostic at the beginning of the sixteenth century. Indeed, the communists define Muenzer's theological concept as a 'variant of pantheism which comes near to atheism'.[1] This Soviet assessment is by no means new, but goes back to Friedrich Engels. Muenzer, said Engels, was a heretic not just in relation to Catholicism, as was Luther, but in relation to Christianity.[2] Luther only dethroned the Church in favour of the Bible, but Muenzer dethroned the Bible in favour of human reason.

Communist praise is bestowed not only on Muenzer but also on all the more extremist Anabaptist groups which emerged after Muenzer's death. A special place of honour in communist history is occupied by the Anabaptist fanatics who in 1553–4 established a rule of terror in the Westphalian city of Muenster. Communist historians refer to the Anabaptist adventure in Muenster by the honourable name of the 'Muenster Commune', putting it on a level with the 'Paris Commune' of 1871 or the 'Canton Commune' of 1927.[3]

It might be supposed that the problem of Anabaptism is for the Soviet communists a rather remote, if not altogether uninteresting, historical problem, but this is not so. They have had to deal with large

[1] *L.S.E.*, vol. xxviii, Moscow 1954, p. 644.
[2] Friedrich Engels, *The Peasant War in Germany*, London 1927, p. 65.
[3] See article *Myunsterskaya Kommuna* (The Muenster Commune), in *L.S.E.*, vol. xxviii, Moscow 1954, p. 641.

and compact groups of descendents of the Anabaptists within the territory of the Soviet Union. The members of these groups have little in common with Thomas Muenzer and the Anabaptist revolutionaries of Muenster. In fact they clearly dissociate themselves from the excesses of the latter. The Anabaptists of Russia trace their origins back to the peaceful, more religious than political-minded wing of the Anabaptist movement of the sixteenth century, and in particular to the Dutchman Menno Simonis (1496–1561), a one-time Catholic priest who left his former Church in 1536. His is the name borne by the largest section of the 'fourth party' in the world to-day — the 'Mennonites'. When the communists took over the government of Russia they found over 100,000 Mennonites under their rule. By the outbreak of the Revolution there were over 365 Mennonite villages whose aggregate land holdings were larger in size than the whole of Ulster.

The Mennonites in Czarist Russia

The first seeds of this large Mennonite colonisation were sown in 1788 when a group of Mennonites landed on Khortitsa, a long, narrow and at that time completely uninhabited island in the river Dnieper. These first Russian Mennonites came from the Danzig region where they found asylum even during Menno Simonis' lifetime. They left that place of refuge because in 1772 Danzig became part of the state of Frederick the Great, who was unwilling to grant them freedom from military service, which they have always held to be essential to their concept of religion. To preserve that freedom the Mennonites never hesitated to leave their familiar surroundings and to settle in strange and unknown lands. It was very largely the promise of that freedom by Catherine II and Paul I which brought them to Russia and again it was very largely the withdrawal of that freedom which drove them out of the country.

A few years after the Mennonite migration to Khortitsa the second and more important Mennonite centre came into being on the river Molochna, now in the Zaporozhe Province of the Ukraine. The first Mennonites settled there in 1803–4. The names which they gave to some of the villages they established reflect the grace and peace they believed they had found in their new homes in the Russian South — Gnadenfeld, Gnadental, Gnadenheim and Friedensdorf. By 1836 there were forty-six villages on the Molochna and by 1863 the number had risen to fifty-seven.

The island of Khortitsa and the Molochna region were the home of what came to be known as the Mennonite 'mother-colonies'. The high

birthrate in these original Mennonite settlements soon necessitated th
foundation of daughter-colonies to absorb the surplus population. Th
establishment of these daughter-colonies was also prompted by certai
religious differences among the Mennonites. It must be pointed out i
this connection that the word 'Mennonite' is a collective term for quit
a number of religious groups who abide by the same doctrine i
essentials but differ in detail. The two main parties were the tradi
tionalist 'Old Mennonites' and the Evangelical revival movement of th
'Community of Mennonite Brethren', who fought against the declin
in religious faith among the Mennonites, many of whom tended t
think of their faith only as a part of their historical background. Th
Mennonite brethren developed under Pietist and Baptist influences
and became an important spiritual force.

In addition to these two principal trends, there were several mino
groups inclined to doctrinal and liturgical eccentricities. It was for thes
eccentrics that the new and more remote Mennonite colonies provide
a welcome outlet. One such extremist group who expected the comin
of the Antichrist hoped to find shelter from his rule in Central Asia. I
about 1880 it founded five villages on the Syr Darya river near Auli
Ata in what is now Southern Kazakhstan and another group migrate
as far as the then semi-independent Khanate of Khiva.[1] Among th
Mennonites who migrated to the Crimea in 1860 was the odd sect o
'breadbreakers' so called because its members insisted on bread bein
broken by the communicants and not given to them in small piece
already cut. The sect forbade the wearing of neckties, starched shirt
polished shoes, lace, ear-rings or any kind of jewellery.[2]

Economic motives alone determined the trek of the Mennonites fror
the Ukraine to the Volga, where another important Mennonite centr
emerged. Its beginnings go back to 1853. Mennonite settlements wer
also established in the North Caucasus region — along the Kuban rive
in 1868 and near the delta of the Terek in 1901. Other daughter
colonies came into being in Siberia, particularly around Barnau
Slavgorod, Pavlodar and Minusinsk. Of all these colonies only th
Terek settlement with its fifteen villages was considered a failur
because the Mennonites were constantly terrorised and robbed by th
Caucasus mountain tribes. The Terek settlement was the only on
which the Soviets did not need to destroy; it was virtually moribun
when the communists established their rule.[3]

---

[1] H. Goerz, *Die Molotschnaer Ansiedlung*, Steinbach, Manitoba, 1951.
[2] C. H. Smith, *Story of the Mennonites*, Newton, Kansas 1957, p. 438.
[3] C. P. Toews, *Die Tereker Ansiedlung*, Rosthern, Saskatchewan, 1947, p. 71.

18. The German Lutheran church in Akmolinsk, Kazakhstan (1958).

19. The Moscow Evangelical Christian/Baptist house of prayer
or 'House of the Gospel'.

20. The Moscow 'House of the Gospel': A Sunday congregation in 1959.

21. Communion service in the House of the Gospel. The service is taken by Jacob Zhidkov, Chairman of the All-Union Council of the Evangelical Christians/Baptists.

It would seem that the Czarist authorities showed a considerable degree of tolerance and benevolence towards the Mennonites, but the Mennonites were in return most valuable citizens who did a great deal not only for the opening up of agricultural land but also for the development of industry. They also performed useful work in the educational sphere. On their own initiative they introduced compulsory education for all children from six to fourteen years.

Despite the continual expansion of the area of settlement and the economic wealth of the Russian Mennonites, many of them began to doubt whether Russia would remain the ideal sanctuary it had seemed to the first Mennonite colonists. These doubts had their roots in the abolition of certain privileges which the Mennonites originally enjoyed. From the beginning of their colonisation in Russia the Mennonites were placed under a special state authority which at first had its headquarters in Yekaterinoslav and later in Odessa. In 1870 this authority — the Welfare Committee as it was called — was abolished and the Mennonites had to deal in future with the ordinary Russian administration, which meant among other things that they had to use the Russian instead of the German language. Deprived of the benevolent supervision of the Welfare Committee the Mennonites feared that military conscription would soon be extended to them. This anxiety led many of them to emigrate to the new world. By 1880 nearly 18,000 Russian Mennonites had left for the United States and Canada. They left Russia without ill-will, and sent an address of thanks to the Government of the Czar expressing appreciation for all the good they had received.[1] The apprehensions of the Mennonites did not prove justified. They were not recruited into the army but a special 'forest service' was introduced for them in 1880. But even if the first emigration proved to have been inspired by a false fear, it ultimately turned out to be of benefit to the whole Mennonite community. It was these first emigrants who later assisted the Mennonite victims of the Soviet régime to build up a new existence on the other side of the ocean.

The Mennonites' Conflict with Communism

The clash between the Mennonites and the communists was inevitable from the outset. It was first of all the usual clash between a group devoted to its religious ideals and an atheistic state, but there were other elements which entered into the situation and complicated it. The Mennonites formed a special sociological group for which neither the communist doctrine of class struggle nor Soviet nationalities policy

[1] H. Goerz, *Die Molotschnaer Ansiedlung*, Steinbach, Manitoba 1957, p. 122.

K

could find any use. In vain did the Soviet authorities try to divide the Mennonite colonies into rich and poor and gain a foothold among the poor. Even the granting of national autonomy was not the way to bring about the Sovietisation of the Mennonites. The communists regarded them as Germans and therefore wanted to incorporate them into various National Districts set aside for the German minority in the Ukraine.

The Mennonites, however, felt that they were in the first place Mennonites and only in the second instance people whose mother tongue was German. They had lived apart from the Protestant and Catholic German colonists and suspected them of being the instruments of communist influence. They also feared the German National Districts as a means of pressing them into the Soviet administrative structure. To counter the Soviet manœuvres and to escape the rule of German communists, the Mennonites declared themselves to be Dutch. They founded an organisation called the 'Association of Citizens of Dutch Origin in the Ukraine' and told the authorities that they would have to send them Dutch communists if they wanted to promote the Soviet cause in the Mennonite villages.[1] This was a clever move which caused considerable annoyance to the Soviet authorities, who had no Dutch communists available. In 1926 the 'Association of the Dutch' was officially disbanded. Historically speaking, it was no more mistaken to refer to the Mennonites as 'Dutch' than to describe them as 'German' without any further qualification. We have seen that the founder of the Mennonite religion was a Dutchman, and many of the original Mennonites were either Dutch or Frisian. For all practical purposes, however, the Russian Mennonites were Germans. Nevertheless, the playing of the Dutch card shows how skilful they were in the defence of their interests. They were also upright and fearless. In 1926 a congress of Mennonites meeting in Moscow submitted a memorandum with eight 'minimum demands'. The fulfilment of these demands would be a matter of course in every democratic country, but the Soviets were bound to regard them as the height of impudence. These demands may be summarised as follows:

1. Freedom for religious meetings in both houses of prayer and private dwellings.
2. Permission to teach the Scriptures and the Faith to the young.
3. The organisation of Children's Homes (*detdoma*) for Mennonite children, where they would receive a Christian education.

[1] A. Reinmarus and G. Frizen, *Mennonity* (The Mennonites), Moscow 1930, p. 49.

4. Freedom to print Bibles and literature including periodicals.
5. Freedom to organise Bible courses for the training of religious teachers.
6. Schools to be recognised as neutral territory where teaching must be neither religious nor anti-religious.
7. No military service for Mennonites, only labour service.
8. There should be no necessity for Mennonites to take the oath. Their promise of loyalty should be sufficient.[1]

The authorities refused all these rights, but the Mennonites did not give up the struggle easily and tried by every means to protect their religious traditions and religious way of life. They upheld the Christian principle that obedience to God comes before obedience to man. For instance, when the official Mennonite Sunday schools were prohibited, smaller illegal Sunday schools were opened in private houses. Nor did Mennonite teachers abide by official instructions that they must educate the children in an atheistic spirit. In Khortitsa, the main centre of Mennonite religious conservatism, they even refused to teach the history of the Bolshevik Revolution.[2] The Khortitsa Mennonites also held out longest in their refusal to serve in the Red Army, but in other less isolated areas, especially in the Crimean settlements, official pressure was such that more and more young Mennonites reported for military service.

However, even in the early years of Soviet rule a large section of the Russian Mennonites realised that resourcefulness and courage alone would not be enough in the long run to withstand an all-powerful tyrannical Government. They came to the conclusion that it would be better to leave Russia than to wait until the atheist State finally crushed the remnants of religious freedom and added another dramatic chapter to Mennonite history. A new wave of emigration to Canada started therefore from the Mennonite colonies. 4,000 Mennonites left Russia in 1925 and as many as 6,000 in 1926, but in 1927 the Soviet Government put difficulties in their way and allowed only 900 to leave; in 1928 only 300 left.[3] Finally, the Soviet Government refused passports altogether. In this new situation the Mennonites stopped at nothing to secure their escape abroad, in spite of all the obstacles which were put in their way. In 1929 about 6,000 German-speaking Soviet citizens, the majority of them Mennonites, the minority Lutherans and Catholics, left their villages and camped in the outskirts of Moscow until exit permits were granted to them. The Mennonites of the party later went

---

[1] A. Reinmarus and G. Frizen, op. cit., pp. 83–4.
[2] A. Reinmarus and G. Frizen, op. cit., p. 67.
[3] C. Henry Smith, op. cit., p. 498.

to Canada, Brazil and Paraguay. Some Mennonites who were not allowed to go legally to America via Europe went there illegally via the Far East, using some newly established Mennonite settlements on the Amur river as the base for their escape. One winter night a group of Mennonites, with fifty-six sledges, made its escape over the ice of the Amur into Manchuria.[1] Nearly 400 Mennonite refugees who had fled from Russia through China settled in Paraguay in 1932, and a smaller contingent was admitted into Brazil.

Although a minority made adventurous escapes, the vast majority of the Mennonites had to share the same ordeals as all other religious groups in Russia under the wave of persecution which descended in 1929. The Mennonites witnessed the closing of their two preachers' training schools in Orlovo (Molochna area) and Chongrav (Crimea), the transformation of their churches into clubs, theatres, and grain stores, and the arrest of nearly all their preachers. The only Mennonite newspaper, *Unser Blatt*, was banned as early as 1927. Its former editor, the preacher Alexander Ediger, was one of the first Mennonite clerics to be arrested. He died in exile on the Arctic Sea.[2]

In their offensive against the Mennonite preachers the Soviet authorities made no distinction between those belonging to the Old Mennonites, the New Mennonites, or the Community of Mennonite Brethren, and the elders of the queer little sects. One of the Mennonite sect leaders victimised by the Soviet police was Hermann Aaron Rempel. The group which he directed, the 'Community of Evangelical-Mennonite Brethren' (as distinct from the 'Community of Mennonite Brethren') was only founded after the October Revolution, in response to the new problems created by the Revolution, and was the last revival movement to emerge among the Russian Mennonites. It insisted on the expulsion from the Mennonite ranks of all godless persons and of all those who took part in dances and worldly entertainments. Rempel soon rallied round him several hundred pious people.[3] The authorities deported Rempel from his home in the Crimea, at first putting him to forced labour in the Stalino coal-mines, later removing him to Siberia, where he died.[4] Not only the preachers, but also the rank and file members of the Mennonite communities were victimised, in particular the recalcitrant Khortitsa Mennonites, 1,500 of whom were deported in the space of ten years.[5] The persecution reached its climax during the

---

[1] Dr. Penner, op. cit., p. 157.   [2] H. Goerz, *Die Molotschnaer Ansiedlung*, p. 121.
[3] Prof. Karl Lindemann, *Von den deutschen Kolonisten in Russland*, Stuttgart 1924, pp. 22–3.
[4] H. Goerz, *Die Mennonitischen Siedlungen der Krim*, Winnipeg, Manitoba 1957, p. 44.
[5] Dr. Penner, op. cit., p. 157.

purge of 1937 when the secret police discovered 'bands of spies and diversionists' in the Mennonite villages of Western Siberia and on Khortitsa island. These alleged bands were charged with preparing an uprising in case Nazi Germany were to attack the Soviet frontiers.[1]

The End — and Rediscovery

There was no Mennonite uprising when war broke out between the Third Reich and the Soviet Union, but that war brought the Russian Mennonites very near to complete annihilation. It resulted in the end of the two mother-colonies, and led to a new Mennonite diaspora. When the nazi armies approached the Mennonite areas in the Ukraine it was the intention of the Soviet Government to deport the whole Mennonite and indeed the entire German-speaking population. However, this intention could be carried out only in part. For instance, out of the fifty-eight Mennonite villages of the Molochna region only twenty-one were entirely cleared of their population. The rapid German advance left the deportation unfinished.[2]

In 1941 the Mennonites were no longer the totally closed community they had been in the twenties. A number of them had turned their backs on religion and some had joined the Communist Party, particularly young people who had gone through a process of indoctrination, as well as a number of teachers.[3] However, the sweeping deportation measures of the Soviet authorities took no account of the 'ideological differentiation' which had taken place in the Mennonite community.

The end of the Mennonites of the Ukraine came in September and October 1943, when the Mennonites of Khortitsa and the Molochna area left their homes and went with the retreating German army. They did not do so out of sympathy with the Nazis but because nazi totalitarianism appeared as a lesser immediate threat to them than communist totalitarianism, of which they had a much longer direct experience. The great westward trek of the Mennonites of the Ukraine proved extremely costly in human lives. Only about a third of the 35,000 who left succeeded in reaching Western Germany. Many old and sick people and children perished on the way, others were overtaken by the advancing Soviet armies and deported to Siberia, or 'repatriated' from the Soviet zone of Germany.[4] Of the survivors 8,000 were absorbed by Canada and 5,000 by Paraguay. In these two countries Mennonite

[1] Kandidov, op. cit., p. 71.
[2] H. Goerz, Die Molotschnaer Ansiedlung, pp. 206–7.
[3] H. Goerz, Memrik, Eine Mennonitische Kolonie in Russland, Rosthern, Sask., 1954, p. 74.
[4] Dr. Penner, op. cit., p. 160; C. Henry Smith, op. cit., p. 526.

refugees from Soviet Russia are much appreciated as exemplary citizens and pioneer settlers.

As to the Mennonites of Russia, complete silence descended until 1956 when they were 'rediscovered' by a delegation of two men: H. S. Bender of the USA, and Preacher David B. Wiens, of Canada. According to the report published by these two American Mennonite leaders, less than one-fifth of the Russian Mennonites were still in their former places of settlement. They live in Siberia, the Altai region and Northern Kazakhstan. In these areas in 1956 there were about 125 Mennonite villages, with a total population of 15,000 to 20,000[1] All the Mennonites have disappeared from the Ukraine. They have been scattered and resettled over the whole vast area of Siberia and Central Asia, from the Arctic Sea to the Chinese border. Karaganda, the polyglot city of exiles in the heart of Kazakhstan, has become one of the biggest of the new Mennonite centres. It has about 1,000 Mennonites among its multinational population. There are also a few small Mennonite groups in the Northern part of European Russia, three of them being in the forests east of Vologda. Mennonite religious life was for twenty or twenty-five years as thoroughly suppressed as any religious activities of Russia's German Lutherans. There were no Mennonite religious meetings, no baptisms and no church weddings. Very few preachers have survived the hardships inflicted on them. Others have abandoned their former faith and only two are able to exercise their ministry. As so many men have perished, Mennonite women direct religious meetings and give Bible lessons to the young.[2] For many years now there have been no schools where the mother-tongue is taught. So the next Mennonite generation will have Russian, not German, as its main language, and if the Mennonite Church can survive at all in the Soviet Union it will have to be a predominantly Russian Church. The other alternative for the Mennonite remnants would be to amalgamate with the Russian Baptists, who have readily opened to them their houses of prayer.

*   *   *   *

The three Western Protestant trends of the Lutherans, Calvinists and Anabaptists, were blended in a strange way in the Russian-Ukrainian movement of the Evangelical Christians and Baptists. This movement was to no small extent the outcome of the common though uncoordinated efforts of the various branches of Western Protestantism.

[1] *Der Mennonit*, July 1957, no. 7, p. 86.
[2] *Der Mennonit*, August 1957, no. 8, p. 103.

IX

Western Protestantism II

(Evangelical Christians and Baptists)

———

The movement of the Evangelical Christians and Baptists has become one of the most dynamic religious forces of the Soviet Union. In Russian and Soviet official parlance the two groups are lumped together with many others under the collective term of 'sects' or 'sectarians'. However, this should not delude anyone about the unique importance of the Evangelical Christians and Baptists in Russia. They have understood better than the rest of the 'religious front' how to adapt themselves to life and work under a communist régime, not so much by making peace with it, although they have done this too on a superficial level, but by challenging it on its own ground.

The Beginnings of the Movement

Russia's Evangelical Christian and Baptist movement may be described as a synthesis of Western Protestantism with Russian-Ukrainian piety. We shall get a distorted picture of its character if we leave either of these factors out of account. The Western evangelical preachers might not have been so successful had the ground not been prepared for them by the deep spirituality of the Russian Orthodox God-seekers.

The Evangelical-Baptist movement emerged almost simultaneously in three different parts of Russia — in the Ukraine, in the Caucasus and in St. Petersburg. In the Ukraine the movement came into being under the direct influence of Lutheran and Reformed pastors and Mennonite preachers. Its first stage was known by a name derived from the German, namely 'Shtundism'. The Ukrainian peasants attended Bible lessons, in German 'Bibelstunden', hence the terms 'Shtundism' and Shtundists'. The first Ukrainian Shtundists made their appearance during the period 1858–62 roughly at the time of the emancipation of the Russian peasants. In a certain sense Shtundism and later the Baptist movement were part of this emancipation. The 'new religion' opened the way of escape from the official State Church, the Church of authorities. No doubt, there was both a spiritual-religious and a social-economic side to the emergence of Shtundism. It was the religion of the prosperous German colonists and this alone was sufficient to instil a certain respect for it among the less fortunate Ukrainian smallholders and labourers. The transition from Shtundism to the Baptist faith was accelerated by the visit to Russia of the Baptist leader Johann Gerhard Oncken (1800–84), a German whose religious beliefs were greatly influenced by Scottish Presbyterianism. Oncken came to the Ukraine in 1869 and two years later the first mass baptism of adult Ukrainians took place.

In the Caucasus the preparatory evangelical work was done by a Scotsman, Melville, agent of the British and Foreign Bible Society, and a Syrian Christian, Kasha Yakub; but the first actual propagandist of the Baptist faith was a Lithuanian, Martin Kalveit. He baptised the Russian merchant Voronin in the Kura river near Tiflis. This event took place on September 1, 1867, and is usually considered as the beginning of the Baptist movement in Russia. N. I. Voronin (1840–1905), who became a distinguished Baptist leader, was originally a member of the Russian sect of the Molokans who attached great importance to Bible reading and were therefore most receptive to Evangelical and Baptist preaching. Although Voronin may have been the first Russian Baptist, he was certainly not the first Baptist in the Russian Empire, for Baptist groups had existed in Latvia ever since 1861 when a large group of Latvians received adult baptism in the town of Vindava.

The beginnings of the Russian Evangelical movement in St. Peters-burg were quite different from the beginnings in the Ukraine and the Caucasus. The initiator was an Englishman, Lord Radstock (1833–1913), who had come under the influence of the Plymouth Brethren. His two visits to Russia in 1874 and 1877–8 had a profound influence on certain members of Russian aristocracy. Among his converts there were Pashkov, a Colonel of the Guards, Count Korff, Master of Ceremonies at the Imperial Court and Princess Natalia Lieven. They were all forerunners of the Russian Evangelical Christians who later merged with the Baptists. The most important part was played by Pashkov, who took the movement to the poorer classes of the population. His supporters were known as 'Pashkovites' (*Pashkovtsy*). Among the foreign missionaries in St. Petersburg, two anglicised Germans achieved prominence in addition to Lord Radstock: George Mueller of Bristol

(1805–98) and Dr. Friedrich Wilhelm Baedeker (1823–1906). Notable Russian writers of the period reacted to the strange spiritual awakening in St. Petersburg. Dostoyevsky wrote about Lord Radstock in his *Diary of a Writer*,[1] Leo Tolstoy depicted Dr. Baedeker in his novel *Resurrection* and the novelist Leskov devoted a book with the significant title *Dissent in High Society* to this topic. The young Baptist and Evangelical Christian movements of Russia suffered a great deal of persecution. Pashkov and Korff were forced to go abroad, where both died. Princess Lieven was urgently advised to leave St. Petersburg and retire to her estates. The humbler supporters of the Evangelical revival went into prison and exile. One of the first Russian Baptist leaders, Vasilii Ivanov-Klichnikov, was arrested thirty-one times.

The Union of Russian Baptists was founded in 1884 at a Conference held in the Ukrainian village of Novo-Vasilevka (near the town of Berdyansk, in the Zaporozhe Province). The Union was illegal for twenty-one years, and its effective work could not begin until 1905, when religious toleration was proclaimed. Only then could the Baptists hold their first open congress. This took place in Kiev and was attended by a hundred delegates. In 1907 the first Baptist journal, called *Baptist* appeared, and in 1908 a Baptist publishing company was launched in the Ukraine.

Meanwhile the St. Petersburg Evangelical group was also put firmly on its feet. A journal *Khristianin* had been published in the capital from 1907, a local Evangelical Christian organisation had existed in the city from 1908 and a national organisation was founded in the following year as a result of the 'First All-Russian Congress of Evangelical Christians'.[2]

The Russian Baptists kept in touch with the Baptist World Alliance, which was founded in 1905, and so did the Evangelical Christians, whose recognised leader, Prokhanov, had received his theological training at the Baptist College in Bristol. Although there was no theological difference between the two groups, they hesitated for many years to amalgamate with one another. There were ethnic and social differences and purely personal reasons besides, which stood in the way of union. The Baptists were mostly Ukrainians, the Evangelical Christians predominantly Great Russians. The Baptists were mostly

[1] *The Diary of a Writer*, New York 1954, pp. 264–7.

[2] For the early history of the Evangelical Christian and Baptist movement I am indebted mainly to Waldemar Gutsche's *Westliche Quellen des Russischen Stundismus*, J. G. Oncken Verlag Kassel 1956, to E. G. Karev's treatise, *Russkoe Evangelsko-Baptiskoe Dvizhenie* (The Russian Evangelical-Baptist Movement) in *Bratskii Vestnik*, 1957, nos. 3 and 4, and to J. H. Rushbrook's *Some chapters of European Baptist History*, London 1929.

peasants, the Evangelical Christians drew many of their adherents from the higher classes of society. Moreover, for a long time the Evangelical Christians were under the leadership of a dynamic, some might say despotic, personality — Prokhanov — who wanted to absorb the Baptists into his own organisation rather than merge the two groups on equal terms. This merger came only in 1944, and even then it might not have occurred without the pressure brought to bear on both Baptists and Evangelical Christians by an atheist régime.

How Many?

The question of the numerical strength of the Baptist and Evangelical Christians is perhaps the least important. In a way the Baptists and Evangelical Christians approach the problem of formal membership in the same way as the Communist Party did in the initial period when it was a genuine *élite*. Like the Communist Party in its more heroic years, they are not interested in nominal members. They admit only people who to them appear spiritually mature and morally stable, and, as we shall see later, they impose a number of obligations on their members which the Russian Orthodox Church has not exacted from its supporters.

The Evangelical Christian and Baptist leaders must be credited with never having attempted to exaggerate the numerical importance of their flock. In 1923, J. H. Rushbrooke told the Stockholm Congress of the Baptist World Alliance that there were 1,000,000 Baptists in Russia, including both Baptists and Evangelical Christians.[1] In 1928, the Baptists alone claimed a membership of 200,000.[2] whilst even Soviet estimates of the same year conceded to the two groups an aggregate membership of 400–500,000.[3] By the middle of the thirties it was assumed in Soviet circles that Evangelical Christian and Baptists had lost all their less fanatical members and were reduced to a total of 250,000.[4] It was plain enough that the ranks of the 'Russian Protestants' should have been weakened by the persecution in the thirties and they themselves thought that the number of their supporters was down to 300,000 in 1937. After the war, they increased from 350,000 in 1947 to 545,000 in 1957, but all these members are baptised people over eighteen years of age. When their families are counted as well, Evangelical Christian/Baptist membership reaches an estimated figure of 3,000,000.[5]

---

[1] *Baptist World Alliance, Stockholm Congress*, London 1923, p. 98.
[2] *Baptist World Alliance, Toronto Congress 1928*, Toronto–London 1928, p. 77.
[3] Putintsev, *Politcheskaya Rol i Taktika Sekt* (The Political Role and Tactics of the Sects), Moscow 1935, p. 449.
[4] Putintsev, ibid.   [5] *Bratskii Vestnik*, 1954, no. 3–4, p. 91.

'Sectarians' and Communists

In the early period of the Soviet régime the 'sectarians', especially such active and expanding groups as the Evangelical Christians and Baptists, found themselves in a somewhat advantageous position. They were persecuted by the Czarist régime and were not in any way its instruments. So they could not be easily denounced as counter-revolutionaries and supporters of the *ancien régime*. No external power and splendour was attached to the sects. No influential and elaborate ecclesiastical organisation supported them. The anti-religious measures of the régime, such as confiscation of church property, removal of church bells and closing of churches, hardly affected them. The Baptist and Evangelical presbyters formed no separate social group, and most of them were humble people pursuing a normal secular occupation. So they could not be made figures of fun like the Orthodox 'popes'. In a way the sects benefited from Soviet anti-religious propaganda which concentrated on the externals of the Orthodox Church — its ikons, relics and customs. The sects were able to say: 'The communists are quite right about the Orthodox Church; but look how different we are — no pomp, no ikons, no relics and no popes.' The sects might even be reproached with having taken an unfair advantage of the plight of Orthodoxy and offered themselves to the régime as collaborators.

Both Russian and foreign Baptists originally misjudged the true nature of Communism. At the third Baptist World Congress in Stockholm Dr. W. O. Lewis optimistically referred to a 'new democracy' in Russia and the special duty of the Baptists 'to make a worthy contribution' to Russia's regeneration.[1] In Russia itself at the ninth Congress of the Evangelical Christians in 1924, its leader, Prokhanov, said the Congress was praying to God Almighty that he would help the Workers' and Peasants' Government in its efforts to achieve the welfare of the toiling masses and brotherhood and peace between nations.

The communists found it most difficult to attach the class label to the sects in the same way as to the Orthodox Church, although this was a matter about which there were considerable disagreements within the Russian Communist Party. These internal communist controversies reached a culminating point in 1924 at the time of the thirteenth Communist Party Congress, when the Soviet attitude towards the sectarians had to be defined officially. The disagreements arose very appropriately in drafting the Communist Party's Resolution on the 'Work in the Village', since the vast majority of the sectarians still lived

[1] *Stockholm Congress*, p. 98.

in the countryside. The efficiency of Russian agriculture and the consolidation of the Soviet régime in the village depended to no small degree on the communist attitude towards the sectarians. The problem was one which transcended the limits of the Evangelical Christian and Baptist groups and affected all sectarians — Molokans, Mennonites, Dukhobors, Pentecostals, New-Israelites,[1] Subbotniki, to mention only a few of them.

The main protagonist of the sectarians in the Communist Party was Bonch-Bruevich, who, long before the Revolution, made a detailed and scholarly study of the sectarian problem in its relation to a maturing 'proletarian revolution'. He had the highest opinion of the sectarians on account of their economic efficiency, whilst rejecting of course their religious beliefs. Bonch-Bruevich even went so far as to advocate that all decaying Soviet state farms and communal farms should be handed over to them. In an article published in *Pravda* in 1924 Bonch-Bruevich described the sectarians as 'exemplary toilers' who formed an economic and cultural vanguard in the countryside and said that it would be not only strange but criminal not to use them for Russia's economic reconstruction.[2] According to Bronch-Bruevich the sects were genuinely popular organisations and in 99 cases out of 100 they were in the hands of poor and middle-class peasants. Bonch-Bruevich greatly influenced Mikhail Kalinin, the peasant expert in the supreme Soviet leadership, who submitted the 'Theses' on 'Work in the Village' to the thirteenth Communist Party Congress in May 1924. These 'Theses' had some friendly words to say about the sects which were enshrined in Point 17 of the Congress resolution: 'A specially attentive attitude must be shown to the sectarians, of whom many were cruelly persecuted by the Czarist régime and among whom there is now much activity. Through a skilful approach we must achieve that the considerable economic and cultural potentialities of the sectarians are directed into the channels of Soviet work. As the sectarians are numerous this endeavour has great importance. In approaching this task local conditions must be taken into account.'[3]

[1] In the first years of Soviet power the New-Israelites made themselves conspicuous by a pronounced pro-Soviet attitude. Their theology was rationalistic to the extreme; they attached no historical significance to the Bible but considered it purely as an allegory. The sect was founded by a railwayman, Vasily Lubkov, and hence the sect was also known under the name of 'Lubkovites'. The New-Israelite sect has died out completely in the years of Soviet power.

[2] *Pravda*, 1924, no, 108.

[3] *KPSS v Rezolyutsiakh i Resheniakh Sezdov, Konferentsii i Plenumov Tseka* (The CPSU in the Resolutions and Decisions of Congresses, Conferences and Plenary Sessions of the Central Committee), Institut Marksa–Engelsa–Lenina–Stalina, Moscow 1953, vol. i, p. 858.

Kalinin, urging the adoption of the controversial Point 17, stated that there were ten million sectarians of every kind in Russia. 'It would be ridiculous' said Kalinin, 'if the party did not take into account that the history of the sectarians was one of uninterrupted persecution.' So a moral afterthought was added to the main materialistic argument in favour of the sectarians.

The opportunistic attitude represented by Bonch-Bruevich ideologically, and by Kalinin politically, was resisted by an intransigent group which looked beyond the agricultural difficulties of 1924. It considered, and rightly so from a communist point of view, that Point 17 was unprincipled and a concession to one religious group at the expense of others. This intransigent party faction was led by such staunch anti-religious communist fighters as Yemelyan Yaroslavsky and Skvortsov-Stepanov. Yaroslavsky's contention was that the sectarians were the same 'little bourgeois' as other peasants.[1] He and Skvortsov-Stepanov urged that Point 17 should be deleted. Their opposition was of no avail. Kalinin's resolution was adopted in its entirety, but the fears of the extremist atheists did not materialise. Point 17 did not become the sectarians' charter which it could have become, theoretically speaking. The 'sectarians' were soon to be treated in the same way as the other religious groups. There was to be only a very short respite for them.

Religious Collective Farms

In fairness to the intransigent communist point of view it must be said that the granting of privileges to the sects might ultimately have destroyed Communism, for it would have provided not merely an ideological but also a practical alternative to the communist system. The few concessions which the opportunists in the communist camp were ready to make to the sectarians were sufficient to cause serious embarrassment to the Communist Party. They enabled the sects to challenge the communist State in several vital fields, especially with regard to the collectivisation of agriculture and the education of youth.

The opportunism of the leading communist circles in the years following the Bolshevik *coup d'état* of 1917 was at the origin of one of the greatest anomalies which have ever existed in the Soviet Union, namely the religious communal and collective farms. Again this is a matter which involves other Christians outside the framework of the Evangelical Christian and Baptist movement. The most fantastic aspect of the religious communal farms was that they were not only tolerated by the régime but actively encouraged, even to the point of

[1] *Pravda*, May 23, 1924.

receiving financial grants. The Soviet organ most amicably disposed towards them was the People's Commissariat of Agriculture, which knew better than anybody else what a useful part the religious farms were playing in the Soviet economy.

The first sectarian group actively to engage in communal farming was a teetotal organisation describing itself as 'Trezvenniki' — 'the Sober Ones'. It has now disappeared and most of its members have joined the Evangelical Christians, who likewise propagate total abstinence from alcohol without engaging in the theological eccentricities to which a section of the Trezvenniki was inclined.[1] In their work of saving drunkards and prostitutes the Trezvenniki showed great similarity to the 'Salvation Army', but Bonch-Bruevich considered, not without a certain Russian national pride, that they stood on a higher ethical level than the latter.[2] In the first years of the Soviet régime the communal farms of the Trezvenniki, known under the collective term of 'Trezvaya Kommuna', did a great deal towards supplying food to the starving population. The chairman of the Moscow Soviet, Lev Kamenev, therefore issued on April 24, 1920, a special ordinance stating that all branches of the 'Trezvaya Kommuna' in the Moscow, Tambov and Tver Guberniyas enjoyed the protection of the Moscow Societ. No measures whatever were to be taken against them or their stores, libraries, printing works, gardens, workshops, etc.

Soon there was hardly any part of communist Russia where religious collective farms did not exist. The most famous perhaps were the two communal farms of the Evangelical Christians in the Tver (now Kalinin) region, bearing the Biblical names 'Vifaniya' (Bethany) and 'Gefsemaniya' (Gethsemane). Of these the 'Vifaniya' farm earned particular praise and was even given financial support by the State. In the North Caucasus with its many sectarian villages, the religious farms were especially numerous. The Pentecostal Sect had a communal farm called the 'Commune of the Apocalypse' near the Cossack village of Korenovskaya, the Molokan farm 'Pravda' was located in the Kropotkin District

---

[1] The Leningrad group of the Trezvenniki interpreted the whole Bible in the sense of teetotalism. It was led by Ivan Churikov, a peasant from Samara (Kuybishev) who proclaimed that the Kingdom of God on earth would begin as soon as drunkenness, the beginning of all evils, was overcome. Churikov, whom his supporters considered as 'a second Christ', was a much-discussed personality in the twenties. The 3,000 to 4,000 supporters whom he then had in Leningrad belonged mostly to the working class, and this fact alone earned him bitter attacks on the part of anti-religious propagandists (I. Ya. Eliashevich, *Pravda o Churikove i Churikovtsakh* (The Truth about Churikov and the Churkikovists), Leningrad 1928). Churikov personally initiated the establishment of a number of communal farms.
[2] Bonch-Bruevich, *Iz mira sektantov* (From the World of the Sectarians), Moscow 1922, p. 144.

and the Baptist farm 'Lager' near Armavir. The 'New Israelites' ran a huge stud farm on collective lines. It was situated on the Manych river, which in the North Caucasus forms the geographical boundary between Europe and Asia. It had the record size of 29,000 hectares and owed its existence to an agreement between the sect and the People's Commissariat of Agriculture. The Seventh Day Adventists had several communal farms in the Ukraine, of which one was significantly called 'Commune of Brotherly Love'. Near Moscow there was the communal farm of the Tolstoyans with the name of 'Lev Tolstoy'. To complete the picture there were also Orthodox 'Monastic Communal Farms'. These too were taken under the protective wings of the agricultural authorities, very much to the disgust of the atheist propagandists. One in particular, near the villages of Bulatnikovo and Pokrovskoe of the former Moscow Guberniya, came into prominence because it won a gold medal and a silver jar at the All-Union Agricultural Exhibition.

'The City of the Sun'

The initial tolerance of the Soviet authorities towards religious communal and collective farms was bound to give rise to some short-lived illusions among the sectarians. They began to believe in a peaceful co-existence between Marxist Communism and Christian Communism, a co-existence which could be both ideological and institutional. If Christian communal farms were recognised side by side with secular communal farms, why not build a Christian city in Russia side by side with the new socialist towns of the communist régime?

Unlike the idea of Christian communal farms, which suffered from no denominational limitations, the concept of the Christian city was the exclusive property of the Evangelical Christians and especially of the Chairman of its all-Union Council, Ivan Stepanovich Prokhanov (1869–1935). It is difficult to size up properly and justly this great and controversial personality whom we have already mentioned in the course of this narrative. This man who did so much to introduce a Western creed into Russia was a typical Russian genius; he had all the virtues and all the faults of a great Russian. One of the many strange things about him was that he had both a technological and a theological training. Many of his evangelising activities were carried out when he travelled through Russia as a representative of the American firm of Westinghouse. In his view the Evangelical Christians were not to confine their activities to religion, but they were to leave their mark on every branch of national life including scholarship, agriculture and industry. So it was by no means surprising that he conceived the idea of a Christian township. Even before the Revolution he tried to build such a city near Simferopol in the Crimea, called 'Vertograd' ('The City of the Future'). This experiment miscarried, but Prokhanov tried to revive it after Soviet rule was established.[1] He had in mind to found the city once again in European Russia, in the Southern Ukraine, the Crimea or the Northern Caucasus, but he failed to obtain official support. So he seems to have changed the plan in favour of a more distant virgin soil area in Asia. The most important thing was, after all, not the location of the place but the implementation of an idea — a town where all people would be 'brothers' and 'sisters' living according to the principles of the Bible as the Russian Evangelical Christians understood them. This meant that a kind of Christian Communism was to reign in the town: everything was to be held in common owner-ship except purely personal belongings. In short, the town was to be a little theocracy inside an anti-religious communist dictatorship.[2]

The new town — to be called either 'Evangelsk' or 'City of the Sun' — would have been a genuine communist rural township such as the communists themselves had tried in vain to establish. The Soviet authorities at first showed a certain benevolence to Prokhanov's plan, since it might have led to the opening up of virgin land. The People's Commissariat of Agriculture gave recommendations to an exploratory party of Evangelical Christians so that they could contact various Soviet local government bodies in Siberia in their search for an appropriate place where the 'City of the Sun' could be established. At last the place for the new town was found in the Altai, at the confluence of the rivers Biya and Katun, situated 85° East of Greenwich and 52° 25' North of the Equator.[3] There two Evangelical Christian emissaries, accompanied by the local representatives of Soviet power, inaugurated the new venture with the solemn planting of oak trees. This amazing and perhaps unique event in the history of Russia took place on September 11, 1927.

This happy start fired the imagination of the Evangelical Christians. Their journal *Khristianin* (No. 1, 1928) gave a detailed description of the appearance of the future city. In the centre there was to be an open space, round in shape and two kilometres in diameter. It was to be planted with many trees and was to accommodate various beautiful buildings, including schools, hospitals and houses of prayer. From the central square the streets were to fan out like rays of the sun. Prokhanov expected to receive funds from abroad for the building of the City and

[1] Waldemar Gutsche, op. cit., p. 93.
[2] K. Petrus, *Religious Communes in the USSR*, Research Programme of the USSR New York City 1953, pp. 65–7.
[3] I. S. Prokhanoff, *In the Cauldron of Russia*, New York 1933, pp. 231–2.

with his extensive international religious contacts he might have received them.[1] The bold plan never got beyond the tree-planting ceremony and this fact is hardly surprising. The foundation of a Christian city in atheist Russia would have been an even greater absurdity than the existence of religious communal farms. Such a city might have enjoyed a tremendous popularity since it offered an escape from official Communism. It might even have become a centre of political opposition. The radical wing in the Communist Party, especially the League of Militant Godless, did everything to frustrate the project. It is significant that those campaigning against the City of the Sun did not predict its economic failure. On the contrary, its success was considered a foregone conclusion and it was just the prospect of a successful Christian communist experiment on a vast scale which made the whole venture so dangerous. Spurred on by the League of Militant Godless, the highest Soviet authorities intervened and withdrew all permissions and concessions which the People's Commissariat of Agriculture, guided by narrow departmental interest, had so rashly granted.[2] As the Soviet State had made the building of the Christian city impossible, the author of the project, Prokhanov, left the Soviet Union never to return. He died in Berlin in 1935, cured of his former pro-Soviet illusions.

The End of Religious Collective Farms

The project of the 'City of the Sun' showed the communist authorities what dangers might threaten from the resourcefulness of the sectarians and at the same time it drew attention to the religious communal and collective farms. The régime could put up with them as long as individual farming prevailed in the Soviet Union, that is until the end of the twenties, but it could no longer tolerate them after the collectivisation of agriculture had started on a big scale. Legally there was no obstacle to the existence of religious collective farms, provided they were properly registered. But law counts for little in Soviet Russia and the authorities therefore managed to close down the religious farms one after another under a variety of futile pretexts. Some were forcibly liquidated in 1928-9 because they were allegedly dominated by kulak elements, 'alien to the working class'; others were charged with having engaged in black market activities; others, like the Commune called 'The Kingdom of Light', a creation of the Seventh Day Adventists in

---

[1] A. Kartsev, *Sekta Evangelskikh Khristian* (The sect of the Evangelical Christians), Moscow 1930, p. 44.

[2] Putintsev, *Kabalnoe Bratstvo Sektantov* (The Slave Brotherhood of the Sectarians), Moscow 1931, pp. 112-13.

the Dniepropetrovsk Province, were closed down because they conducted 'active religious propaganda'.[1] The Commune of the Churikov supporters near Detskoe Selo in the Leningrad area was denounced for exploiting its members, treating them as slaves and preventing them from going to cinemas and theatres. The communal farm 'Lev Tolstoy' was disbanded on April 30, 1929, for a reason of which the Soviet authorities had always been aware, namely, that its members were Tolstoyans, i.e. opposed to the Soviet rule of violence and refusing to participate in elections.[2]

However, there were a number of sectarian collective and communal farms ('kolkhozy' and 'kommuny') against which no arguments could be found. They had no kulaks in their midst, they respected the Soviet law to the letter and they were too isolated to exercise any 'hostile' ideological influence on their surroundings. Against them the objection was put forward that they were too perfect, too egalitarian, too communistic. They had refused to admit even such private property as the Soviet State was willing, or rather forced, to concede for the time being. That type of Christian communal farm was obviously the most dangerous. The Soviet régime could not accept the existence of a more perfect Christian Communism outside the official collectivised system, a communism without class struggle and Soviet power. The sectarians, both in their zeal to organise communal living — a zeal which nobody in Russia shared with them to the same degree — and in achieving that communal living far better than others, did not assist the Soviet Government but on the contrary challenged it. These religious collective farms were not a practical implementation of Marxist-Leninist ideology; they rather continued the venture of Christian communal living as expressed in monasticism or in various Utopian experiments. They were similar to such manifestations of Christian community spirit as the Jesuit 'reductions' in Paraguay and the many dozens of communist and co-operative colonies established in the nineteenth century on the North American continent. These religious communal farms were brought into being by a spirit of selflessness and dedication which the communist collective farms had never dreamt of attaining. For instance the sect of the Shakers, who at one time had as many as fifty-eight communes in the USA, laid down the following principle:

'It is an established principle of faith in the Church that all who are received as members thereof do freely and voluntarily, of their deliberate choice, dedicate, devote and consecrate themselves, with

[1] *Pravda*, June 12, 1929.
[2] Putintsev, *Kabalnoe Bratstvo Sektantov*, op. cit., p. 116.

all they possess to the service of God. Each member of the Church renounces all property for himself and his heirs and all rendering account.'[1]

Practically all communist agricultural experiments in North America owed their origin either to direct religious inspiration, like the Shakers and Perfectionists and nowadays the Hutterites, or to the indirect influence of religious ideas, like the experiments of the Fourierists and Icarians.[2] Certainly most of these communist experiments collapsed, but they broke down for the same reasons which would bring about the collapse of Soviet collective farming if the kolkhozy were not kept going by an elaborate system of coercion.

The problem of the sectarian kommuny is now a matter of the past for Soviet Russia, but the spirit which brought them into being still haunts the Soviet régime. Its own collective farms are still far from representing an ideal form of community life. Continuous concessions to the acquisitive instincts of the collective farmer are the only thing that can ease the tensions inside the kolkhozy and the tension between them and the State. Such concessions are also the only way to enhance their economic efficiency. In fact, what has happened with the 'official' collective farms is exactly what a spokesman of Christian sectarian Russia, the Tolstoyan Tregubov, had foreseen in a letter he was bold enough to write to Stalin in 1929 at the time of the collectivisation: 'In many places communal farms are now being formed with unusual rapidity like mushrooms after rain. These communal farms have no religious basis. . . . As they owe their origin to expediency alone and not to any deep conviction, as they are supported by state assistance and not by the energy of the individuals concerned, they will disintegrate with the same rapidity, and even if they continue to exist they will remain a great handicap for the State.'[3]

Both these alternatives foreseen by Tregubov have actually happened. Many of the collective farms did disintegrate and Stalin had to sound a temporary retreat in the collectivisation campaign; and those collective farms which remained in being or were re-established later, did become, and remained, a great handicap to the Soviet State. Stalin paid quite unexpected attention to the statement of a Tolstoyan sectarian about the collectivisation problem, not because he believed in his warning, of course, but because it supplied him with a valuable argument. Tregubov's letter was a striking proof that the sectarians and the

[1] Charles Nordhoff, *The Communistic Societies in the United States*, London 1875.
[2] Charles Gide, *Communist and Co-operative Colonies*, London 1930.
[3] Putintsev, *Kabalnoe Bratstvo Sektantov*, op. cit., p. 92.

right-wing opposition in the Communist Party really held identical views about the collectivisation. Ample use was made of this in the inner-party controversy, especially by the League of Militant Godless, which tried to enhance its importance by asserting that the fight against the sectarians was a fight for the correct party-line.

Even after the disbandment of collective farms founded on religious principles, the authorities could not prevent the existence of kolkhozy where the entire membership consisted of sectarians. This happened for geographical reasons. Several sects lived in compact villages and any collective farm based on their inhabitants was bound to have a 'sectarian' character. Naturally the Soviet régime had it in its power to impose on such collective farms, chairmen and officials of its own choosing to prevent the farms from assuming a religious character.

'Khristomol' versus Komosol

We have already mentioned that the education of the young was another field where the sectarians competed successfully with the régime and its organisations. In the period after the First World War, when drunkenness and immorality grew in Russia, the sects made a determined effort to stop the moral decay, especially among youth, and so became a serious rival of the Young Communist League. The alternative was between Soviet morality and Christian morality. Had there been full freedom of propaganda for both sides, there can be little doubt which of the two would have triumphed. Of course, such freedom did not exist. An All-Russian Union of Christian Youth which had come into being in 1917 was disbanded by the authorities for 'counter-revolutionary activities'. So there was no national organisation to compete with the Young Communist League. There were only small youth groups, each twenty-five to fifty people strong, which were attached to the religious organisations of the Evangelical Christians and Baptists. The sum total of these small Christian groups, working under considerable difficulty and having but a semi-legal existence, was astonishingly large. Although it had all the weight of the state apparatus on its side the Young Communist League feared that it could be outflanked by the religious youth organisations.

It appears from communist sources that the Christian youth organisations very successfully endeavoured to provide for the young people what the Komsomol had only promised to give them. They went out to fight for a new way of life without alcohol, tobacco smoking and swear-words. They fought against hooliganism and unseemly behaviour towards girls. They also propagated a spirit of comradeship which the

Komsomol had failed to achieve. Both at the eighth All-Union Congress of the Komsomol in 1928 and at the sixth All-Union Conference of that organisation in 1929 the problem of religion and its impact on the younger generation was brought up. At the eighth Congress Bukharin, then still a member of the supreme Soviet leadership, made the startling statement that there were organisations in the Soviet Union, Christian organisations, which united in their ranks roughly as many young people as the Komsomol. Their members were largely young workers and young peasants, and in Stalingrad, for instance, 60–70 per cent of their membership were factory workers. Bukharin described these Christian organisations as 'Bapsomol' and 'Khristomol', meaning a Baptist youth organisation and a Christian youth organisation. He might have added a third one, the Trezvomol, the youth organisation of the Trezvenniki sect.[1] These nicknames 'Khristomol', 'Bapsomol' and 'Trezvomol' were presumably chosen to indicate that the Christian youth groups were replicas, and dangerous replicas, of the state youth organisation — the Komsomol. Bukharin spoke of the Christian youth organisations not only with hostility but also with a certain amount of respect and even envy. 'The majority of the sectarian organisations', he said, 'wage a struggle against the drinking of alcoholic spirits, against smoking and against the use of various genuinely Russian swear-words. This makes it understandable that they have attracted both in town and country by no means the worst elements among the youth, and particularly among working girls and peasant girls. From this one must draw far-reaching conclusions with regard to the work of the Komsomol organisations.'[2] This success of the Christian youth organisations in outstripping the Komsomol and assuming a kind of moral leadership was preying very much on the mind of that Old Bolshevik Bukharin. A few weeks before the Komsomol Congress he had attended the foundation meeting of a Society for the Fight against Alcoholism which, incidentally, never became a major success in Soviet Russia and was soon disbanded again. Bukharin addressed that meeting and said that the sectarians who were organising the fight against alcohol on a grand scale would take from the Komsomol the best part of the youth unless the young communists would hit out against alcoholism.[3]

At the sixth Komsomol Conference in 1929, another Politbureau member, Rudzutak, drew attention to a further point where the

---

[1] Roshchin, *Kto takie sektanty?* (Who are the sectarians?), Moscow 1930, p. 133.

[2] Roshchin, op. cit., p. 118.

[3] Eliashvili, *Religiya v borbe za rabochuyu molodozh* (Religion in the fight for working class youth), Leningrad 1928, p. 56.

sectarians seemed to have scored over the Komsomol — the highly-developed spirit of comradeship in the sectarian organisations. He quoted the example of a Russian girl who left the Komsomol and went to the sectarians because, as she put it, she had met finer people there than in the Young Communist League. Rudzutak said this was not an isolated occurrence. The brotherly nearness once to be found in the illegal organisations of the Communist Party had vanished both from the Party and the Komsomol, and so it was perhaps not incomprehensible if young people looked elsewhere for a spirit of comradeship. Rudzutak tried to analyse the feelings of a young man craving for friendship, and looking for it both in the Komsomol and in the Baptist community. The comparison was in favour of the latter. In the Komsomol there was a 'formal attitude' towards the young man; in the Baptist meeting he was received like a real brother and people asked him about his troubles and worries and how he could be helped.[1]

The Challenge of the Bible

The challenge with which the Baptists and Evangelical Christians confronted the communists was not confined to problems of a social order such as the fight against drunkenness and the fostering of brotherly relations between young people. Part of this challenge was tied up with the religious message of the two groups, particularly their zeal in propagating the Bible. The Orthodox Church built monasteries, cathedrals, churches and chapels, and it implanted into the Russian people a deep sense of piety; but there was one thing it failed to give them, a knowledge of the Holy Scriptures. It was the specific contribution of the 'sectarians' to the religious life of Russia that they helped to fill this gap. They carried the Bible into the humble homes of the Russian and Ukrainian peasants and craftsmen.

In fighting the sectarians the Soviet régime found itself face to face with people whose religion was largely rooted in their love and knowledge of the Bible. The anti-religious propagandists, well versed in pouring contempt on the ikons and relics of orthodox Saints, were less prepared to cope with religious groups which based themselves on an infallible book. In dealing with the Orthodox the scantiest knowledge of Bible texts might have been of value and impressed the audiences. But when the same agitators addressed sectarians and resorted to quoting the Scriptures they were easily defeated. Time and again the anti-religious propagandists had to be warned to be careful with

[1] *Pravda*, June 22, 1929.

the selection and use of Bible texts[1] or even that they should ignore the Bible and devote as little time as possible to its study.[2]

It was much safer to attack the Bible in the absence of such persons as were able to refute anti-religious arguments; this was done at a blasphemous 'Trial of the Bible' organised in the Latvian House of Culture in Leningrad early in 1928. The Bible was accused of serving the exploiting classes together with police and prisons, of falsely interpreting the laws of nature and of arrogating to itself the title of the 'oldest book in the world'. Four anti-religious propagandists masqueraded as 'counsel for the defence', one as a rabbi 'defending' the Old Testament and three others as a Lutheran pastor, an Orthodox priest and a Baptist preacher. The Court arrived at the verdict that the Bible was a historical document which had outlived its time and that believers should therefore abandon it.[3]

When this 'trial' was held the problem of the Bible was particularly acute for the Russian communists, especially in Leningrad, the headquarters of the Evangelical Christians who were then still legally entitled to publish the Bible in Soviet territory. Altogether there were four important ventures of Evangelical Christian Bible publishing in the USSR during the twenties: (1) a complete Russian Bible printed in Leningrad in 1926 in an edition of 25,000 copies, (2) an incomplete Bible printed in Kiev in 1927 in 10,000 copies, (3) a New Testament printed in 25,000 copies and (4) a Bible Concordance appearing in 1928 in 10,000 copies.[4] The Baptists too were entitled to publish Bibles in Soviet Russia, but the edition of the Bible they prepared never saw the light of day.

The Baptists and Evangelical Christians also had other legal opportunities for spreading their faith in addition to printing and distributing the Bible. In Leningrad, the Evangelical Christians had since 1924 a 'Bible School' which trained their presbyters, and in 1927 the Baptists were allowed to open a 'Preachers' School' in Moscow. Both Evangelical Christians and Baptists were able to publish hymn books and the Baptists also issued a Concise Guide for Preachers.

Persecution and Survival

The considerable success which the Evangelical Christians and Baptists scored in their propaganda ultimately prompted a complete reversal of the comparative benevolence which the communist authorities showed towards them at first. This volte-face came as a complete

---

[1] Kommunisticheskoe Prosveshchenie, 1927, no. 1, p. 31.   [2] Pravda, June 13, 1929.
[3] Antireligioznik, 1929, no. 5, p. 69.   [4] Bratskii Vestnik, 1957, no. 3, p. 63.

surprise to the Baptists both inside and outside the USSR. Thus, as late as summer 1928, the secretary of the Russian Baptist organisation, Ivanov-Klichnikov, could still make a most optimistic statement on freedom of religion in Russia when addressing the Congress of the Baptist World Alliance in Toronto.[1] Some thought that his speech there was too much of an apology for the communist régime.

A few weeks after his return from the West he was arrested and exiled to Central Asia. Many other leading Baptists shared his fate. These arrests were accompanied by other repressive measures calculated to put an end to dangerous sectarian propaganda. The licence to print Bibles was withdrawn from both the Baptists and Evangelical Christians. It was not renewed until twenty-eight years later. The journal *Baptist* had to cut down its circulation by ninety per cent and after a few months it had to stop circulation altogether.[2] The same fate befell the other two Christian periodicals, *Baptist Ukrainy* and *Khristianin*. No 'sectarian' periodical was allowed to appear for another sixteen years. Finally, both the 'Preachers School' of the Baptists and the 'Bible School' of the Evangelical Christians were closed in 1929.

The most serious blow administered to the Baptists and Evangelical Christians was the law of April 8, 1929, which put religious organisations in the USSR on an entirely new footing. The law prohibited all religious organisations not concerned with religious worship in the narrowest sense of the term. It banned in particular all those organisations which the sectarians had brought into being and which the Communist Party regarded as dangerous competition, namely evening classes for the teaching of writing and reading, sewing and singing circles for girls and women and, above all, special youth organisations. But neither the legal nor the administrative terror could defeat the sectarians, nor could it dispose of the problems which had encouraged the growth of sectarianism and of sectarian youth groups, namely alcoholism, hooliganism, immorality and the existence of an intellectual and spiritual vacuum which Communism was unable to fill. It would be wrong to suggest that the official anti-religious measures made no difference whatever, but they could not paralyse the zeal and devotion of the Evangelical Christian and Baptist rank and file.

All over the world the Baptist movement has grown thanks to the work of lay-people. 'Every Baptist a missionary' has been the Baptists' motto. Deprived of their organisational framework and of many of their presbyters, the Russian Baptists and Evangelical Christians con-

---

[1] *Baptist Times*, October 11, 1928.   [2] *Baptist Times*, April 18, 1929.

centrated all their energy on an individual lay-apostolate which primarily propagated a faith and a way of life and not affiliation to an ecclesiastical body. The skill and success of that lay-apostolate was recognised even by the arch-enemies of the sectarians. 'In the field of individual proselytising,' said Fyodor Nestorovich Oleshchuk in 1929, 'they have achieved very much. Worker-sectarians attach themselves to their neighbours at the bench and work on them. Women-sectarians attach themselves to non-sectarian women in the absence of their husbands.'[1] The sectarians did more or less the same things that the communists would do in a country which denied them a proper legal existence: they penetrated into the organisations of the régime which oppressed them. They joined such 'voluntary societies' as the MOPR (International Society for Assistance to Revolutionaries) or the ODN (Society for the Fight against Illiteracy) to obtain their membership-cards and to establish new personal contacts, to be used for further proselytising.

Above all, the sectarians did not lose their influence on certain sections of Soviet youth. Seven years after the prohibition of the Baptist and Evangelical youth clubs, on May 17, 1937, the organ of the Komsomol, *Komsomolskaya Pravda*, still found it necessary to publish an article 'The sectarian youth and the tasks of its re-education'. The article provided another proof of the resourcefulness of the sectarians. It gave roughly the following picture: sectarian preachers continued to do great harm to the communist cause. Although communists conducted anti-religious propaganda in meetings and clubs, the sectarians defied them. They declared openly: 'We begin work where you end. You work in the clubs and in meetings, and we in the streets outside the clubs and after your meetings.' One could not produce any figures about the strength of the sectarians, but they were considerable. First of all, there was a high percentage of believing youth in the traditional sectarian villages, but in addition there existed groups of young believers in factories, trading enterprises and co-operatives. Illegal 'Circles of Christian Youth' were still in existence, and into them came young people drawn by the Baptists and Evangelical Christians. They were camouflaged as choir and music circles and exploited the love of music among young people. In these circles Christian hymns were sung which, though legally printed under the Soviet régime, were hostile to it. Sectarians also penetrated into educational establishments, e.g., a sectarian group was discovered in a school in Omsk. Sectarians even infiltrated into the Young Communist

---

[1] *Kommunistichekoe Prosveshchenie*, May 1929, no. 5, p. 29.

League itself. Such cases were reported from a village in the Stalingrad Province and a factory in Leningrad.[1]

The Soviet authorities always found it extremely difficult to convict the Baptists and Evangelical Christians of genuine anti-régime activities. *Pravda* once said in a leading article that Baptists were very cautious and not easy to catch in their counter-revolutionary manœuvres[2] and this perhaps accounts for the attempts of the Soviet authorities to charge them with all sorts of imaginary crimes, including the disintegration of collective farms, espionage and sabotage. The only substantiated charge made against them referred to the receipt of financial assistance from abroad, but this help was accepted with the knowledge of the Soviet authorities. The funds reached the Baptists and Evangelical Christians through the Soviet State Bank, which was not displeased whenever it could exchange valuable foreign currency for paper roubles.

The first espionage cases among Baptists were 'uncovered' in 1929 when the Baptist organisations of Volhynia and Kiev were charged with working for Poland, whilst another 'Baptist spy organisation' was found in Byelorussia. In 1936 and 1937 Yezhov's police produced Baptist and other sectarian spies on a much larger scale. Baptists in Leningrad, Moscow, Smolensk and Izhevsk were arrested for espionage in favour of Germany. Siberian Baptists suffered the same fate for alleged spying in favour of both Germany and Japan.[3]

Not every Baptist presbyter and 'activist' could be easily converted into a 'spy'. Another way to render the sectarians innocuous was to transform their virtues into vices. Their closeness to the people, their ready acceptance of Soviet power and institutions, including collective farms, as well as their proletarian character — in short everything that had assisted them in the early twenties — was now turned against them. The harm they caused to the régime was that they professed a 'proletarian religion'. Even the rank and file communist could not see that a Baptist and Evangelical Christian worker was in fact a class enemy. Worse than that, time and again it was reported that communists had succumbed to the influence of the sectarians. So the régime accused the sectarians of using a proletarian mask for purposes of deceit and wrecking activities. The great purge of 1937 offered the long-sought opportunity to strike against this embarrassing working-class sectarianism. The Baptists were made to serve as scapegoats for all sorts of technical and economic shortcomings in industry. In the

[1] *Komsomolskaya Pravda*, May 17, 1937.   [2] *Pravda*, February 9, 1929.
[3] Kandidov, *Tserkov i Shpionazh* (Church and Espionage), Moscow 1938, pp. 71–3.

Kuzbas coal-mining region, for instance, mining was on a primitive level, safety regulations were not observed and accidents occurred. Sectarians were at once declared to be responsible and arrested.[1] Or another example: on a narrow-gauge railway line servicing a timber-trust in the Vyazemskii District (Soviet Far Eastern Territory, now Khabarovsk Territory) about forty accidents occurred in the timber season of 1936–7. At the same time there was discontent among the timber-workers about wages and the timber-plan was not fulfilled. The police 'found' that all the people responsible for the situation were leaders of Baptist organisations. In the Donets coal-mining basin, the authorities tried to prevent any proselytising for the sect by asserting that recruiting Baptist believers was tantamount to recruiting agents of a spy organisation.[2]

Throughout the thirties the Evangelical Christians and Baptists were unable to carry out any proper organisational activities. The last Evangelical Christian congress took place in 1930, and the last plenary meeting of the 'All-Union Council of Evangelical Christians' was held in 1931.[3] The central organisation of the Baptists stopped all activity in 1935 and the Baptist Moscow branch folded up in the following year after the State had confiscated the Baptist house of prayer. This prompted individual Moscow Baptists to join the Evangelical Christian community.[4] Similar instances of Evangelical Christians and Baptists sharing the same house of prayer happened in many other places. It also occurred frequently that Baptist preachers looked after Evangelical Christians and vice versa. So there was at least one positive element in the difficulties to which the two groups were exposed; the hostility of the State brought them closer to one another.

The All-Union Council of Evangelical Christians/Baptists

A new era for the two groups began in 1944, when they were allowed to hold in Moscow a unification conference which was the starting point for a reorganisation and strengthening of the existing Evangelical Christian and Baptist groups throughout the country. The conference was held in Moscow at the end of October 1944. It was attended by forty-five delegates including all the surviving leaders of the two parent bodies, the All-Union Council of Evangelical Christians and the All-Union Council of Baptists. About half the delegates were from Moscow itself. The others came from the provinces. Permission to travel in

---

[1] *Udarnik Kuzbassa*, November 11, 1937.
[2] *Sotsialisticheskii Donbass*, January 11, 1938.
[3] *Bratskii Vestnik*, 1954, no. 5–6, p. 31. [4] *Bratskii Vestnik*, 1957, no. 3, p. 64.

wartime conditions was obtained from the 'Council for the Affairs of Religious Cults', and it was on this body that the future of the Evangelical Christians and Baptists largely depended from now on. The Chairman of the Evangelical Christian/Baptist unity conference, M. A. Orlov, made this quite explicit when he said: 'This Council has its local representatives attached to the Provincial Soviets. These representatives decide the problems of our congregations and take an extremely attentive attitude towards our needs.'[1]

The Conference of October 1944 established the new organisation, the 'All-Union Council of Evangelical Christians and Baptists' a name which soon afterwards was slightly altered into 'All-Union Council of Evangelical Christians/Baptists' to stress the complete unity of the two groups participating in the merger. The Evangelical Christians obtained a slight predominance in the new body; for instance they occupied the posts of Chairman and Secretary-General. This was primarily due to the fact that Evangelical Christians were the more numerous of the two groups. Moreover, the Evangelical Christians were predominantly Russian and it was expedient to have Russian leadership in the new organisation, in line with the general trend of development in the Soviet Union.

The establishment of a united Evangelical Christian/Baptist organisation was in the interest of both the sectarians and the State. It fulfilled the long-felt aspirations towards unity of the former and it simplified the situation on the 'religious front' for the Soviet authorities. The final objective of an atheist government is, of course, the total elimination of religious groups. But as long as such groups are still in being the régime must have a policy towards them. In communist Russia this policy consists of making the existing Churches not only as docile as possible but also as centralised as possible, for a rigidly centralised Church can be more easily compelled to carry out the instructions of the Government. The All-Union Council which provided a rigidly centralised framework was considered a body suitable to serve the State and therefore found favour with the régime. The Soviet Government seemed prepared to grant the new Council the sole right to represent all 'sectarians' of the Soviet Union and it lent its active and passive support to the Evangelical/Christian Baptist body whenever it attempted to extend its influence to other groups. The authorities especially counted on the help of the Evangelical Christian/Baptist leadership to establish a kind of order among the sectarians of the 'new' Soviet territories where they were particularly undisciplined and anti-communist.

[1] *Bratskii Vestnik*, 1945, no. 1, p. 21.

Immediately after the war, when Soviet civilian persons were not usually able to travel in border areas, the emissaries of the All-Union Council enjoyed considerable freedom of movement to bring the various sectarian groups in the former Eastern Poland, Moldavia and the Carpathian Ukraine under its jurisdiction. In this way the All-Union Council gathered together a very heterogeneous crowd of religious believers who recognised its authority only in order to escape persecution. Thus in the Carpathian Ukraine the secretary-general of the Council secured the affiliation of about forty congregations of a so-called 'Free Christian' group which had spread in the twenties under American influence. It opposed the observance of religious holidays and worship in houses of prayer and also refused to register with the authorities. They even rejected baptism and 'breaking of bread'. Despite their anarchist attitude they were quickly persuaded to sign an act of unity with the Moscow Council and to repudiate publicly the most characteristic tenets of their faith. Above all they pledged themselves to act in organisational matters 'in accordance with the laws of the Soviet Union'.[1]

Whatever its weaknesses, the new organisation has achieved a strange synthesis between discipline and sectarianism. The central council in Moscow keeps in touch with the 5,400 congregations throughout the country. This is done with the help of forty-five full-time senior presbyters who look after up to 200 congregations each. These senior presbyters appoint the presbyters of the individual congregations, inspect the latter, settle all disputes between presbyters and their flocks and draw up reports for headquarters. Each congregation pays allegiance to the central council, not only by obeying its orders but also by contributing financially to its upkeep. Five times a year collections are made for the Council: at Easter, Whitsun, the Harvest Festival celebrated on the last Sunday in September, Christmas and the Day of Unity. The latter is a special Evangelical-Christian/Baptist holiday celebrated in Russia only. It commemorates the merger between the two groups and is observed on the last Sunday in October.

The new central Evangelical Christian/Baptist organisation is a spiritually powerful body in Russia because it brings a Christian message to many thousands of people. It gives them a purpose in life and the strength to face the drabness of Soviet reality and, as we shall see later, it continues the most noble traditions of the Evangelical Christians and Baptists of the pre-war period in upholding Christian moral standards in defiance of the atheist régime. Moreover, the new

[1] *Bratskii Vestnik*, 1946, no. 2, p. 42.

Evangelical-Christian/Baptist movement is representative of the Soviet people both socially and ethnically. Socially its membership is based on the collective farmers and the working class. Ethnically, that membership is almost a microcosm of the Soviet Union, at least fifty per cent belonging to non-Russian nationalities. It is amazing how such a comparatively small religious organisation as the Evangelical Christians and Baptists have been able to spread to practically all parts of the Russian Empire, as we can observe when making a quick imaginary trip through Baptist and Evangelical Christian Russia.

Baptist Geography and Ethnography

Let us begin in the Far West of the Soviet Union. Here we find some of the most flourishing 'sectarian' organisations in the whole country, for this is 'new' Soviet territory where the Evangelical Christian and Baptist congregations have not been weakened by the purges of the twenties and thirties.[1] These western border areas annexed from Poland, Czechoslovakia and Rumania include nearly ten per cent of the entire Evangelical Christian and Baptist members inhabiting the USSR. It is a polyglot crowd, including Ukrainians and Byelorussians, Hungarians in the Carpathian Ukraine and Moldavians, Bulgars and Gagauz in the Moldavian Soviet Republic. The Gagauz are a small Turkic people who form most of the Baptist membership in the township of Chadyr-Lunga. As to the Baltic countries, there are ninety-one Baptist churches in Latvia with an aggregate membership of 6,600 and in Estonia there are sizeable Baptist groups in all the towns, even in Kokhtla Järve, a new mining centre developed by the Soviets. The Baptist movement did not previously exist in that place, but was brought there by Moldavian migrant labour. This may be considered a typical case. State-controlled labour direction and semi-voluntary migration have been major factors in the spread of the Baptist movement to areas where it has no tradition.

From the West we must logically proceed to the South, for that is another stronghold of 'sectarianism'. Throughout the Ukraine, especially in the Southern Ukraine, and throughout the North Caucasus region, we find strong sectarian congregations. In the Ukraine we might devote our attention first of all to a little village, Lyubomirka, in the Kirovograd Province. It is the place where simple peasants founded the first Ukrainian Baptist church in 1870. A foundation member of this first Baptist church of the Ukraine was still its presbyter in 1956 when he

---

[1] All data about the spread of the Baptist movement and the figures of local Baptist membership are taken from *Bratskii Vestnik* unless otherwise stated.

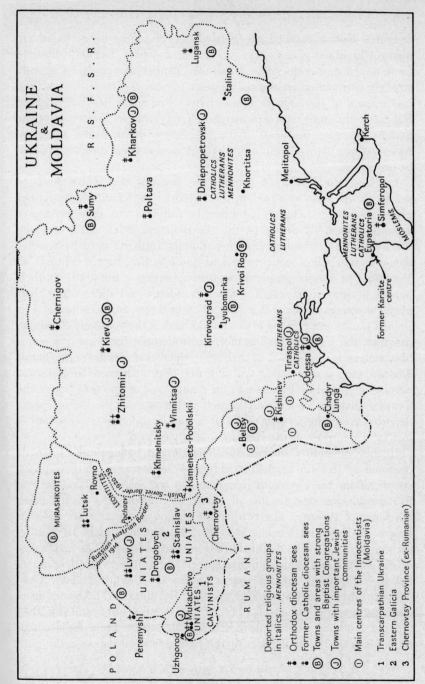

UKRAINE
&
MOLDAVIA

R . S . F . S . R .

‡‡ Lugansk Ⓑ
Ⓑ
• Stalino
Ⓑ Kharkov Ⓙ Ⓑ
‡ Sumy
• Poltava
‡ Dniepropetrovsk Ⓙ
CATHOLICS
LUTHERANS
MENNONITES
• Khortitsa
• Melitopol
• Kerch
Ⓑ Chernigov
Ⓑ Kiev Ⓙ Ⓑ
Kirovograd ‡ Ⓙ
• Lyubomirka
Krivoi Rog • Ⓑ
CATHOLICS
LUTHERANS
• Simferopol
Ⓑ Eupatoria Ⓑ
Former Karaite centre
MENNONITES
LUTHERANS
CATHOLICS
MOSLEMS
‡ Zhitomir Ⓙ
Ⓙ Vinnitsa
‡ Khmelnitsky
‡ Kamenets-Podolskii
Ⓙ Beltsy
Ⓑ
Ⓘ
‡ Kishinev
Tiraspol Ⓙ
LUTHERANS
CATHOLICS
‡ Odessa Ⓙ Ⓑ
Ⓘ
• Chadyr Lunga
Ⓑ
Ⓘ
Ⓑ MURASHKOITES
‡ Lutsk
Rovno
(LEONTITES)
Pochaev
Polish-Soviet Border 1939
U N I A T E S 2
Stanislav
‡ Chernovtsy ‡‡ 3
R U M A N I A
P O L A N D
Peremyshl ‡‡
Ⓑ ‡‡ Lvov Ⓙ
‡‡ Drogobych
U N I A T E S
Ⓑ Mukachevo
CALVINISTS 1
Uzhgorod ‡
UNIATES 1
Ⓑ
Russian-Austrian Border until 1914

Deported religious groups in italics..... *MENNONITES*

‡ Orthodox diocesan sees

‡ Former Catholic diocesan sees

Ⓑ Towns and areas with strong Baptist Congregations

Ⓙ Towns with important Jewish communities

Ⓘ Main centres of the Innocentists (Moldavia)

1 Transcarpathian Ukraine

2 Eastern Galicia

3 Chernovtsy Province (ex-Rumanian)

307

resigned, having reached the blessed age of ninety-five.[1] There are many Ukrainian villages like Lyubomirka where Baptist collective farmers are numerous. The Ukrainian Baptist movement is equally strongly entrenched among the iron-ore miners of Krivoi Rog and the coal miners of the Donets Basin. Krivoi Rog itself has a flourishing Baptist community with 340 members (1953) and in the whole of the Stalino Province, the heart of the Donets coal-mining area, there are seventy-three Baptist communites (1953) some of them directly attached to coal mines.

In Kiev, the Ukrainian capital, the Baptists have two houses of prayer in the town and two on the outskirts. In Kharkov, the former capital, the Baptist church has a membership of 1,650; they worship in a building formerly owned by the Old Believers. Such cases, in which the Baptists are allocated church-buildings 'formerly used by another denomination', do occur here and there — the Baptist church of Voronezh in Russia proper is another example — but most of their houses of prayer are small wooden buildings and quite often their prayer meetings are held in a room of an ordinary dwelling house. The Baptist movement still maintains its foothold in the youngest Ukrainian province, the Crimea; for instance, in Simferopol there are 370 members, in Kerch 170, and in Bakhchisarai, the former capital of the Tartar Khans, 100. Incidentally, the Baptists once managed to attract a number of Crimean Tartars into their ranks and at one time one of the Crimean Baptist leaders was himself a Tartar.[2] As the Tartars were deported from the Crimea lock, stock and barrel, this is now only a historical reminder of the Baptists' missionary zeal.

In the Northern Caucasus, the Baptists and Evangelical Christians continue to live up to their traditions. The strength of their urban congregations there remains remarkable — 500 each in Krasnodar and Pyatigorsk, over 560 in the oil centre of Maikop, 464 in the other oil-centre of Grozny. The two largest groups in the area are those of Rostov-on-Don and Vladikavkaz with 800 members each. In Rostov, the number of Baptists doubled between 1947 and 1954. The nationality of the North-Caucasian church membership is Russian and Ukrainian, but in Vladikavkaz many Ossetins profess the Baptist religion. They were recruited into the sect after the 1917 Revolution. The communists destroyed the traditional way of life of the Ossetins, but for all that, they did not embrace Communism. During the search for a replacement some Ossetins found the sect of the Evangelical Christians, who gave

---

[1] *Bratskii Vestnik*, 1956, no. 5, p. 64.
[2] *Antireligioznik*, 1931, no. 10, p. 59.

22. The newly-baptised members of the Evangelical Christian/Baptist
Congregation of Moscow are presented with flowers.

23. Baptism by total immersion in the Leningrad Evangelical Christian/
Baptist house of prayer.

24. Evangelical Christian/Baptist house of prayer with the presbyter in Rovenki, Voroshilovgrad, Province, Ukraine.

25. Evangelical Christian/Baptist house of prayer and congregation in Mosty, Grodno Province, Western Byelorussia.

them a better reason than the communists could for dropping barbarian customs such as blood feuds.[1] The Transcaucasian republics include many sectarian strongholds but the Baptist movement is faced with a good deal of competition on the part of the more eccentric sects, especially in the countryside. In some of the towns, however, there is a strong Baptist membership, especially in Tiflis where there are 1,000 Baptists of Russian, Georgian and Armenian nationality.

In Central Asia with its mass of Ukrainian-Russian immigrants, the Baptists and Evangelical Christians have acquired a much greater importance than in Transcaucasia. As a matter of fact, Central Asia has become one of the most important centres of the Baptist movement in the Soviet Union. In the five Central Asian Soviet republics there are now astonishingly large Baptist groups, especially in the capitals of Uzbekistan (Tashkent), Kazakhstan (Alma Ata), and Kirghizia (Frunze). In each of the two last-mentioned places there are over 1,000 Baptist members and in Tashkent there are over 1,300. A particularly impressive congregation exists in the Kazakh coal-mining centre of Karaganda. It includes a large number of mineworkers, some of whom are sufficiently wealthy to come to the Sunday services in their own motor-cars. These are attended by about 1,500 people. Other sizeable groups of Evangelical Christians and Baptists can be found in the most unexpected Central Asian places — 270 in Fergana, 300 in Dzhambul in Southern Kazakhstan, 260 in ancient Samarkand and 25 even in Bokhara, that Moslem city once so completely secluded. It is a matter of particular annoyance to the Soviet authorities that Baptists live and work even in Central Asia's 'socialist towns' such as the textile centre of Yangi-Yul (meaning 'New Road') in Uzbekistan[2] and Nebit-Dag, a locality in Turkmenistan's oil-bearing district founded as late as 1933. The last mentioned group has been particularly reproached with most actively recruiting both youth and schoolchildren.[3] The Baptists have also penetrated into the towns of Mary and Bairam-Ali which are situated in an oasis of the Kara Kum desert, into Kuldzha, in Chinese Turkestan (Sinkiang), and into the Autonomous Province of Tuva, until 1944 the Tuvinian People's Republic.[4]

Although the Central Asian Baptists and Evangelical Christians are mostly Russian and Ukrainian colonists, it may be regarded as certain that they have made some converts among the Moslem population. Indeed, a Baptist missionary society was founded in Moscow in

[1] *Kommunistichekoe Prosveshchenie*, 1926, no. 6, p. 35.
[2] *Trud*, August 22, 1954.   [3] *Turkmenskaya Iskra*, April 8, 1958.
[4] A. Dolotov, *Tskerkov i Sektantsvo v Sibiri* (Church and Sectarianism in Siberia), Novosibirsk 1930, p. 123.

L

April of 1927 under the name of 'Friends of the Mission among Heathen and Mohammedans'. In September 1928 the Baptist leader Ivanov-Klichnikov stated that 'seven specially trained evangelists worked among Mohammedans and the Lord has blessed their labour'.[1] This was more than a pious over-optimistic statement, for various Soviet sources confirmed that these missionaries had indeed obtained a certain success. The communist writer of a pamphlet about religion in Siberia complained that the Baptists had 'hundreds of supporters among the Kazakhs' of the Semipalatinsk and Akmolinsk provinces.[2] In Kirghizia too the Baptists preached the Gospel to the native Kirghiz people and were alleged to have worked according to a 'Five Year Plan for the Evangelisation' of the republic.[3] The growth of the Baptist movement in Uzbekistan was likewise attributed to missionary work among Moslems.[4] Such Baptist missionary activities as existed there must have become increasingly difficult with the growth of religious persecution in the Soviet Union. The Baptist missionary society was probably very soon wound up.

The Soviet Far East is another traditional bulwark of Russian sectarianism. In 1929, the Baptists had 193 congregations and the Evangelical Christians 118, in the 'Far Eastern Territory' as it then existed. Persecution of believers was more violent in the strategically important Far Eastern region than in many other parts of the Soviet Union and by 1932 only 85 congregations were left, almost equally divided between the two groups. In the post-war period, the Baptists experienced a strong revival, especially in the Pacific coastal region, the Maritime Territory. The Baptists themselves were rather reticent about their Far Eastern groups, but the local Soviet authorities have disclosed a great deal about their evangelising zeal, their influence on youth and on the working class and the efforts of the régime to counteract Baptist propaganda in such places as Vladivostok, Ussuriisk, Artem, Lesozavodsk and Nakhodka. In 1958 it was announced triumphantly that assiduous communist counterpropaganda had succeeded in reducing by half the attendance at Baptist prayer meetings in Vladivostok and Ussuriisk.[5] In the Soviet Far East the Baptist movement has revived in its traditional centres, where it owed its origin to foreign missions, and it has also made its appearance in new places. In the post-Stalin period new and apparently strong congregations were formed among the convicts of the Dalstroy concentration camps in various parts of the

[1] *Baptist Times*, September 27, 1928.   [2] A. Dolotov, op. cit., p. 122.
[3] *Izvestiya*, 1928, no. 229.   [4] *Pravda Vostoka*, 1927, no. 227.
[5] *Pravda o Sektantakh* (The Truth about the Sectarians), Vladivostok 1958, pp. 132–136.

Magadan Province (Palatka, Duskanya etc.). After having had a house of prayer in Alexandrovsk in Northern Sakhalin for some time, the Baptists also gained a foothold in the Southern part of the island, which was annexed from Japan in 1945. Post-war colonists established a Baptist branch in Yuzhno-Sakhalinsk.

On our way back from the East to European Russia, we come upon another group of Baptist strongholds in Western Siberia and the Altai region. For instance, there is the large Baptist congregation of Novo-sibirsk with 1,000 members (1953) and there are the flourishing Baptist working-class communities in the mining towns of the Kuzbas. In such 'socialist cities' as Leninsk-Kuznetskii, Stalinsk and Kemerovo there are overcrowded Baptist prayer-meetings.

The rehabilitation of the German minority in Russia and the closing down of the special punitive settlements for them has brought many German-speaking people into the larger Siberian towns where they have swollen the ranks of the Baptists and Evangelical Christians. In places like Novosibirsk, Tomsk and Slavgorod the local Evangelical houses of prayer have either organised mixed Russian-German services where hymns in both languages are sung or have arranged separate services for the German part of the congregation.[1]

European Russia, in its narrower sense, is not among the areas where the Evangelical-Christian/Baptist movement is strongest. Church membership in such Russian provinces as Kazan, Penza, Tula and Kaluga is far below the average of the Ukrainian Provinces and is under 1,000 for each. In Russia proper, as everywhere else in the Soviet Union, the communists are still much troubled by the penetration of Baptists and Evangelical Christians into the working class. They have found converts among the steel and metal workers of Izhevsk and Stalingrad and among the textile workers of Vyshnii Volochok where they have over 300 supporters. In Stalingrad, the Baptists were parti-cularly well represented among the workers of the huge 'Red October' steel plant, one of the biggest industrial enterprises of the USSR. Naturally the war weakened the Stalingrad Baptist congregation and its further development was handicapped by the fact that it had no church in the town itself. In 1954 their house of prayer was fifteen miles from the centre of the city.[2] However, even in European Russia we find the Baptists in the most unexpected places such as Syktyvar, the capital of the Komi Autonomous Republic, where they hold their services both in Russian and in the Komi language.[3]

[1] *Bratskii Vestnik*, 1958, no. 4, pp. 75–8.   [2] *Baptist Times*, July 22, 1954.
[3] *Nauka i Religiya* (Science and Religion), Moscow 1957, p. 409.

Finally, there are, of course, the Baptist centres of Leningrad and Moscow. Leningrad, which until 1931 was the headquarters of the Evangelical Christian movement, has 1,500 church members, but it has lost the lead to Moscow, where the Baptist community is 4,500 strong. It has only one church, the 'House of the Gospel', often visited and described by foreign visitors to the USSR. For all of them it is a moving experience to see the crowded services during which not only the aisles and galleries, but even the staircases, are packed.[1] The Moscow Baptist church has become an object of tremendous pride and satisfaction to the world Baptist movement. Dr. F. Townley Lord, the President of the Baptist World Alliance, described it as 'a true church as the New Testament understands churches'.[2]

Baptist geography is not a geography of towns and villages alone. In a way, the Russian Baptists are much more identified with Russia's rivers, in which they are baptised — the Volga, the Don, the Dnieper and even the Irtysh in Siberia. The ceremonies of baptism by 'total immersion' are usually celebrated at an early hour in the morning at a quiet point on the river, not to provoke the attention of the curious and the hostile.[3] Even those who on theological grounds may not agree with insistence on the principle of 'believers' baptism' can easily see that in Russia it has tremendous importance as a personal manifestation of Christian faith. It is obvious that the baptism of adults is much more convincing for the unbelieving onlooker than the infant baptism of the Orthodox Church. This he considers only as a tradition, a superstition and a concession to the older members of the family. In the communist view a collective-farmer who christens his child, but leaves it later without any proper instruction in the Orthodox faith, is much nearer to atheism than a believing Baptist who refuses to baptise his children but prepares them by a Christian education for the acceptance of 'believers' baptism' at a mature age.[4]

The Presbyters

The presbyters are the backbone of the vast network of Baptist congregations existing in the Soviet Union. They are usually simple people who have little secular education and no theological training, but are endowed with great religious fervour and enthusiasm. As collective farmers and workmen they are within the orbit of Soviet life and have

[1] *Baptist Times*, July 22, 1954.
[2] *Baptist World Alliance, Golden Jubilee Congress*, London 1956, p. 66.
[3] In Moscow, Novosibirsk, Izhevsk and all places where there are sufficiently large houses of prayer, baptism takes place in baptisteries which are built into the churches.
[4] *Sovetskaya Etnografiya*, 1957, no. 2, p. 57.

to share its problems and difficulties, but their faith commands them to remain aloof from its temptations. The Evangelical Christian/Baptist Council in Moscow wants them to form an *élite* in every way. Every presbyter is urged to be irreproachable as a human being, spiritual elder and Soviet citizen. What the Council expects of individual presbyters has been summarised in twenty-four commandments of which only a few, which are particularly characteristic, are quoted here:

'2. Your personal life must be pure and holy. You must endeavour to vanquish every sin. Let your heart be the purest in the whole congregation. . . .

5. Try to improve yourself spiritually. Study the Bible: you must know it better than all the other members of the congregation. Study spiritual literature. You must be continually improving your cultural level. . . .

8. Be modest about your material expenses for yourself. Learn to be satisfied with little. . . .

12. Love all your sheep. Avoid having favourites. Love the sheep who are not attractive to you.

13. Know all your sheep. Know their number and have an exact list. Know everyone individually. Know their spiritual situation, their gifts, their joys and sorrows, their family life.

14. Visit the members of the church in their homes. Show special love to the weak, the needy, those in sorrow and the sick.

22. Be clean and neat in your external appearance. A clean body and clean clothing contribute to your authority.

23. Be exemplary in the fulfilment of your civic duties and educate the members of your church in this spirit. Your church must ardently love your country and your people.[1]'

Soviet sources are prepared to admit that the authority of the presbyters over their congregations is very considerable, and this suggests that they try to live up as much as possible to the injunctions of their spiritual superiors. The authorities know that quite a number of presbyters are excellent shockworkers and collective farmers, achieving high agricultural yields, and in some cases they have been forced to enhance their prestige by awarding them orders and medals for their performances on the labour front. The authorities are also aware of the fact that the presbyters look after their sheep very diligently and that they pay great attention not only to members of their own congregation who are in difficulty, but also to any outsider who has

[1] *Bratskii Vestnik*, 1946, no. 3, pp. 28–9.

experienced shock and grief and who is left without help and advice by the communist State and its organisations. 'The Baptist preacher', says a journal of the Soviet Communist Central Committee with dismay, 'by a sincere confidential talk tries to win over such people into the "sect", promising to heal all the wounds of the heart.'[1] Since the presbyter gives a good example of human kindness, the members of the congregations do as he does; they visit the sick and talk to the afflicted and as a result the influence of the Baptists grows and their ranks increase.

No wonder that Soviet anti-religious propaganda sets out to undermine the authority of the presbyter by slander and by taking away his character. Presbyters are said to corrupt youth or to destroy the cohesion of the Soviet family. Time and again the Soviet press has endeavoured to show that the Baptist presbyters by their proselytising activities have sown disagreement and even hostility between man and wife and between parents and children. In some cases Soviet propaganda has tried to make the point that presbyters have profited financially and have been enabled to afford a motor-car.[2] It has frequently been suggested that there were even criminal elements among the presbyters. One would be charged with embezzlement, another would be accused of having betrayed 'anti-fascist believers' to the Gestapo, a third would simply be denounced for having engaged in 'banditism'.[3] The most formidable attack ever published against a Baptist preacher after World War II was directed not against any real person but against a fictitious figure, and was contained not in a newspaper article but in a novel. The novel was called *The Settlement on the Sea* and its author was Vilis Latsis, then Prime Minister of Soviet Latvia. One of the heroes of the novel was the presbyter Theodor Kalnbirze, whom Latsis described as a most important figure among the 'sectarians' of Riga. Latsis did not mention the Baptists by name but all the detail he gave showed clearly that it was they who were meant. The presbyter of Latsis' novel was a thoroughly evil man, who took a very active part in anti-Soviet espionage and sabotage activities, and also killed his own wife in a most treacherous manner. In the end 'Brother Theodor' was arrested, but for a long time the authorities were unable to get any evidence about his being the agent of a foreign power. He was as cunning as a fox. He never spoke an ill-considered word. Whilst carrying out the instructions of his

---

[1] L. Mitrokhin, 'Where the harm of the Baptist creed lies', *V Pomoshch Politicheskomu Samoobrazovaniyu*, June 10, 1958, no. 6.

[2] *Pravda o Sektantakh* (The Truth about the Sectarians), Vladivostok 1958, p. 132.

[3] *Pravda Vostoka*, April 14, 1959; *Partiinaya Zhizn*, 1959, no 14, p. 75; *Sovetskaya Rossiya*, June 16, 1959.

foreign masters, he had created for himself the reputation of a Soviet man.[1] The purpose of this description of 'Brother Theodor' was very transparent. Latsis meant to give a warning to his readers not to believe the sectarian preachers if they profess their loyalty to the communist State.

Baptists and Soviet Patriotism

The anti-Baptist bias of the Latsis novel indicates clearly how difficult the Baptist leaders found it even after World War II to convince the régime of their pro-Soviet attitude. And yet the Baptist leaders have made such great efforts to prove their sincerity. Not only have they produced such statements on foreign policy as the régime required them to make, but they have also carried their self-identification with Soviet internal policy to considerable lengths. They stated that everything connected with the life of the Soviet Union was 'dear and sacred' to the Baptists and that their personal life could not be separated from the civil life of the country.[2] To give a particular proof of their loyalty they exhorted their flock to celebrate the state holidays. The Baptist believers were urged to mark by private prayers the six principal Soviet holidays, including the October Revolution Anniversary of November 7, which established 'religious freedom and equality through the separation of Church and State'.[3] The question of these state holidays has always occupied the minds of the Evangelical Christians and Baptists from the very first days of Soviet power. When the imaginative Prokhanov was still the leader of the Evangelical Christians the attempt was made to 'christen' them. Instead of the 'International Feastday of the Toilers' on May 1, the Evangelical Christians celebrated the 'Day of the Evangelical International'; instead of the Lenin Days in January they held a 'Week of Evangelisation'. Instead of 'International Women's Day' on March 8, there was a 'Day of the Christian Woman' with special meetings.[4] However, the régime regarded these ingenious innovations as offensive and they were dropped long ago. To-day the state holidays are observed by the Baptists unreservedly — at least officially.

However much goodwill the Baptists show to the Soviet régime, Soviet leaders and Soviet ideologists are not prepared to take the pro-régime attitude of the Baptist elders and presbyters as much for granted as the loyalty of the Orthodox Church hierarchy and clergy. In a way this is understandable. On the strength of its historical record

---

[1] *Zvezda*, 1954, no. 2, p. 70.   [2] *Bratskii Vestnik*, 1946, no. 2, p. 13.
[3] *Bratskii Vestnik*, 1946, no. 2, p. 15.   [4] Kartsev, op. cit., p. 18.

and character the Orthodox Church is a Russian Church. The origin
of the Baptist movement exposes it to the charge of being connected
with the West and having pro-Western sympathies which may at times
be pro-Anglo-Saxon, at times pro-German. To invalidate the accusation
of having Western connections, the Russian Baptists during a prolonged
period were forced to pass over in silence some of the most vital chapters
of their religious history or even to distort them. For several years they
tried to prove that their contacts with world Protestantism were
predominantly Slav. They claimed to be continuing on Russian soil the
work of the Czech reformers Jan Hus and Peter Chelčický.[1] It is
significant that between 1945 and 1953 *Bratskii Vestnik* carried only
three articles about foreign ecclesiastical history, and of these one dealt
with Hus, one with Chelčický and only the third with a Protestant
movement of non-Slavonic Europe — namely the Waldensians. It was
only after Stalin's death that the Baptists were able to give a truer
picture of their own spiritual ancestry. The Russian Baptists were then
no longer afraid to admit that their movement had drawn mainly on
two sources — Russian spirituality and German Protestantism. They
rewrote their history accordingly and gave due acknowledgment to
Martin Luther,[2] and to their German connections.[3]

As the pressure of the régime relaxed after 1953 the Baptists were
able to take a more positive attitude towards co-operation with their
foreign co-religionists. The difference between their reactions to the
seventh and to the ninth Congresses of the Baptist World Alliance was
significant. To the seventh Congress held in Copenhagen in August
1947, the All-Union Council sent a letter in which it expressed full
agreement with the social and economic principles of Communism 'as
not contradicting the teaching of our Lord Jesus Christ'. The Council
refused to send representatives to the Congress, fearing that its agenda
might give rise to political discussions, quite apart from the fact that
the Soviet Government might not have granted exit permits. At the
ninth Congress of the World Alliance, held in London in 1955, not only
did a representative Baptist delegation from the Soviet Union appear,
but its leader Ya. I. Zhidkov was even elected Vice-President of the
Alliance. Soviet permission for the Soviet Baptists' international contacts may turn out to be a doubtful blessing. Their membership
in a world-wide religious organisation in which Americans play a
distinguished part has continued to be exploited by Soviet anti-religious
propaganda even in the more liberal post-Stalin period. Atheist agitators

---

[1] *Bratskii Vestnik*, 1948, no. 2, p. 57.   [2] *Bratskii, Vestnik*, 1955, no. 2.
[3] *Bratskii Vestnik*, 1957, nos. 3 and 4.

have taken a delight in reminding people that Baptist tenets were held
by many an American millionaire and warmonger who called for a war
of annihilation against the Soviet Union.

The Baptists and the Red Army

Another deeply ingrained Soviet suspicion against the Baptists refers
to their pacifism. Christian pacifism has very strong roots among the
Russian sects. There was a period when even the Soviet State itself
recognised the anti-militarist frame of mind of the 'sectarians' and
provided them with the alternative of serving in a labour army. But as
communist intolerance increased, the sectarians were more and more
forced to throw their radical Christian pacifism overboard.

In the early twenties both the Baptists and Evangelical Christians
passed resolutions, under official pressure, in favour of military service.
Twelve Baptists who opposed the acceptance of this *volte-face* were
exiled to Siberia.[1] In 1936, cases of 'sectarians' refusing to join the
army for religious reasons were still reported — three Baptists in
Makhachkala (Daghestan), three Trezvenniki in Moscow; and similar
instances occurred 'in other places'.[2]

During the Second World War many Baptists served with distinction
in the armed forces and were decorated with orders and medals. The
Council of Evangelical Christians and Baptists as a whole helped the
war effort by prayers, money collections and appeals urging foreign
Protestant bodies to support the 'second front'. One might have said
there was little difference between the Orthodox and the Evangelical
attitude; and yet there was a difference. The Orthodox Church collected
money for the tank column bearing the name of Dimitry Donskoy, and
the Evangelical Christians and Baptists for a Red Cross plane called
'The Good Samaritan'. This was a subtle and elegant concession to
Christian anti-militarism.

At that time anti-militarism was probably still alive among a section of
the sectarian rank and file. This may be gathered from a statement
which the Praesidium of the Evangelical Christian and Baptist Council
issued about opposition to the carrying of arms having no real basis in
Scripture. The statement warned against a too literal interpretation of
three Biblical quotations from which the opponents of military service
usually took their guidance. The first is the Commandment: 'Thou shalt
not kill'; the second is the words of our Lord: 'All that take the sword
shall perish by the sword' (Math. 26.52); and the third, the Lord's
commandment in the Sermon on the Mount: 'Love your enemies.'

[1] Gutsche, op. cit., p. 97.   [2] *Komsomolskaya Pravda*, May 17, 1937.

Trying to find a Biblical interpretation acceptable to Caesar, the All-Union Council declared that the Commandment and the words of the Lord about not resisting evil referred 'exclusively to our personal enemies, not to the enemies of society and the State'. 'It is in the sphere of our personal relations', said the statement, 'that we have great scope for the display of such qualities as patience, humility, love and charity.'[1] Such a statement, even if directed against Christian pacifism, could not satisfy the communists. True, the Evangelical Christian confined love of one's enemy to private and personal enemies, but even this, as the Marxist communist sees it, is a dangerous and reactionary approach.

In the period after World War II, Baptist conscientious objectors were no problem, for they had ceased to exist altogether; but instead the military authorities had to cope with Baptist infiltration into the army. Time and again astonishing cases came to light from which it appeared that not only soldiers but even officers were followers of the Baptist way. In other instances, Baptist beliefs had crept into the families of higher Soviet officers, and this prompted the political administration of the army to retaliate by a wave of anti-sectarian propaganda.[2]

Work for the State and Work for God

The Russian Baptists were much more successful in countering another accusation which the communists have frequently levelled not only at the sectarians but at all Christians, that is, their alleged attitude of contempt for work. In this respect the All-Union Council has put itself into an almost unassailable position. The Council has urged its members not only to fulfil their duties as workers at the bench and as collective farmers but even to practise a kind of Christian super-Stakhanovism. A message of the Council issued on Victory Day 1946 set the tone. The believers were spurred on to become the best toilers in their profession; the quality and quantity of their work should be the highest. This was to be done not so much for the sake of the state plan, but to demonstrate genuine Christianity through their conscientious toil, and 'to glorify our Lord and Saviour through our good deeds'.[3] It seems that these precepts of the Council were faithfully observed. There are many Baptist shockworkers, or Stakhanovites, as

[1] *Bratskii Vestnik*, 1945, no. 3, p. 51.
[2] *Red Star*, December 28, 1959, *Red Star*, April 5, 1959. Radio Volga to Soviet Armed Forces abroad, March 29, 1959.
[3] *Bratskii Vestnik*, 1946, no. 3.

they used to be called, after the most famous Soviet shockworker, Aleksei Stakhanov.

From a practical point of view little can be done about the Christian Stakhanovite. He has done a good job. Thanks to his efforts the country has received more coal, iron or gold, or whatever he produces. He has contributed to the power and wealth of the Soviet State. But communist ideology has at the same time suffered defeat. Stakhanovism, which, according to the communist definition, is a powerful movement for the building of a communist, godless society, suddenly received a quite different ideological complexion. It became a manifestation of a Christian sacrificial spirit, a way of praising the Lord, and a means of preparing one's passage to heaven. The Communist Party found to its dismay that there were Soviet citizens, men and women of the working class, who had changed the official slogan 'Comrades, forward to Communism!' into 'Brothers and sisters, boldly forward to eternal Canaan!'

The Council not only issued a general ruling about its attitude towards productive work, but reminded its members of their duties towards the State in a more specific way. Perhaps the basic idea of the Council was that the Soviet State often asked for the right thing for the wrong reason, and it wanted its followers to do the right thing for the right reason. A case in point was an appeal to all Evangelical Christians and Baptists to participate in the tree-planting activities to which they were summoned by Soviet economic and social organisations. 'Our brothers and sisters', said the appeal, 'should be in the first ranks of the active participants in communal work aimed at planting trees and shrubs.' This appeal was made when the Soviet State itself prepared its great plan for the planting of forest shelter belts — the plan for the transformation of nature. For the communists this plan was a gesture of Promethean defiance which was to prove that man could change climate and other aspects of nature, and thus direct another blow at religious prejudice. The believers organised in the Council of Evangelical Christians/Baptists took this ideological weapon out of the hand of the régime by proclaiming tree-planting as a Christian duty, an action pleasing to God. Indeed, in recommending the planting of trees the Soviet Baptists quoted the Book of Genesis, where it says 'And Abraham planted a grove in Beer-sheba and called there on the name of the Lord, the everlasting God'.[1] So every tree which a Russian or Ukrainian Evangelical Christian planted as a conscripted labourer in the Soviet afforestation campaign was, from his point of view, a tribute to the Lord.

[1] *Bratskii Vestnik*, 1947, no. 4, p. 52.

The Russian Baptists also tried to take the materialistic and atheistic sting out of another great initiative of the Soviet régime — the building of new dams and canals. The purpose of these projects was to enlarge Russia's agricultural land and increase the food supply of the country. They were to safeguard the final victory of Communism. But before this could be achieved the Russian people had to make heavy sacrifices. They had to work on the construction sites under very primitive conditions, and many thousands of peasants had to move their villages so that the canals could be constructed. Quite a number of Baptists participated in one of these construction works — the building of the Kakhovka power station on the Dnieper in the Ukraine, and an entire Baptist community (Nizhnii Rogarchik) was affected by the mass evacuation of the flooded territory. The Baptist preachers told their flock that they should work on the sites with goodwill, bearing in mind that in so doing they would fulfil the prophecy contained in the thirty-fifth chapter of the Book of Isaiah about the desert which shall blossom abundantly and the waters which shall break out in the wilderness. But everybody whose attention was drawn to the short thirty-fifth chapter of Isaiah read it to the end, and it was probably the last verse which gave him true consolation and hope: 'And the ransomed of the Lord shall return, and come to Zion with songs and everlasting joy upon their heads; they shall obtain joy and gladness, and sorrow and sighing shall flee away.'

A last glance at the Soviet Baptists

However, no amount of constructive work on the part of Evangelical Christians and Baptists can dispose of the basic Soviet objection that they are queer people who will never become properly integrated into Soviet life. It is a depressing thought for the régime that there is no sign of the Baptist ranks dwindling under the impact of Soviet anti-religious propaganda or as the result of social transformations. The Baptists have not suffered from the various social and economic processes which have taken place in the USSR since 1917, but they have turned them all to their advantage, collectivisation, urbanisation and migration to the virgin soil land. Like other sects, the Baptists have both lost and profited from the communist purges, for they have enabled them to hoist the banner of their faith in remote areas where no Baptist missionary would ever have been allowed to go either in Czarist or Soviet times.

The absence of any proper training of presbyters and the dearth of literature are bound to keep the Baptist community in the Soviet Union at a low theological and intellectual level. It will be hard to replace the present leaders of the movement by people of equal quality, although a handful of young Baptists have been allowed to follow theological courses abroad. The dearth of Baptist literature is also a serious disadvantage for the Baptists of the Soviet Union, and will prevent them from developing along Western religious lines. In 1957 a Baptist edition of the Bible was printed in 10,000 copies, but this is but a drop in the ocean.[1] It cannot still the hunger for the Bible existing among Baptists and other 'sectarians' who are prepared to pay up to 300 roubles, a third of the monthly wages of a better-paid worker, to acquire the rare and precious book.[2] The virtual impossibility of buying a copy of the Bible is not altogether to the disadvantage of the Baptists. In a way it stimulates the attendance at Baptist prayer meetings, where the Divine Word can be heard by those who have no chance of reading it.

No real reconciliation between Baptists and Communism is possible as long as Communism remains Communism and Baptists remain Baptists. However loyal the leaders of the All-Union Council may wish to appear towards the Soviet régime, their religious beliefs imply an ultimate disloyalty to any system based on a materialist philosophy. As to the rank and file members of the Baptist movement, they may in many cases hold themselves much further aloof from the Soviet system than their leaders, and live in a kind of internal emigration. They may not wish to challenge the Soviet power by positive action, but they resist passively and keep themselves away from the impact of all Soviet propaganda media.

Whilst little danger may threaten the Soviet Baptists from without, there is danger from within. The gulf between loyal leaders and the not so loyal rank and file may increase, and a section of the rank and file may transfer its allegiance to the extremist sects.

---

[1] *Bratskii Vestnik*, 1958, no. 1, p. 33.
[2] *Neues Leben*, November 17, 1959; *Sovetskaya Rossiya*, June 16, 1959.

X

American Seeds—Russian Harvest

T he United States of America and the Soviet Union are politically
and ideologically at opposite poles, but otherwise they have
much in common — the huge spaces, the unlimited possibilities
for economic development, the intense materialism bred by a rapid
economic advance, and the wish of the people to find a spiritual antidote
to this materialism. This must be strong and powerful and often it does
not seem to be provided by the traditional Churches. Of course, only a
minority, both in America and Russia, is attracted by the more spicy
spiritual nourishment; but this minority is growing and is an essential
feature of the religious scene in both countries. A further attraction of
the more quaint spiritual fare is that it is new to Russia, often as new
or even newer than the social order created by the communists.

There is not only an analogy between the American and Russian
religious situation, there is also some interdependence. Sectarian
America has become the mentor of sectarian Russia. Seventh Day
Adventists, Pentecostalists and Jehovah's Witnesses have penetrated
into both European and Asiatic Russia.

In this chapter we shall tell the story of how the various sects of
American origin became 'naturalised' in Russia and how they blended
with native Russian religious trends.

I. SEVENTH DAY ADVENTISTS

The very name of the Seventh Day Adventists reveals where the
main stress of their religion lies — on the Advent — the second
coming of Christ and on the observance of the Seventh Day of the
week as the Day of the Lord. This day is the Jewish Sabbath. The
latter practice alone distinguishes the Seventh Day Adventists from all
other Christian groups, whether Catholic, Orthodox or Protestant. They
all celebrate Sunday, the Day of the Resurrection of Christ and not the
Sabbath day of the Old Testament.

From the point of view of the Seventh Day Adventists themselves, which day to observe is no small matter. The keeping of the Sabbath expresses for them the greatest loyalty to the Creator. Those, on the other hand who uphold the 'false Sabbath', namely Sunday, avow allegiance 'to a power in opposition to God'.[1]

The Seventh Day Adventists make great demands on their followers. As they observe a different day of rest and worship from most of the population, they expose themselves to inconveniencies and difficulties in many countries. In addition, they are not allowed to drink alcohol, smoke, or eat 'unclean' meat. They must also give one-tenth of their income to their Church. This they consider a divine commandment. There is hardly any other Christian group that insists on such extensive financial sacrifice from its members. The considerable funds obtained by these tithes have enabled the Seventh Day Adventists to build up an impressive network of schools, to conduct missionary activities on a vast scale and to penetrate from the United States, where their community was founded, to virtually every corner of the globe, Latin America, Europe, Africa.

They also came to Russia where, in spite of their small numbers, they have attracted a good deal of attention. The history of the Russian Seventh Day Adventists begins in 1883. In that year a German living in Russia, Philipp Reiswig, returned from America, where he had become an Adventist, to his home in the Crimea. Reiswig began to spread the Adventist faith among the German settlers in Crimean villages. A few years later another Russian German re-immigrant went as an Adventist convert to the Kuban region of the North Caucasus where he propagated Adventism among both German and Estonian settlers. An Adventist source says that the followers of the new religion were severely persecuted; a number of them were imprisoned for their faith and subsequently banished and these, it seems, carried the message with them into their place of exile.[2] This is how Seventh Day Adventism came to Siberia. The Czarist Government unwittingly met the travelling expenses of the Adventist missionaries. The Soviet Government later gave the same 'assistance' to sectarian Evangelists of every persuasion.

The Adventists intended right from the beginning that their faith should spread not only to Germans but to Russians as well and it is this which must have made them suspect to the Czarist authorities. As

---

[1] Ellen G. White, *The Great Controversy*, Mountain View, California 1950, p. 605.
[2] M. Ellsworth Olsen, *A History of the Origin and Progress of the Seventh Day Adventists*, 1926, pp. 478-9.

early as 1889 a printing plant in Switzerland was producing Adventist writings in Russian which were smuggled into the Empire of the Czars.[1] In 1908 the first Russian Adventist was commissioned to preach, a man trained at the Adventist college in Friedensau, Germany.

Adventists and Russian Tradition

Despite its foreign origin Seventh Day Adventism became acclimatised in Russia no less than the Baptist movement. None of its teaching was really alien to traditional Russian sectarianism. This applies in particular to the most striking feature of Adventist theology, observance of the Sabbath. As far back as the fifteenth century Judaising groups in Russia have regarded the Sabbath as sacred, and new groups of Sabbatarians, in Russian, 'Subbotniki' came into being at the end of the eighteenth century.

These Subbotniki survived into Soviet times and the best informed Soviet expert on sectarianism divides them into two groups, namely, cap-less Subbotniki ('Bezshapochniki') and cap-wearing Subbotniki ('Shapochniki'). The latter kept their heads covered during prayers and thus followed more closely the Jewish example.[2] One particularly interesting group of Subbotniki could be found in the Jewish Autonomous Province of Birobidzhan. They felt so strong an affinity with the Jews that they migrated to a province which the Soviet Government had specially set aside for Jewish colonisation. The Subbotniki are an authentic product of the Russian soil. Apart from their observance of the Sabbath they have little in common with the Seventh Day Adventists. Indeed, they no longer have anything in common with Christianity, but have formed a quasi-Jewish sect consisting entirely of Gentiles. They discarded the New Testament in favour of the Old and replaced baptism by circumcision. The Soviet press, however, does not always pay heed to the fundamental difference between the Adventists and the Subbotniki. It sees only the fact that both groups refuse to work on Saturdays. The Russian and Ukrainian Baptists also sometimes use the name 'Subbotniki' when they really mean 'Adventists'. This terminological confusion makes it difficult to obtain a correct picture of the activities and geographical distribution of the two sects. However, as the original Subbotniki are a dying community it may be assumed that this expression now generally refers to the Seventh Day Adventists.

---

[1] Emma E. Howell, *The Great Advent Movement*, Washington, D.C. 1935, p. 157.
[2] Putintsev, *Politicheskaya Rol i Taktika Sekt* (The Political Role and Tactics of the Sects), Moscow 1935, p. 465.

The strict ban on tobacco-smoking which is common to the Adventists, Baptists, Jehovah's Witnesses and other sects of Western origin also has a tradition in Russia of several centuries. It figures prominently among the taboos of the Old Believers. Vladimir Dal's monumental collection of Russian proverbs contains eight warnings against the smoking and sniffing of tobacco. They leave no doubt that the tobacco smoker is no better than a beast. 'He who sniffs tobacco is the brother of the dog' or even 'He who sniffs tobacco is worse than the dog'. Not only was it wrong to smoke but it was even wrong to associate with a smoker: 'With the smoker and sniffer of tobacco and with the clean-shaven man you must not pray, you must not be friends, and you must not even quarrel.'[1] The ban on smoking, whilst difficult to accept for some, may well appeal to others as the expression of a higher moral code and may even give rise to a certain moral conceit.

Strength and Geographical Distribution

According to all Soviet accounts the Seventh Day Adventists are among the most thriving sects and one of the few which have gained ground under communist rule. They certainly prospered in the twenties and increased their numbers again after the Second World War. In 1928, there were 13,405 members in 600 Adventist congregations. They had three newspapers: *Golos Istiny* for the Russian members, *Blagovestnik* for the Ukrainians and *Adventsbote* for the German-speaking population of the Volga German Republic and the Black Sea region. They did a good deal of proselytising but the new recruits often only replaced those who had withdrawn from membership, usually because they found it too hard to give up a tenth of their meagre income to the sect. They therefore transferred their loyalty to other religious groups which did not require such high monetary contributions. But those who did pay tithes no doubt developed a feeling of deep satisfaction for doing more for their religion than any other Christians.

After World War II the number of 'registered' Seventh Day Adventists was 26,000, but it is claimed that the real number is considerably higher. Of the registered Adventists 9,000 live in the Ukraine, their traditional stronghold. There are 115 registered congregations of varying sizes there; the congregation of Kiev, the capital, had 300 members in 1955. One of them was a former Orthodox priest who attended the meetings in a wheel chair.[2] Numerous Adventist communities also exist in the Provinces of Rostov and Kamenets which

---

[1] *Poslovitsy Russkogo Naroda, Sbornik V. Dalya*, Moscow 1957, p. 47.
[2] *The Advent Review and Sabbath Herald*, November 15, 1956, no. 46.

adjoin the Ukraine in the West. Their main centre is the town of Rostov where religious life in general is intense and varied. To judge from broadcasts of the local radio stations, these Rostov and Kamenets Adventists cause the authorities a great deal of trouble. Other Adventist groups exist in Siberia, the Far East, and in an increasing number also in the Central Asian Soviet Republics. The Soviet press has mentioned too the existence of a travelling team of Adventist 'hot gospellers', with headquarters in Stalinabad in Tadzhikistan, who visit with their message Kazakhstan, Kirghizia and Uzbekistan. In Tadzhikistan, the Adventists have houses of prayer in the capital, Stalinabad, in Ordzhonikidzeabad, in Regar, near the Tadzhik-Uzbek border and in other places. Among the members of the sect in this part of the Soviet Union there are medical students, university graduates and well-paid technological experts prepared to jeopardise their jobs for their newly acquired faith.[1] In Northern Kazakhstan the Adventists have a number of churches, particularly in the Konyukhovo district. Their Sabbath services there are attended not only by the older generation but also by some of the younger peasants.[2] The largest single Adventist groups are those of Riga with 900 and Tallin with 600 members. In Moscow the Seventh Day Adventists claim a membership of 500, but they have no church building of their own. They are allowed to use the Baptist church on Saturdays.

For a long time little was known about the life of the Adventist groups in Russia but there is some information about them in a report by a Swiss Adventist pastor, R. Gerber, about his visit to Moscow, Kiev, Rostov and other places in 1956. The report conveys the impression that the Seventh Day Adventists are active and enthusiastic and living an intense spiritual life following the usual Adventist pattern. The Sabbath meeting is divided into two parts — Sabbath school in which a chapter of the Bible is studied, and the actual service with sermon, prayer and choral singing. The Russian Seventh Day Adventists also show the generosity so characteristic of their community in general. In 1955 they collected three million roubles in tithes and offerings, a large amount considering the smallness of the sect and the poverty of its members.

Adventists-Reformists

The All-Union Council of the Seventh Day Adventists, the central organisation set up to supervise the Adventist congregations throughout

[1] *Nositeli Tmy* (Bearers of Darkness), *Kommunist Tadzhikistana*, May 15, 1958.
[2] *Kazakhstanskaya Pravda*, December 8, 1957.

the country is not recognised by all enthusiasts of the 'Advent Message'. The splits which exist in the world-wide Adventist movement are also reflected in Russia. In the Western Provinces of the Ukraine and in Moldavia there are a number of Adventist-Reformist groups[1] which are off-shoots of an American organisation much more radical than the main Adventist body. They carry the prohibitions of the Seventh Day Adventists considerably further and reject not only 'unclean' meat but meat of any kind. It is even said that they are against sexual intercourse and childbirth. In their uncompromisingly negative attitude to the secular authorities they come very close to the Jehovah's Witnesses. In Nazi Germany, for instance, the Adventist-Reformists refused to give the Hitler salute or join the army.[2] It would seem that they are no less intransigent in Soviet Russia. An anti-religious pamphlet published in 1956 and dealing with the religious sects in the USSR singled them out for special attack because of the 'extremely reactionary and anti-social character of their teachings'.[3]

Seventh Day Adventists and the Soviet State

With the exception of this one small group of Adventists-Reformists the Seventh Day Adventists are law-abiding citizens and their leaders at least have often expressed their loyalty to the Soviet State. During the collectivisation period, for instance, they took great care not to become identified with the 'class-enemy'. One Adventist preacher was even quoted as describing the liquidation of the kulaks as pleasing to God since it is said in the Bible, 'Woe to the rich!'[4] In the Volga-German Republic where a very conservative and anti-Soviet atmosphere prevailed in the early years of communist power, the Adventists were the first to preach a more positive attitude towards the new régime. They issued a statement welcoming the decisions of the thirteenth Communist Party Congress and expressing their readiness 'to assist with the cultural undertakings of the Soviet power'.[5] The authorities were more embarrassed than pleased by the support they received from the Adventists and regarded it as a cunning manœuvre.[6]

After the war the situation changed. It was thought that the Adventists

---

[1] *Bloknot Agitatora*, Ukrainian edition, March 1957.
[2] Kurt Hutten, *Seher, Grübler, Enthusiasten, Das Buch fer Sekten*, Stuttgart 1954, p. 59.
[3] I. N. Uzkov, *Chto takoe religioznoe sektantsvo* (What is religious sectarianism), Moscow 1956, p. 11.
[4] *Antireligioznik*, 1933, no. 2, p. 28.
[5] E. Gross, *Avtonomnaya S.S.R. Nemtsev Povolzha*, Pokrovsk, 1926, p. 99.
[6] *Antireligioznik*, ibid.

could be exploited to publicise the Soviet cause abroad and the Soviet propaganda services did indeed distribute a number of declarations and appeals in which the All-Union Council of the Seventh Day Adventists endorsed the objectives and campaigns of Soviet diplomacy. They were the same kind of statements as the Orthodox Church and other recognised communities have periodically to publish. However, it should not be thought that the official Soviet attitude towards the Adventists is in any way tolerant. After World War II and especially after Stalin's death the Seventh Day Adventists received a considerable amount of adverse press publicity. On both ideological and practical grounds the Soviet State could not accept the two main distinct features of their creed, their belief in the approaching end of the world and their observance of the Sabbath.

Adventist eschatology is interpreted as the expression of a deep-seated, fundamental hostility towards Communism. Its exponents are obviously not prepared to wait for the communist materialist millenium. Nor is the Adventist belief in and longing for Christ's second coming only a theoretical challenge; it may also have practical consequences. According to the communist charge it may sow alarm among the workers and undermine their trust in their own strength. The Adventist prophecies divert attention from the construction of Communism. They induce people to neglect their earthly duties and in the rural areas that means a neglect of agricultural production.[1]

Such Soviet apprehensions are not entirely groundless. Sects in Russia are very much given to extremes and on various occasions Russian, Ukrainian and Byelorussian peasants have indeed been seized by a kind of mass hysteria, stopped all work and prepared themselves for the end of the world. As a rule such cases have not been attributable to the official Seventh Day Adventists but they have been reported from the Ukraine and the Russian South, areas where the Seventh Day Adventists are active. The case of the so-called 'Ascensionists' (*Voznesentsy*) in the village of Kitaevskoe, situated in the Stavropol Territory of the Northern Caucasus, made a specially deep impression on the Soviet authorities. In the summer of 1949 a group of peasants expected their ascent to heaven between May 25 and June 15. They left their collective farms, locked their houses and in scanty attire awaited the happy event of their departure from this earth.[2] A similar case, in which the official body of the Seventh Day Adventists was involved, was reported in 1957 from the village of Bukovets in the Transcarpathian

---

[1] *Pravda Ukrainy*, September 27, 1957.
[2] *Literaturnaya Gazeta*, September 3, 1949.

Ukraine. There, too, as a result of a prophecy by the local Adventist leader, peasants expected the 'end of the world'. In the night for which the great cataclysm was announced they were lying on tables dressed in white shirts.[1] Similar 'incidents' occurred in 1957-8 in two different villages of Byelorussia. People prepared themselves by prayer and fasting for ascension to heaven.[2] With such precedents in mind, and there must be others not reported in the press, it is not unreasonable for the Soviet authorities to fear that such happenings may easily recur and to view with particular suspicion any sect whose beliefs might lead to such drastic apocalyptical behaviour.

A more immediate practical conflict between the Soviet State and the Seventh Day Adventists arises out of their Sabbath observance. The crucial fact is that Saturday is a working day in the USSR. This puts the Seventh Day Adventists in Russia in a difficult position. If they were to live fully in accordance with their faith, they would have to work on Sundays instead of Saturdays. They would also have to prevent their children from attending school on the Sabbath Day. The Seventh Day Adventists do their best to sanctify the Sabbath, but with varying success. In most cases they do not manage to keep the children away from school, but there are exceptions; for instance, in Latvia they have secured official recognition of Sabbath observance.[3]

To avoid work on Saturday many Seventh Day Adventists must put up a hard fight and show great firmness but it may be that they occasionally win their point with a lenient factory manager, particularly when they are otherwise efficient and industrious workers. In Tallin, for instance, fifty-three Adventist workmen of the municipal 'Construction and Repair Trust', many of them very young people, persistently stayed away from work on Saturdays. The director of the trust admitted that he did not get far in his attempt to win over his Adventist subordinates: 'We tried to sway them', he confessed, 'but nothing came of it. We finally gave up. Let them work on Sundays.'[4] The newspaper *Trud*, organ of the Soviet Trade Unions, which disclosed the incident, took the tolerant director heavily to task for pandering to religious prejudices and insisted that when freedom of religious cults conflicted with the demands of labour discipline the former had to give way.[5] The letter of the Soviet law can always be invoked against Sabbath observers

---

[1] *Pravda Ukrainy*, September 27, 1959.
[2] *Mohilevskaya Pravda*, January 31, 1958.
[3] The *Advent Review and Saturday Herald*, vol. cxxxiii, November 15, 1956, no. 49, p. 26.
[4] *Trud*, September 15, 1954.   [5] *Trud*, ibid.

who may easily be charged with disrupting production schedules and endangering socialist property.

In the countryside the problem of Saturday observance may give rise to even greater difficulties, as can be gathered from events in the Transcarpathian village of Bukovets, where the Adventists predicted the 'end of the world'. When the Soviet administration was established in the village practically all the inhabitants there were Seventh Day Adventists. The Soviet authorities declared total war on them, asserting that their low production record was due to their refusal to work on Saturdays and holy days. The sect lost members as a result of the pressure brought to bear on it, but a hard core was left. The once united village was now divided between the 'renegades' and the remaining believers. Relations between the two groups deteriorated to such an extent that an ex-Adventist who had joined the Communist Party was killed. One of the villagers was accused of the murder and executed. At the same time the Adventist sect was charged with inspiring the assassination and nobody in the village dared to associate openly with it any more.[1] The whole affair may, of course, have been a piece of deliberate provocation of the kind often employed by the Soviet police in the fight against religion.

II. THE PENTECOSTAL MOVEMENT

What is it?

One of the newcomers on the religious scene of the twentieth century is the Pentecostal revival movement. Unlike other sects, Pentecostalists have no personal founder, they have no rigid single organisation like the Seventh Day Adventists and the Jehovah's Witnesses. Indeed, organisational diversity is characteristic of them. Since 1947 the various branches of the movement have been loosely co-ordinated by a Pentecostal World Conference which meets every two or three years. As its name shows, the sect focuses its attention on the Spirit of Pentecost, the Holy Ghost, the third Person of the Holy Trinity. An offshoot of the Protestant Churches, the Pentecostalists have gone beyond the message of the Reformation. Pentecostal piety, as Kurt Hutten, the Lutheran theologian, points out, is not based on faith but on emotions, on a direct emotional experience of divine power. A Pentecostal meeting has nothing of the sober unspectacular character of a Protestant service. It is a longing and struggling for the presence of the Holy Ghost.[2] Since Pentecostalists often start to tremble when, as they believe, the Holy

[1] *Pravda Ukrainy*, September 27, 1957.   [2] Kurt Hutten, op. cit., p. 391.

Spirit enters into them, they are in Russia also called 'Tryasuny', in English 'Tremblers' or 'Shakers'. Occasionally they are also known by other names such as 'Children of God.'

The Pentecostalists do not accept infant baptism — only adults are baptised, and baptism by water is supplemented by the 'Baptism in the Holy Spirit'. This stress on the miraculous is one of the chief characteristics of the Pentecostalists who are a community of faith-healers, prophets and mass evangelists. This means to say that eccentricity and extremism can easily creep in. The idea of discipline must remain alien to them, for they wish to give free rein to the gifts of the spirit. Among the spiritual gifts which they seek, Pentecostalists attach particular importance to the gift of speaking in a strange tongue, an excited speech understandable only to God. We shall later see that this speaking in tongues plays no small part in Pentecostal practice in Russia.

The Pentecostal theologians are well aware of the dangers which threaten their movement when the 'mentally unstable' use the opportunity for disordered self-expression which Pentecostal meetings offer them. The quality of such meetings depends very much on the persons attending them. They may reach a great depth of piety or they may simply lead to a violent but superficial religious hysteria. Of course, the communist critics of religion find it easy to ridicule such a movement. They do not see that the Pentecostal groups in their search for direct contact with the supernatural are reacting against twentieth-century materialism. It is not doing justice to the Pentecostals to focus all attention on their eccentricities as the Soviet press does.

The Pentecostal Message in Russia

The Pentecostal revival reached Russia a few years after it had emerged, almost simultaneously, in the United States, Britain, South Africa and Scandinavia, in 1906–7. Pentecostal missionaries went from these countries to many parts of the world, especially to Latin America and Africa. In 1954 the Pentecostal movement claimed a membership of ten million scattered all over the world, a figure which a Roman Catholic writer did not consider exaggerated.[1] The Pentecostal organisations most zealous in missionary work were the two principal American Pentecostal bodies 'Assemblies of God' and the 'Church of God.' In 1911 a missionary of the latter group came to Helsinki, then capital of the Grand Duchy of Finland and part of the Czarist Empire. He made the first Russian converts to the Pentecostal movement and in the next year the journal *Khristianin*, organ of the Evangelical Christians,

[1] Maurice Colinon, *Le phénomène des sectes au xx siècle*, Paris 1959, p. 56.

saw itself compelled to warn its readers against the new teaching.[1]

However, the Pentecostal movement only began to spread in Russia after the communists had seized power. In 1922, the Soviet authorities allowed a missionary of the 'Church of God' to enter the Soviet Ukraine. This missionary, Ivan Efimovich Voronaev, of Russian-Ukrainian origin, is described by his co-religionists as 'a great preacher' and 'a born organiser with deep wisdom'.[2] Voronaev's preaching had indeed considerable success, chiefly among the Baptists and Evangelical Christians. By 1926 the Pentecostal movement in the Soviet Union had 350 congregations with 17,000 believers. They were incorporated into an 'All-Ukrainian Council of Christians of the Evangelical Faith' with headquarters in Odessa. In 1928 the Council began the publication of a Russian journal, *Evangelist*, but it was short-lived. Soon the wave of active religious persecution descended on the Ukraine and put a stop to the further development of the Pentecostal revival movement.

There is no evidence of Pentecostal activities in the thirties, but it is certain that many congregations built up by Voronaev's evangelistic fervour continued to exist. The Pentecostal movement in the Soviet Union was strengthened in 1939 when a number of small but very active Pentecostal groups of Eastern Poland came under Soviet rule. Two years later, during the German occupation, the Pentecostal organisations in the Ukraine and Byelorussia came into the open, but the nazi authorities forced them to amalgamate with the Baptists and Evangelical Christians. After the liberation of the Western Soviet territories, the Soviet régime carried on this aspect of nazi religious policy.[3] Both totalitarian régimes desired a simplified and easily supervised religious front. In August 1945 it was disclosed that 400 Pentecostal congregations had joined the Council of Evangelical Christians/Baptists, and the Council itself was in future to include a member of the Pentecostal sect. An unspecified number of congregations in the Ukraine refused to participate in the amalgamation. The 400 groups included not only members of the former All-Ukrainian Council of Christians of the Evangelical Faith' but also Pentecostal groups in the territories which Russia had annexed from Poland. There, as in the Ukraine, the Pentecostal movement had spread at the beginning of the twenties. It had a number of preachers and organisers trained in the Danzig Bible School. Some of them caused considerable difficulties to the Baptist-Evangelical leaders in Moscow.

---

[1] Quoted in *Bratskii Vestnik*, 1957, no. 3, p. 62.
[2] W. Dawidow, 'The Pentecostal Flame in Russia', *Pentecost*, March 1957, no. 9, p. 4.
Gutsche, *Westliche Quellen des russischen Stundismus*, Kassel 1956, p. 120.

Pentecostalists and Baptists

In general, an Evangelical-Baptist-Pentecostal Union was not a working proposition. For the régime to have one large, easily supervised, sectarian organisation was certainly convenient, but for the believers themselves it was most unsatisfactory that they should not be free to conduct services according to their own religious tastes. No wonder there was frequent trouble in the mixed Baptist-Pentecostal congregations and often the Pentecostalists seceded altogether.[1] In the Ukraine, Byelorussia, Moldavia and even in other areas such as Latvia and the Bryansk Province of the Russian Federation it became one of the main tasks of the travelling senior presbyters to mediate in mixed congregations, to curb the zeal of the Pentecostalists, or to bring the independent Pentecostals back into the fold. The Evangelical Christian-Baptist Council in Moscow was repeatedly forced to deal with the 'Pentecostal problem'. In January 1957, over eleven years after the amalgamation, a conference was held in Moscow between the heads of the Evangelical-Baptist movement and the more moderate Pentecostal leaders to discuss theological problems. The conference lasted a week and ended with a new profession of unity.[2] However, this joint statement did not alter the fact that many Pentecostalists remained outside the united body and wished to form an independent Pentecostal Church.

The Soviet authorities were not neutral in the Baptist-Pentecostal controversy. As they saw it, the Baptists were more docile and loyal, therefore more acceptable; Pentecostalists could be dangerous fanatics. In trying to keep the Pentecostalists in their fold the Baptists could therefore count on a certain degree of support. In fact the Government forcibly removed from the Ukraine some particularly successful Pentecostal preachers (for instance, Ivan Panko, a graduate of the Danzig Bible School). Even after the post-Stalin amnesty these Pentecostal leaders were not allowed to return to their homeland.[3]

The Spread of the Pentecostal Movement

It is a paradoxical fact that the Pentecostal movement became an important religious force in the Soviet Union only after its formal amalgamation with the Baptists and Evangelical Christians. A French Catholic priest who has made a special study of modern sects has described the Pentecostalists as the 'most dynamic' of contemporary

---

[1] I. N. Uzkov, *Chto takoe religioznoe sektantsvo?* (What is religious sectarianism?), Moscow 1956, p. 10.
[2] *Bratskii Vestnik*, 1957, no. 1, p. 78.   [3] *Pentecost*, March 1957, no. 39, p. 5.

sectarian movements,[1] and so it is in the Soviet Union too, rivalled only, perhaps, by 'Jehovah's Witnesses'. Moreover, in the communist State the Pentecostalists exercise a dual attraction, a religious and a political one. Membership of the Pentecostal movement is often consonant with a negative attitude towards the state authorities.

Originally confined to the Ukraine and Byelorussia, it invaded many other parts of the country within a few years. The Soviet press has mentioned Pentecostal groups in a large number of provinces and cities of European Russia, in Smolensk, Tula, Kazan, Sverdlovsk, Nizhnii Tagil, Saratov and other places. It has reported on Pentecostal organisations in many parts of Asia, especially the Altai, Kirghizia, Uzbekistan, Kazakhstan and the Maritime Province of the Soviet Far East. The reason for this astonishing spread is twofold. First of all, numerous converts were made in labour camps, where the prisoners met Ukrainian and Byelorussian Pentecostalists who were zealous in preaching and distributing texts from the Bible.[2] After their release from the camps these new recruits founded organisations in new areas. This also brought about an ethnic change: the movement ceased to be a predominantly Ukrainian one, but now embraces a considerable number of Great Russians with a sprinkling of Germans and other nationalities also. The Soviet press claims that these new Pentecostal recruits include a number of criminals and hooligans. If this is true, then they are reformed criminals and reformed hooligans, for the Pentecostalists, like the Baptists, impose a strict moral code on their members.

Secondly, the Pentecostal faith has spread as a result of the deliberate migration of entire Pentecostal groups. Several factors seem to enter into this Pentecostal nomadism — perhaps a certain psychological instability in the Pentecostal believers; then a desire to avoid persecution and to go to new areas where they are unknown and where the local authorities may still be unaware of the 'Pentecostal peril'; and finally the apocalyptic search for a legendary country where the forces of evil do not rule. In this latter respect the Pentecostal migrations are reminiscent of those of the Old Believers who tried to escape the rule of the Czarist Antichrist or the later migration of an extremist Mennonite group to the Syr Darya region and the Khanate of Khiva.

An apostate Pentecostal preacher has given us a most vivid account of a Pentecostal migration. He has told us, albeit in a tendentious manner, the moving story of how a Pentecostal group, led by its preacher, went first from Kirghizia to Barnaul in the Altai and later in 1957 from there to Nakhodka, the new Soviet port on the Pacific

---

[1] Colinon, op. cit., p. 54.   [2] *Sovetskaya Rossiya*, June 16, 1959.

coast. The second migration was particularly long and arduous. The Pentecostalists of Barnaul took with them their belongings and their many children, covering in their travels a distance as far as from London to the Persian gulf. They claimed to have made their long pilgrimage in response to an injunction of the Holy Spirit, who had first told them that the Lord's wrath rested on Frunze, the Kirghiz capital, and then that the Lord had cursed Barnaul. They wanted to find a town where they would be 'safe from the power of the unjust' and chose Nakhodka in the hope that from there they would be able to go to the heavenly kingdom on board an ark which would come from America. So great was the urge of the Pentecostalists to leave for a better place, blessed by the Almighty, that many abandoned good jobs and flats to join the trek. In Nakhodka the Pentecostalists waited in vain for the ark but, whatever their personal disappointment, the Pentecostal movement, thanks to their privation and wanderlust, had for the first time reached the Eastern shore of the Pacific. Pentecostal nomadism also exists on a less spectacular scale. Many Pentecostal families do not stay longer than two or three years in one place and some have lived in as many as fifteen different cities.[1]

The Pentecostal Challenge and the Communist Answer

The Soviet press, basing its reports chiefly on the biased accounts of former members of the sect, describes the Pentecostalists, especially their preachers, as skilful propagandists of their faith. Wherever they are, they make active attempts to spread their faith either through personal talks or with the help of letters to be copied and passed on.[2] The communal life of the Pentecostalists is intense, some groups meeting three times a week. Their meetings are spent in prayer, singing, preaching and the mutual washing of feet, a ritual action particularly dear to them. The members of the sect show a great spirit of sacrifice and much money is collected at the meetings, most of it to be spent on evangelism.

The Pentecostalists make converts entirely from among the poorer members of the community; they are more proletarian even than the Baptists. As a dynamic religious body it can be very attractive to young people. There is something romantic and revolutionary about the Pentecostal movement in the Soviet Union. In the first place, the movement is banned and it demands some courage to belong to it. Moreover, the Pentecostal meetings take place in circumstances which

[1] Fyodor Myachin, *Moy razryv s sektantami tryasunami, Rasskaz byvshego propovednika* (My Break with the Sectarians/Tremblers, The Story of a former preacher), Vladivostok 1958, pp. 38–41.

[2] *Molodoy Kommunist*, May 1959, no. 5, p. 85.

appeal to young people. Some are held in mountains, others in forests, others in half-dark rooms somewhere on the periphery of a city, and all meetings are secret and conspiratorial. What the underground gatherings of illegal political circles did for another generation, the Pentecostal prayer meetings have done for certain young Soviet people in the fifties. At these meetings, of course, the youngsters sing Christian hymns, but they often sing them to the tunes of the revolutionary songs which fired the imagination of their elders but which have lost their revolutionary power now that they are the songs of an established régime.[1]

The attitude of Pentecostalists towards Soviet life ranges from non-committal passivity to outright negation although, as a rule, Pente-costalists are not as openly and provocatively hostile to the State as the Jehovah's Witnesses. Thus they try to avoid service in the army by cunning rather than by obtrusive action and their boycott of the official demonstrations on May 1 or on October Revolution Anniversary Day is very quiet and inconspicuous.[2]

In general, the régime tries to ignore the religious aspect of the Pentecostal movement and to attach disproportionate importance to its hostility to the State, the army, the Party, the trade unions and Soviet education. The Soviet police have not found it difficult to convict Pentecostal leaders in various parts of the country as political criminals. In the Khrushchev era, trials of Pentecostalists have occurred in the Ukraine proper, Byelorussia, Moldavia, the Crimea, Lithuania, the Kaliningrad Province, in the Moscow region, and other areas. The defendants received prison sentences of up to ten years. The preachers and other 'activists' of the sect thus rendered innocuous were usually courageous men who, having spent years in the labour camps under Stalin, were nevertheless prepared to face new risks under Khrushchev. The authorities accused the Pentecostal preachers not only of indulging in dangerous religious fanaticism, alienating young people from Soviet life and committing crimes against the State, but also of all kinds of debauchery; one Pentecostal group called 'Children of God', active in a small village of the Semipalatinsk Province (Kazakhstan) was even said to have declared all women the common property of the sect, allegedly at the Lord's command. This need not necessarily be dismissed as 'Soviet slander'. Extremist sects have frequently invoked divine authority for the strangest practices. For instance, Joseph Smith, the founder of Mormonism, declared that God himself had revealed to him the 'Mormon Law of Polygamy'. However, the Soviets also attribute to the 'Children of God' some atrocities which it is more

[1] Myachin, op. cit., pp. 16–17.   [2] Myachin, op. cit., pp. 17, 37.

difficult to credit. Thus they were charged with trying to murder a woman by nailing her to a cross. She was rescued at the last moment by the gallant local Komsomol organisation. For this attempted murder the two leaders of the sect were put on trial and sentenced to seven and ten years of imprisonment respectively. One of the defendants was the husband of the woman to be crucified.[1]

Judicial trials were not the only means by which the authorities fought the Pentecostalists in the late fifties. Ample use was also made of the weapons of propaganda. Anti-pentecostal newspaper articles were written, communist village teachers organised discussion groups with Pentecostal peasants to convert them to atheism, former members of the sect were encouraged to make public disclosures of various scandals involving Pentecostal preachers. Even a play was written, *The Dead God*, denouncing the 'God of the Pentecostalists' and his servants.

It was not an easy thing for the communists to fight the Pentecostalists. Before World War II the sect was small and was hardly studied by atheist propagandists. The rapid spread of the sect after the war, and especially after the death of Stalin, caught the régime unawares and its agitators were not equipped to meet the challenge. In one case, in the city of Kherson in March 1957, Pentecostalists very nearly wrecked a public anti-religious meeting. A local leader of the sect, a fitter in the Kherson ship-repair yards, came with several Pentecostal believers to the meeting. He came with the definite intention of confounding the atheist lecturer, a former graduate of an Orthodox theological seminary who had apostatised. The Pentecostal elder listened to the anti-religious lecture carefully and after the lecture, when all the questions had been asked, he said to the lecturer: 'I have one more question to ask. You have just said that there are no miracles and that the Pentecostalists cannot speak with tongues. You have not seen it happen, but among us, when the Holy Ghost descends on one of our brothers and sisters, that person speaks an unknown tongue without understanding what he is saying himself. It was in itself a sensation that a member of the despised and ridiculed Pentecostal sect should have found the courage to challenge an anti-religious lecturer. However, what followed was even more unusual; and here we may quote the account which the lecturer himself gave of the event several months later:

'And all of a sudden he (the Pentecostal elder) began speaking in an unfamiliar language. He mumbled something, gesticulated, as if he were trying to convince somebody. The listeners were surprised.

[1] *Komsomolskaya Pravda*, April 28, 1957.

Some 800 people were present at the lecture. You know, they all gasped. I too, I must say, was somewhat at a loss, for nothing of the sort had happened in the practice of atheist propaganda.'[1]

Finally, the lecturer recovered his presence of mind and shouted at the Pentecostal ship-yard worker, who then abruptly brought his performance to an end. But the audience, most of whom were no doubt convinced atheists, must have gone away with a feeling of great uneasiness about the strength of 'religious prejudices' as expressed by the living example of the Pentecostal Elder and his friends.

It is not at all certain whether intimidation and propaganda combined can dispose of the Pentecostalists. Even a greater liberalisation of the Soviet régime would not eliminate them, for they exist in democratic countries too; but they would certainly mellow if the Russian political climate changed. They would lose the halo of martyrdom and with it a good deal of their power of attraction. The same applies, perhaps to an even greater extent, to the Jehovah's Witnesses.

III. JEHOVAH'S WITNESSES

The name 'Jehovah's Witnesses' has been in use since 1931. The members of the sect trace it back to various arbitrarily interpreted Biblical passages, expecially to Isaiah (43.10) 'Ye are my witnesses, saith the Lord, and my servant whom I have chosen. . . .' This is changed into 'Ye are my witnesses, says Jehovah.' Jesus himself was 'Jehovah's Chief Witness'. Until 1931 members of the sect were known by various other names such as 'Bible Students' or 'Russellites' after their founder, Charles Taze Russell, who started the journal *The Watchtower* in 1879. It is still the main organ of the 'Witnesses' and is also published in Russian and Ukrainian editions.

In Russia, where they are usually called 'Yegovisty' — 'Jehovists', the Witnesses found the ground prepared by various sects which from the seventeenth century on had propagated theological views very similar to their own: the denial of the Trinity, the identification of the present world with the dominion of Antichrist, and the belief that only a small number of elect would survive the end of the world. The Judaising tendencies of the Jehovah's Witnesses, their rejection of the Divinity of Christ, their stress on the Old Testament and their insistent use of the word 'Jehovah' itself, are familiar features of Russian sectarian teaching. One might even go further and say that Russia is

[1] Moscow Radio, November 24, 1957.

probably the only country in which Jehovah's Witnesses had spiritual forerunners. In fact a Russian sect of 'Jehovists' existed in Russia long before the American sect of the Witnesses. It was founded in the forties of the nineteenth century by a Czarist artillery officer, Nikolay Sozonto-vich Ilin. Its queer theology was made up of Jewish, Christian and pagan elements. Like the Witnesses, the followers of Ilin made great use of the word 'Jehovah', but applied it to Christ, not to God the Father. Like the Witnesses, too, the original Russian Jehovists con-sidered the rulers of this world as Satanic powers. The sect spread in the North Caucasus, the Volga region and the Urals, where it had followers among the industrial workers. Remnants of Ilin's sect of Jehovists continued to survive into the Soviet period and this produced some confusion among communist anti-religious experts when an American sect of the same name made its appearance.[1]

Russia is a fertile ground for Jehovah's Witnesses, not only because they fit so well into the whole historical pattern of Russian sectarianism but also because they thrive in the grim circumstances created by the Soviet régime, especially in the newly-annexed territories of the Soviet Union. The Jehovah's Witnesses have an easy explanation and an easy consolation for all that has happened since 1914, including the entire tragic history of Russia since the Revolution. They assert that Jesus Christ was enthroned as king over the earth in 1914, but his final victory over Satan will be preceded by world wars, famine and various other calamities. The present world will never return to real stability, in fact it is living through its last days now. Soon the New World Society will be built by Jehovah's Witnesses, then there will be total peace, not only between men but even in the animal kingdom. People will no longer die, nor will they feel pain, sorrow and sickness.[2]

Since Jehovah's Witnesses take a completely negative attitude towards the existing world and existing government, they are bad citizens and have frequently come into conflict with the secular power. In democratic countries they are not taken seriously, but authoritarian states regard them as dangerous political criminals. Hitler subjected them to savage persecutions. Jehovah's Witnesses or 'Earnest Bible Students', as they were called in Germany were a familiar feature of all German prisons and concentration camps. By 1945 the nazi authori-ties had imprisoned 10,000; according to Jehovah's Witnesses' sources 2,000 died, 2,000 re-emerged disabled from the prisons, and 6,000

---

[1] *Nauka i Religiya* (Science and Religion), Moscow 1957, p. 406.
[2] Marley Cole, *Jehovah's Witnesses, The New World Society*, London 1956, pp. 174–5.

returned to preaching.[1] Those who died could easily have escaped their cruel fate by consenting to serve in the nazi army, but with rare exceptions they preferred to perish rather than betray their principles.[2]

The German concentration camps, unbelievable as it may sound, are one of the channels by which the message of Jehovah's Witnesses came to Russia. It was brought there by Russian prisoners in Germany who had admired the courage and steadfastness of the 'Witnesses' and probably for that reason had found their theology attractive. However, the Witnesses entered Russia by another way also: through the territories annexed by the Soviet Union in 1939–40, where there were small but very active groups of Jehovah's Witnesses which were later to give a great deal of trouble to the communist régime.

In democratic countries Jehovah's Witnesses make the utmost use of all the means of propaganda the law allows them, including door to door and street preaching. They always hope that they may convince even the rulers and bring them over to their faith.[3] This has been their aim even in Russia, and in 1947–8 several delegations were sent to Moscow from the provinces to submit petitions to the government explaining the objectives of the Jehovah's Witnesses organisation. This attempt, far from securing freedom for the Witnesses, only drew the attention of the authorities to the activities of the sect.

The rounding-up of Jehovah's Witnesses was carried out in several waves between 1948 and 1951. It seems that up to 1948 the 'Witnesses' were still able to distribute mimeographed copies of the *Watchtower* and other pamphlets, but later this became impossible. Nevertheless, they continued to hold their meetings. At first only the 'activists', such as the members of the delegations which had gone to Moscow, were arrested. The mass arrest of all members followed in March and April 1951 throughout the six Western Soviet Republics where the Witnesses had supporters. The Witnesses themselves estimate that 7,000 persons altogether were deported, to the Urals, Siberia, the Far North (Vorkuta) and Kazakhstan.[4]

This was not the end of the 'Witnesses' in Russia, but only the beginning of a new chapter in their proselytising activities. They even tried to propagate their faith when they stopped at stations on their way into exile.[5] In deporting them the Soviet Government could have done nothing better for the dissemination of their faith. Out of their village isolation the 'Witnesses' were brought into a wider world, even

[1] Marley Cole, op. cit., p. 129.
[2] Ernst Niekisch, *Gewagtes Leben*, Koeln–Berlin, pp. 147–9.
[3] Marley Cole, op. cit., p. 131.   [4] *The Watchtower*, April 1, 1956, p. 214.
[4] *1957 Year Book of Jehovah's Witnesses*, Brooklyn, 1956, p. 253.

if this was only the terrible world of the concentration and slave labour camps. There they met a large number of disillusioned and maltreated people and many were predisposed to accept their promises of a total change in the world's political structure within the lifetime of the present generation.

With the proclamation of the Soviet amnesty in 1955, both the 'Witnesses' of long standing and their new converts either returned to their homes or remained as free labourers in their places of banishment. In this way the Jehovists spread like the Pentecostalists to many parts of the Soviet Union. They reappeared in all the Western Soviet Republics. They established new organisations in the former forced labour areas such as the Far East and the Komi Republic, where there are Jehovist branches along the ill-famed Pechora Railway line with its terminus at Vorkuta. The Jehovists also 'invaded' Siberia and Kazakhstan, where they are particularly numerous. Organisations of 'Witnesses' are to be found in many parts of that vast country — in Ust-Kamenogorsk, in the mining towns of Karaganda and Dzhezkazgan and in Tekeli in the Taldy-Kurgan Province which borders on China. Some of these Jehovist groups owe their existence to the state-organised migration of Moldavians and Ukrainians into the newly developed areas in Kazakhstan.

A Jehovist organisation was also founded in Daghestan. Its leader was a student at the Medical Institute in Makhachkala who conducted successful propaganda activities among young people in various Daghestani towns until the state security police arrested him.[1] In short, the Russian branch of the Jehovah's Witnesses may be regarded as one of the strongest in the world, and there is certainly no branch anywhere which receives so much adverse publicity from the secular power.

A Unique Illegal Organisation

Experience has shown the Soviet authorities that the Jehovah's Witnesses are not just another sect with strange beliefs, but are first and foremost an organisation. Organisational and propaganda work is far more important to the 'Witnesses' than the observance of a religious cult. They believe that their organisation was set up by Jehovah himself. Membership of it is in itself a guarantee of salvation. All Jehovists will survive the battle of Armageddon, foretold in the Book of Revelation, which the 'Witnesses' believe will precede the end of the world. It is these beliefs which give the 'Witnesses' their moral and ideological strength and which have enabled them to form the most

[1] A. T. Moskalenko, *Kto takie Yegovisty* (Who are the Jehovists?) Moscow 1959, p. 19.

M

efficient and widespread illegal organisation that has ever existed under Soviet rule. Former Jehovists have described the rigid discipline in the ranks of the 'Witnesses'. No excuse for non-attendance at meetings is ever accepted. The number of members in each 'Jehovist' group is small, often not more than five or ten.[1] At the meetings the Bible is read and so are articles from the *Watchtower*, either smuggled into the country from abroad or illegally produced in the Soviet Union itself, sometimes in handwritten, sometimes in duplicated form. Pictures of Jehovist duplicating machines and photostat copies of Jehovist publications have often been published in the Soviet press. In Kazakhstan even tape recorders were found, used for recording sermons.[2]

But for the photographs accompanying the press articles against the Jehovists, the public would have found it difficult to believe that anybody in the Soviet Union would dare to produce and distribute anti-régime periodicals. Indeed, no other group in Soviet Russia, whether of religious or political inspiration, has ever thought of embarking on such extensive illegal propaganda and publishing work. The fervour and courage of the Jehovah's Witnesses in propagating their faith has likewise its roots in their strange theology. They believe that when they recruit new members they not only swell the organisation but also save souls from destruction on the 'Day of Armageddon'. The Soviet authorities assume that a good deal of the illegal Jehovist literature pours into Russia from Poland, where the East European Bureau of the Witnesses has its headquarters.[3] This Bureau is believed to direct and co-ordinate the work of the 'Witnesses' in Russia and to collect information about their activities.

The various branches of the 'Witnesses' in the USSR keep in close touch with one another. Contact is maintained with the help of letters in which a simple but highly characteristic code language is used. 'Family' stands for the Jehovist branch organisation, 'mother' for the organisation as a whole, 'food' for Jehovist literature and 'harvesters' for those who receive this literature. The Soviet authorities are given the Biblical name of 'Ammonites'.[4] This last code word was hardly chosen fortuitously. It seems that the Jehovists had in mind a passage of Ezekiel (25.2) 'Son of man, turn thy regard towards the Ammonites and prophesy their doom'.

The Jehovist branch leaders work on the same lines as their opposite numbers in other countries. They keep precise statistics of their members, the literature distributed, the hours devoted to Bible study and even the extent to which the traditional Jehovist door to door propaganda is carried out. It is astonishing that the latter should be possible at all in Soviet conditions, considering the risk which it involves for an illegal organisation. Nevertheless, in at least one of the trials involving Jehovah's Witnesses they were alleged to be molesting peaceful citizens in their homes.[1] The gambit of the Russian Jehovists when they knock at strange doors is much the same as that used by 'Jehovists' elsewhere: 'Good day. Let me come in for a few minutes. I come to you as a Witness of Jehovah and wish to draw your attention to a number of interesting Bible prophecies. . . .'[2] Jehovists in Russia take advantage, as they do elsewhere, of every opportunity to advertise the Kingdom of Jehovah. They try to proselytise wherever they are, in shops and coal mines, in buses and in streets.

Khrushchev's anti-'Jehovist' Campaign

In 1957, the Soviet authorities started a nationwide campaign against the 'Witnesses'. The body primarily in charge of it was the Committee for State Security, the notorious KGB, the successor of the MVD which carried out the anti-Jehovist operations in the forties. The KGB made numerous arrests of 'Witnesses' in various parts of the country. The arrests were followed by trials, especially in the Ukraine, Moldavia, Kazakhstan and the Komi Republic. The Jehovists were among the first Soviet citizens to be condemned under the new Law of December 25, 1958, 'On Criminal Responsibility for State Crimes.' At the same time the population was informed of both the misdeeds and the thought-crimes of the 'Witnesses'. An attempt was made to present the 'Witnesses' primarily as an anti-Soviet organisation, and no mention at all was made of their opposition to all governments in general and to active service in any army. The uninformed public was given the impression that the sect of the 'Witnesses' was specially formed by the Americans to carry out sabotage in the USSR. The Soviet press published sensational 'disclosures' to the effect that the Jehovists were financed by the Americans and the British. The great capitalist Rockefeller himself was said to have given large sums to the organisation, and the 'Witnesses' were alleged to praise the American way of life and have close ties with the ruling circles of American imperialism on behalf of which they engaged in espionage.[3] For this allegation no

[1] *Literatura i Zhizn*, ibid.   [2] *Literatura i Zhizn*, ibid.
[3] *Prykarpatska Pravda*, August 30, 1957.

proof could be supplied, except that the 'Witnesses' had their head-quarters in Brooklyn. Specifically political charges against the 'Witnesses' concerned their refusal to participate in elections or serve in the army, their reluctance to send children to school, or to read newspapers and Soviet books, and their boycott of the appeals of the World Peace Council. They asserted that no international body in the world could prevent war nor bring universal peace against God's will, and so the peace movement was a wicked thing.[1]

Truth and fiction are closely intermingled in the Soviet accusations, but one is outstandingly ludicrous, namely, that the 'Jehovists' were racialists who accepted the nazi philosophy of a master-race. This assertion is based on a distorted interpretation of the Jehovah's Witnesses' allegiance to the biblical Israel which an illiterate Soviet press identified in all seriousness with the present Jewish State. By regarding Israel as a people chosen by God, the Witnesses made themselves guilty of 'rabid Zionism',[2] and justified the barbarian aggression of the Israeli troops against the freedom-loving Egyptian people.[3] In fact, far from being racialists, the 'Witnesses' are more internationally-minded than the communists, for they do not recognise any national and racial barriers among themselves. They consider themselves part of 'Jehovah's Nation of Worshippers' to which their undivided loyalty belongs. One 'Witness' whom a Soviet court sentenced to ten years' imprisonment expressed this supra-national allegiance even when filling in the questionnaire submitted to him in the population census in 1959. He refused to say that he was a 'Soviet Citizen'; instead he described himself as 'Citizen of the New World and the Theocratic State'.[4]

This campaign against the 'Witnesses' pursued several objectives. One was to discourage people from joining the sect, another to induce those who were already members to resign and declare publicly that they had been deceived, and a third to justify the arrest of the leaders of the organisation and the hard punishment meted out to them. Only the future will show whether Khruschev has been more successful in fighting the 'Jehovist' danger than either Hitler or Stalin. Had the Soviet communists a better knowledge of Jehovist theology, they would leave them alone, for persecution is likely to confirm them in their views that the 'satanic powers' will stop at nothing to destroy 'Jehovah's theocratic organisation' in the final stage of world history.

[1] *Prykarpatska Pravda*, ibid.   [2] *Prykarpatska Pravda*, ibid.
[3] *Sovetskaya Moldaviya*, March 1, 1957.
[4] *Sovetskaya Moldaviya*, October 28, 1959.

IV. CHRISTIAN SCIENTISTS

The only American religious organisation which tried in vain to take root in the Soviet Union was Christian Science. Although it made its first appearance in Russia in 1909 it never became popular and remained confined to a few middle and upper-class people. Christian Science organisations in the USSR had a legal existence for five years only, from 1924 to 1929. The main Christian Science centre was Leningrad, another group existed in Moscow and there were some isolated followers in other parts of the country with whom contact was maintained by correspondence. The Leningrad meetings of the Christian Science organisation must have had a certain snob appeal, for at one time they were conducted in English, mainly because there was no authorised Russian translation of Mrs. Mary Baker Eddy's standard work *Science and Health*. Attendance at the meeting was thus necessarily limited to polyglot çi-devants and English language teachers. According to Soviet sources, membership of the Christian Science organisation also offered the material inducement of American food parcels.

In 1929, the Leningrad group was closed because it was 'ideologically harmful' and because it accepted American subsidies, but in 1931 anti-religious propagandists were still being told that they needed to have a clear idea about 'Christian Science' or 'scientism' as it was also called in Russia. It seems that this was the last time the Christian Scientists were mentioned as a problem, however small, of the Soviet religious home front.[1] But there may be a return one day and the last word about American-Soviet interdependence in religious matters has not yet been spoken. A relaxation of the political tension between the two great countries may well lead to interesting and, as yet, unforeseeable developments even in the religious field.

[1] *Antireligioznik*, August 1931, no. 8, pp. 23–7.

XI

Genuine Russian Sects

As we have discussed in some detail the sects imported into Russia from abroad, we may have seemed to belittle the original Russian contribution to religious eccentricity. We shall make up for this omission in the present chapter. We are reviewing here the destinies of those genuine Russian sects of a rationalist, mystical or apocalyptical nature, which for the most part cannot be traced back to the great Russian Schism which produced the Old Believers. These typical Russian sects, native to the country's soil, have survived the political upheavals to a lesser extent than the imported plants. To-day one need not mention many Russian sects which might have figured prominently in a similar analysis undertaken in the early part of the century. We shall only deal with those genuine Russian sects which have played a significant part in the USSR or at least throw some light on certain aspects of the Soviet religious and political scene.

The sects listed in this chapter include both 'survivals of the past' such as the Molokans, Dukhobors and Skoptsy, and sects which were either founded under the Soviet régime such as the Fyodorists, or like the Imyaslavtsy acquired new importance under communist rule. Of particular interest are the sects which the Soviet régime itself has nicknamed 'Red Dragon people', in Russian 'Krasnodrakonovtsy'. A sect of this name existed in Moscow in the twenties. Its agents travelled all over Russia preaching the second coming of Christ, the overthrow of Soviet power and the return of a Czar.[1] Later 'Krasnodrakonovtsy' became a generic term including such groups as the Fyodorists, Imyaslavtsy, Innocentists and others violently and intransigently opposed to the Communist State. The word 'Red Dragon people' is, of course derived from the 'great red dragon' of the Apocalypse (12.3) with which certain extremist sectarians identify the Soviet Government. 'These "Red Dragon" sects', said the Soviet Encyclopaedia in 1948,

---

[1] *Bezbozhnik*, July 5, 1930.

'denounce all state power as the power of Satan. They urge their followers to conduct a ferocious struggle against the authorities.' The *Encyclopaedia* added, of course, that 'such pseudo-religious groups cannot be recognised by the State, and in especially malicious cases their leaders and members are treated in accordance with the Criminal Law'.[1]

If we speak here of 'genuine Russian sects', this is because the Dukhobors and Molokans, not to mention the minor groups, have no real counterpart in any other country, except, of course, where there are refugees from Russia. The term does not mean that they have been entirely immune from foreign religious influence nor that they are confined to the Great-Russian people of the Soviet Union. For instance, the Dukhobors claim that their first adviser and instructor was a foreigner whose name they do not know and about whom they have only the most nebulous ideas. The Imyaslavtsy most certainly received their original inspiration from abroad.

The nursery of extreme Russian sectarianism, like that of the Old Believers, was Muscovy, the nucleus of the Russian State; but later, as a result of persecution and migration, the centre shifted more and more to the South and to the Eastern and Western peripheries. This accounts for the special importance of Bessarabia (Moldavia) and the Far East in Russian sectarian geography. The South has produced the largest number of sects and sectarians. The Ukraine in particular even in the Soviet period has remained a bulwark of sectarianism, both imported and autochthonous. Although some of the newer sects are Ukrainian, Moldavian or Byelorussian in their composition they must still be looked upon as 'genuine Russian sects' since they belong exclusively to the religious scene of Russia, understood in the widest sense.

One has to face two particular difficulties when writing about most of the sects which figure in this chapter. First of all, it is often difficult to feel the same understanding and charity for them as for the other religious communities of the USSR. After all, they represent some of the worst distortions of Christianity, whether in its Catholic, Protestant or Orthodox form. Secondly, we are too much at the mercy of Soviet sources when dealing with the newer sectarian groups and the Soviets have every interest in exaggerating their negative aspects, the absurdities of their teachings and the alleged criminal character of some of their actions. The Soviet State is less entitled than anyone else to express moral indignation at the eccentricities or even the crimes of the wilder 'Red Dragon' sects. It is Soviet power which has provoked an

[1] *Large Soviet Encyclopædia*, vol. SSSR, 1948, col. 1785.

extreme exasperation among simple Russian people and this has given rise to an extreme religious reaction, particularly among the peasants forced into the collective farm system. The communist régime has also created a fertile ground for extremist sects by its treatment of the Orthodox Church. The sect of the Fyodorist Crusaders in particular emerged largely as a reaction to the humiliation and oppression to which Orthodoxy was exposed in the twenties.

New sects appeared in the post-collectivisation period, especially in the Ukraine. On the eve of World War II the League of Militant Godless reported the foundation of twelve new Ukrainian sectarian groups which were particularly fanatical and ascetic and were said to consist of the 'splinters of the liquidated classes'.[1] After the war, extremist sects emerged or re-emerged in the Western Ukraine and Moldavia as a form of social and political protest. One of their main characteristics was opposition to the Soviet 'kolkhoz' which was identified as a tool of Satan. These anti-régime sects in the new border provinces included the Leontiites and Murashkoites in the West Ukrainian Province of Rovno and the Innocentists in Moldavia. The sectarian groups of the postwar period stress their opposition to the 'official' Orthodox Church even more than those which existed before the war. This is not surprising, for uncompromising opposition to the régime is easily extended to a Church which has found a *modus vivendi* with the Soviet Government.

The objective reasons for the emergence of sects — an oppresive atheist Government and an official Church allied to the atheist State — are still present in the post-Stalin period. So new sects have continued to make their appearance especially in areas where the régime's large-scale social engineering caused despair. A case in point was the transplantation of people into the virgin soil areas of Kazakhstan and the Altai where 'the most varying sects' are reported to have come into being.[2] In addition to previously known sectarian groups the Soviet press mentioned a new group called 'Bozhii Korovy' or 'Ladybirds'.[3]

The importance of the 'genuine Russian sects' must not be judged by the numbers of followers but by the amount of irritation they cause to the authorities. Their existence alone is a significant feature of Soviet reality which is often overlooked. These sects certainly correspond as little to our Western religious taste as the Bantu Churches in the Union of South Africa. Oppressive governments of whatever kind

[1] *Antireligioznik*, May 1939, no. 5, p. 22.
[2] *Nauka i Religiya*, Moscow 1957, p. 396.
[3] *Kazakhstanskaya Pravda*, September 1, 1958.

usually generate ugly alternatives. But it would be wrong to blame the Soviet Government alone for the wilder forms of sectarianism in Soviet Russia. The USSR has simply taken over the heritage of Czarist Russia whose social system bred a wide range of rebels, many of them in the guise of religious reformers.

I. MOLOKANS

We are starting our catalogue of the genuine Russian sects of to-day with the Molokans, although this may seem wrong historically since they trace their origin back to the older sect of the Dukhobors. And yet the Molokans have a primary claim to our attention since their position differs basically from that of the other sects mentioned in this chapter. Unlike the others they are a legal religious organisation in the USSR. The Molokans, who go back approximately to the year 1765, have had a remarkable past. At the beginning of this century they still had as many as 1,200,000 followers in Russia, although their total number in the Soviet Union to-day is not very great.

The name of the Molokans is derived from 'moloko', the Russian for milk. It means milkdrinkers, and is a nickname which they received for drinking milk during Lent, a thing forbidden by the Orthodox Church. They themselves prefer to be called 'Spiritual Christians', but they do not reject the more common term 'Molokans' since, in their view, it refers to the biblical spiritual milk which St. Paul for instance, mentions in the First Letter to the Corinthians (3.2). The Molokan movement has had many sub-groups and offshoots, some of them with extreme views and strange practices. There is no point in going into this subject, since with one or two exceptions there is no evidence of the survival of these groups in Soviet Russia. The main body of Molokans believe in the Bible but reject all sacraments, including baptism, and oppose all prayers not contained in the Scriptures.

In the Soviet era the Molokans, like other sects oppressed under the Czarist régime, tried at first to build up a central organisation, but they were not as successful in this as the Baptists and Evangelical Christians. An All-Russian Congress of Molokans, it is true, met in 1920 but did not lay the foundations for a permanent organisational framework. It was three more years before the 'All-Russian Union of Religious Communities of the Spiritual Christians/Molokans' came into being. The statutes of the organisation pledged the Molokans to spread the Gospel and watch over the purity and preservation of Christian principles in all Molokan congregations. The communists attached particular importance to point seven of the statutes which opposed both direct and indirect military service and stated that participation in violence and war was opposed to the convictions of the Molokans since it was contrary to the teachings of Jesus Christ. In response to governmental pressure this intransigent attitude was dropped in 1924 and it was left to every individual member of the organisation to decide about the question of military service according to his own conscience. This was not yet satisfactory to the authorities and the fourth Molokan congress held in 1929 in Vladikavkaz accepted a resolution unconditionally recognising military service in the Red Army. The Chairman of the All-Russian Molokan Union, I. F. Kudinov, tried to cover up this retreat with queer pseudo-religious arguments which only brought disrepute on the Molokans and increased Soviet suspicion of them. Kudinov declared that all believers of whatever class origin should apply for service in the Army to fight the Pope, whom he considered to be Antichrist. The Soviets were as little pleased at the thought of the recruits who might enlist as a result of Kudinov's appeal as they were with the conscientious objectors. Kudinov was charged with trying 'to transform the Red Army into an army of religious fanatics' and to convert the 'anti-religious class struggle into a religious sectarian fight against the Roman Pope'.[1]

The Molokan organisation did not survive its capitulation over military service. The congress which passed the resolution burying the Christian pacifism of the Molokans also decided on the liquidation of the entire All-Russian Union of Spiritual Christians. The reasons given for this drastic step were twofold, first the Five Year Plan and second financial difficulties.[2] 'Five Year Plan' was only a euphemism for things which could not be said in public, namely that official pressure and the anti-religious offensive of the régime had made the life of the central Molokan organisation most difficult. The Pyatigorsk Molokan group was at first supposed to take over the leadership of the scattered Molokan branch organisations but it does not seem that this arrangement worked and each Molokan group was left more or less to itself.

As the Molokans were a declining community even before World War II, Soviet atheist publications did not attack them very often. Still it was considered that some attention needed to be paid to them. A short article about the Molokans which appeared in 1938 in the first edition of the *Large Soviet Encyclopaedia* said that it was 'a topical task

[1] Putintsev, *Kabalnoe Bratstvo Sektantov* (The Slave-Brotherhood of the Sectarians), Moscow 1931, p. 169.
[2] Morozov, *Molokane* (Molokans), Moscow–Leningrad 1931, p. 85.

of anti-religious propaganda' to unmask them. There were still quite a few of the proletariat under Molokan influence, said the article. The main objection to the Molokans was their anti-cultural attitude and their total boycott of every kind of adult education and entertainment provided by the Soviet régime.[1]

For several years during and after World War II nothing was heard of the Molokans. It therefore caused some surprise when the Tass agency reported the appearance of Molokan representatives at the peace conference of the Churches in Zagorsk in May 1952. The two Molokan delegates came from Transcaucasia; one represented the Molokan community of Baku, the other that of Tiflis. This in itself may be considered as proof that it is only in Transcaucasia that the Molokans have remained a major religious factor. It is not unexpected to find them there. Although the Molokan movement originated in Central Russia, Czarist persecution in the first half of the nineteenth century forced them to migrate to the peripheral areas of the Russian Empire, especially to the Caucasus and Transcaucasus, and they are still there to-day, little touched by Communism and its anti-religious propaganda.

The Molokan spokesman at the Zagorsk conference spoke of tens of thousands of Molokan followers in Azerbaidzhan alone and he did not exaggerate. There are compact Molokan villages in the Azerbaidzhani Soviet Republic, curious little islands which have preserved their own way of life despite collectivisation, electrification, cinema, radio and television. There are even members of the Communist Party and the Young Communist League in the Molokan settlements, but the latter try to combine membership in an atheist organisation with psalm singing and the observance of the old traditions. In the large Molokan locality of Khilmili in the Shemakha district which is only sixty miles from Baku, the big proletarian centre and largest city of Soviet Asia, even in 1958 there was not a single marriage at which a Molokan presbyter was not present.[2]

In all Molokan villages there are 'spiritual pastors' maintained by the believers and houses of prayer. It is remarkable that the Molokans of Azerbaizhan preserve their faith even when they move away from their villages into the cities. They have opened houses of prayer in such 'socialist towns' as Sumgait and Mingechaur. Both before and after the war many Molokan groups have failed to register with the authorities, who therefore have no accurate knowledge of their numbers.

---

[1] *Large Soviet Encyclopædia*, first edition, vol. 38, Moscow 1938, p. 707.
[2] 'Passivnye ateisty i voinstvuyushchie sektanty' (Passive atheists and militant sectarians), *Literaturnaya Gazeta*, October 30, 1958.

Molokan villages exist not only in the Shemakha district of Azer-baidzhan but also in the Western part of the republic in the district of Kedabed which is on the Armenian-Azerbaidzhani border. There the Molokans live together with other sectarian groups such as Baptists, Adventists and especially Pryguny or 'Jumpers' an extremist group which has seceded from the Molokans. Their strange name is derived from the ecstatic dancing which is a characteristic of their worship. The sectarian villages in Western Azerbaidzhan have likewise preserved their identity, having their own preachers and houses of prayer. Long after World War II the influence of the sectarians on local youth disturbed the authorities.[1] The same seems to apply to Armenia where both Molokans and 'Jumpers' live in compact villages in the northern part of the country around the large village of Kalinino (previously Voront-sovka) and also in the eastern border district of Krasnoselsk where the sectarian villages have such typical Russian names as Novo-Ivanovka and Novo-Saratovka.[2]

As to the Molokans outside Transcaucasia, Ivan Manayenko, the Chairman of the Baku Molokan community, claimed that the Molokan faith also had supporters in the Volga regions, Siberia, the Far East, Moldavia and other parts of the USSR.[3]

Manayenko's statement can be substantiated only with the help of figures which are very much out of date since they refer to the late twenties. Then the largest single Molokan group was undoubtedly in the Soviet Far East. Putintsev's standard work on the Russian sects recorded the existence in 1929 of 118 Molokan groups there, totalling a membership of 7,433.[4] Another Soviet writer speaks of as many as 20,000 Molokans in the Far-Eastern Territory.[5] The same source gives quite impressive figures, between 1,100 and 3,000, for the Molokan groups in the Okruga, as the administrative districts were then called, of Samara (Kuibyshev), Omsk and Stalingrad. It also refers to large numbers of Molokans in various parts of the Northcaucasus region which Manayenko did not mention and which have probably completely disappeared. However, their disappearance is not a triumph for Soviet atheism. In many places Molokanism had to die so that the Evangelical Christian and Baptist movement could take root. This gradual transition of the Molokans to the Evangelical Christian faith is one of the most interesting developments which have taken place in the camp of Russian

---

[1] *Bakinskii Rabochii*, December 12, 1958.
[2] *Armyanskaya SSR* (Armenian SSR), Moscow 1955, pp. 197, 215, 224.
[3] *Conference in Defence of Peace of all Churches and Religious Associations in the USSR*, Moscow 1952, pp. 122–3.
[4] Putintsev, op. cit., p. 77.   [5] I. Morozov, op. cit., p. 77.

religious nonconformity over the past seventy-five years. It entails a very considerable change in doctrine, for the Molokans, unlike the Evangelical Christians, reject baptism and do not believe in the human nature of Christ.

Many of the leading figures of the All-Union Council of Evangelical Christians/Baptists, including its chairman Zhidkov and its secretary-general Karev, come from Molokan families and are proud of this spiritual ancestry.[1] Some of the largest Evangelical Christian/Baptist congregations, especially those of the Northern Caucasus, owe their particular vitality to the strength of the Molokan tradition in the localities concerned. The Molokan settlements of Transcaucasia, it is true, have been less affected by the advance of the Baptist movement but this is only due to their geographical isolation.

Many Molokans were attracted to the Evangelical Christians and Baptists by the prospect of becoming part of an international Christian movement. In the first years of the Soviet régime in particular, many Russian Christians felt the need to confront the internationalism of the communists with a Christian internationalism. The Molokans too tried to enlist religious allies outside Russia; they worked for the formation of an 'International of Spiritual Christians' together with the Quakers and the Salvation Army, but this did not materialise. Such attempts only earned the Molokans the reproach from the régime that they were looking for 'bourgeois allies' abroad.

II. DUKHOBORS

The Dukhobors ('Spirit-Wrestlers') are the one Russian sect which is better known outside than inside Russia. There is an extensive literature about them in the free world and in Canada, where over 10,000 Russian Dukhobors received sanctuary, their more unpleasant characteristics, especially their negative and unco-operative attitude towards the state authorities are well known.[2]

The Dukhobor sect was founded in the middle of the eighteenth century, slightly earlier than the Molokans who emerged partly as a reaction against Dukhobor extremism. For instance, the Molokans attach decisive importance to the Bible, which is 'inessential' to Dukhobor spirituality. In fact, the Dukhobors have, as it were, completely emigrated from the world of the Gospel. They have found a completely rationalist interpretation for the great mysteries of Christianity. The

---

[1] *Bratskii Vestnik*, 1953, no. 1, pp. 50–1.
[2] The Doukhobors of British Columbia, Report of the Doukhobor Research Committee, Harry B. Hawthorn, Editor, The University of British Columbia, 1952.

Holy Trinity is light, life and peace. Jesus Christ is the Son of God in the sense in which every man is God's son. The Church, as the Dukhobors see it, is not a society of Christians; Jews and Moslems also belong to it if they hearken to the divine inward voice. Government, if needed at all, is needed only for the wicked. To go to war, to serve in the army and to take oaths is forbidden. Their beliefs have a certain similarity to those of the Quakers.[1] But the honourable name of 'Russian Quakers' cannot be applied to them with real justification. Their belief in authoritarian leaders which has given rise to the emergence of such Dukhobor 'dynasties' as the Verigins, and also their self-centred anarchist attitude makes any real comparison with the Quakers impossible. The attitude of the Dukhobors in Canada shows this very clearly. Their resistance to schooling, their defiance of the courts, where they strip themselves of their clothes, and in particular their acts of arson and sabotage have brought them a doubtful reputation.

The Dukhobors are a people condemned to restlessness. Canada, where they first arrived in 1899, is neither their first nor their last destination. They have been on the move ever since the beginning of the nineteenth century. From their original homes in the Guberniya of Kharkov they were transplanted to the Melitopol region on the Sea of Azov in 1801 and in 1842 Czar Nicholas I ordered their deportation to Transcaucasia. From Transcaucasia a large body of Dukhobors crossed the ocean and another section, very likely a minority, stayed behind in Russia. By 1921 all Dukhobors who remained in their old country were at the mercy of an atheist government.

The Soviet Dukhobors, if one can call them this, may be divided into two groups, those who live in closed settlements and those who are in the diaspora. As far as the former are concerned the Dukhobor villages in Southern Georgia have earned the particular attention of the Soviet authorities. There are eight such villages situated along a highway which runs parallel to the Soviet-Turkish border. According to the 1926 census (no later data are available), the villages there totalled 5,000 inhabitants the vast majority of whom were Dukhobors. Under the Czarist Government these Dukhobors were left more or less alone. An Orthodox theologian, Butkevich, who had little love for the Dukhobors or any other sect, spoke ironically of a 'little state' which the Dukhobors had set up in Transcaucasia around the village of Goreloe, where they are still at present.[2] The Soviets did their best to put an end to Dukhobor

---

[1] Aylmer Maude, *A Peculiar People, The Dukhobors*, London 1904, p. 109.
[2] T. I. Butkevich, *Obzor russkikh sekt i tolkov* (Survey of Russian sects and religious groupings), Petrograd 1915, p. 213.

isolationism, but this was a difficult task. The Dukhobors read no
newspapers and ignored all Soviet cultural and educational activities.
An ever-increasing antagonism developed in this Georgian border
district between the Dukhobors and the Armenians who, as state
officials, dealt and interfered with Dukhobor affairs. This much was
discovered in an investigation carried out in 'Dukhoboria' in 1928 by
a Russian communist.[1]

The next report about the eight Dukhobor villages on the Turkish-
Armenian-Georgian border was produced eleven years later, on the
eve of World War II. It still showed the slowness of the Sovietisation
process in Goreloe, Bogdanovka and the other Dukhobor localities and
at the same time proved the strength of Dukhobor resistance. What the
Dukhobors did in Canada under a liberal government, they tried to do
in Soviet Russia under the world's most 'perfect' totalitarian system.
They kept their children away from school and refused to participate
in any adult education schemes. In 1939, when the collectivisation of
agriculture was virtually complete through out the USSR, one-third
of all farmsteads in the Dukhobor villages were still privately owned.
The resistance of the Dukhobors to the Soviet régime also took more
ostentatious forms. Some Dukhobors boycotted the state loan financing
the third Five Year Plan (1938-42), an unheard-of thing, since Soviet
state loans were then compulsory. Other members of the Dukhobor
sect disseminated anti-Soviet letters allegedly emanating from Canadian
Dukhobors and containing 'counter-revolutionary rumours'. Finally,
during the elections to the Supreme Soviet in 1937 or 1938, the
Dukhobors organised a pilgrimage to the tomb of their venerated
woman leader Lukeria Kalmykova — a matter which caused particular
displeasure to the local party authorities. The District Secretary of the
Communist Party had to intervene in person.[2] There is nothing more
known of the exploits of the Dukhobors of Georgia. The Soviet régime
has not deported them but has left them in their villages. Soviet
geographers and ethnographers prefer to speak of 'Dukhobor descendants' rather than of 'Dukhobors' to suggest, presumably in defiance of
the true state of affairs, that the Dukhobor religious spirit has been
overcome.[3]

Another Dukhobor group which lived in the district of Salsk in the
Rostov Province was less fortunate. As the Salsk Dukhobors had
settled in one of the main agricultural areas of the Soviet Union they

---

[1] Putintsev, *Dukhobore*, Moscow 1928.
[2] *Antireligioznik*, 1939, no. 7, pp. 39–40.
[3] *Gruzinskaya SSSR* (Georgian SSSR), Moscow 1956, p. 233.

were far less able to defy the authorities than those of the remote Transcaucasian villages. All went well at first. The 4,000 Dukhobors resettled in the Salsk district after their departure from the Kars area which had become part of Turkey, were granted a vast stretch of land which they organised into a communal farm 'Work and Peace'. For a few years they were allowed to work it in peace but then the communist authorities intervened. At first a number of party men and members of the Young Communist League were sent to the communal farm to 'help' the Dukhobor leaders. Finally, in 1929, the leading posts in the farm were handed over to non-Dukhobors. The communal farm became a fully-fledged Soviet kolkhoz. The main point of dispute between the Dukhobors and the régime was their resistance to all attempts to carry the class struggle into their own ranks. Poor Dukhobors did not wish to agitate against alleged Dukhobor kulaks as Marxist doctrine demanded. The liquidation of the Dukhobor kulaks appeared to the majority of the Dukhobors as an interference with religion, and they protested in Moscow and withdrew their representatives from the village councils. It was in vain; the Dukhobor leaders ended up in the Rostov prison and later in forced labour camps.[1]

Among the Dukhobors who suffered persecution in the Rostov Province there were quite a number of reimmigrants from Canada who believed that a new and better era had dawned in Russia with the advent of Soviet power. When they discovered their mistake it was too late, the Soviet authorities did not allow them to return to North America. It is strange that the Canadian Dukhobors, or rather a minority among them, should make the same mistake twice. In 1958, a group of four Dukhobor leaders from Canada went to Russia to negotiate with the Soviet authorities about a resettlement in the USSR of the extremist Dukhobor group known as 'Sons of Freedom'. Fortunately for the Canadian Dukhobors these negotiations came to nothing.

III. THE SECT OF THE CASTRATED

In 1914, Karl Konrad Grass, professor of theology in Dorpat University, published a 1,000 page work on the sect of the Skoptsy.[2] The formidable size of this book did justice to the extreme eccentricity

---

[1] About the Dukhobors of the Rostov Province see F. M. Putintsev, *Vybory v Sovety i razoblachenie popovshchiny* (The Elections to the Soviets and the Unmasking of Clericalism), Moscow 1938, p. 77, and K. Petrus, *Religious Communes in the USSR*, Research Programme on the USSR N.Y.C. 1953, pp. 54–61.

[2] K. K. Grass, *Die Russischen Sekten*, Zweiter Band, *Die weissen Tauben oder Skopzen*, Leipzig 1914.

of the sect but might give a false impression of its numerical importance. The sect was bound to remain small, for it demanded of its members that they should castrate themseves voluntarily. Herein lies its most distinct feature and the very word 'skopets' means castrated.

There were few provinces of the Czarist Empire where small groups of Skoptsy were not discovered at one time or another. They originated in the Guberniyas of Tula and Orel in the central part of European Russia but spread as far West as Bessarabia and even Rumania and as far East as Yakutia. In the latter territory, where they lived as deportees, they formed entire compact settlements. Remnants of these Skoptsy settlements in Yakutia continued to exist in Soviet times but probably not for long. It may be taken for granted that under the Soviet régime the Skoptsy have died out everywhere. In 1930 it was estimated that the total number of Skoptsy in the whole of Soviet Russia was some-where between 1,000 and 2,000,[1] 500 of whom were in Moscow, including 150 who had been castrated.

If mention must be made at all of this unattractive group it is not because it was at any time a significant religious factor in the USSR, but only because of the part it played in Soviet anti-religious propaganda which has always given the Skoptsy more than their due. They served the authorities as an example that the Soviet régime was not really persecuting religion but only criminal fanaticism in religious disguise. Soviet propaganda literature explaining the attitude of communist Russia towards religion at the time of the worst anti-Church persecution of 1929–30 made great play of two trials of Skoptsy which conveniently took place during this period. One was held in Saratov in December 1929 and the other in Leningrad in January 1930.[2] In a way these trials were only a continuation of many similar Skoptsy trials held in Czarist Russia in the nineteenth and at the beginning of the twentieth century but unlike the Czarist authorities, the Soviets tried to give the proceed-ings against the Skoptsy a political character. They laid less stress on their distasteful self-mutilation practices — castrations still occurred until 1927 — than on their alleged monarchist bias and their 'reactionary propaganda'. The point was almost invariably made that the Skoptsy belonged to the wealthy class. The illustrated journals *Bezbozhnik* and *Bezbozhnik u Stanka* reverted to the subject of the Skoptsy with particular relish. The articles about the Skoptsy were usually accom-panied by pictures showing naked men who had undergone various

---

[1] Gorsky, *Izuvery* (Fanatics), Moscow 1930, p. 5.
[2] M. Sherwood, *Die Wahrheit ueber die Religionsverfolgung in der Sowjetunion*, Moskau 1930, p. 26.

degrees of castration and so provided the readers with a mixture of anti-religious sensationalism and pornography.[1]

IV. THE FYODORIST CRUSADERS

The sect of the Fyodorists has probably been the most dangerous anti-Soviet sectarian group the communist authorities have ever had to deal with. They play no small part in Soviet anti-religious literature and are mentioned as an extreme example of what religion, if unchecked, might ultimately lead to. The remarkable thing about the sect is that it is a product of the Soviet period founded in response to a situation which arose under communist rule.

The Fyodorists are named after a man called Fyodor Rybalkin, officially described as a 'mad monk',[2] but the members of the sect used to describe themselves as 'Fyodorist crusaders'. The Soviet Secret Police arrested and probably executed Rybalkin in the early twenties and he played no part in the development and activities of the Fyodorist sect, which did not start until 1925. The scene of action of the Fyodorists was the 'Black Soil Province' which existed at that time. Their centre was the village of Novaya Kalitva which the Fyodorists called New Jerusalem. It is situated in the present Voronezh Province, not far from the borders of the Rostov Province and the Ukraine. The influence of the Fyodorists extended over a radius of sixty-five miles around Novaya Kalitva.

The Fyodorists are a complicated body. Soviet writers were perhaps not so wrong when they referred to the Fyodorists as a mixture of Ku Klux Klan, underground Orthodox Church and illegal monarchist organisation. It would seem that the Fyodorists never entirely severed their links with the Orthodox Church, they went to Orthodox services even if they prayed their own special prayers there. Until 1925 they referred to themselves as 'Tikhonites' that is supporters of the legitimate Orthodox Patriarch Tikhon Belavin. Only after the Patriarch's death in 1925 did the Fyodorist sect assume that strange physiognomy which put it beyond the pale of Russian Orthodoxy. From that time on, the Fyodorists spread rumours about the forthcoming end of the world and a terrible judgment to be inflicted on all non-Fyodorists.[3] The Fyodorists have not left behind any written material about their doctrines; all we know about them comes from Soviet sources and mainly from the indictment and the proceedings of the trial of the forty-two Fyodorists

---

[1] *Bezbozhnik*, 1931, no. 6, and 1931, no. 23.   [2] *Pravda*, November 11, 1929.
[3] S. Navaginsky, *Tserkovnoe Podpole* (Church Underground), Voronezh 1929, p. 24.

which took place in the 'Palace of Labour' in the city of Voronezh during November 1929.

The indictment stated that the Fyodorists alarmed their fellow countrymen by announcing the coming of the Archangel Michael mounted on a white steed and accompanied by a host of angels all dressed in white to punish the communists and the Soviet Government. According to the Public Prosecutor at the trial, the angels were nothing but White Guards and foreign troops to destroy the Soviet régime. To be spared in this Massacre of St. Bartholomew, which the Fyodorists expected on the eve of some big feastday, they wore embroidered crosses in their clothing, the men's crosses black, the women's white or blue. The higher the status of a person in the sect the more crosses he had on his garments. For the same reason the houses in which Fyodorists lived were specially marked and carried signs very similar to masonic symbols, namely a triangle with the eye of God together with biblical texts and the Russian capital letters 'X.B.'. These letters stand for 'Khristos Voskres' ('Christ is risen') the words with which Russian Christians greet each other at Easter time. The public prosecutor of the Voronezh trial asserted however that they stood for 'khotim voinu' — 'we want war'. Even a Soviet anti-religious pamphlet considered this an unlikely explanation and thought the Fyodorists had taken over the slogan 'Christ is risen' from the extremist monarchist organisation 'Union of the Russian People' in which Orthodox priests used to play an important part.[1]

The Fyodorists' apocalyptic doctrine seemed to have an immediate effect on the common people. By proclaiming all Soviet institutions the work of the Antichrist they caused many peasants and workmen to leave collective farms and industrial co-operatives. In the area under Fyodorist influence children were withdrawn from school and Soviet loans boycotted. Their particular weapon in their fight against the 'Antichrist' was arson. Within a short period as many as thirty buildings in Novaya Kalitva went up in flames and each time the sufferers were people friendly to the Communist Party and the Soviet régime. Fyodorist arson was different from the ordinary sabotage carried out by peasants of all over Russia in their resistance to the Government's agrarian policy. Cases of arson in Fyodorist villages had a ritual character, and usually occurred in connection with religious holidays. The Fyodorists themselves regarded the houses and barns they set on fire as sacrifices to God.[2]

[1] Navaginsky, op. cit., p. 26.
[2] A. Lunin, *Fyodorovtsy-Krestonostsy* (Fyodorists-Crusaders), Moscow 1930, p. 37.

The Fyodorists had one other, more harmless, peculiarity which infuriated the Soviet authorities as much as the serious anti-Soviet actions they committed. This was the symbolical importance they attached to the onion. The leader of the sect, the hermit Dmitry Parkhomenko, urged his followers to eat onions. Onions were bitter and provoked tears and were thus characteristic of the Soviet régime. The big ceremonial banquets which Parkhomenko organised had onions as the first dish and honey as the last to indicate that sweetness — the coming victory over the Antichrist — would follow the bitter struggle of the present.[1]

This question of the anti-Soviet Fyodorist onions also came up at the trial, one of the strangest ever conducted in Russia — which, of course, is saying a good deal. The Fyodorist leaders, instead of answering questions put to them by the Public Prosecutor, fell on their knees, crossed themselves and exclaimed ecstatically 'Christ is risen'. The hermit Parkhomenko repeated invariably 'I don't know, only the heavenly Father knows'. In the end the Public Prosecutor admitted defeat and conducted the trial in the absence of the leaders, which made it easier to obtain confessions from the rank and file sectarians.[2] Even before the evidence was produced, the communists had decided the outcome of the trial. Its proceedings were interrupted by deputations from Soviet factories and Red Army units urging the judges to pass death sentences on the main defendants.

The judges acceded to these 'popular demands'; of the forty-two defendants fourteen were sentenced to death including Parkhomenko, only three acquitted and the remainder sentenced to terms of imprisonment up to ten years, with subsequent banishment and confiscation of their belongings. The executions were carried out at the end of January 1930.[3] Not only the leaders of the sect were victimised. Immediately after the trial the Soviet authorities instructed the Executive Committees of the District Soviets to round up all rank and file members of the Fyodorists and to banish them with their families to outlying provinces of the USSR.[4] This must have affected many hundreds of people, for even official estimates put the total number of Fyodorists as high as 2,000.

One would have thought that this action might have been sufficient to wipe out the Fyodorists as an organised community. However, Putintsev, the communist expert on sects, reported in 1938 that

[1] Lunin, op. cit., p. 35.   [2] *Pravda*, November 14, 1929.
[3] *The Times*, January 28, 1930.   [4] *The Times*, November 28, 1929.

remnants of them continued to exist, only their tactics had changed.[1] More surprising is it that the sect survived the Second World War, though no longer under the name of 'Fyodorists' and 'Crusaders'. Its members simply call themselves 'Genuine Orthodox Christians' which is much in line with Fyodorist tradition. The name implies a denunciation of the 'betrayal' of the official Orthodox Church from which the Fyodorists detached themselves when it abandoned its original anti-Soviet militancy.

Thirty years after the great trial of the 'Crusaders' the survival of the Fyodorists was discovered in a rather strange way, almost by accident. It came to light when a young man domiciled in the 'Fyodorist area' of the Voronezh Province burnt his driving licence and all his military documents. When summoned before the authorities he showed the same evasive, fanatical and at the same time courageous attitude with which the original Fyodorists had astonished the whole of Russia. The following conversation took place between a Soviet army officer and the young 'Genuine Orthodox Christian':

'You are subject to military service?'
'I am a Christian.'
'You are a citizen of the Soviet Union.'
'No, I am a man of God.'
'If you believe in God please do. But you must abide by Soviet laws.'
'I abide by the laws of God.'
'According to Scripture "all power is from God"? Is this not so?'
'It is so.'
'So Soviet power is from God too?'
'It exists by God's sufferance.'
'This means that you as a believer must submit to this power?'
'It is not given to us sinners to know about this.'[2]

It is from the further course of this interview that the new name of the Fyodorist sect became known as well as the fact that, though it no longer uses arson in the fight against the régime, it still looks upon service in the army as a sin and 'the work of the devil' and considers all Soviet documents satanic. It also seems that the members of the sect have not given up their reluctance to work in Soviet institutions, including collective farms.[3]

---

[1] F. M. Putintsev, *Vybory v Sovety i razoblachenie popovshchiny* (Elections to the Soviets and the Unmasking of Clericalism), Moscow 1938, p. 79.
[2] *Komsomolskaya Pravda*, April 15, 1959. In the original 'God' is written in small capitals.
[3] *Komsomolskaya Pravda*, ibid.

V. THOSE GLORIFYING THE HOLY NAME (IMYASLAVTSY)

Soviet anti-religious literature usually brackets the 'Imyaslavtsy' with the Fyodorists and from the Soviet point of view this may indeed be justified. The two sects look back to Czarist Russia and were 'unmasked' at about the same time. In other respects, however, the two movements differ greatly from one another. Whatever the antecedents of the Fyodorists, there is no doubt that the Imyaslavtsy have a most respectable theological ancestry. They can trace their origin back to Mount Athos where, under the influence of Byzantine mysticism, many Russian monks adopted the teaching that God's name should be the object of special veneration. The teaching was rejected on Mount Athos and the monks who subscribed to it migrated shortly before the First World War to the North Caucasus region.[1] The Russian Orthodox Church too disapproved of the views held by these monks and so a new sect was reluctantly born, the sect of those glorifying the Holy Name or, in Russian, Imyaslavtsy.

As to the further development of the Imyaslavtsy after World War I and the Russian Revolution we must once again rely entirely on information supplied by Soviet anti-religious propagandists. From this it would emerge that the mystics of the original sect joined hands with the remnants of the White Army who were still at large in the twenties in the mountains and ravines of the Caucasus. Under the influence of the new recruits, who included officers of the White Army, the esoteric and peaceful monastic group became a monarchist fighting organisation using religious cover. In the religious field it pursued no narrow sectarian aims but thought of itself as a reform movement aimed at rescuing the Orthodox Church.

Even with their increased membership the Imyaslavtsy maintained a monastic discipline in their ranks. Marriage or sex relations were strictly prohibited. Every member had to take an oath pledging himself to absolute secrecy regarding everything pertaining to the Imyaslavtsy. It is further claimed that the same oath covered the solemn promise to fight Soviet power, not to join the Red Army, not to subscribe to newspapers nor to read them, not to visit Soviet reading rooms and not to pay any taxes. The Imyaslavtsy were concentrated in the North-caucasian districts of Armavir and Maikop and the Autonomous Karachai-Cherkess Province. In the latter, in particular, they managed to remain hidden because the local population was particularly hostile

---

[1] Robert Stupperich, *Russische Sekten*, Wernigerode am Harz 1938, p. 21.

to Soviet rule. The centre of the movement was in the village of Babuk-Aul, twenty-five miles North-East of the Black Sea port of Sochi. It was in Babuk-Aul that the 'Council of Twelve' of the Imyaslavtsy had its headquarters. This Council enjoyed great authority among the members of the sect and was entitled to impose draconic punishment for all violations of discipline. On the lower level the members of the sect were organised in groups of from five to sixty persons.[1]

When the Soviets found out about this solid and elaborate organisational structure they were not only incensed at the 'religious-counter-revolutionary plot' but also felt a good deal of admiration for the skill in conspiracy of their enemies. The suppression of the Imyaslavtsy by the GPU took place in 1927. It was very cruel and ended with the execution of its leaders, among whom two brothers Grigorovich, one a former colonel and the other an ex-cavalry officer, were particularly mentioned. Nevertheless this strong emphasis of the Soviets on the military and political character of the Imyaslavtsy in the post-revolutionary period seems somewhat suspect. Had the movement been purely political the persecution of 1927 would have finished it once and for all. And yet, the Imyaslavtsy like the Fyodorists survived World War II. In 1948 the Orthodox parish priest of Maikop denounced the Imyaslavtsy, also known under the new name of Solyanovtsy, as 'underground anti-Patriarch agitators'.[2] If this phrase has any meaning it would indicate that the Imyaslavtsy still look upon themselves as Orthodox but are fighting the Orthodox Patriarch because of his collaboration with the communist régime. Later it became known that the Imyaslavtsy have adopted the same name as the Fyodorists — 'Genuine Orthodox Christians'. In 1960 the Imyaslavtsy were still firmly entrenched in several villages of the North Caucasus region and showed the same hostility towards collective farms and Soviet society as their leaders and martyrs in the twenties.[3]

VI. IOANNITES

The sect of the Ioannites continued its anti-régime activities until 1938. It too is a product of the twentieth century although its deeper roots go back at least to the middle of the seventeenth century when the Russian peasant Danila Filipovich proclaimed a new, distorted

[1] *Antireligioznik*, 1930, no. 1, pp. 18–22.
[2] *Zh.M.P.*, January 1948, no. 1, p. 77.
[3] Literaturai Zhizn, December 14, 1960.

form of Christianity and gave his own twelve commandments superseding those of the Scriptures. The supporters of the new heresy became generally known as 'Khlysts' ('Flagellants') and called themselves 'People of God'. They gained notoriety by many eccentricities, one of which was their rejection of married life. A further characteristic feature of the Khlysts is that although they venerate the biblical Jesus Christ, they really believe in a plurality of Christs just as they believe in a plurality of 'Mothers of God'. 'Christs', 'Mothers of God', and also Prophets of the Old Testament and Apostles of the New therefore found perpetual reincarnation in the members of the sect and appeared in many parts of Russia right into the twentieth century. The Khlysts are really not one single sect but an amalgam of sects. Some offshoots of the Khlysts have played a certain part during the Soviet régime, including in the first place, the Ioannites.

The Ioannites derived their name from a pious Orthodox priest Ivan Ilich Sergiev (1829–1908). Under the name of Ioann of Kronstadt he became the object of a widespread cult. Pictures of him were venerated equally with ikons. The worshippers of Ioann were most industrious propagandists and at one time even published a weekly '*Kronshtadtskii Mayak*' ('The Kronstadt Lighthouse'). All this caused alarm among the Orthodox hierarchy, who repeatedly condemned as 'heretical' and 'blasphemous' the Ioannite teaching about the divine character of Ivan Sergiev. A special Ukaz to this effect was issued by the Holy Synod in December 1908.[1] Although anathematised by the Orthodox Church and persecuted by the Czarist Government, the Ioannites survived and were as hostile to the new secular power as they had been to the old. The Ioannites and even more the sect of the Enochians[2] which also venerated Ioann of Kronstadt considered that Nicholas II was an impostor and Antichrist, that St. Petersburg and Moscow were Sodom and Gomorrha and that the real Czar would come in the person of Mikhail Romanov, the founder of the Dynasty.[3] However, after the October Revolution, the Ioannites turned against the new régime, identifying the latter as Antichrist and thus taking an attitude similar to that of the Fyodorists and Imyaslavtsy. But unlike

---

[1] T. I. Butkevich, op. cit. p. 153.

[2] The Enochians, who like the Ioannites appeared at the turn of the century, believed that Enoch, Elias and St. John the Evangelist had come to the earth again in the guise of various humble Russian figures. They took Ioann of Kronstadt for St. John but other Enochians thought he was the Holy Spirit. They were disbanded under the Czarist régime and exiled to Poland. Their belief that the end of the world was near induced many Enochians to join the Seventh Day Adventists. The Enochians have played no part in the Soviet period.

[3] F. M. Putintsev, *Politicheskaya Rol i Taktika Sekt* (The Political Role and Tactics of the Sects), Moscow 1935, p. 458.

the latter, they did not have one single stronghold, but were scattered over a number of places. Nevertheless the Ioannites showed themselves extremely enterprising and resourceful.

Even in the late thirties groups of Ioannites existed in the Kirov Province in the northern part of European Russia, in the town of Tver (now Kalinin) in the two Autonomous Republics of Udmurtia and Tartaria and in the Caucasus region. Contact between all these groups was maintained with the help of travelling nuns. Members of the Ioannite sect also showed a special interest in work in hospitals, where they seem to have achieved some success. In the words of the newspaper *Bezbozhnik* they approached sick people who had little resistance power and indoctrinated them with religious and anti-Soviet ideas.[1]

The final 'unmasking' of the Ioannite sect and presumably its destruction took place in 1938. In that year the secret police discovered the Tver group of the Ioannites. It found that it operated under the guise of a co-operative called 'Red Toilers' and that it was in reality a monarchist conspiracy. The police not only found pictures of Ioann of Kronstadt which the Ioannites had printed illegally but even portraits of members of the Romanov family. Most surprising of all was that the Ioannites contrived to print a small illegal periodical. Branded as monarchist plotters, the Ioannites were arrested everywhere and as *Bezbozhnik* put it, received their 'well-deserved and just punishment'.[2] The influence of the sect did not disappear completely. 'Ioannite' literature was still illegally distributed long after the Second World War.[3]

VII. INNOCENTISTS

The Innocentists (Innokentevtsy) have followers on both sides of the Dniester — both on its left bank, which came under Soviet rule after World War I, and on its right bank (Bessarabia), which Russia annexed in 1940. The sect was founded in the last years of the Czarist régime by Innokentii Levizor, a monk of the Orthodox monastery of Balta, now situated in the extreme West of the Ukraine. Innokentii became a miracle-worker attracting a considerable number of supporters who claimed that their idol was the personification of the Holy Spirit. This however was only a modest beginning. In their short history the Innocentists, who are really another branch of the Khlysts, boasted of many 'Mothers of God', 'Archangels' and 'members of the Holy Trinity', all simple Ukrainian and Moldavian peasants.

---

[1] *Bezbozhnik*, February 12, 1939, no. 5.   [2] *Bezbozhnik*, ibid.
[3] Pravda Vostoka, November 13, 1960.

Innokentii died in 1917 but his supporters remained together venerating their founder and praying to him. In Innokentii's lifetime, they had founded a collective engaged in fruit growing and viticulture. It was said that among its members there prevailed promiscuity of the worst kind, a charge frequently levelled at the various branches of the Khlyst sect. The Innocentist Collective which called itself pretentiously 'Paradise' was confiscated by the Soviet Government, which transformed it into a communal farm called 'From Darkness to Light'. The former members of 'Paradise' formed a new community and built a house of prayer. In 1926, a Soviet monograph on the Moldavian Autonomous Soviet Republic listed Innocentism among the local religious trends and complained that many peasants and especially the womenfolk still took part in the cult of Father Innokentii, particularly on Sundays. It was therefore surprising when the newspaper *Bezbozhnik* triumphantly reported four years later that Innocentism had been finally stamped out in Moldavia.[1] The paper added, however, that the sect was still active in Bessarabia, then under Rumanian rule.

After 1940, these Bessarabian Innocentists, now incorporated into the USSR, caused the Soviet authorities particular difficulty. They were accused of resisting the collectivisation of agriculture and sabotaging the state plan for agricultural deliveries. This they allegedly did by burying grain in pits or concealing it in special hiding places.[2] Opposition to the collective farm system in Moldavia was not confined to the Innocentists; it was common to peasants of all religious creeds. A much more original charge brought forward against the sect was that it preached the restoration of the Romanov dynasty. This charge was substantiated with a wealth of detail. One of the Innocentist preachers, Ivan Georgitsa, allegedly spread the rumour that Czar Nicholas II was still alive and that he would soon come to power again. This prediction was only the prelude to even stranger happenings. One member of the sect, who was incidentally called Romanenko, posed as the Czarevich Aleksei and another as the Grand Duchess Anastasia. The two wore special 'imperial' garments and the rank and file members of the sect fell on their knees before them and kissed their hands and feet.[3] All this happened in 1945–6 and sounds almost too fantastic to be believed and yet this impersonation of members of the imperial family has had its precedents in the history of Russian sectarianism. The most famous case was that of Conrad Selivanov (1732–1832), the founder of the

---

[1] *Bezbozhnik*, 1930, no. 20.
[2] 'Kto takie Innokentevtsy? (Who are the Innocentists?, *Sovetskaya Moldaviya*, July 3, 1957.
[3] *Sovetskaya Moldaviya*, ibid.

Skoptsy sect, who for many years posed as Czar Peter III, the husband of Catherine II, murdered in 1762. More recently, at the beginning of the twentieth century, a peasant Nikolay Myshkov, acting under the influence of the Enochian sect, proclaimed himself Czar Nicholas II and was, of course, arrested. So the behaviour of the Innocentists was not without its parallels. The most remarkable thing about their attachment to the Romanov dynasty was that it remained unimpaired by the long Rumanian rule over Bessarabia.

The fate of the Bessarabian peasants who impersonated the unhappy children of Czar Nicholas II is not known. We may assume that it was very harsh since the Stalinist administration showed little mercy to people in the newly annexed territories who manifested hostile anti-Soviet views. After 1946, Soviet sources do not speak of direct manifestations of Innocentist monarchism. However one wonders whether the latter was not camouflaged in the cult of the Archangel Michael which was so popular among the Innocentists that part of the sect became known as 'Archangelists'. This cult the Innocentists have in common with the Fyodorist Crusaders. It was said that in Fyodorist theology the Archangel Michael was identical with Czar Michael, the founder of the Romanov dynasty (Mikhail Fyodorovich) and there may have been a similar association in the minds of the Innocentists.

The Innocentists were alleged to have continued their resistance to the Soviet régime in various forms until the late fifties. They urged the collective farm workers not to work on holy days and there were as many as a hundred holy days in the Innocentist calendar. There were further complaints that the Innocentists sabotaged elections and during the polling for the local Soviets in March 1957 an Innocentist woman was accused of setting fire to a ballot box.[1]

For several years the oppressive measures of the régime against the Innocentists seemed to be of no avail. In 1946–7 the authorities arrested various Innocentist leaders including an Archangel Michael and a 'Mother of God' but this did not discourage the sectarians. From their midst there emerged in the tradition of the Khlysts ever new 'holy persons', in the end even an entire 'Holy Trinity' consisting of three Innocentist women. Local Innocentist preachers assumed various holy names as a matter of course.

The Innocentists were not confined to one particular district of Moldavia; according to Soviet sources, they lived in many parts of the Republic, in the north near the town of Beltsy, in the district of Oloneshty on the Dniester near the Ukrainian border, in the district

[1] *Sovetskaya Moldaviya*, ibid.

of Bulboki not far from the Moldavian capital and in the district of Karpineny near the Rumanian border. Altogether there must have been several hundred Innocentists, if not several thousand. This may account for the very intense campaign which the authorities conducted against the sect in April and May of 1957 when a new set of Innocentist leaders was arrested. This wave of persecution received wide local publicity. Not only were long newspaper articles written against the sect but a film was produced denouncing its alleged misdeeds.[1] Rank and file sectarians were induced in various ways to leave the Innocentist groups. In the first place they were told that their leaders were not only religious fanatics but impostors and criminals guilty of burying alive several people including children. They were also promised that they would not incur any punishment themselves and Soviet power would generously forgive them their membership of an illegal and counter-revolutionary sectarian organisation. Even so the sect was still in existence in 1959.

VIII. OTHER 'RED DRAGON' SECTS

It is impossible to give a full list of the sects which have played a part under the Soviet régime, only a few more examples may be quoted to show the extreme types of religious opposition to which the anti-Communism of the Ukrainian and Russian peasant has given birth.

Opponents of Soviet Money

Such an extreme sect was, for instance, that of the Chernokhristovtsy, or 'followers of the Black Christ' who avoided everything Soviet, not only Soviet newspapers — this is a feature common to many sects of the USSR — but also money. In this they were similar to another strange sect near the Ukrainian town of Zvenigorod whose members were simply known as 'People ignoring numbers'. They too would not recognise money and rejected any calculation and any plan worked out in figures. They did not join collective farms because membership would have immediately involved them in figures, quotas and accounts. 'Where there are accounts and figures', they used to say, 'there is also deceit and violence. We are God's people and don't want this.' Their asceticism was expressed in the wearing of sack-like clothes. They could not always live up to their rigid principles and from time to time they bought something on the market but admitted that in doing so they were committing a grave sin.[2]

[1] *Sovetskaya Kultura*, April 4, 1959.   [2] *Antireligioznik*, May 1939, no. 5, p. 22.

Molchalniki and Skrytniki

Two sectarian groups, both relics of the pre-revolutionary period which have exasperated the Soviet authorities, not by active counter-revolutionary opposition but by the powerful weapon of passive resistance, are the Molchalniki and the Skrytniki. Both groups observe a negative attitude not only to the State but to everybody who does not belong to them. Theologically Molchalniki and Skrytniki have not the same origin. The Molchalniki are a Khlyst group and the Skrytniki are an extreme Old Believer sect. The names of the two groups speak for themselves. Molchalniki means 'The Silent Ones' and Skrytniki 'Those hiding themselves'. Faithful to their name, the Molchalniki did not talk to any outsider, not even to their neighbours, and they never visited anyone, never received any visits. Also their children did not play with other children, until this became impossible, they did not go to school. In one village in the region of Rostov on Don the Molchalniki lived mostly by cutting reeds and selling them but they said not a word to the customers. They only lifted a finger to show that one parcel of reeds cost a rouble.[1] At election times they outwitted the communists who wanted to take them to the polls. Anticipating what was going to happen, they left the village on the eve of the elections and locked their houses.

The Skrytniki, who are also known as 'genuine Christians' ('Istinnyie Khristyane') abhor participation in Soviet public life no less than the Molchalniki. Following an old tradition of their own, they have always refused to give their names to the authorities, nor would they disclose their residence or their place of birth. If they did so, they believed they would surrender themselves to the Antichrist who rules the world. The Skrytniki upheld this tradition also under the Soviet régime and even at the elections to the Supreme Soviet of 1937 they still acted as their fathers and grandfathers had done. When asked for their name they simply answered 'Slave of God Ivan' or 'Slave of God Iosif'. This was reported from Karelia but there were other groups of Skrytniki in the Ukraine and Siberia,[2] and also in the Komi Republic where they at one time had illegal monasteries.[3] The Soviet authorities put the Skrytniki in prison but this was of little avail. Even there they refused to be called by their family names. The warders had to call them 'Slave of God' if they hoped for any attention.[4]

[1] *Bezbozhnik*, September 1, 1938.
[2] F. M. Putintsev, *Vybory v Sovety i Razoblachenie Popovshchiny*, Moscow 1938, p. 19.
[3] *Bezbozhnik*, April 21, 1929.
[4] Alex Weissberg, *Conspiracy of Silence*, London 1952, p. 407.

'Brethren of Holy Zion'

A sect under this name made its appearance in the Rovno Province, one of the eight provinces annexed by the Ukraine during and after World War II where the population has shown particular hostility to the Soviet régime, a hostility which has assumed both political and religious forms. The 'Brethren of Holy Zion' existed even before the war. The followers of the sect are also called 'Murashkoites' after their founder Ivan Murashko who described himself as 'Father of Sion' and 'the Prophet Elias'. He went to Brazil and his place as leader of the sect was taken over by a Ukrainian woman, Lyubov Ushenko, who was venerated by her followers as a divine person. The theology of the Murashkoites is a mixture of Christian, Jewish and pagan elements, but what interests the Soviet authorities above all is the sect's militant anti-Communism. They look upon the Murashkoites as an underground movement which incites the local people against the measures of the régime and forecasts 'the inescapable doom of Soviet power'. The Murashkoites even had a youth organisation, called 'Army of Christ' whose members were not allowed to mix with youngsters outside the sect.[1] From the Rovno Province the sect spread to Odessa and to Kustanai. It was in this Kazakh town that its leaders took refuge after being released from prison under a post-Stalin amnesty. In 1959 they were tried once again and severe punishment was meted out.[2]

The 'True Orthodox Church'

In the Southern part of the Rovno Province there spread another sect, the Leontiites, which looks like a secession from the Orthodox Church, not unlike the Fyodorists. The sect did not exist before the war, and is one of the youngest of the Soviet Union. It was founded by a man called Leontii Gritsan whom the Soviet authorities denounced as a horse-thief but whom his supporters regard as a saint. Gritsan went from village to village and proclaimed the foundation of the 'True Orthodox Church', also called the 'Leontii Church'. The 'old Church' he said could no longer be considered as 'true' since it did not fight the order established by Satan. The Leontiites observe the same extensive list of taboos as most 'Red Dragon' sects. In a word they boycott everything Soviet, whether the army, the collective farm or elections. The Leontiites even urge their women supporters not to accept state grants given to mothers. Leontii was arrested and exiled,

---

[1] *Chervony Prapor*, Rovno, May 14, 1958.
[2] *Kazakhstanskaya Pravda*, November 29, 1959.

to judge from a sarcastic remark in a Soviet newspaper.[1] This resulted in Leontii being venerated by his followers as a martyr. Even Leontii ikons have been distributed.

Their faith commands the Leontiites not to carry any Soviet indentity papers, and not to work at all but to lead a vagrant way of life in prepartion for the end of the world, which they consider imminent. This way of life has allowed the Leontiites to spread their faith. According to Soviet sources they have gained a foothold in the monastery grounds of Pochaev, where they conduct successful proselytising activities among the pilgrims visiting the holy place of the Ukrainian Christians. It has been asserted that the Leontiites are even enjoying the active sympathy of some Pochaev monks.[2] This is not altogether incredible. A section of the West Ukrainian Orthodox Christians, including members of the clergy, may well prefer the militancy of the Leontiites to the meekness and loyalty of official Orthodoxy.

It would be wrong to dismiss the Leontiites as a purely local phenomenon. They represent a type of sect which is likely to become more widespread as long as Russia continues to be half-slave and half-free and as long as the Patriarchal Church remains in fetters. There is not enough freedom to enable that Church to maintain an attitude of independence towards the State but terror is being sufficiently relaxed to make illegal religious activities less risky than they were under Stalin. The search for the 'true' or 'genuine' Church which is usually found in the shape of small illegal organisations is therefore characteristic of the religious situation in post-Stalin Russia. Not only Leontiites, Fyodorists and Imyaslavtsy, but also other underground groups operating in various parts of the country, have labelled themselves 'true' and 'genuine' Orthodox Christians. The Soviet authorities discovered groups of 'Genuine Orthodox Christians' in the Tambov Province, the Mari Republic, the Altai, Uzbekistan and Kazakhstan, where the 'Genuine Orthodox Church' maintained an underground monastery near Temir Tau. All these groups regarded Patriarch Tikhon as the last legitimate leader of Russian Orthodoxy. All were violently anti-communist and the groups in Kazakhstan and Uzbekistan were denounced for monarchist leanings. Their members suffered arrest and exile and children of 'Genuine Orthodox Christians' were taken away from their families and put into boarding schools.[3]

---

[1] *Sovetskaya Kultura*, January 13, 1959.   [2] *Trud*, July 9, 1960.
[3] Pravda Vostoka, October 19, 1960, Nauka i Religiya, Nr. 3, 1960 pp. 53/56; Sovetskaya Kultura, January 7, 1961.

XII

The Secularisation of Soviet Jewry

Jehovah, at thee contempt I fling,
And I in Babylon am King.
HEINRICH HEINE

The Theory of Soviet Anti-Judaism

A study of the Soviet attitude towards religious Judaism is complicated by the dual character of the Jewish problem in Russia. Usually it is only the national, not the religious, aspect of the problem which receives attention and in a standard work on the Jews in the Soviet Union the fate of religious Judaism is treated only as a minor matter.[1] However, much of the national oppression to which the Soviet Jews have been exposed is rooted in the communist assessment of Judaism as a reactionary religious force. Lenin himself described the demand for Jewish national culture as a 'slogan of rabbis and bourgeois' which shows that he attached to Jewish culture predominantly religious meaning.[2] The existence of world-wide religious Judaism invalidates from the start the Soviet communist thesis that the word 'Jews' is no more than the collective term for various heterogeneous national groups or rather national splinters which trace their origin back to the ancient Hebrews.[3]

According to Soviet anti-religious theory Jewish monotheism was invented by the Prophets to endow the Jews with a kind of religious exclusiveness and so to silence the class contradictions in their midst. Whilst attacking the luxury and rapacity of the rich, the 'prophets' failed to call for a real fight against social injustice. Their appeals to wait for the arrival of the Messiah were intended to put a brake on the activity of the exploited lower classes.[4] Soviet sources add that the Jewish 'nationalist propaganda' contained in the Old Testament, namely about the Messiah routing the enemies of Israel, has been very actively

[1] Solomon M. Schwarz, *The Jews in the Soviet Union*, Syracuse University Press, 1952.
[2] Lenin, *Sochineniya* (Works), vol. xx, p. 9.
[3] *Large Soviet Encyclopædia*, second edition, vol. xv, Moscow 1952, p. 377.
[4] *Large Soviet Encyclopædia*, second edition, vol. xix, Moscow 1953, pp. 157–8.

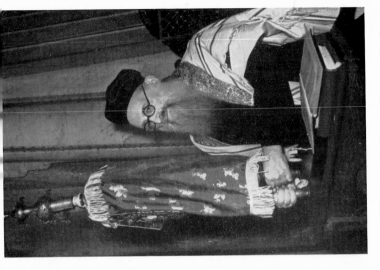

27. Shloime Schliefer, Rabbi of the Moscow synagogue and President of the Jewish Community of Moscow.

26. Joseph Isaac Schneersohn, the Rabbi of Lyubavichi.

28. Students at the Moscow yeshivah.

exploited at the present time by the State of Israel, that puppet in the hands of foreign, especially American, imperialists.[1]

The attacks levelled at religious Judaism by anti-religious propagandists have differed but little from the attacks on other religions. The Jewish religion, it has been said, preaches anti-scientific ideas about nature and society; the priesthood has cruelly persecuted such philosophers as Spinoza and Uriel d'Acosta as well as many other progressive scholars and writers;[2] Judaism preserves all that is backward in Jewish life, it is an enemy of the revolutionary movement; it has been kept alive artificially by the bourgeoisie 'with the aim of diverting the toiling Jews from the fight against both Jewish and non-Jewish exploiters'.[3] Judaism has proved a counter-revolutionary factor under Soviet rule; its reactionary teaching has aimed at maintaining chauvinism and national barriers among the Jews of the USSR and at obstructing the communist education of the workers in the spirit of friendship between peoples.[4]

In the period following the Second World War Judaism has been attacked above all as the 'official religion of the bourgeois state of Israel'. Soviet anti-religious propagandists have usually credited the Israeli rabbis with a 'great political influence' which, in the view of religious Jews, they do not possess.[5]

Soviet Anti-Judaism in Practice

Soviet anti-Jewish practice, however, has always had a slightly different character from the rest of the communist anti-religious offensive. In the first place, a good deal of the day-to-day agitation has been aimed less at wiping out religious Judaism, although this is of course a communist objective, than at depriving the Russian and Ukrainian anti-Semites of a favourite argument. In the early years of communist rule there were many people in the Soviet State who identified communist power with the Jews and who looked upon the anti-God movement not as an instrument of anti-religious propaganda in general, which in fact it was, but as an agency especially created for the persecution of the Christians and above all the Orthodox Church. To prevent the anti-Christian campaign from losing its vigour the

---

[1] I. A. Kryvelev, 'O tak nazyvaemykh svyashchennykh knigakh' (About the so-called 'sacred books') in Nauka i Religiya, Moscow 1957, p. 313.

[2] Pravda Ukrainy, September 21, 1957, quoting a pamphlet by T. K. Kichko published in Kiev in 1957 on 'The Origin and Essence of the Jewish religion'.

[3] Large Soviet Encyclopædia, vol. xix, Moscow 1953, p. 158.

[4] Pravda Ukrainy, ibid.

[5] M. I. Shakhnovich, O proiskhozhdenii i klassovoi sushchenosti iudeiskoi religii (About the origin and class nature of the Judaist religion), in Nauka i Religiya, Moscow 1957, p. 370.

N

communists intensified the fight against Judaism, thus bearing out
Sigmund Freud's famous dictum that 'hatred of Judaism is at the
bottom hatred of Christianity'.[1]

Anti-Semitism was kept in check by being diverted into the channels
of anti-religious propaganda against religious Jews. The weekly newspaper *Bezbozhnik* published a regular column under the heading
'Down with the Rabbis!' and every action against Christian groups was
immediately paralleled by a similar anti-Jewish action. Cartoons and
posters vilifying the Christian faith were matched by cartoons and
posters showing unattractive looking rabbis with huge crooked noses.
Whatever the original intention of the initiators of this propaganda may
have been, it is obvious that it played up to anti-Jewish sentiments.

This remains true despite the fact that anti-religious propaganda
among Jews was conducted almost exclusively by Jewish communists,
members of the 'Jewish sections' (Yevsektsii) set up inside both the
Communist Party and the League of Militant Godless. The latter had
a total of 40,000 Jewish members in 1929, the year when the anti-
religious campaign was at its peak.[2] These 'Jewish sections' were much
despised by the bulk of Russia's Jewry. Their members were regarded
with as much contempt as the Jewish renegades who turned persecutors
of their own brethren in the Middle Ages.

The hardships which the 'Jewish sections', in co-operation with other
Jewish institutions, inflicted on the religious Jews of Russia in the
twenties and thirties can no longer easily be seen in true perspective.
They have become overshadowed by the nazi extermination of six
million Jews. Nevertheless, to the contemporaries of the earlier and
less violent communist persecutions, they appeared savage and indeed
unparalleled in the twentieth century. Although there was much anti-
Semitism in countries like Rumania and Hungary, there was at least no
interference with Jewish religious practices. It was only Soviet Russia
which had declared war on religious Judaism.

The Anti-Sabbath Offensive

Perhaps the most striking single feature of the Soviet offensive against
Judaism was the fight against the Sabbath and the Jewish religious
holy days, especially the Passover, Rosh ha-Shanah (the Jewish New
Year) and Yom Kippur (Day of Atonement). If the Jews could be
persuaded to give up the Sabbath and their holy days, so the anti-
religious agitators argued, then the battle against the Jewish religion

---

[1] Sigmund Freud, *Moses and Monotheism*, London 1939, p. 148.
[2] *Antireligioznik*, 1929, no. 4, p. 116.

would be won. The history of anti-Jewish propaganda among Soviet Jews is, therefore, very largely an account of the ways and means by which this 'persuasion' was effected. The régime was determined to make refusal to work on the Sabbath day morally impossible for all but the lowest categories of workers. However, there were also special 'Work on the Sabbath' campaign, deliberately calculated to shock religious Jewry. These campaigns consisted of public exhibitions of young communist Jews who on the Sabbath purposely engaged in such work as sweeping streets or carrying fuel into public buildings.

The fight against the Sabbath was comparatively easy in places where the Jews lived and worked as a minority in predominantly Gentile surroundings, but it was much more complicated in the Ukrainian and Byelorussian townships (in Yiddish *shtetl*) where the Jews formed a very substantial proportion of the population. There the Jewish communists infiltrated into the local co-operatives (artels) of artisans and bullied them into deciding by majority vote that Saturday should be made an ordinary working day obligatory for all members. One can well imagine what dismay the first desecrations of the Sabbath caused among the simple religious Jews of Soviet Russia's Western border areas. They regarded in great bewilderment this blasphemy which meant the collapse of the world of their ancestors. The Soviet anti-religious press has given very vivid descriptions of these first working Sabbaths. People crowded around tailors' and shoemakers' co-operatives, looked through their windows to see with their own eyes the new communist monstrosity — work on the Day, which for thousands of years pious Jews of all lands had sanctified. Some of the onlookers even cursed the working co-operative members and jeered at them. In this way the Sabbath work introduced a sharp division among the Jewish people of every locality and it also interfered with the internal harmony of Jewish family life. The men could often be persuaded to work on the Sabbath but their wives continued to observe the ancient religious traditions and urged their children to do the same.[1]

The Campaign against Holy Days

Jewish communists who were prepared to desecrate the Sabbath often found it hard to part with 'religious prejudices' as far as Passover or Yom Kippur were concerned. Even if these holy days had no religious significance for them, they still observed them for motives of filial piety in order to attend the Memorial Service for the Dead which is embodied in the liturgy of these festive days. So the fight against the

[1] *Bezbozhnik*, September 22, 1929, no. 39.

Jewish holy days had to start within the Communist Party itself. Careful records were kept of party members who went to the synagogue and those discovered doing so were penalised in various ways. In some cases mock trials were staged against such pious communists, in other cases the culprits were enrolled into compulsory political indoctrination classes; and incorrigible offenders were expelled from the Party. In later years religious attendance on the part of a party member became *ipso facto* a ground for expulsion. Observance of Jewish holy days by communists ceased as time went on, but this was not the end of the trouble. Many Jewish communists, whilst ceasing to believe and practise their religion, did not wish to be involved in active propaganda against the Jewish holy days. This passive attitude was denounced as 'right-wing opportunism'.[1]

Among the mass of the Jewish people, observance of the holy days was to be fought by means of lectures about the harm they did and their truly reactionary essence. Often these lectures were delivered on the eve of the holy days themselves. For several years demonstrations were held in the vicinity of synagogues at the time of the holy days with the special purpose of burlesquing the Jewish religious rites. These anti-Passover and anti-Rosh ha-Shanah manifestations were simply an adaptation of campaigns against Easter and Christmas. Whenever the intensity of these anti-Christian manifestations was relaxed the Jewish holy days too came in for more lenient treatment. Every year the League of Militant Godless issued detailed instructions for the campaign against the observance of the Passover and the Jewish autumn holy days and stated which slogans were to be used. The main accent was usually on the class character of the holy days.

Apart from conducting negative propaganda the League of Militant Godless tried to keep the Jews busy during the holy days. For instance in 1932 the Jewish communist mouthpiece *Der Emes* asked for special efforts on the labour front. During the holy days Jewish craftsmen were to produce more than was originally planned, and Jewish collective farmers were to organise 'Red Convoys' carrying grain to the assembly centres for agricultural deliveries.[2]

Not only additional work but also additional entertainment was to undermine the observance of the holy days. Communal meals were organised on the Day of Atonement when pious Jews are expected to fast.[3] During the Passover period the Jewish sections of the Communist Party provided concerts and other cultural attractions. They were timed

---

[1] *Antireligioznik*, 1932, no. 23–4, p. 28.   [2] *Antireligioznik*, 1932, no. 23–4, p. 28.
[3] *Bezbozhnik*, September 10, 1930, no. 59.

in such a way as to coincide with the Seder ceremony held in symbolic commemoration of the ancient meal at which the paschal lamb was served together with unleavened bread (matzot) and bitter herbs.[1]

The question of unleavened bread provoked a yearly struggle. During the period of the New Economic Policy, when private enterprise was able to exist in Soviet Russia within certain limits, matzot could be obtained without much difficulty in most places and in 1928 half a million pounds were sold in Moscow alone during the Passover period. By 1929 the situation had completely changed and matzot had to be imported from abroad. To this the Soviet Government gave its agreement in order to relieve the food crisis at that time. A customs duty was fixed at five kopeks per kilogram of matzot, but when the bread arrived the Soviet authorities raised the duty tenfold.[2] In the next year the difficulties increased still further. The League of Militant Godless agitated against the import of foreign matzot 'the counter-revolutionary bread' as it was styled, and the central organisation of Soviet co-operatives forbade the sale in its shops of both matzot and all other Passover food. In response to this situation the rabbis of Russia issued an emergency statement relaxing the ritual requirements for matzot baking. Later in the thirties, the régime became for a short period slightly more liberal. In 1934 the Chief Rabbi of Moscow was empowered to supervise the production of matzot provided the flour for it was bought in the Torgsin shops for either gold or foreign currency.[3] In 1936 Jewish organisations abroad reported for the first time that the baking of matzot in the Soviet Union was no longer subject to any restriction. However, the concession was nullified in the following year and moreover the number of Jews insisting on the full observance of their holy days had by this time dwindled to a minority. As early as 1929 the anti-religious propagandists asserted that among the Jewish working class there were almost no believers[4] and this was of course even more true of the sizeable group of Jewish civil servants. By the middle of the thirties this withdrawal from religious Judaism had become still more pronounced, although only in the growing Soviet cities.

The Jewish Agricultural Colonies — Bulwarks of Religion

In the country, however, the secularisation of Soviet Jewry proved a failure. In fact, the new Jewish agricultural settlements and collective farms in the Ukraine and the Crimea turned out to be bulwarks of

[1] *The American Jewish Yearbook 5690*, Philadelphia 1929, p. 68.
[2] *The Times*, April 4, 1929.
[3] *The American Jewish Yearbook 5659*, Philadelphia 1934, p. 236.
[4] *Bezbozhnik*, July 13, 1929.

religious life. This is what officials of the American 'Joint Distribution Committee' reported about the inhabitants of the new Jewish agricultural colonies late in 1925. 'A new settler comes to the land to become a peasant, but a Jewish peasant. The Sabbath and all the Jewish holy days are observed. Removed as they are from the influences which are affecting the life of the cities and the towns, the colonies afford an opportunity for closer family life. The strong influence exercised in the colonies by the father over his children results in a higher religious and Jewish life than in the city and town. The lack of interference on the part of the Government officials makes it possible for them to develop their schools and institutions along Jewish lines.'[1]

This statement from the middle twenties remained true, at least to some extent, throughout the thirties and perhaps even until the liquidation of the colonies during the war. In October 1931, the communist press still complained that wives of Jewish colonists had their poultry slaughtered by shohetim, the ritual Jewish butchers. But even worse things were reported; new synagogues were springing up, weddings were held according to Jewish religious customs and circumcisions were performed.[2]

In 1932, the League of Militant Godless conducted an enquiry into the observance of holy days in Jewish national districts and collective farms and the result was disheartening for the atheist propagandists and encouraging for the believers. In the Dzhankou district of the Crimea hundreds of Jewish collective farmers failed to turn up for work on festival days. Religious preachers and rabbis seemed to have free access to the collective farms. In the Fraydorf district, also in the Crimea, the 'Black Agitprop' (meaning the representatives of religious Judaism) were said to hold entire groups of collective farmers under their influence. Although there were cells of the Militant Godless organisation in Fraydorf they did nothing at all. In the Novozlatopol District in the Ukraine even members of the collective farm management did not work on religious holy days.[3] Four years later, in 1936, complaints were still being made about the popularity of Jewish holy days among the collective farmers of the Jewish agricultural settlements, particularly in the Jewish National District of Kalinindorf in the Ukraine. Even many tractor drivers who, theoretically at least, belong to the communist vanguard in the Soviet village, stayed away from work.[4]

[1] The American Jewish Yearbook 5687, Philaeelphia 1926, pp. 54–5.
[2] The American Jewish Yearbook 5693, Philadelphia 1932, p. 79.
[3] Antireligioznik, 1932, no. 23–4, pp. 30–2.
[4] Antireligioznik, 1936, no. 6, p. 41.

The Jewish agricultural colonies were able to maintain a certain Jewish religious spirit in their midst because they enjoyed the protection of some more moderate communists. This tolerance with regard to the Jews in the agricultural colonies was perhaps like that shown originally to the collective farms of Christian sectarians. Agricultural production was given priority over anti-religious propaganda, very much to the annoyance of the atheist propagandists. The organisation which held a protecting hand over the Jewish agricultural colonists was the Komzet (Committee for the Agricultural Settlement of Jewish Toilers.) On one occasion it went so far as to suggest that they might postpone the celebration of the official 'Day of Industrialisation' to avoid its coinciding with the Jewish 'Day of Atonement'. The leader of the godless organisation did not fail to point out that this was a 'right-wing opportunist mistake'.[1] The persistence of religious feelings in the Jewish agricultural colonies in the Crimea and the Ukraine must have been one of the reasons which determined the Soviet authorities not to re-establish them after World War II.

The Jewish School

Apart from the agricultural colonies there was yet another bulwark of religious Judaism in the twenties and even in the thirties, namely, the Jewish schools. A minority of religious Jews defended them most heroically against communist encroachments. At first, the Soviet authorities showed some hesitation in closing Jewish religious schools, because no secular counterparts could be made speedily available, but by the end of 1922 an intense campaign against Jewish schooling had started. Two types of schools were involved, the traditional religious elementary schools, called hedarim, and the religious academies, called yeshivoth. The latter imparted higher rabbinical learning, but they were not true rabbinical seminaries since their graduates might become religious functionaries of every kind (ritual slaughterers, circumcisers, religious teachers) or embrace secular professions.

When the State closed the hedarim and the yeshivoth the believers reopened many of them in secret. This in turn led to the arrest of rabbis and religious teachers. Throughout the twenties the Soviet press reported many trials of teachers maintaining hedarim clandestinely and even humble Jewish women were sentenced to imprisonment for teaching prayers to small groups of children. A close watch was kept on all former Jewish religious teachers and on several occasions they

---

[1] Yaroslavsky, *Protiv Religii i Tserkvi* (Against Religion and Church), vol. iv, Moscow 1935, pp. 83–4.

were forced to sign formal pledges that they would not engage in maintaining illegal schools. Some local authorities devised other ways of fighting religious schooling. In the town of Kamenets Podolsk, for instance, brigades of schoolboys were organised to 'discover illegal Hebrew schools which cripple the children's minds' and to denounce Hebrew teachers to the State.[1]

American Jewish sources reported that by the end of 1929 about 12,000 Jewish children were still receiving illegal religious instruction and 800 students in 22 localities were attending yeshivoth. The network of illegal Jewish educational establishments remained in being until about 1936.[2] Soviet sources give, if anything, a much more impressive picture of the illegal Jewish religious education system. They asserted for instance that in 1930 yeshivoth were attached to virtually every synagogue of the Byelorussian Republic. Each of these yeshivoth was said to have about fifty students. Religious schools of a lower order existed even in quite small towns.[3] A few illegal hedarim and yeshivoth must have survived until the beginning of 1938, for in April of that year the Yiddish communist newspaper *Der Emes* published the disclosures of a Jewish boy who had just run away from an underground yeshivah.[4]

The 'Pietists'

It was to a very considerable extent due to the activities of the 'Pietists' that Jewish religious learning was kept alive in the Soviet Union and that Jews went on studying the works of their sages in cellars and attics and even in the Siberian taiga. The 'Pietists' or Hassidim, who were the heart and soul of Jewish religious resistance to communist atheism, derive their name from the Hebrew word 'Hassid' meaning pious. The movement started in the eighteenth century in what to-day is the Western Ukraine and Western Byelorussia. It is essentially a mystical brand of Judaism which puts the main emphasis on a personal ecstatic contact with God. Hassidism originated in Jewish Byelorussian and Ukrainian townships such as Braslav, Medzhibozh, Lyubavichi and others where their great rabbis, also called 'Tsadikim' ('the righteous ones') lived and taught. By the end of the nineteenth century Hassidism had about 250,000 active adherents in Russia and comprised between

[1] *The American Jewish Yearbook 5691*, Philadelphia 1930, p. 120.

[2] Lucy S. Dawidowicz, 'What future for Judaism in Russia?' *Commentary*, November 1956, p. 405.

[3] F. Oleshchuk, *Borba Tserkvi protiv Naroda* (The Fight of the Church against the People), p. 59.

[4] Oleshchuk, op. cit., p. 61.

one-fifteenth and one-twentieth of Russian Jewry.[1] However, the spiritual and moral importance of Hassidism was greater than this figure might suggest and this is particularly true for the Soviet era.

The little Jewish township which by its radiating spiritual power proved a particular handicap to anti-religious work among Soviet Jewry was an insignificant little Byelorussian place on the Berisina river, called Lyubavichi. It was once the residence of Schneur Zalman ben-Barukh (1747–1812), the famous Tsadik who founded Lithuanian-Byelorussian Hassidism. One of his descendants, Joseph Isaak Schneersohn (1880–1950) played an outstanding part in the early years of the Soviet period. Operating first from Rostov-on-Don and later from Leningrad, Rabbi Schneersohn did a great deal to secure the religious survival of Russian Jewry. He promoted illegal Jewish education and sent teachers to the remotest Jewish communities of the Soviet Union. He supported rabbis through loans and subsidies. He founded a committee which helped Jewish artisans to keep the Sabbath as a day of rest. He helped religious Jews to get out of Russia to receive religious training in Poland.

The Soviet communists soon realised the great importance of Rabbi Schneersohn as the driving power behind religious Judaism. They arrested him in July 1927 and sentenced him to death. Owing to the colossal interest which not only world Jewry but also leading foreign statesmen showed in the fate of the 'Lyubavicher', as he was commonly called, he was released and even allowed to leave the country together with his family. He went first to Latvia, later to Poland and finally to the United States. From Latvia he continued his efforts to assist Judaism in Russia by raising funds for religious activities and providing the Russian Jews with matzot. Even after his departure from the country the communists continued to regard him as the supreme spiritual leader of Soviet Jewry. When in the spring of 1931 the Yiddish atheist journal *Der Apikoires* (the talmudic word for 'heretic') appeared for the first time, it made the significant promise that it would give battle 'to both the Pope of Rome and the Rabbi of Lyubavichi'.

Persecution of Rabbis and the Closing of Synagogues

The arrest of the Rabbi of Lyubavichi was but the prelude to the more general measures taken against other rabbis in the late twenties and thirties and to the closing of synagogues. Rabbis have not the same importance for Jewish religious practice as priests have for the

---

[1] S. A. Tokarev, *Etnografiya Narodov SSSR* (Ethnography of the Peoples of the USSR), Moscow 1958, p. 209.

observance of the Catholic and Orthodox religions. Nevertheless, the Soviet régime was bound to devote its attention to the rabbis, in view of the influence they exercised on the believers and their efforts to preserve the Jewish faith in the Soviet Union. Like all other members of the clergy, the rabbis were deprived of civic rights, but this in no way affected their prestige in Jewish eyes and religious Jews provided amply for their maintenance. Throughout the twenties the rabbis were most active. They created Jewish medical aid societies, organised recitals of sacred music in the synagogues and founded special study circles for the reading of religious books and the reciting of psalms.[1] They were particularly eager to encourage private charity among the Jewish population. An anti-religious pamphlet of the period pays this significant tribute to the rabbi of a Jewish township in the Ukrainian Province of Kamenets Podolsk: 'The rabbi very rarely refuses help to anyone and among the masses there is the impression that he is not only a man of piety but also kind-hearted.'[2] It was not the rabbis alone who caused concern to the authorities but also the travelling preachers or 'magids' of whom it was said that they went 'from synagogue to synagogue with an anti-Soviet repertory'.[3]

The obvious way of eliminating rabbis and magids as serious ideological opponents was, of course, by destroying their strongholds, the synagogues, and the attitude of the Soviet authorities to these was much like their attitude to Christian churches. Individual Jewish houses of worship were closed even in the early years of Soviet power, but a large-scale campaign for their conversion into all kinds of secular institutions started only after 1927. In 1928 no less than fifty-nine synagogues were shut, more than ten per cent of the 'cult buildings' of all religions liquidated in that year. But even this was only a modest beginning. In the following year the number of confiscated synagogues had to be counted not in dozens but in hundreds. This wholesale closing of synagogues was prompted by the very narrow materialistic outlook of the communists. Until the end of the twenties, the Soviet régime saw a certain need to consider the feelings of the Jewish traders and merchants whom they regarded as forming the class basis of the Jewish religion. With the beginning of the period of long-term economic planning and the resulting total destruction of private enterprise it was no longer necessary to pay any attention to these people. The synagogues could, therefore, be closed on the grounds that they were 'clubs of

---

[1] *Bezbozhnik*, January 27, 1929, no. 5.
[2] I. Veitsblit, *Derazhnya — sovremennoe yevreiskoe mestechko* (Derazhnya — the contemporary Jewish township), Moscow 1929.
[3] *Bezbozhnik*, February 10, 1929, no. 7.

profiteers' or clubs of 'Nepmen', the *nouveaux-riches* benefiting from
the 'New Economic Policy' (NEP) which the Soviet Government
introduced in March 1921, or that they were places where traders
discussed methods of concealing their operations from financial
inspectors.[1]   A good idea of the vicious character of the anti-synagogue
campaign may be obtained from a poem by the well-known communist
poet Nikolay Aseev who later became a Stalin Prize winner. The poem
entitled 'The Synagogue' differs little from similar products of nazi
versification.

> The synagogue: house of the living god . . .
> Gleam, oily eye! Cheek, be suffused with red!
> The pathway to its portals is well trod
> By all the dealers that devoutly tread.
> Within its walls you may with unbowed head
> Glorify god, while joy your being fills;
> Push out your belly, sleek and nobly fed,
> And handsomely discount your notes and bills.
> But for the synagogue, what would avail?
> Elsewhere you'll feel disconsolate, depressed!
> Let ancient talith from your shoulders trail,
> And here, but only here, your soul will rest.
> The synagogue's the place: to get the best
> Of prices: for a coat, a ring, a fake;
> The synagogue is, soberly assessed,
> The best of clubs for nepmen on the make.[2]

Soviet propaganda represented the closing of the synagogues as a
yielding of the authorities to an irresistible Jewish popular movement.
In some instances the newspapers simply reported something like the
following: 'The Crimean Central Executive Committee has granted the
request of the Eupatoria Jews for the liquidation of the empty merchant
synagogue and its transformation into a club.'[3] In other places the
closing of the synagogues was either preceded or followed by anti-
religious manifestations during which Jewish communists appeared
before the building of a local Soviet often with a band and demanded
the surrender of a given synagogue to a craftsmen's co-operative or to
a cultural or educational institution. The size of the manifestation was
usually in direct proportion to the size of the coveted building and in

[1] M. Shakhnovich, *Komu sluzhit religiya Izraila* (Whom does the Religion of
Israel serve), Leningrad 1929, p. 24.
[2] *Bezbozhnik u Stanka*, 1926, no. 12, p. 17. Translated by Dr. W. A. Morison.
[3] *Bezbozhnik*, August 4, 1929, no. 32.

the case of the large choral synagogues of Minsk, Kiev, Odessa and Kharkov, particularly large crowds assembled. For instance, in the autumn of 1929, when the Rosenberg Synagogue in Kiev was transformed into a club, 5,000 'toiling Jews' were reported to have celebrated the 'victory over clericalism' and a huge red poster was displayed at the synagogue with the slogans 'Down with religion! Long live Soviet power and proletarian culture!' However, it was also reported that the 'clericals' and the 'zionist-rabbinical clique' did not accept these provocations unchallenged but distributed leaflets protesting against what they considered to be an anti-Jewish measure.[1] By 1932 the closing of the synagogues had made such headway that the well-known anti-Jewish communist Jew David Zaslavsky was able to write that the remaining ones existed 'only for the old and the remnants of the Jewish bourgeoisie clinging to the past'.[2]

In closing the synagogues the Soviet authorities always honoured the principle of 'parity'. Soon after they had closed a Christian cathedral they would seize a large synagogue. Exceptionally a Jewish synagogue already secularised was restored to its congregation if in the same place the Christians had retained their house of worship. The policy of 'equal injustice' was even applied to such things as candlesticks. In 1929–30 candlesticks were confiscated from the synagogues to balance the confiscation of Christian church bells carried out during the same period.[3]

There was however one feature of their policy in the Christian camp which the authorities failed to reproduce in Judaism, namely, the establishment of a schismatic pro-régime religious body. The attempt was made in the Ukraine and Byelorussia, it is true, to found a 'Living Synagogue',[4] which was to imitate the 'Living Church' schism in Russian Orthodoxy. However, the 'Living Synagogue' or 'New Synagogue' never seems to have gone beyond the starting point although one 'living synagogue' existed for a short time in Poltava.

From the Big Purge to the 'Great Patriotic War'

At the time of the purge of 1937–8 the measures against synagogues and rabbis were no longer said to be on account of their class-alien character but because of their alleged espionage activites on behalf of fascist intelligence services. Such a charge was made, for instance,

---

[1] *Bezbozhnik*, September 29, 1929, no. 40.
[2] D. Zaslavsky, *Yevrei v USSR* (Jews in the USSR), Moscow 1932, p. 45.
[3] *The Times*, January 17, 1930.
[4] *Uchebnik dlya rabochikh antirelioznykh kruzhkov* (Textbook for workers' anti-religious study circles), Moscow 1930, p. 339.

when in 1938 the NKVD discovered a 'hostile rabbinical nest' in the central synagogue in Moscow[1] which led to the arrest of the Rabbi Melade and of some of the Jewish lay leaders. The charge 'spying on behalf of the fascist intelligence service' was made indiscriminately against the servants of all religious cults in Russia. In the case of the rabbis it seemed even more senseless than in other instances, since the fascist intelligence service tacitly understood to be the driving force behind every political or religious opposition in the USSR was that of Nazi Germany. The professional anti-religious propagandists did not wish to admit that the Nazis engaged in the indiscriminate persecution of the Jewish national and religious group. All they were willing to concede was that German Fascism persecuted the Jewish workers whilst concluding a 'touching alliance with the Jewish bourgeoisie'. This was stated by the journal *Antireligioznik* in November 1938, the very month in which the nazi Jew-baiting reached a tragic climax. In the same issue it was alleged that the German rabbis had proclaimed their loyalty to the Hitler Government and supported the fascist régime of starvation, misery and ruin. Together with the fascists 'the rabbis were spreading slander against the Soviet Union'. The journal even made the absurd assertion that there existed a special rabbinical organisation, apparently operating from Nazi Germany, which helped saboteurs and spies to infiltrate into the USSR.[2]

The religious Jews gained no advantage from the hostility between Soviet Russia and anti-Semite Nazi Germany and derived nothing but misery from the Nazi-Soviet Pact in force between 1939 and 1941. As a result of the political developments ensuing from this pact many more than two million East European Jews came under Soviet rule — 1,600,000 in Eastern Poland, 145,000 in Lithuania, 93,000 in Latvia, 4,800 in Estonia and 330,000 in the Soviet-occupied territories of Rumania — 250,000 in Bessarabia and 80,000 in Northern Bukovina.

Although the situation of the Jews in these countries and territories left much to be desired and Jewish civic rights were limited in both Poland and Rumania, the Jews had been able to practise their religion freely in all these areas annexed by the USSR. Indeed, they included several outstanding Jewish religious centres such as Kishinev, which at one time had as many as forty Jewish houses of worship, and Vilnius, the 'Jerusalem of Lithuania' as it used to be called. The nazi occupation of Vilnius destroyed the majority of local Jewry and, before that, a few months of Soviet occupation in 1940–1 were sufficient to reduce Jewish religious life in the city to a minimum. It brought an end to the famous

---

[1] F. Oleshchuk, op. cit., p. 61.   [2] *Antireligioznik*, November 1938, no. 11, p. 54.

Vilnius Yeshivah, to many synagogues and to a vast number of so-called 'klausen', houses for prayer and study combined.[1]

The same process was repeated throughout the newly-annexed territories. The almost immediate result of the establishment of Soviet rule was the closing down of Jewish religious schools, including the yeshivoth in Lomzha, Slonim, Novogrodek, Brest Litovsk, Grodno, Baranovichi and Mir, the imposition of heavy taxes on rabbis and synagogues and the fostering of anti-religious education for the Jewish people. Sabbath work was forced upon a reluctant older generation.

Before all these measures could mature, war broke out between Soviet Russia and Nazi Germany. For sheer lack of time the secularisation of Jewry in Eastern Poland, Bessarabia and the Baltic states was still incomplete, and this provided Soviet propaganda with some impressive statistics. When trying to dispel the misgivings of Russia's new allies about the plight of religion under Communism, Soviet spokesmen were able to state that at the outbreak of the Nazi-Soviet war there were as many as 2,559 rabbis in the USSR and 1,011 synagogues.[2] The vast majority of these were in those areas which had seen communist religious persecution for a few months only.

From the 'Great Patriotic War' to the Death of Stalin

The war between Russia and Germany which hastened the physical extermination of East European Jewry was a complicated phenomenon. What appears to be a single war was really several wars waged at the same time. There was the war between two hostile totalitarian systems, the war for the defence of Holy Mother Russia and the war fought by the Soviet Jews for self-preservation. In the early part of the war even official Soviet and communist sources stated frankly that religious Jews supported the Soviet war effort for reasons of their own and not out of love for communist Russia, which had oppressed them for so long. 'Many rabbis', says a communist propaganda publication of the period compiled by Professor Hyman Levy, 'have joined the partisans, angered particularly by the deliberate destruction by the Nazis of synagogues and the holy Scrolls of the Law.'[3] The same pamphlet was honest enough to admit that some of these rabbis were really ex-rabbis and one elderly Jew reporting to Red Army headquarters for service in a guerilla detachment was quoted as saying: 'I was once rabbi of this

---

[1] Israel Cohen, Vilna, Philadelphia 1943, pp. 488–9, 514.
[2] Statement published by the Press Department of the Soviet Embassy in London, August 22, 1941. Stanley Evans, Churches in the USSR, London 1943, p. 89.
[3] Professor H. Levy, Soviet Jews at War, London, April 1943, p. 21.

town but for some years I have been engaged chiefly in gardening.'[1]

From Professor Hyman Levy's pamphlet, which is based on information supplied by the Jewish Anti-fascist Committee in Kuibyshev, there also comes a moving story testifying to the ardour of Jewish religious feeling in Russia despite nearly a quarter of a century of relentless anti-religious propaganda. It is the story of the Scrolls of the Law from the synagogue of Piryatin, a small town in the Province of Poltava. Mendel Matlin, the fifty-year-old manager of a flour mill, rescued these Scrolls from the burning synagogue and brought them to Stalingrad where he deposited them in the synagogue for safe keeping. When a nazi bomb was dropped on the synagogue Matlin risked his life a second time to save the Scrolls. They were ultimately taken to Kuibyshev on a barge carrying a number of refugees down the Volga. In Kuibyshev the Jews formed a procession behind their Scrolls which were carried in a large case covered with red velvet. One of the Scrolls was so badly burnt that it had to be buried in Kuibyshev according to Jewish rites. The ceremony was attended by a large number of practising Jews.[2]

During the war an important Jewish religious leader was allowed to come into greater prominence, the Moscow Rabbi Shloime Schliefer. His speeches and messages were the main link between the religious Jews of Russia and their brethren in other countries. From Tashkent, whither the Moscow Jewish community was evacuated, he addressed his greetings to the Jews in the West on the occasion of the Jewish New Year. After his return to Moscow he spoke at an 'anti-fascist meeting of the representatives of the Jewish people' which was primarily intended to impress foreign countries. The other speakers were mostly atheists of Jewish extraction, Communist Party officials, soldiers on active service and writers using either the Yiddish or the Russian language as their medium. Alone of all the speakers, Rabbi Schliefer made a profession of faith in religious Judaism, expressing confidence in God who would never abandon the people of Israel. As an example to his contemporaries, Schliefer recommended the 'great Rabbi Schneur-Zalman who at the time of the war with Napoleon spared no effort to persuade the Jews to help the Russians in every way in the fight against the enemy',[3]

When Rabbi Schliefer made this and other statements in support of the Soviet military effort he probably expected that religious Jewry in

[1] Professor Levy, op. cit., p. 22. [2] Professor Levy, op. cit., p. 22.
[3] *Yevreiskii narod v borbe protiv fashisma* (The Jewish people in the fight against fascism), Moscow 1945, p. 37.

Russia would receive better treatment once the war was ended. These hopes seemed justified at first since Stalin had embarked in general on a more positive religious policy. It soon became clear that Stalin would not extend to the Jews the concessions he was prepared to grant to other religious communities. From a purely Machiavellian point of view this discrimination was not without logic. The proletarisation and eastward migration of Soviet Jewry in the period between the wars, followed by the nazi extermination measures during the war, inflicted a severe blow on collective and sociological Judaism as it once existed in the Ukraine, Byelorussia, Bessarabia, Lithuania and other Western borderlands of the USSR. A large percentage of the Jews who survived the war lived far from the traditional centres of Jewish life in Russia and, scattered among Gentile surroundings, were often reluctant to manifest their Jewishness. In these circumstances Stalin had no reason to see in religious Judaism a factor which could be usefully exploited in the interests of Soviet home and foreign policy. He anticipated that religious Judaism would disappear much more quickly than other religions which had preserved their sociological roots and he was determined to hasten this natural process as effectively as possible. The Jewish religious community was not outlawed like the Catholic Church of the Slavo-Byzantine Rite but it was relegated to a position inferior to that enjoyed by other religious organisations. Thus the authorities denied the Jews the right to publish any religious literature and refused them any facilities for the training of rabbis and ritual slaughterers. In many places with Jewish minorities the authorities withheld permission to re-open synagogues.

In the last years of Stalin's lifetime the situation of religious Judaism in the Soviet Union deteriorated still further on account of two events — one was the establishment of the State of Israel with which religious Jewry was, in Soviet eyes, closely connected, and the other was the persecution of all manifestations of so-called 'Jewish bourgeois nationalism'. There is no doubt that the presence in the Soviet capital of the first Israeli ambassador, Mrs. Golda Meyerson (later Mrs. Meir), made a very considerable impression on religious Jewry, particularly when she appeared in the Moscow central synagogue to participate in the celebration of the Jewish New Year. This well-meant gesture brought no good to Soviet Jews. The ambassadress was the centre of a friendly manifestation in front of the synagogue. There even exists a photograph of the event in which the faces of some of those cheering Mrs. Meyerson are clearly recognisable.[1] It must

[1] Léon Leneman, *La Tragédie des Juifs en URSS*, Paris 1959, p. 288

have been invaluable to the MVD, which arrested quite a number of the bystanders, who were later to be found in various concentration camps.

It is most difficult to see why Stalin's stern measures against 'Jewish bourgeois nationalists' should have had any repercussions on religious Judaism, for these alleged 'bourgeois nationalists' were in reality communists who propagated a Jewish culture which though Jewish in form was Marxist in content. The Jewish cultural and political leaders whose arrest and execution were ordered by Stalin had been more prominent in anti-Judaism than in Russian Judaism. This applies to the most distinguished victim, Salomon Lozovsky, the main Soviet government spokesman during the war, and former Secretary General of the communist Trade Union International 'Profintern', to most members of the 'Jewish Anti-fascist Committee' which was disbanded in 1949 and to the leading Yiddish writers, Peretz Markish, Itzik Feffer and David Bergelson, who were executed in 1952. All three wrote works 'against the synagogue and God' although, under the influence of the war, they took a more positive attitude towards the Jewish national heritage and Bergelson seems to have returned to the religion of his childhood.[1] Even though Stalin's anti-Jewish terror was primarily aimed against Jewish communists and atheists suspected of nationalist or simply pro-Western leanings, it had a paralysing effect on Jewish religious life as well. It discouraged Jews from displaying their Jewishness and many refrained from attending synagogue services during the holy days. It was during this anti-Jewish period of terror that the very mention of Judaism was expurged from the history text books of Soviet schools. The textbook by Professor Michulin still in use in 1946 devoted two and a half pages to ancient Israel and Judea[2] whilst the next textbook by Kovalev completely dispensed with ancient Jewry.[3] It even managed to avoid any reference to the Jews when explaining the emergence of Christianity.

The few rabbis exercising their function in the Soviet Union in the post-war period were apparently not affected by the anti-Jewish purge. Only Rabbi Levi of Kharkov was arrested for alleged 'subversive activities'.[4] Rabbi Schliefer remained unscathed; fortunately for him he was never made a member of the Jewish Anti-fascist Committee. Otherwise he might have shared the fate of its functionaries.

[1] Wolf Blattberg, *The story of the Hebrew and Yiddish writers in the Soviet Union*, Institute of Jewish Affairs, New York 1953, pp. 13–17, p. 24.
[2] Professor M. A. Mishulin, *Istoriya Drevnego Mira*, Moscow 1946, pp. 54, 56–7.
[3] Kovalev, *Istoriya Drevnego Mira*, Moscow 1954.
[4] *New York Times*, November 9, 1955.

Judaism under Stalin's Successor

Jews benefited from the general relaxation of religious persecution in Soviet Russia after the end of the Stalin rule. The anti-Jewish policy conducted in the last years of Stalin's lifetime had the immediate result of intimidating the Soviet Jews but it had also the long-term effect of reviving to a certain extent both personal and collective religious Judaism. It brought some Jews back to their religion, particularly in the former areas of compact Jewish settlement, the Western borderlands. When the new collective leadership abandoned Stalin's anti-Jewish policy quite a number of Jews were inclined to manifest their religious allegiance more openly, and the new Government was confronted with something like a Jewish religious revival. Although the revival affected only a small minority, both Soviet 'religious policy' and communist anti-religious propaganda had to take it into account. As the expectation of a speedy disappearance of religious Judaism had turned out to be erroneous, a few concessions were at last made to it as they had been to other religious communities. These included the opening in 1956 of a small yeshivah in Moscow with the intake of students as strictly limited as in all other religious training establishments of the USSR; greater facilities for obtaining kosher food and the publication in Moscow of a Jewish prayerbook in an edition of 4,000 copies.[1] The prayerbook — called *Peace Prayerbook* (*Molitvennik Mir*) — could probably only be published because its authors were willing to put it into the service of the peace campaign, in which the Jewish religious leaders took part along with the hierarchy of the Christian Churches. Thus on each Sabbath morning Rabbi Schliefer recited a prayer in the Moscow synagogue which started with the words 'Our Father who are in heaven, bless the Government of the Soviet Union, the defender of peace throughout the world . . .'.[2]

The Soviet Government itself publicised religious Judaism in the interests of its own propaganda. For instance, in March 1955 *Izvestiya* printed an appeal against atomic warfare and in support of the World Peace Council which was signed by the rabbis of eight large Jewish communities of the USSR, namely, Moscow, Kiev, Odessa, Riga, Kutaisi, Minsk, Vilnius and Kaunas.[3] In November 1956 another statement was signed, this time by the rabbis and Jewish community leaders of eighteen Soviet towns. The latter comprised all those previously mentioned except Kutaisi together with Lvov, Tashkent,

---

[1] Moscow Radio, October 18, 1958.   [2] *The Day—Jewish Journal*, April 5, 1957.
[3] *Izvestiya*, March 18, 1955.

Baku, Kaunas, Tallin, Sverdlovsk, Rostov, Dniepropetrovsk, Kursk, Penza, Kishinev and Omsk. This was the first occasion on which so many rabbis appeared to act jointly and publicly. However, this joint action was not in defence of Jewish interests. On the contrary, its purpose was to put on record that religious Soviet Jewry condemned the policy pursued by the Jewish State and in particular the Anglo-French-Israeli action against Egypt.[1]

Although political pressure brought to bear on religious Jews thus remained strong, they nevertheless began to breathe more freely under Stalin's successors. Various local Jewish communities, emboldened by the political thaw, held an increasing number of prayer meetings. Money was collected for the building of new synagogues and houses of prayer. In some cases building actually started, if not with the direct permission, at least with the connivance of the authorities. Here and there Jews resorted to baking matzot privately. As no printed Jewish calendars existed, handwritten ones were produced and sold and perhaps one or more illegal yeshivoth even may have come into existence.

All this prompted the Soviet authorities to strike once again at religious Judaism. Until 1957, the Soviet anti-religious propagandists of the post-war period usually overlooked the Jewish religion, or dismissed it with a few summary remarks, but in that year the situation changed. As in the twenties, it was communists of Jewish origin who were foremost in attacking the Jewish faith. At the Moscow anti-religious conference which was held in May 1957 two such Jewish-born communists gave the signal for a new offensive against Judaism. The first was Academician Mitin, one of the very few Jews still occupying a high political post in the Soviet Union. He complained that the rabbis had 'become noticeably active again' and that attendance at synagogues had 'increased considerably'. The other speaker who mentioned Judaism was Shakhnovich, Deputy Director of the Leningrad Museum of Religion and Atheism. He delivered a whole lecture entitled 'The origin and class character of the Jewish religion'.[2]

Following the Moscow atheist conference the Soviet authorities fought Judaism first only by propaganda — atheist pamphlets designed specially for religious Jews were published both in the Ukraine and Moldavia — but very soon by direct action as well. In 1959 increasing evidence reached the free world of the limitations which the Soviet authorities were once again imposing on Jewish religious life. New

[1] *Izvestiya*, November 29, 1956.
[2] *Nauka i Religiya* (Science and Religion), Moscow 1957, pp. 352–70.

instructions were issued centrally to local government bodies to adopt a sterner attitude towards Jewish religious congregations. As a result the various Town Soviets in the Ukraine, Byelorussia and, to a lesser extent, in other Soviet republics, confiscated synagogues and ordered them to be used for secular purposes, as a warehouse in Voronezh, as a reading room in Simferopol, and as a concert hall in Uzhgorod. Even small prayer meetings in private houses were prohibited. Money collected by pious Jews for the building of new synagogues was confiscated. Applications for the opening of synagogues were rejected and the signatories of such applications were interrogated and intimidated by the authorities.[1] New obstacles were also put on the distribution of matzot except in the larger cities frequently visited by foreigners. Those baking and selling matzot were accused with transgressing Soviet Penal Law.[2]

The number of Jews in the Soviet Union — there may be as many as 3,500,000 although the official census of 1959 records only 2,268,000 — gives no indication at all as to the extent of Jewish religious practice in the USSR. Only a very small number of Jews have the possibility of living fully according to the precepts of the Orthodox Jewish faith, keeping the Sabbath and the Jewish dietary laws, but even those who observe some of the Jewish religious rites may not exceed 500,000, an estimate provided by an official of the Soviet 'Council for the Affairs of Religious Cults'.[3] However, there is a large number of Soviet Jews who have preserved certain remnants of Jewishness, for instance by keeping Hebrew prayer books and other religious objects in their homes, if only as souvenirs of days gone by.[4]

The majority of Soviet Jewry is now concentrated in the large cities where religious loyalties are weak and where the synagogues attract only a small part of the Jewish population. Moscow not only has the largest religious community in the Soviet Union; it is, in all probability, still the second largest 'Jewish city', after New York, with a larger Jewish population than Tel Aviv, even. On the great Jewish holy days services in the Moscow central synagogue are crowded, but this means very little, since the synagogue has a normal seating capacity for only 2,000 people. Apart from the central synagogue, two or three smaller ones have been open at various times during the post-war period. The total number of Jewish Muscovites attending any religious service on Jewish New Year day was estimated at 12,000 in one of the years of

[1] *New York Times*, May 22, 1959. *Jews in Eastern Europe*, 1959, no. 1, pp. 5–6.
[2] *Sovetskaya Moldaviya*, July 23, 1959.   [3] *Le Monde*, January 17–18, 1960.
[4] *Current Events in Jewish Life*, series xi, July–September 1958, no. 2, pp. 2–3.

the 'thaw' period.[1] In Leningrad, where the Jewish population has been estimated as being between 150,000 and 300,000, the main synagogue attracted 6,000 to 7,000 people on feast days, whilst a smaller number of persons prayed in other lesser places of worship.[2]

Very sizeable Jewish communities live in the various Ukrainian cities, but facilities for Jewish religious worship are insufficient and the number of practising Jews is accordingly small. An official Soviet report mentioned that there were 'dozens of synagogues functioning in the Ukraine', including those of Kiev, Odessa, Lvov, Kherson, Nikolayev, Berdichev, Dniepropetrovsk and Kirovograd.[3] Even a few dozen synagogues is little compared with the 934 which existed at the beginning of 1929 in the then much smaller Ukrainian Soviet Republic. In cities like Kiev and Odessa where, even according to the lowest estimates, the Jewish population is well over 100,000, there is only one synagogue. In Minsk, the capital of Byelorussia, Jewish believers use one small wooden building as their synagogue. Its services are poorly attended and an American visitor counted not more than 150 faithful at the celebration of the Feast of Tabernacles,[4] although no fewer than 40,000 Jews may be living in the town.[5] Much larger Jewish congregations have been reported from such 'new' Soviet cities as Vilnius, Lvov and Kishinev.

Little is known about the life of those Jewish religious communities which have sprung up in the Urals, Siberia, Kazakhstan and Kirghizia as a result of Soviet social engineering and internal migration. The so-called Jewish Autonomous Province of Birobidzhan in the Soviet Far East can be mentioned only in a negative way as far as religious Judaism is concerned. The Soviet Jewish Autonomous Province was to be built 'without Torah and God' and its settlers were largely recruited from among the younger communist generation. Only a few of them went into agriculture, the majority were directed as industrial and transport workers into new socialist towns and workers' settlements such as Birobidzhan city, Obluche, Londoko, Nikolaevka and Birakan. In this way the Jewish Province became one of the most urbanised and proletarian regions of the Soviet Far East and therefore also one of its least religious ones. The only synagogue which it is reported to have

---

[1] The American Jewish Yearbook, 1957, Philadelphia 1957, p. 417.
[2] Jewish Chronicle, September 28, 1956.
[3] Moscow Radio in English for North America, September 3, 1959.
[4] The feast marks the completion of the harvest, to be celebrated according to the Book of Exodus 'when all is gathered in' (Exodus 23.16 and 34.22). Later the Festival came to serve as a commemoration of the booths in which the Israelites dwelt during their wanderings after leaving Egypt.
[5] New York Times, October 3, 1955.

is 'a small ramshackle barrack without a rabbi'.[1] On Friday nights and Saturday mornings prayers take place there for not more than thirty persons, the majority women.[2]

Soviet Oriental Jews

The Soviet Empire includes a number of oriental Jewish communities who deserve to be treated separately for both historical and topical reasons. These communities, who live at some distance from the chief administrative and economic centre, have been able to withstand the secularisation of Judaism and the impact of anti-religious propaganda and action to a greater extent than the Jews of Russia proper. Moreover, marriages with Gentiles, so frequent among the Jews of the large Russian cities, are rare in the oriental Jewish communities where the cohesion of the Jewish family is being preserved.

1. *Georgian Jews.* Almost throughout the Soviet period the Georgian Jews have provoked the astonishment of such foreign visitors as have come into contact with them. A Jewish communist from Central Europe who toured all the Jewish settlements of the USSR in 1930 found that Georgian Jewry obstinately resisted and defied Soviet anti-religious policy. He told the story of the Jews of the town of Kutaisi who obtained from the local Soviet permission for the rebuilding of their synagogue, destroyed by a big fire in the Jewish ghetto in 1928. This was achieved at a time when synagogues were beginning to be closed all over Russia. After this catastrophe too, the town council wanted to move the Jews to the other side of the Rion river which cuts Kutaisi into two. The Jews refused to accept this, since it might have involved them in a desecration of the Sabbath, and in the end they were allocated new tenements near the houses which had been burnt down.[3]

Many years later foreign visitors still found that the small group of Georgian Jews, and especially those of Kutaisi, continued to excel in religious devotion and viewed the future with greater confidence than Jews in most other parts of the Soviet Union. A delegation of rabbis from the USA was most impressed by the fact that 1,200 out of the 2,000 Jewish families in Kutaisi still celebrated the Feast of Tabernacles by spending eight days in temporary huts.[4] In both Kutaisi and Tiflis Jewish parents find it less difficult to instruct their children in their ancient faith than in European Russia, and they also seem to have greater facilities for obtaining kosher food. It was in Kutaisi that a

---

[1] *Jewish Chronicle*, July 13, 1956.   [2] *New York Times*, May 2, 1959.
[3] Otto Heller, *Der Untergang des Judentums*, Wien–Berlin 1931, p. 314.
[4] *New York Times*, August 8, 1956.

delegation of American rabbis saw the first kosher butcher shop since their arrival in the Soviet Union.[1] It is in keeping with the fervent religious spirit of the Georgian Jews that Georgians were among the first to enter the new Moscow yeshivah.

2. *The Bokharan Jews.* The Soviet census of 1926 recorded the existence of 18,600 Bokharan or Central Asian Jews who speak either Tadzhik or Uzbek as their native language. About one-third may have lived in the city of Bokhara itself and the rest in other parts of the former Emirate of Bokhara as well as in various towns of the present Uzbek Republic such as Tashkent, Samarkand, Andizhan, Kokand and Osh. How many of these have remained faithful to the Jewish religion it is impossible to say. However, an indication that the Bokharan Jewish community continues to be of some importance was given by the Soviet authorities themselves in the autumn of 1956 when they publicised a statement attributed to the Bokharan Jews denouncing Anglo-French Middle Eastern Policy. Foreigners who have visited Bokhara have likewise testified that local Jews are still practising religion in their ancient way and studying the Talmud.[2] About five hundred people attend service in the Bokhara synagogue on holy days and two hundred on Friday evenings.[3] Another urban community of Bokharan religious Jews exists in Stalinabad, the capital of Tadzhikistan, known as Dyushambe in the days of the Bokharan Emir. A foreign journalist visiting Stalinabad asserted that there were two synagogues there, one small, the other of medium size.[4] In 1958 the Jewish religious community of Stalinabad was without a rabbi, but a fairly young man born under the Soviet régime conducted services 'as best he could'. That the Jewish religion should survive in Stalinabad at all is in itself amazing for, until the beginning of the war, it suffered particularly heavy persecution. The last local rabbi and the Jewish orthodox slaughterer were not even left in peace by the régime after they had been forced to take on the humble work of shoe-shiners.[5]

3. '*Mountain Jews*'. No foreign visitor has been able to enlighten us about the survival of religion among a third group of oriental Jews — the Mountain Jews (Dag Chufut). They are among the oldest inhabitants of the Caucasus and speak a Persian dialect. According to the 1926 census there were 26,000 Mountain Jews in the Soviet Union, of whom the greater part lived in Daghestan, both in mountain villages (auls) and in the towns of Derbent, Buinaksk and Makhachkala. There

[1] *Jewish Chronicle*, August 10, 1956.   [2] *New York Times*, October 10, 1953.
[3] Levine, *The Red Russia*, London 1959, p. 372.
[4] *National Guardian*, November 10, 1959.   [5] *Antireligioznik*, 1939, no. 11 p. 60.

are smaller groups of Mountain Jews in Azerbaidzhan and the Northern Caucasus. Those of the Northern Caucasus, being nearer to Russian communist influence, were the first to be drawn into the orbit of anti-religious propaganda and the synagogue of the Mountain Jews of Grozny was closed at an early date. The Azerbaidzhani group was able to defend its beliefs far more tenaciously and therefore provoked a mighty anti-religious propaganda campaign conducted in 1936 on the occasion of the Jewish autumn holy days. As many as twenty-three lectures and seventeen performances by atheist propaganda teams were organised and were said to have reached 10,000 people, which is roughly the total of the Mountain Jewish community of Azerbaidzhan.[1]

As to the Mountain Jews of Daghestan, a Soviet ethnographic symposium about this country published in 1955 claimed that religion there, although extremely strong in the past, has for the most part been successfully eliminated. There were no synagogues and no rabbis left in the auls. Both seem to have disappeared towards the end of World War II. Since then marriages have no longer been arranged nor weddings celebrated according to the old customs with the rabbi's participation. Only the older generation still clings to certain religious customs, and circumcision especially is practised in such families as have elderly relatives. These isolated cases have been unable to influence contemporary life.[2] One wonders whether this is not too rosy a picture from the communist point of view. Religious Jews are not likely to be helpful to a Soviet investigation party, even if composed of bona fide ethnographers. There may be no outward signs of religious life among the Mountain Jews and yet such life may go on, for it is not dependent on the existence of synagogues and the presence of rabbis in the auls.

What is known of the history of the Mountain Jews prior to World War II makes it plain that the annihilation of Judaism in Daghestan must have been carried out in the face of very stubborn resistance. As late as 1932, Soviet sources gave a very vivid description of the power of the Daghestani rabbi who was at one and the same time judge, lawyer, doctor and leader of the synagogue. The rabbis in Daghestan gave great trouble to the authorities. They led public feeling against the introduction of the Latin alphabet in place of the Hebrew script and they opposed the collective farms, and when this failed, insisted on these farms being built on the basis of complete equality, a principle the communists are known to reject. The rabbis rendered the life of

---

[1] *Antireligioznik*, 1936, no. 6, p. 41.
[2] *Narody Dagestana* (The Peoples of Daghestan) Academy of Sciences of the USSR, Institute of Ethnography, Moscow 1955, pp. 238–40.

the non-believing Jew difficult by expelling him from the Jewish
national community, for they held that a Godless man was 'no Jew at
all'. At that time there were still only a very few Mountain Jews who
were prepared to become communist 'activists', and Jewish women
joining the Party or the Young Communist League were the exception.
In the early thirties it was still noted as something remarkable that
there were certain Mountain Jewish collective farmers who desecrated
the Sabbath by smoking quite openly.[1] As late as 1938, at the height of
Soviet police terror, the Jewish religion had still survived not only in
remote auls but also in the town of Derbent where as many as seventy
courageous Jews signed a petition for the reopening of the synagogue.[2]

4. *The Krimchaks.* The smallest of the Jewish oriental communities,
the Krimchaks, have virtually ceased to exist as a result of the nazi policy
of extermination. As their name indicates, they used to live in the
Crimea. Before World War I, they numbered 7,500. Their main centre
was the small town of Karasubazar, whilst other Krimchak groups
existed in Simferopol, Sevastopol, Kerch, Eupatoria and Feodosia.
They spoke the Tartar language, which they wrote in Hebrew letters.
They felt little kinship with the non-Tartar-speaking Jews whom they
nicknamed 'Poles'. From a religious point of view, however, the
Krimchaks were not only orthodox Jews but excelled in piety. They
held their rabbis in high honour and their family life was irreproachable.
After the Soviet régime had applied to them the same repressive
measures as to other religious Jews, the Reichssicherheitsdienst of the
SS exterminated the great majority of them, although there were some
German minority experts who tried to rescue the picturesque little race.
Only individual Krimchaks survived the Second World War.[3]

Soviet Judaism in Perspective

The late Chief Rabbi of Britain, Dr. H. J. Hertz, coined as early as
1927 the prophetic phrase about 'the strangulation of the soul' of
three million Russian Jews.[4] No better term could be found to epitomise
what has happened to Russian Jewry under Soviet rule. And yet it
would be wrong to blame the spiritual strangulation entirely and solely
on the communists. To a certain extent the Jews of the USSR have
but shared a process which Jews all over the world have undergone in

[1] *Antireligioznik*, 1932, no. 1, pp. 31–35.
[2] *Antireligioznik*, 1938, no. 12, p. 16.
[3] Rudolf Loewenthal, 'The Extinction of the Krimchaks in World War II' in *The American Slavic and East European Review*, vol. x, 1951, pp. 133–6; Ben Zwi, *The Exiled and the Redeemed*, London 1958, pp. 109–11.
[4] *The Times*, September 27, 1927.

varying degrees, the secularisation of Judaism. A large proportion of Jews in Britain and the United States have either withdrawn altogether from participation in Jewish religious life, or participate only for reasons of national heritage and family ties, and no longer from religious conviction.

Had there been a liberal Russia instead of an illiberal Soviet Union the problem of religious decline among Jews would still have existed, only then it would have been due entirely to such sociological factors as assimilation, inter-marriage with Gentiles and the triumph of a purely political and nationalistic Jewish concept. Nevertheless, it is fair to say that official Soviet anti-religious doctrine and practice have driven the secularisation of Judaism in the USSR much further than it could and would have gone under a 'normal' régime. In London, for instance, between one-third and one-half of all adult Jewish men are still synagogue members.[1] This may be a low percentage compared to that which a Jewish community of Galicia and the Transcarpathian Ukraine might have boasted before World War II but it is high by comparison with the probable percentage of practising believers among the secularised Jews of Moscow or Leningrad.

Moreover in Soviet Russia the Jews have had all the disadvantages of secularisation without any positive compensation; whereas in democratic countries they have been able to strengthen their national ties even when their religious loyalties have weakened. However questionable the value of such a compensation may be from the Jewish religious point of view it certainly prevents the annihilation of the Jews as a conscious national entity. In Soviet Russia the process of de-nationalisation of the Jews has gone hand in hand with the destruction of their religion. The religious Jew of Russia, unlike many of his co-religionaries in the West, is not transformed into a religiously indifferent (or even non-religious) but staunchly national, Jew. He becomes a nondescript hybrid without religion, and without proper nationality, a second-class citizen not entitled to cultivate the history, language and culture of his ancestors. But one thing is still left to him, hope for the future. Devout Jews will outlive Communism in the same way as devout Christians. To give a final example of that orthodox Jewish religious spirit which is braving communist materialism, one may quote the following true story about the Rabbi of Lyubavichi. One day, three members of the Soviet secret police rushed into the synagogue guns in hand, to arrest the rabbi. Facing these armed and

---

[1] Maurice Friedmann, *A Minority in Britain*, London 1955, p. 230.

determined men, he affirmed that he would under no threat of compulsion give up his religious activities. When one of the police agents pointed a gun at him saying, 'This little toy has made many a man change his mind', the Rabbi of Lyubavichi calmly replied: 'This little toy can intimidate only that kind of man who has many gods — passions — and but one world — this world. Because I have only one God and two worlds, I am not impressed by this little toy,'[1]

[1] Rabbi J. I. Schneersohn, *Some Aspects of Chabad Chassidism*, New York 1957, p. 11.

NOTE: In this chapter we have not been concerned with theological problems but with a factual situation. Therefore we have accepted the view that religous Judaism is the only spiritual expression of the Jewish people. The possibility of the Jewish people of the Soviet Union accepting another religion than Judaism, Christianity, for instance, is remote. Nevertheless such a possibility exists and in a number of cases Russian Jews have adopted the Christian religion. We are not speaking here of baptism as a means to escape persecution or as a means towards assimilation but of those rare instances in which Jews become convinced Christians whilst continuing to identify themselves with the Jewish people. Small congregations of Hebrew Christians or Jewish Christians existed in Czarist times in Kishinev and in the Soviet period in Moscow, Dniepropetrovsk, Kiev and Odessa (I. S. Prokhanov, *The Cauldron of Russia*, New York 1933, p. 236). The Soviet Communists themselves were aware of the existence of such Hebrew Christians and on July 7, 1929, *Bezbozhnik* published a sarcastic article about four 'Jewish' Evangelical Christian groups in Odessa.

XIII

Islam[1]

'. . . with false arguments the unbelievers
seek to confuse the truth, scoffing at My
revelations and My warnings.'

THE KORAN

Introduction

None of the numerous religious factors of Soviet Russia is as difficult to evaluate in its importance as Islam. According to the Soviet census of 1959 there were over 24,000,000 persons in the USSR who belonged to nationalities traditionally professing the Islamic faith. What this figure means in terms of religious allegiance and religious observance cannot be answered, even approximately. The Moslems of the Soviet Union live in areas which foreigners are mostly not allowed to visit or where they are usually permitted to stay only for a very short time. Most of their impressions are highly superficial and refer to a few administrative and tourist centres. The Soviet Moslems themselves make hardly any contribution to our knowledge of their problems; they have produced no informative literature in any way comparable to that issued by the Russian Orthodox Church, the Council of Evangelical Christians/Baptists or the Armenian Church. Owing to these circumstances, most contradictory opinions have been put forward about Soviet Islam. Some have considered it a *quantité*

---

[1] Material for this chapter was mainly obtained from the anti-religious and general Soviet press for the period before World War II and from the *Soviet War News* for the wartime period. The most important single primary source of information about Soviet Islam after 1945 is the Moscow Radio reports for the consumption of foreign Oriental audiences. They were taken from the BBC Summary of World Broadcasts, Part I (Soviet Union). Information about Soviet Islam is also scattered over a large number of works by Western authors, though some understood the term 'Moslem' in a secular rather than a religious sense. Of particular relevance to our subject are Vincent Monteil, 'Essai sur l'Islam en URSS', *Revue des Études Islamiques*, Paris 1952; Vincent Monteil, 'Supplément à "l'Essai sur l'Islam en URSS"', *Revue des Études Islamiques*, Paris 1953 and for the earlier period Alexander Parks, *Bolshevism in Turkestan 1917–1927*, and Richard Pipes, *The Foundation of the Soviet Union*, Cambridge, Massachusetts, 1954. A useful compilation about Moslems in Russia covering the years 1945 to 1952 was issued under the title 'L'Islam en URSS après 1945' by a French government agency (*Notes et Études Documentaires*, Direction de la Documentation, December 1953, no. 1812).

négligeable no longer to be reckoned with; others have regarded it as a powerful anti-communist force. What we do know about Soviet Islam from communist sources would tend to prove that institutionalised Islam has declined in the years of Soviet power, but this is not tantamount to a weakening of the Moslem religion. Mohammed did not found a Church like Christ, he gave birth to a faith. Islam can, therefore, and does, exist quite independently of all institutionalised forms. Questions of hierarchy and ecclesiastical jurisdiction, so important to most Christians, have been immaterial to the survival of the Islamic religion. One could not tell the history of the Catholic Church without making the fullest mention of the Popes, nor could one give an account of the history of the Orthodox Church without talking of its Patriarchs and the Metropolitans. With Islam it is different. Mullahs and sheikhs, however distinguished they may be, are of little relevance and in describing the fate of Moslem religion in the USSR we must look primarily beneath the surface, where Islam continues to live without registered mosques and officially approved mullahs. It continues to live in the faith of the basic tenets of the Koran, in the observance of holy days, in the cult of saints and in many other ways. Islamic and pre-Islamic beliefs may often exist side by side, but there is no contradiction between them, for the people have always reconciled them with one another, notwithstanding the opinions of theologians and anthropologists. The division between official and unofficial Islam in the Soviet Union seems to be the only one which is of decisive importance. The other customary divisions on theological lines have much less significance for Soviet Russia.

Divisions of Soviet Islam

Ninety per cent of all Moslems in Soviet Russia are Sunnites and the rest are Shiites. Most of the latter belong to the main body of the Shiah sect, believing that Mohammed's succession was taken by twelve spiritual leaders called Imams. The Sunnite Moslems live in many parts of the Soviet Union. In European Russia and Siberia they form diaspora groups. In the Volga region, in Soviet Central Asia and in the North Caucasus area they live in large compact communities. There is a considerable number of Sunnite Moslem nationalities in the Soviet Union, of which the larger ones are the following:

Uzbeks	6,004,000
Tartars	4,969,000
Kazakhs	3,581,000

Tadzhiks	1,397,000
Turkmenians	1,004,000
Bashkirs	983,000
Kirghiz	974,000
Chechens	418,000
Circassians	314,000
Karakalpaks	173,000
Ingush	100,000
Uighurs	95,000
Karachai	81,000

To this there must be added apart from smaller nationalities, the peoples of the polyglot Daghestan, amounting to 945,000, as well as the Moslem sections of those ethnic groups whose religious loyalties are divided, especially the Ossetins (410,000) half of whom used to be Moslems prior to 1914.

The Soviet Shiites form small minorities in Daghestan as well as in such Central Asian cities as Samarkand, Bokhara, Ashkhabad and Chardshou. However, their main strength lies in the Soviet Republic of Azerbaidzhan, where between 80–85 per cent of the Moslems belong to the Shiite faith.[1] The ethnic groups of the Soviet Union who to a greater or lesser extent belong to the Shiite religion are: the Azerbaidzhani Turks (70 per cent out of 2,929,000), the Talyshi (90 per cent out of 77,000), the Taty (28,000) and also parts of the Kurdish minority in Azerbaidzhan. Finally there is a small Georgian group in Western Azerbaidzhan called Inghilos who were converted to Shiite Islam at the beginning of the seventeenth century. The differences between Azerbaidzhan's Shiite majority and the Sunnite minority are now no longer as important as they used to be even in the first years of communist rule. Soviet anti-religious policy is directed against both of them. Shiites and Sunnites form a single 'Spiritual Administration of the Moslems of Transcaucasia', of which the Chairman is the Shiite Sheikh-ul-Islam, whilst the Vice-Chairman is a Sunnite.

A comparatively small number of Soviet Moslems adhere to the Ismailite, or more precisely the 'Neo-Ismailite' variety of Shiite Islam. They all belong to small Iranian nationalities of the Western Pamir, which is administratively part of the Gorno-Badakhshan Autonomous Province of Tadzhikistan. These Ismailite mountaineers, whose villages lie between 5,000 and 7,000 feet above sea-level, are frequently referred to as 'Mountain Tadzhiks' but a more proper name would be

[1] *Large Soviet Encyclopædia*, vol. xlix, 1957, p. 35.

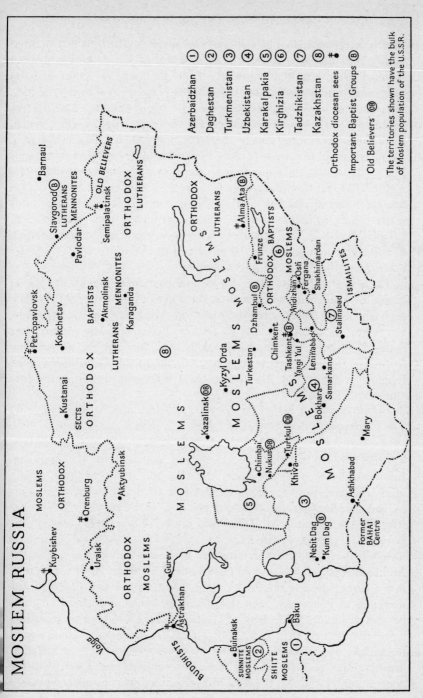

MOSLEM RUSSIA

① Azerbaidzhan
② Daghestan
③ Turkmenistan
④ Uzbekistan
⑤ Karakalpakia
⑥ Kirghizia
⑦ Tadzhikistan
⑧ Kazakhstan

‡● Orthodox diocesan sees
Ⓑ Important Baptist Groups
⒪Ⓑ Old Believers

The territories shown have the bulk of Moslem population of the U.S.S.R.

403

'Pamir nationalities'. Their literary language is Tadzhik but in their homes they use their ancient Iranian dialects. The following distinct national groups in the Pamir are from the religious point of view Ismailites: Shugantsy (12,000), Rushantsy (5,500), Vakhantsy (4,500), Ishkashimtsy and Gorantsy (2,000). The Neo-Ismailites consider the Aga Khan as their religious leader. He traces his origin back to Ismail ibn Djafar, the alleged son of the sixth Shiite Imam, Djafar al-Sadiq. From Ismail there runs, according to neo-Ismailite beliefs, a continuous line of Imams down to our time — the present Imam being the forty-eighth. The fact that their religious head lives outside the Soviet Union has made them particularly vulnerable to communist attacks, since this made it easy to accuse them of imperialist connections. Nevertheless, despite all attacks, the Ismailites have been protected by the isolation of the Pamir mountains and so preserved their faith to a much greater extent than the Shiites of Azerbaidzhan.

There are still some other Shiite groups represented in the Soviet Union in smaller numbers, such as the adepts of the extremist Ali-ilahi sect which has about 3,000 followers in Azerbaidzhan and Armenia. Large groups of Ali-ilahi live in Turkey, Persia and Afghanistan. The name Ali-ilahi means 'those who deify Ali', for it is the outstanding feature of the sect that it considers Ali, the fourth Calif, a god. The religious cult of the Ali-ilahi betrays strong syncretist, including Christian, elements.

The Communist Interpretation of Islam

Marxism-Leninism, being an ideology which originated in Europe, has had little to say about Islam. It was axiomatic for the Marxists-Leninists that they should reject and denounce Islam as much as any other religion, but it was more difficult to decide what arguments to use in attacking the Moslem position or even what the proper Marxist interpretation of Islam was to be. These difficulties of the Soviet Marxists and anti-religious experts have been reflected in a number of contradictory communist theories about the origin of the Mohammedan religion and its class basis. The theory most widespread in the early period of the Soviet régime, because it was in line with the teachings of Pokrovsky, then the official historian, considered Islam to be the creation and ideology of Arab merchant capitalism. According to another theory, that of N. A. Roshkov, the triumph of Islam meant the victory of feudalism. A further hypothesis, soon to be dismissed as 'un-Marxian', pointed out that Islam was originally the ideology of the poor peasantry and that the state of Mohammed was originally a peasant state, although power soon got into the hands of the tribal aristocracy. All these theories were expounded in Soviet books and periodicals, especially in the anti-religious press.[1]

Nor is there agreement about the assessment of the prophet Mohammed himself. The *Large Soviet Encyclopaedia* describes him as a 'religious preacher considered as the founder of Islam'.[2] The leading Soviet orientalist, Professor Tolstov, only speaks of a 'myth of Mohammed', which, he says, was based on pre-Islamic shamanistic myths.[3] More determined in his rejection of Mohammed is Klimovich, Soviet Russia's most prolific anti-Islam author, who states: 'Mohammed is that imaginary personality with whose help the origin of Islam was explained and is explained to this day.'[4]

It is from Professor Lutsyan Klimovich's numerous articles in the Soviet press that we get a fairly up-to-date and authoritative Soviet view of Islam. This is the definition which Klimovich gives:

'Islam is an anti-scientific reactionary world concept, alien and inimical to the scientific Marxist-Leninist world concept. Islam is in opposition to the optimistic and life-affirming materialistic teaching; it is incompatible with the fundamental interests of the Soviet peoples: it prevents believers from being active and conscientious constructors of the communist society.'[5]

About the Koran, Klimovich says that it was 'compiled to please the Calif's feudal lords and merchants' and its stories about paradise and hell were a 'means of converting the workers into will-less slaves'.[6] The Moslem religious holy days, Kurban Bayrami and the Ramadan fast in particular, were survivals of a past when man 'believed that by magic he could bribe the evil spirits or gods'.[7] Klimovich defines the hajj, the pilgrimage to Mecca as a 'source of income for the merchants and feudalists of Arabia' and an 'opportunity widely used by the imperialists for the recruitment of spies and diversionists'.[8] These more offensive statements, it is true, were not included in an anti-Islam pamphlet which Klimovich published in 1956 both in Russian and the languages of the Soviet Orient.[9]

---

[1] N. A. Smirnov, *Ocherki Istorii Izucheniya Islama v SSSR* (Essays on the History of the Study of Islam in the USSR), Moscow 1954, pp. 181–201.

[2] *L.S.E.*, vol. xxviii, p. 599, Moscow 1954.   [3] Smirnov, op. cit., p. 206.

[4] Smirnov, op. cit., p. 203.

[5] *Zarya Vostoka*, October 10, 1954.   [6] *Zarya Vostoka*, ibid.

[7] *Zarya Vostoka*, ibid.   [8] *Pravda Vostoka*, June 28, 1951.

[9] L. I. Klimovich, *Islam, ego proiskhozhdenie i sotsialnaya sushchnost* (Islam, its origin and social essence), Moscow, 1956.

O

Occasionally, nationalistic arguments would also be invoked against Islam. In addition to being 'conservative', 'reactionary' and 'anti-scientific' it is denounced as 'anti-Russian', whilst Central Asian Moslems in particular would be told that Islam was an 'alien' religion forcibly imposed on them, first by Arab invaders, later by the Tartar clergy and finally by the Czarist administration.[1] This kind of argument is addressed in particular to the Kazakhs who it was intended should be flattered by the statement that their ancient religion, shamanism, was 'less harmful' than the foreign Moslem religion which superseded it.

The presentation of the Soviet case against Islam always undergoes some slight changes in accordance with the tactical switches in communist policy towards the Islamic nations inside and outside the USSR. What can never be a question of discussion is the fundamental ideological incompatibility between Islam and Communism. The day-to-day attitude which the communists observe towards Moslems is, however, quite a different problem. During the years of Soviet power the communists have applied the most contradictory policies. There were some situations which demanded from the communists toleration and friendly understanding towards the Moslem religion and there were other times when an all-out offensive against Moslem religious 'prejudices' was called for. In their 'Moslem policy' the Soviet communists were guided by their usual system of priorities, putting the general cause of the proletarian revolution first and the fight against a particular 'hostile' and 'reactionary' ideology second. If one bears in mind that Soviet atheism is not a concept complete in itself but only part of a wider ideological system — Marxism-Leninism — one will not be surprised by even the most sensational tactical *volte-face* on the 'Moslem front'.

The Waiting Period

When the Russian Bolsheviki took over the government of Russia, they were anxious to postpone the unavoidable conflict with the Moslems of the Soviet East. They were too much preoccupied with establishing power in Europe to be able to tackle the question of Islam. They had to break the influence of the Russian Church before they could take up the question of Moslem religious law or Moslem religious education in the North Caucasus and Turkestan. They also lacked allies within the Moslem camp. The number of Moslem communists in the

[1] A. Iskakov, *Chokan Valikhanov o reaktsionnoi roli Islama* (Chokan Valikhanov about the reactionary role of Islam), in *Izvestiya Akademii Nauk Kazakhskoi SSSR*, March 1957, pp. 59–65.

first few years of Soviet power was minute and those prepared to conduct anti-religious, i.e. anti-Moslem propaganda was even smaller. Moreover, the Russian communists expected that the 'World Revolution' might quickly extend to other countries with a Moslem population. For all these reasons religious tolerance towards the Moslems was the only conceivable policy during the first years of the Soviet régime.

This initial communist approach towards Islam also suffered from a certain confusion of terminology. Originally the Russian communists used the word 'Moslems' in a secular sense — a meaning which this term has also acquired in other parts of the world. 'Moslems', as the Soviets understood it, were simply people belonging to the Moslem world in a historical and cultural sense, but were not necessarily believers in Mohammed's religion. For instance, when in November 1917 Lenin and Stalin appealed to the 'Moslems of Russia' and the 'Moslems of the East', asking them for 'fullest moral and material support in the rebuilding of the world', they thought of them as oppressed colonial peoples, not as devout sons of the prophet. Although Lenin and Stalin did not mean to address religious Moslems but 'political' and 'national' Moslems the former may have gathered from the appeal that the communist leaders were their friends.

To Lenin, in particular, Islam and the Moslems were a great unknown force to which he showed the grudging respect which the unknown so often receives. His attitude was shared by Zinoviev, the first president of the Communist International, and Mikhail Kalinin, a man who, for a communist, had a most cautious and tolerant attitude towards religious problems. At the eighth Congress of the Russian Communist Party in March 1919, Lenin formulated the original Soviet policy towards Islam. It can be summed up in a single word: 'Wait!' This is what Lenin said: 'What can we do in relation to such people as the Kirghiz, Uzbeks, Tadzhiks and Turkmenians, who are still under the influence of their mullahs? Here in Russia, the people's memory of their unhappy experience of the *popes* has helped us to throw these off. But you know how badly the decree about civil marriage is still being carried out. Can we go to those nations and tell them "We shall get rid of your exploiters"? We cannot do that because they are completely subservient to their mullahs. We just have to wait for the development of each particular nation and that differentiation of the proletariat from the bourgeois elements which is inescapable.'[1]

In the usual communist way, Lenin completely identified religion

[1] V. I. Lenin, *O natsionalnom i natsionalno-kolonialnom voprose* (On the National and National-Colonial Question), Moscow 1956, pp. 478-9.

with exploitation, and the clergy and the mullahs with the 'bourgeois elements'. But the meaning of his words was nevertheless clear. He admitted that in the first years of the Soviet régime the communists had neither the power nor even the opportunity to tackle the problem of Islam. Some communist leaders went a step further than Lenin. They considered that the fight against Islam must be postponed to a later date and also that there could even be co-operation between the Soviet power and the 'mullahs'. So a rather absurd situation developed. In the Christian areas of Russia an all-out merciless struggle against religious institutions was waged, whilst in some Moslem areas, for instance in Daghestan, the communist authorities were still prepared to recognise the Shariat courts. Abroad the Russian communists were attacked for this opportunistic attitude, for instance, by that most orthodox Marxist party of the Independent German Social Democrats (USPD) which Moscow wanted to recruit to the Third International. Zinoviev himself went to a congress of that party held in Halle in October 1920. The German left-wing extremists reproached the Soviets for their softness towards the 'mullahs of Khiva', a term which must be understood metaphorically rather than literally. But Zinoviev insisted, in the face of a hostile audience, that the 'prejudices of these peoples' (meaning the Moslems of Soviet Asia) must be respected and that communists must bring enlightenment also to the 'mullahs of Khiva' and lead them.[1]

It was easy for the German Marxists to decry the 'mullahs of Khiva'. For the Soviets, they were a most difficult problem, both in the metaphorical and literal sense and even more so the 'mullahs of Bokhara', which was the most important centre of 'religious obscurantism' in the whole of Moslem Central Asia. It was the mullahs of Bokhara who supported the armed struggle against Soviet power almost to the bitter end. It is hard to say when this end came. Large-scale fighting went on until 1924, especially in the Eastern part of the former Emirate of Bokhara. Dyushambe (Stalinabad) which later became the capital of Tadzhikistan, was still in anti-communist hands until the summer of 1922. Smaller skirmishes between Soviet forces and nationalist Moslem bandits occurred until 1928, when the band of the Khivan Dzhunaid Khan was routed.[2] There was a last flare-up of fighting in 1931 when a force of Bokharan Moslem refugees invaded Tadzhikistan from Afghan bases.

[1] G. Sinowjew, *Die Weltrevolution und die dritte Kommunistische Internationale*, Berlin 1920, p. 37.
[2] L. Klimovich, *Sotsialisticheskoe stroitelstvo na vostoke i religiya* (Socialist construction and religion in the East), Moscow–Leningrad 1929, p. 50.

The 'Old Mosque' and the 'New Mosque'

Although the situation in the Moslem parts of the Soviet Union greatly differed from that in the Christian areas, there were also certain similarities. One of them was the divisions inside the religious camp. The split between the 'Old Church' of Patriarch Tikhon and the 'Living' or 'Renovated' Church within Russian Orthodoxy had an almost exact equivalent within the camp of Soviet Islam. On the one hand, conservative Moslem dignitaries continued to fight stubbornly against the atheist régime, whilst 'progressive' Moslems called for support for Soviet power, often in a demonstrative and enthusiastic way. The conservatives were as extreme in their hostility to Communism as the reformists were in their servility to the new rulers and their policy, but both invoked the Koran in support of their attitude. The North Caucasus region remained for a long time the main bulwark of the conservatives — and, in some areas, such as the Karachai territory and the Chechen-Ingush Republic, the intransigent anti-Soviet Moslem trends were not vanquished until World War II. The reformists were most influential in Tartaria, Bashkiria and other areas of the Russian Federation more strongly exposed to European and communist influence. In Azerbaidzhan at an early stage there emerged a collaborating Moslem faction. In the Central Asian Republics the two trends existed side by side and the attitude of the local Moslem dignitaries varied from one town to the next. In Fergana, the chief of the Moslem ecclesiastical administration still urged believers as late as 1927 to boycott Soviet medical services, whilst in the same year the Moslem religious dignitaries of Kokand wanted to take part in the communist demonstration celebrating the tenth anniversary of the October Revolution.[1] Even among the Ismailite religious elders there were some 'reformists' who said that the Soviets came from God and that Lenin was a son of the Aga Khan.[2]

From the point of view of the Soviet régime the 'conservatives' were a major menace. They incited the people against the Government and fomented disobedience or even outright revolt. But the 'reformists' or people of the 'New Mosque' (Novomechetniki) as they were nicknamed, were also a very mixed blessing to the communists. It was, of course, pleasing to the Party that authoritative Moslem bodies issued statements endorsing various facets of Soviet policy and thus helped the consolidation of communist rule. The Soviet authorities also welcomed the fact that these same bodies put on record their hostility

---

[1] *Bezbozhnik*, no. 4, 1927.   [2] Klimovich, op. cit., p. 95.

to British imperialism in the most outspoken manner. With the support of the Moslem clergy, England was to be built up as the main enemy of Islam, whilst Soviet Russia was to appear as the saviour of the Moslems. Indeed, a statement by the Baku Moslem clergy in 1923 praised the Soviet régime for having saved Persia and Turkey from 'predatory England' and appealed to the Moslems of the world not to yield to 'English intrigues'.[1] A Moslem ecclesiastical conference held in Tashkent in the following year adopted a similar declaration, asserting that the Soviets would bring liberation to the peoples of the East, whilst the imperialists of England were sucking the blood of the oppressed people and bringing slavery.[2]

The 'New Mosque' people also proved their usefulness to the authorities when the latter carried out land reform in Soviet Central Asia in the winter of 1925-6. The reform was facilitated by various mullahs declaring that the measure was compatible with the Islamic religion and the teachings of Mohammed. Even the Moslem Ecclesiastical Administration of Turkestan issued a statement to this effect, but it could hardly have been to the liking of the communists. Whilst advising people to obey the land reform decree of the Government, it urged landowners to anticipate the reform 'by a voluntary hand-over of land and property'. The person following the advice would then be treated as a 'benefactor in the world beyond'.[3] This statement, which transformed a communist social reform into a religious gesture, showed that a Moslem supporter of the Soviet régime could be more dangerous than a Moslem opponent. Against the latter the punitive organs of the State could be mobilised, against the former there was no protection. The 'New Mosque' Moslem was an awkward ally of the régime, for he gave a religious motivation to the actions of the Government and so caused tremendous confusion among the first Moslem communists, who politically were almost completely illiterate.

The Moslem Communists

The Moslem communist of the first years of the Soviet régime was a strange phenomenon. He still believed in Allah and he observed religious rites. At first it even happened that regional Central Asian Party conferences were interrupted at prayer-time. Even later, it could still be observed that during Party meetings people suddenly walked out in order to pray. The very idea of anti-religious propaganda horrified the

---

[1] *Zarya Vostoka*, August 17, 1924.   [2] *Pravda*, December 28, 1924.
[3] Statement of December 20, 1925, B. Hayit, *Turkestan im 20. Jahrhundert*, I. W. Leske Verlag, Darmstadt 1956, p. 270.

first Moslem communists. When the question was raised for the first time before the Communist Party organisation of Tashkent in 1923, the Uzbek communists showed themselves more perturbed than even the mullahs themselves. They asked the atheist lecturer such questions as 'Who created you if not God' or 'How can one live without religion?' They also said that an Uzbek opposing religion was selling himself to the Russians and demanded a brand of Communism 'compatible with Islam'.[1] As late as 1927, Yaroslavsky, the chief of the League of Militant Godless, stated that a substantial part of the communists of Moslem origin (in Daghestan, Bokhara and other areas) continued to carry out religious rites and were members of religious organisations.[2] However, Yaroslavsky thought that after ten years of Soviet power the time had come to enforce stricter rules for the Communist Party branches in the Moslem areas, and to demand from every party member a clear break with religion. For this demand the time was not yet ripe. In the North Caucasus region even atheist communists posed as devout Moslems and went to the mosque in order to maintain their authority among the population.[3] In the Pamir mountains Communist Party members continued to pay the gold tribute ('zakat') to the Aga Khan, like all the other Ismailite faithful throughout the world.[4]

Those who wanted to be Moslems and communists at the same time stubbornly adhered to the theory that Communism and Islam were really identical, notwithstanding all the pronouncements made by authoritative party spokesmen. This view coincided with that expounded by the 'New Mosque' people, of whom some went as far as to equate the Koran with the Communist Manifesto.[5] Quite naturally, there existed a kind of alliance between the religious Moslem communists and the 'New Mosque' clergy. The 'anti-religious' activity of some Communist Party branches in Central Asia simply consisted of appointing 'progressive' mullahs in place of reactionary ones.

Persecution and Resistance in the Late Twenties

The peculiar frame of mind of the Moslem communists considerably delayed the introduction of a fully-fledged Soviet system in the Moslem

---

[1] *Pravda Vostoka*, 1928, no. 277.

[2] Yaroslavsky, *Protiv Religii i Tserkvi* (Against Religion and Church), vol. ii, 1933, pp. 219–20.

[3] *Pravda*, 1926, no. 200.

[4] The continued collection of this tribute after the establishment of the Soviet régime was one of the strangest things which happened in the Islamic territories of the USSR. The collectors travelled from India to the remotest villages, first with frontier passes, later illegally. The authorities tried to discourage the payment of the tribute by denouncing the collectors as 'spies' (*Antireligioznik*, 1937, no. 8, p. 38).

[5] Yaroslavsky, op. cit., vol. iv, p. 373.

territories. It also delayed the annihilation of Islam, which confronted the régime not only as a religion but also as a legal framework, a way of life and as a whole network of institutions. In fighting all these various facets of Islam the Soviet régime was unable to proceed at the whirlwind pace at which it usually solved social, economic and ideological problems. For once it had to choose a slow and gradual approach. This applies particularly to the way in which the régime wrested from the Moslem peoples their three main legal-institutional and at the same time religious assets, namely, first the Vakufs, the religious endowments, mostly in the form of church land, which provided the means for the upkeep of mosques and religious schools; second, the Koranic schools and, third, the religious and Shariat courts.

The Vakufs were, in theory, abolished by the Soviet decree of January 23, 1918, which separated the Church from the State, but their last remnants continued to survive until the end of the twenties. In fact, the Vakufs were needed as long as Koranic schools or 'old method' schools, as they were officially called, were allowed to remain in being. The Soviet régime obviously could not afford to disband these schools before being able to provide a secular alternative. In Turkestan, the authorities even saw themselves compelled to authorise the establishment of a special Moslem educational society called 'Makhkamai Shariya' which worked for a compromise between religion and Communism in the sphere of education. It was entitled to own Vakufs for financing its activities. Both clergy and parents fought hard for the preservation of the Koranic schools, but in vain. As for the Shariat courts, their competence was persistently curtailed and their number reduced from year to year. In 1925, as many as eighty-seven such courts were still in being in Uzbekistan alone. By 1926 this number was reduced to twenty-seven. In 1927, only seven Shariat courts were left and in the next year not a single one remained in the whole of Soviet Central Asia.[1] The official abolition of Moslem schools and courts did not mean that they passed out of existence altogether. In the more remote parts of the country, for instance, in the Daghestani mountain regions, they continued to survive for a certain time.[2] Even secular education in the Moslem areas was originally not necessarily an atheist affair. Some of the textbooks used in the Soviet state schools were compiled by religious-minded people and among the first Soviet 'secular' teachers were a considerable number of mullahs.

The liquidation of the Moslem religious schools was part of a whole

[1] Klimovich, *Sotsialisticheskoe stroitelstvo na vostoke i religiya*, p. 121.
[2] *Bezbozhnik*, September 20, 1929.

series of measures by which the situation in the Moslem territories of the Soviet Union was brought into line with that prevailing in the rest of the country. In the long run the centralised Soviet empire could not afford to have two religious policies, one more lenient for the Moslems and another, most intolerant, for the Christians. It was logical for this discrepancy to be brought to an end. This was achieved by the big atheist offensive which began in 1928 and reached its full vehemence in 1929. A very large number of mosques were closed, destroyed or secularised and the Moslem clergy was drastically reduced in numbers. Proportionately, the losses suffered by the Moslems were greater than those of the Christians, since before the religious persecution there were considerably more mosques and mullahs per head of population than there were Christian churches and priests. The way in which the Moslem houses of worship were taken away from the believers hardly differed from the manner in which the churches were confiscated. Meetings of citizens were convened in towns and villages which were bullied into deciding 'voluntarily' that the local mosques should be converted into schools, clubs, cinemas and reading rooms. Other mosques were transformed into prisons and hotels, whilst the most ancient and artistically most remarkable ones became museums.

As to the Moslem clergy, vast numbers became redundant through the closing of the mosques after they had already lost much of their income through the nationalisation of the Vakufs. Some were persuaded to resign their offices in a dramatic way by publicly denouncing themselves as 'deceivers of the working people'. Others, especially the members of the higher clergy, were put in prison; as for instance, the entire supreme ecclesiastical administration of Central Asia, headed by its Chairman and Chief Shariat Judge. It seems that their arrest was carried out under article 156 of the Uzbek Penal Code which did not figure in the Penal Code of Russia proper and was especially designed to fight Islam. The article dealt with: 'Exploitation of religious prejudices of the masses with the aim of overthrowing the Workers' and Peasants' government or of provoking resistance against its law and decrees.' The punishment envisaged for this crime ranged from three years of imprisonment if there were mitigating circumstances, to the 'highest measure of social defence', namely, death by shooting. The leaders of any active religious movement in Uzbekistan challenging communist anti-religious education could easily be accused of 'exploitation of religious prejudices' in the sense of article 156 of the Code.[1]

[1] *Ugolovnyi Kodeks Uzbekskoi SSR* (Penal Code of the Uzbek SSR), Tashkent 1954, p. 66, p. 28.

O2

It is difficult to give any figures as to the precise extent of the havoc caused to Islam by the atheist campaign, which began in 1928-9 and went on for several years, but it is certain that it reduced the numbers of both the mosques and the Moslem clergy to insignificance. In Bashkiria, for instance, the number of mullahs declined between 1929 and 1932 from 3,000 to 300.[1] Such a drastic decrease must also have taken place in other Moslem areas of the USSR.

The Soviet Moslems did not capitulate easily to communist atheism. There was a good deal of local resistance of every kind. Illegal religious-inspired organisations were founded and in some places armed revolts broke out. The fight for the preservation of the Moslem faith was probably the most important single motive of these anti-Soviet movements and activities, although they also pursued political and economic objectives. In Tartaria, the mullahs founded a religious Youth League called 'Star of the Truth', ('Zvezda Pravdy'), which even published a newspaper *Child of Islam*. The leaders of the organisation were arrested and put on trial in 1929.[2] A particularly original form of religious opposition was discovered in Bashkiria. There, devout Moslems propagated a so-called 'Testament of Mohammed'. This was a skilful device whereby local Moslem leaders tried to warn the people against the anti-religious policy of the communists. Mohammed's 'testament' was of an apocalyptic nature; it forecast the coming of doomsday, and predicted that the Koran and faith in God would be taken away from the people. Terrible misfortunes were to come, and they would reach their culminating point in 1937, but Mohammed would protect those who carried his testament from town to town, village to village, mosque to mosque. The 'testament' had its effects. More people went to the mosques, a number of Moslem youngsters left the Komsomol and some parents even stopped sending their children to the Soviet school.[3] Needless to say, those who propagated the 'testament' came into sharp conflict with the Soviet punitive organs.

In the Caucasus, Moslem resistance took particularly violent forms. For instance, in the Kabardino-Balkar Autonomous Province, a rising broke out in June 1928, and lasted five days. A whole district of the province, that of Baksan, fell into the hands of the insurgents. Officially the insurrection was attributed to the 'kulaks and the reactionary mullahs of the Baksan district' some of whom were alleged to have been in contact with 'the centres of militant Moslem reaction abroad'.[4]

[1] *Antireligioznik*, 1932, no. 9, p. 35.   [2] *Antireligioznik*, 1929, no. 4, p. 63.
[3] *Bezbozhnik*, May 12, 1929.
[4] *Istoriya Kabardy* (History of Kabarda), Publishing House of the Academy of Sciences of the USSR, Moscow 1957, p. 243.

Another rising took place in the Adzhar Autonomous Soviet Republic
in the April of 1929. The Moslems of Adzharistan, which lies on the
Soviet-Turkish border, were exasperated by Soviet anti-religious policy
and attacks on Islamic customs. This led to guerilla-fighting, which had
to be put down by Russian troops.[1] Much fiercer still was the Moslem
opposition in Chechnia. Various anti-communist Imams made their
appearance and proclaimed a Holy War against the enemies of Allah.
The last religious rising of this kind recorded in the Soviet press was
that of Imam Saadtsev, whose base was in the aul (mountain village) of
Cheberda. The authorities seized the Imam and put him and his
principal associate in prison. The hillmen, however, refused to believe
that a man who held his commission from Allah could be taken away
so easily, so the rumour spread that he had evaporated. Thereupon the
authorities took several hundred hillmen to the town of Grozny to see
that the Imam really was in their power. They produced him at a trial
and sentenced him and his chief lieutenant to death.[2]

In Central Asia the act of Moslem resistance which the communists
still denounced three decades after it had happened was the violent
death of the communist leader, Hakim Zade (1889–1929), who became
the first and principal martyr of atheism in Russia's Moslem territories.
In August 1928 Hakim Zade was sent on an important assignment. He
was entrusted by the Party with stamping out religion in a picturesque
Uzbek village high up in the mountains, which was then called Shah-i-
Mardan. According to a popular legend the Moslem saint buried in the
village is none other than Calif Ali.[3] Small wonder that Shah-i-Mardan
had become one of Central Asia's most famous places of pilgrimage.
Hakim-Zade, the rare type of communist fanatic who had severed every
tie with Islam, went out to transform the holy place of Shah-i-Mardan
into a bulwark of atheism. He campaigned for the closing of the local
mosque and the stoppage of all pilgrimage to the village. To provoke
devout Moslems even more he had a Lenin monument erected in the
very centre of Shah-i-Mardan. In March 1929, Hakim-Zade was
killed by 'mullahs and sheikhs' who literally tore him to pieces.[4] As
many as fifty-four people were put on trial for being implicated in the
murder of Hakim-Zade, whose fame as a Soviet hero has continuously
increased with the passing of the years. Shah-i-Mardan, the scene both
of his atheist outbursts and of his assassination, was called after him

---

[1] *The Times*, April 11 and May 14, 1929.   [2] *Bezbozhnik*, October 15, 1930.
[3] According to Shiite Moslem tradition Ali was buried in Najaf, south of Baghdad.
Najaf has therefore become a great, if not the greatest, Holy Place of Shiah Islam
(Dwight M. Donaldson. *The Shiite Religion*, London 1933, p. 64).
[4] *Bezbozhnik*, April 28, 1929.

'Hamzabad'; 'Hamza' being the literary pseudonym under which he became famous. His reputation as a writer and poet is largely posthumous: in his lifetime he was primarily known as a schoolteacher. The literary works from his pen are saturated with an anti-religious bias which makes him the first atheist writer of Soviet Central Asia.

The 'Attack' ('Hudjum')

Much of the Moslem resistance to communist atheism was tied up with a vast campaign which started in the spring of 1927 and became known as 'Hudjum' or 'attack'. This was the struggle for the emancipation of Moslem women and became primarily a campaign for the discarding of the veil. The question of the veil was not equally important in all Moslem territories of the Soviet Union, but it had quite exceptional significance for Uzbekistan, Tadzhikistan, Turkmenistan and Transcaucasia.

The 'Hudjum' was a clever move on the part of the Soviet communists. It was as clever as the campaign for the confiscation of church treasures carried out in the Christian territories of the Soviet Union in 1922. This confiscation brought the Christian opposition against the Soviet régime into the open. The Orthodox hierarchy was made to defend not religion as such but material interests against a government which championed the cause of a starving people. It was the purpose of the 'Hudjum' to focus public attention on a similar side-issue. The Soviet power very cunningly manœuvred its Moslem opponents into a position where they defended not religion but an out-of-date reactionary point of view about women. The alternative, as put by the communists, was not for or against Islam but for or against women's equality, for or against women's rights. The Moslem religious opposition fell into the communist trap. It used up much of its energy in resisting the emancipation. This resistance brought many setbacks to the communists, and resulted in a good deal of suffering for the emancipated women, but in the long run it nevertheless led to a weakening of the religious camp.

The problem of the emancipation of the Moslem women is not one which concerns the Islamic regions of Russia alone. It has become an issue in all Moslem countries which have reached a certain degree of modern development. Although the Koranic teaching on divorce, polygamy, concubinage and the status of women in general was an immense advance on the situation in pre-Islamic Arabia, there is little doubt that it is quite incompatible with a democratic society. The

Moslem world has become increasingly aware of this problem. Moslem writers and poets of various nations — Turks, Egyptians, Iraqis, Tunisians amongst others — have pleaded for an elastic interpretation of the Koran and urged that distinction must be made between the divine and human elements of the Shariat.[1] So the fight against out-dated customs in general and an out-dated attitude towards Moslem women in particular is nothing essentially communist. On the contrary, Communism seems hardly fit to fight for a modernisation of Moslem society and for the emancipation of Moslem women, because it is a force extraneous to Islam.

To make the emancipation fully effective, painless and widely acceptable it would have to come from inside the Islamic camp or, at least, it would have to be proclaimed on behalf of a higher moral principle. It is doubtful whether the communist State can claim to represent higher moral principles than the ones enshrined in Islamic teaching. The Koran, it is true, grants the husband the right to divorce his wife without any misbehaviour on her part and without having to give any reason for his step. But this does not mean that the devout Moslem looks upon divorce as something commendable; he regards it as the most hateful thing to God of things permitted. To this Islamic teaching about divorce Communism does not oppose the sanctity of marriage. Communist family legislation in its original form (that in force at the time of the emancipation of the women of Soviet Central Asia) did not make divorce more difficult than the Koran had; it only made it equally easy for men and women. From a thing permitted but hateful to God divorce became something on which the all-powerful state looked with indifference.

Official Soviet historians refer to the emancipation of the Oriental women of the USSR with tremendous pride, but in reality it was a most costly operation. It was hastily imposed on all ill-prepared public opinion, reluctant to accept the overthrow of ancient customs, and so turned against those whom Communism was pretending to help — the emancipated women themselves. Indeed, the Soviet emancipation campaign resulted in more fatal casualties than many a colonial war conducted by the Western imperialists.

March 8, 1927, the communist 'International Women's Day', marked the actual beginning of the 'Hudjum'. Big women's meetings were organised in a theatrical fashion. During these meetings a large number of Moslem women took off their veils and afterwards a solemn *auto-da-fé* took place during which the collected, abandoned veils were burnt. For

[1] H. A. R. Gibb, *Modern Trends in Islam*, Chicago 1947, pp. 91–3.

a moment, but only for a moment, it seemed as if the campaign was eminently successful. In Uzbekistan alone, as many as 100,000 women renounced the custom of the veil — but most of them did so for a single day only. Once the celebration of International Women's Day was over, all but 5,000 women resumed the wearing of the veil. The whole action provoked fanatical opposition among the Moslem population. So great was the indignation at the unveiling of the women that some people stooped to murder. Fourteen Uzbek women pioneers of the communist-directed 'emancipation' drive were killed. Others were subjected to various attacks and raped. Widespread opinion simply equated unveiled women with prostitutes.[1]

On March 8, 1928, the performance of the preceding year was repeated on an even larger scale. Again there were big women's demonstrations and 'unveiling' meetings. But the violence of popular reaction grew at an even quicker pace than the impetus of the 'Hudjum'. In 1928, the number of officially registered anti-feminist murders in Uzbekistan exceeded 200, and there were 45 death sentences for terrorist attacks on women.[2] The victims of the assassinations were, in the first place, women who had accepted posts in village councils and so had identified themselves particularly closely with the very régime which had challenged the conservative religious feelings of the bulk of the people. Those assassinated included not only women, but also a few men who had approved the unveiling of their womenfolk. How general the resistance to the unveiling was may be gathered from the fact that in 1928 an unveiled woman communist was still unable to walk unmolested across the Registan, the famous central square of Samarkand, then the capital of the Uzbek Soviet Republic. Beatings-up of unveiled Komsomol girls and women activists used to be a frequent occurrence there. The Moslem militiamen not only did not protect the women but even encouraged the crowds in their hostility against 'the unbelieving she-dogs'.[3] One can well imagine the situation in small Moslem townships, not to speak of the remoter villages, if this happened in the capital city.

Again there came March 8, International Women's Day, with new unveiling actions which were soon to demand new victims. In the first half of 1929 the number of anti-feminist murders soared to 169 in Uzbekistan alone.[4] The régime was running amok over the question of the emancipation of women and it almost looked as if the initiators of

---

[1] Fannina W. Halle, *Frauen des Ostens*, Zurich 1938, pp. 150–2.
[2] *Istoricheskie Zapiski*, Moscow 1954, no. 48, p. 189.
[3] *Bezbozhnik*, January 6, 1929.
[4] T. N. Kary-Niyasov, *Ocherki Istorii Kultury Sovetskogo Uzbekistana* (Essays on the History of the Culture of Soviet Uzbekistan), Moscow 1955, p. 159.

the 'Hudjum' experienced a kind of perverse satisfaction at the large number of casualties which the unveiling of the women provoked. The victims were useful to the Government and the Party, because they provided them with ammunition against the religious Moslem opposition. It is significant in this connection that at the second Congress of the League of Militant Godless in 1929 the unfortunate assassinated women were mentioned among the 'many fighters of the anti-religious front' who had 'fallen in battle'.[1]

According to the official Soviet thesis it was the mullahs who inspired or instigated the assassination of many women pioneers of the emancipation. This accusation may well be true, though only in an indirect sense. Many mullahs could not but denounce the emancipated women, inasmuch as their taking off the veil was a deliberate affront to religion. In those parts of Moslem Russia such as Bashkiria and Tartaria, where the wearing of the veil was not customary, the mullahs were able to act more shrewdly. Far from opposing the women's emancipation, they proclaimed that the latter would not come from the Soviet power but from Islam itself.[2] In practice a great deal was done to show that this was not an empty claim. The Moslem Central Administration in Ufa co-opted a woman member. Throughout Tartaria and Bashkiria women were admitted to mosques. Special women's meetings were organised either in the homes of mullahs or in the mosques themselves. Communist sources even accused the mullahs of inciting devout Moslem women to break up meetings which were summoned by the communist women's departments ('zhenotdely').[3]

From the 'Hudjum' to the Great Purge

Throughout the 'Hudjum' the organisers of the emancipation campaign were somewhat handicapped by the unco-operative attitude of a section of the Communist Party and Young Communist League membership. The Central Asian Bureau of the party, its North Caucasian Territorial Committee and the Central Committee of the Azerbaidzhan party made it incumbent upon all party members to take off the veils of their wives, their sisters and the other female members of their family. But instead of doing this they often agitated together with the mullahs against the discarding of the veils.[4]

Many communists recruited in the Moslem areas continued to fail in support of the Party with regard to the wider problems of anti-religious propaganda and action also. It was the fault or, from the point

[1] *Pravda*, June 12, 1929. [2] *Kommunisticheskos Prosveshchenie*, 1927, no. 4, p. 76.
[3] *Kommunisticheskoe Prosveshchenie*, ibid. [4] *Bezbozhnik*, February 3, 1929.

of view of the believers, the merit of the Moslem communists that the League of Militant Godless in Soviet Russia's Moslem territories continued to remain a farce. Membership figures produced from time to time by certain 'Moslem' branches of the League could hardly be taken very seriously, for they showed tremendous and quite inexplicable fluctuations from one year to the next. A sensational membership boom was often followed by a disastrous decline or by a statement that the branch in question had ceased to exist altogether. For instance, in Azerbaidzhan the ranks of the League increased from 3,000 in 1930 to 70,000 in 1931.[1] At the beginning of 1936 the League had virtually closed down, but at the end of the same year it once again boasted 15,000 members.[2] By the end of 1938 membership had gone up to 85,000.[3] In Daghestan, the country par excellence of Moslem fanaticism, the League claimed 49,000 members in 1931, over five per cent of the population, whilst it was admitted six years later that membership was below 1,000.[4] These ups and downs of the League are hard to explain, but it seems fair to assume that its members, and even the native Moslem Soviet officials, were not fully aware of its real significance and programme. Indeed, in 1929 the Ministry of the Interior of the Daghestan Autonomous Soviet Republic made an official enquiry as to whether the League was a religious or a scientific organisation.[5]

Moscow, and Moscow means first of all the Soviet police and the security apparatus, probably had an even poorer opinion of the anti-religious fervour of the local Moslem communists than they deserved. By the second half of the thirties quite a number of native communist officials in Central Asia and Transcaucasia had not only severed every external connection with Islam, but in all probability had broken away from Moslem religion altogether. In many cases the NKVD, always suspicious, did not believe the sincerity of such conversions. It considered that the continued existence of religious life in the Moslem territories was only due to the connivance of communist prime ministers, ministers and party officials of Moslem origin who took mullahs and sheikhs under their protection and secretly favoured the survival of religious superstitions which they publicly condemned. In the end, practically all the prominent leaders of the Soviet Moslems, including the Prime Ministers of Tadzhikistan, Turkmenistan, Uzbekistan, Bashkiria and the Party Secretary of Daghestan were accused of serving foreign intelligence services, and moreover of working hand in

---

[1] *Antireligioznik*, 1931, no. 8, p. 101. [2] *Antireligioznik*, 1936, no. 6, pp. 37-8.
[3] *Antireligioznik*, 1938, no. 12, p. 56.
[4] *Caucasian Review*, Munich 1958, no. 7, p. 48. [5] *Bezbozhnik*, October 10, 1929.

glove with mullahs and ex-mullahs. They were charged with having appointed these religious men to leading posts, sabotaged the work of the League of Militant Godless and built and repaired mosques out of official funds.[1] Some of these charges were quite fantastic and had not the remotest relation to reality, but they indicated the dissatisfaction, if not rage, with which the Kremlin regarded the unsettled situation in the Moslem areas and the survival of Islam in particular. It was clear that the situation required scapegoats, and the police found them in vast numbers. Throughout 1937 and still in 1938 the NKVD discovered one nationalist-clerical conspiracy after another and the alleged conspirators disappeared for ever, irrespective of the high posts they occupied.

The purge of 1937–8 not only served to eliminate those communist leaders who had shown themselves too lenient in the fight against the Moslem religion, but was also directed against certain functionaries who had gone too far in the anti-religious struggle and so helped to bring it into discredit. This was one of the crimes imputed to Akmal Ikramov, the First Party Secretary of Uzbekistan. He and his associates were accused of offending the toiling Moslems by their atheist extremism, particularly by resorting to administrative measures when fighting against the veil.[2] Nearly twenty years after his execution, which took place in March 1938, Ikramov was rehabilitated; and if he was ever over-zealous in his anti-religious campaign, this is now posthumously condoned. Nevertheless, it is significant that the régime found it necessary to pin the excesses of the anti-veil campaign on Ikramov, for this alone would show that ten years after the launching of the 'Hudjum' its success still remained in doubt.

On this point there is a good deal of evidence, going right up to World War II, from Soviet sources. Whenever in 1937, 1938 or even 1939, the League of the Militant Godless or the Communist Party examined the situation in the Moslem areas, especially in Soviet Central Asia, it found that the emancipation of women was suffering constant setbacks or that it was entirely fictional. Even the Moslem women working in the largest industrial undertakings of Central Asia could not be considered emancipated. The 2,000 Tadzhik and Uzbek girls in the Leninabad silk combine nearly all wore the veil.[3] In the textile plant of Tashkent things were little better. There the women workers took off the veil in the factory itself but put it on again when

---

[1] Boris Kandidov, *Tserkov i Shpionazh* (Church and Espionage), Moscow 1938, pp. 94–6.
[2] *Antireligioznik*, 1938, no. 12, p. 14.   [3] *Pravda*, September 15, 1937.

leaving in the evening for their homes on the outskirts of the city.[1] Complaints that husbands forced their wives to wear the veil never ceased. Even attacks on women who had discarded the veil continued to be reported from Uzbekistan, Turkmenia and especially Tadzhikistan, where ten emancipated women were killed in 1939, including the woman activist Rafieva, who was assassinated in Stalinabad by her own husband.[2]

Soviet Islam on the Eve of the 'Great Patriotic War'

The purge of 1937–8, as far as it affected the Moslem problem, was directed not only against communists whose attitude towards religion was too opportunistic or too extremist, but also against many members of the Islamic clergy. Humble mullahs in the Moslem villages of Daghestan, Azerbaidzhan and Tadzhikistan were as savagely victimised as the big sheikhs and imams, who occupied leading positions in the Moslem ecclesiastical administration. The mullahs were charged with petty sabotage of Soviet agriculture, with inciting anti-feminist murders and with joining anti-Soviet bands. The higher Moslem leaders were denounced for much more hideous crimes, such as collecting secret information for the Japanese and German intelligence services, preparing terrorist and diversionist acts, infiltrating into the defence industry for the purpose of sabotage and collusion with the communist inner-party opposition.[3] These and similar accusations were put forward against Mufti Tardzhemanov, the head of the Moslem ecclesiastical administration, which had its headquarters in Ufa, as well as against the Moslem religious leaders of Azerbaidzhan and the Northern Caucasus.

The communists probably overrated the significance of the persecution of the Moslem clergy as much as they had over-estimated the lasting impact of the closing of the mosques. Communists are naturally inclined to consider the strength of an opponent on the basis of the 'cadres' at his disposal and the institutions over which he holds power. However, a few shrewder Soviet observers, mostly ethnographers familiar with Islamic society, had given a timely warning that the hold of religion on a Moslem country could not be measured in terms of numbers of mosques and mullahs.[4] By the beginning of World War II the Soviet authorities were perhaps able to manipulate the younger generation in the Moslem territories more easily than before, but the

[1] *Antireligioznik*, 1938, no. 12, p. 15.　　[2] *Antireligioznik*, 1939, no. 12, p. 31.
[3] *Antireligioznik*, 1938, no. 8–9, p. 66.
[4] *Sovetskaya Etnografiya*, 1932, no. 5–6, p. 190.

middle-aged and older people for the most part still remained under religious influence and observed religious holy days and fasts. Islam remained alive in many ways, tangible and intangible. Traditional places of pilgrimage in the open air replaced the mosques, and ordinary farmers and craftsmen were venerated as 'religious elders' and took the place of mullahs. As the religious life could not find any normal outlet, devout Moslems became more and more interested in miraculous visions and apparitions.

The League of Militant Godless has always been much less well-informed about the extent of the religious survival in the Moslem territories than about the religious situation in the Christian territories of Russia, but occasionally it has produced quite startling disclosures, which showed how strong religious Islam was in virtually every part of Moslem Russia. From Tartaria there came news that religious influences were very much alive among the 'backward sections of the population', whether Moslem or Christian.[1] From Kazakhstan it was reported that there was underground agitation for the re-opening of mosques.[2] About Kirghizia Yemelyan Yaroslavsky himself said that there was no village without believers. Yaroslavsky made known the fact that in Kirghizia the religious enemies of Soviet power had in 1938 as many as 106 mosques, in addition to 43 churches and 102 sectarian houses of prayer. But even in places without mosques or churches there were still groups of faithful.[3]

From the remoter parts of Moslem Russia there came strange tales about the strength of religious fanaticism which illustrated the complete helplessness of anti-religious propaganda and communist indoctrination efforts. In the Pamir mountains, the 'roof of the world', there was in 1939–40 real religious unrest because the local Ismailite Moslems believed that the Aga Khan, their leader, had appeared and given them various instructions. A young man even claimed that the Aga Khan, the 'Living God', as he is also called, had appointed him as his deputy.[4] An anti-religious conference held in Khorog, the capital of the Pamir, in 1940, looked into this matter. It came to the conclusion that the autonomous Pamir province contained 'hundreds of holy places, mosques and shrines visited by both young and old'.[5]

The lowlands of the Tadzhik Soviet Republic to which the Pamir province belongs, also showed great religious fervour right up to the beginning of the war. Bobozhdan Gafurov, Secretary for Agitation and

[1] *Pravda*, July 19, 1940.   [2] *Kazakhstanskaya Pravda*, May 17, 1940.
[3] *Antireligioznik*, 1938, no. 7, p. 23.   [4] *Antireligioznik*, 1939, no. 12, p. 31.
[5] *Kommunist Tadhikistana*, October 22, 1940.

Propaganda of the Communist Party of Tadzhikistan, revealed in 1938 that in one single tiny district of the Tadzhik Republic, that of Ura Tyube, as many as fifty mosques had been counted; of these only twenty-nine were registered with the authorities, whilst twenty-one were illegal.[1] How many such illegal mosques must there have been in all the forty-nine districts of Tadzhikistan, throughout Soviet Central Asia and throughout all the Moslem territories of the Soviet Union?

In 1942, when it was in the Soviet Government's interest to give an optimistic picture of the religious situation in the USSR, the statement was made that there were only 1,312 mosques in the whole territory of the USSR.[2] This was less than half the number of mosques existing up to 1927 in the small territory of Bashkiria alone. This figure of 1,312 mosques was in all likelihood confined to officially registered mosques only. Also in 1942, the Soviet Government informed the world that there were 8,872 mullahs, sheikhs and other Moslem religious dignitaries in the USSR. This figure too was ridiculously low, considering that there were 9,000 clergy in Bashkiria before the religious persecution of the twenties, whilst the clergy of Daghestan numbered 40,000.[3] But again the Soviet Government was in no position to produce any reliable data for it could speak only of those of the clergy who were officially registered, not of the *de facto* and clandestine clergy, about which the authorities had but a vague notion.

This applies, for instance, to the 'seyyids', who exist all over the Moslem world. They are a class of people who consider themselves to be descendants of the Prophet and who are therefore held in especial honour. The ordinary Moslem regards them with awe and values their advice and their services as peacemakers. After their death they are frequently venerated as saints.[4] Seyyids usually live together in villages. Such Seyyid villages still existed in the thirties in Soviet Azerbaidzhan, and this fact prompted an anti-religious writer to say that not the mullahs, but the seyyids were 'the curse' of the country.[5] The mullahs, being class-alien elements, could easily be outlawed, disfranchised and later, when the disfranchising of the clergy ceased, at least supervised. Against the seyyids, who lived the lives of ordinary peasants, the régime was more or less powerless. The authorities resented, in particular, that these seyyids moved about the country and even had the temerity to appear in the proletarian city, Baku, itself. Nobody in Soviet Russia, whether chief mufti or supreme police chief, could have said even

[1] *Antireligioznik*, 1938, no. 12, p. 32.   [2] Soviet War News, May 16, 1942.
[3] Klimovich, *Sotsialisticheskoe stroitelstvo na vostoke i religiya*, p. 57.
[4] Samuel M. Zwemer, *Heirs of the Prophet*, Chicago 1946, p. 112.
[5] *Sovetskaya Etnografiya*, 1932, no. 5–6, p. 190.

approximately how many seyyids and other clandestine Moslem clergy
there existed in the country at any given moment.

All attempts to size up properly the situation on the Moslem religious
front in Soviet Russia also meet with an obstacle in the strange Shiah
Moslem principle of *takiya*, namely, the obligatory concealment of
religious opinions to escape harm, even at the price of assenting to
improper words and actions. Whatever moral objections one may have
to *takiya*, it is certainly a useful weapon in dealing with a hostile secular
power and it may have served Moslem believers well under the Soviet
régime.

Realising the strength of religious survivals in Russia's Moslem areas,
the League of Militant Godless, in the months before the German
invasion, made unprecedented efforts to intensify its work among the
Islamic population. New branches of the League were founded
wherever possible. In Uzbekistan, as many as 100,000 new members
were recruited within two years,[1] and in Tartaria membership went
up from 26,000 in 1938 to 45,000 in 1940.[2] An anti-religious museum
was opened in Tashkent 'containing interesting material on the reactionary role of the Moslem priesthood in Central Asia and their slavish
subservience to the Czarist colonisers'.[3]

The 'Red Muftis'

This new anti-Moslem offensive might have gone to great lengths
had not the nazi invasion of June 22, 1941, forced the Soviet Government to put a stop to all anti-religious propaganda. A new era began in
the relations between the Soviet power and Islam. It cannot be said
without qualification that this new era was better; in some ways it was
more depressing than the preceding one. Up to the war the régime was
clearly out to destroy official institutionalised Islam. As from 1941,
when the new Moslem policy of the Kremlin started, Islam was allowed
to vegetate and by becoming an instrument of government policy forced
to discredit itself in the eyes of the believers.

The Islam which was resurrected in 1941 is an Islam of statements
and appeals in favour of the atheist communist régime. It might be
argued that the same could be said about the Russian Orthodox Church,
the main beneficiary of the new religious policy on which the Kremlin
has embarked since the war. To draw such a parallel would be unfair
and incorrect. In the first place, the Russian Church is naturally
inclined to take up a patriotic attitude towards any Russian state even

[1] *Pravda Vostoka*, February 16, 1941.   [2] *Pravda*, July 19, 1940.
[3] *Pravda*, March 22, 1941.

if it is communist and atheist. The Church may go too far in its loyalty statements and may take an uncharitable attitude towards states more worthy of Christian sympathy than the Soviet Union, but usually there is an element of sincerity in the verbal support which the Patriarchal Church gives to the Soviet Government. This sincerity is extremely doubtful in the case of the Moslem community, to which only minority races belong. Moreover, as far as World War II was concerned, the Russian Orthodox Church leaders had much more reason than the Moslem dignitaries to support the Soviet Government. In a certain sense the Church shared in the victory and was able to extend her jurisdiction as a result of Russia's military triumph. Soviet Islam, on the other hand, was defeated in the war; evidence of this is the wholesale deportation of five Moslem peoples, who may have been small numerically but were passionately devoted to the Islamic faith. Finally, the Russian Orthodox Church obtained for its loyalty a number of genuine concessions. It even became a power in the state, exercising effective spiritual jurisdiction over millions of believers. The concessions which official Soviet Islam obtained in exchange for similar services were minute. It never became a power, only a façade. The leaders of the Orthodox Church, though carrying out a policy of collaboration, and receiving a good deal of official publicity, were nevertheless personalities in their own right. Their Moslem opposite numbers, the 'Red Muftis', as one might call them, were almost entirely created by the Soviet propaganda services. They were generals without soldiers.

The first of the Red Muftis to achieve prominence was Abdul Rahman Rasulayev of Ufa. At the beginning of the war he was described as 'Chief of the Central Council of Islamic Religious Centres in the USSR', but popularly he was called the 'Soviet Mufti'. Especially in the early part of the war, the régime was in need of a man to issue pro-Soviet and anti-Nazi statements on behalf of all the Moslems of the USSR. Rasulayev discharged this task most satisfactorily, but it is doubtful whether he exercised much real jurisdiction outside Bashkiria and Tartaria. Rasulayev's patriotic activity began soon after the nazi invasion. On July 18, 1941, he addressed his first appeal to the Moslems of the Soviet Union, calling on them to 'rise up in defence of their native land, to pray in the mosques for the victory of the Red Army and to give their blessing to their sons, fighting in a just cause'. This was followed up six weeks later by a second appeal, in which Mufti Rasulayev urged the Moslems of the Soviet Union to defend the country 'in the name of religion'.[1]

[1] Stanley Evans, *The Churches of the USSR*, London 1944, p. 158.

Soviet radio transmissions and other Soviet propaganda for foreign consumption took great pains to build up Rasulayev as an important Moslem personality to counter the nazi and axis propaganda for Haj Amin el-Husseini, the Grand Mufti of Jerusalem. In an interview triumphantly published under the heading 'Soviet Mufti exposes Hitler Mufti' Rasulayev denounced his fascist counterpart as a man who had turned traitor to the faith of his ancestors and who voluntarily worshipped the nazi god Wotan.[1]

In May 1942 Rasulayev was the host of a conference of eighty-five sages and spiritual leaders of Islam in the Soviet Union. Its main purpose was to support the war effort by issuing a statement to the faithful, who were told, in the words of the Koran, 'seek not reconciliation with the enemy and thou shalt conquer' and 'kill the enemy wheresoever thou findest him'.[2] At the same conference, so Rasulayev reported later, 'dreadful accounts' were given about nazi atrocities in the Crimea, where the Nazis were accused of the very deeds which the communists had perpetrated before, namely, of having 'wrecked mosques', 'removed holy symbols', 'banned public prayers' and 'outraged national and religious customs in every imaginable way'. They were further charged with having destroyed religious books and with forbidding infants to be named according to Moslem custom.[3] The participants at the Ufa meeting must have been well aware that it was the communists who on the eve of World War II had virtually exterminated Islam in the Crimea, the most Western Moslem territory of the Soviet Union. There was no religious life left which the Nazis could possibly have destroyed in the territory. In fact, Crimean Tartar nationalists secured the opening of about fifty mosques from the German occupation authorities.[4] When the Soviets took the Crimea back from the Nazis these mosques were closed and the entire Crimean Tartar Moslem population was deported to Soviet Asia, particularly to Uzbekistan.

In 1943, Mufti Rasulayev and Ufa, his headquarters, were to lose their leading positions. In October of that year the Moslem clergy and believers of the five Central Asian Soviet Republics held a Congress in Tashkent at which was founded the Ecclesiastical Administration of Moslems of Central Asia and Kazakhstan. This represented the majority of the Moslems of the Soviet Union and became the most important Islamic body of the USSR. In future the Central Asian

---

[1] *Soviet War News*, October 24, 1942.   [2] *Soviet War News*, May 20, 1942.
[3] *Soviet War News*, October 24, 1942.
[4] Edige Kirimal, *Der nationale Kampf der Krimtürken*, Emsdetten 1952, p. 307.

Moslem administration was the main medium for issuing statements in support of Soviet policy. Rasulayev lost his status as the principal spokesman of the Soviet Moslems and two other 'Red Muftis' came increasingly to the fore, namely, the Chairman of the Central Asian Moslem organisation, Mufti Ishan Babakhan Ibn al-Majid Khan, and the Vice-Chairman, his son and successor, Zia al-Din Babakhanov. In May 1944 the Transcaucasian Moslems made themselves likewise independent. They held a congress (Kurultai) in Baku, which was attended by sixty delegates from Azerbaidzhan, Armenia and Georgia. The congress adopted a particularly servile message of allegiance to Stalin, who was described as the 'God-sent and wise head of the Soviet Government'.[1] The founding of a Moslem Council for Transcaucasia led to the emergence of another 'Red Mufti', namely the Sheikh ul Islam Ahund Aga Ali Zade, whom the Soviet Government used chiefly to propagate its point of view among the Shiite Moslems of Persia and Iraq.[2] Yet a further Moslem Council was founded at the end of the war for the Moslems of the North Caucasus and Daghestan. It began its activities under particularly unfavourable auspices, since the Soviet authorities had just deported a very considerable proportion of its potential flock, namely the members of the Balkar, Karachai, Chechen and Ingush peoples. Although these nationalities had primarily incurred the displeasure of the Soviet authorities for alleged co-operation with the Germans, they have always been highly suspect to the communists because of their unswerving adherence to Islam. With the establishment of the three Moslem Councils in Tashkent, Baku and Buinaksk (Daghestan), the jurisdiction of the Ufa Mufti became confined to the Moslems of the Volga-Ural region, Siberia and the Moslem diaspora in the big Russian cities. This restored the situation which had prevailed in Czarist times, when the Mufti of Ufa was the supreme ecclesiastical authority for all Russian Moslems outside Russian Central Asia, Transcaucasia, the North Caucasus region and the Crimea. The institution of the Mufti of Ufa or Mufti of Orenburg, his original title, goes back as far as 1784, when Catherine II was Empress of Russia.

Soviet Islam for Export

The official recognition extended to various Moslem bodies during the war, though born out of the necessities of a wartime situation, also pursued certain long-term objectives. The war saw the expansion of

[1] *Soviet War News*, May 31, 1944.
[2] See Interview with Sheikh ul Islam of Transcaucasia, *Soviet War News*, October 11, 1944.

diplomatic relations between the Soviet Union and a number of
Moslem countries, such as Egypt, Iraq and Syria, as well as a revival
of relations with Saudi Arabia. A loyal Moslem hierarchy spreading
the legend about freedom of Moslem religion in the Soviet Union
could play a most useful part in strengthening Russia's influence in
the Moslem world. The reports about the Moslem Congresses held in
the Soviet Union provided valuable propaganda material for the Soviet
diplomatic missions, particularly in Cairo and Teheran. The favourable
response to these reports showed the Kremlin that Soviet Islam might
prove in future a valuable export article and this is what it became in
the post-war period.

The leaders of the Soviet Moslems, although enjoying little prestige
in the Soviet Union itself, were persistently used by the régime to put
across to the peoples of the East the Soviet propaganda line on every
important topic. The political statements issued by the Moslem bodies
of the USSR and the leading Muftis and Imams on various international
issues are very numerous, and all one can do is to give samples of their
tone and bias. These statements usually contained such forceful
expressions as are characteristic of communist polemical writings on
international affairs. They spoke of 'United States and British warmongers', 'monstrous crimes of American soldiery', and 'American
barbarians committing ever new crimes against humanity' — this
referred to the Korean War.[1] They accused the Western powers of
'flagrantly violating international treaties under the pressure of American
aggressors' and concluding a 'shameful deal' to revive German militarism
in Western Germany.[2] Soviet Moslem statements protested against
NATO, SEATO, the Baghdad Pact and the San Francisco peace
treaty with Japan. They supported every single initiative of the World
Peace Council; all its appeals and all its Congresses. In 1956, they
condemned the Anglo-French—Israeli attack on Suez as a 'shameless
crime committed against the behest of the Most High'.[3] In 1957, they
protested against a 'Turkish armed aggression in Syria' which existed
only in the imagination of Soviet propagandists.[4] Then again in 1958
they denounced the persecution of Algerians as 'the worst possible
crime' and demanded for them the very independence which Moscow
denies to the Moslem peoples of the USSR.[5]

Some of these statements were sent out by the Soviet propaganda
services, but others were read over the radio by the 'Red Muftis' in

[1] Tass report, June 20, 1951.   [2] *Izvestiya*, January 5, 1955.
[3] Tass report, November 11, 1956.   [4] Moscow Radio in Arabic, October 25, 1957.
[5] Moscow Radio in Arabic, October 7, 1958.

Arabic and Persian, so as to enhance their publicity value. Besides being addressed to the Moslems of the non-Soviet Orient generally, they also mentioned by name a number of specific Moslem ecclesiastical dignitaries in other countries. The purely political diatribes contained in the statements were usually interspersed with quotations from the Koran, with the appeal to Allah to punish the enemies of the Soviet Union, to drive the 'dark powers' (Britain and the United States) from the territories of the Arab nations, or even culminated in the wish that Allah would submit Britain, France and Israel to 'tortures'.

For a long time only purely verbal contributions were expected from the Moslem leaders of the Soviet Union, but as Soviet and communist intrigues grew in the Moslem states, more services came to be exacted from the 'Red Muftis'. They had to play their part in welcoming foreign guests from Moslem countries, they were sent on propaganda tours abroad, usually in the guise of pilgrimages, and the Imam of the Moscow mosque was even invited to certain diplomatic functions which Moslem delegations attended. They were allowed to send monetary gifts to Moslems in foreign countries, if this was likely to create a favourable impression, for the victims of the 'Suez aggression' and for the casualties of the floods in Pakistan. A meeting with the Chief Mufti of Central Asia and Kazakhstan became almost a matter of routine for every Moslem statesman going to Tashkent, including President Soekarno of Indonesia, who was there in 1956,[1] and President Gamal Abdel Nasser, who visited the city in May 1958.[2]

The chief mufti whom Nasser saw was Zia al-Din Babakhanov, whom we have already mentioned, and whom one might call the 'Moslem Metropolitan Nikolay', for he has proved to be as versatile and as active a collaborator with the Soviet régime as his Orthodox Christian opposite number. There are few religious figures in the Soviet Union who have been as useful to the Soviet Government as he — first as the real power behind his father, who died in 1957 at the age of ninety-eight, and later as the elected head of the largest Moslem body of the USSR. As Babakhanov has been *persona grata* with the Kremlin he has been able to play a part in various semi-official Soviet organisations such as the 'Soviet Society for Friendship with Arab countries' which was founded in 1958 and to travel abroad on official and semi-official business. He went to Damascus to award the Soviet Peace Prize to a left-wing Syrian sheikh, to Stockholm for a communist-sponsored Disarmament Conference and to Delhi for a World Congress of Religions. He also went to Mecca and Medina on the hajj; permission

[1] *Pravda Vostoka*, September 5, 1956.   [2] *Pravda*, May 5, 1958.

for this being granted by the Soviet Government, not only to Babakhanov but also to quite a number of other Soviet Moslem functionaries.

The resumption of the hajj after many years of interruption was one of the most interesting features of the New Moslem Policy of the Soviets. The first group of Mecca pilgrims were allowed to leave the USSR in November 1944 and since then there were annual pilgrimages until 1947 when a cholera epidemic made the hajj impossible. In the last years of Stalin's lifetime the pilgrimages were stopped again, but under Stalin's successors they have been not merely permitted, but encouraged and surrounded with a great deal of publicity. The Soviet pilgrimages to Mecca never assumed a mass character, but were usually confined to better-known Moslem figures who were collaborating with the Soviet régime and could be trusted to use their trip to the Holy Places for spreading Soviet propaganda. From the official information available it would appear that the Government never granted more than two or three dozen exit permits to would-be pilgrims at a time and those who obtained them were, in all likelihood, most carefully chosen.

The propaganda which Soviet pilgrims carry into the Arab world is of a triple nature. In the first place the Soviet pilgrims proclaim to their co-religionists of other countries that there is full freedom of religion in the Soviet Union, an assertion which not infrequently meets with scepticism among the non-Soviet Moslems.[1] The second task of the pilgrims from Russia is to tell the Moslems of other countries that their brethren in the USSR are wealthy and provided with cultural amenities of every kind.[2] Thirdly, and finally, the pilgrimages are used to boost the Soviet Union as a bulwark of peace and to induce the Moslems all over the world to join the Soviet-sponsored peace campaign. On their way back from the Holy Places the pilgrims have often stopped in Cairo, visiting Al Azhar University and giving press conferences and receptions — all with the obvious intention of creating goodwill for the Soviet Union as a power showing respect to the Moslem religion.

Soviet Post-War Islam on Home Ground

Official institutionalised Islam in the Soviet Union has eked out a precarious existence, but there has been a certain improvement ever since the Kremlin became more active in the affairs of the Middle East. As an immediate result of the new religious policy which Stalin initiated during the war a number of mosques were re-opened. By the end of 1944 mosques existed again in Gorky, Omsk, Novosibirsk and other

[1] *Soviet News*, December 9, 1954.   [2] 'Pilgrims to Mecca', *New Times*, 1953, no. 36.

Russian cities with a Moslem minority, mostly of Tartar nationality. Altogether, Mufti Rasulayev could boast of ten new mosques added to his jurisdiction; this was a small 'bakshish' in return for his policy of total collaboration with the régime. In the years which followed, more mosques were re-opened or had their existence legalised. Polyansky, the Soviet official in charge of the non-Orthodox religious groups, stated in 1947 that there were 3,000 mosques in the Soviet Union, which would have meant an increase of nearly 1,700 since the beginning of the war.[1] The Chief Mufti of Central Asia repeated this figure three years later to foreign visitors.[2] There was a further increase in the number of mosques after Stalin's death and in 1957 Mufti Babakhanov was able to announce the 'recent' opening of fifty 'new grand mosques' in Central Asia alone.[3] In the same year, an official Soviet organ stated that there were about 8,000 'Moslem communities' in the Soviet Union.[4] It does not seem that 'communities' can necessarily be identified with 'mosques' but only with groups of Moslem believers. Details about existing and re-opened mosques are scanty, often unreliable, and contradictory, as oriental statistics usually are, but if the existing data about Soviet Islam in the fifties are treated with caution and checked against one another the following picture emerges:

In a considerable number of predominantly Russian cities the religious spirit of the Moslem minorities has been so strong that the Soviet authorities have been forced to re-open the mosques closed in the years of religious persecution. Of particular importance is the mosque of Ufa, still the main religious centre of European Russia and Siberia, as well as those of Moscow and Leningrad. Prayers in the Ufa mosque are attended by 3,000 to 4,000 people on important holy days. The Moscow mosque can accommodate about 2,500 people and foreign visitors have found it crowded even on ordinary Fridays. It would seem that this one Mosque is insufficient for Moscow's Moslem population, which may be as large as 100,000. The Moscow mosque plays a major part in Soviet propaganda to the Moslem world. Its services are attended regularly by representatives from Moslem diplomatic missions accredited to the USSR Government and it is frequently visited by delegations from Moslem countries.[5] The Moscow Imam is therefore an important personality within the general framework of Soviet Moslem policy. His sermons always have a strong political bias and it stands to reason that he co-operates with the authorities even more closely than other Moslem

---

[1] *Alger Républicain*, October 7, 1947.   [2] *Alger Républicain*, December 20, 1950.
[3] Tass report of October 19, 1957.   [4] *Moscow News*, March 13, 1957.
                              [5] *Moscow News*, March 13, 1957.

dignitaries. The Leningrad mosque, which in Czarist times was built by the Emir of Bokhara, was repaired and re-opened in 1956 at the time when the Soviet régime began to pay more heed to public opinion in the Moslem countries. The régime was quite indifferent to the religious needs of the Leningrad Moslems, but it was not in its interests to ignore the susceptibilities of the foreign Moslem delegations, who often included Leningrad in their itinerary. Small wonder that the Leningrad Imam became a régime propagandist, almost as frequently quoted by the Soviet radio as his opposite number in Moscow.

Facts about Moslem religious life in the Caucasus and Transcaucasia have rarely been released by official Soviet sources and the Shiite Moslems of Azerbaidzhan in particular have been allowed fewer contacts abroad than their Sunnite brethren. From this, one need not conclude that Islam in the Caucasian and Transcaucasian areas is a negligible quantity. Also the observations of foreign travellers are misleading: they refer only to a few places open to visitors, such as Baku, where they have recorded an almost total disappearance of all signs of religion.[1] The Soviet authorities know better. They know that there are 'tenacious religious survivals' among a section of the Baku population and its hinterland, the workers' settlements on the Apsheron Peninsula.[2] The authorities are also aware of the fact that 'illegal' mullahs are going around in the streets of Baku and that they receive in their homes believers to whom they preach and with whom they pray. Very surprisingly, some of the most resourceful illegal mullahs, who even use tape-recordings for their religious seances, are women.[3]

Much more than in the proletarian and internationalised capital of Azerbaidzhan, Moslem religion has maintained itself in the remoter parts of the country never to be visited by a foreigner. There are various 'black spots' on Azerbaidzhan's map where the population is being persistently denounced for its backwardness and its observance of religious customs. These are the areas of the country where women still wear the veil, where the mullahs and religious elders have preserved their influence and where even the communists cannot be trusted. These areas include the Nakhichevan Autonomous Republic which is separated from Azerbaidzhan proper by a wedge of Armenian territory, the towns of Nukha and Kuba in Northern Azerbaidzhan and the three districts of Lenkoran, Lerik and Yardymli in the South-Eastern tip of the country on the Persian border.[4]

The official evidence shows that Azerbaidzhan, years after World

[1] *New York Times*, November 11, 1955.   [2] *Bakinskii Rabochii*, May 25, 1956.
[3] *Bakinskii Rabochii*, September 26, 1959.   [4] *Bakinskii Rabochii*, January 27, 1956.

War II, still remained the country of *takiya*, concealment. The communist authorities in Baku found, time and again, that they could not rely on local functionaries to set a good example to the 'backward population'. Some of these preach atheism in public, but in their own life uphold the religious heritage of their fathers. Whenever such cases of ideological dualism are disclosed, they cause consternation in the communist headquarters; but they also give us real insight into the complexities of the communist struggle against Islam. There was a lecturer on atheist subjects who privately resorted to the services of a mullah to drive out the 'evil spirits' who had taken possession of his boy.[1] There was the case of the First Secretary of a Komsomol town committee who married, according to all the rules and ceremonies prescribed by the Shariat, a woman teacher employed at a teachers' training college.[2] One wonders how many similar incidents may have taken place without receiving publicity in such Soviet newspapers as are available for export. And if these incidents happened in the 'advanced Soviet Republic of Azerbaidzhan' how much more frequent and glaring must they have been among the mountain peoples of the Northern Caucasus, known for their conservatism.

These North Caucasus Moslems may be divided into two groups, those who were deported in 1944 to Central Asia and re-settled in their mountain homeland during and after 1956 and those who were spared this bitter experience, such as Circassians and the peoples of Daghestan. In both groups of North Caucasus Moslems Islam has survived, among the peoples whom Stalin ear-marked for genocide, even to a greater extent than those who remained comparatively unscathed. The Chechens and Ingush were treated for over a decade as pariah peoples; they were used as agricultural labourers on collective and state farms in Kazakhstan, but they were not considered worthy of political indoctrination and frequently their children did not go to school. When they returned to the Caucasus after twelve years of exile, their negative attitude towards Soviet power had not diminished, nor had their adherence to Islam become weaker. The resurrected Chechen-Ingush Autonomous Republic had to cope once again with 'reactionary elements, especially supporters of old customs and the Shariat'.[3] A feature of Moslem religion peculiar to the Chechen-Ingush Republic is the existence of a strange sect called the Kunta Hadji people. The sect was founded by a Moslem sage called Kunta Hadji at the end of the nineteenth century. The Soviet authorities found it difficult to

---

[1] *Bakinskii Rabochii*, December 11, 1952.   [2] *Bakinskii Rabochii*, June 20, 1954.
[3] *Groznenskii Rabochii*, January 31, 1958.

combat the sect for its supporters were mostly poor people who joined the red partisans during the Civil War. Far from declining under Soviet rule the Kunta Hadji sect was able to extend its influence and even survived the deportation of the Chechens to Central Asia. After their repatriation to the Caucasus the sect remained a major problem for the local anti-religious propagandists.

As to the survival of Islam among the non-deported mountaineers, conditions in the comparatively small town of Derbent may be considered typical. The mosque of this town has room for 5,000 people and it is usually filled to capacity on Fridays.[1] From this, conclusions may be drawn as to the liveliness of Moslem religious feeling in the Daghestani mountain villages, where people are far less within the scope of anti-religious propaganda than they are in Derbent. The Soviet authorities seem to be aware of the fact that Islam will continue to have a strong grip on the Daghestani, as long as they remain in their mountain abodes and this seems one of the reasons why in 1958 the Government began the resettlement of certain groups of Daghestani hillmen in the plains.

In Central Asia, where the majority of the Moslem population of the Soviet Union lives, the picture shows considerable local variations. In Kazakhstan, with its strong European population, institutionalised Islam is weaker than in any other Central Asian Soviet Republic. The local ecclesiastical dignitaries themselves admit that there are only twenty-six official mosques in the Republic, most of them in towns such as Alma Ata, Semipalatinsk, Turkestan and Dzhambul. The mosque of Alma Ata, the only surviving one of eighteen, is a small wooden building recognisable as a mosque by the crescent on its highest point. Congregations in the few Kazakh mosques are small even on the big Moslem holy days and confined to old people. This does not necessarily mean that the suppression of Islam in Kazakhstan was more drastic than elsewhere and recovery, therefore, more difficult. The weakness of the Moslem religion in Kazakhstan is largely due to the fact that it never had as deep roots among the previously nomadic Kazakhs as among the settled population of Central Asia, especially that of Uzbekistan.

That country is still the very heart of Central Asian Islam and perhaps of Soviet Islam as a whole. It would even be true to speak of a timid revival of Uzbek Islam. According to the most optimistic estimates by foreign visitors the city of Tashkent contains seventeen large and fifty small mosques, that is less than one-third of the 230 Moslem

[1] Moscow Radio in Arabic, November 23, 1959.

houses of worship which existed on the eve of the first World War. Other estimates put the number of mosques in Tashkent at not higher than ten or even less. During important holy days, as many as 10,000 faithful attend prayer in the Central Mosque of Tashkent, the Tillah Sheikh Mosque, where the Chief Mufti of Central Asia officiates.[1] On ordinary Fridays up to 3,000 people may come to the same mosque.[2]

In Samarkand, that ancient holy city of Islam, only seven mosques have remained open to the public for worship out of 105 which previously existed. It is not so much the mosques which attract the religious fervour of the local Moslems but the Shah-i-Zind Mausoleum. According to a legend, the mausoleum contains the mortal remains of a cousin of Mohammed, Kusam-bin-Abbas, who brought the Islamic religion to Samarkand. For this reason, the Shah-i-Zind, or 'Living Shah', mausoleum has remained one of the most remarkable monuments of Islam in the Soviet Union, despite all official attempts to transform it into something of interest only to scholars, sightseers and tourists. An official Moslem statement which Soviet propaganda services themselves made available to the world, said that as many as 20,000 people assembled in 1954 in front of the Shah-i-Zind mausoleum to celebrate the end of the Ramadan fast.[3]

Very little Moslem religious life is left in the other holy city of Uzbekistan, Bokhara. At the outbreak of the first World War it included within its walls 354 mosques and 138 religious schools. Of these, only four mosques are now open, and one medreseh, the Medreseh Mir-i-Arab, which for several years was the only Moslem teaching establishment in the whole of the Soviet Union. This is all that remains of officially recognised Islam in Holy Bokhara. Many, though by no means all, of the ancient Islamic buildings of Bokhara still exist, but they serve no religious purpose, and the streets in which they are situated are called after the Paris Commune, Lenin, Stalin, Karl Marx, Marat, Klara Zetkin, Thaelmann and other representatives of Western godlessness. There is even a street which is called outright 'Bezbozhnaya', the 'Godless' street.[4]

Most of the other places in Central Asia which are occasionally mentioned as the scenes of important Moslem religious activities on holy days are also situated in Uzbekistan, such as Andizhan, Fergana,

[1] Statement by the Moslem Board of Central Asia and Kazakhstan, Tass report, June 3, 1954.
[2] Peter Scholl Latour, 'Sowjetzentralasien und der Islam', Aussenpolitik, 1959, no. 6, p. 273.
[3] Tass report, June 3, 1954.
[4] Bukhara, Kratkii Spravochnik–Putevoditel, (Bokhara Short Reference and Guide Book), Tashkent 1956, pp. 77–81.

29. Moslems of Tashkent at the Tillah Sheikh Mosque on a Moslem holy day.

30. The congregation of the Moscow mosque in November 1956. The Imam calls upon the faithful to donate money for the 'Egyptian people's aid fund'.

32. The Chief Lama of the Mongolian People's Republic, Erdenpil, in his tent in the Gandang

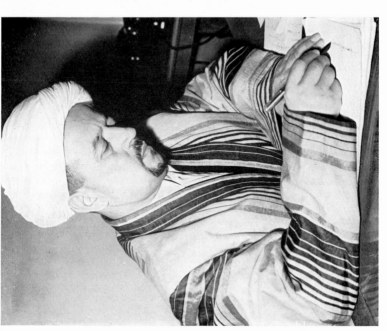

31. Mufti Zia-al-Din Babakhanov, head of the Moslem organisation of Central Asia.

Kokand, Khiva and Chimbai in the KaraKalpak Autonomous Republic. All these towns have mosques attracting a considerable number of worshippers. Religious life also seems comparatively strong in Tadzhikistan. Between 6,000 and 10,000 devout Moslems have been reported as attending service on special occasions in the Shah Mansur mosque of Stalinabad.[1] Whilst these figures were triumphantly quoted to foreign audiences, a 'home consumption' account stated with regret that the Stalinabad mosque was visited by 'youths and girls' and that even children of school age were brought there.[2]

The real bulwark of religious life in Central Asia is not the towns but the countryside, over which the official Moslem administration with its headquarters in Tashkent has very little influence. Official Soviet reports show that the Moslem religion is firmly entrenched in the Central Asian village and the Central Asian collective farm. There is a large number of 'unregistered but active mosques', the existence of which the authorities ignore, since administrative measures against them might stir up local discontent and trouble. 'Many dozens' of such illegal mosques were discovered in one Province of Kirghizia alone.[3] The situation is not very different in Tadzhikistan, where Western tourists were informed that there was a mosque in virtually every 'kishlak' (village), and in Turkmenistan, where the Soviet press and radio warned the peasants against obeying the Moslem clergy when they called upon them to pray and carry out religious rites.[4]

The 'unregistered' mosques are served by an illegal or semi-legal clergy and there are also many itinerant preachers and roving mullahs unattached to mosques and catering for collective farmers in their homes.[5] Some of these mullahs also preach in the open air and attract vast audiences. The authorities take a serious view of such illegal religious meetings and even during Khrushchev's liberal era did not hesitate to put such popular preachers under lock and key. In Turk menistan two of them were sentenced to twenty and seventeen years in gaol respectively.[6] This is in striking contrast to the pliable and opportunistic attitude of the officially recognised muftis and imams. Even some collective farm chairmen have realised what a power the Moslem clergy still represents in the Central Asian village. On some occasions, they have enlisted the mullah's support to raise labour discipline and to increase the output of their kolkhoz. Whenever such instances of

[1] Moscow Radio in Arabic, May 13, 1956.
[2] *Kommunist Tadzhikistana*, July 27, 1958.
[3] *Sovetskaya Kirgiziya*, April 19, 1959.
[4] Ashkhabad Radio: talk, 'Islam and its reactionary role', August 12, 1954.
[5] *Sovetskaya Kirgiziya*, ibid.   [6] *Turkmenskaya Iskra*, July 25, 1958.

P

collaboration between kolkhoz management and Moslem rural clergy came to light, they were bitterly resented by the higher communist authorities.[1] How could one ever hope to stamp out Islam in the Central Asian village, if even the kolkhoz chairman recognised the mullah's authority? Some of the village muftis astonish the authorities not only by their influence over the people but even by their spirit of enterprise. Even after four decades of Soviet rule it was possible for a mullah in Kirghizia to find the courage to transform a Soviet elementary school into a mosque. Obviously such a bold action could not have been carried out by the mullah alone without the assistance of a section of the population or without the connivance of some local communists. Indeed, when the mullah was finally compelled to give up the school building he received sufficient help from the people of the surrounding villages to build a mosque, and among the friends of the mullah there was even the secretary of a party organisation. He was found among the gathering at a religious feast (toi), where the Koran was recited.[2]

Holy Places

From the communist point of view Islam is a many-headed monster. The official mullahs and their mosques are perhaps the least obnoxious head. The main foe is the popular piety of the simple Moslem, which expresses itself in countless religious observances and taboos. A study of Soviet anti-religious literature pertaining to Islam shows which of these practices worries the authorities most. It is the cult of the 'Holy Places' and the cult of the 'mazars' or sacred tombs. Soviet anthropologists have described the cult as pre-Islamic rather than Moslem. They assert that only the name of the venerated saint and the legend connected with him belongs more or less to Islam, but many of the actions carried out during the pilgrimages have their roots in more ancient beliefs. These beliefs are influenced by animistic concepts and magic elements connected with the cult of nature.[3] That the cult of the sacred tombs results from a mixture of Islamic and pre-Islamic beliefs is no consolation for the authorities, who are faced with the existence of 'Holy Places' all over Central Asia and Azerbaidzhan. People attribute to pilgrimage and to the mazars, miraculous effects. They believe that sickness or health, rain or drought depends on the saints they worship. To some mazars reverence is paid because the saint in question might help in the case of an eye-disease, others are mostly

---

[1] D. Kishbekov, *O feodelno-baiskikh perezhitkakh i ikh preodolenii* (On feudal-bai survivals and how to overcome them), Alma-Ata 1957, pp. 55–6.
[2] *Sovetskaya Kirgiziya*, ibid.   [3] *Sovetskaya Etnografiya*, 1957, no. 2, pp. 61–7.

visited by women suffering from barrenness. Earth from the tombs of
the saints is considered miraculous, and healing qualities are attributed
to it.

It is usually the Soviet press itself which draws attention to the
popularity of certain pilgrimages by complaining about the crowds
thronging certain mazars and Holy Places, for instance, the Mazar of
Hodja-Obi-Garm and the Gissar fortress, both in Tadzhikistan,
Kunya-Urgench in Northern Turkmenistan and, of course, Shah-i-Zind
in Samarkand, which has already been mentioned. Also in Samarkand
there is a huge marble stand for the Koran in the yard of the Bibi
Khanum mosque. There women can be seen crawling in the hope that
they will be able to bear children afterwards. Almost in the same class
as Shah-i-Zind as a pilgrimage centre is the mausoleum of Ahmed
Yassaui in the town of Turkestan, which belongs to the Kazakh Soviet
Republic. Yassaui, a Moslem Saint and author of learned religious
works, died in the second half of the twelfth century and Tamurlane
built a magnificent mosque in his honour. The Soviet authorities
closed the mosque but they could not prevent Yassaui's fame continuing
to attract many thousands of pilgrims every year. They hold their
devotions not far from the mausoleum in a smaller nearby mosque
which the State has left to the believers.[1]

Also the mountain called 'Takht-i-Sulayman' (Throne of Solomon)
near the town of Osh in Kirghizia enjoys great popularity with devout
Moslems, who believe that King Solomon prayed and died there. It is
thought to be a miraculous mountain where people expect to be cured
of all sorts of ills. The Soviets were unable to stamp out the cult of
Takht-i-Sulayman and even in the late fifties there were still about
twenty sheikhs living there guiding the steps of pilgrims and advising
them how to make the best of their visit to the mountain.[2]

The cult of the 'Holy Place', widespread in Central Asia, has remained
an important feature also in the local religious life of Azerbaidzhan.
Even the young Soviet generation, including members of the Young
Communist League, were reported to take part in pilgrimages.[3] The
tomb of a local saint called 'Mohammed effendi', near the town of
Nukha, continued to attract wedding processions long after the Second
World War and many 'Soviet brides' have prayed there before setting
out to the home of their bridegrooms.[4] This was not an isolated local
occurrence, for in 1957 Mustafayev, the Azerbaidzhani Party Secretary,
urged 'public organisations and party activists' to 'put an end to the

[1] *Partiinaya Zhizn Kazakhstana*, 1959, no. 8, p. 32.   [2] *Sovetskaya Kirgiziya*, ibid.
[3] *Bakinskii Rabochii*, August 27, 1954.   [4] *Bakinskii Rabochii*, June 20, 1954.

worship of Holy Places'.[1] Similar prohibitions of pilgrimages had also been suggested for various parts of Central Asia. In some instances the prohibitions were actually carried out 'on popular request'. The authorities also tried to undermine faith in the power of the various Moslem saints by conducting anti-religious propaganda near the monuments and mazars which are the object of special veneration. Yet another way of discouraging the pilgrimages is to take administrative measures against the self-appointed guardians of the 'Holy Places' and to expel them under various pretexts from the district where the saint's tomb is situated.

The most awkward aspect of the problem of the 'Holy Places' from the communist point of view is that it is not a 'survival of the past' which is doomed slowly but surely to die out. In fact, new 'Holy Places' have come into being during the Soviet era, such as the tomb of the Seyyid Ali Et-Aga in a village near Baku. Ali Et-Aga died in 1950 and the people now venerate him as a saint, even though the professional anti-religious propagandists have denounced him as a 'sorcerer' who had speculated for many years in ignorance and super-stition.[2] In 1957, another new 'Holy Place' appeared near the town of Tashkent by the roadside, where a young man had been killed by lightning.[3]

Observance of Holy Days and Other Moslem Customs

Pilgrimages to the Holy Places usually reach their climax at the birthdays of the saints whose tombs are visited by the faithful, and during the great Moslem fasts and holy days. The observance of these holy days by the Soviet Moslems has always worried the communist State as much as the cult of the mazars. The fight against the observance of the principal Moslem holy day, the Kurban Bayrami, 'The Feast of the Sacrifice', which is also called Kurban Ait or Id al-Adha, has been characteristic of the atheist campaign in Moslem territories, just as the fight against Christmas and Easter was characteristic of anti-God propaganda in the Christian parts of the Soviet Union. In addition to Kurban Bayrami, Soviet atheist propagandists have always violently denounced Ramadan, the month of fasting when devout Moslems eat only during the night. Both Kurban Bayrami and Ramadan have been fought by the régime with every means communist propaganda has been able to design: satirical poems, pungent cartoons, mass meetings and plays performed on the stage. The great day of mourning of the

[1] *Bakinskii Rabochii*, April 6, 1957.   [2] *Literaturnaya Gazeta*, July 11, 1959.
[3] L. I. Klimovich, 'The Cult of Saints in Islam', *Nauka i Zhizn*, no. 9, 1958.

Shiite Moslems, the tenth day of the Moslem month of Moharram, also came in for bitter attack.[1] On this day the Shiites commemorate the death of Hussein and Hassan, the sons of Calif Ali and the chief martyrs of the Shiah faith. The day used to be observed by mourning processions, called 'Shakhsei-Vakhsei' during which the participants indulged in ghastly forms of self-mutilation. It was therefore by no means immoral for the communist Government to prohibit the processions. Persia, the Shiite country par excellence, did the same. However, the Soviet régime was not satisfied with putting an end to a savage centuries-old religious practice, but exploited the processions to vilify the Shiite creed and to question the entire spiritual basis of Islam. Other Moslem holy days did not supply Soviet propaganda with such convenient anti-religious arguments as the Tenth of Moharram, nor could they be banned. They continued to be supported by hundreds of thousands and even millions of Soviet Moslems. Soviet propaganda had to make a virtue of an awkward situation by advertising the widespread celebration of Kurban Bayrami in the Soviet Union as evidence of the religious freedom alleged to exist under communist rule.

Communist opposition to the observance of Kurban Bayrami is motivated not only by atheist arguments but also by the damage it is said to cause to the national economy. This 'harm' results from the non-appearance of the Kurban Bayrami observers at their work and from the mass-slaughter of livestock which is offered as a sacrifice to Allah. The Soviet press has not infrequently recorded how many sheep or head of cattle this or that collective farm or rural district wasted on the Kurban Bayrami observance. Also the month of Ramadan comes in for criticism not only as a religious fast but also for having a deleterious effect on people's health and so decreasing their ability to work properly.

The Moslem administration for Central Asia and Kazakhstan has skilfully countered the arguments put forward against both the Kurban Bayrami and the fast of Ramadan. A decree (fatuah), which the Tashkent Chief Muftiate issued in 1954 ruled that the slaughtering of livestock on the occasion of Kurban Bayrami was not obligatory, and that prayers in the mosque during religious holidays should take place early in the morning, before the beginning of agricultural work. As to the Ramadan fast, another decree of the Moslem leaders of Soviet Central Asia stipulated that it should not apply to sick people, travellers, nursing-mothers, and persons engaged in heavy manual labour.[2]

---

[1] D. Hadjibeyli, *Antiislamistkaya propaganda i yeyo metody b Azerbaidzhane* (Anti-Islamic propaganda and its methods in Azerbaidzhan), Munich 1959, pp. 24–36.
[2] Kishbekov, op. cit., pp. 60–1.

As the old arguments against the Moslem feasts became outdated the communists looked for other and more constructive ways to oust them. They introduced local secular or rather agricultural holidays, in Bashkiria and Tartaria the 'Feast of the Plough' ('Sabantui'), in Daghestan the Festivals of Spring, of Flowers, of the Cherry-tree and the First Furrow, and in Uzbekistan the Feast of Cotton-growers ('Pakhta-Bayrami'), for which a great success was claimed, from the time of its introduction in 1956.[1]

The régime finds it equally difficult to wipe out other Moslem customs still stubbornly adhered to by many Moslems of the Soviet Union. Circumcision is one of the customs which die hard. Even communists have attached great importance to having their children circumcised and when challenged by the authorities they have denied that circumcision had any religious significance. They claim to carry it out for hygienic or traditional reasons. The Party, always suspicious of religious survivals, has never condoned the widespread practice. From the very beginning it has stated most emphatically that there could be no 'Red Circumcision' and that the practice was reactionary even if only party members were invited to the family feast celebrating the occasion.[2] The basic communist ideological objection to circumcision is that it produces a physical difference between Moslems and people of another faith. However, communist writers themselves have admitted that this argument is untenable since circumcision has been practised not only by Moslems and Jews but by many peoples who have nothing to do with Judaism or Islam such as Polynesian or American ethnic groups.[3]

In line with Koranic teaching Russian Moslems also continue to regard the pig as an unclean beast. Moslem collective farmers can only with difficulty be persuaded to keep pigs, however much the Government tells them that pig-breeding is the most profitable branch of animal husbandry. In one Kazakh district (Suzak) pig-breeding was not introduced until 1956.[4] Even Moslem cattle-breeders who are prepared to supply pigs to the state will not consent to eat pork-meat themselves.

Religious and Anti-Religious Training in Moslem Territories

Soviet policy towards Islam in the period after World War II was no longer endeavouring to smash the Moslem religion by drastic action but to destroy it by a systematic anti-Islamic indoctrination of the people. The régime thought it could achieve its purpose by means

---

[1] *Nauka i Religiya*, op. cit., p. 342.   [2] *Pravda Vostoka*, 1927, no. 277.
[3] *Nauka i Religiya*, February 1960, no. 2, p. 43.   [4] Kishbekov, op. cit., p. 57.

of an army of anti-Moslem agitators and flood of anti-religious pamphlets, books and newspaper articles, to which the devout Moslems could oppose only a small handful of theologically-trained persons and practically no religious literature whatever. However, the suppression of all Moslem theological training and of all Moslem literature seemed inadvisable. Both were necessary to keep up the pretence that there is equality in religious matters for Moslems and Christians. Both served Soviet propaganda abroad and the only two Medresehs of the Soviet Union, the Mir-i-Arab Medreseh of Bokhara and the Barak Khan Medreseh of Tashkent, became important show places for foreign visitors. Although a large number of foreigners have inspected the two establishments, information about them is vague and contradictory. The Bokhara Medreseh was the first to be opened and the Tashkent Medreseh, though planned since 1948, was not inaugurated until 1956. Since then, Moslem theological students have spent only the first five years of their training in Bokhara, making their final studies in Tashkent. The curriculum of Bokhara includes 'Tafsir', the interpretation of the Koran; 'Mashkat', the study of the prophets; history of Islamic Law; Soviet constitution; Russian and Uzbek, which is the mother-tongue of about half the students.[1]

One of the most striking features of the curriculum at the Bokhara Medreseh is the great attention it pays to the study of the Arabic language. Over one-third of the time (4,392 out of 12,081 hours) throughout the five-year course is devoted to Arabic. The language is taught in three separate sections — morphology, syntax, and practical conversation. The fact that so much Arabic is taught in the resuscitated Medreseh Mir-i-Arab may suggest that at least a certain number of the graduates are to be used by the régime for the conduct of Soviet propaganda in the Arab world. It is also interesting that the curriculum devotes 384 hours to Persian, which was not taught in the higher Moslem schools existing in pre-Soviet times.[2] So the teaching of this language in the Medreseh Mir-i-Arab may likewise serve objectives which have nothing to do with the official religious purpose of the school.

In all likelihood the student body of the two Medresehs contains both régime agents and devout religious young people with genuine vocations. That the latter category should exist at all displeases the authorities and the Turkmenian Communist Party chief once stated regretfully that

---

[1] Other nationalities are represented among the students in the following order: Tadzhiks, Tartars, Kazakhs, Kirghiz and Turkmenians.
[2] *Oriente Moderno*, August–September 1954, p. 403.

'some young people, educated in our Soviet schools, go to study in Moslem ecclesiastical training establishments'.[1] In reality the Soviet leaders have little reason to worry about the two Medresehs, for the number of their students is small. In the case of the Mir-i-Arab Medreseh it has never exceeded the 100 mark and in the case of the Barak Khan Medreseh it is smaller still.

The situation is even more precarious for Moslem religious literature than it is for Moslem religious training. After World War II it was announced that the Central Asian Moslem administration was publishing a journal of its own, but only two copies of it seem to have appeared. Apart from this short-lived publishing venture, Soviet sources have reported from time to time the existence of annual Moslem calendars which come out in Tashkent in editions ranging from 2,500 to 10,000 copies and a book *Islam and Worship* in the Tartar language written by the Mufti of Ufa and comprising sixty-eight pages.[2] In addition, two editions of the Koran were printed, one in Ufa and one in Tashkent. The Tashkent edition came out in fewer than 5,000 copies. Although Moslems in Russia itself have difficulty in obtaining the 'Soviet Koran', 'many copies' of it have been presented to foreign Moslem visitors or sent to Moslem religious leaders in foreign countries.[3]

Anti-religious propaganda in the Moslem territories of the Soviet Union has been concentrated since 1947 in the hands of the All-Union Society for the Dissemination of Scientific and Political Knowledge. The propaganda has had its ups and downs and there has been periodic criticism that not enough was done to spread atheism among the local people. The anti-religious work of the Society in the Moslem areas is not very different from what it is in other parts of the Soviet Union. It publishes atheist pamphlets, mostly translated from the Russian into Uzbek, Tartar, Kazakh, Tadzhik and other languages spoken by Soviet Moslems. The Society also trains anti-religious lecturers in seminaries and these lecturers are expected to impart their newly-acquired knowledge to a wider public. The training of anti-Islam experts in the Soviet Union was greatly stepped up in 1956, when two big inter-Republic, anti-religious conferences were held in Moslem Russia, one in Baku for the Caucasian and Transcaucasian territories and the other in Tashkent for the Central Asian Republics. In the following years it was considered that the seminaries and lectures alone were insufficient and that more

[1] *Turkmenskaya Iskra*, February 17, 1957.
[2] *Soviet News*, March 23, 1957. See also C. Quelquejay, 'Documentation sur la Religion Musulmane en Union Soviétique depuis 1945', *Cahiers du Monde Russe et Soviétique*, May 1959, no. 1, p. 187.
[3] Moscow Radio in Turkish, February 13, 1959.

permanent atheist propaganda institutions were required. In Alma Ata a so-called 'House of the Atheist' was established. In Baku an 'Atheist's Study' ('Kabinet ateista') was set up in the city's 'House of Political Education'. In Ashkhabad a 'University of Scientific Atheism' was founded, the first to be opened in the Soviet Union after World War II.[1] All these institutions aimed at making Soviet anti-Moslem propaganda more varied, more detailed, more hard-hitting.

With the passing of time anti-religious propaganda in Moslem territories has not become any easier. If non-Moslems conduct this propaganda they are bound to be ineffective and even atheist agitators coming from a Moslem family may fail and be misunderstood by the comparatively unsophisticated audiences which they address. People in the Orient want to hear stories and the Oriental communist lecturer in the attempt to make his talk more attractive may be carried away and describe religious festivals and rites and talk about the 'legends of the Koran'. He is doing this, of course, with the intention of refuting the Moslem religion, but he has lost his case. The more he seems to know about Islam, the more will the audience shower him with questions as to how one should celebrate this or that Moslem festival or for what reason this or that Moslem prophet or saint is famous. So instead of promoting the cause of atheism, an atheist lecturer may involuntarily contribute towards the spread of religious propaganda. The champions of atheism in Moslem Russia themselves are painfully aware of the fact that, unless they are extremely careful, they may show the people the way to Allah and Mohammed.[2]

Summing-up on Soviet Islam

If one glances back over the many years during which the Soviet communists have fought Islam one easily discovers that much of the fight has been concentrated on the secondary aspects of the Moslem religion; the veil of the Moslem women; the pilgrimage to a sacred tomb, often of doubtful historicity; the wasteful ways in which Moslem feasts are celebrated; circumcision often carried out in unhygienic conditions. These seem to be the main targets of communist anti-Moslem propaganda. At first glance, Communism does not come out too badly from this battle. It appears as the advocate of light against darkness, as the defender of a new progressive and hygienic way of life against reaction and obscurantism. However, the questions of detail to which Communism gives prominence in its struggle against Islam only

[1] *Kommunist Turkmenistana*, October 1958, p. 63.
[2] *Turkmenskaya Iskra*, February 7, 1958.

confuse the picture. Communism is not concerned with the abolition of certain religious practices but with the extermination of religion itself. The real communist targets are not the things which provide convenient short-term anti-religious arguments, such as the excesses of the Shakhsei-Vakhsei processions and the harm to health caused by the fast of Ramadan. The real target is the central idea and message of the Koran, that there is one God, merciful and compassionate, 'The sovereign of the heavens and the earth, the witness of all things and the all-knowing, all-powerful creator of all things.' It is the mighty Allah, says the Koran, 'who on the Day of Judgment will reward the righteous and the believers and punish the unbelievers.' The Koran is not a dead book for the devout Moslems who read it in Russia. It has a topical meaning which must give them the strength to resist the atheist onslaught. It tells the sons of the Prophet in Russia that the rule of unbelief is transitory. 'The unbelievers', says the great Moslem Book, 'expend their riches in debarring others from the path of Allah. Thus they dissipate their wealth, but they shall rue it, and in the end be overthrown. The unbelievers shall be driven into Hell.' There are many similar passages in the Koran all urging Moslems to show patience and fortitude and assuring them of the final triumph of belief over unbelief.

However, Moslem faith in Russia is able to derive nourishment from sources which are not only purely spiritual. Islam is a world religion, and what happens in one part of the Moslem world cannot remain without effect on other lands and peoples with a Moslem background. The emergence of so many new states in which Islam is a powerful factor, the new role of the Moslem religion as a link between the peoples of Asia and Africa, the prestige which certain Moslem statesmen enjoy in the USSR, notwithstanding their attachment to the faith of Mohammed — all this is pleasing to Russia's religious-minded Moslems. At the same time the growing importance of the Moslem world is bound to exercise a certain influence even on such Soviet Moslems as have thrown religion overboard. Even some of the younger 'Soviet Moslem' intellectuals who are committed to the communist atheist cause may see themselves compelled to reconsider their attitude towards Islam. They must ask themselves whether the Moslem religion, which supplies a strong spiritual backbone to the various Afro-Asian national emancipation movements, can be so simply dismissed as a 'reactionary' ideology. These intellectuals may yet grow proud of their Islamic heritage and become prepared to accept Moslem religion in a modernised and enlightened form, an Islam without the Shariat. The example of modern Turkey may perhaps prove not without relevance to the Moslems of the USSR. Their communist leaders consciously imitated the policy of extreme and fanatical secularisation which young Kemalist Turkey carried out in the twenties and thirties. Having reached a more mature stage in its development, official Turkey became reconciled with Islam and, without losing the character of a modern state, once again granted it an honourable status in Turkish society. Such a development may be desirable also for the Soviet Moslem territories but it could happen there only in the event of a far-reaching liberalisation of the Soviet régime. The Moslem countries which acquired their national independence more recently have an even greater lesson to teach the Soviet Union and the Soviet Moslems than the Turkish Republic has. The example of the young Moslem states shows that the transformation of Moslem society can proceed without any anti-religious bias at all and without any hardships to the individual believers. Tunisia in particular has tackled in a painless way all the revolutionary changes which in the Moslem territories of the Soviet Union were achieved only at the price of very heavy sacrifices. The Tunisian government has relaxed the Ramadan fast, emancipated Moslem women and secularised education but at the same time preserved everything which is timeless in the Moslem heritage and Moslem spiritual values.

XIV

Buddhism

―――

The Soviet attitude towards Buddhism has been in many respects similar to the Soviet approach to Islam; which means that Russian communist hostility towards the Buddhist religion has been tempered by opportunism. Winning Asian support has seemed at times more important to the Kremlin than conducting an all-out attack on Buddhist beliefs and institutions.

It took the Soviet communists several years to work out a proper Marxist-Leninist approach to Buddhism, and the longer the Soviet State lasted the more hostile did the official Soviet view of Buddhism become. The first edition of the *Large Soviet Encyclopaedia* still admitted that the philosophy of Buddhism contained 'individual elements of great value'.[1] The second edition of the same Soviet work of reference, published after World War II, no longer made this concession. Its rejection of Buddhism was unqualified. The communist analysis of Buddhism, like the communist evaluation of any other religion, moves within the narrow limits of a proletarian utilitarianism which attempts to explain the supernatural in terms of a materialistic ABC. Thus, the *Soviet Encyclopaedia* describes the Buddhist doctrine of reincarnation as serving to protect the interests of the ruling classes and to stifle the class protest of the toiling masses. Particularly objectionable from the communist point of view is the Buddhist rejection of violence, which is incompatible with communist revolutionary tactics. In the communist view, Buddhism, by preaching non-resistance to force, defends the coercion of the oppressed by the exploiters and serves as the ideological weapon of the oppressors.[2] Soviet scholarship claims priority in discovering 'the roots, the historical path and the reactionary nature of Buddhism' and in pointing out 'its true role in the exploitation of the toiling masses'.[3] Soviet communists have

―――

[1] *Large Soviet Encyclopædia*, first edition, vol. vii, Moscow 1927, pp. 777–92.
[2] *Large Soviet Encyclopædia*, second edition, vol. vi, Moscow 1951, p. 229.
[3] *Large Soviet Encyclopædia*, second edition, ibid.

identified Buddhism with every enemy of the Soviet Union and of
Communism in Asia — at first with Japanese militarism, then with the
'Anglo-American imperialists' — in particular with the American
occupation authorities in Japan — and also with the 'Kuomintang
reactionary clique'.

In Soviet Russia itself the problem of Buddhism is of minor importance if we take as our yardstick numbers alone. Buddhists in the Soviet
Union have never exceeded half a million people, but in proportion to
their numbers the Soviet Buddhists have suffered at least as much as
any other religious group under Soviet rule. The combined national
and religious persecution inflicted on the Buddhist peoples of the
Soviet Union may be considered as something unsurpassed. There are
three distinct Buddhist peoples under Soviet rule. The first and most
important are the Buryat-Mongols living near Lake Baikal in Eastern
Siberia. Since 1938 they have no longer been included in a single
administrative territory but have been split up between the Buryat-
Mongol Autonomous SSR, which comprises the bulk of the Buryat-
Mongol people, the Ust-Ordynsk National Okrug in the Irkutsk
Province and the Aga National Okrug in the Province of Chita. The
last-mentioned is of particular importance to us as it contains within
its boundaries one of the main centres of Buddhism in the Soviet Union.
In 1958 the name of the Buryat-Mongols was changed to Buryats and
the name of their territory from Buryat-Mongolia to Buryatia, presumably because it was felt that the old term encouraged pan-Mongolian
and pan-Asian trends among local intellectuals.

The second Buddhist people are the Kalmucks who, together with
Volga Germans, Crimean Tartars and various Moslem nationalities of
the Caucasus, were among Soviet Russia's pariah nations in the last
years of Stalin's lifetime. Having languished in Siberia for over twelve
years they were re-allocated in 1957 the area South-West of the Volga
Delta which they had previously occupied. Since 1958 this territory
has been known once more as the 'Kalmuck Autonomous Republic'.
Finally, there are the Tuvinians, annexed by Soviet Russia in 1944 and
living in the Tuvinian Autonomous Province, originally an integral part
of the Chinese empire.

Even this short enumeration of the three Buddhist peoples of the
USSR shows that their lot has been harder than that of any other
cultural-religious group of Soviet nationalities. One Buddhist people
had its territory dismembered and was forced to change its name, the
second was decimated by deportations and narrowly escaped complete
genocide, and the third lost its independence under Soviet rule. The

religion of these three peoples suffered even more grievously than their national aspirations.

Buryat Buddhism before the Communist Offensive

Buddhism penetrated into Buryat-Mongolia from the seventeenth century onwards, but it was only in 1712 that Tibetan missionaries arrived in the country in large numbers. Buddhism came to the Buryats in the form in which it ultimately triumphed both in Tibet and in Mongolia proper, namely, in that of the Ge-luk-pa or Yellow Hats sect. Being connected with Buddhism primarily through Tibet and to a lesser extent through Mongolia the Buryat converts became part of the spiritual empire of the Dalai Lama. It was Russian overlordship over Buryatia and the expansion of Russian missionary work which prevented the country from becoming a theocracy like Tibet or Outer Mongolia. Buddhism or Lamaism never became the religion of the entire Buryat people. About fifty thousand Buryats, or about one-fifth of the whole nation, became Christians, even if only superficially converted, and at least ten thousand remained attached to Shamanism, the old Buryat religion.

In Buryatia as in Tibet the monasteries became the most important expression of the Buddhist faith and the chief instrument of its power. The year 1741, which saw the foundation of the first two monasteries in the Russian Transbaikal region, was therefore one of the most important landmarks in the history of Buryat-Mongol Buddhism. The two monasteries of Tsongol and Gusinoe Ozero (Goose Lake) were both situated close to the present capital of Buryatia, Ulan Ude, the former Verkhneudinsk. They became the spiritual and administrative centres of Buddhism in Russia and served in turn as the seat of the Chief Lama of the Buryat Buddhists. Gusinoe Ozero fulfilled this function until 1930 when the monastery ceased to exist. The hierarchical head of Buryat-Mongol Buddhism — the Bandido Hambo Lama — received recognition by the Russian Government in 1764 and from then on Buddhism continued to gain in influence until the communists launched their full-scale anti-religious offensive at the end of the twenties.

Generally speaking, it would be true to say that the history of Buryat-Mongol Buddhism is the history of its monasteries ('datsans'). The latter were at the same time spiritual institutions and centres of learning; they provided health services and in a sense they even formed the political backbone of the Buryat-Mongol people. In the end there was an entire network of ecclesiastical schools closely connected with the monasteries. In addition to schools for children, called 'shadda', there was a type of school of a more monastic character, the 'dubda', where a limited number of adults obtained training. The highest level of learning was reached by the 'tsanit' faculty, specialising in the study of Buddhist religion and philosophy, whilst the 'manba' faculty trained the doctors of Tibetan medicine.[1]

Without taking into account the power, influence and prestige of the 'datsans', the magnitude of the struggle between Communism and Buddhism cannot be properly understood. Considering the numerical smallness of the Buryat-Mongol people, Buryat Buddhism was perhaps the best organised religious force in the whole Soviet Union. The original strength of lamaism, namely, its branching out into the fields of education and medicine, which made it such a powerful factor in the life of the people, ultimately turned out to be its weakness when facing communist totalitarianism. Total destruction was the inescapable fate of a religion which was so firmly entrenched on the institutional side as Buryat-Mongol Buddhism.

Let us first give a short survey of the 'assets' which the Buddhist community possessed on the eve of the communist accession to power and in the first years of the Soviet régime. Only then can we appreciate the magnitude of the losses which the Buddhists of Buryat-Mongolia suffered. In 1917, the Buddhists had as many as thirty-seven monasteries of various sizes. The largest included the two already mentioned, the Tsongol Datsan and the Datsan of Gusinoe Ozero, as well as the Aga Datsan near Chita, founded in 1811, which ranked first from the educational point of view. Each of these datsans had about a thousand inmates. The Czarist Government when issuing its 'Ordinance concerning the Lama Clergy in Eastern Siberia' in 1853 provided the datsans with land, the Datsan of Gusinoe Ozero with 1,500 desyatins (4,050 acres), and the two others with 1,400 desyatins each (3780 acres.)[2] The Datsan of Atsagat, with three hundred inmates, was particularly famous for its school of Tibetan medicine. On the other hand there were also some very small datsans, especially those of the Irkutsk Province, where Buddhism is weak as a result of the evangelising activities of Orthodox Christian missionaries. Less than ten people each were attached to the Irkutsk datsans, which are more comparable to churches than to actual monasteries. The total number of lamas on

[1] N. N. Bogdanov, *Ocherki Istorii Buryat-Mongolskogo Naroda* (Essays on the history of the Buryat-Mongol People), Verkneudinsk 1926.
[2] *Istoriya B.M.A.S.S.R.* (History of the B.M.A.S.S.R.), Ulan Ude 1954, p. 214.

the eve of the 1917 Revolution was 14,000, a more than threefold increase since the middle of the nineteenth century, when it was 4,546.

The Early Years of Soviet Power

The year 1917 did not mark the beginning of Soviet rule over Buryatia. Until the end of 1922, the land of the Buryats was divided between Soviet Russia proper and the buffer-state of the Far-Eastern Republic, a Soviet satellite country but not a fully-fledged Soviet state. In the period between 1917 and 1923 there was no anti-Buddhist and anti-lamaist campaign in Buryatia but, on the contrary, a religious revival took place. New temples were opened, new datsans were even founded and the old ones repaired. The number of lamas increased to 15,000. Only in 1923 was the whole of Buryat-Mongolia put under a single communist administration, and not until that year did the Soviet authorities begin to face the problem of Buddhism. Even after 1923 they had to proceed very cautiously. At first there could be no question of suppressing the monasteries or of suspending their teaching and medical activities. Any such drastic measures would have created a vacuum which the Soviet régime was unable to fill.

It was years before the communists were in a position to provide an adequate replacement for the monastic education and the 'Tibetan medicine' and during the intermediate period, which continued until 1930 and even later, the teaching and healing Buddhist clergy competed successfully with the educational and health authorities of the communist State. Their success can be proved, even statistically. Thus in 1928 there were 119 state schools in Buryatia, compared with 73 monastic schools. The network of state schools was obviously not sufficient to make the religious schools unnecessary. The lack of medical personnel was even more serious than the shortage of teachers. In the Selenga district, which forms the heart of the Buryat-Mongol Autonomous SSR, there were in 1929 still eight times as many lama doctors as Soviet medical workers. However, much of the influence of the lamas in Buryatia at the end of the twenties did not depend upon their medical and educational activities but was intangible and spiritual. As late as 1930 the average Buryat, according to a communist testimonial of the period, still saw 'gods, demons and spirits' everywhere and the lama — and in some parts of Buryatia also the Shaman — was the link with this spiritual world.[1]

A further handicap for any kind of ideological offensive was that the Soviet régime in Buryat-Mongolia had practically no influence on the

[1] *Bezbozhnik*, September 1930, no. 17–18.

Buryat people, for its administrative apparatus was run by Russians. In the late twenties only fifteen per cent of the administrative jobs were in Buryat hands. If anti-Buddist measures were to be effective they had to wait until there was a sufficient number of ex-Buddhist renegades available to initiate them formally and to carry them out.

The Soviets were too impatient to wait for that more opportune moment. Throughout the Soviet Union the year 1929 was the year of the great offensive against ideological and class opponents and Buddhist Buryat-Mongolia had to be included in the campaign, whether local conditions were ripe for it or not. The campaign against Buddhism was unsuccessful to the extent to which it was based on persuasion and successful as far as it was implemented with the help of administrative terror. The attempt to extend the activities of the League of Militant Godless to Buryat-Mongolia ended in a fiasco. A branch of that organisation had existed in the BMASSR since 1928. However, it was officially admitted that the organisation was completely useless. Its intellectual level was low, it did 'nothing but harm to anti-religious work' and 'encouraged religious fanaticism by its excesses'.[1] At the headquarters of the godless organisation in Moscow the failures of the Buryat-Mongol branch were explained by the fact that Buddhists themselves had become members of the organisation by claiming that they did not believe in God.[2] An atheist journal specialising in the fight against Buddhism was founded under the pretentious sounding title 'Science and Religion' (*Erdem-Ba-Shadzhin*) but it was discontinued after a few issues and was not heard of after 1929. The next attempt at producing anti-Buddhist literature was made in 1932 when the first two anti-Buddhist pamphlets in the Buryat-Mongol language were issued. One was called *The Origins of Buddhism*, and the other *Lamaism and War*. They were printed in editions of 2,600 and 2,000 copies respectively and were simultaneously published in Russian for non-Buddhists in somewhat larger editions. The two pamphlets had bad reviews in the more serious Soviet periodicals. The pamphlet on the *Origins of Buddhism* in particular was criticised for being divorced from Buryat-Mongol reality and talking mostly about India. In other words it did not attack Buddhist monasticism in the BMASSR and, therefore, defeated its own purpose.

Communist-Buddhist Symbiosis

In the fight against Buddhism the communists were obstructed not only by their own ideological poverty but also by the shrewdness of

Antireligioznik, 1930, no. 8–9, p. 56.   [2] *Antireligioznik*, 1930, no. 6, p. 68.

their opponents, who succeeded in adapting themselves to the new situation and turning it to their advantage at least as long as the authorities allowed them the tiniest scope for manœuvre. The Buddhist community in Russia was split into a conservative and a reformist group, as most other Churches were in the early years of Soviet power. The reformist party among the lamas represented only a comparatively small minority, less than one-fifth of the total. A larger proportion belonged to the 'conservatives', whilst over half took no part in the controversy and were classified as 'passive'.[1] The reformist minority comprised, however, the most articulate section of the Buddhist clergy, and it entirely dominated the Congress of Soviet Buddhists which took place in January 1926. The congress, which accepted the idea of the quasi-identity of Buddhism and Communism, sent a telegram to the Dalai Lama praising the Soviet nationalities policy.[2] Although representing a minority, the Buddhist reformers were more representative of Soviet Buddhism than the 'Living Church' was of Russian Orthodoxy, for they were led by the legitimate ecclesiastical superior of the Buddhist community, the Bandido Hambo Lama, Agvan Dordzhiev.

Agvan Dordzhiev was a personality of great calibre, whose historical significance transcended by far the limits of the Buryat territory. He had played an important part in the history of Inner Asia long before the Russian Revolution, and it is relevant to state that it was a pro-Russian part he played. For a long time Dordzhiev stayed in Tibet as tutor to the eighth Dalai Lama. Sir Charles Bell, who was British Representative in Lhasa at that time, said that Dordzhiev's influence there was outstanding 'for to his great store of knowledge he added strong driving power'.[3] Dordzhiev spread the belief that Russia was identical with the legendary messianic kingdom of Shambala, which would destroy all heretics and usher in a new period of Buddhist prosperity. The Czar was, according to Dordzhiev, a reincarnation of the founder of the Tibetan Buddhist sect of the Yellow Hats.[4] Dordzhiev's pro-Russian influence on the Dalai Lama was one of the reasons prompting the British intervention in Tibet in 1904.

A man of such stature, who already occupied a place in world history, was more than a match for the local communist bureaucrats in Irkutsk or Verkhneudinsk. Dordzhiev propagated a most dangerous theory,

---

[1] Klimovich, *Sotsialistichekoe stroitelstvo na vostoke i religiya* (Socialist construction in the East and Religion), Moscow, Leningrad 1929, p. 68.
[2] Klimovich, op. cit., p. 68.
[3] Sir Charles Bell, *The Religion of Tibet*, Oxford 1931, p. 165.
[4] Robert A. Rupen, 'Mongolian Nationalism', in *Royal Central Asian Journal*, vol. xiv, p. 15.

which for a while alarmed the communist leadership and in particular the anti-Buddhist propagandists. He proclaimed that there was no conflict between Soviet power and Buddhism either on the ideological or on the practical political level. His disciples went even further; they said that the spirit of Buddha lived in Lenin, and asserted even that Buddha, not Lenin, was the founder of Communism and that Lenin himself held a high opinion of Buddha.[1] Such extravagant statements were not put forward by Dordzhiev himself, but the Chief Lama did believe that the building of a socialist society was compatible with the continued existence of Buddhist monasteries as national cultural centres.

As a forceful personality, Dordzhiev was bound to exercise considerable influence even on Buryat communists.[2] In public disputes conducted in Ulan Ude he was able to hold his own, especially since he could quote in his support various learned Soviet authorities, who were afterwards denounced as taking up an erroneous attitude towards Buddhism. They included Ivan Maisky, author of a book on *Contemporary Mongolia*, and Professor Reisner, the well-known Soviet orientalist. No wonder that the Militant Godless considered the reform movement in Soviet Buddhism a most serious menace, and great pains were taken to point out that 'Buddhist atheism has nothing to do with militant atheism based on the Marxist appraisal of the laws of nature and society'.[3]

Agvan Dordzhiev made a serious attempt to counter the argument that Buddhism was unscientific. He stressed the importance of the study of natural and social sciences and tried to 'wed' Tibetan medicine with European medicine in order both to make it more efficient and to rescue it from communist persecution. It was over this question of Tibetan medicine that a particularly sharp conflict arose between Agvan Dordzhiev and the Moscow authorities, but even in this conflict he could count at first on local Buryat communist support. For instance, the lama doctors were allowed to organise a congress and to set up in 1926 a special 'Central Council for Tibetan Medicine', having a semi-official status. At a time when acute religious persecution was raging all over the Soviet Union and when all religious organisations not directly connected with worship were disbanded, the Council continued to function for a short time. It was responsible for running the school for Tibetan medicine attached to the Atsagat Datsan, situated only thirty-two miles from Ulan Ude. In 1931, there were still five 'Tibetan doctors' in that school, teaching ten pupils who were undergoing a

[1] *Bezbozhnik*, September 1930, no. 17–18.
[2] *Revolyutsionny Vostok*, 1932, no. 11, p. 244.   [3] *Antireligioznik*, 1930, no. 6, p. 66.

six-year course. The school was most popular with the surrounding people, and its dispensary had up to five hundred patients a month. Payment for treatment was very modest, averaging three roubles, and only in very rare cases was a higher charge made.[1]

Destruction

It was obvious that the local authorities would be unwilling to take any action against Tibetan medicine in general and against the Atsagat school in particular, and so a commission, ostensibly scientific, was sent to Ulan Ude from Moscow. The commission recommended the closing of the school and the disbandment of the Central Council for Tibetan Medicine, but it was undecided whether the Atsagat school should be destroyed by direct administrative interference or by indirect pressures, such as high taxation and the prohibition of the import of medical supplies from China.[2]

After the commission had submitted its report the days of the school of Atsagat were numbered. The school was liquidated as part of the programme of the gradual suppression of all datsans and all establishments attached to them. First to be affected were the new monasteries which had sprung up after the Revolution. In 1929 the first monastery, the Alar Datsan, was closed, allegedly in response to a popular vote by 'Buryat toilers'. By that time the number of lamas in Buryat-Mongolia had already been reduced to 6,900 as compared to the peak figure of 15,000 in the early twenties. But the greatest blows were yet to fall on Buryat lamaism. In 1931, the Tsongol Datsan was abolished after nearly two hundred years of existence.[3] At the beginning of the thirties, one datsan after the other disappeared, the reason given by the Soviet authorities being increasing counter-revolutionary activity on the part of the lamas. In 1935, the Party Secretary of Buryat-Mongolia was able to report to the Kremlin that the number of lamas had fallen to nine hundred and that six monasteries were closed down, whilst twelve had been disbanded by the lamas themselves.[4]

A particularly great loss to Buddhism was the suppression of the Aga Datsan, which had produced many outstanding Buryat educationalists. Most of the lamas of the Aga Datsan were arrested and deported to concentration camps.[5] The remnants of Buryat-Mongol monasticism

[1] *Sovetskaya Etnografiya*, 1932, no. 5–6, p. 223.
[2] *Sovetskaya Etnografiya*, 1932, no. 5–6, p. 228.
[3] *Sovetskaya Sibirskaya Entsyklopedia*, vol. iii, Moscow 1932, p. 15.
[4] *Antireligioznik*, 1936, no. 2, p. 9.
[5] Prof. N. Poppe, *The Destruction of Buddhism in the USSR*, *Bulletin*, Institute for the Study of the USSR, July 1956, p. 19.

were destroyed in 1937 when the Soviet authorities closed the small
Buddhist temple in Leningrad and arrested and executed the few lamas
attached to it.[1] Agvan Dordzhiev himself was forced to leave the
BMASSR in 1934 so that he should no longer exercise any influence on
his Buryat kinsmen. He lived near Leningrad as an exile, but in 1937
he was arrested and transferred to a prison in Ulan Ude, where he died
the following year.

The persecution of the Buddhists during this period was motivated
less by anti-religious arguments than by the assertion that Buddhism
was 'in the service of Japanese militarism'.[2] In the name of Buddha,
said the propaganda line of the period, the lamas justified all the
atrocities of fascist aggression and all the Japanese plans for seizing
and enslaving China.[3] The lamas were also charged with having given
an anti-Soviet and pro-Japanese twist to the Buddhist legend of
Shambala, the mythical country defending the Buddhist religion. It
was asserted that Buddhist propaganda in Buryatia identified Shambala with Japan.[4] Even Dordzhiev was accused of being a 'Japanese
agent'. The external annihilation of Buddhism could not and did not
satisfy the anti-religious propagandists. They felt that Buddhism could
continue to exist without lamas and lamaseries. Quite a number of rites
and religious precepts could be carried out directly by the faithful
within the family circle, however great the anti-religious persecution.

The outbreak of the war must have made things worse for the Soviet
Buddhists before they became better. The fact that Japan, always
identified as the power exploiting Buddhism for its own ends, was
an ally of Germany must have increased the Kremlin's suspicions of its
Buddhist subjects, but ultimately they benefited with other believers
from Stalin's 'New Religious Policy'.

Revival

Little was heard of the Soviet Buddhists in the immediate post-war
period apart from the fact that there existed a Buddhist Central Council
under the direction of the new Bandido Hambo Lama, Lobsan Nipa
Darmaev.[5] Only when Chinese Communism was firmly established on
the Asian mainland and when Moscow grew more interested in co-
operation with Asian countries did the Soviet Buddhists receive greater
publicity. The communist Government rediscovered what it had

---

[1] *Bulletin*, op. cit., p. 20.   [2] *Izvestiya*, June 5, 1938.
[3] *Antireligioznik*, 1938, no. 8–9, pp. 29–30.
[4] G. D. R. Phillips, *Dawn in Siberia, the Mongols of Lake Baikal*, London 1942,
p. 168.
[5] *Large Soviet Encyclopædia*, first edition, volume USSR, Moscow 1948, p. 1790.

forgotten, namely, that the Buddhist community in the USSR could have its propaganda uses. It was useful for the Kremlin to have at its disposal a few high lamas who could be shown to the world, especially to Asia, and who were ready to endorse any action taken by the Soviet Government.

Soviet Buddhism was exploited in particular in connection with the peace campaign. In August 1950 the 'Buddhist Central Council' of the USSR — a body composed at that time of five full and two deputy members — denounced 'the bloody crimes of the American aggressors in Korea'. In the person of its Chairman, Darmaev, the Council also took part in the second and third All-Union Peace Conferences as well as in the Ecclesiastical Peace Conference in Zagorsk in May 1952. On the latter occasion he was accompanied by the Lama Zhizhgitov, dean of the Aga temple, one of the few Buddhist places of worship left or restored to the Buddhists of the USSR. The speech of the Bandido Hambo Lama at the Zagorsk Conference showed the extent to which he and his collaborators have been mobilised both for supporting the foreign policy of the Soviet Government and for exhorting their followers to fulfil the Five Year Plan. The Buddhist priesthood, said the Chief Lama, campaigned energetically for signatures to the Stockholm Appeal to ban the atomic weapon, and to the appeal of the World Peace Council demanding the conclusion of a Peace Pact between the five Great Powers. Lamas from Buddhist temples and members of the Central Buddhist Council of the USSR 'travelled up and down the valleys of the Baikal region, across the vast expanses of the Aga steppes and into the gorges of the Sayan mountains, urging the faithful to fight for peace and to labour to increase the wealth of our great country'.[1]

Three years after making this statement the Chief Lama was once again summoned to Moscow, but this time for a more subtle Soviet propaganda effort. He was to meet U Nu, the Prime Minister of Burma, who had come to Russia on a state visit and who, as a devout Buddhist, was greatly interested in the fate of the Buddhist community in the USSR. The Chief Lama was even invited to the receptions given in honour of the Burmese statesman both in the Kremlin and at the Burmese embassy. In the official list of guests as issued by the Tass agency, Darmaev's name figured before those of the Chief of Protocol of the Soviet Foreign Office and the commander of the Moscow garrison[2] — an indication of the length to which Soviet propaganda is

---

[1] *Conference in Defence of Peace of all Churches and Religious Associations of the USSR*, Moscow 1952, p. 216.
[2] *Izvestiya*, October 23 and November 3, 1955.

prepared to go to make a show of religious freedom and even respect for religion to impress a distinguished foreign visitor. The climax of Darmaev's stay in Moscow was a personal meeting between him and U Nu. It lasted over an hour. The Chief Lama gave U Nu various souvenirs and received from him an offering in money to be spent on Buddhist religious purposes in Russia.[1] It was the first time that any religious personality of the Soviet Union openly accepted financial help from a foreign statesman. Darmaev feared at first that acceptance would meet with official Soviet disapproval and he was, therefore, inclined to refuse the gift until a Soviet official present at the meeting urged him to accept it.[2]

Darmaev informed U Nu that the Buddhist priests and faithful in Soviet Russia 'fervently preserve the rites, dogmas and traditions of Buddhism'. Darmaev's account to U Nu as published by the Soviet Information Bureau conveyed the impression that in a certain sense the situation of Russia's Buddhists was better under the Soviets than it had been under the Czars, for now the Bandido Hambo Lama was elected whereas previously he had been appointed by the authorities. As compared to the total annihilation of institutionalised Buddhist religion, the post-war and especially the post-Stalin situation of the Buddhist community in the USSR could, of course, be described as a 'revival', but it remains a revival within very narrow limits. Only two datsans have been re-established, those of Aga and Ivolga; the latter, a very modest building, serves as the residence of the chief lama.

The Soviet authorities, apparently content with the success of Darmaev's visit to Moscow, started to release news more frequently about Buddhism in the USSR for foreign consumption so that the legend of communist religious tolerance and friendliness towards the Buddhist faith should spread more widely to the Buddhist countries throughout Asia. A particular occasion on which Soviet Buddhist activities were reported to the world was the celebrations organised in Ivolga and Aga for the 2,500th anniversary of the Birth of Buddha.[3]

In the autumn of 1956 an event took place which became a further important landmark in the history of Soviet Buddhism and its exploitation by the Soviet authorities. This was the election of a new Bandido Hambo Lama in the person of Eshi-Derji Sharapov. The election was held in the Ivolga datsan and attended by 150 representatives of the Buddhist communities throughout Russia.[4] The reason given for the

[1] *Izvestiya*, October 25, 1955.
[2] Soviet Information Bureau report, October 28, 1955.
[3] Tass report of May 26, 1956.
[4] *Soviet Land*, published by the USSR Embassy in New Delhi, 1957, no. 1.

election of a new chief lama was Darmaev's failing health. However, it looked as if the authorities had had a hand in the matter because not only was Darmaev himself replaced, but his deputy also. The Soviet Government was interested in having a chief lama who could be absolutely trusted and who could be sent abroad, especially to those Buddhist countries of Asia which both Moscow and Peking were anxious to win for the communist cause.

Soon after his election it became clear that Sharapov was expected to play a role similar to that of Metropolitan Nikolay as a religious *commis voyageur* of the Soviet régime. At the beginning of November 1956 he headed the Soviet Buddhist delegation to the fourth Buddhist World Conference in Katmandu, from whence it proceeded to India.[1] In June of the following year Sharapov went to Colombo to attend the session of the World Peace Council as a member of a Soviet delegation of twelve. In August 1958 he was able for the first time to entertain a foreign visitor at the headquarters of the Soviet Buddhists in Ivolga, which had meanwhile been embellished. A hotel and a garage had been erected, trees and shrubs had been planted, and the territory of the Ivolga pagoda was fenced off. The first foreign visitor to Ivolga was well chosen. He was the Ceylonese Buddhist monk Udakendawala Saranankara, founder of the Ceylonese Peace Council, member of the World Peace Council and a holder of the Lenin Peace Prize. He could be relied upon not to look behind the façade of the Soviet Buddhist Potemkin village.

In line with the change in the political situation in South-East Asia and especially in view of Burma's drift towards the right, the Soviet Buddhists had to shift the emphasis of their foreign contacts from Burma to other countries, especially to Ceylon. In April 1959 the head of the Soviet Buddhists was encouraged once again to go from Ivolga to distant Moscow for talks with the Ceylonese ambassador. The picture of Soviet Buddhism which Sharapov put across to him was even more optimistic than the one which Darmaev had painted for U Nu's benefit.[2]

The most objectionable and immoral piece of exploitation to which the Soviet Buddhists were subjected occurred at the time of the Tibetan rising in the spring of 1959. The Bandido Hambo Lama was forced to issue a statement expressing 'anger' at the 'imperialist activities', and the 'behaviour of the reactionaries' in Tibet. The statement further called upon the Dalai Lama to leave the reactionaries and to

---

[1] Tass report of November 11, 1956.
[2] Moscow Radio in English for South East Asia, July 7, 1959.

return to Lhasa. However, the Bandido Hambo Lama managed to smuggle into his pronouncement a passage indicating his disapproval of Chinese intervention, expressing the conviction that the Tibetan nationalist would be 'strong enough to suppress the reactionary rebels' whilst in actual fact the suppression could not have happened without the most active Chinese interference.[1] Taken as a whole, however, the statement of the Chief Lama took sides against the most representative forces of Tibetan Buddhism and it was typical of Soviet policy to fight religion with the help of religion, Christians with the help of Christians, Jews with the help of Jews, Moslems with the help of Moslems and Buddhists with the help of Buddhists.

Whilst exploiting Buddhism for purposes of foreign policy the regime really feels uneasy about the extent to which Buddhism has survived, and the Buryat communist intellectuals are distressed that they have failed to make a decisive impact on their kinsmen living in the country-side. The Ivolga datsan attracts hundreds, and, six times a year, on festive days, even thousands of pious visitors to whom the 'senseless and fanatical rites' performed there are still full of meaning. It pains the materialist admirers of modern technology quite particularly that motor cars and aeroplanes are put into the service of religion and make it easy for pilgrims to travel from every part of Buryatia to the last remaining centres of Buddhist 'obscurantism' in the Soviet Union.

Throughout Buryatia there are also numerous sacred trees and stones. The sacred trees can be recognised by the coloured ribbons and wisps of material attached to their branches. Underneath the sacred stones the faithful hide coins and banknotes intended for the lamas who keep alive the glory of the sacred places. The innocent ribbons to which the communists greatly object as symbols of the survival of Buddhism can be found not only along the roads of Buryatia but also in the villages. There they are attached to poles erected over the dwellings of the collective farmers. The ribbons are covered with what the communists consider 'incomprehensible inscriptions' but in reality are Buddhist prayers. The collective farmers themselves value the ribbons as a token of supernatural protection which keeps harm away from their families and their cattle.[2] It is from supernatural power and not from communism that even a prosperous collective farmer expects his happiness.

What we have said up to now about Soviet Buddhism applies directly only to the Buddhists of Buryat nationality. Although the Buddhist Central Council and the Buryat Chief Lama now hold jurisdiction also

[1] Moscow in Burmese, April 4, 1959.   [2] *Trud*, November 27, 1960.

over Kalmucks and Tuvinians their destinies and problems are different
from those of the Buryats and must, therefore, be considered separately.

The Spiritual Genocide of the Kalmucks

When the communists came to power, Buddhism in Kalmuckia was
flourishing. Both the 1905 Revolution and the February Revolution of
1917 had led to a religious upsurge among the Kalmuck people. The
year of 1905 saw the foundation of the Choira, a kind of Buddhist
ecclesiastical high-school. It was founded by Agvan Dordzhiev in the
little township of Gashun Burguste in the Manych ulus. Thanks to the
Choira the numbers of the Kalmuck clergy and Buddhist monasteries
increased. In 1916 there were 1,603 'gelyuns' as the Kalmuck priests
were called, and seventy monasteries, or 'khuruls', six more than there
were in 1908.[1] The liberal atmosphere created by the February
Revolution gave Buddhism further encouragement. At the second
All-Kalmuck Congress in Astrakhan it was decided that the Buddhist
religion should be taught in all elementary and secondary schools of
the Kalmuck country.[2] The number of khuruls and priests increased
again and the latter exercised considerable if not a dominant influence
on the social and political life of the Kalmuck people to which the
Revolution had given an enormous impulse.

In the first years of Soviet power the Kalmuck Buddhists were
treated with no less consideration than their co-religionists in Buryatia.
In 1923, at the time of the first congress of the Buddhist clergy of the
Kalmuck Autonomous Province the seventy khuruls were still in
existence but the number of the Buddhist ecclesiastical persons had
grown to 2,840. In 1925, at the second congress of the Kalmuck clergy,
they were still able to brave the régime. The Chairman of the Kalmuck
Executive Committee, the highest representative of Soviet power in
Kalmuckia, wanted the Congress 'voluntarily' to renounce the training
of youth in Buddhist ecclesiastical schools, but the 'gelyuns' did not
yield to the communist pressure.[3]

By the time of the summoning of the third congress of the Kalmuck
clergy in 1929 the situation had become more critical. Arrests of
gelyuns had started and the life of those remaining in liberty had become
more difficult, especially because of high taxes. This third congress
elected the last chief lama of the Kalmuck Buddhists in the person of
Lubsan Sharab Tepkin, a very learned man who had received his

[1] T. Borisov, *Kalmukiya*, Moscow 1926, p. 26.   [2] Borisov, op. cit., p. 12.
[3] D. Arbakov, *O presledovanii Budiiskoi Tserkvi v SSSR* (About the Persecution of
the Buddhist Church in the USSR), manuscript.

education in Tibet and who had taught for three years at the Leningrad Institute of Oriental Languages. It was his fate to become a helpless onlooker at the annihilation of Kalmuck Buddhism by the Soviet régime. Soon after his election the communist anti-religious offensive in Kalmuckia gathered momentum. The khuruls were closed down one by one and an ever-increasing number of gelyuns were put into prison and deported. By 1936 the number of the Buddhist clergy was reduced to seventy, all very old and sick people. The most decisive blows inflicted on the Kalmuck Buddhist community were the closing of the Choira and the arrest of the Chief Lama Lubsan Sharab Tepkin and his deputy Ogdzhan Garya. The former was sentenced to ten years imprisonment and died as deportee, but the latter after a long exile in Central Asia, returned in 1941 to his homeland where he concealed his identity and lived as a simple shepherd.[1]

The closing of the khuruls had to be legalised by decisions of the Buddhist believers themselves. They were taken at meetings carefully stage-managed by party and police officials. At first the 'activists' of a given locality were summoned to a special conference where the larger 'mass meeting' was prepared. At that second meeting the atmosphere of intimidation was such that the vote to abolish the khurul and to transform it into a secular building was usually carried unanimously. Before the meeting the police authorities devoted special attention to the clergy and especially to the 'baksha' or head of the khurul, who was made to renounce his office publicly. The authorities saw no objection to speakers at those meetings using quite unconventional and un-Marxian arguments, e.g. that there was no difference between Buddhism and Communism and that it was, therefore, quite in order if the veneration of Buddha was replaced by that of a new bearded god, Karl Marx, the founder of Communism.[2]

On December 27, 1943, the Soviet Government issued a secret ordinance by which the Kalmuck Autonomous Republic was disbanded and the Kalmuck people deported to an unknown destination. This action had a disastrous effect for the Kalmucks — between 1939 and 1959 their number decreased from 134,000 to 106,000 — but it did not touch upon the fate of the Buddhist religion in Kalmuckia, which was destroyed before the Soviet genocide measures. Also the re-establishment of Kalmuck autonomy in 1957 and the resettlement of the Kalmucks in the steppe south-west of Astrakhan did not restore to them those spiritual values of which the Soviet régime had robbed them in the thirties. Only one small temple has been reopened and a

---

[1] D. Arbakov, op. cit.   [2] D. Arbakov, op. cit.

few gelyuns have spontaneously re-emerged in the Kalmuck villages. Local communist functionaries are closely watching their activities.[1]

Splendour and Eclipse of Tuvinian Buddhism

In Tuva, as in Buryat-Mongolia, Buddhism was introduced comparatively recently — in the second half of the eighteenth century. It never fully ousted the original religion, Shamanism, and shamanist and lamaist rituals always co-existed in the country. The religious history of Tuva for the period stretching from the foundation of the Tuvinian People's Republic in 1921 over its annexation by the USSR in 1944 to the present time shows two significant features: the original strength of Buddhism in the country and its subsequent thorough extermination.

In the first eight years of its existence the small Soviet satellite state of Tuva not only did nothing to fight religion but actually took Buddhism under its protection. The lamaseries of Tuva enjoyed respect, and even privileges. The chief lamas had extensive disciplinary powers which they could use in particular whenever their subordinates wanted to leave monastic life. The Prime Minister of the Republic during this early period, a man called Tonduk, was himself a former lama, and it was under his auspices that a Tuvinian Buddhist Congress was held in April 1928. The congress was financed by the Government which later expressly ratified its decisions.[2] More than that, a few weeks after its conclusion the Government issued a law which, in imitation of the Soviet model, called itself 'Law about the Separation of Religion from the State', but which in reality was a Law for the protection of Buddhism. It made anti-religious propaganda a criminal offence.[3]

As Tuva was completely dependent on the Soviet Union, this state of affairs could not go on for long. The Buddhist Congress of 1928 was the climax of the co-operation between Buddhist monasteries and the Tuvinian authorities and at the same time the swansong of religion in Tuva. It showed the Soviet overlords how much out of step Tuva was. They were particularly alarmed at the prospect that this theocratic state would be perpetuated in the next generation. Indeed the Deputy Secretary General of the Tuvinian People's Revolutionary Party, in theory an ally of the Soviet Communist Party, told the Buddhist Congress that the youth should be educated 'in the spirit of lamaist traditions'.[4] The Soviets had taken the precaution of interfering directly

[1] *Nauka i Religiya*, no. 6, 1960, p. 23.
[2] V. M. Iezuitov, *Ot Tuvy feodalnoi k Tuve sotsialisticheskoi* (From the feudal Tuva to the socialist Tuva), Kyzyl 1956, p. 66.   [3] Iezuitov, op. cit., p. 67.
[4] S. A. Soizhelov, *Tuvinskaya Narodnaya Respublika*, Tuvinian Peoples Republic, Moscow 1930, p. 86.

with the education of the Tuvinian youth, but in an anti-religious sense. A 'substantial number' of young Tuvinians were taken to Moscow to the 'Communist University of the Toilers of the East' and upon their return the older generation had to hand over to them the Party and the Government. Official Tuvinian policy was switched from support of Buddhism to the active fight against religion. The landmark of this change was the eighth Congress of the Tuvinian People's Revolutionary Party in October–November 1929. At that time there were still twenty-two lamaseries in Tuva and, of a total population of 60,000, 2,000 were lamas.

The young hotheads who had taken over the administration of the country instituted such a repressive anti-religious policy that they roused the people against them. As a Soviet historian puts it, 'It happened that there was jeering at the religious feelings of the believers and that there were arrests of lamas who carried out religious rites. This led to a strengthening of the influence of the feudal and theocratic elements. . . .'[1] Moscow intervened and counselled moderation to the Tuvinian rulers, and the violent anti-religious policy had to give way to greater leniency. The result was new concessions to religious believers. Thus, in 1933, the Tuvinian People's Revolutionary Party adopted a resolution to the effect that religious beliefs were no obstacle to party membership. This was again at variance with the practice of the Soviet Communist Party, even if the same resolution added that the Party 'should endeavour to overcome the religious prejudices of its members through educational work and by raising their cultural level'. Nevertheless, the Party was again open to religious believers, and it seems that they were once again able to influence its policy.[2] However, the previous situation could not be restored, the monasteries remained closed and secularised and the conduct of atheist propaganda continued to be safeguarded by the Constitution of 1930, the fourth Constitution the country had within nine years. A further victory over religious elements in Tuva was achieved during the purge of 1937 although even after that some doubts must have remained in the Soviet mind about the ideological outlook of the members of the Tuvinian People's Revolutionary Party. When the party was disbanded after Tuva's absorption into the Soviet Union, its members were not automatically taken over into the Soviet Communist Party. Every member had to apply individually for transfer and it may be assumed that those indulging in 'religious prejudices' were rejected outright.

[1] Iezuitov, op. cit., pp. 79–80.   [2] Iezuitov, op. cit., p. 84.

Buddhism was not wiped out altogether, even with the transformation of the semi-independent Tuvinian Republic into an Autonomous Province of the Russian Soviet Federation. At the time of the collectivisation of agriculture, which in Tuva occurred much later than anywhere else in the Soviet Union, i.e. between 1949 and 1954, the lamas were still offering resistance. A Soviet publication mentions them among those elements in the country who tried to undermine working discipline among the collective farmers and spread all kinds of rumours to sabotage the government-ordered transfer of the Tuvinians from nomadic tents into houses. One of these rumours was that various diseases might befall people in their new abodes.[1] As the lamas were officially classified among the 'enemies of the people', they were no doubt very harshly treated during the collectivisation period. What is still left of Buddhism in Tuva after this must be very insignificant remnants. It is perhaps characteristic that a Soviet ethographic expedition investigating the Tuvinian Province in 1956 paid much more attention to shamanist than to lamaist practices. The decline of Tuvinian lamaism resulting from the anti-religious policy of both the Tuvinian left-wing and the Soviet communist régimes may have given encouragement to a recrudescence of the pre-Buddhist religion of the country. Nevertheless one hundred Tuvinian lamas were still surviving in 1960.[2]

The Christian religion of the Russian settlers in Tuva has resisted the onslaught of communist atheism to a much greater degree than Buddhism. It is one of the strangest aspects of communist domination in Tuva that institutionalised Christianity has been preserved to a most remarkable extent, whilst Buddhism is all but destroyed. It is an irony of history that under Soviet rule Kyzyl, the Tuvinian capital, received for the first time the visit of an Orthodox Metropolitan. He was the Metropolitan of Novosibirsk and Barnaul, to whose vast diocese the Tuvinian Autonomous Province belongs. In 1958 he celebrated a solemn liturgy in Holy Trinity Church in Kyzyl in the presence of five priests and three deacons. Nothing comparable had happened in Kyzyl as long as it was called Belotsarsk — town of the White Czar.[3]

The International Significance of Soviet Anti-Buddhism

The study of the problem of Buddhism in Soviet Russia would be less important than in fact it is had Soviet anti-Buddhism not become

---

[1] L. V. Grebnev, *Perekhod tuvinskikh aratov kochevnikov na osedlost* (The transition of the Tuvinian nomadic arats to a settled way of life), Kyzyl 1955, p. 58.
[2] *Nauka i Religiya*, no. 6, 1960, p. 23.   [3] *Zh.M.P.*, 1958, no. 8, p. 11.

an article of export. It has been exported not only into the tiny puppet republic of Tuva which Russia has swallowed up, but also into the Mongolian People's Republic (MPR) which can claim to be the first Asian state to be transformed into a socialist country. This transformation was very largely achieved by the destruction of the country's religious foundations — lamaist Buddhism — but, as in Tuva, the Soviet advisers had to proceed with caution, for many of their local collaborators continued for a considerable period to be 'prisoners of religious superstitions'. The Mongolian People's Revolutionary Party, the organisational backbone of the pro-Soviet Mongol régime, neither wished nor dared at first to proclaim open hostility to the Buddhist faith. All the party could do in the early period of its existence was to agitate for 'a purer Buddhism'. This seemed a strange position for an organisation which was an associate member of the Communist International to take, and yet the party had no choice. In the early twenties, when the Mongolian national-revolutionary régime was born, the Mongolian capital Urga, now Ulan Bator, was, after Lhasa, the most important centre of Lamaist Buddhism. In fact it would be correct to say that then Urga was not a town at all but a big monastery.[1]

Although Soviet overlordship over Mongolia dates from 1921, until 1924 the Soviet-controlled country was still a theocracy under the Jebtsun Damba Khutukhtu, also called 'the Khan of Mongolia'. He was almost the exact Mongol equivalent of the Tibetan Dalai Lama, a holy and infallible ruler. Only on May 20, 1924, when the eighth incarnation of the Jebtsun Damba Khutukhtu died, could there be any question of destroying the theocratic character of Mongolian society. The authorities, acting no doubt on Soviet instigation, did not allow the search for a new incarnation of Mongolia's spiritual ruler to take place. There was to be no ninth incarnation of the Jebtsun Damba Khutukhtu. The attitude of the authorities was at variance with the wishes of the vast majority of the people at the time, and the widespread desire for a new reincarnation led to considerable unrest over a number of years. But the cause of secularisation had won, although only very gradually did it become the cause of atheism.

Even after the Mongol theocracy as such was swept out of power, the friends of lamaism still remained in high places until the latter part of 1928. It was only then that things started moving. In October 1930, a Mongol League of Militant Godless was organised on the Russian model, and soon boasted 5,000 members. In 1932, the Government

---

[1] V. Maslennikov, *Mongolskaya Narodnaya Respublika* (Mongolian People's Republic), Moscow 1955, p. 14.

carried out large-scale confiscations of the property of Buddhist monasteries. In 1933, the foundation of new monasteries was forbidden and government commissars were appointed for those which remained open. In 1935, there came the great trials of Buddhist functionaries, far exceeding even Soviet trials in ferocity. In 1937 and 1938 alone over 2,000 lamas from forty-eight monasteries were tried and shot for organising counter-revolution.[1] These mass trials were not the only means by which the resistance of the lamas was broken. A real military offensive was launched against the lamaseries in 1937. Both Mongol and Soviet troops took part in this action, in which both tanks and aircraft were used. This fully-fledged military offensive resulted in some 37,000 lamas being killed, After this massacre, in 1940, the Mongolian People's Revolutionary Party adopted a new statute stating that the Party's foremost task included the organisation and implementation of 'broad anti-religious propaganda' and 'explaining the harm caused by religion to the toilers'.[2]

To what extent was this offensive against Mongol lamaism successful? Foreign travellers to the MPR can tell us only that the outward signs of lamaism have been almost completely swept away 'except for some remnants, mainly maintained to impress foreigners'.[3] As one visitor put it, Buddhism is now 'a dying feature of Mongol culture'. In 1958 there were only five active monasteries in the whole country, including the Gandang monastery in Ulan Bator which has been returned to the faithful.[4] A communist traveller refers to these few remaining monasteries as 'living museums' and 'zoos of the past' and adds that for the young Mongolians, lamaism has ceased to be an issue and has become something absurd and a little embarassing.[5] The precarious remnants of Mongol Buddhism are exploited by the Government, which induces the chief lamas to serve on the Mongol Peace Committee and the Mongol Committe for Afro-Asian Solidarity.[6] All this is far from meaning that religion is dead in the hearts and minds of the Mongol people, especially outside the few urban settlements, and the Mongol press prints occasional warnings against the harm caused by 'religious prejudices' although these may refer as much to primitive shamanist beliefs as to Buddhism.

The attitude which both the Soviet communists and their Outer

[1] I. Zlatkin, *Mongolskaya Narodnaya Respublika*, Moscow 1950, p. 227.
[2] *Mongolskaya Narodnaya Respublika*, Academy of Sciences of the USSR, Moscow 1952, p. 367.
[3] Robert A. Rupen, 'Inside Outer Mongolia', *Foreign Affairs*, January 1959.
[4] Charles Bawden, *Three Weeks in Mongolia*, London 1958, mimeographed.
[5] Ivor Montagu, *Land of the Blue Sky*, London 1956, p. 48.   [6] Bawden, op. cit.

33. Gandang temple buildings in Ulan Bator, reopened after the Second World War. Photo Charles Bawden.

34. Congregation of the Gandang temple 1959. Photo Charles Bawden.

35. Temple buildings of Erdeni Joo, the 'St. Peter's of Mongol Lamaism', ruined during the anti-religious offensive of 1937 and no longer in use. Photo Charles Bawden.

The monthly *Journal of the Moscow Patriarchate*

Bratskii Vestnik, the organ of the Evangelical Christians/Baptists. Published six times a year.

These two journals together constitute the whole 'religious press' in the Russian language existing in the Soviet Union.

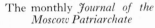

Echmiadzin, the organ of the Armenian Church, largely produced for export.

The first issue of the Soviet atheist periodical *Science and Religion*, founded in September 1959.

36. Religious and anti-religious periodicals.

Mongolian disciples have assumed towards Buddhism in practice, throws significant light on the ultimate aims which Chinese and any other brand of Orthodox Marxist-Leninist Communism pursues with regard to the Buddhist religion. Indeed, the Chinese communist régime, learning from Soviet experience in so many fields and copying it in many ways, was bound to assimilate Soviet anti-religious tactics as applied to Buddhism. Tuva and Outer Mongolia with their former theocratic societies provide China with far more instructive lessons than Buryatia, where the power of Buddhism had already been weakened through Christian missionary activities. From the example of Tuva, the Chinese communists could learn above all how to settle the religious problem by playing off the younger generation against the old. As Russia trained young Tuvinian Buddhists at the Moscow 'University of the Toilers of the East', the Chinese communists are indoctrinating young Tibetan Buddhists at the 'Nationalities' Institute' in Peking from which they send them back to their homeland as communists emancipated from the religious traditions of their people. The Chinese communists can be expected to be aware of the particularly close parallel existing between Outer Mongolia, once the state of the Khutukhtu, and Tibet, in theory, still the state of the Dalai Lama. By their dealings with the lamas and monasteries of Mongolia the Soviets have supplied the Chinese communists with a complete blue-print as to how to undermine a theocratic state and how to destroy the theocracy by a combination of patient work, re-education and persecution.

Q

XV

Scattered Groups

═══════════

S everal small religious groups represented in the Soviet Union do not fit into any larger context and, therefore, have not yet been considered. Such groups are the Baha'i, who have their roots in Islam without being Moslems, the Karaim, who profess a Judaic faith without being Jews in the accepted sense ,the Yezidis who have a special syncretist religion of their own, the Zoroastrians of the Tadzhik mountains and the Nestorian Christians who, on account of their theological peculiarities, could not be dealt with in connection with any other Christian community. Theologically, there is a world of difference between these groups but they have one characteristic in common, their geographical origin. Their home is either Persia or Mesopotamia.

I. BAHA'IISM AND COMMUNISM

Islam, both in its Shiite and Sunnite form, is attacked by the communists because it is 'reactionary', encourages nationalist narrowmindness and obstructs the education and emancipation of women. Baha'iism has incurred communist displeasure for exactly the opposite reasons. It is dangerous to Communism because of its broadmindness, its tolerance, its international outlook, the attention it pays to women's education and its insistence on equality of the sexes. All this contradicts the communist thesis about the backwardness of all religions. In the political sphere social reformers appear to the communists more harmful than 'reactionaries', and in the religious field an outlook which is mindful of modern social problems is thought to be more obnoxious than out-of-date obscurantism. This is perhaps why Baha'iism has attracted the attention of the Soviet communists to a much greater degree than might be warranted by the numerical strength of its supporters.

Baha'iism has its roots in Shiite Islam and, more precisely, in the messianic expectation of the second coming of the Twelfth Imam,

which plays such a central role in Shiite beliefs. The movement goes
back to a Persian, Mirza Ali Mohammed, called 'Bab', 'the Gate',
meaning the gate to or forerunner of the Mahdi, the redeemer. His
supporters were subjected to cruel persecution and 20,000 of them
died for their faith in the 'Bab', who was himself executed in 1850.
This martyrdom fired the imagination of Mirza Husayn Ali (1817–92)
who, under the name of Bahá u'lláh (Glory of God), took over the
leadership of the Babist movement and changed its character. It was
Bahá u'lláh who transformed the Shiite sect of 'the Bab' into a modern
syncretist religion. Babism became Baha'iism. The new religion was
further modernised and indeed Westernised by the son and successor
of Bahá u'lláh, called Abdu'l Bahá, 'the Son of Glory'.

As an up-to-date ethical teaching almost devoid of theological
accessories and as a unitarian religion rejecting priesthood, Baha'iism
has satisfied the spiritual needs of thousands of people in many countries
who either had become estranged from the religious beliefs they
originally held or were complete agnostics. Baha'iism penetrated to
India, Egypt, Europe and the United States; but it was in the Russian
Empire that the first Baha'i temple was built, in the town of Ashkhabad
which is situated just across the Persian border and is now the capital
of the Turkmenian Soviet Republic. Persecuted in Persia, the Baha'i
found sanctuary in the Russian Empire. Not only were they able to
build their 'unusually beautiful temple' but they also organised a
special missionary school on Russian soil.[1] Russian Orthodox missionaries were somewhat jealous of Baha'i successes and uttered warnings
against the new movement, asserting that it violated 'the feelings of
loyalty towards the Russian White Czar'. Notwithstanding such charges,
the Baha'i sect continued to flourish under Czarist rule and even during
the first years of the Soviet régime it seemed to prosper. A Baha'i youth
organisation which the communists nicknamed 'Bekhamol' was set up
in Ashkhabad. On account of its extensive cultural activities and supra-
national tendencies it was a serious competitor of the Komsomol.[2]

The first major blow to be inflicted by the Soviet authorities on
Baha'iism came in 1928. In that year the Soviet régime confiscated the
temple of Ashkhabad and the Baha'i had to pay rent for it after that.
The Ashkhabad temple was then still the only one the Baha'i had
anywhere in the world, for their second temple at Wilmette, a suburb
of Chicago, was not opened until 1931. The Soviet authorities also

---

[1] Krymsky, *Istoriya Islama* (History of Islam) vol. iii, Moscow 1912, pp. 17–9.
[2] L. Klimovich, *Sotsialisticheskoe Stroitelstvo na Vostoke i Religiya* (Socialist
Construction in the East and Religion), Moscow–Leningrad 1929, p. 140.

thought it appropriate to warn the people against Baha'iism with the help of anti-religious propaganda. This seemed necessary because the Baha'i faith was not confined to the original Baha'i immigrants from Persia but had succeeded in proselytising certain people to whom Islam seemed too reactionary and Communism too devoid of spiritual content. To stop the growth of the Baha'i movement two anti-Baha'i pamphlets were published in 1930. One, called *Baha'iism* by A. M. Arsharuni, was produced by the publishing house of 'Bezbozhnik'. The other was entitled *Baha'iism — a New Religion of the East*. It was brought out by the Leningrad Oriental Institute. The two pamphlets assessed Baha'iism as the ideology of the Persian trading bourgeoisie. They saw its particular harmfulness in the alleged Baha'i claim that socialist teachings could be traced back to Baha'iism. The article on Baha'iism which the *Small Soviet Encyclopædia* published in 1933 took the same line of denouncing 'the new religion' for allegedly camouflaging itself as 'socialism'. Baha'iism, the *Encyclopædia* added, was one of the 'fashionable religious philosophical systems which the bourgeoisie uses in its fight against the ideas of Socialism and Communism'.[1]

As time went on Soviet charges against the Baha'i became more violent. In 1938, an anti-religious pamphlet made the monstrous accusation against Baha'i leaders that they were 'closely linked with the leaders of Trotskyite-Bukharinist and Dashnak-Mussavat bands'.[2] From the wording of this accusation we might gather that the Baha'i suffered persecution not only in Turkmenistan, where their temple was situated, but also in Transcaucasia, once the scene of action of the Dashnaks and Mussavatists. It was in 1938 that the Ashkhabad temple was finally closed for religious worship and transformed into an art gallery. Over 500 Baha'i were arrested, most of them expelled to Persia but some ended up in Siberian labour camps.

In the post-war period Soviet propaganda attacked Baha'iism primarily because of its cosmopolitan character. The second edition of the *Large Soviet Encyclopædia* objected to Baha'iism because it denied the principle of national independence and of state sovereignty. It supported the anti-national idea of the abolition of national boundaries and the creation of a 'united world state'. This was an idea beneficial to reaction. American and British imperialists — said the *Encyclopædia* — have supported the Baha'is in every conceivable way ever since the end of the nineteenth century. They have subsidised them and assisted

---

[1] *Small Soviet Encyclopædia*, first edition, vol. i, Moscow 1933, p. 895.
[2] Boris Kandidov, *Tserkov i Shpionazh* (Church and Espionage), Moscow 1938, p. 94.

the foundation of Baha'i communities in the United States and Britain. Baha'iism was one of the instruments serving the spiritual disintegration of the peoples of the Middle East.[1] It is another proof of the similarity of the various totalitarian régimes of our time that Nazi Germany argued on similar lines against the Baha'i. The Baha'i movement in the Third Reich was disbanded on June 9, 1937, because of its 'international and pacifist tendencies'.

The attacks on the Baha'i in various Soviet works is not the only indirect evidence that the Baha'i faith in the Soviet Union has continued to exist after the Second World War. In the southern parts of the USSR it still happens that Soviet Baha'is approach foreign travellers asking them for information about the Baha'i movement abroad.

II. KARAITES

The Karaites or Karaim, who speak a Turkic language may be described as a heretical Jewish sect, although they themselves would resent this identification. Nevertheless, their connection with Judaism, though not necessarily with the Semitic race, has never been disputed. They are the 'Protestants' of Judaism. They separated from the main Jewish body in the eighth century, and what distinguishes them from the Orthodox Jews is their rejection of the oral tradition of the Talmud, that great depository of Rabbinical wisdom. The basis of the Karaite faith, like that of Orthodox Judaism, is the Torah. The Karaim derive even their name, which was originally a nickname, from this rejection of the Talmud. The word 'Karai' may be freely translated as 'he who adheres to the written Law to the exclusion of the oral Law'.

The Karaim appeared in the territory of the present Soviet Union first in the North Caucasus region, later in the Crimea and then in Eastern Galicia and finally at the end of the fourteenth century also in Lithuania. But this is not the place to go into the long and complicated history of the Karaite people; what is important and significant within the context of this book is the fact that the Karaim enjoyed a high degree of toleration both under the Czarist régime and under the Polish 'bourgeois' governments of the period between the two wars. Soviet power, on the other hand, very nearly annihilated them as an ethnographic and especially as a religious entity. In 1837 the Czarist authorities created the 'Taurian Karaite Spiritual Administration' (Tavricheskoe Karaimskoe Dukhovnoe Upravlenie). It was called 'Taurian' because most of the Karaim of the Russian Empire lived in the

---

[1] *Large Soviet Encyclopædia*, second edition, Moscow 1950, vol. v, p. 129.

'Government of Tauria' which included, in the first place, the Crimean Peninsula. The largest Karaite community was in the town of Eupatoria, which very appropriately served as the headquarters of the Taurian Karaite Spiritual Administration. The head of this body was the Haham, who supervised the work of the hassany, the Karaite rabbis. In 1857 a second Karaite 'Spiritual Administration' was created for the small Karaite congregations in the Western territories of the Russian Empire, with headquarters at Troki (Trakai) near Vilnius. Nevertheless, Eupatoria remained by far the more important Karaite centre and, in 1884, its prestige was further enhanced by the opening there of a training college for hassany. Karaite synagogues, also called 'kenasy', existed in all the cities with sizeable Karaite minorities, including Feodosia, Simferopol and Bakhchisarai in the Crimea; Odessa, Kherson, Kiev and Nikolayev in the Ukraine and in Moscow.

After the October Revolution the Karaite people of Eastern Europe who, except for the small community of Halich (Galicia), had up till then been subjects of the Russian Czar, were split up by the new frontiers. The larger portion, including all the Karaite groups of the Crimea and the Ukraine, except those of the West Ukrainian town of Lutsk, came under Soviet rule. Those of the former Western border provinces found themselves in Poland and Lithuania. In Soviet Russia there remained 8,300 Karaim, in Poland there were about 1,000 and in Lithuania a few hundred, mostly in the town of Panevezhys. However, the small Polish and Lithuanian Karaite groups were able to conduct national-cultural and religious activities on a scale out of all proportion to their numerical significance. In Vilnius, a Polish journal called *Mysl Karaimska* ('Karaim Thought') was founded, as well as a 'Society of the Friends of Karaite History and Literature'. In Lutsk another journal, known as *Karaj Awazy* ('Voice of the Karaim') appeared in the Karaite language and a third journal came out in Panevezhys under the title of *Onarmach* ('Progress').[1] The religious status of the Lithuanian Karaim was still determined by the old Czarist legislation, whilst the Polish parliament passed a special law in 1936 for the protection of the Karaite community.

The larger Soviet Karaite community was in a much less favourable position. It enjoyed no legal protection as a religious unit. Its religious training colleges in Eupatoria and Odessa ceased to exist. Its kenasy were secularised; that of Kiev, for instance, was turned into a cinema.[2]

---

[1] Simon Szyszman, 'Die Karäer in Ost-Mitteleuropa', *Zeitschrift fuer Ostforschung*, 1957, no. 1, p. 50.

[2] *Bezbozhnik*, January 27, 1929, no. 5.

Karaite cultural activities, on the other hand, were not completely suppressed but, unlike those conducted in Poland and Lithuania, they were based not on the acceptance of Karaite religious thinking but on the rejection of it. The Karaite political-literary journal *Bizym Iol* ('Our Road'), which started to appear in Simferopol in 1929, served the purposes of a completely secularised Karaite national culture. It is not known for how long it was able to exist.

As a result of Russia's territorial annexations in 1939–40, virtually all Polish and Lithuanian Karaim came under Soviet rule. There was no question of the Karaite press of Vilnius, Lutsk and Panevezhys continuing, and Karaite religious life also suffered. The cohesion of the community of Troki was more or less preserved and the local kenasa remained in being after the war, presumably the only one existing anywhere in the Soviet Union. Karaite folklore can still be studied in the Karaite Historico-Ethnographic Museum in Vilnius.[1] The Karaim of the Crimea were reduced in numbers by the war. They escaped, it is true, the usual extermination measures of the Nazis because the latter, after some wavering, did not consider the Karaim as Jews but as a Turkic nationality. This proved to be their undoing when the Soviets returned to the Crimea. Jews who were not exterminated by the Nazis were *a priori* suspect. When the communist authorities deported the Crimean Tartars from the Crimea to Soviet Asia many Karaim were affected by the operation. The language of the Karaim is identical with the Crimean Tartar language and this alone may have determined the Soviet police not to discriminate between the two groups.[2] According to a statement by the Odessa rabbi, 300 Karaim were still living in Eupatoria in 1956, and this was about one-quarter of the city's previous Karaite population.[3] Such Karaim as are still left in the Crimea are no longer entitled to any special cultural amenities, for in the present Soviet view they are completely Russified.[4] Indeed, according to the Soviet census of 1959 only 1,000 Karaim considered the Karaite language as their mother-tongue as against 3,000 in the early years of the Soviet régime. The census also revealed that during thirty-three years of Soviet rule, from 1926 to 1959, the Karaite people decreased from 8,300 to 5,900.

Many Karaim have been well aware of the fact that they can expect nothing good of the communist régime and have, therefore, emigrated from Soviet Russia. The first wave of Karaite emigration took place

[1] *Sovetskaya Etnografiya*, 1948, no. 1, p. 228.
[2] Leon Léneman, La Tragédie des Juifs en URSS, Paris 1958, p. 188.
[3] *Jewish Chronicle*, August 3, 1956.
[4] *Large Soviet Encyclopædia*, second edition, vol. xx, Moscow 1953, p. 110.

immediately after the October Revolution and the second in 1946–7 within the framework of the Polish-Soviet exchange of populations. The Karaim emigrating after World War II hailed from the Western territories of the USSR only. They tried to rebuild Karaite cultural and religious life in Poland but were not numerous enough to do so. Only two issues appeared of the revived Karaite journal *Mysl Karaimska*.[1] It seems sad that the Karaite groups in the free world are too scattered and too small — the largest single Karaite group outside the communist world is in Israel — to ensure the survival of this very interesting religious-ethnic community.

III. YEZIDIS

The strange eccentric religion of the Yezidis, who live mostly in Iraq and to a smaller extent in Turkey, Syria and Iran, also has its adepts in the Soviet Union, among the Kurds of Transcaucasia. The majority of the Kurds of Armenia and virtually all the Kurds of Georgia are Yezidis.[2] There are also some Yezidis in Azerbaidzhan living in the Lachin district on the Armenian-Azerbaidzhan border. According to the census of 1926, the total number of Soviet Yezidis was 14,500.

The Yezidis have a syncretist religion if there ever was one. From the Christians they have taken baptism and they regard Christ as an angel who had taken the shape of man. From Islam the Yezidis have adopted the custom of circumcision, to avoid persecution by the Moslems, who used to be their mortal enemies, and they recognise Mohammed as a prophet. From the Jews they accept the Old Testament, especially the Book of Genesis, which they hold in greater respect than either the Koran or the New Testament. They also venerate Abraham as a prophet, but the main prophet of the Yezidis is Sheikh Adi, who is said to have founded the sect in the twelfth century. Zoroastrian dualist ideas are predominant in the religious beliefs of the Yezidis. Like the Zoroastrians, the Yezidis hold that the world is ruled simultaneously by a good god whom they call Yezda or Yezdana (the Zoroastrian Ormuzd), from whom they derive their name, and the evil spirit Malak-Tauz (the Ariman of the Zoroastrians) who is identified by Christians and Moslems as Satan. This is why the Yezidis have also been described as devil-worshippers.[3]

It has often been asserted that the Leninist-Stalinist nationalities policy has produced a profound effect on the Yezidis, and Soviet

[1] Szyszman, op. cit., p. 51.   [2] *Sovetskaya Etnografiya*, 1958, no. 6, p. 138
[3] Joachim Menont, *Les Yezidis, Épisodes de l'Histoire des Adorateurs du Diable*, Paris 1882.

sources have given us to understand that the old way of life of the Soviet Yezidis has gone and with it also their peculiar religious views and customs.[1] There is no doubt that the Soviet authorities have discouraged the survival of the religion of the Yezidis and done their best to destroy their clergy. Moreover, pilgrimages to their Holy Place in Iraq, the tomb of Sheikh Adi near Mosul, have been forbidden. Even supporters of the Soviet régime feel not altogether happy about the destruction of this strange sect, for it has become clear that the colourful folklore and folk art of the Yezidis could not be preserved without its religious foundations. Much of this folk art has been lost in the Soviet era. When in 1926 the Soviet woman writer Marietta Shaginian visited Kandakhsaz, a village of the Yezidis of Armenia, she not only met a sheikh there who was both the spiritual and secular head of the community, but she also saw some primitive but powerful artistic monuments which made her pay tribute to the 'inborn sense of beauty' of the Yezidis and their sense of style and form.[2] When Madame Shaginian returned to Kandakhsaz twenty years later, the sheikh had gone and the old customs were disappearing, especially the burial customs and with them the desire of the Yezidis to erect sculpture of great originality over the graves — a custom which had made all their cemeteries into places of artistic interest.[3] Nevertheless, remnants of the religion of the Yezidis have remained alive in the USSR. It is certain that there are not only believers but also propagandists of their faith, as could be gathered from an attack which a Soviet newspaper published as late as 1959 on a 'mullah' — faqir or gawwal would have been more appropriate terms — who was charged with spreading the Yezidis' creed.[4]

IV. ZOROASTRIANS

The ancient Zoroastrian religion, of which such strong elements have survived in the faith of the Yezidis, does not exist in the Soviet Union in the pure form in which it has been preserved in India, where its followers are the Parsees of Bombay, and in Persia, where they are called Guebers. However, Zoroastrian influence is still present in the customs and beliefs held by the people of the Tadzhik mountains,

[1] Marietta Shaginian, *Puteshestvie po Sovetskoi Armenii* (Travel through Soviet Armenia), Moscow 1951, p. 239.
[2] Marietta Shaginian, *Sovetskoe Zakavkazie* (Soviet Transcaucasia), Tiflis 1931, p. 39.
[3] Shaginian, *Puteshestvie*, op. cit., p. 239.
[4] *Bakinskii Rabochii*, September 12, 1959.

especially in the Darvaz and Karategin areas. According to the eminent Soviet ethnographer, S. A. Tokarev, the name of Zoroaster is still known to the majority of the Tadzhik hillmen.[1] They know that their forefathers were fire worshippers and remnants of the veneration of fire have still been preserved. This is why Soviet ideologists and propagandists cannot afford to consider Zoroastrianism a completely extinct religion as far as the USSR is concerned. In books on the history of Tadzhikistan, Zoroastrianism is still attacked as a 'stupefiant like any other religion' giving its blessing to the rule of the aristocrats and priests over the toiling masses.[2]

The people of Darvaz and Karategin, who were the main bulwark of Zoroastrian survivals, were for the greater part transplanted after World War II to the cotton-growing plain of Southern Tadzhikistan. This provides an interesting parallel to the transplantation of the pagan Khevsurs to the Georgian plain mentioned in Chapter III and the transfer of the Moslem hillmen in Daghestan referred to in Chapter XIII. Several tens of thousand of people were affected by the Tadzhik resettlement action.[3] The action was officially justified by economic considerations, but all the same it had considerable sociological and ideological importance. The complete Sovietisation of the Tadzhik hillmen and the uprooting of their ancient religious customs could obviously be achieved only by their removal to the plain.

V. THE SYRO-CHALDAEAN CHURCH

The origin of this Church goes back to the great heresies of the first Christian centuries. The particular heresy which the Syro-Chaldaean Church holds, the Nestorian heresy, with its exaggerated emphasis on the human nature of Christ, was condemned as early as A.D. 431 by the Council of Ephesus. Not until A.D. 499 did the Syro-Chaldaean or Nestorian Church come formally into being. This Church has had a fascinating and dramatic history. In the Middle Ages it penetrated as far as India, Sumatra, Ceylon and China. At one time it seemed as if the Nestorian Church might become the most important Christian Church of Asia. However, the Church was unable to preserve its original spiritual conquests. It suffered disastrous setbacks almost

---

[1] S. A. Tokarev, *Etnografiya Narodov SSSR* (The Ethnography of the Peoples of the USSR) Moscow 1958, p. 343.
[2] B. G. Gafurov, *Istoriya Tadzhikskogo Naroda* (History of the Tadzhik People), Moscow 1952, pp. 27-30.
[3] Academy of Sciences of the Tadzhik SSR, *Tadzhikskaya SSR*, Moscow 1956, p. 204.

everywhere and by the nineteenth century only a few insignificant groups had survived, mostly in the inaccessible mountain regions of Kurdistan. Although these remnants of the ancient Nestorian Church in the Kurdish mountains were Assyrians the Church does not represent the whole Assyrian nation. In the middle of the sixteenth century a Chaldaean Church came into being which is in communion with the Holy See in Rome. Its head is the Patriarch of Babylon and its flock is slightly more numerous than that of the Nestorian Church.[1]

The Assyrian Nestorian Christians have been in touch with Russia since the thirties of the nineteenth century, when the first Assyrian groups emigrated from Persia into the Transcaucasian territories which were put under the rule of the Czar in 1828. A much larger number of Assyrians sought Russian protection during the First World War and in the early years of the Soviet régime the number of Assyrians living in the USSR exceeded 50,000. Among them there was an Orthodox and perhaps even a Catholic minority but the vast majority belonged to the Syro-Chaldaean Church. Relations between Soviet power and the deeply religious Assyrians proved difficult and the extensive cultural and political work which the Soviet régime conducted among the 'Soviet Assyrians' bore little fruit. There were constant complaints that persons upholding the national and religious traditions of the Assyrian nation infiltrated into Assyrian collective farms and craftsmen's co-operatives. Even Assyrians who had joined the Communist Party or the Young Communist League were apparently unable to rid themselves of these traditions. The opposition of the Assyrian Christians to the communist Government was expressed in their emigration or flight from the Soviet Union. By 1939 their number had shrunk to less than half of what it originally was.[2] The Syro-Chaldaean Church in the Soviet Union never had a bishop but in 1930 it still had a number of priests (meliks) and deacons (chamats).[3] They officiated mostly in Transcaucasia and the North Caucasus region, where the bulk of the Soviet Assyrians were living.

---

[1] Donald Attwater, *The Catholic Eastern Churches*, Milwaukee–London 1935, pp. 229–31.
[2] Walter Kolarz, *Russia and her Colonies*, London 1952, pp. 249–50.
[3] *Bezbozhnik u Stanka*, 1930, no. 12.

XVI

The Future of Religion in Russia

<hr>

The struggle between Communism and religion which is the main subject of this book will not continue *ad infinitum*, not because religion will ultimately disappear, as the communists themselves too readily assume, but because Communism, like every other political system, will have an end as it had a beginning. To see the present struggle in its true perspective, let us leave the present and try to look at Communism as people are likely to regard it in fifty or even a hundred years time. What position will the Russian October Revolution then occupy in the minds of the nations of the world? What will they think then of Marx, Engels, Lenin and Stalin? It is not an unfair assumption that the October Revolution will by then have come to occupy a similar position to that of the American and French Revolutions in the minds of the present generation. This is to say that the October Revolution will still be looked upon as an important historical landmark by the men and women of the year 2050 and beyond, but it will be only one event among many others. As to Karl Marx, his name will convey even less to the twenty-first century than it does to the mid-twentieth. Lenin and Stalin will still be recognised as great Russian historical figures, but their theoretical writings will be forgotten and ignored, as products of a bygone epoch, without any message for the generations to come. Lenin's polemics against Karl Kautsky will have no more lasting value than the polemics of Friedrich Engels and Karl Marx against their liberal opponents. Whatever the strength of religious feelings in a hundred years' time, there can be little doubt that the Holy Scriptures of the great religions will still be read and studied and at least to some extent venerated by a generation which will know, at most, the titles of some of the so-called classics of Marxism-Leninism.

The end of Communism will come either in a revolutionary way or, much more likely, through evolution. Individual atheist communists have shown that they are not incapable of change. Even some party officials and professional propagandists of Communism have thrown off the doctrine of Marxism-Leninism and embraced a religious belief.

However, Communism will be overcome less by spectacular personal conversions than by a more general and long-term re-interpretation of communist ideology. The communist movement in its entirety or at least essential parts of it seem capable of transformation. The urge to redefine the communist dogma has steadily gathered momentum in the communist camp since Stalin's death. It has found expression in the shape of various heresies and 'revisionist' trends. The heresies have affected the most important ideological issues of Communism, including the communist attitude towards religion. Many Hungarian and Polish 'revisionists' may have been no less anti-religious in their philosophical outlook than orthodox communists, but they had a less optimistic idea than the latter about the length and intensity of the struggle between the religious and the communist world outlook. The revisionists of the future may go one step further yet, and consider it expedient for atheism to become the private affair of every citizen, even if he happens to belong to the communist upper-class. Those who will put forward this idea may do so not in order to abandon the communist ideology but to rescue it. At one stage, the communists may discover that the anti-religious concept prevents the formation of a society of equal human beings and this, after all, is the final objective of Communism. They may realise that the old inequalities between haves and havenots have been superseded by a new inequality existing between believers and unbelievers. Communist anti-religious policy has indeed created a new depressed class whose members, in view of the beliefs they hold, are unable to take any part in directing the political life of the nation or occupy any posts which bring them into contact with the education of the young.

Discrimination on religious grounds not only diminishes the rights enjoyed by the individual Soviet citizen but it is also prejudicial to the collective rights of national groups. National rights and religious rights are inseparably interconnected. The Tartar or Uzbek ethnic group of the Soviet Union cannot fully unfold itself unless Islamic teaching and the practice of the Moslem faith can proceed without any official impediment. The Lithuanians and the Poles of the Soviet Union cannot be considered as free nations as long as the Catholic religion is in fetters and as long as the Catholic Church is not allowed those normal activities which it carries out in non-communist countries. Nor will the Russians, Georgians and the other Orthodox peoples of the USSR be in full possession of their national personality as long as the Orthodox Church is subject to the indignities under which it has suffered under communist rule both under and after Stalin. Nowhere in the vast Soviet

Empire can the communist régime be truly popular as long as it fails to recognise that religion is a genuinely popular phenomenon deeply rooted in the soul and the traditions of every people. To be really free, a nation needs more than schools, libraries and literature in its mother tongue, it needs spiritual freedom, free access to its holy places, the recognition of its religious heritage and its national Church.

Once it is understood that atheist Communism obstructs freedom and equality of men by making discrimination against believers compulsory, Communism will change its character. The idea that a new society need not necessarily be built without God but that it can be built with God may, therefore, become increasingly attractive to the communist mind. This idea has cropped up in communist circles practically since the beginning of an international communist movement. Indeed, one of the first great controversial debates in the Communist International turned on this very question. The debate was started by a Swedish communist leader, Zacharias Hoeglund, an important figure of the labour movement in his country, of whom it was said that the whole Swedish working class listened to his voice. In an article on Communism and Religion published in 1923 Hoeglund said, in substance, that it was a matter of indifference whether capitalism was overthrown in the name of God or man. The Communist Party should not declare that faith is counter-revolutionary and reactionary. If atheism were proclaimed obligatory communist teaching, the Communist Party would sink down to the level of a sect. The biggest guns of Soviet Communism, Zinoviev, Bukharin and Radek, were mobilised to reject and denounce the view of Hoeglund, who was soon to leave the communist for the social-democratic camp.[1] One day, perhaps, Hoeglund's old heresy will become the new communist orthodoxy but, if it does, Communism will have retained no more than its name: it will have ceased to be the atheist-materialist doctrine which has been forcibly imposed on the Russians and other nations.

A transformation of Communism may also be expected for yet another reason, one which the great Russian philosopher Nicholas Berdiaev outlined long ago. He thought that the fulfilment of the communist economic programme, rather than the collapse of the communist system, would bring about a revival of religious thinking even in quarters which are alien to it to-day. Once the urgent economic and social problems of the human individual were solved, the unsolved moral problems of man would demand greater attention. Communism

[1] Yaroslavsky, *Protiv Religii i Tserkvi* (Against Religion and Church), vol. ii, Moscow 1933, pp. 544–5.

in its present form could not answer these deeper personal needs but religion could.[1] This idea, that religion might make an impact on the citizens of a fully-fledged communist society, might have seemed absurd to the active participants in the October Revolution, but it is no longer absurd to the second and third communist generation, which either readily or grudgingly recognises that religion can exist quite independently of a society's economic foundations.

From all this one should not draw the conclusion that the end of Communism, whether reached by revolutionary upheavals, evolutionary developments or even by the fulfilment of parts of its programme, would automatically place religion in a significant or even predominant position. Only an emotional Russian messianism, blind to the facts of social and economic developments and entirely dominated by irrational feelings, could assume *a priori* that religion in a post-communist or differently communist Russia would be a more important factor than it is to-day in any of the major non-communist countries.

How important religion will be in a future Russian state will depend on many things. The decisive factor will be the further steadfastness and piety of the Russian believers in the face of renewed persecution, iniquities, anti-religious propaganda and temptations. In the past not all religious groups have resisted atheist pressure to an equal degree and in future too there will be considerable differences in their respective attitudes towards the disintegrating influences of state and party inter-ference. If genuine freedom of religion were established in Russia we should probably see a certain regrouping of the religious forces existing within her boundaries. The Russian Orthodox Church, whilst gaining in depth, and obtaining the free access to Russian youth of which she is deprived at present, might lose in width. It might suffer a certain curtailment of jurisdictional scope through the emergence of national Orthodox Churches and through the resurrection of Eastern Catholic Churches in those border areas where they have a tradition. Freedom of religion in Russia would also bring into the open certain sects which under Soviet rule are either condemned to illegality or have to camou-flage their organisational and theological identity by membership of a legal and officially recognised church body. On the other hand, a number of extremist sects which thrive in an atmosphere of political tyranny and are in fact a reaction against the latter would gradually loose their *raison d'être* if the atmosphere in the Soviet Union were more relaxed. At least these sects would lose their main appeal, that of

[1] Nicolas Berdiaev, 'Personne Humaine et Marxisme' in the symposium *Le Communisme et les Chrétiens*, Paris 1937, p. 202.

being an irreconcilable opposition force which, unlike the recognised Churches, refuses to come to terms with the 'communist Antichrist'.

But how far should the future of religion in Russia be seen in conventional terms as an uneasy co-existence of rival groups and how far can it be visualised in a new light? In other words, how far has religion in Russia been cleansed by the purgatory of Communism, how far has it become more ecumenically minded? In this respect the situation does not seem to be entirely discouraging. Religious-minded people who have gone through bitter experiences in the Soviet Union, including prisons and concentration camps, have reported an ecumenism of suffering which has united Christians of various denominations and on occasion also Christians, religious Jews and Moslems. The ecumenism of suffering is likely to have a deeper long-term effect on the religious life of Russia than the officially organised ecumenical activities in which various Russian Churches, especially the Russian Orthodox Church, have been allowed to take part at certain times. But how far it will exercise an immediate practical influence is, of course, a different matter. The division of Christianity exists quite independently of encouragement by communist secular interests. In fact, taking the world and its history as a whole, Communism counts for little or nothing in the split between Western and Eastern Christendom. If Russia and the whole world had overcome Communism, the problem of Christian unity would be somewhat different from what it was before the communists took power, just as the Protestant-Catholic relationship in Germany is not the same before and after Hitler. The ecumenism of the camps introduced a new element of charity and understanding into the relations between Protestants and Catholics. Theoretically and theologically speaking, it should even be easier to establish closer bonds between Orthodox and Catholics than between Catholics and Protestants. However, it is not so much theology which divides Orthodox and Catholics as nationalism, which seems to have a vested interest in making the lowest theological barriers insurmountable. Metropolitan Platon of Kiev once stated that the walls separating Orthodox and Catholics 'do not reach up to heaven', but of the walls separating rival national aspirations it may be said that they reach down to hell. Only if the role of national pride as an obstacle to Christian unity is clearly understood on all sides will its danger diminish and means be found to overcome it.

Whilst religion will not die out in the Soviet Union, even if communist rule continues for a very long time, it may find to an ever-increasing extent such outlets as every genuine religious believer will consider undesirable and reject as superstitions. The Soviet communists, in agreement with atheists of ages past, usually state that there is no difference between religion and superstition. In fact, all religions are *ipso facto* superstition in the communist view. This, however, is only theory. In practice the Soviet communists do discriminate between genuine religion and mere superstition. They are prepared to look more benevolently at a properly conducted religious service than at a pilgrimage to a 'holy well'.

The problem of superstition is, of course, not confined to Russia; it is universal, but there are certain situations and circumstances in which superstitions flourish quite particularly. For instance, super- stitions are particularly rife in territories where the Christian faith is new and where it still competes with non-Christian beliefs and also in countries where Christian Churches have inadequate power and opportunity to conduct a determined struggle against superstitious views and practices. However, even in countries where Christianity is of long standing, superstitions based on pre-Christian folklore die hard and re-assert themselves over and over again. All these situations can be found in Russia. The country includes many peoples and tribes superficially evangelised and therefore given to primitive superstitious beliefs. Among the Russian-Ukrainian population pre-Christian folklore has remained alive.[1] And last, but not least, the anti-religious persecu- tion and the plight of the teaching Church has made existing super- stitions more widespread and has proved a feeding ground for new ones. As long as there is a shortage of priests in Russia and religious instruction remains inadequate, superstition must grow at the expense of genuine religious faith. Saint Jean Vianney, better known as the Curé d'Ars, said that people will finish by adoring beasts if their parish is left without a priest for twenty years. This applies to twentieth- century Russia probably much more than to nineteenth-century France. There is a thirst in the human being for the supernatural and, if this thirst cannot be satisfied by normal religious means, he turns to all kinds of *ersatz*. His imagination starts to work and to produce 'miracles'. It is quite possible and even natural that this quest for the miraculous and supernatural should be exploited by unscrupulous and mercenary persons, as the Soviet press often asserts. However, one must not simplify the problem of superstition in Russia by considering it merely as something to which a person resorts who is frustrated in the exercise

[1] A survey of these folk beliefs is contained in S. A. Tokarev, *Religioznye verovaniya vostochnoslavyanskikh narodov XIX nachala XX veka* (Religious beliefs of the Eastern Slavonic Peoples of the 19th and beginning of the 20th century), Moscow 1957.

of proper religious practices. Superstitions of the most primitive type are rife among a section of Soviet youth which has had no past connection with real religion.

Official Soviet spokesmen have often alleged that religion in Russia continues to exist mainly because the victory of Communism has not yet been achieved on a world-wide scale and because religious influences are penetrating into the Soviet Union from the outside. Up to a point this seems to be true. Religion in Russia finds encouragement through the prestige which religious thinking, religious organisations and religious personalities enjoy outside her boundaries. The religious forces of the non-communist world come into contact with the Soviet Union partly in an entirely legal way and, even with the help of the communist Government itself, which is trying to neutralise the Churches of the 'capitalist world' and to draw them over to the communist side. With this end in view foreign ecclesiastical delegations are admitted into the Soviet Union, Soviet Church delegations are allowed to go abroad and foreign religious dignitaries are being awarded Soviet 'Peace Prizes'. There is a comparatively small but growing and qualitatively important group of Soviet citizens who, as a result of cultural, economic and other exchanges, come into touch with religion outside the Soviet Union more or less by accident, but this contact may stimulate them towards independent thinking. The Soviet citizen who has the privilege of visiting a non-communist country is able to realise on the basis of first-hand impressions what an important factor religion has remained in the life of certain nations which he is inclined to regard as 'progressive' in view of their outstanding cultural, technical and economic achievements. He may even reach a further stage in this rethinking process where, without beginning to believe himself, he may question some of the cheaper anti-religious arguments about the reactionary character of religion and its pernicious influence on progress.

Although Soviet anti-religious literature speaks so much of the influence of 'capitalist surroundings' on keeping religion alive in the communist State, it may be asked whether the free world really does enough for religion in the Soviet Union, for its survival and rebirth and, whether in its present frame of mind, the free world is at all in a position to do anything. The situation certainly requires a serious examination of conscience. The things which can be done are primarily beyond the sphere of the tangible and the material, even if purely material help is thinkable; for instance in the form of religious broadcasts or the dispatch of Bibles and prayer books to the Soviet Union — provided they pass Soviet censorship. However, religious people and institutions can help the peoples of the Soviet Union infinitely more by way of example, first of all by the fervour and sincerity of their own religious beliefs and their loyalty to their own religious principles. Great and striking manifestations of religious faith or the attachment of a whole nation to the beliefs of its fathers are things which filter through even in a country like the Soviet Union where the means of mass communication are strictly regimented. There is no doubt, for instance, that a section of Soviet public opinion is well aware of the resistance which the Catholic Church in Poland has put up to assert itself against the atheist communist régime. Many facts about religious life in the West reach the Soviet citizen only through the distorting mirror of anti-religious propaganda, but nevertheless he can draw his own conclusions from the biased reports and give them his own interpretation. He may read, for example, about vast evangelising campaigns and he may disagree with the methods they use as much as many people in the West do and yet he may see in them an illustration of the tremendous interest in religious problems and of that search for God which is taking place in the non-communist world. Also outstanding religiously-inspired efforts in the intellectual field, such as books of particular merit, become known in the Soviet Union, even if only through polemics written by official reviewers. Nevertheless the Soviet reader sees from them that the religious opponents of the materialistic world outlook are active and that the alleged dilemma 'science or religion?' in fact does not exist.

Whether the Christians of the free world (and the same applies to Moslems and Jews) can be of help to their co-religionists in the communist world depends to a major degree on the extent to which they are able to cope with the urgent economic, social and racial problems of the time. Communism is the bad conscience of mankind. It has come into being very largely because religious-minded people have been slow in answering the various challenges facing their generation, slow in providing religiously inspired answers to its many needs. The more positive the contributions of religious people to the problems of peace, poverty, colour and race the less *raison d'être* there will be for the 'spectre of Communism'. As far back as 1848, Karl Marx and Friedrich Engels said that the 'spectre of Communism' was haunting Europe. This simile is still true to-day with the difference that the spectre of Communism is now haunting the whole world. However, it can haunt only an evil world and not one where man is prepared to do God's will by keeping peace and treating his fellow human beings as brothers. Nothing could accelerate more the evolutionary disintegration of Communism of which we have spoken above than the Western world's clearer recognition of the Fatherhood of God, with its consequence, the brotherhood of man. If Western man, on the other hand, fails to acknowledge by his deeds this dual fundamental relationship he may prolong the sufferings of people living under Communism and help materialism to assert itself at the expense of religious belief both in Soviet Russia itself and in the countries which are her satellites and allies. More than that, the inability of the West to live up to religious standards is the surest means of allowing Communism to spread to other parts of the globe before it has fully spent its force in its country of origin.

Appendix

THE PEOPLES OF THE SOVIET UNION AND THEIR RELIGIOUS BELIEFS

Nationality	Numerical Strength (unless stated otherwise according to the 1959 census)	Geographical Distribution	Majority Religion or Church	Minority Religions
Great Russians	114,588,000	In all 15 Soviet Republics especially in RSFSR (97,845,000) Ukraine (7,400,000) Kazakhstan (4,000,000) Uzbekistan (1,100,000)	Russian Orthodox Church	Old Believers, Baptists, Dukhobors, Molokans and other sects.
Ukrainians	36,981,000	Ukraine (31,852,000) RSFSR (3,377,000) Kazakhstan (762,000) Moldavia (421,000)	Russian Orthodox Church	Catholics of Slavo-Byzantine Rite (dominant among Western Ukrainians), Baptists, Seventh Day Adventists, Pentecostalists and other sects.
Byelorussians	7,829,000	Byelorussia (6,444,000) RSFSR (845,000) Ukraine (291,000)	Russian Orthodox Church	Strong Catholic minority, Baptists, Pentecostalists and other sects.
Uzbeks	6,004,000	Uzbekistan (5,026,000) Tadzhikistan (454,000)	Sunnite Moslems	
Tartars (including Crimean Tartars expelled from the Crimea in 1944)	4,969,000	In many parts of the USSR, especially in the Tartar and Bashkir Autonomous Republics and in Uzbekistan (Crimean Tartars)	Sunnite Moslems	About 100,000 Tartars, the so-called 'Kryashens', are Orthodox Christians.

Kazakhs	3,581,000	Kazakhstan (2,755,000) RSFSR (383,000)	Sunnite Moslems	Sunnite Moslems (30%)
Azerbaidzhani Turks	2,929,000	Azerbaidzhan (2,481,000) Armenia (108,000) Georgia (157,000)	Shiite Moslems	
Armenians	2,787,000	Armenia (55·7%) Georgia (15·9%) Azerbaidzhan (15·8%) RSFSR (chiefly North Caucasus) (9·2%)	Armenian Church	Small groups of Catholics and Baptists
Georgians	2,650,000	Georgia	Georgian Orthodox Church	Shiite Moslems (Inghilo), Sunnite Moslems (Adzharians), Pagans (Khevsurs), small groups of Catholics and Baptists
Lithuanians	2,326,000	Lithuania	Roman Catholic Church	Lutherans, Calvinists
Jews	2,268,000 (About 3,000,000 according to unofficial Jewish estimates)	RSFSR (875,000) Ukraine (840,000) Byelorussia (150,000) Uzbekistan (94,000) Moldavia (95,000) Georgia (52,000) Baltic States (62,000)	Judaism	Insignificant groups of Evangelical Christian converts in the Ukraine, and converts to Islam, the so-called 'Chala' in Central Asia.
Moldavians	2,214,000	Moldavia (1,887,000) Ukraine (239,000)	Russian Orthodox Church	Baptists, Innocentists, Jehovah's Witnesses and other sects.
Germans	1,619,000	About half in Siberia and other half in the Central Asian Republics, especially Kazakhstan	Lutherans	Strong minority of Roman Catholics, also Mennonites, Baptists and smaller groups of Seventh Day Adventists.

NATIONALITY	NUMERICAL STRENGTH (unless stated otherwise according to the 1959 census)	GEOGRAPHICAL DISTRIBUTION	MAJORITY RELIGION OR CHURCH	MINORITY RELIGIONS
Chuvash	1,470,000	Chuvash ASSR	Russian Orthodox Church	
Latvians	1,400,000	Latvia	Evangelical Lutheran Church	Strong minority of Roman Catholics, small groups of Orthodox and Baptists
Tadzhiks (including Pamir nationalities)	1,397,000	Tadzhikistan (1,051,000) Uzbekistan (312,000)	Sunnite Moslems	Ismailites
Poles	1,380,000	Byelorussia (539,000) Ukraine (363,000) Lithuania (230,000) Kazakhstan (53,000)	Roman Catholics	Orthodox
Mordvinians	1,285,000	In the eastern parts of European Russia, especially in the Mordvinian ASSR	Russian Orthodox Church	
Turkmenians	1,004,000	Turkmenistan	Sunnite Moslems	
Bashkirs	983,000	Bashkir ASSR	Sunnite Moslems	
Kirghiz	974,000	Kirghizia	Sunnite Moslems	
Estonians	969,000	Estonia	Evangelical Lutheran Church	Fairly strong Orthodox minority, smaller groups of Baptists and Methodists

Peoples of Daghestan including Avars Lezghins Darghinians Kumyks Laki Nogay Tartars Tabasarans Aguly Rutuls Tsakhurs	945,000 268,000 223,000 158,000 135,000 64,000 41,000 35,000 8,000 7,000 6,000	All in the Daghestan ASSR. There are about 48,000 Lezghins in Azerbaidzhan	Sunnite Moslems	
Udmurts	623,000	Udmurt ASSR	Russian Orthodox Church	Small Moslem minorities, remnants of pagan beliefs, especially Kugu Sorta sect among the Mari.
Mari	504,000	Mari ASSR	Russian Orthodox Church	
Komi and Komi Permyaks	431,000	Komi ASSR Komi-Permyak National Okrug	Russian Orthodox Church	
Chechens	418,000	Chechen-Ingush ASSR	Sunnite Moslems	
Ossetins	410,000	About one-third in Georgia, two-thirds in RSFSR (North Caucasus)	Religious allegiance divided between Orthodox and Sunnite Moslems. Remnants of pagan beliefs. Small Baptist groups.	
Bulgars	324,000	Ukraine and Moldavia	Russian Orthodox Church	
Koreans	314,000	Uzbekistan (139,000) Kazakhstan (74,000) RSFSR (91,000)	Russian Orthodox Church	Methodists

NATIONALITY	NUMERICAL STRENGTH (unless stated otherwise according to the 1959 census)	GEOGRAPHICAL DISTRIBUTION	MAJORITY RELIGION OR CHURCH	MINORITY RELIGIONS
Circassians (Soviet statistics divide them up into 'Cherkess', 'Adyge' and 'Kabardinians')	314,000	Northern Caucasus region (Kabardinian-Balkar ASSR, Karachai-Cherkess and Adyge Autonomous Provinces)	Sunnite Moslems	
Greeks	310,000	Ukraine (104,000) Georgia (73,000) RSFSR (43,000) Kazakhstan	Russian Orthodox Church	
Buryats	253,000	Buryat ASSR, Chita and Irkutsk Provinces of RSFSR	Buddhists	In the Irkutsk Province, Orthodox Christians and Shamanists.
Yakuts	236,000	Yakut ASSR	Russian Orthodox Church	Shamanist survivals.
Karakalpaks	173,000	In Uzbekistan, especially Karakalpak ASSR	Sunnite Moslems	
Karelians	167,000	Karelian ASSR Kalinin Province (RSFSR)	Russian Orthodox Church	
Hungarians	155,000	Transcarpathian Province of Ukraine	Calvinists	Roman Catholics, small Baptist groups.
Gypsies	132,000	About half in RSFSR, half scattered over other Soviet Republics	Nominally Orthodox	Central Asian Gypsies (5000) are Moslems.

Nationality	Population	Location	Religion	
Peoples of the North', including: Nentsy Evenki Khanty Chukchi Eveny Nanai Koryaks Mansi Selkupy Nivkhi Ulchi Saami (Lapps) Udege Eskimos Itelmeny Kety Orochi Nganasany Yukagiry Aleuts	128,000 25,000 24,000 19,000 12,000 9,000 8,000 6,300 6,000 4,000 4,000 2,000 1,800 1,400 1,100 1,100 1,000 800 700 400 400	European Arctic, Northern Siberia, Far East, especially Amur Valley, Kamchatka, Sakhalin Island and Aleutian Islands	These nationalities practise or practised until recently every kind of worship characteristic of primitive peoples anywhere in the world — adoration of the sun, ancestor worship, cult of inanimate objects (fetishism), cult of animals (totemism). Usually the peoples of the North are referred to as Shamanists in view of the important role played by the Shaman, the Siberian witch-doctor. At the time of the establishment of Soviet power, the peoples of the North found themselves in various stages of Evangelization. The Lapps (Kola Peninsula) and the Itelmeny (Kamchatka) may be considered as Orthodox Christians. Certain groups of Evenki have been under Buddhist, others under Orthodox influence.	
Gagauz	124,000	Moldavian ASSR and Odessa Province of Ukraine	Russian Orthodox Church	Baptist groups
Rumanians	106,000	Transcarpathian and Chernovtsy Provinces of Ukraine	Russian Orthodox Church	
Kalmucks	106,000	Kalmuck ASSR	Buddhists	
Ingush	106,000	Chechen-Ingush ASSR	Sunnite Moslems	
Tuvinians	100,000	Tuvinian Autonomous Province	Buddhists	Shamanists

NATIONALITY	NUMERICAL STRENGTH (unless stated otherwise according to the 1959 census)	GEOGRAPHICAL DISTRIBUTION	MAJORITY RELIGION OR CHURCH	MINORITY RELIGIONS
Uigurs	95,000	Kazakhstan, Kirghizia, Uzbekistan	Sunnite Moslems	
Finns	93,000	Leningrad Province Karelian ASSR	Lutherans	
Karachai	81,000	Karachai-Cherkess Autonomous Province	Sunnite Moslems	
Talyshi	77,000 (1926)	Southern parts of Azerbaidzhan Soviet Republic	Shiite Moslems	
Abkhazians	74,000	Abkhazian ASSR	Religious allegiance divided between Sunnite Islam and Georgian Orthodox Church.	
Kurds	59,000	Armenia (26,000) Georgia (16,000) Azerbaidzhan	Armenian Kurds are Yezidis and Sunnite Moslems; Georgian Kurds are Yezidis; Azerbaidzhani Kurds are Shiite Moslems.	
Khakassians	57,000	Khakassian Autonomous Province	Russian Orthodox Church	Shamanist survivals
Altaitsy (Oirots)	45,000	Autonomous Province of the High Altai	Russian Orthodox Church	Remnants of 'Burkhanism', a nationalist-messianic faith and Shamanist survivals
Balkars	42,000	Kabardino-Balkar ASSR	Sunnite Moslems	
Czechs and Slovaks	40,000	Ukraine	Their religious background is Catholic and Protestant but many may have adopted the Orthodox faith.	

Turks	35,000	Scattered mainly over Transcaucasia	Sunnite Moslems	
Taty	28,000 (1926)	Azerbaidzhan	Shiite Moslems	
Chinese	25,000	Presumably scattered all over USSR	Their religious background is Confucianism and Buddhism, but nothing is known about an organised Chinese religious life in the USSR. Half of the Soviet Chinese do not speak the Chinese language and they are bound to be estranged from their national and religious traditions as well.	
Assyrians	22,000	Armenia	Nestorian Christians	Orthodox
Dungans	21,000	Kirghizia Kazakhstan	Sunnite Moslems	
Persians	21,000	Scattered over towns of Transcaucasia and Central Asia	Shiite Moslems	Bahai
Abaza	20,000	Karachay-Cherkess Autonomous Province	Sunnite Moslems	
Vepsians	16,000	Karelian ASSR Leningrad Province	Russian Orthodox Church	
Shorians	15,000	Kemerovo Province (Southern Siberia)	Russian Orthodox Church	Shamanist survivals
Arabs	8,000	Uzbekistan	Sunnite Moslems	
Baluchi	7,800	Southern Turkmenistan	Sunnite Moslems	
Karaites	5,900	Lithuania, Ukraine and scattered over other parts of USSR	Karaite Religion	

INDEX

R

PRINTED IN GREAT BRITAIN BY ROBERT MACLEHOSE AND CO. LTD
THE UNIVERSITY PRESS, GLASGOW